Logistics and Supply Chain Management

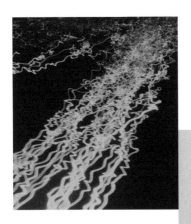

Logistics and Supply Chain Management

Patrik Jonsson

The McGraw·Hill Companies

London   Boston   Burr Ridge, IL   Dubuque, IA   Madison, WI   New York   San Francisco
St. Louis   Bangkok   Bogotá   Caracas   Kuala Lumpur   Lisbon   Madrid   Mexico City
Milan   Montreal   New Delhi   Santiago   Seoul   Singapore   Sydney   Taipei   Toronto

Logistics and Supply Chain Management
Patrik Jonsson
ISBN-13 978-0-07-711738-2
ISBN-10 0-07-711738-7

McGraw-Hill
Higher Education

Published by McGraw-Hill Education
Shoppenhangers Road
Maidenhead
Berkshire
SL6 2QL
Telephone: 44 (0) 1628 502 500
Fax: 44 (0) 1628 770 224
Website: *www.mcgraw-hill.co.uk*

British Library Cataloguing in Publication Data
A catalogue record for this book is available from the British Library

Library of Congress Cataloguing in Publication Data
The Library of Congress data for this book has been applied for from the Library of Congress

Acquisitions Editor: Rachel Gear
Development Editor: Karen Harlow/Jennifer Rotherham
Marketing Manager: Mark Barratt
Senior Production Editor: James Bishop

Cover design by Jan Marshall
Printed and bound in Great Britain by Bell & Bain Ltd, Glasgow

ISBN-13 978-0-07-711738-2
ISBN-10 0-07-711738-7

The *McGraw-Hill* Companies

Brief Table of Contents

v

Detailed Table of Contents

Guided Tour

Figures and Tables:

Each chapter provides a number of figures, illustrations and tables to help you to visualise the examples. Descriptive captions summarise important concepts and explain the relevance of the illustration.

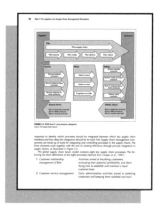

Packed with Examples:

Eah chapter includes short boxed examples which show how a particular concept or idea is used in practice. Where appropriate **quantitative examples and exercises** have been included to help explain planning and control concepts and analysis tools. Full solutions are provided in the appendix.

Mini Cases:

The book includes many **mini cases** to illustrate current practice and key concepts defined and described in the book.

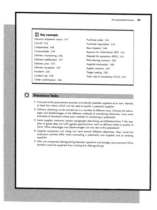

Discussion Questions:

These questions encourage you to review and apply the knowledge you have acquired from each chapter.

Conclusion and Summary:

The briefly reviews and reinforces the main topics that you will have covered in each chapter to ensure that you have acquired a solid understanding of the key topics. Use it as a quick reference to check you've understood the chapter.

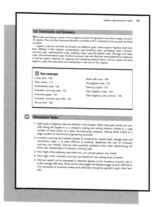

Key Concepts:

These are highlighted the first time they are introduced, alerting you to the core concepts and techniques in each chapter. A full explanation is contained in the glossary at the end of the book.

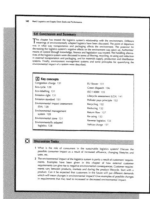

Glossary of Key Concepts:

At the end of the book a glossary of key concepts in alphabetical order provides full definitions of all the main terms that have been introduced throughout each chapter. The numbers of the pages on which key term definitions appear are colour-highlighted in the index.

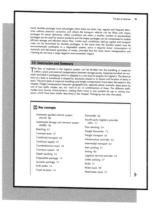

Technology to enhance learning and teaching

*Visit **www.mcgraw-hill.co.uk/textbooks/Jonsson** today*

Online Learning Centre (OLC)

After completing each chapter, log on to the supporting Online Learning Centre website. Take advantage of the study tools offered to reinforce the material you have read in the text, and to develop your knowledge in a fun and effective way.

Resources for students include:

- *Glossary*
- *Weblinks*
- *Learning objectives*

Also available for lecturers:

- *Lecturer manual*
- *PowerPoint slides*
- *Short abswers to discussion questions*
- *Quantitative and qualitative cases with solutions*

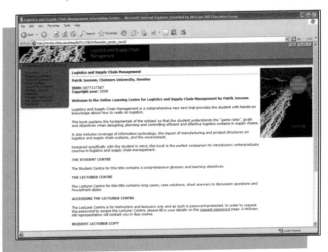

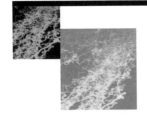

Custom Publishing Solutions: Let us help make our content your solution

At McGraw-Hill Education our aim is to help the lecturer find the most suitable content for their needs and the most appropriate way to deliver the content to their students. Our **custom publishing solutions** offer the ideal combination of content delivered in the way which suits lecturer and students the best.

The idea behind our custom publishing programme is that via a database of over two million pages called Primis, www.primisonline.com the lecturer can select just the material they wish to deliver to their students:

Lecturers can select chapters from:

- textbooks
- professional books
- case books – Harvard Articles, Insead, Ivey, Darden, Thunderbird and BusinessWeek
- Taking Sides – debate materials

Across the following imprints:

- McGraw-Hill Education
- Open University Press
- Harvard Business School Press
- US and European material

There is also the option to include material authored by lecturers in the custom product – this does not necessarily have to be in English.

We will take care of everything from start to finish in the process of developing and delivering a custom product to ensure that lecturers and students receive exactly the material needed in the most suitable way.

With a **Custom Publishing Solution**, students enjoy the best selection of material deemed to be the most suitable for learning everything they need for their courses – something of real value to support their learning. Teachers are able to use exactly the material they want, in the way they want, to support their teaching on the course.

Please contact *your local McGraw-Hill representative* with any questions or alternatively contact Warren Eels e: warren_eels@mcgraw-hill.com.

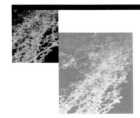

Acknowledgements

Our thanks go to the following reviewers for their comments at various stages in the text's development:

Dotun Adebanjo: University of Liverpool
Eirll Bo: BI Norwegian School of Management
Ben Clegg: Aston Business School
Linda Englyst: Aalborg University
Jens Horluck: University of Aarhus
John Lindegren: University of Gävle
Christer Lindh: Kth Royal Institute of Technology
Luc Muyldermans: University of Nottingham
Mikael Ronnqvist: Norwegian School of Economics and Business Administration
Chris Savage: University of Huddersfield
Hugo van den Berg: University of Johannesburg
Robert van den Berg: Nelson Manadela Metropolitan University.

Every effort has been made to trace and acknowledge ownership of copyright and to clear permission for material reproduced in this book. The publishers will be pleased to make suitable arrangements to clear permission with any copyright holders whom it has not been possible to contact.

Author's Acknowledgements:
This book is an extension of the book *Logistik*, published in Swedish by Studentlitteratur, and co-authored by Patrick Jonsson and Stig-Arne Mattsson. I therefore, first of all want to acknowledge Stig-Arne Mattsson for his co-operation in writing the book *Logistik*. I also want to acknowledge Dr Magnus Blinge, Professor Lars-Erik Gadde, Professor Mats Johansson, Professor Kenth Lumsden, Dr Lars Medbo and Dr Johan Woxenius at Chalmers University of Technology and Dr Andreas Norrman at Lund University for contributing with case studies, exercises, background material and comments to separate chapters. All companies allowing me to use their material in case studies and illustrations also need to be thanked. I am also thankful to the lecturers and students who have used the Swedish book *Logistik* in courses and have given input to the work with this book. Finally, I am grateful to all reviewers who have provided valuable feedback and suggestions on semi-finished book chapters, and to the editorial team at McGraw-Hill; Rachel Gear, Karen Harlow and Jennifer Rotherham who have supported me in a great way during the entire development process of the book.

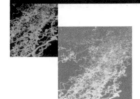

About the Author

Dr Patrik Jonsson is Professor of Operations and Supply Chain Management at Chalmers University of Technology, Sweden. He holds a PhD in production management from Lund University and is CFPIM and CSCP certified through APICS. At Chalmers he is currently Head of the PhD programme at the Department of Technology Management and Economics and lecturers in master's and executive training programmes in Supply Chain Management. He has during the last 15 years co-ordinated and taught numerous logistics and supply chain management courses and programmes at Växjö University and Chalmers University of Technology and in executive and further education programmes for people working in industry. His research which mainly has dealt with manufacturing planning and control, information systems, supplier structures and relations, outsourcing and performance management in supply chains has been published in journals such as *Journal of Operations Management, International Journal of Operations and Production Management, International Journal of Production Research, International Journal of Production Economics, Supply Chain Management: An International Journal* and *International Journal of Physical Distribution and Logistics Management.* He is currently on the editorial advisory boards of logistics and business journals.

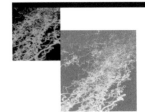

Preface

The aim of the book is to provide a fundamental understanding of all subject fields of logistics and supply chain management. The focus is on designing and controlling efficient and effective material flows through individual companies and in chains and networks of companies. The changing business conditions as results of globalisation, outsourcing of production processes to low cost countries, consolidation of logistics service providers and manufacturing companies, information technology development and improved environmental consciousness and customer satisfaction focus have grown the importance of logistics and supply chain management to be a strategic discipline with crucial significance for a company's competitiveness. These issues together with several traditional and general industrial conditions have been important starting points when designing and writing this book.

The choice of topics is first of all based on their industrial relevance. Emphasis is on issues and knowledge that should be of vital importance for companies. The book should therefore be as relevant for further education in industries as in university courses. The book is primarily written from a European manufacturing company's perspective but some sections and chapters take a distribution company's perspective. Still, most perspectives on logistics and supply chain management are general and the structure and content should thus be relevant for all types of companies dealing with flow of goods and being located on different continents.

The book is considered to be used in under-graduate university courses in logistics and supply chain management, and together with some complementary readings in introductory courses on graduate level. It treats all the component areas in logistics, both from an intra-organisational and inter-organisational supply chain perspective. The contents and chapters are divided into five parts:

Part I: The logistics and supply chain management disciplines
Part II: Logistics and supply chain goals and performances
Part III: Logistics and supply chain structures
Part IV: Logistics and supply chain planning and control
Part V: Extended perspective on logistics and supply chain management

The **first part** of the book describes the starting points of logistics and supply chain management and defines the various parts and perspectives of the logistics system. It also describes how storage, handling of materials, freight transport and packaging affect the physical flow of materials.

The **second part** treats the performance variables of the logistics system, which represents the goal and measurement system of logistics and supply chain management. The areas of customer service, costs, tied-up capital and environmental aspects are covered.

In the **third part**, about logistics and supply chain structures, different aspects of the products and items which flow through the supply chain are discussed. It also treats the usual supply strategies and their significance for the logistics system, as well as aspects of choice and design of supplier structures. The existing production conditions are described from the viewpoint of logistics and their significance for achieving efficient and effective flows. Alternative methods of organising production are also described, as are resource strategies in production. This part concludes with distribution strategies and distribution structures. The utility values contributed by distributors and the principal alternatives that can be applied to the design of distribution structures are included.

Part four, about logistics and supply chain planning and control, describes the customer order process, and processes and methods for forecasting. It treats materials management and contains different methods and aids to control the flow of materials and stocks. Some general and fundamental starting points and principles for this control are discussed, as well as the de-coupling functions for different types of stocks in the flow of materials. It also looks at different planning and control issues that are specific for manufacturing and distribution companies respectively. Included are principles of production activity control, transport planning and procurement.

The last **fifth part** of the book describes different emerging practices in supply chains and information systems for logistics and supply chain management. Various planning and execution systems are described, as well as communication and identification systems, and e-commerce. This part supports the previous chapters and is closely related to the issues described in Parts III and IV.

The book contains several mini cases illustrating current practices of key concepts defined and described in the book. Each chapter ends with discussion tasks and key terms with glossary, suggested further readings and when appropriate also quantitative exercises with full solutions in appendix. The instructors' manual contains teaching suggestions, power point presentation slides with all figures and tables in the book, suggested case studies and answers to all end of chapter discussion tasks.

PART 1
The Logistics and Supply Chain Management Disciplines

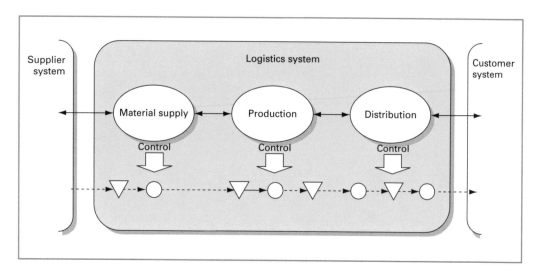

The first part of the book contains three chapters. The first two chapters describe the starting point of, and define different parts and perspectives of, logistics and supply chain management. The third chapter describes how packages, storage, materials handling and freight transport make up the physical flow of material.

Part Contents

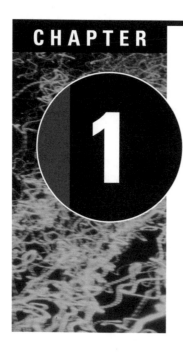

CHAPTER 1

Introduction to logistics and supply chain management

As consumers, we want to be able to visit a shop or an Internet website to buy clothes, food, furniture, books and so on. In much the same way, industrial companies require access to materials and components in order to manufacture products. Not only do customers demand the right functions and appearance in a product – it must also be available at exactly the place and time demanded and, moreover, at a reasonable price – preferably a very low one. In the case of, for example, clothes, wood products and electronics it is not unusual for raw materials to come from one continent, production to take place in another, and the product sold in a third. Thus, there is a great deal of transportation, handling and storage of the product and its component parts in the supply chain before it reaches the buyer. In the same way a great deal of information will have moved between those involved in activities related to material flows. **Logistics**, or the management of companies' supplies of materials, production and distribution, often plays a decisive role for many businesses in their attempts to satisfy customer needs efficiently, and indeed creates competitiveness.

The purpose of this book is to provide a fundamental understanding of the subject fields of logistics and supply chain management. The focus is on logistics in individual companies and in supply chains. This chapter contains an introduction to the subject and its in-depth treatment in subsequent chapters. Logistics and supply chain management are defined and described in terms of systems. Later, the goals of logistics and what is meant by efficient logistics are taken up, and in what ways contradictory goals may arise. Finally, the role of logistics and its significance in creating competitiveness are discussed.

1.1 What is Logistics and Supply Chain Management?

Logistics may be described as the science of the efficient flow of materials. It is a generic term for all the activities which together ensure that materials and products are at the right place at the right time, that is, create place and time utility. In common with all corporate financial interests, logistics is also aimed at increasing financial gain for the parties concerned. For the individual company this takes place through increased profitability, that is, through more income, lower costs and less working capital. Environmental demands, among others, are made on logistics from the social economic perspective. The term **supply chain management** is sometimes used to describe something similar to but not the same as logistics.

Definitions of logistics and supply chain management

Logistics is often described in terms of an approach, meaning that logistics is not only a number of techniques, methods or tools. Here, the logistics definition of the Council of Supply Chain Management Professionals (CSCMP; www.cscmp.org) is used:

> Logistics management is that part of supply chain management that plans, implements and controls the efficient, effective forward and reverse flow and storage of goods, services, and related information between the point of origin and the point of consumption in order to meet customers' requirements. Logistics management activities typically include inbound and outbound transportation management, fleet management, warehousing, materials handling, order fulfillment, logistics network design, inventory management, supply/demand planning, and management of third party logistics service providers. To varying degrees, the logistics function also includes sourcing and procurement, production planning and scheduling, packaging and assembly, and customer service. It is involved in all levels of planning and execution – strategic, operational, and tactical. Logistics management is an integrating function which coordinates and optimizes all logistics activities, as well as integrates logistics activities with other functions, including marketing, sales, manufacturing, finance, and information technology.

Logistics can be studied as an individual part of one company or as an integrated flow of **materials** through several companies. In the above definition, the flow of materials is from raw materials to end-user and includes the return flow of defective products, reusable packages and the recycling of used products, to name some examples. It is often necessary to have a wider perspective of the logistics system than within an individual company, since there is an interdependence between customers and suppliers, and synergies can be achieved if consideration is taken to the conditions and consequences for those outside the individual company.

Logistics can be divided into issues related to either structure or control. Structural issues are related to how systems for products, distribution, production and supply of materials should be designed for specific conditions. For example, they may dictate how much of the finished product is to be manufactured, the proportions of completed components to be purchased, who the suppliers will be, how deliveries will take place, how production layout and production organisation will be designed, whether the finished products will be stored or distributed directly to customers, and how transportation to customers will take place. The issues of control are related to planning and implementing efficient flows of materials starting with existing structures. Included in that work is the overall planning and execution of inbound deliveries, production and outbound deliveries so that the overall goals of the company and logistics can be achieved. In the shorter perspective this means planning quantities and timing for various items to be delivered to and from stores and production units, and initiating real transportation of materials.

In recent years the concept of supply chain management has come to be used as a similar concept to logistics. The overall aim of using this concept is to emphasise the significance of integrating flows within the individual company with other companies in the supply chain. Intra-organisational supply chains are also discussed – that is, supply chains which integrate flows in several internal units in a company. The Council of Supply Chain Management Professionals (CSCMP) defines supply chain management in a similar way to logistics:

Supply Chain Management encompasses the planning and management of all activities involved in sourcing and procurement, conversion, and all logistics management activities. Importantly, it also includes coordination and collaboration with channel partners, which can be suppliers, intermediaries, third-party service providers, and customers. In essence, supply chain management integrates supply and demand management within and across companies. Supply Chain Management is an integrating function with primary responsibility for linking major business functions and business processes within and across companies into a cohesive and high-performing business model. It includes all of the logistics management activities noted above, as well as manufacturing operations, and it drives coordination of processes and activities with and across marketing, sales, product design, finance and information technology.

In the definition of the Global Supply Chain Forum, "supply chain management is the integration of key processes from end user through original suppliers that provides products, services, and information that add value for customers and other stakeholders (Lambert, 2004)".

The above descriptions and definitions of logistics and supply chain management have the same integrated view of logistics and flows. In the CSCMP definition, however, logistics constitutes one part of the supply chain process. Supply chain management is not only concerned with the integration of material flows over company borders. It also involves more processes and activities in a company than those related to logistics, such as product development, marketing and so on. However, many processes interact and consequently processes not directly related to logistics can have an indirect impact on the logistics.

To create efficient logistics it is necessary to have both efficient and effective internal material flows and efficient and effective flows between companies. The supply chain focus in logistics underlines the significance of these external relationships and flows. Another important point made by CSCMP in their definition is the importance of information flow in creating efficient and effective logistics. The term "supply chain" is slightly misleading since it implies a linearity that is often not the case. The term "supply network" is therefore often used to emphasise that the actual flows are related in networks rather than in chains.

This book on logistics and supply chain management treats all the component areas in logistics, both from an intra-organisational and inter-organisational supply chain perspective. The contents are divided into five parts:

Part 1 – The logistics and supply chain management disciplines: The first part of the book consists of three chapters. The first two chapters describe the starting points of logistics and supply chain management and define the various parts and perspectives of the logistics system. The third chapter describes how storage, handling of materials, transport of goods and packaging affect the physical flow of materials.

Part 2 – Logistics and supply chain goals and performances: The three chapters in the second part treat the performance variables of the logistics system, which represents the goal and measurement system of logistics. The areas of customer service, costs, tied-up capital and environmental aspects are covered.

Part 3 – Logistics and supply chain structures: In the first chapter of the third part, different aspects of the products and items which flow through the supply chain are discussed. The second chapter treats the usual supply strategies and their significance for the logistics system, as well as aspects of choice and design of supplier structures. The third chapter clarifies existing production conditions from the viewpoint of logistics and their significance for achieving efficient and effective flows. Alternative methods of organising production are also described, as are resource strategies in production. This part concludes with a chapter on distribution strategies and distribution structures. The utility values contributed by distributors and the principal alternatives that can be applied to the design of distribution structures are included.

Part 4 – Planning and control of logistics and supply chain systems: This part consists of five chapters. The first describes the customer order process, and processes and methods for forecasting. The second treats materials management and contains different methods and aids to control the flow of materials and stocks. Some general and fundamental starting points and principles for this control are discussed, as well as the de-coupling functions for different types of stocks in the flow of materials. The subsequent two chapters look at different planning and control issues that are specific for manufacturing and distribution companies respectively. Included are principles of production activity control and transport planning. The last chapter describes the purchasing process from a logistics perspective.

Part 5 – Supply chain, IT and improvement aspects of logistics: The last part of the book contains two chapters. The first describes different emerging practices in supply chains. The second is about information systems for logistics and supply chain management. Various planning and execution systems are described, as well as communication and identification systems, and e-commerce. Both chapters support the previous chapters and are closely related to the issues described in Parts III and IV.

Logistics as a system

A system is constructed on subsystems which in turn contain a collection of interrelated **components**. An open system has an exchange with its surroundings, whereas a closed system does not. Logistics is often described as a system. It is always open: that is, it has an exchange with its surroundings. Exactly where the limits of the logistics system lie will vary from case to case. In the same way, the subsystems and components included also vary. If the limits of the logistics system correspond to those of the company then it is common to include the subsystems for supply of materials, production and distribution.

The relationships between the subsystems and components included, and between the system and its surroundings, take the form of co-ordination and exchange of materials and information. The relationships between subsystems and components in the system give rise to synergy effects, meaning that the combination and co-operation of subsystems and components can produce a higher total system effect than that possible from the individual components and subsystems.

The aim of the system is to supply customers efficiently with their required products. Each subsystem controls the size and timing of the flow of materials through the system via storage, transportation and various stages of handling and product value adding, as illustrated in Figure 1.1. In the materials **supply system**, for example, consignments larger than the exact quantity required for manufacturing a batch of products are often purchased. The surplus not used directly when it arrives from the supplier is placed in storage. During the operational steps in the manufacturing process there are also cases of temporary storage in the form of buffers and queues ahead of certain groups of machines. When a product's manufacture is completed it may be placed in finished goods stocks before it is delivered. Efficient distribution may also make temporary storage in central and regional warehouses advantageous. Transportation between storage points takes place, and during the production process value adding is carried out in which materials are processed into components and products. Product value adding sometimes takes place during distribution – for example, in the form of repackaging.

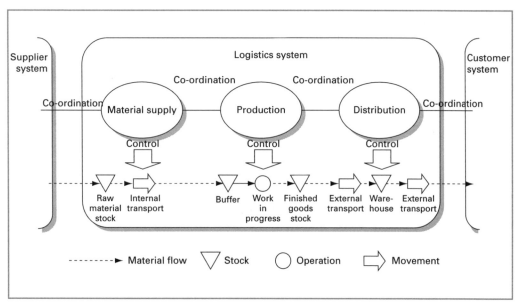

FIGURE 1.1 Logistics systems with the company as a limit. It consists of the subsystems' material supply, production and distribution

The distribution system

Distribution has a close relationship to the overall market strategy, which originates in the market's and customers' needs, and determines what delivery service distribution must achieve, among other things. For example, a market strategy that aims at supplying a number of consumers daily with inexpensive standard products over a large area will require a different distribution structure from one aimed at occasionally distributing complex manufacturing equipment with customer-specific functions to industrial companies. In the first case, consolidated shipment, temporary storage and sales through retail outlets may be necessary to minimise costs and enable sufficiently short delivery times. In the second case, distribution costs and delivery times may be less significant and distribution direct to the customer company and installation in the customer's plant may be part of a suitable distribution structure. If the limits of the logistics system correspond to the limits of the company, then the subsystems of distribution will be main related to the downstream environment – the company's customers. It is necessary to understand that the vending company's distribution must be adapted to customer needs and that commitments do not end on dispatch from the company, but only when the customer's needs have been satisfied. This may mean that distribution is extended as far as the customer's warehouse shelves or production line, or that it continues until the equipment delivered is installed and fully functional.

The production system

From the perspective of logistics, production means those structures and systems that control the flow of materials in production through supplying production resources with information on where and how much is to be produced by machines and personnel, and to ensure access to materials and components. Thus, the logistics of the production system co-ordinates machines, personnel and materials to achieve an efficient production process. The **production system** is closely integrated with the material supply system. When materials are supplied to a raw material store, the interface is set between the two subsystems on outbound delivery from the raw material store. When materials are supplied directly to a production line, materials supply merges into production when the material is accessible at the company premises. The interface with the distribution system is at the inbound delivery of finished products in the finished goods store or, if they are not stored, at the dispatch to customers.

The material supply system

The purpose of materials supply is to supply production with raw materials and components. Materials supply is directly connected with the supplier's distribution system and the individual company's production system. In the same way as in other subsystems, it cannot operate independently of other subsystems and surroundings. Information on the needs of customers and production must be the basis of materials supply. For example, information is required on material needs for future planned production and demands on size of shipments and delivery frequencies to be adapted to assembly work in production. Materials supply must also be adapted to suppliers' distribution and production. If the demand for small and frequent inbound deliveries gives rise to an increase in tied-up capital at the supplier, for example, since the supplier cannot manufacture such small batches as the customer demands, total tied-up capital and costs will increase.

Logistics system and the supply chain

Logistics systems do not only consist of flows of materials, components and products which are processed and distributed to customers, but also include supply chain flows of spare parts and return flows of defective and used products and packaging.

It has become increasingly important to regard the logistics system as a supply chain, not confining the logistics system to the company's boundaries but including the entire material flow from raw material to end-users in the same system. There is a striving towards optimal efficiency and effectiveness in the entire supply chain and not only for individual companies. In practice, however, it is often difficult to identify one clear supply chain. Instead, companies are part of a network of many supply chains. The most common approach is to include direct suppliers and customers in the same logistics system, but not secondary and tertiary level suppliers, as shown

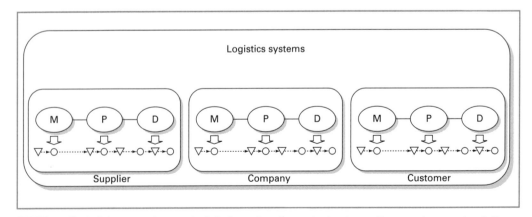

FIGURE 1.2 The logistics system in a supply chain. It consists of several subsystems with companies as system limits

in Figure 1.2. As a result of the interdependence of customers and suppliers, this broader perspective nearly always gives rise to increased efficiency and effectiveness from the individual company's perspective, also. The flow of materials in a supply chain is often compared with a flow of water. If the company being studied is placed in the middle, the flow of materials on the supply side is referred to as upstream, and on the customer side, downstream. Suppliers that deliver directly to the company being studied are called tier 1 suppliers, those that deliver directly to tier 1 suppliers are called tier 2 suppliers, and so on. The boundaries between the logistics system and logistics in supply chains are described in more detail in the next chapter.

1.2 Goals and Performances of Logistics

The purpose of logistics is to create competitiveness and high performance by improving companies' efficiency and effectiveness so as to positively affect profits, but in an environmentally friendly way. Performance can be expressed in terms of different performance variables, each one representing a particular aspect of performance. By setting up goals defined by performance variables, measuring them and following them up, it is possible to formulate a business approach that supports competitiveness and which accords with the company's overall strategy and goals. The logistics system's influence on performance can be expressed with the aid of variables that affect the company's revenue, the company's costs, the company's assets and the environment. There are also variables that indirectly measure the capacity of the logistics system to fulfil performance goals. The system's time and flexibility characteristics are examples of such variables. Logistics' main performance variables and their interrelationships are shown in Figure 1.3. Several of the performance variables are inversely proportional to each other and must be internally prioritised and related to the company's overall goals. The prioritised performance variables then become the starting points when establishing the goals of logistics, and indeed are the basis of a logistics strategy.

Customer service

The influence of logistics on revenues takes place by creating good customer service, which is brought about with the help of activities related to customer contact and delivery of products and services. The logistics system can contribute to **customer service** by creating a good delivery service, supplying information on material flows or other logistics services.

Customer service consists of a mix of different service elements which are more or less important in different situations. In the case of deliveries from finished stocks, the warehouse service level – the extent to which an item is accessible in the warehouse for direct delivery – is

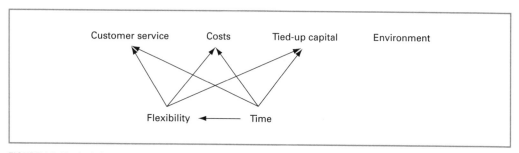

FIGURE 1.3 The logistics system's performance variables. Arrows indicate links between variables

an important measure of the quality of the customer service offered. The period of delivery time and the reliability of promised delivery times are important customer service elements in most situations. **Delivery flexibility** is another service element. This means the capacity to adapt to and comply with changed customer requirements in agreed and ongoing orders. For example, it could mean changing delivery times or ordering quantities at short notice, which is not an uncommon demand for many suppliers.

To create customer service with the help of information on material flows is about enabling the exchange of information with the aim of decreasing uncertainties in planning for the parties involved. Many products are also combined with peripheral services, whose structure can have a positive effect on customer service. It could include giving the product a customer-specific package or label, handling it in the customer's packaging solution, packaging it together with other products, affixing bar codes for subsequent handling by the customer, etc.

Costs

The logistics system influences a number of cost items. The physical handling, moving and storage of materials give rise to costs in terms of personnel, materials, operation and deprecia-tion. The logistics system also incurs costs for administrative personnel and information systems whose purpose is to plan and control the physical flow of materials. **Tied-up capital** along the flow of materials also creates logistics costs. When an order cannot be delivered in accordance with agreement, shortage costs and delay costs arise if measures are necessary to compensate for the missing or late delivery. Warehouse costs, shortage costs and delay costs are to some extent the trade-off for costs in increased capacity. This is the case if buffer stocks are replaced by over-capacity in the production plant to deal with fluctuations in demand.

Tied-up capital

A company's assets can be divided into fixed assets and current assets. Investing in assets ties up capital. Tied-up capital affects a company's cash flow and solvency, but it also incurs costs equiv-alent to the potential returns on invested capital if it had been used in another way; for example, deposited in a bank account.

Fixed assets are those assets which are utilised over a long time period such as buildings, machines, computer systems and so on. They give rise to costs in the form of depreciation. The degree of capacity utilisation affects the unit cost, since at a lower utilisation level a smaller number of products must bear the same fixed costs of a manufacturing machine.

Current assets refer to assets of a more temporary nature such as materials in stock, in pro-duction or transport, and accounts receivable. The capital tied up in accounts receivable is due to the flow of payment, which may partly be affected by logistics. Late deliveries, for example, can give rise to delayed settlement. Tied-up capital from a logistics perspective normally refers to capital involved in the flow of materials, that is, materials that are held in raw material and component stocks, in production, in finished stocks or distribution stocks and in transport.

Flexibility

As described earlier, delivery flexibility is an important part of customer service which can create value for the customer. It has also been mentioned that the capacity to vary production and delivery volumes by deciding to invest in overcapacity may incur flexibility-related costs, which can lead to lower tied-up capital and increased customer service. The flexibility of the logistics system, then, has an indirect influence on the performance variables of customer service, costs and tied-up capital. 'Agility' is a word sometimes used to describe a logistics system that is dynamic and adaptable to rapid external changes, i.e. is flexible. Due to its increasing signifi-cance in many logistics systems and its influence on other performance variables, flexibility is dealt with here as a separate performance variable. A distinction is normally made between delivery flexibility, **product mix flexibility** and **volume flexibility**.

- *Delivery flexibility* is an expression of the ability, when required, to make changes in deliveries in order to adapt to customers' changing needs. The ability is determined by factors such as length of promised delivery times, throughput times, set-up times and batch sizes in production.

- *Product mix flexibility* means the ability within the existing capacity to rapidly adapt production and material supplies to shifts in demand between existing products and product variants. This ability is affected by factors such as delivery times for purchase items, size of batches in production and the length of throughput times.

- *Volume flexibility* expresses the ability to rapidly increase or decrease production and delivery volumes independently of any simultaneous mix changes. The ability is deter-mined by delivery times for purchase items, the size of stocks of raw materials, throughput times, batch size in production and the degree of overcapacity, or utilisa-tion of capacity in the existing plant.

Time

The focus on time is central in the logistics system since time influences the other performance variables. Without a time-efficient logistics system it is difficult to create a totally efficient logis-tics system. The significance of short and reliable delivery times as part of the delivery service and rapid deliveries of spare parts after delivery have already been discussed. Delivery time is sometimes called **time-to-customer (TTC)**.

To make possible short delivery times to customers in the case of engineer to customer order or production to customer order, throughput times and set-up times in business activities must be short. Without short throughput times for those activities which are carried out after receipt of order until dispatch, there is a risk that delivery times will become longer than what is accept-able to customers, more capital will be tied up in the flow and it will take longer to react to changes in customer requirements. The fact that materials with a long throughput time are tied up for longer also increases the risk that the product cannot be sold when it eventually becomes available: in other words, the risk of obsolescence increases. Without short set-up times it is not defensible in terms of cost to manufacture small batches required for manufacturing directly to customer orders. In addition, long set-up times give rise to large manufacturing batches, which in turn result in higher levels of tied-up capital. Short throughput, set-up and delivery times for purchase items also improve all the other flexibility variables, since it is faster and less costly to make changes in orders already accepted.

The innovation capacity of a company is also affected by time. A short product development time, called **time-to-market (TTM)**, or the time from product concept to product launch, can provide a time advantage on the market with respect to competitors. This lead can be increased further with the help of short delivery times.

It is also important to have time-efficient order cycles, which can be achieved through the simplification and automation of parts of the customer order process. Orders of standard items can, for example, be generated automatically in the customer's system when a certain stock level of the items has been reached, and sent to the supplier's system which automatically approves and registers the order. Such a procedure means not only that the order process is faster than a manual process, but that it is also more cost-effective. The logistics system is also dependent on high-quality planning information in the form of sales statistics, forecasts, stock balance information and so on. The quality of information deteriorates when such information is conveyed with time lags. When decision-makers involved have real-time access to necessary information both from their own activities and from other companies' activities in the supply chain, this has a positive influence on efficiency and effectiveness.

Environment

The environmental demands which society, industry, public administration and customers put on industrial and public activities have direct consequences for logistics systems. The environmental impact of logistics systems is through pollution, emissions, noise from transportation, high-energy consumption, poor handling of waste and recycling and so on. The environment is affected by most parts of the logistics system such as production, distribution, after-market, return flows, packaging, product development and overall system design.

An example of logistics-related measures aimed at minimising environmental impact is the adaptation of technical systems through the use of alternative vehicles, engines and fuels which

---

CASE STUDY 1.1: SCOR MEASURES

The Supply Chain Operations Reference-model (SCOR) was developed by the Supply Chain Council (SCC). As part of the model, five supply chain performance attributes and nine related measures were defined:

Attribute	Measure
Supply chain reliability	*Perfect order fulfillment:* Percentage of orders meeting delivery performance with complete and accurate documentation and no delivery damage.
Supply chain responsiveness	*Order fulfillment cycle time:* Average speed at which the supply chain delivers products to customers.
Supply chain flexibility	*Upside supply chain flexibility:* Number of days an organization requires to achieve an unplanned sustainable 20% increase in quantities delivered.
	Upside supply chain adaptability: Amount of increased production an organization can achieve and sustain in 30 days
	Downside supply chain adaptability: Reduction in quantities ordered sustainable at 30 days prior to delivery with no inventory or cost penalties.
Supply chain costs	*Supply chain management costs (SCMC):* All direct and indirect expenses associated with operating SCOR business processes across the supply chain.
	Cost of goods sold (COGS): Supply chain expenses not measured in supply chain management costs.
Supply chain asset management	*Cash-to-cash cycle time:* Time required for an investment in raw materials to flow back in an organization.
	Return of supply chain fixed assets: Return an organization receives on capital invested in supply chain fixed assets used in plan, source, make, deliver, and return activities.

Source: Supply Chain Council, *Supply-Chain Operations Reference-model Version 7.0.*

are more environmentally friendly. They may also involve combined transport, such as flexible road transportation with environmentally friendly railroad transport, or consolidating goods from several customers with the aim of increasing the load fill rate and decreasing the number of transports. Financial controls may be applied with the purpose of encouraging the logistics system to be more environmentally friendly. Road tolls and environment taxes are examples of such measures.

There are a number of tools and environmental management systems whose purpose is to facilitate, structure and evaluate companies' environment work. Most of them can be utilised to adapt the logistics system to long-term environmental sustainability.

CASE STUDY 1.2: LOGISTICS AND SUPPLY CHAIN GOALS AT VOLVO TRUCKS CORP.

Volvo Truck has nine own assembly plants worldwide. In addition, trucks are assembled at eight plants not owned by Volvo. The company continuously monitors the logistics and supply-chain performances. These are examples of logistics and supply-chain-related goals at Volvo Trucks:

♦ **Leadtime** reduction from order to delivery (average number of days)

♦ Inbound delivery precision (proportion of deliveries on promised day)

♦ "Direct runners" (proportion of totally assembled products without failures direct from assembly)

♦ Product quality (max points based on the number of failures and the criticality of the failures)

♦ Inventory turnover rate (number of days in stock)

♦ Sustainability (e.g. energy consumption)

Logistics and profitability

Since one long-term goal for all companies is to maintain a high return on capital invested in the company, it is natural to view the logistics system as a mechanism for creating high returns. A company's yield is usually measured as annual profits in relation to its total capital tied up in assets and is called profitability or **return on capital employed (ROCE)**, and is calculated using the following formula and expressed as a percentage:

$$\text{Return on capital employed} \ = \ \frac{\text{Profit}}{\text{Total capital employed}} \ = \ \frac{\text{Revenues} - \text{Costs}}{\text{Total capital employed}}$$

The logistics system affects yield through the variables of customer service, costs and tied-up capital. By focusing on and decreasing the total tied-up capital in stocks, production and transport, it is possible directly to improve the rate of return on capital employed. In a corresponding fashion, decreases in unnecessary costs in the flow of materials caused by long set-up times, unnecessary purchasing administration or low fill rates in transport vehicles would lead to an immediate decrease in return on capital employed. Customer service will also affect a company's yield. By raising service in those areas critical to customers and reducing it in areas which are less crucial – for example, by giving priority to important customer service elements, customers and product groups, the company can offer a better overall delivery service at only a marginally

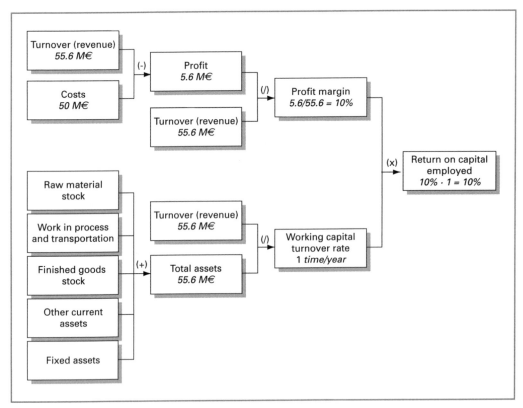

FIGURE 1.4 The DuPont model

higher cost or possibly even a lower cost. The improved delivery service will have an indirect influence on the return on capital employed since it is aimed at creating added value for customers and increasing total revenue in the long term. One way of illustrating these effects on the return on capital employed is to use the DuPont model, as in Figure 1.4. Revenue of €55.6 millions, total costs of €50 millions and total capital tied up in assets of €55.6 millions result in a profit of €5.6 millions, a profit margin of 10 per cent and a working capital turnover rate of one time per year. The return on capital employed is calculated by multiplying the profit margin and working capital turnover rate, in this example 10 per cent multiplied by 1, resulting in 10 per cent return on capital employed.

The return on capital employed is a product of the profit margin (the profit in relation to turnover) and working capital turnover rate (average tied-up capital in relation to turnover). Thus, to achieve a higher return on capital employed percentage it is necessary to increase the profit margin and/or the working capital turnover rate. Customer service and direct cost reductions will influence the profit margin through their effects on profit. Tied-up capital caused by tied-up materials constitutes part of the total capital and therefore exerts an influence on the working capital turnover rate.

In many situations measures for improvement can have a positive impact on both profit margins and working capital turnover rate. Such is the case, for example, when set-up times in production are reduced. If a company succeeds in shortening set-up times the result will be better utilisation of machines' capacity, since less time is taken by non-value-added set-up and more time can be utilised for production. Through the increase in available capacity it is possible that overtime work and other costly practices can be decreased, which will result in lower production costs per unit and increased profit margins. Shortened set-up times will also increase the financial possibility of manufacturing small, customer-specific batches, which can increase customer service and thereby generate additional sales or make a higher sales price possible. This will also give rise to increased profit margins. Shortened set-up times will also influence tied-up capital, since they enable the manufacture of smaller batches. Such measures have an influence on tied-up capital both during production and storage. The reduction in tied-up capital results in an increased working capital turnover rate and therefore increased return on capital employed.

However, it is not the case that all improvements have such a direct and major impact on both profit margins and working capital turnover rate. It is therefore necessary to give priority to certain improvements to achieve the best possible effects on profitability. If a company with a return on capital employed of 10 per cent has a profit margin of 10 per cent and a working

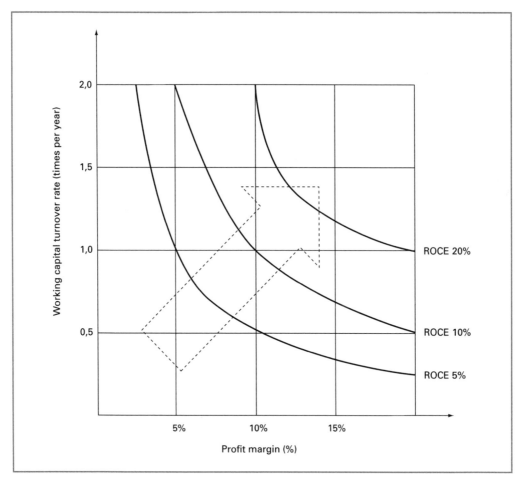

FIGURE 1.5 Example of a profitability diagram showing the relationship between profit margin and working capital turnover rate
The arrow shows the direction of increased profitability measured as return on capital employed

capital turnover rate equivalent to once per year, a rationalisation of costs that decreases the total annual costs from €50 million to 49 million will mean that the profit margin increases to 11.8 per cent and that the return on capital employed also increases to 11.8 per cent. If, on the other hand, the company was to make the same rationalisation with a return on capital employed of 10 per cent but a profit margin of only 1 per cent and the working capital turnover rate was 10 times per year, the resulting profit margin would be 3 per cent whereas the return on capital employed would be 29.8 per cent. The same decrease in costs in absolute terms results in different levels of profitability improvements. This is because the percentage profit increase is higher in the latter case. In the same way, the influence on profitability of capital rationalisation depends on whether the original working capital turnover rate was high or low. A low working capital turnover rate and a high profit margin require less capital rationalisation in absolute terms than a high working capital turnover rate and a low profit margin. The opposite relationship also exists; when a company has a high working capital turnover rate and a low profit margin, a relatively low absolute increase in profits is required to achieve a relatively high improvement in profitability. The relationship between profit margin and working capital turnover rate is illustrated in Figure 1.5.

Conflicting goals in logistics

The aim of a logistics system is naturally that it should have high quality with respect to goals and performance variables. However, it is necessary to be aware of the conflicting nature of individual variables and that they may be assigned different levels of importance by different people in a company.

A majority of performance variables are, in fact, conflicting. As a result of these inverse relationships, certain priorities must normally be assigned to the variables. It is not a question of optimising one individual performance variable, but rather striving towards the best overall **performance** based on the **trade-off** between several variables. One example of conflicting variables is that high levels of customer service, which can be created through large finished goods stocks, will in turn demand much tied-up capital and high storage costs. Short throughput time in production can be achieved by small manufacturing batches, but this creates low capacity utilisation and high manufacturing cost per unit due to set-up times. It is especially important to balance the trade-offs between customer service, costs and tied-up capital. The three variables have direct profitability impact. The goal should be to create an optimum balance of the three variables, and not to increase one variable at the expense of the other, if that doesn't result in improved total performances.

There are not only goal conflicts between performance variables but also between a company's different departments. The reason is that many companies operate as functional organisations, that is, different departments are specialised and focus on their own well-defined tasks, each striving to minimise its own costs and tied-up capital without considering the whole flow of materials and acting in the best overall interest. Such an approach easily leads to sub-optimisation – individual departments are optimised at the cost of overall performance. Another effect is that employees tend to focus on their own particular tasks to satisfy the manager instead of the customer. The focus then tends to be on efficient use of resources rather than customer value. Table 1.1 provides some examples of common goal conflicts between functions.

One picture of demands which is common for many companies is to have good cashflow, high flexibility, short delivery times and many product variants. At the same time it is becoming more common to have material flows that lead directly from external supplier to component production, from component production to final assembly, and from final assembly to customer without interim storage. In such situations functions become more interdependent, and there are

	Purchasing	**Production**	**Market**	**Finance**
Goal?	Low purchase prices	Low manufacturing costs	High revenues	High profits, good cash flow, low tied-up capital
Customer service?	Large batches and long delivery times to customers are preferable: we then have time for purchases and can gain quantity discounts.	We cannot decrease batch sizes because this causes too much set-up time, which decreases available production capacity.	Customers demand very small and frequent deliveries with short delivery times.	Smaller batches are positive: tied-up capital in stocks decreases, which gives positive effects on cash flow.
Size of stocks?	We can gain quantity discounts if we purchase large quantities.	Large stocks of raw materials decrease the risk of shortages in input material, and since large production batches reduce the number of set-ups, this is preferable.	Customers demand short delivery times, necessitating that all products are available in finished goods stocks.	Large stocks cost too much and cause poor cash flow. They must be kept to a minimum.
Transport and production costs?	"Unnecessary" transportation costs too much. Goods must be consolidated into larger shipments.	By manufacturing larger batches, production costs per unit can be minimised.	Customers demand short delivery times. Consolidated deliveries are not possible since we must send the goods as soon as we get the order. We must be able to manufacture small batches with short leadtimes so that unique customer orders can be quickly supplied.	

TABLE 1.1 Examples of goal conflicts between the functions of purchasing, production, market and finance

higher demands on co-ordination between the different areas of responsibility. The functional organisation, focused on specialisation and use of resources, is seldom the best form of organisation in this case. A more flow-oriented or process-oriented distribution of responsibility and organisation is required, where the focus is on the processes of logistics aimed at efficiently creating value for the customer instead of optimising the use of resources within one particular function. This type of focus normally demands increased co-operation and contributions from many of the traditional functions as in Figure 1.6, where the flow and process orientation illustrates a focus on processes which cut across the functions instead of focusing on individual functions as isolated silos.

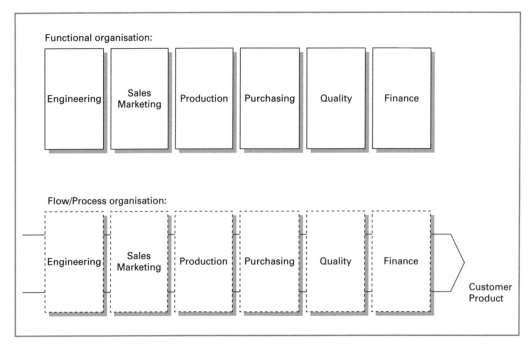

FIGURE 1.6 Function-oriented versus process-oriented organisational structures

1.3 Logistics as a Means of Competition

A well-designed and well-utilised logistics system can create efficiency in different ways for an organisation. However, it is not sufficient only to perform efficient logistics activities. In order to create competitiveness for the company it is also essential that the right type of logistics solutions is performed and the right performance variables are given priority, i.e. the efficiency is turned into effectiveness. Performance variables are variables that impact the efficiency and effectiveness and the success of a company. There is no point in being good at something which is not appreciated by customers or other key stakeholders, such as suppliers, owners and employees. To decide on logistics solutions and how to execute them in order to create competitiveness, the logistics strategy must be aligned with the organisation's other strategies. The starting point for strategic logistics planning is to focus on the customers and group the performance variables into **order-qualifiers** and **order-winners** for products and services.

Order-qualifiers and order-winners

To prioritise different performance variables it is necessary to understand how they influence a company's competitive situation. A common and practical way of doing this is to distinguish between variables which are **order-qualifiers** and those which are order-winners.

Order-qualifies are those variables which open doors to a market but which in themselves do not mean that a customer buys a **product**. They may be seen as a minimum level of performance required for a customer to even consider buying offered products and services. Order-winners are those variables which are decisive for a customer choosing a product or not. It is thus essential to ensure the necessary performance of qualifying variables and to prioritise order-winning variables to be more competitive. For many products and markets, for example, it is necessary to offer almost perfect product quality, short delivery times and a reasonable price, at the same time as it must be simple for a customer to place a purchase order if he is even going to consider buying a product. In such a situation, these variables are order-qualifiers. It may subsequently be the total purchase costs (including the purchase price) and the ability to adapt at short notice to changes in delivery times and delivery volumes that are decisive for whether the customer purchases the product or chooses a competitor. Total costs and delivery flexibility will then be order winners and will determine which supplier the customer finally chooses.

Which variables are order-qualifiers and which are order-winners may vary between a company's different products and sometimes also between different markets for the same product. For a clothes manufacturer, quality and delivery service may be qualifiers and the price an order-winner for a standard garment, whereas a maximum price and delivery service are qualifiers and product characteristics are order-winners for a fashion garment. Logistics with small resources, small stock levels and cost-effective flows of standard fabrics and garments are therefore important logistical challenges for standard garments, whereas being sufficiently cost-effective and being able to adapt very quickly to changes in customer demands for different product models and types of fabric are logistical challenges for fashion garments.

Order-qualifiers and order-winners do not only vary between products and markets. They also change over time. At the start of a new product's lifecycle, when supply is not very large and volumes relatively small, maximum price is often a qualifier and must be held under a certain maximum level so that customers can afford to buy the product. In the same way, delivery service is a qualifier and must not be too poor even if the customer in this situation is prepared to wait for the product. It is the unique product characteristics which are order-winners. When the product has come into the maturity phase of its lifecycle, or when volumes have increased and the competition is tougher, the variables of order-qualifiers and order-winners change. Many of the previous order-winners now become order-qualifiers. Product characteristics are seen as a matter of course and must be offered for the customer to even consider purchasing. Instead it is often costs and certain differentiated customer service characteristics, such as responsiveness, which become order-winners.

Logistics strategy

A strategy consists of those plans or patterns of actions that integrate an organisation's primary goals, policies and activities into a coherent whole. A well-formulated strategy helps to utilise all the resources of an organisation and create value based on its internal competence and shortcomings with respect to the external environment. A strategy may be planned down to the finest detail and far in advance in order to fulfil specific goals. A strategy can also evolve as a consistent pattern of action in business activities, without necessarily having been planned in advance. Most strategies are partly planned and partly evolved.

A logistics strategy consists of those plans or patterns of actions that relate to the flow of materials. It is sometimes called a *functional strategy*. In concert with other functional strategies it is aimed at supporting current order-qualifies and order-winners so that competitiveness can be created according to a defined business strategy, and by extension, so that the long-term goals of growth and yield can be achieved.

A strategy must be focused to some extent, meaning that it is not possible to support too many conflicting performance variables. For example, it is often difficult using the same system to competitively offer both high-volume products demanding low costs at the same time as low-volume products with many variants. The two types of products normally put far too many different demands on the various systems of a business, not least the logistics system. For this reason it is

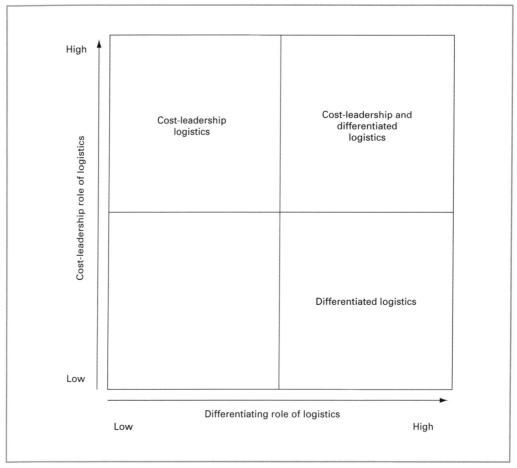

FIGURE 1.7 The role of logistics in cost-leading and differentiated strategies

usually said that a strategy must be focused and aimed at certain performance variables, making it possible to specialise activities. Competitive advantage is achieved by knowing the performance variables relevant for the key stakeholders and developing superior performance on these variables.

A common method of focusing a business strategy is to determine to what extent the company will be a cost-leader or will offer unique, differentiated products and services. Different logistics solutions will be necessary if the business strategy is to be a cost-leader, differentiated with respect to products and customer service commitment, or if it will be a cost-leader at the same time as demands are put on differentiated customer service, as in Figure 1.7. A logistics cost-leadership strategy may focus on minimising the physical logistics costs for transportation, storage, etc. A differentiation strategy may focus on short leadtimes and quick response to fluctuating customer demands. Combining cost-leadership and differentiation may require parallel-focused logistics systems that support different performance variables. For example, outsourced production to low-cost countries could focus on creating cost capabilities for the assortment and volumes with high forecast accuracy, and in-house production close to the markets could focus on creating quick response and flexibility capabilities for the volumes with fluctuating demand.

It is also important to underline the significance of co-ordination of logistics strategies between different organisations that are active in the same supply chain so that they do not use systems with different goals and conditions. The point is not only to align logistics strategies with the company's other strategies, but also to co-ordinate them with customers and suppliers in the supply chain. Superior logistics and supply chain management strategies are often achieved through structural changes of the supply chain, such as specific supplier and customer relationships, allowing for efficient information and material flows or technical developments and innovations. Competitiveness is no longer only conducted between companies. It is to a greater extent groups, chains or networks of companies that together form an enterprise structure and develop competitive advantage and compete with other groups, chains and networks of companies. Thus, competition takes place between supply chains, which calls for supply chain strategies.

1.4 Conclusion and Summary

This chapter has introduced and defined the subjects of logistics and supply chain management, from the starting point of how logistics can create efficiency and effectiveness in a company and supply chain. The goal from a corporate financial perspective is to create profitability through high customer service, low costs, low tied-up capital, high flexibility and short times. From a social economic perspective, environmental aspects are important.

Trade-offs arise between different logistics goals, both between individual performance variables and between goals in the company's different departments. To develop competitive strategies it is important to be aware of these conflicting trade-offs, to consider equally all performance variables and to create forms of organisation which as far as possible eliminate conflicts between departments.

🔑 Key concepts

Components 6	Production system 7
Customer service 9	Product mix flexibility 11
Delivery flexibility 10	Products 18
Distribution system 7	Return on capital employed (ROCE) 13
Leadtime 13	Supply chain management 4
Logistics 3	Supply system 6
Materials 4	Tied-up capital 10
Order-qualifier 18	Time-to-customer (TTC) 11
Order-winner 18	Time-to-market (TTM) 11
Performance trade-off 16	Volume flexibility 11

Discussion Tasks

1 Some organisations use the terms *value chain*, *demand chain* and *supply network* as substitutes to logistics and supply chain management. Compare these terms by, for example, searching on the Internet.

2 Goal conflicts are not uncommon between the marketing and production functions of a company. Identify some of these conflicts and give examples of how they could be eliminated.

3 Goal conflicts are not uncommon between different companies in a supply chain. Identify some of these conflicts and give examples of how they could be eliminated.

4 The performance variables with impact on a logistics system vary for different products, markets, and phases of the product lifecycle. Discuss which variables should be order-qualifiers and order-winners for computers, chocolate bars and building materials.

5 A logistics system can be the basis of cost-leading and differentiated strategies. Give examples of a situation (product, market, etc.) in which logistics supports a cost-focused and a differentiated strategy at the same time.

Further reading

Alvarado, U. and Kotzab, H. (2001) "Supply chain management: the integration of logistics in marketing", *Industrial Marketing Management*, Vol. 30, pp. 183–198.

Cooper, M., Lambert, D. and Pagh, J. (1997) "Supply chain management: more than a new name for logistics", *International Journal of Logistics Management*, Vol. 8, No. 1, pp. 1–13.

Hill, T. (1999), *Manufacturing strategy*. McGraw-Hill, New York.

Lambert, D. (2004) "The eight essential supply chain management processes", *Supply Chain Management Review*, Vol. 8, No. 4, pp. 18–26.

Lambert, D., Cooper, M. and Pagh, J. (1998) "Supply chain management: implementation issues and research opportunities", *International Journal of Logistics Management*, Vol. 9, No. 2, pp. 1–19.

Larson, P. and Halldorsson, A. (2002) "What is SCM? And, where is it?", *Journal of Supply Chain Management*, Vol. 38, No. 4, pp. 36–44.

Mentzer, T., Min, S. and Bobbitt, M. (2004) "Towards a unified theory of logistics", *International Journal of Physical Distribution and Logistics Management*, Vol. 34, No. 8, pp. 606–627.

Web links box

The Association for Operations Management (APICS):

www.apics.org

Council of Supply Chain Management Professionals (CSCMP):

www.cscmp.org

European Logistics Association (ELA):

www.elalog.org

Supply Chain Management Council (SCOR):

www.supply-chain.org

CHAPTER

02

The logistics system

As described in the book's introductory chapter, logistics can be expressed as a system consisting of the subsystems materials supply, production and distribution. Logistics management is part of supply chain management. From a supply chain perspective, logistics refers to a system that integrates the flow of materials between several companies. Such descriptions of logistics activities apply in most situations and for most companies. The meaning of logistics is not unambiguous for everybody, however.

To deepen the understanding of logistics and supply chain management, this chapter provides concise definitions and descriptions of logistics and supply chain-related processes, functions, flows and players. Different perspectives of the logistics system are also presented, with an explanation of how the subjects of logistics and supply chain management emerged and developed.

2.1 The Processes and Functions of the Logistics System

A process consists of the result of logical and conditional interrelated activities that are repeated time after time and have a clear beginning and end. A process transforms input to output. The goal of a process is to create value that satisfies customers and consumes minimal resources. A company may be described as a network of processes in which output from one process becomes input to another. The process perspective consequently motivates the wider definition of supply chain management. In the same way, a supply chain is made up of a set of linked processes which transform materials into products for distribution to customers. Processes are parts of a hierarchy in which one process may consist of several sub-processes. A logistics system can be characterised as a set of processes. Correspondingly, a logistics system may be described in terms of its main functions, that is, what primary output or function each subsystem is intended to generate.

Processes

Processes may be classified in different ways. One frequent classification is to differentiate between *core processes, support processes* and *management processes*. Core processes are those that directly contribute to customer value. They are often multifunctional and involve several departments or organisations. One important characteristic of a core process is that it is initiated by an event. A low stock level in the raw materials store may, for example, initiate the start of the core process supply. Support processes are aimed at aiding core processes so that they can be carried out in an efficient manner and contribute indirectly to customer value. For the core process of manufacturing to be carried out efficiently it must normally be supported by a maintenance process, which will ensure that disruptions in production equipment are kept to a minimal level. The supporting maintenance process may be initiated by events such as a vibration meter that indicates when vibrations from a machine bearing exceed a set point, but may also be plan-initiated, meaning that the maintenance process is initiated at certain time intervals. Management processes is the third class of processes. They may also directly affect customer value and are normally initiated by plans. Long-term strategic and business planning are examples of management processes.

From a logistics perspective, core processes are central to achieving an operative perspective, and management processes are central to achieving a strategic perspective. Certain support processes are extremely central for logistics. Planning and demand forecasting are examples of such process types. Core processes for the majority of manufacturing and distributing companies can be divided into the following eight fundamental types, or combinations of these types:

1	*Product development*	From identified need on the market to launched product
2	*Sales*	From identified prospect to agreement with customer
3	*Order-to-delivery*	From customer order received to invoiced dispatch
4	***Supply***	From identified material need to received and approved delivery
5	*Manufacturing and service*	From identified need to performed, accessible and approved added value
6	***Distribution***	From physically accessible product to distribution of product on site to customer
7	***After sales***	From delivered product or service performed to expiry of guarantee or agreement
8	***Return***	From identification of return need to received return consignment at recipient.

Several processes of the same type normally occur in one and the same company: purchasing processes, **manufacturing processes** and so on. For example, different purchasing processes are required for the acquisition of high-value equipment such as offer procedures, single customer orders for unique items, low-value standard products with frequent needs and expendable supplies. In certain situations a core process will also function as a sub-process in another core process. When manufacturing-to-order, the purchase of items specific to the customer order and manufacturing will be included as sub-processes in the **order-to-delivery processes**, whereas they are not when manufacturing-to-stock.

All core processes influence or are influenced by logistics. In the description below, however,

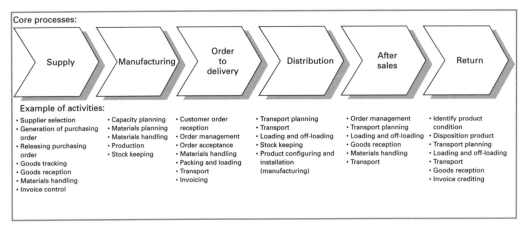

FIGURE 2.1 Processes in the logistics system

the main focus will be on the six later processes which are normally most central to logistics. Figure 2.1 lists examples of logistics activities for each of these six core processes.

Two common process models used to describe and design supply chains are the SCOR model and the Global Supply Chain Forum SCM model.

Supply chain operations reference-model (SCOR)

The Supply-Chain Council (SCC) (www.supply-chain.org) has developed the process model called **Supply-Chain Operations Reference-model (SCOR)** to describe, measure and evaluate supply chains. The model starts in an individual company and continues for several steps upstream and downstream in the supply chain. It does not describe all business processes or activities in the supply chain. For example, it does not include sales and marketing (demand generation), research and technology development, product development, and some elements of post-delivery customer support and information technology. The model is built on the following five business processes:

1 *Plan*   Processes that balance aggregate demand and supply to develop a course of action which best meets sourcing, production and delivery requirements

2 *Source*   Processes that procure goods and services to meet planned or actual demand

3 *Make*   Processes that transform product to a finished state to meet planned or actual demand

4 *Deliver*   Processes that provide finished goods and services to meet planned or actual demand, typically including order management, transportation management, and distribution management

5 *Return*   Processes associated with returning or receiving returned products for any reason. These processes extend into post-delivery customer support

Figure 2.2 describes the five standard processes in a supply chain consisting of an individual company, two levels of suppliers and two levels of customers. The company itself is in the centre.

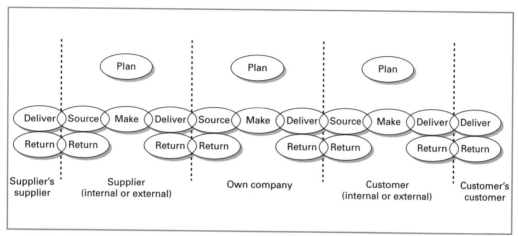

FIGURE 2.2 SCOR based on five standard business processes
Source: The Supply-Chain Council.

Directly to the right of the company is the first-level customer, which may be either an internal or external customer. To the right of the first level customer is the customer's customer, or the second-level customer, which may be a retailer. Similarly, the first-level supplier, which may be internal or external, is to the left of the company. To the left of the supplier is the supplier's supplier, or the second-level supplier, which may be a raw materials supplier. All five process types are performed by the supplying company, focal company and customer company in the middle of the model. But the units at each end of the chain only perform two processes. The customer's customer carries out source and return, and the supplier's supplier carries out delivery and return.

The SCOR model is an approach for describing the five processes in a standardised way and can be applied at different levels of detail. It is also a framework for relations between standard processes, definitions of standard measures for the measurements of process performance and a set of measures for best-in-class benchmarks. The model can be applied at different levels of detail.

Level 1 describes which units and process types are included in the supply chain and what the overall objectives for the whole chain are. Level 2 configures each process type in a set of core process categories. This is done by stating precisely the format of each of the five standard process types. For example, the sourcing process can be specified as source stocked products, source make-to-order products and source engineer-to-order products. In a corresponding fashion, the plan, make, deliver and return processes can be specified as in Figure 2.3. At levels 3 and 4, activities are described and measured in greater detail.

Global supply chain forum process model

The **Global supply chain forum (GSCF)** model is another process model for describing and supporting the design of supply chains. The model starts with three related elements: supply chain network structure, supply chain business processes and supply chain management components. Supply chain structure is made up of the members of the supply chain and links between them. To create efficient supply chains according to the model, the key members of the supply chain between which the processes can be integrated must first be identified. Supply chain business processes are those activities that produce the output which creates value for customers. It is

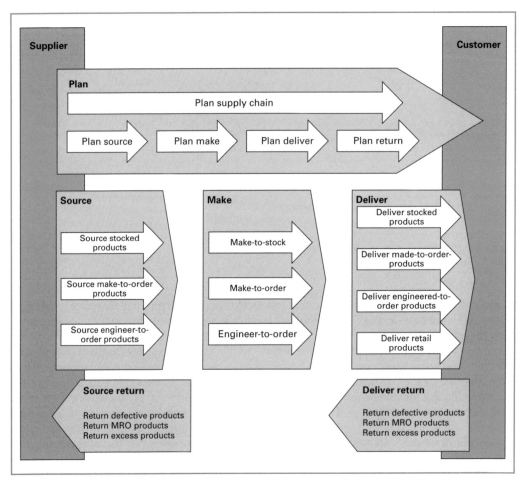

FIGURE 2.3 SCOR level 2: core process categories
Source: The Supply-Chain Council.

important to identify which processes should be integrated between which key supply chain members and how deep the integration should be for each link. Supply chain management components are made up of tools for integrating and controlling processes in the supply chains. The three elements work together with the aim of creating efficiency through process integration in supply chains, as illustrated in Figure 2.4.

The global supply chain forum model contains eight key supply chain processes. The following are short definitions of the eight processes (derived from Cooper et al., 1997):

1 *Customer relationship management (CRM)*	Activities aimed at localising customers, evaluating their potential profitability and identifying how to establish and maintain a loyal customer base
2 *Customer service management*	Daily administration activities aimed at satisfying customers and keeping them satisfied and loyal

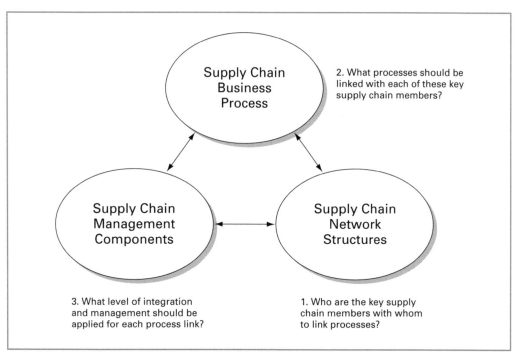

FIGURE 2.4 Elements and key decisions in the GSCF process model
Source: Cooper et al., 1997.

3 *Demand management*	Forecasting and customer order administration activities aimed at describing the demand picture
4 *Order fulfilment*	Activities aimed at delivering the right product at the right time in the right quantity at the right address after receiving an order
5 *Manufacturing flow management*	Manufacturing process that gives rise to desired product at the right quality and at the planned time
6 *Supplier relationship management (SRM)*	Activities aimed at developing long-term relationships with suppliers
7 *Product development and commercialisation*	Activities which develop new products and establish them on the market at the right time
8 *Returns management*	Activities that deal with repairs, return flows and exchanges, and develop preventive strategies that decrease the number of repaired and returned products

Customer relationship management (CRM) and supplier relationship management (SRM) processes are related to developing deep and long-term relationships with customers and suppliers. These processes create links between supply chain members and thus enable integration of other processes in the supply chain.

General process mapping and analysis

Many of the business processes at a company and in a supply chain play a decisive role in the performance of the logistics system. The execution of business processes means that resources are consumed and thus different types of costs are incurred. Executing business processes takes time and therefore affects leadtimes in material flows in the company and between the company and its customers and suppliers.

To be able to improve performance in business processes, it is generally appropriate to map the current status of the processes in question. The reason for performing this mapping is that personnel involved often have limited knowledge of how the processes are structured as a whole. In a functional organisation every individual is expected to have good knowledge of activities which are carried out in their own department. One of the characteristics of processes related to logistics and supply chain activities is that they cross functional, departmental, and sometimes also corporate borders. It is not at all certain that there is anybody at the company who has an overall view of the structure of these processes. This knowledge is an important point of departure for the analysis and improvement of existing methods of working. The SCOR model provides a standardised set of processes and best-practice measures to use for process mapping and improvement. Often the design and function of processes are unique for specific companies and supply chains. Therefore, more general process-mapping tools and forms may be suitable for mapping and analysing processes. Here, two such tools (**process analysis chart** and **function flow chart**) are described.

Process analysis chart

The process analysis chart is used for mapping and documenting which activities are carried out in the process and in which order they are performed. Figure 2.5 illustrates the general appearance of a form for carrying out this process mapping. Process mapping of this type is useful above all for studying time and costs for performing different activities in a process.

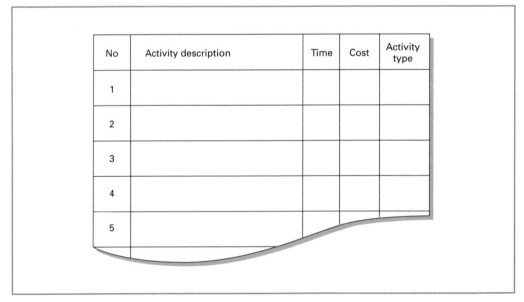

No	Activity description	Time	Cost	Activity type
1				
2				
3				
4				
5				

FIGURE 2.5 Illustration of a process analysis chart for mapping processes

The activities in the process are noted down in the chart in the order in which they are performed. Times and costs for performances are also noted. The time taken may refer to working hours consumed in performing activities, or throughput times required for the activities, i.e. the time taken from the start of an activity to its completion, including waiting time and other breaks when no value-adding activities are taking place. In the chart in the example there is a column for type of activity, i.e. what type of activity or break is referred to. With the aid of these activity times and activity costs as registered in the process analysis chart, the total time taken and costs for performing the process can be calculated.

When all activities have been mapped and data of different types have been collected, the mapped process can be examined and analysed critically. This is done by systematic questioning based on the words *what, where, when, who,* and *how,* as well as *why* for each one of these preceding questions. The aim of each question is summarised as follows:

- *What?* Purpose of the activity
- *Where?* Place of the activity
- *When?* Sequence of the activity
- *Who?* Person who performs activity
- *How?* Way of performing activity

- *Why* must it be performed ?
- *Why* must it be performed there?
- *Why* it must be performed then?
- *Why* must it be performed by him?
- *Why* must it be performed like that?

The overall purpose of posing these questions for every activity is to attempt to eliminate, combine, change or simplify the different activities in the process to be made more efficient.

Function flow chart

Another type of tool for mapping and analysing business processes is the function flow chart. This chart not only shows which activities are performed in a process and in which order they

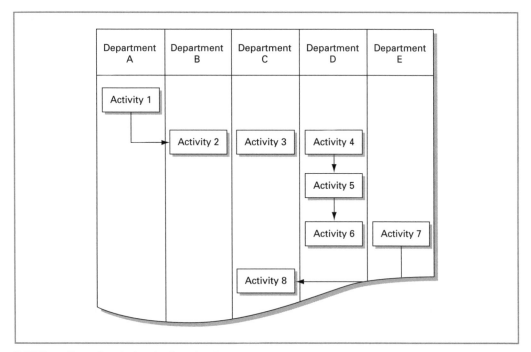

FIGURE 2.6 Illustration of a function flow chart for mapping processes

are performed, but also who performs them. "Who" in this case may be an individual or a department in a company or supply chain. The general illustration of a function flow chart is shown in Figure 2.6. In this figure, activity 1 could represent sales to a customer, activity 2 the registration of an order including reservation of materials, activity 3 dispatch planning, activity 4 printout of picking list, activity 5 picking from stocks, activity 6 packing the picked product and activity 7 delivery.

Function flow charts are especially useful in providing a picture of how many individuals and departments are involved in a process and what is done by different individuals and departments. A good overview of the complexity of a certain process is given by the chart. It is above all the "where?" and "who?" questions which are processed with the help of a function flowchart. For this reason it is a valuable aid in making processes more efficient by redistributing or combining activities involving different individuals. This is of great significance for the reduction of lead times, since they are to a large extent dependent on the number of individuals and departments shared by a process.

Functions

It is also possible to describe the logistics system as consisting of a set of functional subsystems. A functional system is defined by its result, i.e. its function or output. A production system is, for example, a system that produces products, a storage system that stores components, a transport system that transports goods, a forecast system that produces forecasts and so on. The following are examples of common logistics-related functions.

Forecasting

A flow of materials is initiated by a demand for the goods in question. The unknown part of the demand must be estimated, which is called *forecasting*. This is normally carried out with different degrees of detail, depending on the aim of the forecast. Long-term forecasting may be aimed at predicting several years of business cycles for the industry as a whole, whereas short-term forecasting may aim at predicting sales volumes of specific product ranges for the coming week.

Customer order management

The known demand factor in a company consists of customer orders received. The function of customer order management includes responding to an offer request, receiving and processing delivery plans, order confirmation and the registration of customer orders in the company's planning system. The design of the function is influenced by the forms of co-operation and relationships with customers.

Production and materials management

Long-term materials and production management consists of planning the timing and quantities of end products and/or product groups to be dispatched, and to ensure the efficient use of resources in the manufacture of these volumes. Medium-term planning is more limited in time and more detailed. It has the same aims but its starting point is the components included in an end product. Medium-term planning is the basis of operative workshop planning, acquisition of materials and management of material flows to and from stocks. For a manufacturing company it means that manufacturing orders and purchasing proposals are generated by medium-term planning. The sizing of order quantities and times for replenishment and withdrawal of material from stocks are also examples of planning activities. Short-term planning and execution of shop floor activities are normally also included in this function.

Transport planning

Transport planning refers to those planning activities prior to external transport. They include the choice of means of transport and the transporter, route planning, sequencing of routes, load planning, choice of places for unloading and reloading, etc. In the same way as materials and production management, transport planning issues are of long-term, medium-term, short-term planning and execution natures.

Procurement

Procurement is the function that ensures that necessary materials arrive at the production system when required. Purchasing is used as synonymous to procurement. The function can normally be divided into strategic and operative procurement. Strategic procurement includes selecting a supplier and drawing up contracts and long-term agreements with suppliers, and providing suppliers with long-term needs information. Operative procurement is aimed at identifying sourcing needs on a more repetitive basis, creating and transmitting purchase orders to suppliers, and ensuring that deliveries take place as agreed.

Materials handling and internal transport

Materials handling is the function that manages and moves goods internally at a plant. It includes among other things goods reception, arrival checks, internal movement of goods, stocking, picking, packaging, marking and dispatching of goods.

Production

The production function provides a product with an actual value. It may be manufacturing, in which case it consists of those activities that affect material flows in a workshop. The performance of the function is influenced by the manufacturing strategy, the factory layout and organisation of work, among other factors. However, production is not necessarily only manufacturing in the traditional sense. It may also be simple sorting tasks and packaging activities at a distributor.

Storage

Storage is the physical stock-keeping of goods in a store or warehouse. It includes the physical layout of the warehouse and its design (based on methods and principles for where and how different items will be stored). Sizing of material flows to and from a point of storage is one part of medium-term planning, and the physical inbound deliveries and withdrawals from a warehouse are part of the materials management function.

Freight transport

Freight goods transport is a consequence of transport planning. It includes the physical performance of transport, which is influenced by which mode of transport is selected – road, rail, sea, air or a combined multimodal transport solution.

2.2 Flows in the Logistics System

Logistics is sometimes called the science of the efficient flow of materials. However, material flows are not the only flows which are central to logistics. The efficient flow of information is very much an important condition for material flows. From the flow of materials and information comes the flow of monetary payment. The three flows are illustrated in Figure 2.7.

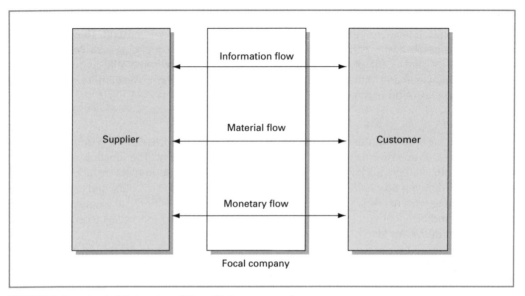

FIGURE 2.7 Flows in a logistics system within and between companies

The flow of materials

The flow of materials from original source to end-user has traditionally been seen as the primary flow in logistics. It represents large values, has a direct impact on the environment and in many situations requires great resources to be carried out. In a manufacturing company, raw materials and components flow in and through the company, while products flow out of the company to customers. The flow of materials in the opposite direction – from customer to supplier or upstream through the production system – consists of returns from claims and recycling. This flow is also called reverse material flow.

The physical flow of materials can be linked to four different systems components, depending on what type of flow is referred to. These are transport, materials handling, storage and packaging. Physical movement may take place between plants or within a plant. Transport refers to movement of materials between plants, for example between a manufacturing company and central stores. Materials handling in connection with goods reception, deposit and withdrawal from stores and loading onto external means of transport are movements within a plant. Transport and materials handling take place between different types of stores, which are therefore components related to the flow of materials. Materials which flow in the system are covered by some sort of packaging. The design of packaging has a direct influence on transportation, materials handling and storage. Packaging can therefore be seen as another materials flow-related component of the logistics system.

Information flow

An efficient flow of materials utilises resources efficiently and corresponds exactly to customer demand. To balance the access and use of necessary resources in both the long term and short term requires information about customers' needs, available capacity, work in process and materials at the individual company, and suppliers' capacity to deliver. Information flow in a logistics system is therefore a prerequisite for the efficient flow of materials.

Information on current and future demand consists of sales information, forecast information and customer order information, among other things. This information is generated internally in the company by sales forecasts, but it is also conveyed from customers in the form of customer orders, sales statistics, delivery plans and so on. The need for demand information in a logistics system gives rise to several flows of information. If a customer is a shop, then information on sales of items will be important demand information to convey to suppliers. If the customer is a manufacturing company, quantities and times for planned future purchases and consumption of stock items will be important information.

Information on suppliers' delivery capacity is also necessary to enable efficient flows of materials. This information is required so that planning and execution of added value can be carried out as efficiently as possible, but also to be able to maintain a good supply service to customers. Information may consist of stock balance information, order confirmation, delivery notification, etc. In an efficient logistics system this type of information is transferred between companies in the system by some form of automatic information transfer, for example electronic data interchange (EDI).

A large amount of information is gathered and registered in the company's databases. It may include, for example, registration of deposits and withdrawals from stocks, completion reports for manufacturing orders, identification of goods unloaded from trucks and so on. The use of a laser scanner, which reads barcodes on packaging, is an example of how such identification can be made efficient in terms of both registration errors and working time.

Monetary flow

As a result of the flow of materials from a supplier to a customer, a flow of payment arises in the opposite direction. Payment is initiated by an invoice or other agreed mechanism. Claims arising from products sold may initiate the flow of payment from the supplier to the customer in the form of invoice crediting. The monetary flow is not only operative. Financing supports to a supplier is one example of monetary flow of a more strategic and individual nature. Monetary flows are not treated in detail in this book.

2.3 Players in Logistics

The logistics system involves many players (see Figure 2.8). Customers and society are the external players that put demands on the system's design and performance. Goods owners and goods movers are the players responsible for performing processes in the logistics system.

The customer

As stated above, the logistics system can be described in terms of processes and activities. For each process there is a customer. The customer could either be an external customer outside the own function, firm or logistics system but also an internal customer located in the same function, firm and logistics system. In many situations it is difficult to clearly identify a customer since there is often more than one obvious purchaser and one interested party in the process' output. For this reason it is not uncommon that processes are aimed at creating value for more than one customer, for example by creating inputs for several different processes. Possible customers for a distribution process of a certain type of item may be, for example, the purchasing unit at the customer company whose purchase order has initiated the distribution process, the materials handlers at the customer company who will unload and stock the delivery, the production

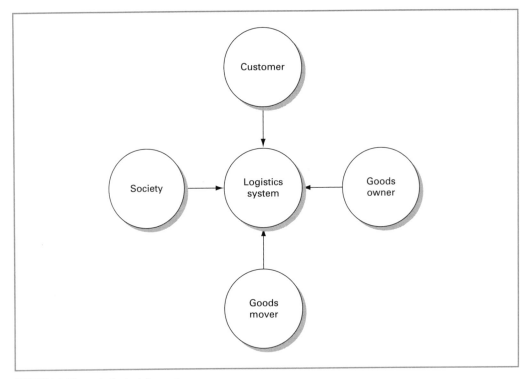

FIGURE 2.8 Players in the logistics system

department which will use the item as input goods in its production, and the end consumer of the product in which the distributed item is included.

The primary customers are the owners of the processes for which the process in question is a direct input. In many situations, though, it is also necessary to have information about which other customers will be affected by the process' output in the future. In a logistics system it is the end-user of the product and service in question who determines whether the earlier processes were efficient. The fact that a product, whose components have been manufactured by different supplies and transported between and stored in several places in the supply chain, sells less well or is perceived as less attractive than expected may be caused by any of the processes involved. Since the end consumer is the party that finally decides what revenues this logistics system will generate, he should always be identified as the customer even though he is not the recipient of the process' primary output.

According to the above argument, it is the customer who places demands on logistics processes and evaluates how well they have been performed. Putting the customer in the centre is just as important in logistics as in all other business activities.

Society

The customer puts demands on the logistics system through being the purchaser of its processes, but society also puts demands on and influences the logistics system. The physical location of manufacturing plants and warehouses may be influenced by regional political measures such as start-up subsidies in sparsely populated areas or low corporation tax in certain countries. Laws and directives on emissions are other examples of how society puts demands on and influences the design and performance of the logistics system.

The goods owner

If the customer is the purchaser of the logistics system's processes, then the goods owner and the goods mover are the two categories of player who are responsible for and perform the logistics processes. When a supplier sells an item to a purchasing company the ownership rights of the item are transferred. Ownership normally changes hands several times in a logistics system. Ownership changes, for example, when a raw material is sold to a company that processes the material into a component and when the component is subsequently sold to a final manufacturing company. Those who own the goods which are produced, stored and transported in the logistics system are called **goods owners**. Manufacturers and distributing companies are in general goods owners.

The goods mover

The ownership of goods is transferred through purchase and sales agreements. It is not necessarily the party that physically moves the goods who also owns them. In a shop which sells goods to consumers, the goods are sometimes owned by the shop but in many cases they are still owned by the supplier, who is paid when the goods are sold. In a similar way, many transportation and storage activities are carried out by players who do not own the goods but who are merely responsible for moving them between two companies' loading platforms, sometimes in combination with other activities such as interim storage, reloading, repackaging, etc. These activities are carried out on commission to the goods owner who then becomes a customer for these processes. Players who are responsible for moving activities, but who do not always own the goods, are called **goods movers**.

It is possible to distinguish between physical goods movers, who are responsible for and carry out physical handling such as transport and storage, and administrative goods movers who, on commission to the goods owner, are responsible for moving the goods but do not carry out the process themselves. The task of the administrative goods mover is to create an efficient goods-handling solution, procure the services from physical goods movers and be responsible to the goods owner for the efficient performance of the service.

2.4 Perspectives on Logistics

Perspectives on the logistics system may vary between different players, but an individual player may also have different perspectives on the same system. Depending on the time perspective when a decision is made, a distinction is made between strategic, tactical and operative perspectives. If, instead, the starting point is where the limits of the logistics system lie, it is possible to distinguish between the internal, external and network perspectives of the logistics system.

Time perspective

A decision may be made with different time perspectives. A decision whose effects stretch far into the future, often several years, will have a strategic perspective, whereas most short-term decisions are operative in nature. Decisions with a medium-term perspective are called *tactical decisions*. These types of decision are illustrated in Figure 2.9.

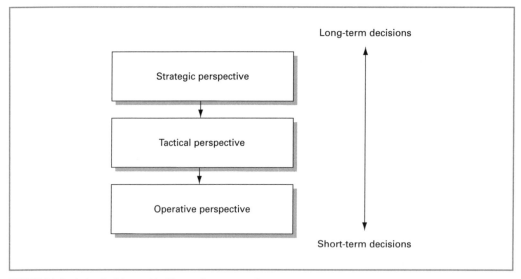

FIGURE 2.9 Logistics decisions with different time perspectives

Strategic perspective

Strategic decisions are aimed at creating the best possible conditions for future high performance in the logistics system. They affect resource investments, contain policy-related standpoints and are connected with the system's relationship to the company's strategy and players around it, such as customers, competitors and suppliers. The decisions are therefore long term and may reach several years into the future. They may concern the continuation of internal production or outsourcing to an external supplier, centralisation and fewer manufacturing and storage units, physical location of warehouses and factories, changes to the layout of factory premises, differentiation of delivery service to different customer groups, decisions on manufacturing-to-order instead of manufacturing-to-stock of a specific product, etc.

Tactical perspective

Tactical decisions are aimed at increasing the performance of the logistics system through reorganising and developing resources at the disposal of the company. The time perspective is not as long term as in strategic decisions, and is normally around a month. Choice of supplier for a specific item, determining workforce levels, determining production levels, principle decisions on order quantities for items to be purchased and in production, and changes in the location within an existing warehouse of a specific item are all examples of logistics-related decisions with a tactical perspective. In many cases tactical decisions are limited by strategic decisions.

Operative perspective

Operative decisions are aimed at creating high performance within the existing resources of the logistics system. They are mainly short-term decisions. Typical operative decisions are specifying and placing a purchase order, releasing and prioritising manufacturing orders in production and deciding transport routes for distribution vehicles. In many cases operative decisions are limited by tactical decisions.

It is not always possible to distinguish between decisions at different levels, since the different levels interact. Some decisions in a certain context may seem to be of a "simple" operative nature whereas they may have strategic significance in other contexts. A simple change of packaging size, for example, may have important consequences for a customer's handling of the goods. Customers' handling systems are perhaps unable to manage the increase in packaging size, and as a result the company and supply chain may find they have greater costs and lose sales. Another example of a situation in which an operative decision may have similar consequences at the strategic level happens where a shortage of input goods to a manufacturing process is created when a supplier cannot fulfil agreed supplies. A decision may be made to delay the manufacturing of the order in question until a supplier can deliver the items required and to re-plan and manufacture products for which input goods are available instead. Such a decision will result in a high utilisation ratio for the manufacturing plant. If the delayed product is a component in a customer's manufacturing process, however, this course of action may result in low utilisation of the customer's plant and possibly decreased sales in the short term and loss of market share in the long term. If, instead, extra costs are paid to obtain the missing input goods from the supplier or from an alternative supplier, and the delay is minimised, sales-related losses and the supplier's stoppage costs can be minimised.

Optimising an individual decision without considering the repercussions outside the system is usually called *sub-optimisation*. To avoid sub-optimisation it is sometimes necessary to upgrade decisions which initially appear to be operative to the usual decision maker to the level of tactical or strategic decisions.

Systems perspective

Depending on where the limits of the logistics system lie, it is possible to distinguish between internal perspective, external perspective and network perspective.

Internal perspective

In an internal perspective of the logistics system, system limits correspond to the company limits for the company being studied (see Figure 2.10). Suppliers and customers are external components in the system's environment. They can influence the logistics system under study, but not

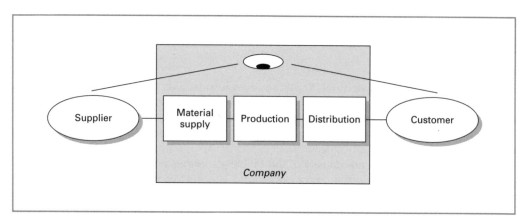

FIGURE 2.10 Internal perspective of the logistics system. The own company is the starting point

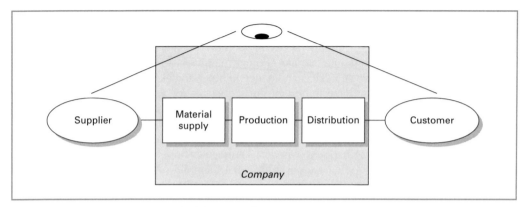

FIGURE 2.11 External perspective of the logistics system. The company, direct suppliers and direct customers are the starting points

control it. In an internal perspective the logistics system is limited to an internal supply chain consisting of materials supply, production and distribution, which are interconnected through internal customer–supplier relationships. The flow of materials, information and payment through the company and with external customers and suppliers takes place using internal resources, based on internal conditions and internal goals.

In an internal perspective it is central to focus on co-ordination between materials supply, production and distribution with the aim of creating efficiency and minimising sub-optimisation within the company, i.e. decisions made in individual units do not negatively affect the company as a whole.

External perspective

In an external perspective of the logistics system, system limits are extended so that they also include direct suppliers and customers (see Figure 2.11). The focus is not on internal company co-ordination and efficiency, which was the case with the more limited internal perspective. This means that efforts are made to find solutions and optimise efficiency for more than one single company at the same time. This striving to create efficient flows of materials, information and payment also involves the direct suppliers and customers and takes place with the help of available resources in all of the companies in the system. Since the majority of companies today have strong ties with suppliers and customers, it is often necessary to use this broader spectrum of logistics instead of the internal perspective.

Network perspective

A further extended perspective of the logistics system is to include the suppliers' suppliers and the customer's customers in the limits of the system. From this perspective, all players from raw materials suppliers to end-users are included, and the logistics system then comprises a complete supply chain. From this perspective it is not companies that compete with each other; competition takes place between supply chains.

It is necessary to create co-ordination and efficiency within and between relatively independent units in the supply chain. For a decision to be effective it must create value for the supply chain as a whole, and the supply chain's end-customers are the only customers that influence revenues in the system. For such a perspective to be possible no single player can make profits at the expense of another player – profits made by one player must be shared with

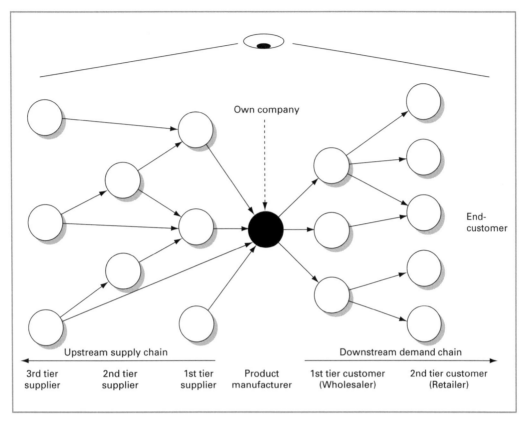

Own company

End-customer

| Upstream supply chain | | | | Downstream demand chain | |

| 3rd tier supplier | 2nd tier supplier | 1st tier supplier | Product manufacturer | 1st tier customer (Wholesaler) | 2nd tier customer (Retailer) |

FIGURE 2.12 Network perspective of the logistics system. The company as part of a network

all the players in the supply chain. If, for example, an end-manufacturer can decrease its tied-up capital by receiving smaller but more frequent quantities of input materials from suppliers, at the same time as suppliers cannot manufacture such small quantities due to high set-up costs and must instead manufacture larger quantities to stock, the purchase price must be raised to compensate the supplier for increased inventory costs. In this way the improvement in efficiency creates value for the end-customer but also a division of profits between players affected in the supply chain.

A company is not only part of one single supply chain. It will normally have several suppliers and several customers that represent different chains. For an individual company it is usually more correct to talk about a network of supply chains. Figure 2.12 illustrates such a network for a company that manufactures products. The supplier network to the left of the product manufacturer is sometimes referred to as being located upstream or as the company's supply chain or supply network. The network to the right of the company is referred to as being located downstream towards the end-customer or as the company's demand chain or demand network.

2.5 The Growth of Logistics and Related Disciplines

The view of logistics has not always been static and the subject has developed over time. From once having been a relatively narrow subject it has evolved to include several different areas of theory. The broadening of logistics also means that it has much in common with related academic disciplines.

The historical growth of logistics

Logistics has changed as a result of new conditions in conducting business, including the rise of a global market and new knowledge and development of computer and information technology. The development of logistics can be divided into the following four time phases:

- Phase 1 – Transport and warehouse optimisation
- Phase 2 – Materials administration
- Phase 3 – Logistics strategies
- Phase 4 – Supply Chain Management

Phase 1 – Transport and stock optimisation

Until the 1960s there were two major streams of logistics applications; one focusing on the procurement, storage, transportation and maintenance of military material and one on the storage and transportation of non-military material. The focus was primarily on separate logistics activities. Much interest was shown in the search for mathematically optimal solutions, with the help of operations research models, for transport organisation and planning of material flows to and from stocks. Logistics referred above all to the material flow of products from manufacturer to customer, i.e. what is now usually called *distribution*. The focus was on the efficiency of individual activities: materials handling, packaging, storing and transport. The inbound flow of goods and materials during the manufacturing process had lower priority, especially the non-military applications.

From the 1960s onwards there has been a gradual development towards a broader view of logistics. An important step towards a holistic view of logistics was taken when *total logistics cost analysis* was introduced. This meant, for example, that when a choice was to be made on the means of transport, the costs for all logistics activities affected by that decision were studied. On the basis of such an analysis it was possible to weigh high transport costs against low tied-up capital costs and choose the transportation option which had the lowest costs in total terms. With the introduction of total logistics cost analysis, logistics began to be seen as a system built on interconnected subsystems such as materials supply, production and distribution. From this systems viewpoint it was no longer sufficient to only study one subsystem. To achieve efficiency it was necessary to create internal co-ordination between subsystems.

Phase 2 – Materials administration

During the 1960s and 1970s a broadening of the view of logistical efficiency took place. Previously, logistics activities had been mostly seen as cost-driven and, thus, the main focus had been on minimising costs and tied-up capital. Now it became increasingly clear that logistics also influenced revenues. Customer service became increasingly important. The solution which provided the lowest total logistics costs was not necessarily the optimal solution; the more costly solution could be advantageous if it gave rise to added sales or made possible an increased sales price through good customer service. The fact that logistics came to be used as a means to influence revenues through customer service also meant that it had a more strategic significance for companies. People began to see logistics as a method of creating competitive advantage.

The widening analysis of a company's entire materials flow meant that suppliers' and customers' influence on these flows received more and more attention. In addition to the total cost analysis, more financial measures and methods of measurement were developed to govern logistics activities. The significance of co-operation and integration with suppliers and customers also became clear. Logistics no longer focused only on the distribution of goods; materials supply and manufacturing was now involved in the logistics system and a more holistic view of the flow of materials was taken. This view was sometimes called **materials administration** and studied the entire flow of materials from the generation of raw materials to the end-user, instead of merely a number of methods or techniques for bringing efficiency to separate parts of the logistics system. In the 1970s and 1980s the term business logistics was becoming more common and physical distribution less common. It was distinguished from military logistics but also emphasised the importance of logistics in the business firm and business strategy. In 1985 the leading American logistics organisation, the National Council of Physical Distribution Management, changed its name to the Council of Logistics Management and formulated a similar definition of logistics.

Phase 3 – Logistics strategy

During the 1980s logistics was above all affected by strong influences from the Japanese car industry and its focus on concepts such as **just-in-time**, total quality management and **Toyota production system**. Until then the majority of companies had manufactured large batches to stocks, but advantages were now seen in manufacturing products directly to customer orders. By manufacturing and delivering small batches, stocking standard components and manufacturing products to customer orders, a relatively high degree of variation could be maintained at the same time as lead times were shorter. The focus was on customer satisfaction, short lead times and the use of a minimum of resources, including minimal stock levels. To enable such a low resource and customer-adapted flow it was necessary to take increased logistical consideration to areas such as product development and purchasing and production by designing products based on standard items and modules from which customer-specific products could be configured and manufactured. Improvements were also made by radically decreasing set-up times in production, thus making the production of small batches possible and developing partnership relations with a smaller number of suppliers, which in turn facilitated the integration of flows between companies and enabled more small and frequent flows. Logistics was now perceived as central to a company's ability to create competitiveness.

During the 1980s and even more so in the 1990s there were revolutionary developments in the area of computers and information technology. As a consequence, the focus changed onto the introduction of computer-based systems for inventory control, production planning, transport planning, design and information transfer. There was a transition from computerised MRP to ERP systems, and communication technologies such as electronic data interchange (EDI) and the Internet were introduced and fast increased in use. This development has been of crucial significance in the ability of many logistical processes to improve efficiency.

Phase 4 – Supply Chain Management

The development towards a global market and tougher competition during the 1980s and 1990s increased the awareness of costs, and contributed to companies increasingly focusing on their core competence and outsourcing activities which could be carried out more cost-effectively by other companies. Many companies outsourced large parts of their external transport and storage activities to specialised logistics service provider companies, whose role in the logistics system increased radically. It was also more common for manufacturing companies not located in low-cost countries to move parts of their manufacturing processes to more cost-effective manufacturers in Eastern Europe, South America and Asia. This trend towards outsourcing has led to more players becoming involved in the logistics system and as a result it has become more important to concentrate on connections and flows in the interfaces between companies to achieve logistical efficiency. Parallel with this restructuring towards fewer manufacturing players – each being responsible for a smaller share of an end-product's total added value – was a corresponding restructuring of the distribution side from decentralised warehousing to central warehouses and direct distribution.

During the 1990s and the beginning of the 2000s the widening of the logistics concept continued. Terms such as *supply chains* and *the extended enterprise* were used to reflect the fact that the limits of the logistics system involve considerably more than one individual company. The significance of information flow in creating effective logistics was increasingly recognised. There was a clear focus on sharing information within and between companies with the help of well-developed partnership relations among players in the logistics system and the use of information technology to simplify and automate the flow of information. To quickly satisfy changing customer demands is another important characteristic of logistics systems in the twenty-first century. With short product lifecycles and demand for many customer variants and short delivery times, it has become increasingly important, as far as possible, to delay the configuration of customer-specific product variants. Strategies building on long-term relationships between functions, processes and firms and allowing for mass customisation and postponement were developed. This, for example, means that logistics service provider companies that were previously responsible mainly for storage and transport now play an additional role in creating variants and adding value through packaging and final assembly. As a consequence of this extended view of logis-

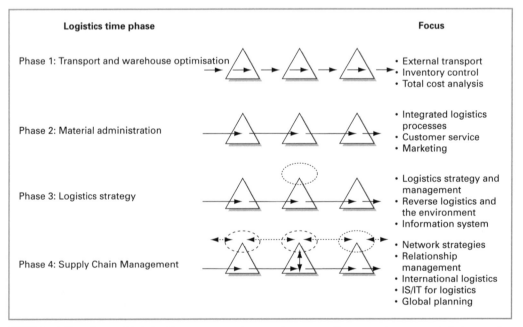

FIGURE 2.13 Time phases of logistics. From separate to integrated processes. From operative to strategic features and solutions in networks of companies

The triangle represents a company. Solid arrows show the focus of material flows. Section-lined areas and arrows show strategic focus.

tics, in 2005 the American association CLM changed its name to the Council of Supply Chain Management Professionals (CSCMP).

The impact on the environment of logistics systems was paid more attention during this phase. This has had consequences for the choice of transport mode, the design and recycling of packages and products, and how production and distribution are carried out. The challenges of distribution are no longer focused entirely on supplying the end-user with a product. Reverse logistics, designing and recycling of packages and products after use is increasingly involved. The vulnerability of acting as one of several players in a supply chain has also increased the importance for supply chain risk management. In recent years supply chain management has to greater extent been viewed from the perspective of the entire chain or network of facilities and companies. Companies like Dell and Zara have, for example, created world-class competitive advantages by designing integrated supply chains. The focus is thus changing from competition between companies to competition between supply chains.

The historic development of the subject of logistics has been extensive. Logistics has grown from being an operative toolbox of optimising models to a strategic discipline with crucial significance for a company's competitiveness. Views of logistics have widened from covering a company's internal resources and activities to include adaptation and co-ordination of networks of companies. The changing perspectives of logistics have also meant that the flow of information is nowadays frequently seen as being more central than the flow of materials in achieving logistical efficiency and effectiveness. Changes in logistics since the 1960s are summarised in Figure 2.13.

Logistics-related disciplines

As the subject and discipline of logistics has grown wider and included more areas of theory it has also gained more in common with a number of related disciplines.

Logistics originated in military activities where there was a need to move and provide equipment and troops in the field, as well as storing, moving and maintaining material and equipment. This branch of logistics is now called **logistics engineering** or **integrated logistics support (ILS)**. Its aim is to create high levels of reliability for a system, and through planning and design of new technical systems, to ensure that they are dependable, that it is simple to discover and remedy faults and, with the help of maintenance personnel repair equipment, to efficiently supply and perform the necessary maintenance to the system to ensure its high reliability. Reliability must be maintained at the lowest possible cost and generate the highest possible revenues during the whole lifecycle from acquisition through operation to disposal. The concept of lifecycle cost/lifecycle profit is often used for this approach and analysis. The area is mainly built on operations research theory and models, mathematical modelling and management accounting, but also on production engineering.

In the USA logistics was for a long time synonymous with physical distribution and activities related to the movement and storage of products between companies. There was a clear goods-handling perspective, and the roles and problems of transport and distribution companies were discussed. When a broader view of logistics began to be established, one other natural consequence was the broadening of the roles of distribution and transport companies, which resulted in the term *third-party logistics* being coined. The theoretical pillars were operations research and the technology of transport, handling and packaging.

Marketing theories and models of distribution channels are also closely related to logistics. A **distribution channel** may be defined as a set of independent organisations involved in the process of making a product or service accessible for consumption or use. The essential aspect is to create customer utility through different structures and roles for intermediaries, such as wholesalers and retailers, and between production and customer. A development of studies of distribution channels is the *industrial network theory*, which instead of seeing material flows as distribution channels studies the divisions of activities, roles of actors and the usage of resources that takes place in networks of companies. The focus is primarily on relationships between organisations, both from the perspective of suppliers, customers and the entire network. The supply side and suppliers are equally important as the demand side and customers.

Operations management is another established discipline with a clear connection to logistics. It has its starting point in production of products and services. The aim is to create competitive advantages through the design of products and production processes, and the control and development of the production process itself. The area was originally built on operations research (mathematical modelling), organisation theory (work organisation and strategy) and production engineering. Logistics engineering is sometimes regarded as part of operations management. In contrast to physical distribution, which mainly studies material flows outbound from companies or downstream towards customers, the focus is on the flow of materials input, from suppliers, and through the company.

Common to the disciplines of logistics, distribution channels and operations management is that they have all broadened from a relatively narrow focus to wider network perspectives. In all of these disciplines, supply chain management is now used as a concept to describe a holistic perspective on the flow of materials in which inter-organisational relations, information sharing and information technology have all gained increased significance. Since the disciplines have different starting points, the definitions of supply chain management tend to vary somewhat.

Logistics can be described, then, as a discipline which has much in common with other areas of knowledge (see Figure 2.14). From the area of organisation theory it is above all the areas of

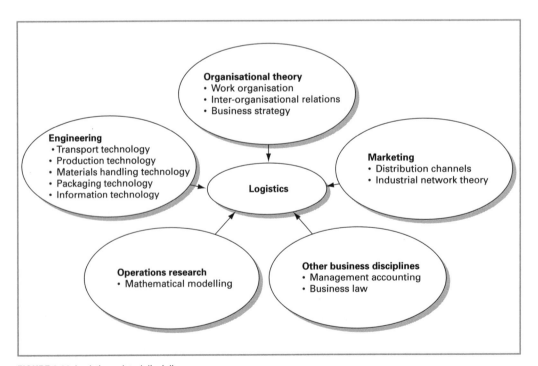

FIGURE 2.14 Logistics-related disciplines

strategy, work organisation and inter-organisational relations that are central to logistics. Equally important to describe and analyse the logistics system are distributional channels and industrial network theories from marketing. Operations research models have for a long time been important for optimising logistics problems. Management accounting and business law are other important business-related disciplines in performance-oriented and global logistics and supply chain solutions. Logistics is, however, not only a business-related subject; it also has many technical applications. Theories and models from technical areas such as transport technology, production engineering, materials handling and packaging technology, as well as information technology, are all important to the discipline of logistics.

2.6 Conclusion and Summary

In this chapter the logistics system has been described from different points of departure. One description starts with a set of processes. Order-to-delivery, sourcing, manufacturing and service, distribution and post-delivery are processes with clear connections to logistics. In a similar fashion, the logistics system can be described as a set of functions.

The aim of the logistics system is to create efficient flows of materials, but for that to take place efficient flows of information are also required. One further flow, monetary, arises from the first two.

The logistics system consists of a set of players. Customers exist at different levels in the system. In addition to society, they put demands on the system's results. The goods owner is the party that owns goods which flow in the logistics system, and the goods mover is responsible for movement of goods within or between different goods owners and customers.

If the logistics system is described in terms of different time perspectives, we can distinguish between strategic, tactical and operative perspectives. If the perspective used is the limits of the logistics system, we can distinguish between internal, external and network perspectives.

Finally, the development of logistics as a subject was discussed, from having earlier been focused on transport, inventory management and cost optimisation to becoming more inclusive and described in terms of supply chain management with clear interfaces to a number of other disciplines.

🔒 Key concepts

After-sales process 25	Just-in-time 43
Distribution channel 45	Logistics engineering 45
Distribution process 25	Manufacturing process 25
Function flow chart 30	Materials administration 43
Goods mover 37	Operations management 46
Goods owner 37	Order-to-delivery process 25
GSCF process 27	Process analysis chart 30
Integrated logistics support (ILS) 45	Return process 25

SCOR model 26	Toyota production system 43
Supply process 25	

 ## Discussion Tasks

1 A company sells furnitures on the Internet. What sub-processes take place from ordering a sofa to delivery at the customer's house?

2 What processes are influenced most in a company which changes from an internal to an external logistics focus? Why?

3 Compare the SCOR model with the GSCF model. What are the similarities and differences between these models?

4 What are the differences between a process and a function? Explain what is meant by a forecasting function and a forecasting process.

5 The historical growth of logistics was described above in terms of four phases. How far have different industries got in their development towards the Supply Chain Management phase? Describe the development of different industries and/or companies towards Supply Chain Management.

Further reading

Anupini, R., Chopra, S., Deshmukh, S., van Mieghem, J. and Zemel, E. (1999) *Managing business process flow.* Prentice Hall, Upper Saddle River.

Ballou, R. (2007) "The evolution and future of logistics and supply chain management", *European Business Review,* Vol. 19, No. 4, pp. 332–347.

Cooper, M., Lambert, D. and Pagh, J. (1997) "Supply chain management: more than a new name for logistics", *International Journal of Logistics Management,* Vol. 8, No. 1, pp. 1–13.

Croxton, K., Garcia-Dastogue, S. and Lambert, D. (2001) "The supply chain management process", *International Journal of Logistics Management,* Vol. 12, No. 2, pp. 13–36.

Harrington, J., Esseling, E. and Nimwegen, H. (1997) *Business process improvement workbook.* McGraw-Hill Professional, New York.

Lambert, D. (2004) "The eight essential supply chain management processes", *Supply Chain Management Review,* Vol. 8, No. 4, pp. 18–26.

Lambert, D., Cooper, M. and Pagh, J. (1998) "Supply chain management: implementation issues and research opportunities", *International Journal of Logistics Management,* Vol. 9, No. 2, pp. 1–19.

Mentzer, J., Min, S. and Bobbitt, M. (2004) "Toward a unified theory of logistics",

International Journal of Physical Distribution and Logistics Management, Vol. 34, No. 8, pp. 606–627.

Supply-Chain Council (2005) *Supply-chain operations reference-model: SCOR version 7.0 overview.* Supply-Chain Council, Brussels.

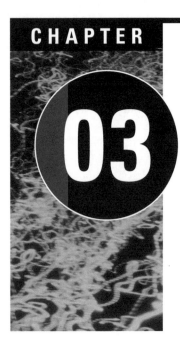

CHAPTER

03

The flow of materials

The flow of materials in the logistics system consists of transportation, handling and storage of goods. The goods that flow through the system are normally enclosed in packaging. Internal transportation and handling of goods in the logistics system's plants (stores, terminals, manufacturing plants, etc.) is called materials handling. Freight transportation is the external transport of goods between plants. The movement of materials takes place between different storage and

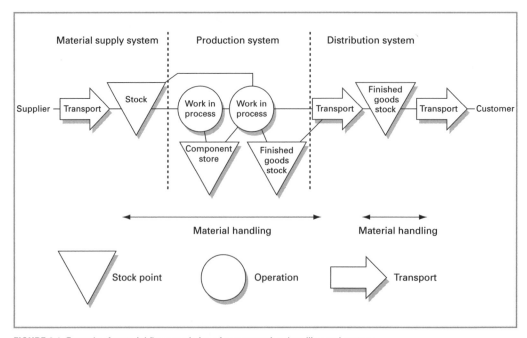

FIGURE 3.1 Example of material flow consisting of transportation, handling and storage

handling points. Examples of handling are sorting and repackaging. Storage itself is also an important part of the flow of materials. Figure 3.1 gives examples of stores (stock points), materials handling and transportation in the flow of materials. This chapter describes considerations made in the selection and design of stores, materials handling, freight transportation and packaging.

The issues described in the chapter are fundamental starting points for several of the following chapters. There are direct links between this chapter and Chapter 8 (especially Section 8.5 about delivery patterns), Chapter 10 (especially Section 10.5 Changing conditions for intermediaries, Section 10.6 Postponement and speculation strategies, and Section 10.7 Value-adding distributors), Chapter 12 (especially Section 12.2 Stock functions), Chapter 14 Transport planning, and Chapter 17 (especially Section 17.1 about warehouse management systems and transport management systems, Section 17.2 about information communication and Section 17.3 about data capture systems).

3.1 Storage

The flow of materials normally takes place to and from some sort of store. It may be a finished product store in a manufacturing company, or a distribution warehouse, or a shop store. The conditions and principles for storage are different for storage of whole **pallets** and picking stores, from which picking takes place from pallets. When designing a physical store, inventory carrying costs and handling costs are kept to a minimum by maintaining a high fill rate and low running costs. This can be achieved by utilising as much as possible of the storage volume for storage, without complicating handling. For example, there must be sufficient space for transport paths and a certain number of empty storage places in order to accommodate variations in the need for storage. Unnecessary movement of goods can be avoided by adapting the layout of the store to the processes carried out in the store; for example, by locating high-frequency items so as to minimise the transport distance, and allowing low-frequency items to have a longer transport distance in the store. However, it is not only the physical transport distance that affects the costs of handling items, but also the ease of finding an item, accessing it and moving it. High-frequency items are located in the most accessible spaces for this reason. A unique item kept in store is called a **stock-keeping unit (SKU)**. The total number of SKUs consequently equals the total number of stored item numbers.

Layout considerations

The goal in designing the layout of a store is to enable flows that are as rational as possible at the same time as a high rate of utilisation. There is consequently a trade-off between movement efficiency and space utilisation. Linear flow is arranged by locating goods reception at the opposite side of the store from dispatch and outbound loading, as shown in Figure 3.2a. All goods flow through the entire store. Using this design, all goods are transported approximately the same distance, which may involve an unnecessary amount of handling work and high costs. Differentiating the location of items with different frequencies of **stock withdrawal** will not have a great effect. Flows through the plant will be very clear, however, which facilitates the use of automated handling systems. When handling large volumes of few items this may be a favourable layout.

A U-shaped layout, as in Figure 3.2b, has goods reception and loading in the same end of the plant. The shared goods reception and outbound loading also make possible more efficient handling. The linear and U-shaped layouts are generalised solutions for store layouts. In reality, there are many combinations and variants of the two layout types.

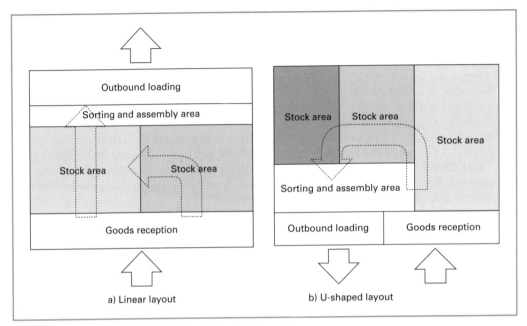

FIGURE 3.2 Examples of stores layout using linear and U-shaped flows
Dashed arrows indicate the flow of materials

Other considerations include to what degree the height of the store should be used for storage and how wide the **transport aisles** should be. The storage cost per unit area decreases with the height of the store, but a high store requires special handling equipment for items stored and retrieved. The wider the transport aisles are, the easier it is to manoeuvre trucks in the aisles. On the other hand, the area available for storage decreases, which also results in longer transport distances in the stores. A rule of thumb in designing stores is that handling efficiency is given higher priority than utilisation of area.

Zones in the store

Dividing a **store** into **zones** involves creating a number of smaller stores, called zones. Figure 3.3 illustrates the principle of a store divided into zones. By placing items with similar handling requirements in the same zone, handling work can be minimised. Zone division gives the largest payoff if the store has a U-shaped layout, since the transport distances for different zones are considerably larger than in linear layouts. The items in stock may have similar handling requirements in different ways, and for this reason there are different principles for division into zones.

If the majority of picking orders only contain items from one product family, this is an indication that it may be favourable to locate such items in their own zones to decrease transport distances. Picking orders that contain order lines from different product families will require especially high amounts of transport and handling work since the picking process will necessitate moving between different zones or consolidating partial pickings from different zones to one unit.

The **retrieval** frequency for each **stock** item refers to how many times per unit of time (for example, 1 week) an item is removed from the store. A relatively small number of stock items normally accounts for a large proportion of picking activities. If items are sorted by their retrieval

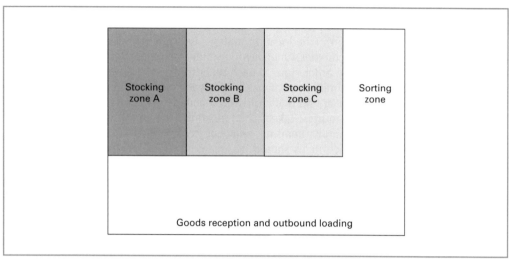

FIGURE 3.3 Example of zone-divided store layout

frequency, it is not unusual that 5 per cent of items may account for up to 50 per cent of picking activities, that 20 per cent of items may account for about 80 per cent of picking activities and that the remaining 80 per cent of the item range is picked very infrequently, amounting to around 20 per cent of the total picking work. An ABC analysis (see Appendix A) can be conducted in order to identify how to differentiate storage strategy according to the picking frequency. The basic principle is to simplify as much as possible the handling work required for those items which are picked most frequently. This may be achieved by automating picking activities and by locating such items in the most accessible spaces in the store.

Zones in a store can also be created on the basis of storage conditions required by the physical characteristics of stock items. One group of items may consist of metal constructions of high volume and weight; another may be high-value electronics; a third may require lower storage temperatures than other items. A group of items may also be differentiated by requiring special handling equipment. In this case efficient storage will necessitate that groups of items are divided into zones so that each zone can use purpose-designed storage and handling systems.

Location of items in the store

The physical location of items in the store can be based on different generalised considerations. One is to apply the principles of **fixed** or **random location** storage systems. Fixed location means that one type of item is stored in a predetermined, fixed place in the store. Random location means that items do not have designated storage places, but are located wherever space is free. An administrative warehouse management system keeps track of where each item is located. The disadvantage of fixed store locations is that a larger total storage volume is required compared with random location, since storage space must be sized for maximum storage volumes for each item. The advantage is that the store layout is simpler to adapt, so that items which are handled or picked infrequently can be placed deep within the store, whereas high-frequency items are located near to the inbound and outbound loading areas. In this way the total handling work can be minimised and the utilisation of the store is improved. It is also possible to combine fixed and random systems. For example, it is common to use fixed store locations for picking sites, from which items are picked for customer orders, and random location is used for buffer stores from which items are taken to replenish picking sites.

Another general consideration in the location of items is to decide which items are suitable for close physical storage to each other. One way to minimise handling work is to locate items that normally follow in the same order close to each other in the store. This is called *correlated location*. Locating items with a similar appearance beside each other can be an advantage if they come from the same supplier or are normally ordered together by customers and are included in the same picking order. Care must be taken when locating items in this way, since the risk of errors increases dramatically if similar items are adjacent to each other.

A third consideration is which items should be located at floor level and which at higher levels in the store. Floor level, or just above, is the most accessible for material handlers and retrieval can take place with or without the help of simple trucks. Storage places located higher up require more advanced trucks and normally take more time for storage and retrieval. One example is to locate items picked in quantities less than whole pallets at floor level and those that are handled as whole pallets at higher levels. Weight and volume also affect location. Heavy goods are normally located on the floor and low-frequency, lighter goods higher up. It is also common to use lower levels as picking stores and higher levels as buffer stores.

Unit loads in stores

If the majority of orders are for quantities less than one whole pallet, the total handling work can be rationalised by creating **unit loads** that are smaller than whole pallets. The optimal solution is that items are loaded into these smaller units when manufactured. If this is not possible for suppliers or manufacturers, repacking in terminals or stores will be necessary after goods reception and before storage.

By offering quantity discounts for the equivalent of quarter, half or whole pallets, customers who had intended to order smaller quantities may be encouraged to order full unit loads, which in the long term will mean simplified handling work in the store. The disadvantage of storing smaller unit loads is that extra repacking work may be required and that space utilisation will be somewhat lower compared with storage of larger units.

Storage systems

Storage systems refer to equipment used for the physical storage of items in a warehouse. A storage system may be manual or semi-automated, i.e. a system which without human aid stores and retrieves goods ordered from a warehouse. Different types of storage systems can be identified irrespective of the degree of automation.

The storage principle with the highest utilisation of warehouse space is to place goods in **depth** directly on the floor and to **freely stack** them on top of each other at several levels, as illustrated in Figure 3.4. Only the outermost units will be directly accessible using this principle, and if access is necessary to a unit further in the stores, much handling work will be required. For this reason the principle is most useful if large volumes of the same item are stored and if shelf life is not a problem. The units last put into the warehouse are those removed first, and units farthest in may remain there for a long time.

Rack storage refers to a system in which items are stored on a load carrier, normally a pallet, which is located in slots in a special construction, called a *pallet rack* (see Figure 3.5). There are many different variants of the pallet rack. They may be adapted to different unit loads, goods in stock, handling equipment, heights, etc. The aim is that all load carriers must be directly accessible from transport aisles. This type of layout provides high flexibility since all items are directly accessible, but low utilisation of warehouse volume since it requires more area for transport aisles.

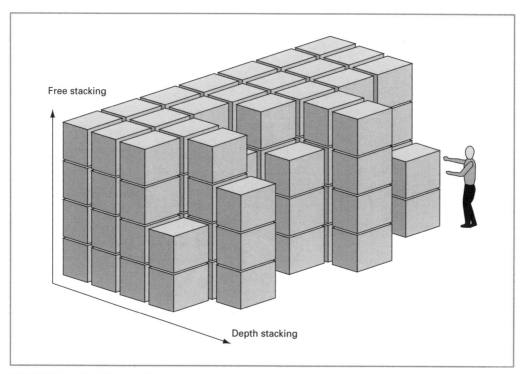

Free stacking

Depth stacking

FIGURE 3.4 Depth and free stacking. Packages stacked freely in depth and on each other

FIGURE 3.5 Rack storage system. This enables storage of goods on pallets in different slots

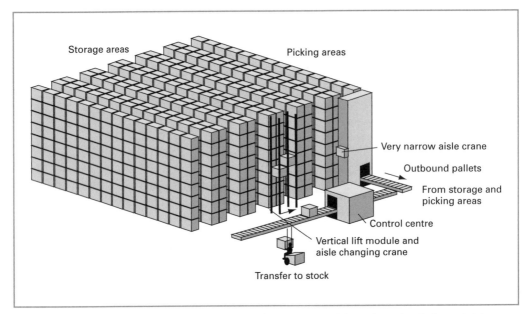

FIGURE 3.6 Example of AS/RS. An automatic crane moves along a transport aisle, storing and retrieving material automatically from the different compartments of the racks

Automatic warehouses utilise **automated storage and retrieval systems (AS/RS)**. This normally consists of several rows of high racks. An automatic crane moves horizontally and vertically along the rows of racks and handles all storage and retrieval of stocks as shown in Figure 3.6. Picking from whole packages or opened packages can also be automated to a greater or lesser degree. But fully automatic picking, including both gripping and counting items, is often difficult to realise technically and economically.

Shelving section storage enables items to be stored in boxes or compartments in a shelf construction, as shown in Figure 3.7. This storage principle is particularly useful when storing input materials for production with very low volumes, spare parts stores and tools stores, but also in picking stores with many items in small volumes.

FIGURE 3.7 Shelving section storage. Shelving design with small compartments and boxes

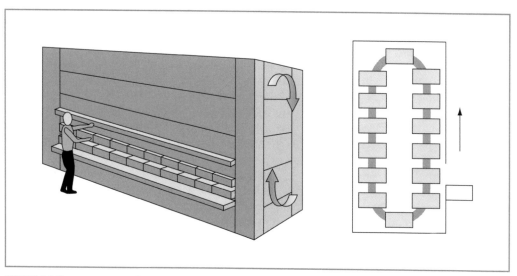

FIGURE 3.8 Paternoster store. Seen from anterior and lateral cross-sections

A more automated form of storing items from opened packages is called the **paternoster store** or **carousel store**, illustrated in Figure 3.8. A large number of items are stored in compartments in a store. No item is directly accessible; a computer controls the exposure of the correct storage compartment. This storage technology is useful when storing many small items. When picking different items at the same time, the picker does not need to move between shelves. In this way transport distances related to **order picking**, i.e. picking ordered items from storage locations, can be minimised. A *pick-to-light system* is a more automated paternoster store system that utilises lights to indicate the correct picking location and number of units to pick.

CASE STUDY 3.1: WAREHOUSE LAYOUT AT TAMRO HEALTHCARE

Tamro is a pharmaceutical distributor, delivering pharmaceuticals, healthcare products and medical products to pharmacies, hospitals, health centres and veterinarians. The company does not manufacture or market pharmaceuticals. The role is purely stocking and distribution. Tamro has a 6500 m² central warehouse from where the Scandinavian market is supplied.

All items have fixed picking locations and random buffer storage locations. The fixed picking locations are based on the picking frequencies in order to minimise the total materials-handling work.

For one part of the assortment, picking is conducted for each individual customer order. For another part, picking is conducted for several orders in order to fill up full distribution vehicles. Every day about 1600 orders, 2600 order lines, 5500 packages, 160 pallets and 40 tons of goods are handled in the warehouse. Fifteen people are working with order picking.

The following diagram shows the warehouse layout of Tamro.

Shelf section storage (465 shelf sections)

Storage of chemicals and dangerous goods

Packing area

Packing area

Rack storage (about 3600 pallet places)

Free stacking of bulky goods

Deep stacking (6 pallets deep, Totally 300 pallet places

Inbound goods

Outbound goods

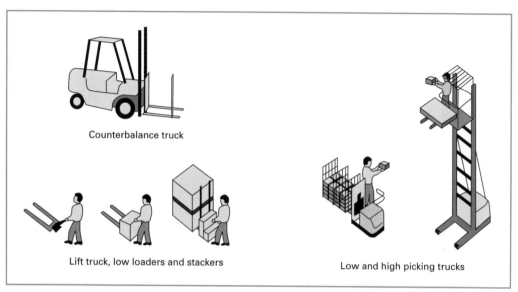

Counterbalance truck

Lift truck, low loaders and stackers

Low and high picking trucks

FIGURE 3.9 Examples of modern truck types

3.2 Materials Handling

Materials handling consists of the handling and moving of materials internally in a plant. The design of the materials-handling system depends on a number of factors, including the number of places to retrieve and store goods, flow frequencies, distances over which goods are moved, and the type of goods. Normal handling equipment and principles for retrieval of materials from stores are described below. Materials handling is normally an integrated part of the storage system, and in many cases it is impossible to separate the two. This section is thus closely associated with the previous section on storage.

Handling systems

Handling equipment may be automated to a greater or lesser degree. The most common equipment for moving materials in functionally organised manufacturing processes with flows of varying frequency is some type of manned **pallet truck** that can lift and transport packages, and manned pallet trucks in combination with trailers to move larger volumes. There are a large number of manual and powered truck types for handling in different types of goods and storage and retrieval situations. Figure 3.9 shows examples of modern truck types. Lift trucks, low loaders and stackers are examples of equipment for handling pallets. Using special picking trucks, the operator can move vertically and horizontally to reach different pallet stations. The **counterbalance truck** is used for heavier lifts. Different types of braced trucks, container trucks, terminal tractors and so on are also involved in common handling systems in warehouses and terminals. Different types of cranes are used for heavy lifts, such as containers in harbours.

Different personnel may retrieve materials from stores and deliver it to production and outbound loading. The person who picks materials in the store will transport it to a distribution point. The material is fetched there by another truck driver, who transports it to a reception area in production or to an area for packaging and loading for external transport. The reception area in production may be a parts market, a common picking place for several production units where

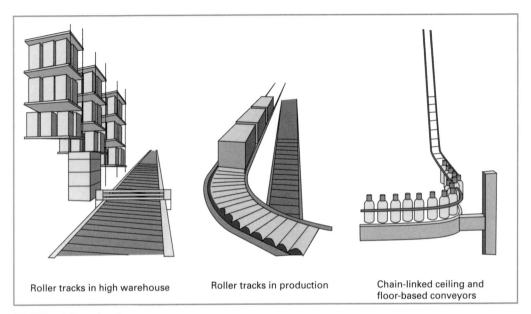

Roller tracks in high warehouse   Roller tracks in production   Chain-linked ceiling and floor-based conveyors

FIGURE 3.10 Examples of conveyor systems

The figure to the left shows roller tracks in a high warehouse. The middle figure shows roller tracks in production, and chain-linked ceiling and floor-based conveyors in production are shown to the right.

operators fetch materials as needed. It may also be a materials facade or other area directly connected to a production unit.

For more frequent and standardised material flows it may be an advantage to use automated handling systems. **Conveyor systems** move materials in the plant in a more or less automated fashion. A powered system means the materials are automatically moved between various stations and vehicles, while an unpowered system uses gravity feed, i.e. the movement of material follows the angle of the conveyor system, or requires manual control. Conveyors can be equipped with scanners to read bar codes on items travelling on them. There are different technical solutions for conveyor systems, such as floor-based rolling tracks, belt conveyors, chain conveyors or ceiling-mounted suspension conveyors. Some of these systems are illustrated in Figure 3.10.

Unmanned truck systems, also called **automatic guided vehicle systems (AGVS)**, are yet another way of moving materials along fixed loops in the plant, controlled by optic tape or magnetic strips in the floor. Figure 3.11 shows one AGVS. In comparison with conventional pallet truck systems, AGVS minimise labour costs and allow for efficient operations in narrow aisles and can provide access to high shelves. Automated handling systems are especially common for moving products in production between different work centres, but are also used for moving materials to and from stores. Compared with automatic conveyor systems, AGVS are more flexible. Transport routes can be changed, and faulty trucks can be quickly replaced with others, or with manual trucks. At the same time as being an automatic storage system, AS/RS is another example of an automatic handling system.

Retrieval of materials from stores

To retrieve materials, information is required about which materials are to be picked and to what address they should be delivered. This information is conveyed in a *picking order*. It may be generated by a manufacturing order, in which case the materials will be delivered to a specific place in the manufacturing plant; it may be a store replenishment order, in which case the material will

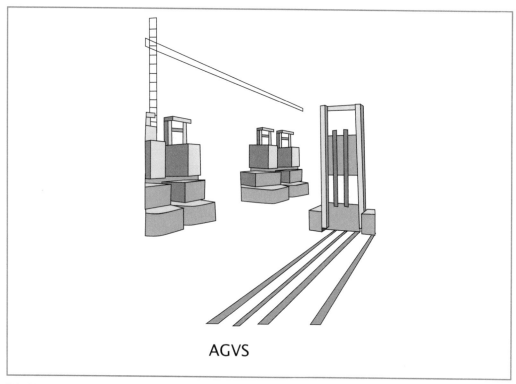

AGVS

FIGURE 3.11 AGVS. Unmanned truck moving along a fixed loop

be delivered to the store downstream; or it may be a dispatch order, in which case the materials will be delivered to a loading area for loading onto an external transport vehicle to the customer.

When retrieving materials for supply of input material to a manufacturing process, a number of different principles can be distinguished. **Kitting** means that the material for the object to be manufactured is retrieved from a store and delivered as a kit to the production address where the material will be consumed. **Batching** is another principle, meaning that larger packages of the selection of items that will be consumed during a certain time period are moved to the production unit. The same items are moved as in the process of kitting, but they are not picked into special kits. A third principle is **continual supply**, which means that small packages of a large number of items are moved to the production unit. The small packages are replaced as they are consumed. This method entails all items which may be required at the place of consumption to be exposed, which demands large areas. Similar principles, except for kitting, are also used for replenishment of stores.

When retrieving materials for supply to an external customer, the exact number of items on the customer order is always picked. However, **item picking** may be performed according to two different principles. The first principle involves transporting the material to special picking sites where picking takes place, called *material-to-man*. Transport of the material to the picking sites may be automatic, for example, with the aid of AS/RS or a paternoster warehouse, but the picking itself is carried out manually. Movements of the picker in the warehouse are thus minimised. This is a superior method when picking large volumes and a few order lines per order. Other methods will give rise to a large number of internal movements of materials and waiting times for the picker. If the orders either contain full pallets or loose boxes, meaning parts of a pallet, it may also be an advantage to separate picking areas for whole pallets and less-than-pallets. In a similar way, it may sometimes be better to separate picking areas for whole boxes and item-picking from opened packages.

The second fundamental principle for picking is that one or several people move around in the warehouse and pick items required directly from their locations, known as *man-to-material*. The picking activity for this principle depends on the number of order lines per order and the number of units and packages per order line. In the case of many small orders with one order line – often the case for spare parts stores – it is often better to bundle together several orders and pick items for several orders on each picking occasion. The order of picking is best decided in terms of the items' location in the store so that the total transport distance is minimised. If there are many order lines per order, and/or the items to be picked have a large volume, it may be difficult to pick several orders in one round of picking. Wholesalers that pick from warehouses and deliver to supermarkets often have orders with many order lines. The process is most efficient if the order can be picked directly in its transport packaging or on the final load carrier. This is called *picking/packing*. When the picker is ready, the labelled goods are left at the designated site for onward delivery to the customer.

One further possibility, if the order is very large and/or involves picking from different zones, is to divide it into several smaller picking orders – one per zone – and consolidate them by subsequent sorting. The advantage of this picking method is that the total transport distance in the warehouse is minimised, especially if the items picked are stored in different warehouses. Handling work can also be rationalised, especially if different handling systems are required for moving the goods in the different zones. In this way the picking activity itself can be made more efficient, but the subsequent sorting activities must be added. In food warehouses, for example, there are freezing zones, chilling zones and ambient zones. **Zone picking** in this case will involve a common picking strategy.

Picking of individual items also occurs; for example, the daily requirement of each item is retrieved from a warehouse at one location. The items are then transported to a sorting site where items for each customer order are identified and packed. Retrieval and transport to sorting sites can in many cases be automated to some extent, using trucks or conveyor belts, for example. This method also means that sorting activities are supplementary. The picking principles above, based on personnel moving in the warehouse, are illustrated in Figure 3.12.

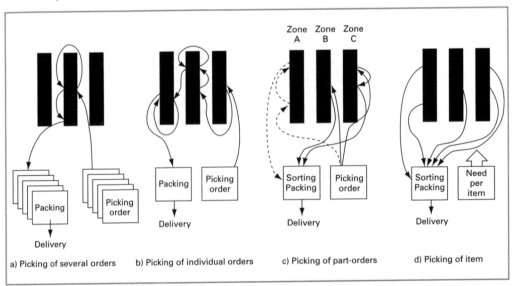

FIGURE 3.12 Four principles of manual picking: a) picking of several orders, b) picking of individual orders, c) picking of part-orders, d) picking of items

CASE STUDY 3.2: PICK BY VOICE AT LOGIA OY (Hinkka and Lehtinen, 2006)

Logia is a subsidiary company of the Finnish Post, which offers full warehousing services to dozens of companies in several industries. Logia is one of the biggest third-party logistics companies in Finland. In the warehouse forklifts bring the incoming pallets, replenish the active place, and then collectors pick the orders.

Staff used to pick the order items with the help of paper-based picking lists. The lists showed the name, location and number of ordered items. After picking a line, the worker marked the line that had been picked. To improve picking efficiency, Logia introduced pick-by-voice. The pick-by-voice system informed the worker of the location of an item while he was walking, When the worker found the right place in the warehouse, he read the last two digits of the bar code of the actual package. If the bar code was correct, the system informed the worker of the number to be picked and the worker responded by repeating the amount after picking.

The following effects of voice picking were achieved: voice-directed picking was faster than picking by paper. The possibility of human error decreased, and the worker had better working ergonomics and safety.

3.3 Freight Transportation

Goods transportation refers to transportation between geographically separated plants, but not internal transport within a plant. This can be carried out in different ways. The four main traffic modes are sea, rail, road and air. A fifth type often included is pipeline. It is also possible to combine different traffic modes for one consignment; for example, a container may be transported on a truck for the first part of the journey and transferred to a goods train for the second part. Using more than one type of transport is called combined transportation. The different traffic modes have different characteristics, which influence how logistical and supply chain goals are achieved, such as rapid, inexpensive, environmentally friendly transportation combined with high levels of customer service.

For each traffic mode there is a variety of vehicles. Road transport, for example, may use a truck-trailer combination or just a semi-trailer, which are two different types of vehicle. Transportation requires functioning infrastructure in the form of terminals, harbours, railway tracks, roads and airports. Infrastructure often takes a long time to develop and is normally owned by the public sector and not the company performing the transportation. Thus, infrastructure constitutes a limitation and a precondition for the performance of a high-quality transportation service. The fact that the use of heavy goods vehicles has increased rapidly while the road network has not expanded at the same pace has resulted in over-utilisation and congestion on the roads, leading to delayed deliveries and increased exhaust emissions.

The transportation system also includes a number of players. **Logistics service providers** such as **forwarders**, third-party logistics operators and agents organise movement, while transportation is carried out by **transport operators** and **infrastructure providers** are responsible for the necessary infrastructure.

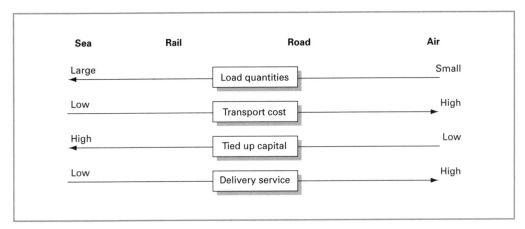

FIGURE 3.13 Comparisons between the four traditional traffic modes

Traffic modes

A continued description of **freight transport** is provided for each of the four common types of transport: sea, rail, road and air, as well as combinations of **traffic modes**, known as **combined transport**. The characteristics of these traffic modes make them more or less suitable for transportation of different types of goods and between consignors and consignees. Figure 3.13 illustrates some of these characteristics. Environmental concerns of different traffic modes are described in more detail in Chapter 6.

Sea transport

Sea transport is generally the slowest of the commonly available traffic modes, enabling transport between ports but only directly to and from suppliers' and customers' plants if they have direct port access. In almost all situations sea transport has the lowest operating cost per ton-kilometre (i.e. the quantity of goods in tons multiplied by the kilometres transported). Large loading capacity is the great advantage of ships over other traffic modes, but flexibility in transport routes afforded by the sea may be regarded as another strength. In central Europe, for example, inland waterway transport of commodities such as cement, chemicals and agricultural products may also be environmentally favourable compared with road transport. Inland waterway transport is especially common in, e.g., certain regions of Asia where there is a lack of developed road and rail infrastructure. Another advantage of this mode is the low cost of maintaining infrastructure for transportation – waterways themselves are normally free. The largest competitive advantages for sea transportation lie in the shipping of low-value bulk loads over long distances where sea routes are available. The only other real alternative for this type of transportation is by rail. Petroleum products are the dominant type of goods in sea transportation, but bulk goods such as sand, lime and ore are also common. A particular sector moving also medium-value goods is container shipping.

Ships, more than other vehicles and vessels, are specially adapted for specific types of goods and transport routes. The use of specialised container ships ensures a high utilisation of the ship's transport capacity since containers can be stacked on top of each other, close to each other and also on the deck. However, not all ports are equipped with cranes that can handle containers, and economies of scale concentrates the flows to major container ports with facilities for loading and unloading the large ships used for trans-ocean container shipping. RoRo (roll-on-roll-off) vessels in particular are built on the principle that goods are loaded onto rolling units for ease of loading and unloading. All types of rolling load carriers, such as trucks, trailers, cassettes and railway wagons, can be loaded onto RoRo vessels. The rapid and inexpensive loading and unloading is an advantage of this type of vessel, but one disadvantage is the relatively large unutilised load space between decks. Container ships and RoRo ships can be used for transporting similar types of goods. Container ships are primarily used for transport between continents whereas RoRo ships are used for transport within continents. Bulk ships and tanker ships are designed to transport solid, dry goods (e.g. ore, coal and cement) and liquid bulk loads (e.g. oil) respectively. Loading and unloading times for such bulk transport ships are often relatively short. There is also a variety of combinations of the above type of ship.

Rail transport

Rail transport is advantageous over road transport when it comes to transporting large quantities of high-volume goods over long distances. This is a natural consequence of being able to join a large number of wagons into one freight train. Almost any type of goods can be transported by rail, but because of relatively long transport times, high-value goods will generate large amounts of tied-up capital, and are therefore less suitable for rail transport. This mode normally allows good transport speeds over long distances, but transport times are still often longer than for the equivalent road transport. For this reason rail is preferable for the transportation of large quantities of high-volume goods of lower value over long distances. To give an example, rail transport has a large proportion of the market for timber products over very long distances, and also for transportation of ore. Rail transport of post and packages over medium distances is also competitive.

Departures by rail are generally less frequent than by road. The railway network is not as well developed as the road network and cannot compete in terms of flexibility in time and geography. However, this competitive disadvantage can be eliminated by combining traffic modes; for example, by transporting goods in containers, swap bodies or semi-trailers, which can be easily transferred from trains to trucks for transportation from terminals to customers' plants. Combined transport will be further discussed later in this chapter. One important competitive edge for rail transportation is its environmental cleanliness – it can transport large volumes without direct exhaust emissions, although eventual indirect emissions through electricity production will have an environmental impact. It is also the most energy-efficient traffic mode. Measured in ton-kilometres, rail transport is the largest mode in certain areas of the world, including USA. One competitive downside for rail transport in Europe is the lack of a uniform standard for electric power system, rail gauge and signalling systems.

Rail transport often uses railway wagons specially adapted to the goods being transported such as containerised goods, palletised consignments, timber, bulk transport etc.

Road transport

Road transport by trucks is common for transport over short as well as long distances. It is, in principle, the only traffic mode that can offer accessibility to all suppliers' and customers' plants on the same continent. Its relative advantages are therefore greatest for transportation in widely scattered markets. Other traffic modes normally ship goods between terminals and offer direct transport to suppliers' or customers' plants only in exceptional cases. Almost any goods can be transported almost anywhere by road transport. Size, goods value, weight and transport distance are of little significance to its potential. For example, it is almost always possible to tailor a transport route for individual consignments as long as there is a reasonable road. Road transportation is thus more flexible than solutions using other modes.

Road transport normally competes with air freight for small volumes and high-value products, and with railways for large volumes and low-value products. Road transport can also be a

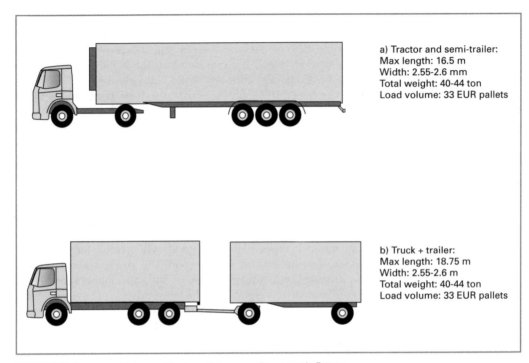

a) Tractor and semi-trailer:
Max length: 16.5 m
Width: 2.55-2.6 mm
Total weight: 40-44 ton
Load volume: 33 EUR pallets

b) Truck + trailer:
Max length: 18.75 m
Width: 2.55-2.6 m
Total weight: 40-44 ton
Load volume: 33 EUR pallets

FIGURE 3.14 Common vehicles used for long-distance road transport in Europe

competitive alternative for both short and long distances, but it tends to have economic disadvantages in comparison with rail transport and sea transport in the case of very low-value goods, and delivery time disadvantages in comparison with air freight for very high-value goods. Environmental consequences in the form of exhaust emissions, noise, road safety and traffic congestion are competitive disadvantages for road transport compared with sea and rail transport.

There are different types of road transport vehicles. For long-distance transport in Europe the maximum weight is 40 tons. The normal combinations are a tractor hauling a so-called semi-trailer, or an articulated truck, which is also referred to as *truck and trailer combination*. These configurations are illustrated in Figure 3.14a. One advantage of the semi-trailer solution is that the tractor can be separated from the load carrier, enabling different tractors to be used to move the load carrier to and from terminals. Truck and trailer combinations illustrated in Figure 3.14b are also known as *wagon and drag*.

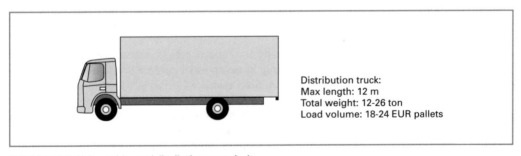

Distribution truck:
Max length: 12 m
Total weight: 12-26 ton
Load volume: 18-24 EUR pallets

FIGURE 3.15 Vehicle used for road distribution at terminals

In distribution between terminals and a number of customers or suppliers, there are many loading and unloading points in the distribution network. Distribution trucks are often used in this situation with a rear lifting device as shown in Figure 3.15.

Air transport

Air transport provides a very fast service over long distances, but in common with sea and rail transport it is limited to terminals and cannot provide direct transport to and from suppliers' and customers' plants. This mode has the highest cost per ton kilometre and for this reason is not normally chosen for low-value, high-volume goods. Air transport is generally used for goods of high value and/or low weight, time-sensitive express goods and emergency deliveries, as well as packets and post over long distances. The very short transport time over large geographical distances is the greatest advantage of air transport. Increasing demands on fast, safe transportation have rapidly raised the demand for air freight in recent years. The trends towards outsourcing production and purchasing more high-value goods from suppliers on other continents have also increased the competitiveness of air freight, which competes primarily with container ships between continents and road transport within continents.

Air freight is carried both in specialised freight aircraft and in the cargo hold of passenger aircrafts, referred to as belly freight.

Combined transport

Combined transport is any single journey that uses a combination of several traffic modes, for example rail and road transport. Combined modes can offer the advantages of their component modes, the most efficient for one leg being combined with the most efficient for another leg. A container may be transported by truck from a consignor's plant to a terminal in Northern Europe, where it is transshipped to a railway wagon for transport to a terminal in southern Europe, and is from there transferred to another truck for delivery to the consignee's plant. This combination exploits the low transport costs and low environmental impact of railways with the flexibility of road transport for local distribution. Environmental consequences in particular are often used for marketing combined transport solutions. Because of the demand for transportation of goods along the whole route from the supplier's to the customer's plant, a combined transport solution is often necessary for using sea, rail and air transport.

When two or more modes take part in transportation, efficient interfaces between them are necessary. This can be achieved by using standardised unit loads such as containers, swap bodies and semi-trailers, which with the help of standardised handling equipment can be directly transferred between traffic modes without the load being opened or repackaged. From the customer's viewpoint the movement of goods is similar to direct transport, and cargo handling during transport is minimised. The movement of goods in one and the same loading unit or vehicle which uses successively several modes of transport without handling the goods themselves in changing modes is called **intermodal transport**.

For an intermodal transport solution to be competitive against all-road transport, the costs for extra terminal activities in the transfers between modes must be lower than cost savings through less expensive long-distance transport by rail or sea. Terminal activities must also be time-efficient to avoid any competitive disadvantages related to transport time. Combined road–rail transport is currently competitive at relatively long distances, in general above 500 kms in Europe and Japan and 500 miles (800 kms) in the USA. Efficient handling is particularly critical for competitiveness for medium-distance transport in the range 200 to 500 kms.

CASE STUDY 3.3: INTERMODAL ROAD-RAIL TRANSPORT IN THE EUROPEAN UNION (Woxenius and Bärthel, 2007)

The European intermodal road-rail transport flows have grown substantially and doubled the volumes between 1990 and 2000. The competitiveness of intermodal road-rail transport depends on geographical and demographical conditions. Studies show that conventional intermodal operations characterised by transshipments of unit loads by use of gantry cranes and

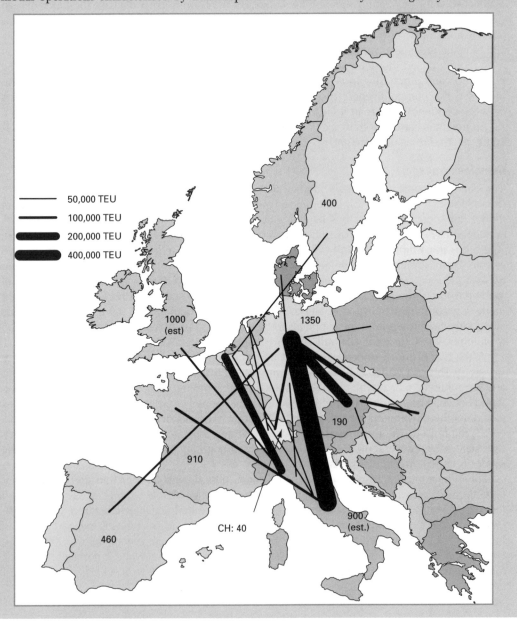

reach stackers, full train night-leaps directly between terminals and services offered to shippers through intermediaries, are generally competitive at distances above 500 kms. For container shuttles to and from ports, the distance is slightly shorter.

Germany holds a dominant position with almost half of Europe's domestic intermodel road-rail transport. France also shows figures for substantial domestic intermodal operations. Many countries, e.g. Belgium, the Netherlands and Denmark, do not have the geographic extensions needed for competitive domestic intermodal road-rail transport. Peripheral countries, like Italy, Spain, the UK and Finland, have fairly substantial domestic networks with border-crossings defined as gateways to other networks.

A few relations across the Alps dominate border-crossing intermodal road-rail transport in Europe. Partly because of Swiss and Austrian regulations and tax policies, intermodal road-rail operations have large market shares for the flows between Italy and Germany/Benelux, e.g. 50 per cent between Italy and Belgium. Examples of other markets shares are between Sweden and Italy with 60 per cent, Belgium and Spain with 30 per cent and Sweden and Belgium with 30 per cent. The dominated intermodal road-rail transport flows in the European Union are shown in the map (domestic in figures and bilateral in lines).

Players in the transport system

In a transport system the players responsible for arranging the transport, physical movement and infrastructure co-operate with the aim of creating a transport service.

Shippers

Comparatively few manufacturing and trading companies carry out physical transport on own account. Instead they buy these services from logistics service providers. The term **shipper** relates to the actor buying transport and logistics services; it should not be confused with shipping as in sea transport. It is hence a term relating to the market for transport services but it is often related to the actor who owns, has owned or will own the goods. The shipper is most often either the one sending the goods, the consignor, or the one receiving the goods, the consignee.

Logistics service providers

Logistics service providers (LSP) are companies normally without their own transportation resources. Their role is to arrange and execute transport by planning and subcontracting necessary transportation resources. They carry out other more stationary activities along the transport chain, such as storage and terminal activities. Depending on the extent of their responsibilities, we can distinguish between forwarders, **third-party logistics providers (3PL)** and **fourth-party logistics providers (4PL)**.

Forwarders

A forwarder operates as a mediator of transport services, i.e. it identifies and enters into agreements for transportation services on behalf of the shipper. Services traditionally arranged by forwarders are transport, reloading, storage, insurance, customs clearance and so on. Forwarders do not normally carry out the transportation itself, but engage carriers who act in the name of the forwarder. To some extent, however, forwarders may also own and operate resources for physical transport.

Facts and figures 3.1: The size and character of European freight flows (European Commission, 2005)

The transport work in the European Union increased from 1.4 trillion ton/kms in 1970 to 3.8 trillion ton/kms in 2005. 50 per cent of this work regards involves distances between 150 and 500 kms and 20 per cent distances over 500 kms. The market share for road transport increased from 35 per cent in 1970 to 44 per cent in 2005. Intra-European sea transport increased its share to 39 per cent. The transport volumes of domestic sea, inland waterways and rail was fairly stable, implying significantly reduced market shares. Rail has decreased from 20 per cent to 10 per cent. Transport flows in the EU between 1995 and 2005 are shown below:

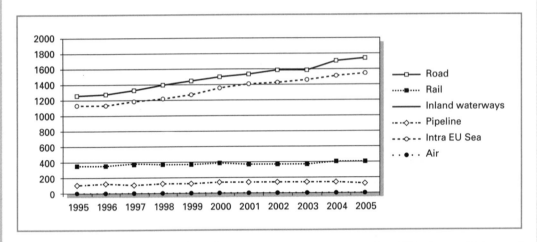

The volume of transport work in the European Union compared to USA, Japan, China and Russia is shown below:

	EU-25 (2004)	USA (2003)	Japan (2002)	China (2004)	Russia (2003)
Road	1684	1845	312	762	173
Rail	379	2341	22	1827	1669
Inland water-ways	130	467		2872	71
Oil pipeline	124	861		7	2273
Sea	1484	424	236		65

Forwarders specialise in developing and arranging logistics services, including transportation, storage and terminal services, and a forwarder will control or have access to a number of terminals. By taking responsibility for the flow of goods from many different customers, a forwarder is able to consolidate the flows at the same time as it can adapt suitable transport arrangements for specific customers. The aim of a freight forwarder's activities is that through specialisation in his role as co-ordinating third party, the forwarder is able to carry out transportation and storage activities more cost-efficiently and generate better customer service than if they had been arranged by a manufacturing company. The freight forwarding business is characterised by a few large international companies with well-developed international networks for most traffic modes. There are also many forwarders operating in niches for different traffic modes, industries, etc.

Third and fourth party logistics providers

Nowadays many forwarders take a larger overall responsibility for arranging logistics in addition to the traditional organisation of transportation between two parties. This may be achieved by taking over a number of tasks from the purchasing companies' storage, terminal and logistics planning functions. The term *third party logistics provider (3PL)* often refers to the fact that the task of the logistics service provider involves warehousing and transportation.

The term *fourth-party logistics (4PL)* provider also exists, which refers to a player that carries out services corresponding to those of a third-party logistics provider. In contrast to a third-party provider, however, a fourth-party logistics company does not necessarily own resources for the physical handling of goods, but purchases these from other players. The consultancy firm Accenture originally coined the term *4PL*. They define it as "an integrator that assembles the resources, capabilities and technology of its own and other organisations to design, build and run comprehensive supply chain solutions". In accordance with the Accenture definition, the tasks undertaken by a fourth-party logistics provider are sometimes defined as somewhat broader and more strategic than those of a third-party logistics provider.

CASE STUDY 3.4: IKEA'S OUTSOURCED DISTRIBUTION SETUP (Stefansson, 2006)

IKEA outsourced part of its distribution to Celexor. Celexor was responsible for co-ordinating replenishment from nine European suppliers to 15 of IKEA's European stores and 11 European DCs. The distribution setup included a cross-docking terminal that a large portion of the shipments goes through. The logistics services that Celexor conducts were:

1 Transport-related services:
  - tendering and contracting carriers
  - forwarding services
  - track and trace of in-transit movements

2 DC and terminal operation services:
  - cross-docking in terminals
  - consolidation and deconsolidation
  - picking according to order and packaging (pick and pack)
  - assembly of components
  - operating vendor-management inventories in stores or stock-keeping facilities
  - recycling with waste handling and reconditioning
  - packaging, re-packaging and labelling
  - labelling
  - unpacking and quality control
  - return of goods

- storage with good reception
- preparing for delivery and packaging
- delivery from storage

3 Administrative services related to DC and terminal operations:
- order administration and customer service
- forecasting and inventory management
- administration of minimum and protective inventories
- purchase and call-offs
- stocktaking
- claims handling
- export clearance and import clearance
- delivery planning and management and follow-up
- track and trace information
- exception management
- insurance services
- payment services

4 Administration of logistics activities not directly related to physical goods movement:
- design of individual logistics setups
- implementation of logistics setups
- operation of the customers' logistics setups
- provision of one-stop logistics service purchasing
- tendering and contracting logistics service providers
- tendering and contracting carriers
- forwarding services
- advanced information services
- track and trace with exception management
- customs services
- financial services
- payment services
- insurance services

Transport operators

Freight forwarders, like third and fourth party logistics providers, do not use own vehicles for carrying out physical transportation. Instead they subcontract services from different transport carriers that specialise in different traffic modes.

Road hauliers transport goods using goods vehicles. The haulage industry is characterised by a mix of a large number of small companies with only one or a few trucks, and some larger hauliers with hundreds of trucks.

European railway companies are dominated by a few large, state-owned companies, but in recent years some smaller railway carriers have been established.

Shipping lines transport goods by sea. The ships are often designed with certain types of goods and transport routes in mind. Ship-owners or shipping lines still often design the ships which are then built in a shipyard. In this way, ship-owners and shipping lines gain relatively central roles for shaping efficient logistics arrangements. It is also common for shipping lines to specialise in the transportation of certain types of goods.

Air freight is carried either by airlines that specialise mainly in passenger transportation, or by freight-only companies.

Infrastructure providers

An important prerequisite for carrying out transportation is access to the necessary infrastructure. Road use is generally charged for by a fixed vehicle tax combined with a fuel tax and in some cases by road tolls. The use of railway tracks, navigation routes and air corridors generally involves user fees. The players are almost exclusively national infrastructure bodies such as a national road administration, a national rail administration and a national civil aviation administration. Road terminals are often owned by forwarders and sometimes by shippers (manufacturing companies or wholesalers), while ports and airports are made available by public or private terminal operators through port and airport charges.

3.4 Packaging

Material flow within or between companies does not only consist of the goods themselves. To enable efficient handling and storage, to protect the materials and environment during handling, and to identify the material in question, it is generally enclosed in some sort of packaging or put onto a load carrier.

Unit loads

The packaging in which a product is stored and marketed to the end customer is called *primary packaging*. It is important that the primary packaging can be packed into larger packages to make it easy and safe to handle. In this way the material flow of finished products to the end-customer is made efficient, with high utilisation of transport and storage places, efficient handling and a minimum of handling damage. This also applies to the handling and movement of items which are not finished products and which do not have any real primary packaging. It is not unusual to have several levels of packaging.

Packaging handled in the flow of materials must correspond to so-called *unit loads*, that is, larger standardised packages which can be handled as single units. In general, the larger the packaging handled, the more efficient is the handling process. Consideration must also be given to the number of items which from other viewpoints is appropriate to transport to a certain storage and handling point, so that repackaging is avoided.

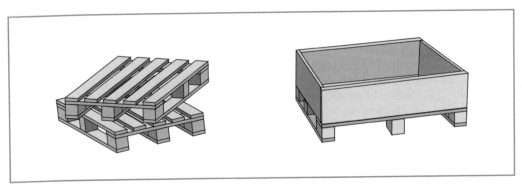

FIGURE 3.16 EUR pallet
The left figure shows a EUR pallet and the right shows a EUR pallet with a pallet collar.

The pallet is a common unit load. Full pallets can be combined to make full container loads. The container is thus a unit load at a higher level than the pallet. To utilise unit load and means of transport efficiently, a size relationship is often required between the different levels of unit loads. The aim should be for a certain number of items to be contained on the pallet, and a certain number of full pallets should fit exactly into a container so that the loading volume is utilised completely and movement without transportation damage can be ensured.

Using standardised unit loads of the same size and shape, such as pallets and containers, is important to facilitate handling. There is a standardised pallet system in Europe. It is based on packages built in modules which are wholly divisible by 400 × 600 mm and placed on a Europallet (**EUR pallet**) which measures 800 × 1200 mm (see Figure 3.16). In the fast-moving consumer goods and mechanical engineering industry it is not unusual to use half-pallets, or half a Europallet (600 × 800 mm). Not all companies use Europallets as a standard, however, and many have developed their own pallets and other unit loads. Some countries have different measurements as the dominating standard, while others have yet to arrive at a dominant standard.

Specially adapted packages are often expensive, which means that for financial reasons they must be returned to the sender after delivery and a return flow of packages is thus created. When EUR pallets or other internationally standardised unit loads are used, it is not necessary to construct a separate return flow system for the units since they can be exchanged or sold after use. Instead of returning empty pallets after delivery they are exchanged between different users through so-called pallet pools.

Disposable and durable packages

In the choice and design of packages, a major consideration is whether **disposable** or **durable packages** will be used. There is no straightforward answer to this question. The optimal solution is determined under specific conditions for the product in question and the flow involved. Some important criteria to consider in such a choice are seasonal variations, transport distances and cycle time for the packages.

In the case of large variations in demand, great transport distances and long cycle times, it is often very difficult to create an economically feasible system for durable packages, since in this case the total amount of capital tied up in the packages and the demand for efficient return flow will increase. Durable packages are normally larger, heavier and more expensive than disposable packages, and they tie up more capital and are more expensive to transport. On the other hand, durable packages have advantages when there are short, fast, regular and frequent deliveries without seasonal variations and where the transport vehicle can be filled with empty packages for return deliveries. Other conditions are when a smaller number of standardised packages can be used for several products and the empty packages can be compressed to enable efficient storage and efficient return flow. Under such conditions, tied-up capital and transport costs can be minimised for durable packages. At the same time the durable system may be environmentally preferable to a disposable system, since it requires lower consumption of materials and decreased quantities of waste, provided that the extra return transportation and cleaning do not have a large negative environmental impact.

3.5 Conclusion and Summary

The flow of materials in the logistics system can be divided into the handling of materials within a plant and external transportation between storage points. Materials handled are normally enclosed in packaging which is adapted to a unit load to simplify the logistics. The physical form of a store or warehouse is shaped by decisions related to its layout and location of items in stock. The principles of materials handling and freight transportation have been discussed in this chapter. Freight transportation between geographically separate plants normally takes place by one of four traffic modes: sea, rail, road or air, or combinations of these. The different traffic modes have diverse characteristics, making them more or less suitable for use in various situations which have been briefly described in the chapter. Packaging was also discussed.

Key concepts

Automatic guided vehicle system (AGVS) 60

Automated storage and retrieval system (AS/RS) 56

Batching 61

Carousel store 57

Combined transport 64

Continual supply 61

Counterbalance truck 59

Conveyor system 60

Depth stacking 54

Disposable package 74

Durable package 74

EUR pallet 74

Fixed location 53

Forwarder 63

Fourth-party logistics provider (4PL) 69

Free stacking 54

Freight forwarder 70

Freight transport 64

Infrastructure provider 63

Item picking 61

Kitting 61

Logistics service provider 63

Order picking 57

Pallet 51

Pallet truck 59

Paternoster store 57

Rack storage 54

Discussion Tasks

1 It is possible to distinguish between goods in a whole logistics system which are handled as unbroken whole pallets, and goods which are put into smaller units than whole pallets. Summarise the most important differences when transporting, handling and storing the two types of goods.

2 The container is sometimes mentioned as one of the most important inventions of the twentieth century. Discuss why that is so.

3 Discuss the pros and cons of fixed and random storage location.

4 Which traffic mode is most suitable for moving sheet steel from the steelworks to a workshop industry, heavy steel constructions between two workshop industries, foodstuffs from manufacturer to shops, electronics components from subcontractors to product-manufacturing companies? Discuss the advantages and disadvantages of using each traffic mode in the different situations.

5 Combined transportation means combining two traffic modes. The combination of railway and road transport is often cited. Discuss the possibilities and effects of combining other traffic modes.

Further reading

Ballou, D. (2003) *Business logistics/supply chain management.* Prentice Hall, Upper Saddle River.

Bardi, E., Novack, R. and Coyle, J. (2004) *Transportation.* Thomson Learning, London.

European Commission (2005) *European Union – Energy and transport in figures, 2005.* Directorate-general for Energy and Transport in co-operation with Eurostat.

Frazelle, E. (2001) *World-class warehousing and material handling.* McGraw-Hill, New York.

Hinkka, V. and Lehtinen, J. (2006) "Testing voice technology in the supply chain". In Arlbjorn, J. (ed.), *Nordic case reader in logistics and supply chain management*. The Nordic Logistics Research Network, University Press of Southern Denmark, Odense.

Jessop, D. and Morrison, A. (1994) *Storage and supply of materials*. Prentice Hall, Upper Saddle River.

Koster, R., Le-Duc, T. and Roodbergen, K. (2007) "Design and control of warehouse order picking: a literature review", *European Journal of Operational Research*, Vol. 182, No. 2, pp. 481–501.

May, G. (2005) "Transport in Europe: where are we going?", *Insight*, Vol. 7, No. 6, pp. 24–38.

Murphy, P. and Wood, D. (2004) *Contemporary logistics*. Prentice Hall, Upper Saddle River.

Schary, P. and Skjott-Larsen, T. (2001) *Managing the global supply chain*. Copenhagen Business School Press, Copenhagen.

Stefansson, G. (2006) "Collaborative logistics management and the role of third-party service providers", *International Journal of Physical Distribution and Logistics Management*, Vol. 36, No. 2, pp. 76–92.

Tomkins, J., White, J., Bozer, Y. and Tanchoco, J. (2003) *Facilities planning*. John Wiley & Sons, Hoboken.

Woxenius, J. and Bärthel, F. (2007) "Intermodal road-rail transport in the European Union". In Konings, R., Priemus, H. and Nijkamp, P. (eds) *The future of intermodal freight transport: concepts, design and implementation*. Edward Elgar Publishing, Cheltenham.

PART 2
Logistics and Supply Chain Goals and Performance

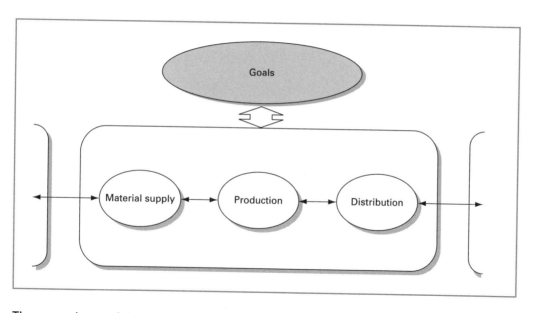

The second part of the book contains three chapters. These discuss the performance variables, representing the goals and performances of logistics and supply chain systems. Customer service, costs, tied-up capital and environmental aspects are covered.

CHAPTER

04

Customer service

A product that is sold and delivered to a customer normally comprises a mix of physical goods and service. The goods may consist of a sheet of glass, while the service is that the size of the glass sheet is ordered to measure, that it can be easily ordered on the supplier's website, that the sheet is delivered directly to the building on the construction site where it is to be installed, that the delivery takes place at the exact time when the sheet of glass is to be installed, and that the supplier also installs the glass on delivery. In this type of situation it may well be that the peripheral services are even more important than the goods themselves when a customer chooses a certain supplier on the basis of their perception of good quality.

For many products and markets, the proportion of goods and services in the total product has changed over the years. In many situations today it is difficult to create added value through changes in the product. Instead, it is the peripheral services in conjunction with the purchase which provide added value to the customer. In certain situations it is even possible to say that

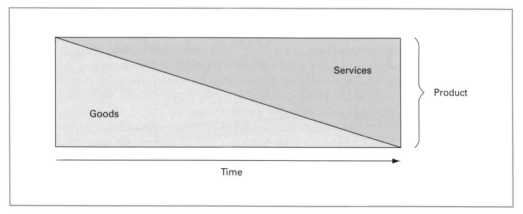

FIGURE 4.1 The product as a mix of goods and services. Development towards increased proportion of service and decreased proportion of product

the product itself is a special function. In a maintenance agreement, for example, it may be the responsibility of the maintenance company to ensure that an engine will operate for a certain number of hours during a time period. In this case it is the function of "serviceability" which is sold. The function consists partly of a number of engine components which are continuously replaced, but also the service of replacing them at the right time and at the right cost. Figure 4.1 illustrates graphically how a product mix of goods and services has changed over time.

Customer service is used as an overall concept for all the peripheral services which are offered to the customer and which take place in conjunction with a business agreement. Customer service can be described as a number of activities involving the purchaser, the vendor and third parties, which aim to add value to the product. It may involve activities and values that are carried out and added in conjunction with transactions and delivery, but it may also include activities and values that are created with the help of more long-term relationships, agreements and contracts.

The capacity of the logistics system to influence revenues is through services in conjunction with the delivery of a product to the customer. By understanding the customer's need for services on delivery, goals for customer service can be determined. These goals, together with others, must be the basis for the design and control of the logistics system.

This chapter describes the role of logistics in creating good customer service and customer satisfaction. Logistics influences customer service before, during and after the delivery itself. A more detailed description is given of commonly used delivery service elements. The process of determining total customer service commitment for customers and products and for developing customer satisfaction is then discussed.

The chapter is closely related to the three other chapters in Part II of the book. There are also direct links to Chapter 10 (especially Section 10.7 Value-adding distributors), Chapter 12 (especially Section 12.5 Safety stock determination) and Chapter 17 (especially Section 17.2 Information exchange, Section 17.4 Electronic marketplaces and businesses, and Section 17.5 Information quality).

4.1 Customer Service and Customer Satisfaction

To achieve appropriate behaviour towards a customer a company must, as far as possible, perform what the customer expects of it. In order to do this the company's performance must be measured and followed up. In this perspective it is possible to distinguish between customer service and customer satisfaction. Customer service starts in the company's performance for customers. The company itself defines what is appropriate customer service, measures its customer service on the basis of these definitions and follows up its performance itself. The goal is to fulfil internally defined standards. Customer satisfaction involves first finding out what it is that really satisfies a customer and what the customer expects. Not until then can measurement units be defined and performances measured by asking customers directly about their perceptions of delivery performance. The approach is to fulfil specified expectations.

The Kano model, described in Figure 4.2, separates customer satisfaction into three groups: basic needs, expected needs and exciting experiences. The basic needs are often unspoken and considered obvious. It could for example be to receive the ordered product in the right quantity and quality. These needs are necessary to satisfy in order to make the customer happy. It is, however, never enough to satisfy only these needs. The expected needs are such needs that the customer is aware of and would like to have satisfied, but they are not absolutely necessary to satisfy to make the customer happy. Examples of expected needs are short delivery times, frequent deliveries of small batches and mounting of bar codes on the customer packages. The

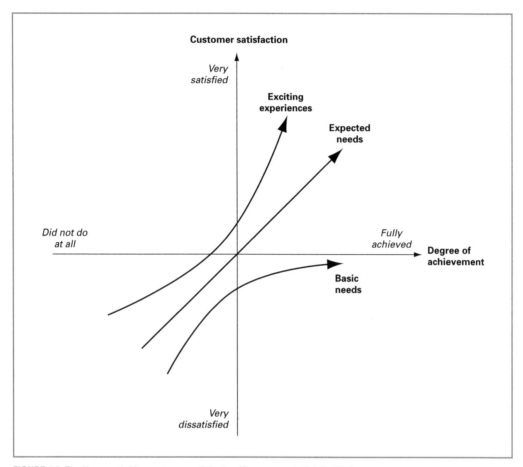

FIGURE 4.2 The Kano model for customer satisfaction (Bergman and Klefsjö, 2004)

decision of what expected needs to satisfy may be a result of a negotiation with the customer where costs and practical issues are considered. Exciting experiences are such that the customer is not aware of and the supplier must find out by itself. These are consequently also unspoken. Offering an exciting experience may make the customer delighted. Unexpected, fast and flexible complaint handling may for example make the customer delighted but other unexpected services could also result in exciting experiences.

Satisfying customers is of great significance for several reasons, but above all to retain them, which in turn is closely tied to a company's profitability. There is a strong correlation between customer loyalty and profitability. It is a good deal more costly to sell to new customers than to existing ones. A good marketing ambition should therefore be to retain existing customers and develop them into lifelong customers. This could be achieved by being a high-performance supplier, supplying different forms of post-delivery service and rectifying as quickly as possible any deficiencies which may have arisen in deliveries carried out, despite all efforts made to avoid them.

Retaining customers is also an important prerequisite for creating the necessary conditions for integration and co-operation in supply chains. Certain minimum demands are required for establishing long-term relationships. The more loyal a customer is, the greater is the probability that they will continue to be a customer, so that relationships once established can be retained. One necessary condition for creating loyalty and long-term customer relationships is a high degree of customer satisfaction being achieved. It is not simply a question of gaining satisfied customers, but customers who are delighted with the performance and service supplied, and who feel that they have received more than their expectations in the exchange, i.e. have achieved exciting experiences according to the Kano model. In this chapter the term *customer service* is used to describe what has been variously defined as both customer service and customer satisfaction.

4.2 Customer Service in Different Time Phases

From the logistics point of view, customer service includes all those activities related to the flow of materials which create added value for customers. These activities do not only take place during the delivery process itself, but can be divided into the four time phases of the business deal: pre-order, from order to delivery, at delivery and post-delivery (see Figure 4.3). Logistics can influence customer service in all of these phases.

Pre-order customer service includes the conditions required for a customer to place an order, including clear and clarifying information about these conditions so that the customer is able to plan his activities around them. Examples are delivery times, current stock levels and so on. Openness and the supply of logistics-related information are important in creating good customer service during this phase.

Customer service from order to delivery refers to the ease with which an order may be placed and to what extent the supplier can facilitate this process for the customer and adapt to the customer's preferences in terms of order procedures. It includes conveying information at an early stage about any delays in delivery times and the supplier's ability to handle changes in customer requirements at short notice; for example, changes in delivery times and delivery volumes – in other words, the supplier's *delivery flexibility*.

Customer service during delivery itself is the service normally included in the logistics system's customer service. Examples of this are length of delivery times and to what extent promised delivery times can actually be achieved.

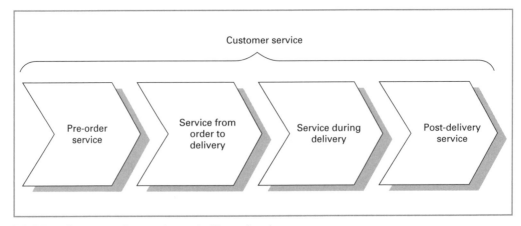

FIGURE 4.3 Customer service commitments in different time phases

Post-delivery customer service includes the possibility of tracking the original materials used in products delivered, obtaining spare parts when needed, handling of claims and returns, and the processing and recycling of used products and packages.

4.3 Delivery Service Elements

Service related to carrying out the order-to-delivery process is usually called **delivery service**, and takes place primarily during the phases order-to-delivery and delivery itself. Delivery service can be expressed in terms of a number of service elements or as a total weighted index of several elements. They vary in significance in different situations. The following is a list of the most common delivery service elements:

- *Inventory service level* – to what extent stock items can be delivered directly from stocks to customer from customer orders
- *Delivery precision* – to what extent the delivery takes place at the delivery time agreed with the customer
- *Delivery reliability* – a measurement of the quality of delivery in terms of the right product being delivered in the right quantity
- *Delivery time* – the time elapsed from receipt of customer order to delivery
- *Delivery flexibility* – the ability to adapt to and comply with changes in customer requirements in agreed and already ongoing orders

Inventory service level

The **inventory service level** is also called service level or **fill rate**, and describes to what extent stock items are actually available in stock when they are demanded. It is a measurement of the probability of being able to directly deliver from stocks to customers from customer orders. It measures the delivery ability of the warehouse and is an important delivery service element in make-to-stock and delivery from stock situations.

There are several different ways of defining the inventory service level. The interpretation of a service level of 99 per cent, for example, is not entirely self-evident. A customer-oriented definition would be the proportion of completely delivered customer orders directly from stocks. This is the most stringent way of measuring inventory service level, especially when a customer order contains many order lines (each unique item number represents an order line on the order). The definition is appropriate when the entire customer order must be delivered completely to create customer value. Another common definition is the proportion of **order lines** that can be delivered directly from stocks. One order line corresponds to one item number and for this reason the definition is oriented towards product-based follow-up of delivery capability. This definition is appropriate when split deliveries of full order lines are acceptable, but not split deliveries of individual order lines. The third and more tolerant definition is to measure the proportion of order value that can be directly delivered, i.e. to accept split deliveries of single order lines.

In the practical application of the first two definitions, split deliveries accepted by the customer are often included and for this reason are not considered as poor customer service. Deliveries with one or two days' delay are sometimes accepted as correctly delivered in calculations.

Example 4.1

During one time period a company has received three customer orders with six, two and three order lines for direct delivery from finished goods stock. Deliveries were as follows:

Order	Item number	Units ordered	Units delivered
Order A	1225	200	150
	1501	10	10
	2301	50	48
	4507	300	200
	5135	250	250
	6287	75	75
Order B	1501	15	10
	3321	125	125
Order C	1501	20	20
	4112	100	100
	4117	100	90

None of the three orders is delivered complete. Six of eleven order lines are delivered directly from the stock but five are not available in stock. 1078 of the totally 1245 ordered units are delivered directly from stock. Consequently, the company's service level can be expressed as a percentage that varies between 0 per cent and 87 per cent depending on how it is defined. It is possible to use the following definitions:

$$\text{Percentage complete orders delivered directly from stocks} = \frac{0}{3} = 0\%$$

$$\text{Percentage complete order lines delivered directly from stocks} = \frac{6}{11} = 45\%$$

$$\text{Percentage of items delivered directly from stocks} = \frac{1078}{1245} = 87\%$$

Delivery precision

Delivery precision is also called **on-time delivery**, and is a measurement of the degree to which deliveries take place at the times agreed with the customer. In contrast to inventory service level, this variable is primarily related to the delivery capacity for non-finished stock items which are assembled or manufactured directly to customer orders, i.e. items delivered with a time delay from receipt of order. Deliveries which are too early or too late are defined as low precision. In businesses with small safety mechanisms, the consequences of low-delivery precision may be very significant. An entire assembly plant may be forced to shut down if a certain component is not delivered at the agreed time.

Delivery precision can be defined as the number of deliveries made at the agreed time in relation to the total number of deliveries. Using this definition, order-based comparisons can be made over a desired measurement period. The promised delivery time may be defined as a day or a time window, the latter meaning that one or two days' early or late deliveries are acceptable. Acceptance and definition of the time window depends on the type of product and demand situation. For example, if the product is bulky or has a high value, early delivery would perhaps not be desirable. If, on the other hand, delivery must be co-ordinated with other deliveries as part of an assembly operation, late delivery would not be acceptable. One measurement issue that arises is how to handle deliveries whose time of delivery has been changed by agreement with the customer. Such deliveries can be defined as deliveries on time if the change in delivery time is a customer requirement, but should not fall into that category if the customer has been forced to accept a new delivery time as a result of the supplier's problems.

CASE STUDY 4.1: DELIVERY PRECISION MEASUREMENT AT HALDEX BRAKE PRODUCTS

Haldex Brake Products makes brake systems and components for on-road and off-road vehicles. It is world market leader in its segment. Its customers are OEMs in the automotive industry but also component manufacturers. The largest customer segment is European heavy truck manufacturers. Finnveden is an example of a single supplier of two components, including about 20 different variants. The components have high volume but not high value, thus being typical "B" items in an ABC analysis. Because of the single source and relatively high volume by value of the two components, Finnveden is considered a strategically important supplier. Haldex is considered a strategically important customer for Finnveden.

Haldex's customer orders are based on delivery schedules/call-offs and on specific customer orders received from its customers. The accuracy of the forecasts received from OEMs is considered high, but the forecasts of the other customers' demand are less accurate. Still, the demand for Finnveden's components is quite even and stable. Haldex sends annual forecasts and 12 weeks rolling delivery schedules to Finnveden. The schedules are frozen within the one-day transportation time plus one day.

Deliveries are bought with Incoterm (see Chapter 15) Exworks, i.e. Haldex is responsible for the transportation but the supplier books the transport.

Delivery precision is the most important delivery service measure at Haldex. It is defined and measured per order line and acknowledged day (i.e. the delivery is on time if the arrival day is the same as the acknowledged delivery day). Several internal measures are also used: for example, inventory turnover rate, production after schedule, takt time and delivery precision to customer.

Haldex's delivery precision target on its suppliers is 98 per cent. This is the same requirement as the OEMs put on Haldex. Finnveden prioritises Haldex as a customer and performs an average delivery precision of almost 100 per cent.

Haldex continuously monitors the supplier delivery precision and internal performance measures. The measurement is used internally in order to take the necessary action. The main measurement focus is on the internal productivity measures and its own delivery service to customers. These measures are monitored and communicated internally on a daily basis. Daily war room meetings are used to identify the causes of low performances. The supplier delivery service measures will be sent to low-performing suppliers on a monthly basis and to all suppliers on a quarterly basis.

Delivery reliability

Delivery reliability measures the quality of delivery in terms of the right product being delivered in the right quantity. Low delivery reliability gives rise to activities which are otherwise unnecessary. High delivery reliability can eliminate much of the work which would otherwise be carried out at the customer's goods reception.

Delivery reliability is normally defined as the number of customer orders delivered without complaints from the customer in relation to the total number of delivered customer orders. Complaints may include the items delivered not corresponding with the agreed number stated on the delivery note, or items delivered not fulfilling quality requirements stipulated. Reasons for incorrect quantities, for example, could be that the wrong item or the wrong number of items has been picked and packed at the supplier. Quality errors may arise in the supplier's processes and remained unidentified in the supplier's quality control, or they may be caused during transport and handling after delivery from the supplier.

Delivery time

Delivery time is the time that elapses from a customer order being received to completed delivery. It consists of administration and order processing times, dispatch and transport times and, in the case of engineer or make to order, engineering or manufacturing times. Whether or

---

CASE STUDY 4.2: LEADTIME DEFINITION AT IKEA

IKEA has defined its leadtime from when the need for stock replenishment is detected in an IKEA store until this need is satisfied, i.e. the stock is actually replenished. The total leadtime consists of the following five sub-leadtimes. The starting and ending of the sub-leadtimes are defined and measured by IKEA.

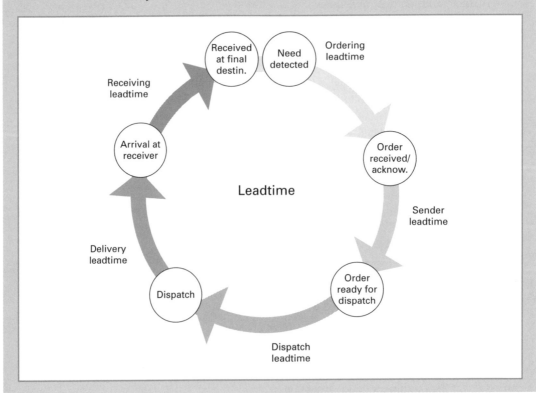

not transport time is to be included in delivery time is determined by the responsibility limits for the delivery. Since there are different transport times to different customers, however, it is appropriate to define delivery time up until dispatch and then add to that the customer-specific transport time.

Delivery time is normally expressed in weeks or days. Long delivery times have many negative consequences; among these, decreased flexibility due to extended response times for the order. Capital tied up and its associated costs also increase since the materials are in transit for a longer period.

Delivery flexibility

Delivery flexibility refers to the capacity to adapt to and comply with changes in customer requirements in agreed and ongoing orders. It may be a question of changes in delivery times, order quantities or contents and performance of products delivered.

We can distinguish between delivery flexibility before orders and delivery flexibility during orders, i.e. from receipt of order to delivery. Delivery flexibility before orders refers to the possibility of accepting delivery times that deviate from those normally used, deliveries of smaller quantities than stated minimum quantities, product requirements that deviate from normal, and so on. Delivery flexibility during orders puts higher demands on the short-term capacity to adapt to changes in customer requirements. This could be bringing forward dispatch, or delivering larger quantities of an order already in production, or making product changes to a product already in production.

Delivery service index

Perfect delivery service means that an order is delivered at the agreed time and contains no quantity errors or quality faults. To gain an indication of the proportion of all customer orders for a special customer category of product group that are perfectly delivered, a **delivery service index** can be calculated by multiplying the percentages of delivery precision and delivery reliability, and possibly other relevant delivery service elements. In this measurement it is also possible to weigh in delivery service performance after delivery; for example, the proportion of correct invoices and proportion of customer orders without returns. A situation with 80 per cent delivery precision, 95 per cent delivery reliability, 99 per cent perfect invoices and 96 per cent of customer orders without returns for a special customer category will mean that 72 per cent of orders have been perfectly delivered, i.e. $0.80 \times 0.95 \times 0.99 \times 0.96 = 0.72$.

In the delivery service index described above, all delivery service elements are weighted equally. It is also possible to calculate an average index with differentially weighted service elements as in Table 4.1. Such an index does not express the proportion of perfect orders, but can function as a measurement of the average delivery service performance.

Delivery service element	Weighting %	Performance %	Weighted performance %
Delivery precision	40	80	32
Delivery reliability	40	95	38
Perfect invoices	5	99	4.95
Orders without returns	15	96	14.4
		Weighted index:	89.4

TABLE 4.1 Delivery service index with weighted service elements

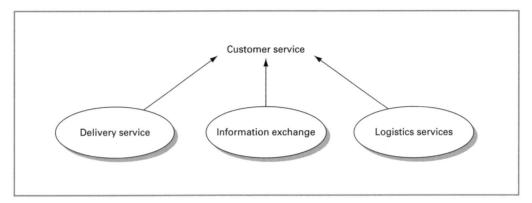

FIGURE 4.4 The influence of logistics on customer service

Customer service is influenced through delivery service, exchange of information and logistics services.

In the example given in Table 4.1 using weighted service elements, the service index is 89.4 per cent. The elements of delivery service precision and delivery reliability have been given the highest weights since they are perceived as having the greatest significance for the customer category in question.

4.4 Exchange of Information and Logistics Services

In addition to creating good delivery service, the logistics system can influence customer service by supplying information on the flow of materials and offer logistics-related services as a complement to delivery of the physical product. The potential of logistics to influence customer service is shown in Figure 4.4.

Information on the flow of materials refers to all information that may provide added value to the customer. Before the order this includes providing the customer with information on delivery times, delivery quantities and stock balance. From order to delivery and during delivery it includes information on any delivery delays and processing status in production, and the location of the consignment during transport. Information after the delivery may include, for example, information about spare parts.

Logistics-related services which can provide customer value are, for example, the ease with which a customer can place an order, the option of having products packed in the customer's packages, supplying packages with bar codes to facilitate the customer's handling work, and so on.

4.5 Determining Total Customer Service Commitments

Customer service can be created during different phases of a business deal, and it is possible to modify service through different delivery service elements, exchange of information and performance of logistics services. However, it is usually more costly to provide high customer service compared with low customer service. It is therefore important to balance the costs of providing customer service with the revenues the service is expected to generate. It is necessary to give the "right" service to different customers. To decide on appropriate customer service strategies, a thorough analysis will be required of customer needs, the relevant customer service performance, competitors' performances and costs and revenues for different customer service commitments. Using this analysis it will be possible to determine customer service commitments for different categories of customers and products.

Customer analysis

The starting point when determining what customer service will be offered to different customers is an understanding of customers' needs for different customer service performance. This involves identifying what customer service – for example, what delivery service elements, what exchange of information and what logistics services – is most important from the customer's perspective. For each of these customer service performances we should also distinguish between what the customer says he wants and what he really needs. In certain situations a customer may demand more than necessary, and in other situations he may not be aware of his needs. Customer service offered should be based on real needs.

Existing customer service performance

To be able to improve total customer service performance, a supplier needs to know how well the present customer service commitment corresponds to the customer's needs. Continuous follow-up and measurement of the supplier's performance is required for this reason.

To be able to compare customers' perceived customer service performance with the supplier's perceptions it is necessary that both parties use the same definitions and make measurements in similar ways. This is not always the case, however. There is often a discrepancy between the supplier's and the customer's perception of customer service performance. This may be due to their customer service goals being unco-ordinated, but may also arise as a result of different definitions being used. Such variations between a supplier's and customer's goals and performance perceptions of customer service must be eliminated if the supplier is to know how to develop total customer service commitment.

Market analysis

By comparing customer needs and the supplier's customer service performance with competitors' customer service performance it is possible to gain an impression of whether a company's performance is too good or too poor. Supplying customer service which is considerably higher than competitors' performances may be unnecessarily costly in relation to additional revenues generated. Service which is poorer than competitors' is not competitive in the long term. Unfortunately, it is not always possible to compare all customer service performances with competitors since not all information is available.

Cost and revenue analysis

Customer service has a direct influence on costs. For example, a higher stock service level requires larger safety stocks, i.e. stocks kept to hedge against uncertainty in demand and replenishment lead time, which incur higher inventory costs. Shorter delivery times may mean that a company is forced to stock an item in several regional warehouses close to customers instead of in one central warehouse. Higher delivery flexibility may mean that continual overcapacity is required in the form of extra machines and personnel, which will also cause higher costs. The normal relationship between costs and customer service is illustrated as in Figure 4.5. The marginal cost increases dramatically as the level of customer service approaches 100 per cent. For

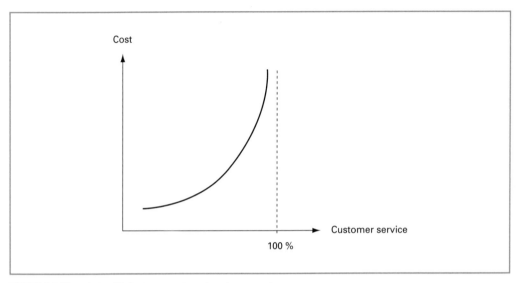

FIGURE 4.5 The relationship between costs and customer service

example, larger increases in safety stocks will be required, and it will be more costly to raise the inventory service level from 97 to 98 per cent than from 70 to 71 per cent.

Revenues are also affected by customer service. This is obviously the reason for wishing to raise levels of customer service in the first place. Estimating how changes in customer service influence revenues is much more difficult than judging the costs of changed service. Only if raised customer service enables a higher sales price will the change in service have an immediate effect on revenues. If, on the other hand, customer service is raised to improve competitiveness and increased sales in the long term, there will be no immediate influence on revenues. If competitors also raise their customer service there may be no noticeable effect at all, but if the increased service levels lead to an advantage over the competition it is possible that customer satisfaction will increase in the future and that a rise in sales may result. The relation-

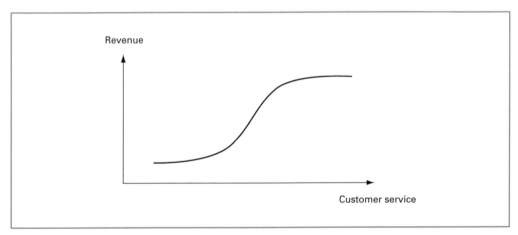

FIGURE 4.6 The relationship between revenues and customer service

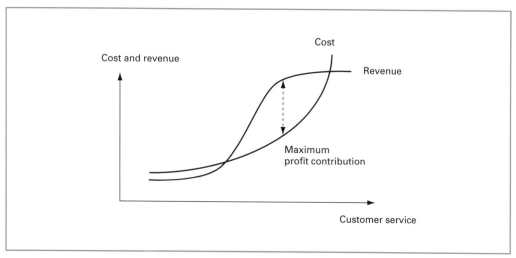

FIGURE 4.7 The relationship between profit contribution and customer service
The dashed line shows the level of customer service that gives the maximum profit contribution.

ship between revenues and customer service is usually illustrated by an S-shaped curve, as shown in Figure 4.6.

The reason for small expected revenues at low levels of customer service is that the service is seen as unacceptably low and uncompetitive. The service bracket in the steepest regions of the curve corresponds to expected customer service and customer service provided by competitors. An increase in customer service in this bracket will generate additional revenues since there is an improvement compared with competitors. Above this bracket we cannot expect a radical increase in revenues by further raising customer service levels. The company already has the highest customer service on the market and it is perceived as satisfactory by customers. Further increases in customer service are over-performance, which costs more than it generates in added value and revenues. By combining the curves in Figures 4.5 and 4.6, as shown in Figure 4.7, the relationship between costs and revenues can be illustrated at different levels of customer service.

Since it is difficult to trace exactly the relationship of costs and customer service, and almost impossible to derive the relationship between revenues and customer service, in practice it is not possible to identify optimal customer service as shown in Figure 4.7. However, it is important to understand how an increase or decrease in customer service offered may be expected to influence revenues and costs. This is made possible by knowing how the current customer service is related to customer needs and competitors' performance. If it is desired to change the total customer service, it is also important to know the expected effects and resources required for different measures aimed at this change.

Establishing a customer service strategy

As described above, customer service influences both revenues and costs. To achieve a good relationship between improvements wanted and resources required for these, it may be desirable to have differentiated control of what measures are to be taken. These may be in the form of differentiated measures between different customer service dimensions or between customers and products.

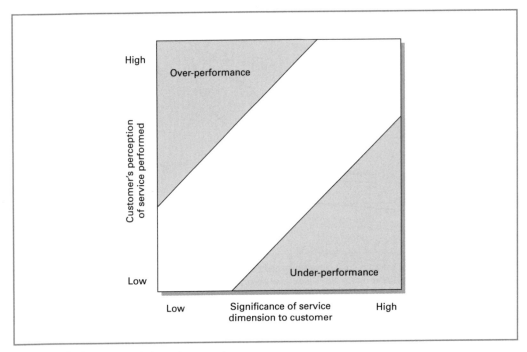

FIGURE 4.8 Performance matrix for customer service
Customer service dimensions in the shaded areas of the figure should be adjusted.

Differentiation of customer service dimensions

Differentiation of customer service dimensions may mean that the focus is on dimensions that are significant to customers and which at the same time have the lowest competitiveness. A small increase in the performance of such a dimension may generate great added value for a customer. It is possible to identify some customer service dimensions that are less costly to improve than others and which also have more significance for customers.

Performance matrices as shown in Figure 4.8 can be used to facilitate priorities in customer service dimensions and determine suitable levels of customer service. The one axis of such a matrix is the significance of service dimensions to the customer, and the other axis is the customer's perception of service performed. By filling in the matrix for each service dimension an indication is gained of which dimensions of current performances are higher than necessary and justified, and in which dimensions current performances are insufficient. Areas of over-performance and under-performance should be rectified first in order to optimise use of resources in relation to their significance for customers.

Differentiation of customers and products

Establishing a customer service commitment also involves deciding on total customer service goals and performances for different customers and products. A uniform service for all customers and for all products will mean unreasonably high costs or service performance that is far too low. High priority customers and products would receive relatively poor service whereas customers and products with low demands and needs would receive too high and costly service. The company would then risk losing demanding but profitable customers and instead would retain more unprofitable ones. In the same way there is a risk of losing sales of profitable products.

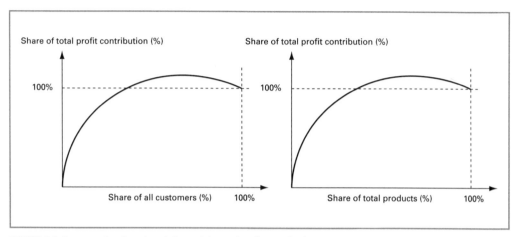

FIGURE 4.9 Customers' and products' share of the total profit contribution

By differentiating customer service commitments and concentrating on profitable customers and products, added value can be created for these important customers and products at the same time as total costs for logistics are reduced. It is often the case that a small number of a company's customers account for a large part of the company's total profit contribution. Similarly, there are normally a small number of products which generate a large part of the total profit contribution. The relationships between products, customers and profit contribution at a company are usually represented by the curves in Figure 4.9.

It is not uncommon for 20 per cent of customers or products to account for 80 per cent of the profit contribution. By grouping customers and products in different classes, and by analysing the Pareto effect with the aid of a so-called **ABC analysis** as described in Appendix A, based on their share of the total profit contribution, customer service strategies can be differentiated between groups. The product groups with the highest proportion of profit contribution can, for example, be given priority by assigning them the highest inventory service levels and thus larger safety stocks in the finished goods stocks than the product groups with lower proportions of profit contribution. When differentiating safety stocks it is also important to consider that items with high volume and value tie up more capital and are more costly to store than those with low volume and value. Volume by value could therefore be combined with profit contribution when grouping customers and products in different priority groups. Another strategy for prioritising this product group could be to stock them in regional warehouses close to customers to enable short delivery times, while other items are stored in a central warehouse at greater distances from regional markets. Customer service costs are increased for the most important products and customers, but by decreasing the costs for other groups the total costs remain unchanged or actually decrease.

The above classification and differentiation can be done for individual products and customers. It is also possible to carry out a combined product and customer classification, as shown in Figure 4.10.

The A groups represent products and customers with the highest proportion of total profit contribution. B represents the next highest and C the lowest. Accordingly, the area A-A represents the combination of products and customers which generate the highest share of profit contribution, while the area C-C represents the combination of products and customers which

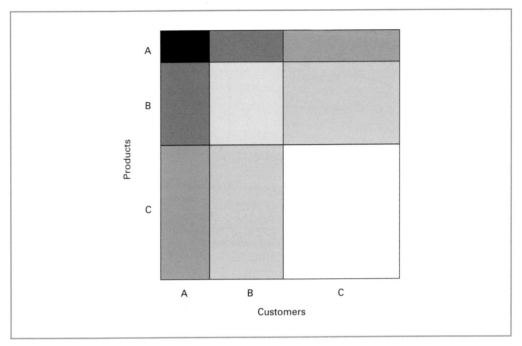

FIGURE 4.10 Combined product and customer classification
A products and A customers generate the highest proportion of the total profit contribution, while C products and C items generate the lowest.

generate the lowest share. If A products correspond to 20 per cent of the products which generate 80 per cent of the total profit contribution and A customers correspond to 20 per cent of the customers that generate 80 per cent of the profit contribution, the A-A group will comprise 4 per cent of the customers/products (20 per cent × 20 per cent) which generate 64 per cent of the total profit contribution (80 per cent × 80 per cent). One conceivable order of priority for customer service between the different groups in the matrix could be A-A, B-A, A-B, B-B, etc.

Differentiating customer service through one of the above analysis models should be seen as a first blunt instrument for deciding priorities. The process should be supplemented with detailed assessments and adjustments. For example, adjustments to the selection of customer service strategy may be needed for those products/customers that are in area C-A, since this area also includes products for important customers. It may also be advantageous to prioritise products at the start of their lifecycle which have the potential to create future profits.

The above analyses are based on products' and customers' capacity to generate profit for the company. They focus less on customers' needs for high customer service for different products. For example, there may be products which generate low profit contributions for the company but which are given high priority by customers. To consider how critical a product is for a customer, an **analysis of critical value** can be made as shown in Table 4.2.

From the analysis of products' critical value for customers in the example in Table 4.2, we can see that product E, ranked as the next lowest priority for its share towards profit contribution, will have a higher priority when its significance to the customer is also weighed in. Similarly, product F will have a lower priority since it is not perceived as critical by customers. This analysis, too, must be seen as an initial, coarse instrument for deciding priorities and must also be supplemented by detailed assessments.

Product	Profit contribution (rank order)	Critical value for customer			Rank order × profit contribution	Order of priority for customer service
		1	**2**	**3**		
C	1		x		2	1
G	2		x		4	3
A	3	x			3	2
D	4			x	12	5
F	5			x	15	7
B	6		x		12	5
E	7	x			7	4
G	8		x		16	8

TABLE 4.2 Example of a critical value analysis

4.6 Conclusion and Summary

Customer service in the logistics system has the potential to influence a company's revenues. This influence occurs in four phases in a business deal: before the order, from order to delivery, at delivery, and after delivery. The influence operates in three principal ways: through delivery service, exchange of information and logistics services.

High delivery service is created and measured through different delivery service elements, whose significance to the logistics system varies in different situations. For example, inventory service level is important in certain situations while delivery precision and delivery flexibility may be more important in others.

In order to determine optimum customer service in a specific situation, an analysis will be required of the customer's needs, the current customer service performance, the competition situation and the expected effects on costs and revenues of the customer service performance. Different methods of establishing customer service strategies for different products and customers have been presented in the chapter.

🔒 Key concepts

ABC analysis 95

Cost/revenue analysis 91

Critical value analysis 96

Customer service 82

Delivery flexibility 89

Delivery precision 86

Delivery reliability 87

Delivery service 85

Delivery service index 89

Delivery time 88

Fill rate 85

Information exchange service 90

Inventory service level 85

On-time delivery 86

Order line 85

Perfect delivery service 89

Discussion Tasks

1 Customer service can be defined as a philosophy, a goal, an activity or a measurement of performance. What does each definition signify? What units in the organisation of a manufacturing company should be responsible for each definition? What are the pros and cons of each type of definition? How would you define customer service?

2 We can distinguish between customer service commitments during the phases of pre-order, order to delivery, during delivery and after delivery. Service during these different phases varies in importance in different situations. Identify situations in which service in each phase can be considered as essential for overall customer service.

3 Discuss how ABC analysis could be used for improving the customer service.

4 In a situation where we measure the delivery precision of goods sent to a customer and the customer measures the same delivery precision of goods received from us, there is a risk that we and the customer have different perceptions of how good the service is. Why could that be so?

5 The significance of different delivery service elements varies between situations. How important would you expect each element to be in the following situations? 1) Delivery of copying paper to central stores at a university. 2) Just in time deliveries (i.e. frequent deliveries in small batches) of components to a final assembly plant in the automobile industry. 3) Delivery of a spare part to an oil platform.

Exercises

Exercise 4.1

A wholesaler wants to estimate how different service levels affect its costs and revenue. Calculate which service level to use.

	Service Level					
	50%	60%	70%	80%	90%	95%
Revenue (M€/Year)	45	50	60	70	90	110
Distribution cost (M€/Year)	15	17	19	20	26	47

Exercise 4.2

Stovecase AB has a range of only five products. Still, they have problems with back orders. They deliver their products to many customers, which results in high transportation costs. Moreover, they know that their customers appreciate to receive complete orders. This is considered more important than a short delivery time.

Now, they have decided to develop a new customer service policy, where they differentiate products and customers (i.e. using ABC classification). They also need to develop their information system in order to get more accurate measures on customer service. The service level is calculated in the following way:

Number of completely delivered order lines of product X / Total number of order lines of product X

Product	Service level/Order line
A	95%
B	92%
C	89%
D	85%
E	86%

They also have information about the historical orders, in terms of ordering frequency and included products.

Products in order	Frequency
A	0.05
B	0.01
C	0.01
D	0.02
E	0.01
All five products	0.50
A+B+C	0.20
A+B+D	0.10
A+B	0.05
B+D	0.05

How well does Stovecase deliver complete orders to its customers?

Exercise 4.3

Conduct an ABC analysis based on the gross contribution of the following products. You know the sales and ratio gross contribution/sales.

Product	Sales (MSEK)	Gross contribution/sales (= gross contribution margin)
A	62	0,6
B	920	0,7
C	7500	0,5
D	176	0,3
E	300	−0,1
F	5213	0,3
G	8200	0,002
H	245	0,5
I	4503	0,5
J	200	−0,05
K	712	0,7
L	2342	0,1
M	150	0,5
N	900	0,25
O	7000	0,01

Further reading

Ballou, R. (2006) "Revenue estimation for logistics customer service offerings", *International Journal of Logistics Management,* Vol. 17, No. 1, pp. 21–37.

Bergman, B. and Klefsjö, B. (2004) *Quality from customer needs to customer satisfaction.* Studentlitteratur, Lund.

Christopher, M. (2005) *Logistics and supply chain management.* Prentice Hall, London.

Christopher, M. and Peck, H. (2003) *Marketing logistics.* Butterworth-Heinemann, London.

Forslund, H. and Jonsson, P. (2007) "Dyadic integration of the performance management process: a delivery service case study", *International Journal of Physical Distribution and Logistics Management,* Vol. 37, No. 7, pp. 546–567.

Lambert, D. and Stock, J. (2001) *Strategic logistics management.* McGraw-Hill, New York.

Mentzer, J., Flint, D. and Kent, J. (2001) "Logistics service quality as a segment-customized product", *Journal of Marketing,* Vol. 65, pp. 82–104.

CHAPTER

Logistics costs and tied-up capital

05

Logistics costs and **tied-up capital** are two performance variables in a logistics system internally in companies and in supply chains. As described by the Du Pont model in Chapter 1, tied-up capital has a direct effect on profitability and costs.

It is important to balance logistics costs and tied-up capital with other logistics goals, but it is also important to identify a system's existing logistics costs and logistics-related tied-up capital in order to measure and follow up current performance and evaluate the effects of rationalisation measures on costs and capital.

This chapter will describe the different types of logistics costs. In addition it will present some common measurements of costs and tied-up capital and introduce methods for mapping material flow, and assessing tied up capital and total logistics costs.

The chapter is closely related to the three other chapters in Part II of the book. There are also direct links to Chapter 2 (especially Section 2.1 about general process mapping and analysis) and Chapter 12 (especially Section 12.5 about financial aspects of safety stocks).

5.1 Logistics Costs

Logistics costs are those costs that can be attributed to logistics activities. These include direct costs for a physical handling, transportation and storage of goods in the flow of materials, costs for tied-up capital along this flow, and also administration costs for planning and controlling the flow of materials. Capacity and shortage costs are indirect costs which are also influenced by the logistics system, and when it is appropriate and possible these are also included in logistics costs. Logistics costs can be defined for an individual process, an organisation, or for a chain or network of companies. Irrespective of where the limits are drawn for a logistics system, total logistics costs can be broken down into the following cost types:

- Transportation and handling costs
- Packaging costs
- Inventory-carrying costs

■ Administrative costs

■ Ordering costs

■ Capacity-related costs

■ Shortage and delay costs

■ Environmental costs

The above division of costs into eight types is not completely consistent. Many partial costs can be attributed to more than one type of cost, and depending on the type of business activity and perspective, some modifications to this division may be appropriate. When looking at total logistics costs it is important to ensure that no costs are counted twice by being included in more than one type of cost.

The size of total logistics costs for a company depends, among other things, on what are defined as logistics costs, in which industry and country the company has operations, the role of the company in the logistics network and the structure of the network. Direct logistics costs for a manufacturing company usually vary between roughly 10 per cent and 30 per cent of the turnover, but could be higher or lower for different companies and industries.

Transportation and handling costs

Those costs related to the moving of goods originate from internal and external freight transportation, packaging and damages to goods during handling. Internal transportation within a company refers primarily to picking, internal movements and packaging, i.e. the materials handling activities. These costs are sometimes included in what is termed inventory carrying or storage costs. The transportation cost is normally a small proportion of the total logistics costs but is higher in industries where the value of the transported goods is high.

The main activities in external transportation are loading, moving, reloading and unloading of goods in movement between the company's own plants and to and from external suppliers and customers. External transportation may be performed by internal vehicles and staff, or may be outsourced. When goods are purchased and delivered free to the company's own plant, it is sometimes difficult to break down the costs for transportation activities since they are hidden in the product price.

During transportation the goods in transit represent tied-up capital. Costs for capital tied up in transported goods are thus a part of total transportation costs.

Packaging costs

Packaging costs include all costs related to packaging materials and the processes of packing and marking goods. In the case of reusable packages there will also be costs for administration, storage, return transport and reconditioning of packages, assuming that these costs are not included in any of the other categories of logistics costs.

Inventory carrying costs

The costs for keeping goods in stock are called **inventory carrying costs** and depend on the stored quantity, and are made up of a financial fraction, a physical fraction, and an uncertainty fraction. The financial costs are equivalent to the required return the company puts on capital which is tied up in stocks. The costs for physical storage are the operating costs for the physical stores, and uncertainty costs are related to the risk associated with keeping materials in stocks. Inventory carrying costs are in many companies the largest single logistics-related cost items.

In order correctly to estimate inventory carrying costs, each of the following three cost components must first be estimated:

1 Capital costs
2 Storage costs
3 Uncertainty costs

Capital costs: one way of valuating the inventory carrying costs is to treat materials in stock as an investment in current assets. Inventory carrying costs will then be the equivalent of the alternative required return for capital tied up in stocks. If it had not been tied up in stocks it could have been invested and generated revenue for the company in another way. Bank interest is the absolutely lowest alternative required return for a profit-making company. Every company determines what required returns it has on invested capital, and this may differ considerably between companies.

Storage costs: storage costs refer to the costs for the store premises and storage-related activities that the items in stock require. These include costs for stores personnel, depreciation on plants, storage and handling equipment, stores administration, internal transportation and energy. In rented storage space, costs are often determined by the number of pallet slots used. The exact cost is also influenced by demands on cooling, heating, space, light, and so on.

Uncertainty costs: keeping items in stock involves uncertainties and risks. When storage volumes increase, there is a tendency for more units to be broken as a result of increased handling. The average storage time for stored units is longer for high storage volumes, which may involve an increased risk of returned perishable items. Items which are not sold within their shelf life, or which for other reasons are in stock and cannot be sold (for example, products with short product lifecycles) will become obsolete and must be scrapped or sold at a reduced price. Stock items may also disappear from stores without any sales taking place. This may be due to theft through burglary, customers or the company's own personnel. A poor storage and order administration system may also cause losses of stock. If the wrong items or the wrong number of items are delivered to a customer, there will be added costs in correcting the error (for example, extra picking, administration and freight costs). Wrongly delivered items may also "disappear" at the customer's premises and not be returned at all. When the items are kept in stock in different stores (for example, different regional warehouses), shortages may arise in one of the warehouses and items must be transferred from one of the others. The reason for shortages is that demand allocation did not follow forecasts. Costs for re-localisation are also part of total uncertainty costs. The size of uncertainty costs varies a great deal depending on which items are involved. Insurance costs are also part of uncertainty costs. In contrast to the other uncertainty costs, insurance costs are simple to determine, but they often amount to only a small proportion of the value of goods.

When making lot-sizing decisions, it is the incremental inventory carrying costs that are of interest. **Incremental costs** are those costs of making extra units above the number already planned – in this case, a decision on whether to increase or decrease average stock volumes. Incremental inventory carrying costs are thus one part of total inventory carrying costs. Incremental inventory carrying costs are often expressed as an inventory carrying interest rate and refer to the annual incremental inventory carrying costs as a percentage of the average stock value. For example, at an inventory carrying interest rate of 15 per cent, the annual incremental inventory carrying cost for an item with a value of €100 will be €15. On the basis of the inventory carrying interest and the item's stock value, the incremental inventory carrying cost can be determined. Stock valuation principles and the definition of the incremental inventory carrying cost are described in Appendix B.

Administrative costs

Administrative costs include all those costs which are associated with long-term planning and operative management of material flows. These are primarily costs for administrative personnel, such as those required for order processing, planning, stock reports and so on. This category of costs also includes costs for procurement and operation of computer and communication systems for logistics activities.

Ordering costs

Ordering costs are those costs which can be attributed to the processing of purchase and manufacture orders. Ordering costs in many cases can be attributed to some other types of identified costs, and order administration may fall under administrative costs, loss of capacity caused by set-up times may fall under capacity-related costs, and transportation costs related to a purchase order may fall under transportation costs.

In decisions related to lot sizing, it is the incremental ordering cost which is of interest. Certain parts of ordering costs can be considered as dependent on the number of order occasions, i.e. they may be treated as incremental costs in the same way as incremental inventory carrying costs. Incremental ordering costs, in other words, constitute that part of the total ordering costs which are changed when order quantities, and consequently the total number of order occasions, are changed. Incremental ordering costs can be divided into four cost components:

1 Re-tooling and dismantling (set-up) costs

2 Costs for capacity losses

3 Material-handling costs

4 Order processing costs

In a manufacturing situation, re-tooling and dismantling costs are costs for the time it takes to change the manufacturing process from one manufacturing order to another, i.e. conducting the set-up. In addition to costs for **set-up time**, there will be costs for any scrapping involved and slowdown in manufacturing when a new batch is started up.

The size of costs for capacity losses will depend on the utilisation of capacity in the production process and the purchasing organisation. At full capacity, the time spent preparing new orders represents not only increased direct costs for personnel and consumables but also an alternative cost for loss of capacity. The time spent could have been used for another value-adding activity. At less than full capacity, there is no capacity loss.

Material-handling costs are costs related to handling of materials in conjunction with orders started or orders completed. Examples are costs for goods reception, arrival controls, placing in stores, retrieval of materials and transportation of finished products to and from stores.

Order processing costs in a purchasing situation include costs for processing orders for the planning department, accounts department, and purchasing department, transferring the order to a supplier by post, fax or other electronic method, and freight charges if these are not included in the purchase price. In a manufacturing situation, costs are primarily related to planning, order release and recalling of an order.

Capacity-related costs

Available plants, vehicles and machines, along with personnel, constitute available capacity. Annual depreciation and costs for maintenance and operation of plants constitute capacity costs. Capacity costs may be influenced by the degree of utilisation of equipment. Since capacity costs are primarily fixed costs, a higher degree of utilisation will mean that the same cost can be divided over a larger number of units, and thus reduce items' cost price.

Capacity costs normally increase if the utilisation of capacity in a production plant or a traffic mode, e.g. rail or truck, varies over time. It will be more difficult to have a minimum capacity investment in production equipment, stores, terminals, vehicles and personnel in the case of high utilisation of capacity. Instead the company may be forced to use overtime work, shifts, sub-contracting, and carry out more transportation and have lower fill rates in vehicles than would otherwise be the case. Consequently, the capacity-related costs increase.

Shortage and delay costs

Shortage costs arise when a delivery cannot take place in accordance with a customer's wishes. Thus, this cost has a direct connection with customer service undertakings and the opportunities of creating value and generating revenues. The worst case scenario for disruptions in deliveries is when lost sales also means that the customer also is lost. A less serious situation may lead to the current sale being lost, but the customer being retained. This may be the case if easily replaceable consumer products are not available at a retail outlet. For items which are more difficult to replace, delivery disruptions do not necessarily mean lost sales. However, extra costs may arise through delivery taking place using alternative distribution solutions or as a result of overtime work in manufacture, or extra costs for express transportation or movement between warehouses. Costs for damages may also arise as a result of delayed delivery.

Costs for lost sales are often difficult to estimate. Order delay costs are also difficult to assess in advance since the activities which arise as a result of delays vary from case to case.

Environmental costs

Environmental costs arise for different reasons. The selection and performance of external transportation influences the environment through emissions, congestion, tyre wear, load on infrastructure, noise, etc. Products, the form of packages and their characteristics influence their transportation, but also have an impact on the environment when they are transformed into waste after consumption.

Environment-related costs in the logistics system are difficult to estimate in many ways. This is because the effects are long term and many aspects have an indirect effect on the environment.

Total costs of the logistics system

Studying the total costs of the logistics system means that the impact of logistics decisions on **total logistics costs** is taken into account, rather than minimising costs for individual logistics activities. If costs are minimised for one activity, this may result in costs for other activities increasing even more. For this reason it is necessary to have an overall perspective on costs when making logistics decisions. If, for example, a company considers replacing three regional warehouses with one central warehouse, inventory carrying costs will in all probability decrease as a result of scale benefits and the evening-out of regional demand variations, but transportation costs will increase due to longer, more frequent and faster transportation being required. For the change to be cost-effective, it is necessary that savings in inventory carrying costs are greater than increased transportation costs.

Different logistics solutions do not only result in costs for performing different physical activities; they also give rise to different customer service levels and effects on the environment. When switching over from a slow and infrequent transportation alternative, it is not only the costs for transportation and tied-up capital which are influenced, but in many cases delivery precision

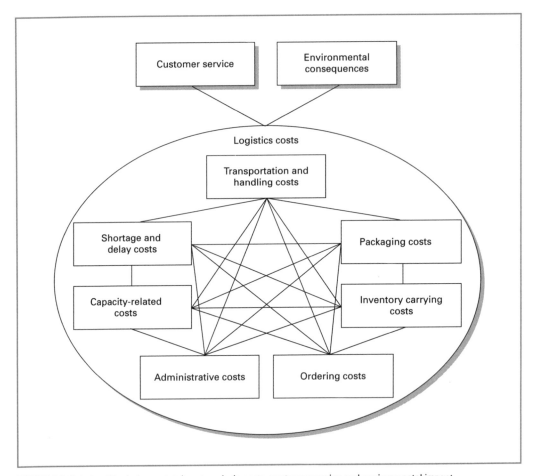

FIGURE 5.1 Relationships between total cost analysis costs, customer service and environmental impact

and the ability to quickly react to changes in customer requirements are improved too. Thus, it is important not only to compare the total costs for physical logistics activities, but also take into account the changed customer service levels and their impact on revenues. One way of doing this is to include in the calculation what are called *market mediating costs*, i.e. costs for shortages in stocks and obsolescence. This type of cost is, however, often very difficult to quantify.

The impact on the environment of different logistics solutions should be valuated as far as possible, but as in the case of customer service, it is not easy to quantify. It may be better to supplement total cost calculations with qualitative customer service and environment impact estimates which indicate the potential influence of the logistics solutions on revenues. In such a situation the **total logistics cost analysis** can act as a model for identifying a balance between high customer service, low logistics costs and favourable environmental consequences as shown in Figure 5.1.

5.2 Tied-up Capital

Acompany's assets can be divided into fixed assets and current assets. When investments are made, capital is tied up, which affects the company's cash flow and solvency. The material that flows through the supply chain is part of the current assets and as such influences the total capital tied up in the company.

Tied-up capital directly affects profitability, but also indirectly through its effects on delivery service. In order to measure and analyse logistics performance it is also necessary to calculate the amount of capital tied up. The average tied-up capital expresses how much capital is tied up in material flows in total, or divided into stores, work-in-process, stocks of finished products and transportation, etc. It may be expressed as capital tied up in absolute figures, **inventory turnover rate (ITR)** or average **throughput time** in current storage points.

Tied-up capital in absolute figures

Expressing tied-up capital in absolute figures means that the stock value is directly stated in a currency. If a new logistics set up is referred to, i.e. if there are no historic data to show stock values, tied-up capital must be calculated in another way. One analytical approach is to draw an **inventory graph** as in Figure 5.2 and from that is derived the average number of tied-up goods. Tied-up capital is obtained in absolute figures by multiplying the average stock expressed in quantities per item with goods value per item.

Inventory turnover rate

If it is wished to compare tied-up capital between different stocks and between departments and companies, it is not possible to use tied-up capital in absolute figures. The same is true if a company wishes to compare tied-up capital over time periods. Instead the *inventory turnover rate (ITR)* can be used. This is easily measured, and enables direct comparisons to be made between different points of measurement and different items at the same measurement point.

The inventory turnover rate refers to how many times per year average stocks are turned over. It expresses the value of the total flow of materials during a certain time period, often one year,

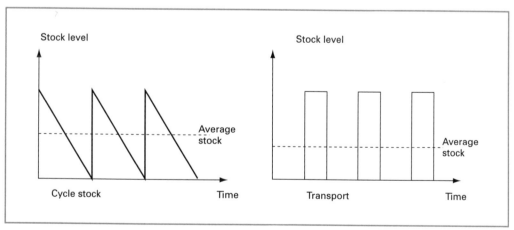

FIGURE 5.2 Inventory graph
The broken line indicates average stocks.

in relation to the average capital during the same time period that was tied up in material flows. The measurement can be applied to different parts of material flows. Inventory turnover rate for an individual item can be calculated using the following formula:

$$\text{Inventory turnover rate} = \frac{\text{number of units consumed annually}}{\text{average number of units in stock}}$$

It is often more interesting to calculate the inventory turnover rate for a group of items or for all items in stock, rather than for one individual item. This is based on the turnover expressed as the outbound delivery value for a time period and the average capital tied up. One practical problem which arises in the calculation of the inventory turnover rate is that the annual turnover is often expressed using the goods' value based on their sales price, while capital tied up is expressed as the stock value based on their cost price. To correctly calculate the inventory turnover rate, the same valuation principle is required for turnover and goods tied up (i.e. costs for goods sold and not the sales price). One effect which is noticeable if turnover is expressed in sales price and capital tied up as cost price is that the inventory turnover rate increases if the sales price increases, while average stocks remain unchanged – which is obviously incorrect. To calculate the average inventory turnover rate correctly, the following formula is used:

$$\text{Inventory turnover rate} = \frac{\text{annual turnover expressed as cost of goods sold}}{\text{average capital tied up in material flow}}$$

If, for example, the delivery value expressed as cost of goods sold during one year is €23 million and the average tied-up capital in material flows is €4 million, the inventory turnover rate will be 23/4, i.e. 5.7 times per year. We say that the inventory is turned over 5.7 times per year. The higher the rate of inventory turnover, the lower is the tied-up capital.

Stock throughput time

Average **stock throughput time** is an alternative expression for inventory turnover rate. If the inventory turnover rate increases, throughput time will decrease and vice versa. Average stock runout time or cover time is sometimes used as an alternative term for average throughput time.

$$\text{Average throughput time} = \frac{\text{average tied-up capital in flows} \cdot 52}{\text{delivery value per year}} = \frac{1 \cdot 52}{\text{inventory turnover rate}}$$

The reason that the factor of 52 is used in the formula numerator is that the throughput time is usually expressed in the unit of weeks. Without the factor 52, throughput time is expressed in the unit of years. Using the same example as for the inventory turnover rate, the average throughput time will be $4 \cdot 52/23$, i.e. 9 weeks. Expressed as **cover time**, we can say that stocks will cover nine weeks' delivery requirement value on average. The principles of making an analysis of tied-up capital with examples in logistics systems are explained later in this chapter. The following examples illustrate how average stocks, tied-up capital and throughput time can be calculated for different types of stocks:

Example 5.1

A company replenishes its stocks once per year. The quantity of replenishment is equivalent to the annual consumption (AC) and consumption of the goods is distributed equally over the year. What is the inventory turnover rate and the average idle time in stocks?

The diagram of stocks will have the following appearance:

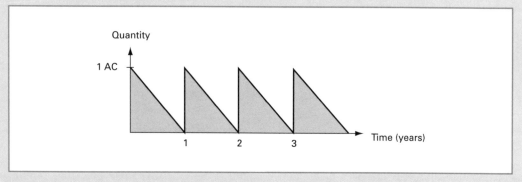

$$\text{Inventory turnover rate} = \frac{\text{annual number of units consumed}}{\text{average number of units tied up}} = \frac{1\ AC}{0.5\ AC} = 2 \text{ times per year}$$

$$\text{Average throughput time} = \frac{\text{average number of units tied up}}{\text{annual number of units consumed}} - \frac{0.5\ AC}{1\ AC} = 6 \text{ months}$$

Example 5.2

Demand for a product is 150 pieces per week. The demand is even and has no seasonal or other variations. The manufacturer's rate of production is the same as the demand, i.e. 150 pieces per week.

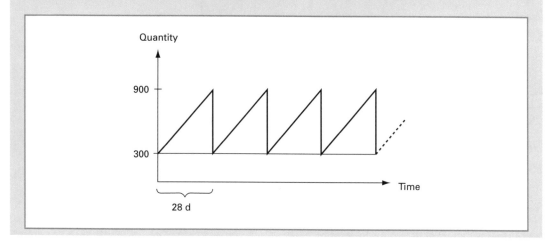

Manufacturing the product in question takes place continuously, with equal quantities produced each day. Safety stocks equivalent to two weeks' demand are kept in finished goods stocks. Withdrawals from finished goods stocks are 600 pieces every 28th day. The value of the products in finished stocks is €200. How large is the average stock, the average tied-up capital and the average idle time in stocks?

$$\text{Average stock} = \text{safety stock} + \frac{\text{order quantity}}{2} = 300 + \frac{600}{2} = 600 \text{ pieces}$$

$$\text{Average tied-up capital} = 600 \cdot 200 = 120\,000 \text{ Euro}$$

$$\text{Average throughput time} = \frac{\text{average stock}}{\text{demand}} = \frac{600 \text{ pcst}}{150 \text{ pcs/week}} = 4.0 \text{ weeks}$$

Example 5.3

When the 600 pieces are withdrawn from stocks in example 5.2, they are loaded onto a ship for transportation. The ship leaves every 28th day and transportation takes place throughout the year. The shipping time is 21 days. The value of the product during transportation is €210. How large is the average stock, the average tied-up capital and the average idle time in stocks?

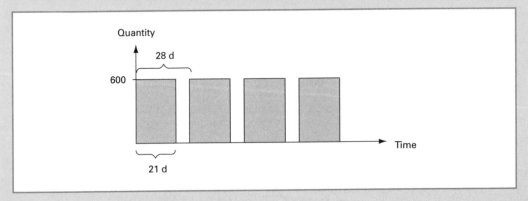

$$\text{Average stock} = \frac{21 \cdot 600}{28} = 450 \text{ pieces}$$

$$\text{Average tied-up capital} = 450 \cdot 210 = 94300 \text{ Euro}$$

$$\text{Average throughput time} = \frac{21 \text{ days}}{7 \text{ days/week}} = 3 \text{ weeks}$$

Example 5.4

When the ship in Example 5.3 docks in a port to unload the 600 products, one quarter of the load, i.e. 150 pieces, is reloaded directly onto an aircraft for further transportation. Let us assume that the flight departs with the first part-delivery at the same time as the ship docks in the port. Thus, the time to reload the goods between the means of transport and the warehouse is considered to be zero. The remainder of the delivery is put into the warehouse. Transportation by air is repeated once a week, so withdrawals from stock can be expected at the rate of 150 pieces per week. Stock is kept at as low a level as possible, i.e. there is no safety stock. The value of the product in stock is €220. How large is the average stock, the average tied-up capital and the average idle time in stocks?

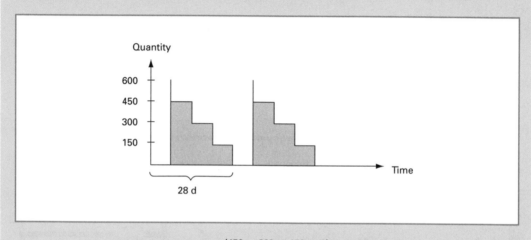

$$\text{Average stock} = \frac{(450 + 300 + 150 + 0)}{4} = 225 \text{ pieces}$$

$$\text{Average tied-up capital} = 225 \cdot 220 = 49500 \text{ Euro}$$

$$\text{Average throughput time} = \frac{225 \text{ pieces}}{150 \text{ pcs/week}} = 1.50 \text{ weeks}$$

5.3 Mapping Material Flows

Material flow mapping is a natural starting point for analysing tied-up capital and logistics costs in a supply chain. Material flows within a company can be mapped and analysed with the help of different types of charts, as a basis for further reducing throughput times to achieve lower tied-up capital, total logistics cost and more rational flows with respect to materials handling and internal transport.

When a process chart is used for material flow mapping, a number of standardised symbols are often used for the different types of activities which occur. The aim is to gain better clarity and readability. Examples of common symbols and activities which they represent are shown in Figure 5.3.

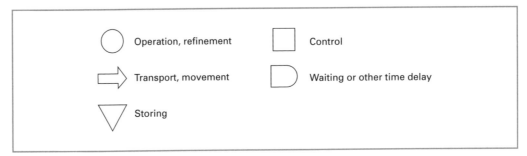

FIGURE 5.3 Examples of common symbols for mapping material flows

If the object of mapping is primarily to gain an overall view of the flows of materials in a workshop, a complement to this process chart could be to use a material **flow chart**. This could be the case when a more rational layout is needed, or when an existing layout must be changed as a result of a modification of production methods. The material flow chart is a scaled-down

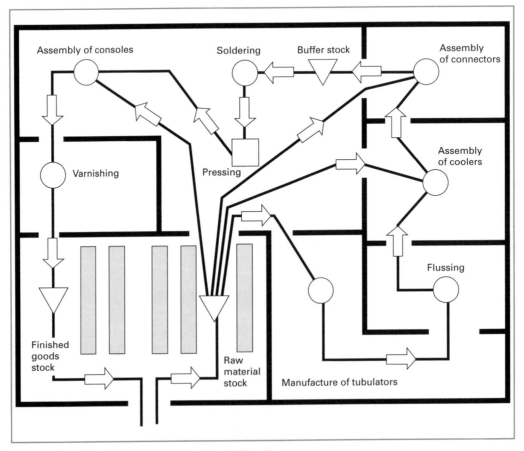

FIGURE 5.4 Material flow chart for the manufacture of oil coolers

drawing of the workshop. The drawing includes different stores, production activities and movements of materials that take place, from the withdrawal of raw materials and purchased components to delivery of finished products to stock or to customers. The symbols shown in Figure 5.3 may be used. Figure 5.4 illustrates an example of material flows in a workshop that manufactures oil coolers.

5.4 Mapping Tied-up Capital

Tied-up capital exists in all companies along the entire flow of materials from supplier to customer. It occurs in different forms along this flow, in stocks of incorporated raw materials and purchased components, in work in process, in stocks of finished products in distribution stores and in goods in transit. Mapping is required to be able to study in a structured and methodical way where tied-up capital exists and where it is concentrated in order to take measures to reduce it.

Flow charts

To carry out this mapping, it is necessary to collect information about which items move in which sub-flows, and which stocks, production operations and transportation occurs in the flow of materials. Information will also be required on how large the flow of each item is per time period (which can be measured as consumption over time), average quantities in stocks and the value of items in the flow. On the basis of this information a flow chart can be produced which will show the different sub-flows expressed in monetary figures. In general terms, the same

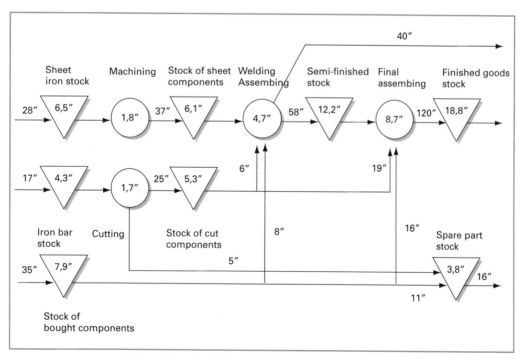

FIGURE 5.5 Example of value flows and stocks in an engineering company

approach and method of describing flows is applied whether the mapping is of flows within a company or between companies.

Figure 5.5 provides an example of what value-flows may look like in a company. The enterprise is an engineering company that purchases sheet steel and bars which are made into semi-finished products, welded together as sub-units which are finally assembled with purchased components of different types into finished products. These products are put in stock for delivery to customers as customer orders are received. There is some subcontracting to other companies, which means that welded sub-units are also sent directly to customers. Some of the purchased components and semi-finished products produced internally are sold and delivered as spare parts.

The figures stated refer to tied-up capital in the different stocks and products in work, and how large the flows are in million euro annually between different stocks and points of production. Flows and stocks can be valued at standard costs for internally produced items and as an average purchase price for purchased items. In general this information can be easily obtained from the planning system used at the company. Based on the estimated value stated in the flow chart, idle time in stocks and average throughput times in production can be calculated with the help of formulas described in section 5.2 earlier in this chapter.

In a similar way it is possible to produce a flow chart that shows monetary flows and tied-up capital in flows between companies, including external freight transportation. Example 5.5 illustrates how tied-up capital can be calculated in such flows. In this example, calculations are not based on stock values retrieved from the planning system; instead, tied-up capital is calculated theoretically on the basis of used order quantities and safety stocks, applying the methods described in section 5.2.

Example 5.5

A company in China manufactures a product for a European distribution company. The material flows from the factory in China to a central warehouse in Europe are shown in the figure below:

The following information is available regarding demand, rate of production, order sizes and delivery times:

- Demand for the product, i.e. outbound deliveries from the central warehouse, is 150 pieces per week. Demand is relatively even and has no seasonal variations.
- The manufacturer's rate of production is the same as the distribution company's demand: 150 pieces per week. Manufacture of the product in question is continuous with the same quantities made every day. A safety stock equivalent to two weeks' demand is kept in the factory stores.
- Every 28th day a batch of 600 pieces is sent by ship to a transshipment terminal in Asia – exactly the

quantity expected to be produced since the last delivery. Sea transport takes 36 days. The products are reloaded in Asia and forwarded by air.

◆ Once every week 150 items are flown to Europe. Since the terminal receive quantities of 600 pieces and outbound deliveries are 150 pieces, interim storage is necessary. This is kept at a minimum level. The flight leaves with the first sub-delivery when the ship docks in the port. A negligible amount of time is taken to reload the goods between the two modes of transport.

◆ The flight arrives at an airport in Europe where the goods are cleared through customs and transported by truck to a central warehouse in Europe. The time taken for the flight, customs clearance, terminal handling and road transport to the central warehouse is three days in total.

◆ The product inventory turnover rate in the central warehouse is 10 times per year.

Calculate the size of total stocks and tied-up capital in finished products in the entire flow of materials from the factory store at the manufacturing company in China via transportation and transshipment terminal to the central warehouse in Europe. The cost price of the product is €200 at the factory store, €210 during sea transport, €220 at the transshipment terminal, €350 during air transport, customs clearance and road transport, and €480 at the central warehouse. Calculate the total average idle time for a product through the same section of the distribution chain.

The flow of distribution can be seen as a number of sub-flows and storage points. To determine total average stocks, tied-up capital and idle time in the entire flow, calculations are first made for each sub-flow/storage point.

1 Factory store:

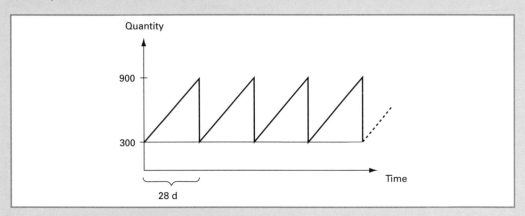

$$\text{Average stock} = \text{safety stock} + \frac{\text{batch size}}{2} = 300 + \frac{600}{2} = 600 \text{ pcs}$$

$$\text{Average tied-up capital} = 600 \cdot 200 = €120\,000$$

$$\text{Average throughput time} - \frac{\text{average stock}}{\text{demand}} = \frac{600\,\text{pcs}}{150\,\text{pcs/week}} = 4.0 \text{ weeks}$$

3 Transport stocks during sea transport:

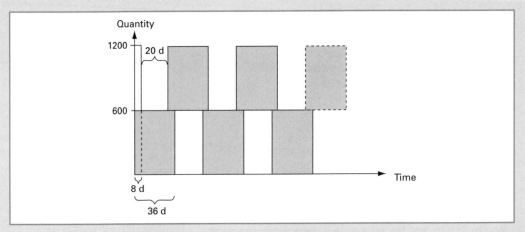

$$\text{Average stock} = \frac{8 \cdot 1200 + 20 \cdot 600}{28} = 771 \text{ pcs}$$

$$\text{Average tied-up capital} = 771 \cdot 210 = €162\,000$$

$$\text{Average throughput time} = \frac{36 \text{ days}}{7 \text{ days/week}} = 5.14 \text{ weeks}$$

3 Interim storage in Asia:

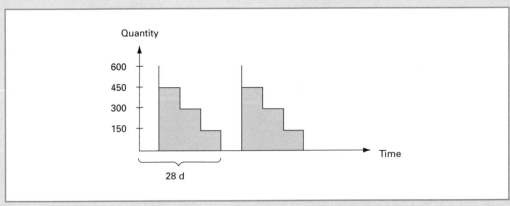

$$\text{Average stock} = \frac{(450 + 300 + 150 + 0)}{4} = 225 \text{ pcs}$$

$$\text{Average tied-up capital} = 225 \cdot 220 = €49\,500$$

$$\text{Average throughput time} = \frac{225 \text{ pcs}}{150 \text{ pcs/week}} = 1.50 \text{ weeks}$$

4 Stocks during air transport etc:

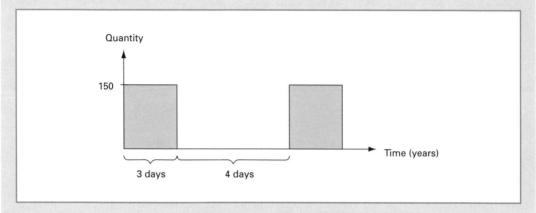

$$\text{Average stock} = \frac{150 \cdot 3}{7} = 64 \text{ pcs}$$

$$\text{Average tied-up capital} = 64 \cdot 350 = €22\,500$$

$$\text{Average throughput time} = \frac{3 \text{ days}}{7 \text{ days/week}} = 0.43 \text{ weeks}$$

5 Central warehouse:

$$\text{Inventory turnover rate (times/year)} = \frac{\text{demand (pcs/year)}}{\text{average stocks (pcs)}}$$

$$\text{Inventory turnover rate} = 10 \text{ times/year}$$

$$10 = \frac{150 \cdot 52}{\text{average stock}} \Rightarrow \text{average stock} = 780 \text{ pcs}$$

$$\text{Average tied-up capital} = 780 \cdot 480 = €374\,400$$

$$\text{Average throughput time} = \frac{780 \text{ pcs}}{150 \text{ pcs/week}} = 5.20 \text{ weeks}$$

	Interim stocks	Tied-up capital (euros)	Idle time
Factory	600 pcs	€120 000	4.0 wks
Sea transport	771 pcs	€162 000	5.1 wks
Interim storage	225 pcs	€49 500	1.5 wks
Air transport etc	64 pcs	€22 500	0.4 wks
Central warehouse	780 pcs	€374 400	5.2 wks
Total:	2440 pcs	€728 400	16.2 wks

TABLE 5.1 Summary of calculations

A summary of the size of stocks in items, tied-up capital and idle time in the different sub-flows and storage points in the flow, together with their totals, is shown in the table.

The total tied-up capital in the entire flow is just over €700 000, and the average idle time for the product is approximately 16 weeks. Thus, it takes on average 16 weeks from completed manufacture of the product until it is delivered from the central warehouse.

Diagram of tied-up capital

To be able to assess possible changes in the flow with the aim of minimising tied-up capital, it may be of interest to see how an increasing amount of capital is successively tied up in the product as it passes through production and distribution. This can be done with the aid of a diagram of tied-up capital, as shown in Figure 5.6. The average tied-up capital in euros per time unit is given on the y-axis, and the average idle time for each sub-flow on the x-axis. The product of x and y values (the area under the graph) illustrates the average tied-up capital per sub-flow. Capital rationalisation can be carried out in two different ways, in principle. Either the length along the x-axis is decreased by cutting lead times in the flow, or the height along the y-axis is decreased by postponing cost-demanding activities which contribute to increased tied-up capital.

A diagram of tied-up capital in example 5.5 is illustrated in Figure 5.7. The y-axis tied-up capital in Euros per week is calculated by dividing the product of the goods' value and the interim store by the average idle time. Tied-up capital in Euros per week during sea transport will be 30 000 euro at the beginning of the route and €31 500 at the end. From these figures it can be seen that the capital tied up each week due to changes in the value of the goods increases as the product is moved from factory stores to the central warehouse. Storing the product for one

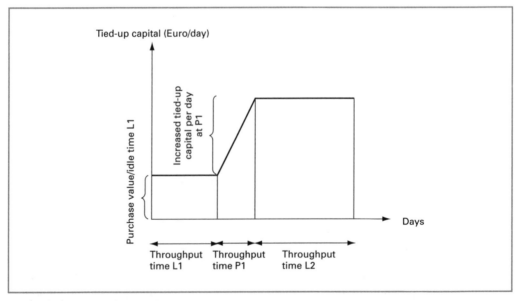

FIGURE 5.6 Diagram of tied-up capital

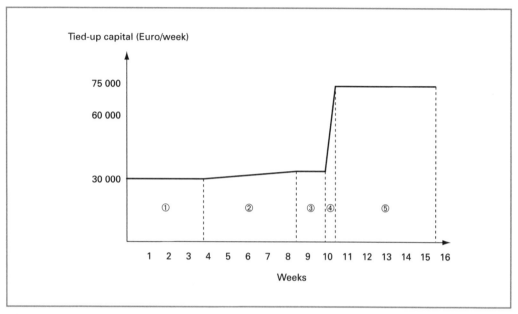

FIGURE 5.7 Diagram of capital tied up in flows in example 5.6
Figures 1–5 refer to each sub-flow/storage point.

week in the central warehouse means twice as much tied-up capital as the same period in the factory stores. Since the product incurs costs in conjunction with storage, transportation and handling activities along the flow of materials, its cost price increases from €200 in the factory store to €450 in the central warehouse. The greatest changes in cost price take place during transportation, as clearly indicated in the figure.

Products tie up more capital downstream in the flow towards customers. For this reason it is always better from the viewpoint of tied-up capital to store products as far upstream as possible. In the same way, lead-time reduction downstream and closer to end customers has a greater impact on tied-up capital than lead-time reduction earlier in the flow.

5.5 Total Logistics Cost Analysis

Activities carried out in the logistics system bring about the consumption of resources and thus costs. It is therefore an advantage to eliminate as far as possible activities which are not necessary for achieving a certain performance, to replace resource-demanding activities with those that demand less, or to perform activities that are necessary with the minimum consumption of resources. If, however, costs are decreased by eliminating or changing a certain activity or by doing it in a different way, costs for other activities may increase instead. If storage is centralised in a distribution network, storage costs will decrease but transportation costs may increase at the same time. It is always necessary to have an overall perspective and to consider all the costs that will be influenced when making changes to the logistics system. To ensure that this is the case, a total logistics cost analysis should be carried out before choices are made between different ways of designing the logistics system. This approach means that for every alternative, all costs influenced are calculated. A total logistics cost analysis is illustrated here with the help of example 5.6.

Example 5.6

A sawmill in Northern Europe exports cut timber products in special dimensions to a distribution centre in Italy. These dimensions are only delivered to the Italian customer. Every year, 12 000 cubic metres of timber are distributed. The sawmill saws the timber before each delivery. Sawing takes place at a rate of 200 cubic metres per day. After sawing, the timber must be dried for seven days.

There are two alternatives for transportation. The first is by sea, with departures every fourth week and a total transport time of 21 days. Freight transport costs are €280 per cubic metre. The second alternative is by rail with departures every second week and a total transport time of 9 days. Freight transport costs in this case are €300 per cubic metre. At the Italian distribution warehouse, in addition to an inevitable turnover stock, there must be a safety stock for the rail alternative equivalent to two weeks' normal sales. In the case of sea transport the safety stock needs to be twice as large. Demand at the distribution centre is assumed to be reasonably constant over time.

What is the total cost of the transport alternatives given the following cost assumptions? The cost price per cubic metre of timber at the sawmill is €1000. The inventory carrying cost of the timber is estimated to be 15 per cent of the annual goods' value at the sawmill and 25 per cent in Italy. The inventory carrying costs for both transport alternatives during transportation are estimated at 10 per cent of the goods' value.

The costs that are influenced by and which differ between the two modes of transport are:

1 Inventory carrying costs in the finished goods stocks/drying at the sawmill.
2 Inventory costs in transit.
3 Inventory costs in the distribution store.
4 Freight costs.

The following cost calculation can be made for the railroad alternative:

1 Inventory-carrying costs in the finished goods stocks/drying at the sawmill:

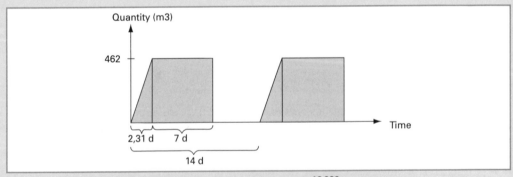

Departure every second week = 26 times/year $\rightarrow q = \dfrac{12\,000}{26} = 462\ m^3$

Production rate = 200 m³/day $\rightarrow$ Number of production days 462 m³: $\dfrac{462}{200} = 2.31$ days

Average stock = $\dfrac{462 \cdot 7\ 1\ 462 \cdot 2.31 \cdot 0{,}5}{14} = 269\ m^3$

Inventory carrying cost = $269 \cdot 1\,000 \cdot 0.15 = 40\,350$ Euro/year

2 Storage costs in transit:

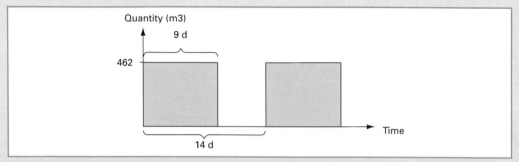

Interim stocks, $\phi_L = 462 \cdot \dfrac{9}{14} = 297 \ m^3$

It is assumed that transport costs of €300 per cubic metre will cover all costs for transport activities incurred by the items freighted. If these €300 are distributed over the items delivered continuously during the transport time, the average goods value during transport will be:

$$\left(1000 + \frac{300}{2}\right) = €1\,150$$

Inventory carrying costs $= 297 \cdot \left(100 + \dfrac{300}{2}\right) \cdot 0.10 = 34\,155$ Euro/year

3 Inventory carrying costs in the distribution store:

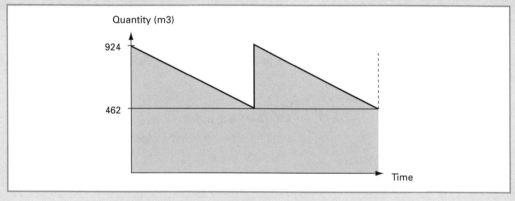

Average stock $= 462 + \dfrac{462}{2} = 693 \ m^3$

Inventory carrying costs $= 693 \cdot (1000 + 300) \cdot 0.25 = 225\,225$ Euro/year

4 Freight costs

Freight cost: $12\,000 \cdot 300 = 3\,600\,000$ Euro/year

Total cost: $40\,350 + 34\,155 + 225\,225 + 3\,600\,000$ euro $= 3\,899\,730$ Euro/year

Cost calculations for sea transport are made in the same way as for the railroad alternative. The total costs for the two transportation alternatives will be:

Costs	Railroad (euros)	Ship (euros)
Inventory at sawmill	40 350	46 027
Inventory in transit	34 155	78 923
Inventory in distribution	225 225	443 007
Freight	3 600 000	3 360 000
Total:	3 899 730	3 928 027 Euro

It can be seen from the above total logistics cost calculations that the freight cost is €240 000 lower for sea transport but that inventory carrying costs are just under €270 000 higher than the sea alternative, since the quantities are larger and transportation times longer. The calculations carried out show that the railroad alternative will have lower total logistics costs. This is on the assumption that all cost estimates and interest rates are correct. If there is a high uncertainty level in these variables, it is appropriate to carry out sensitivity analyses, i.e. alternative calculations in which the cost and interest variables vary between minimum and maximum values. To determine which mix is the most favourable overall in terms of costs, the total cost analysis must be supplemented with valuations of environment, customer service effects and other importance performance variables.

CASE STUDY 5.1: LANDED COST CALCULATION AT IKEA

IKEA wants to select the most cost-efficient supplier and distribution set-up for supply and distribution of goods through the supply chain. As input to these decisions the company uses a total cost model, based on forecast sales volumes, existing supply and distribution structures and the following costs:

Costs included in the cost model (1–7):

(1) The supplier's price for the product

(2) Customs costs

(3) Goods consolidation costs

(4) Inbound transportation to IKEA

(5) Handling and storage costs

(6) Outbound transportation from IKEA warehouses

(7) Store costs

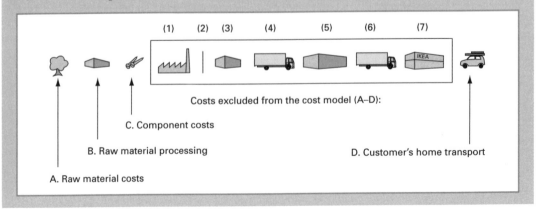

Costs excluded from the cost model (A–D):

A. Raw material costs

B. Raw material processing

C. Component costs

D. Customer's home transport

5.6 Conclusion and Summary

The costs and tied-up capital which a logistics system brings about have direct impact on profitability. They are thus important performance variables and it is essential to set up goals for these variables.

Logistics costs can normally be divided into different types. Some types of logistics costs have been defined in this chapter: transportation and handling costs, packaging costs, inventory carrying costs, administrative costs, ordering costs, capacity-related costs, shortage and delay costs, and environmental costs. Inventory turnover rate and idle time were presented as measures of tied-up capital. Methods for mapping and analysing material flows, tied-up capital and total logistics costs were described and exemplified in the end of the chapter.

🔑 Key concepts

Cover time 108	Stock throughput time 108
Flow charts 112	Throughput time 107
Incremental costs 103	Tied-up capital 101
Inventory carrying costs 102	Total logistics costs 105
Inventory graph 107	Total logistics cost analysis 106
Inventory turnover rate (ITR) 107	
Set-up time 104	

Discussion Tasks

1 Eight types of logistics costs are defined in this chapter. What cost types would you consider being the largest in a) a company making and selling fashion clothes to a large number of retail stores, b) a steel manufacturing company making sheet metals to a large number of mechanical engineering factories?

2 Inventory carrying cost interest consists of components' capital costs, storage costs and uncertainty costs. It is often difficult to correctly determine the size of inventory carrying cost interest. Discuss what practical problems arise when determining the three cost components of inventory carrying costs.

3 How high is the ordering cost when you, as a private person, buy food?

4 How high is the inventory carrying cost interest for you storing food at home?

5 Tied-up capital can be expressed in absolute figures, as the inventory turnover rate or as the average idle time. What are the advantages and disadvantages of each definition? Give examples of situations where each definition should be applied to gain clear benefits.

Exercises

Exercise 5.1

During the last five months 513 pieces of item B712 have been picked from stock. The stock balances in the end of the last six months were 282, 175, 620, 340, 243 and 195, respectively. Determine the average inventory turnover rate (ITR) for the item.

Exercise 5.2

A sub-supplier manufactures a product in batches of 2000 pieces to finished goods stocks. Demand is even and annual consumption is 52 000 pieces. A safety stock of 1000 pieces is maintained in finished products stocks. The rate of production is 1000 pieces per day and products are moved to finished stocks as they are manufactured. Deliveries of 1000 pieces are made each week to a terminal by rail transport. Manufacture of the products takes place as late as possible to keep finished product stocks at a minimum. The first 1000 manufactured products can be loaded onto railcars as soon as they are finished. The remaining 1000 pieces are put in stock until the next outbound delivery. When the production equipment is not being used for manufacturing this particular product it can be utilised for other production.

Railroad transportation from the sub-supplier to a receiving terminal takes 3 days. Products are re-loaded at the terminal onto a truck for onward transport to a distribution centre. The truck delivers twice a week (with 3.5 days between each departure). The quantity delivered in each truckload is 500 pieces and the transport time is one day. There is a safety stock equivalent to one week's consumption kept in the terminal. In other respects the stock levels at the terminal are kept as low as possible.

The inventory turnover rate for the product in the distribution centre is eight times per year.

The product has the following goods value in the different parts of the flow:

- Sub-supplier's finished goods stocks: €1000
- Interim storage in terminal: €1100
- Distribution warehouse: €1200

An inventory carrying interest of 15 per cent is estimated along the entire flow, except during rail transport when it is 17 per cent. The amount of time taken for loading, putting in stocks, withdrawing from stocks and unloading of goods is negligible in the context of the overall time taken, and for this reason the time is not included in the analysis.

What is the total capital tied up in absolute figures, costs for tied-up capital and average throughput time during the entire material flow?

Exercise 5.3

A small company in Poland exports its product Baby Seat to a wholesaler in France. It operates at maximum capacity, producing seven days a week, which makes 50 000 Baby Seats per year (to make it simple, we assume that a year has 50 weeks). This product is distributed to France, where it is sold to the customers. The cost of Baby Seat is €100. There is no safety stock in Poland. The cost of capital is estimated to 20 per cent. The cost for holding inventory is 15 per cent, which gives a total inventory carrying percentage of 35 per cent.

There are two distribution alternatives to choose between, either rail or truck. The rail alternative means a dispatch every 14 days. The transportation time is one week, and the cost is €4/piece. The truck alternative means a dispatch every week. The transportation time is two days, and the cost is €5/piece.

In France the wholesaler has a safety stock corresponding to half a week of sales. Which distribution alternative gives the lowest total cost when considering transportation cost and inventory carrying cost (in Poland, during transportation and in France)? Which other aspects should be taken into consideration when choosing transportation mode?

Exercise 5.4

A company is considering closing down their regional distribution centres and instead only operating from a central distribution centre. Before finally deciding about closing the centres they want to compare the total costs of the alternative distribution system. Calculate the total costs of the two alternatives, but also discuss other aspects that should be considered when choosing system.

The distribution system right now:
The annual sale is expected to be €330 million. To distribute their products to the customers in Europe, the company has a central distribution centre in the Netherlands and two regional centres, one in Sweden (with annual sales of €55 million) and one in France (with annual sales of €120 million). The annual cost for tied-up capital is estimated to 20 per cent of the product value. All products are stored in the Netherlands. The contribution margin averages 18 per cent. Right now, the turnover rate in Sweden is 7.5 times per year, while the turnover rate in France is 9.5 times per year. In the Netherlands, the turnover rate is 6.5 times per year. The low turnover rates are one of the most important causes for discussing closing the centres. The following annual costs are expected:

M€/Year	Netherlands	Sweden	France
Salaries/wages	4.8	1.2	2.9
Rental costs	5.6	1.8	4.5
Transportation costs	8.6[1]	2.8	4.1
Other costs	2.0	0.5	1.2

Transportation to regional distribution centres included

Suggested change:
By closing down the regional distribution centres, the following changes are expected to occur. The turnover in the central distribution centre will increase to 9 times per year, due to better information about the consumption and decreased demand fluctuations. The salaries/wages in the Netherlands are estimated to increase to €5.2 million. The rental costs in the Netherlands will not be affected, as there is some spare capacity. It will be easy to let the facilities in Sweden and France.

The transportation costs are estimated to total €16.5 million. Other costs will be €2.9 million. A new order processing computer system will be necessary. The investment will be €2.9 million. It will be depreciated in four years.

Further reading

Lambert, D. and Stock, J. (2001) *Strategic logistics management.* McGraw-Hill, New York.

Silver, E., Peterson, R. and Pyke, D. (1998) *Inventory management and production planning and scheduling.* John Wiley & Sons, New York.

Vollmann, T., Berry, W., Whybark, C. and Jacobs, R. (2005) *Manufacturing planning and control for supply chain management.* McGraw-Hill, New York.

Environmental aspects of logistics

From the business viewpoint, companies strive to achieve high customer service, low costs and low tied-up capital. The environmental consequences of the logistics system can in certain situations constitute part of customer service through customers making specific demands for environmentally friendly products and services. Environmental demands may become order qualifiers, i.e. to qualify as a supplier to a customer, a minimum demand may be that a company implements an environment management system or that certain demands for environmentally adapted products and services are fulfilled. Environmental impact may also be one part of total costs, but in many situations it is difficult to estimate financial consequences for the environment.

Environmental impact is one of the logistics system's performance variables and goals, but there are often trade-offs between traditional financial goals and environmental goals. For example, faster and more frequent transportation may lead to lower costs, lower tied-up capital and a better delivery service, but at the same time it may involve more transport work, since higher frequencies may mean that vehicles' fill rate is lower, with higher emissions per unit transported as a result.

Demands for short delivery times may mean that faster transportation is given priority rather than low environmental impact transport. Emissions generally increase with the speed of vehicles. Development towards a larger number of more geographically remote suppliers also results in longer transportation distances. Demands on minimising transportation damage and attempts to reduce the need for quality controls on purchased items may also result in a greater number of bulkier or specially designed packaging materials being used, which in turn can lead to bulkier goods and an increase in waste products. Thus, the overall demands on customer service, costs and tied-up capital which are an everyday reality for companies often have negative environmental consequences. It is therefore necessary to balance environmental goals with traditional financial goals and add in environmental consequences in the total performance of the logistics system.

This chapter describes how the logistics system influences the environment. The reduction of environmental impact with the aid of regulations and logistics-related alternatives is discussed, as is reverse logistics. **Environment management systems** and methods for **environmental impact assessments (EIA)** are described at the end of the chapter.

The chapter is closely related to the three other chapters in Part II of the book. There are also direct links to Chapter 14 Transport planning.

6.1 Environmental Impact of the Logistics System

The physical flow of materials influences the environment in different ways. The selection and performance of external transportation affects the environment through emissions, congestion, tyre wear, load on infrastructure, noise and so on. The form and characteristics of products and packages influence how transportation is carried out, as well as their impact on the environment when they become waste products after use.

Environmentally adapted logistics

Environmentally adapted logistics may have many different aspects, depending on which factors set limits for what is regarded as being environmentally adapted. Limiting factors include the environment, as well as financial, technological and social conditions.

If the environment is set as the limiting factor, environmentally adapted logistics could mean "logistics which does not affect the environment at all". If finance sets the limits, it may mean "logistics in which environmental investments are made as long as they are financially profitable". If the limiting factor selected is technology, the definition may become "logistics with the best commercial technology with respect to the environment". Social conditions as the determining factor will dictate the maintenance of material and psychological welfare, the preservation of the structure of society and trust in the political system. From this viewpoint, environmental considerations would mean "logistics that assures material and psychological welfare and preserves the structure of society and trust in the political system". For example, trust in the political system would be undermined if transport companies were forced to make such high investments in environmental measures that the demand for transport services was to decrease significantly. Sometimes the concept of sustainable logistics is used to describe a system that at the same time takes into consideration the environment, finance, and social conditions as limiting factors.

Environmental impact of transport

External transport involves direct impacts on the environment through exhaust emissions and evaporation/transfer of fuel into the air, water and ground. Emissions that affect water and the ground also take place when there are spillages, leaks, accidents, maintenance/cleaning, and as a result of normal operations – tyre wear on trucks and abrasion of ships' antifouling paint are two examples. Emissions consist mostly of nitrogen oxides, carbon monoxide, carbon dioxide, sulphur oxides, hydrocarbons and particles. They result in the following environmental threats:

- Greenhouse effect/impact on the climate
- Acidification
- Over-fertilisation
- Depletion of the ozone layer
- Ground-level ozone

- Impact of metals
- Broken chemical/biological cycles
- Exploitation of the natural environment
- Specific urban problems

All combustion engines at present produce carbon dioxide and water. Carbon dioxide from fossil fuels increases the greenhouse effect with climate change as a result.

Combustion at higher temperatures produces nitrogen oxides when nitrogen in the air reacts with oxygen. Sulphur dioxide is formed when fuel containing sulphur is combusted. Emissions of sulphur oxides and nitrogen oxides result in increased acidification of ground and water. A surplus of nitrogen and phosphorus in the natural environment leads to over-fertilisation.

The ozone layer in the upper atmosphere provides essential protection from the sun's UV rays. Emissions of Freon and similar substances have depleted this protective layer of ozone, with the consequence that damaging ultraviolet radiation from the sun now reaches the Earth's surface. Ozone also exists in the lower atmosphere, but here the gas has no protective effect. Ground-level ozone, in contrast, may even be toxic to living organisms. Ground-level ozone is produced when hydrocarbons and other organic compounds react with nitrogen oxides in the presence of sunlight. There are consequently two problems associated with ozone: there is too little ozone in the upper atmosphere and too much in the ground-level atmosphere.

Increasing levels of heavy metals such as mercury, cadmium and lead in the ground raise the risk of these leaking into groundwater, rivers, lakes and seas. These elements are dangerous in that they cannot be broken down; they are absorbed by organisms and reach high toxic concentrations.

The **eco-cycle** means that natural resources are returned to the environment at the same rate as they are extracted. If more resources are extracted than returned or that can be reproduced in the environment, the natural eco-cycle is broken. The use of fossil fuels such as oil, coal and natural gas involves consumption which is far higher than replacement, and thus the eco-cycle is broken.

Exploitation of the natural environment for the construction of plants and infrastructure also affects the environment. Expanding transport requirements result in increased road and motorway construction through valuable areas of nature. Habitation impacts on the landscape and changes conditions for flora and fauna.

In addition to the effects on the environment, transport may also influence individuals' physical, psychological and social well-being. This is a particularly urban problem. Gases such as carbon monoxide, nitrogen oxides and particles result in various health problems. Nitrogen oxides and particles contribute to asthma, impairment of lung functions and cause respiratory tract diseases. Carbon monoxide impairs the uptake of oxygen in the blood. Particles and hydrocarbons may be carcinogenic. Noise, among other things, can cause stress and impaired hearing. As well as the direct effects on people, animals and the environment, transport also has a direct impact on the environment through its consumption of non-renewable resources.

Different types of traffic account for a considerable proportion of total emissions of nitrogen oxides, carbon monoxide, carbon dioxide, sulphur oxides and hydrocarbons. Their impact on the environment takes place locally, regionally and globally, as shown in Table 6.1. Local effects include emissions that affect the environment in the short term and in the proximity of the source of emission. They are often short-lived and since they are concentrated in the immediate area of the emission they are often easier to identify and reduce. Emissions with regional impact travel for longer distances and affect the environment in a longer time perspective. They are more difficult to identify and reduce. Carbon dioxide is one example of an emission with global impact.

Local threats	Regional threats	Global threats
■ Heavy metals	■ Over-fertilisation	■ Ozone layer depletion
■ Noise	■ Ground emission of hazardous waste	■ Greenhouse effect
■ Smell	■ Landscape changes	
■ Air pollution		

TABLE 6.1 Local, regional and global environmental threats

This type of emission spreads quickly over the earth, regardless of the source of emission, and gives rise to more long-term effects than regional emissions.

Road traffic accounts for a large proportion of transport emissions of carbon dioxide, nitrogen oxides, hydrocarbons and particles. Diesel and petrol engines produce emissions of nitrogen oxides and particles (soot, tyre particles, etc.) as well as carbon dioxide. Road transport may also cause noise problems.

The environmental impact of railways depends on whether the locomotives are diesel or electric. In some European countries most railways are electrified, but in Europe as a whole there are more diesel-driven locomotives. The use of electricity has an indirect impact on the environment through its production. Noise may also be a problem associated with rail traffic. In comparison with road traffic, however, rail traffic consumes less energy per trailer transported. The total consumption of energy per transported unit will depend on the fill rate, however.

The emission of greenhouse gases is the most serious problem associated with air transport, but nitrogen oxides and noise are other environmental problems in this mode. In addition to the environmental impact of flights themselves, de-icing of runways and aircraft causes further negative consequences for the environment.

At low speeds, sea transport is a relatively low-energy method of transporting goods. Calculated per transported ton-kilometre, emissions are small. In relation to the consumption of energy, however, emissions are relatively high. Sea transport produces emissions of carbon dioxide, sulphur oxides and nitrogen oxides. Faster ships cause more overload on the environment since fuel consumption increases dramatically at higher speeds. One environmental advantage of sea transport is that there is no exploitation of land, little congestion and noise in comparison with other modes of transport.

Environmental impact of products and packages

Products and packages in the logistics system affect the environment through their influence on transport and the resulting waste after their use. Their form and characteristics may simplify or complicate materials handling and influence the potential of efficient transport. Recyclable products and reusable or recyclable packages must be transported from the customer back to the supplier after use. This may result in increased transport. Bulky, hazardous or easily damaged goods may put such specialised demands on transport that the most environmentally friendly alternatives are no longer possible. They may also bring about lower fill rates in load carriers.

In addition to products and packages giving rise to more transport, after use they become waste products which also require handling and transport. Waste may be recyclable or environmentally hazardous to a greater or lesser degree.

6.2 Environmental Regulations

Authorities have different means of control at their disposal to influence the environmental impact of logistics. It is possible to distinguish between control through information, control through financial measures, and control through legal measures.

Control through information means that users are informed of the environmental impact of the logistics system and, if possible, their behaviour is changed to prevent negative environmental consequences. This may be through directives to increase the percentage of recyclability of products and materials. There are also **eco-labelling** systems to environmentally approve products and transportation. Within the EU there is the **EU flower**. There are also country-specific labels, such as the Nordic Swan and the German Blue Angel. The principle behind eco-labelling is that a producer can apply for its products to be environmentally approved. Independent assessors determine the environmental demands for different product groups, and if the products in question comply with these demands they will be marked with an eco-symbol such as the Swan. Specific eco-labelling may refer to goods transportation and include restrictions on the use of non-renewable energy, emissions of nitrogen oxides and sulphur oxides, emissions of hydrocarbons and waste products from load bearers. Since it is the responsibility of the producer or transport provider to apply for environmental approval, an item or service may fulfil stipulated environmental requirements even if it is not eco-labelled.

Financial measures of control are generally taxes and subsidies which have the aim of allocating public finance environment costs to those who cause them, and to prioritise preventive environmental measures. Specific environment taxes are imposed within the EU on petrol and diesel. Products which are less harmful to the environment may be more expensive to manufacture and to regulate their consumer prices, production costs may be offset by lower tax rates. On the basis of specific emissions and noise requirements, there are also **emission standards** for vehicles. **Vehicle charges** and road tolls are other financial means of control. Drivers of vehicles which do not comply with specified environment classification requirements may be forced to pay special charges when they use roads. **Congestion charges** are levied during time periods when the road network is most used in order to even out the density of traffic at different times of the day. The aim is to control traffic so that it flows better and, if the existing road network is utilised more efficiently, this can provide gains in time and may prevent over-dimensioned infrastructure. From the individual's perspective, the goal is to make other forms of transport more attractive and to encourage shared transport through lower charges or other advantages.

Emission rights trading is another financial measure to reduce emission of pollutants. A domestic government agency sets a limit on the total amount of pollutant that can be emitted in the actual country. Companies or other groups that emit the pollutant are given credits or allowances which represent the right to emit a specific amount. Companies that pollute beyond their allowances must buy credits from those who pollute less than their allowances or face heavy penalties. This means that the buyer is being fined for polluting, while the seller is being rewarded for having reduced emissions.

Authorities may also use legal measures to minimise the negative environmental consequences of the logistics system. Direct regulations stipulate limitations on emissions and noise. Other examples include time restrictions for distribution, special regulations for vehicles with consolidated loads such as special pallets or permission to drive in bus lanes in cities. It is also possible to introduce zones with special conditions to improve the environment in urban areas. Only heavy goods vehicles which comply with specific environmental classifications will be allowed to drive in **environmental zones**. This would prevent older vehicles from driving into inner-city areas.

Information measures	Financial measures	Legal measures
■ Information	■ Environmental taxes	■ Limitations on emissions and noise
■ Education	■ Emission standards	■ Regulations
■ Marketing	■ Environmental charges	■ Environmental zones
■ Eco-labelling		■ Polluter pays principle

TABLE 6.2 Authorities' means of control for reducing the environmental impact of the logistics system

The **polluter pays principle** is applied in most OECD and EU countries, meaning that the party responsible for pollution must also be responsible for dealing with it and paying for its environmental consequences. The OECD defines this principle as

> a policy in which the producer's financial and/or physical responsibility for a product is extended to the post-consumer stage of the product's life cycle. It specifically focuses on reducing the environmental impacts of a product at the post-consumer phase. There are two key features to the policy: the responsibility for a product at its post consumption phase is shifted upstream in the production–consumption chain, to the producer; and it provides incentives to producers to incorporate environmental considerations into the design of their products.

The principle is applied to different product types, including packages, recycled paper, cars and electronics. Packaging manufacturers must supply suitable collection systems and make it easier for consumers to separate packages from other waste products. Products must be designed so that they can easily be processed and recycled after use. Environment taxes have been proposed as a means of implementing this principle. Table 6.2 summarises authorities' means of control for reducing the environmental impact of the logistics system.

6.3 Alternatives for Environmental Measures

The entire logistics system influences the environment and there are various alternatives for measures to improve consideration of the environment in the different parts of the system. We can distinguish between three types of measures:

■ Filtering

■ Re-using and recycling

■ Reducing

The filtering alternative means that environmentally harmful substances are collected before they are spread in the environment. For hauliers, for example, this could be a filter in the exhaust system that collects sulphur. The filter alternative is a reactive strategy and does not result in total elimination of environmental impact but rather a postponement or shifting of it.

Re-using, **recycling** and **reducing** represent a higher level of reduction of environmental impact. Re-using is related to products and components and recycling is related to materials. Products can be designed so that the materials and components can easily be separated for re-use or recycling. Re-using items may mean designing products so that materials and components can easily be separated and re-used, or designing products that can be easily upgraded and in this way given an extended lifespan. Purchasing, transport and disposal costs can be eliminated through the application of this strategy. Charging rechargeable batteries is an example of this category. The recycling alternative is relevant when a product cannot be re-used after its lifespan, but must be processed into recycled materials which can be used in the manufacture of a new product. An example of this is the retreading of truck tyres with recycled rubber, which is then used for a further period of time.

Reduction is a preventive alternative and is aimed at minimising the use of resources and the creation of residual products. Reducing the use of resources is the most responsible alternative and should be prioritised. Examples of reducing measures are designing products and packages so that a minimum of resources are utilised in their manufacture and use, designing distribution structures with the emphasis on low-resource usage, powering locomotives with electricity produced by hydropower, or by using cleaner engines and catalytic converters.

Reverse logistics is a common generic term for logistics systems that support the re-use of products and components and the recycling of materials. It includes collecting and moving used, damaged, unwanted or outdated products, as well as packaging materials from the point of consumption to the point of origin for the purpose of recapturing value or proper disposal. This measure often includes reducing the use of resources in reverse logistics. The logistics system for reverse logistics, in the same way as the traditional logistics system, must handle the flow of information, materials and money in a resource-efficient manner. Reverse logistics systems are dependent on reusable resources – for example, containers.

The practical relevance of these measures is to a large extent determined by customers' behaviour. In many situations, customer demands for small, frequent and rapid transport combined with low costs limit the possibilities for environmental improvements. In the description that follows below, measures are grouped with respect to transportation and packages, and the sub-systems of material supplies, production and distribution.

Transport

The impact on the environment caused by the use of transport may be decreased with the aid of technological improvements to engines, vehicle design, wheels, tyres, infrastructure, alternative fuels, post-combustion treatment of exhaust gases and changes in driving styles, to name a few options.

Technical developments in the case of goods vehicles have led to lower emissions thanks to more efficient and cleaner engines, decreased wind resistance and rolling friction and lighter vehicles. Through the use of catalytic converters, for example, and filters for cleaning exhaust gases, emissions can be further reduced. Quieter vehicles and tyres have been developed to reduce the amount of noise pollution from road traffic. For sea traffic, the application of better designs for vessels, propellers and engines can reduce the consumption of energy. Slower speeds will also result in lower fuel consumption. Emissions may also be cut with the aid of technological measures to engines, the use of more environmentally friendly fuels and the application of exhaust emission controls. Technical improvements for aircraft are aimed at reducing fuel consumption and emissions through lighter designs of aircraft and improvements to the energy conversion processes in aero-engines. The technical development of aircraft has also decreased noise levels. Emissions from rail traffic may be decreased by replacing diesel locomotives with electric models, and the utilisation of technical solutions that make diesel versions more ecological. By giving locomotives and carriages a more aerodynamic design with lower wind resistance, the consumption of energy can be decreased and the speed of transport increased. Technical measures applied to wheels, brakes and rails can decrease noise levels.

Technical changes to vehicles and infrastructure aimed at reducing negative consequences for the environment are never free, however, and may involve large investments that result in higher transport costs. Thus, environmental transport alternatives may mean higher costs, at least initially.

Another approach to decreasing the environmental impact of transportation is the use of alternative fuels such as methanol, ethanol, RME (rapeseed methylester), natural gas, hydrogen, reformulated petrol and synthetic diesel. The production of alternative fuels may be more costly than traditional fossil fuels. Because of the small quantities produced, vehicles that use alternative fuels are still often more expensive to purchase than traditional vehicles.

Transport does not only affect the environment through the use of vehicles. The production of vehicles, fuels and infrastructure inevitably causes emissions and demands large amounts of energy. Any environmental gains from the use of certain fuels must be weighed against the losses accrued in their production if the total environmental consequences are to be fully understood. For example, the production of alternative fuels and energy may be carried out in environmentally unfavourable ways. Production of electricity through the combustion of fossil fuels produces carbon dioxide emissions that are proportionally as great as internal combustion engines. Slightly higher efficiency levels may be achieved in large power plants, but the differences in emissions are not large in comparison with modern vehicle engines. Electricity produced through nuclear power has no direct emissions, but the processes of enrichment and mining cause levels of emission. Nuclear power also has its particular problem of the final storage of waste products, and its operation is not adapted to eco-cycles.

Driving style also has an effect on the environment. For all types of traffic, better maintenance and lower speeds reduce emissions and the consumption of energy. Particularly for road transport, fuel consumption can be further reduced by smoother driving, and noise can be decreased through lower speeds and avoiding nighttime traffic in sensitive areas.

Packages

Packages make up a large part of the total waste in society, while at the same time the design of packages affects efficiency, environmental handling and transportation. Environmental measures for packages are aimed at technical solutions for the design of packages, but also involve their re-use and recycling.

According to the polluter pays principle, companies that manufacture packages must also provide appropriate collection systems and ensure that it is easy for users to sort packages from other waste. The producer must also make sure that the sorted packages are transported, re-used, recycled or processed in an environmentally acceptable way. In the manufacturing process, the producer must ensure that packages are designed so that they can be recycled and the amount of waste minimised. Directives also include those parties that use packages by setting demands for them to sort them from other waste and return them to collection systems provided by the producer. The aim is to control the design and handling of products and packages so that they can be re-used or recycled with minimum impact to the environment. The aim is also to drive the development of smaller and lighter packages so that the amount of waste is decreased.

One method of reducing the amount of waste and the environmental impact of waste is to cut down the use of packages, reduce the amount of material in packages and pack more items into larger packages. Ambitions to decrease the materials used in packages may conflict with requirements to cut down damages in transit, however, which may demand more robust packages. The transition to packages that enable recycling and packaging materials that are easier to recycle also has environmental consequences. By using materials that facilitate more compact loads, the load rate of vehicles can be increased and the indirect environmental impact decreased. Packages should be and often are adapted to the products they are intended to contain. One way of decreasing the environmental impact of packages is to change the form of the products themselves so that smaller and simpler packages can be used. To give two examples: products may be delivered in concentrated or unassembled forms.

Materials supply system

The materials supply system influences environmental impact through the choice of supplier and the demands that are put on suppliers and deliveries.

One way of influencing the environmental impact in the whole supply chain is to demand that suppliers work in a focused manner with environment issues – for example, by only engaging suppliers that are **ISO 14000** certified. In the selection of suppliers there may be a conflict between environmental alternatives and the most cost-effective. It may be a question of choosing between buying services from a geographically remote low-cost supplier or from local suppliers whose deliveries involve less transport or from environmentally approved but more expensive suppliers.

When purchasing, it is also possible to demand that items purchased are environmentally approved and comply with environmental marking principles. However, since it is up to the producer to decide whether the product will be assessed for environmental approval, there may be products that fulfil these demands without being marked as such. In a purchasing situation, environmental-demand specifications may be included in a request for quotation to suppliers. Purchasing large quantities may also bring about positive environmental effects, since this can lead to less transport work. On the other hand, it will involve more tied-up capital, longer throughput times and increased risk of obsolescence.

CASE STUDY 6.1: ENVIRONMENTAL ASSESSMENT WHEN CHOOSING DISTRIBUTOR AT TETRA LAVAL GROUP

Tetra Laval Group is a corporation focusing on systems for processing, packaging and distribution of food and accessories for dairy production and animal husbandry. The group has about 60 manufacturing sites worldwide and is represented in more than 165 countries. The Tetra Laval Group has a central support function, Tetra Laval Group Transport & Travel, that manages the freight transport flows of the group.

Tetra Laval Group Transport & Travel makes annual supplier assessments of all suppliers used. These are example of environmental issues included in the assessments:

- Does the company have an environmental policy?
- Does the company have operative programmes for the environmental work?
- Is there an organisation for the environmental work in the company?
- Is the company ISO 14001 certified or is any other environmental documentation used?
- Are the personnel educated in environmental issues?
- Are environmental assessments carried out at the company's plants?
- Does an annual environmental assessment report exist?

Production system

The production system's logistics environmental consequences are related to the layout of production and how efficient the materials-handling and storage systems are. Resource-efficient production systems that eliminate wastes in the form of unnecessary transport, loss and risk of obsolescence will have small negative environmental impact in production. However, if they are based on small order quantities and frequent deliveries of components they may lead to transportation with low load rates, giving rise to negative environmental impact caused by extra transport and emissions.

The polluter pays principle also has an effect on production. It means that products must be easily disassembled, returned and recycled after use. It is therefore important to consider the environment as early as the product development stage and design products for recycling.

Distribution system

The distribution system aims at moving goods over geographically widespread areas. The environmental impact of the system can be influenced by decreasing the total need for transportation, changing to environmentally friendly types of transport, or by decreasing the environmental impact of the mode of transport used as described in the Chapters 3 and 14 – for example, by increasing truck fill rate through larger transportation networks and consolidation. Reverse logistics strategies is another way for the distribution system to decrease negative environmental impacts.

Transport system efficiency

The total need for transport can be decreased by the efficient use of a transport system that is often designed for demand peaks but is used for smaller goods volumes. This means that the environmental impact of road transport can potentially be halved through better transport and load planning. Making fewer deliveries and using vehicles' full load volumes may be contradictory to common delivery service requirements, however. Some examples of strategies to decrease total transportation needs are:

- *Green dispatch*: one example of less frequent deliveries is that of **green dispatch**, meaning that the distributor delivers goods to the customer company when they have space in the vehicle going to the place in question. The uncertain delivery frequency caused by this strategy means that the customer must keep more safety stocks of the items in question, and so this is only applicable to low-value items.

- *Fixed time delivery days*: another alternative is to only allow deliveries on fixed delivery days, which simplifies transport planning.

- *Consolidated distribution*: another way of increasing the fill rate without cutting back on delivery service is to apply consolidated distribution. This means that goods from different shippers and often for different recipients are loaded onto the same vehicle. The recipient then receives deliveries from several suppliers at the same time of delivery.

- *Breakpoint distribution*: in the case of consolidated distribution, goods are consolidated by reloading at terminals, which results in extra handling work and the method demands extra resources. A distribution system that has many flows of goods co-ordinated between terminals, so-called *breakpoints*, is called *breakpoint distribution*.

- *Milk runs*: milk runs mean that a vehicle driving on a loop collects small consignments for delivery to a terminal, where the consignments are consolidated into larger loads.

- *Balancing return flows*: if the quantity of goods to transport into a region is not as large as the quantity of goods transported out from the region, there will be an imbalance between inbound and outbound transportation. Increasing the fill rates in **return flows** by, for example, taking goods that would have been transported in another fashion is one way of decreasing the total transport kilometres of the distribution system.

- *Route and load planning*: using an efficient route planning and load planning, often performed with the aid of a computerised transport management system (see Chapter 17), it is possible to optimise routes and load rates and thus carry out distribution with a smaller number of vehicles and fewer total transport kilometres.

- *IT systems*: IT based planning and ordering systems, and closer co-operation and exchange of information between suppliers and customers, also increases the possibilities of planning and carrying out co-ordinated deliveries.

- *Local suppliers*: another measure to decrease total transportation need is to minimise the transport distance by engaging local suppliers. This goes against the trend to prioritise low-cost suppliers, irrespective of whether they are in the geographical vicinity or further away.

- *Vehicle design*: the design of vehicles that allow increased load volumes is one more way of decreasing transport kilometres.

Intermodal transportation

Choosing intermodal transport solutions is a further way of decreasing the negative environmental impact of distribution systems. By using railways for long-distance land transportation, emissions are eliminated and allow the increased use of alternative fuels on the short-distance transport between customers, terminals and suppliers. However, intermodal transport requires investments in the form of standardised load carrier systems and adapted handling systems at terminals.

Reverse logistics

Developing distribution systems for reverse logistics is another method of decreasing negative environmental impact. In many supply chains, there has been an increased return flow of products, packaging waste and handling and packaging equipment. This is, for example, a result of governmental directives for recycling of package waste, EU directives for retrieving end-of-life products for refurbishment and remanufacturing, increased use of reusable handling and packaging equipment, growth of home shopping where a large proportion of the merchandise is returned, etc.

Distribution systems for primary products and reverse distribution differ in a number of ways. A reverse system is seldom as time-critical as a normal distribution system, since the value of goods and therefore capital tied up is lower, and the durability of the goods is long. Time is important for the systems that recycle or re-use returned goods, however, since shortages may arise. Reverse systems must be "environmentally profitable". If the profits that are made in the reversed logistics system are not greater than the increased load as a result of collection and transport, the system is not environmentally profitable. Problems may arise when old and new goods are mixed in the same load space in terms of damage to the newly produced goods, and customers may refuse to purchase goods that are transported together with used ones.

	Filtering	**Re-using & recycling**	**Reducing**
Transportation	Exhaust emission control	Recycling of vehicles, engines, tyres, etc.	More efficient and cleaner engines Lighter vehicles with less wind resistance and road friction Quieter vehicles, tyres and roads Better design for vessels, propellers and airplanes Eco-driving, reduced speed Improved vehicle maintenance Environmental friendly fuel Use of environmental friendly energy
Packages		Polluter pays principle Re-usable packages	Resource efficient package design Product design requiring less packaging material
Material supply system			Environmental approval suppliers Environmental approved items Environmental demand specifications
Production system	Exhaust emission control	Polluter pays principle	Eliminate waste
Distribution system	Discharge emission control	Reverse logistics	Intermodal transportation Higher fill rate Full truck loads and fewer transports Minimise transport distance

TABLE 6.3 Alternative methods of handling to decrease the environmental impact of the logistics system

Reverse logistics is common in the case of empty bottles, plastics, metals, paper and glass. Empty bottles are collected by breweries when they deliver full bottles to shops. In this way, empty-return transport back to the breweries is eliminated. Plastics, metals, paper, glass and so on are collected at recycling centres, transported to recycling companies and are then included in the production flow of new products. In many cases, the distribution system for reverse flows is not as well developed and efficient as for "traditional" flows. This may be because it is not possible to use packages that minimise load space required, or that transport only takes place when space is available on the vehicle's return. Sorting activities, too, can be very resource intensive. Another obstacle to reverse logistics is international variations in approaches to packaging waste recovery.

Alternative methods of handling to decrease environmental impact of the logistics system's different parts are summarised in Table 6.3.

CASE STUDY 6.2: DESIGN FOR SUSTAINABILITY – THE SMART TOWN CAR (Genes, 2002)

In the production park in Hambach, Daimler Chrysler produces the compact town car, Smart. The challenge and aim of the Smart project was from the beginning to design an "environmental-friendly" car. Local and global environmental protection is integrated in all the company's activities, from the development of individual components, to the construction of the production facilities and the use and recycling of the car.

The car is designed in modules for easy disassembly, so that individual parts can be replaced if necessary and discarded parts can be recycled. 85 per cent of the components used for assembly a car are recyclable. Recycled material is also used in the car, for example, in the instrument panel that contains 12 per cent recycled plastic. The designers continually try to improve each component from an ecological perspective, to use recycled and sustainable materials as much as possible.

Fuel consumption is low, as are emissions into the atmosphere. The car is very compact (with room for only two) and materials used in the car are chosen to reduce the overall weight of the car. This means that less fuel is used.

Several sustainability measures are taken in the production process. The chassis is, for example, painted with an environmentally friendly technique, and surplus painting material is recycled. Also the production layout and flow of inbound material are designed in as efficient a way as possible in order to ensure smooth and efficient material flows.

In addition, the facilities in the production park in Hambach are designed to be environmentally friendly. No construction material contains substances that are harmful to the environment. The buildings facades are lined with a material from fast-growing European woods. All buildings have heat insulations and, when possible, heat recovery. Not only the waste heat is re-used but also the rainwater.

6.4 Environment Management Systems

An environment management system is a tool to organise environmental work in a company. It may be designed in different ways, but it will include a policy, goals, an action plan and the execution of environment work. One basic condition for all companies is that current environmental legislation is complied with. In other respects there are no particular requirements for emissions or use of energy, for example.

As guidance for companies and consumers that make environmental demands, requirements for environment management have been stipulated in various standards and regulations. ISO 14000 is an extension of the quality standard ISO 9000 and relates to work in designing, executing, following up and improving environment management systems. To hold ISO 14000 certification means that a company has developed processes which handle, follow up and continuously improve environmental requirements and goals. In the same way as other quality standards, the standard does not state how good the company is at environment work or which environmental goals are worked towards, but it shows that the company works in a structured fashion with environmental issues.

CASE STUDY 6.3: WAUSAU PAPER & ENVIRONMENTAL PROTECTION
(http://www.wausaupapers.com/ (Date: 2007-09-10)

Wausau Paper is a larger producer of fine printing and writing, specialty products and towel and tissue papers. The company has the following environmental policy:

"At Wausau Paper, we work hard to safeguard natural resources for future generations. Being responsible environmental stewards is good for the communities in which we operate — and good for the future of our business.

♦ **Waste** — Each of our facilities works to minimize emissions and wastes that negatively impact the environment. We adhere to the Reduce, Reuse, Recycle, Recover philosophy.

♦ **Facilities** — Painting, housekeeping and outside storage standards help ensure that the facility appearances meet community values.

♦ **Air Quality** — Not all emissions can be eliminated, reused, or recycled. Sources of these byproducts are monitored, evaluated, and controlled for minimum environmental impact.

♦ **Water Conservation** — The water management programmes we have in place are designed to maintain potable and process water system integrity.

♦ **Wastewater Management** — Our facilities are designed to eliminate, reduce, or recycle their wastewater streams. Wastewater treatment systems help maintain effluent quality.

♦ **Storm Water** — Segregating drainage water reduces water contamination potential. As an added safety measure, our facilities also have containment and control systems in place.

♦ **Spills** — Containment facilities for process, transfer, and storage spills are maintained to protect area surface water and groundwater from toxicity and other potential dangers.

Our employees are encouraged to comply with the spirit as well as the letter of the laws protecting the environment. Only through continuous, diligent effort can we be certain that Wausau Paper is maintaining the highest standards of environmental protection."

6.5 Environmental Impact Assessment (EIA)

To enable complete comparisons between environment goals and cost goals, it is necessary that environmental impact be quantified in monetary terms. However, there are many difficulties involved in putting a correct price tag on environmental impact. This is because the effects are of a long-term nature and because many factors have an indirect effect on the environment. Environmental impact is therefore normally reported as a combination of quantified estimates and qualitative descriptions of actions carried out.

Emissions from transportation vehicles are normally quantified. Other emissions are not usually taken into account. Determining factors for a vehicle's emissions are the type of engine, fuel consumption and fuel type. For electrically powered vehicles, particularly locomotives, environmental impact consists of the consumption of resources and environmental impact when the electricity was produced. So-called "green electricity" means that only environmentally friendly methods of production such as hydropower were used for producing the electricity. If a combination of different sources of electricity is used, the emissions value for the average annual production can be calculated. In the case of sea transport, emissions are to a large extent influenced by the speed of the vessel. At higher speeds, small changes in speed will have a larger impact on fuel consumption than at lower speeds. Two different emission pictures emerge in the case of air transport. The first is related to emissions during take-off, landing, initial and final flight at low levels. The second is during flight at high levels. Different calculation models have been produced and are available for estimates of emissions from different types of transport.

However, it is not sufficient to calculate total emissions per kilometre for transport; they often need to be broken down into products transported, or per customer commission, etc. This breakdown of total emissions is in many cases considerably more difficult than calculating total emissions.

The costs for emissions can be calculated from the point of view of public finance, which means that the costs may be equivalent to the tax and charge levels imposed. They may also be calculated from the company financial perspective. **Lifecycle assessment (LCA)** is one method that is used as a basis for such evaluation.

Lifecycle assessment is a tool used to create a picture of the total environmental impact of a product, "from the cradle to the grave", or its total lifecycle. This analysis identifies how much energy, emissions and other loads on the environment are required to extract raw materials for the product, for transportation, production, maintenance, re-use, recycling and scrapping of the product, i.e. all factors that affect the environment during its entire lifecycle. For example, the transporting of a product may cause more environmental impact than its manufacture. Similarly, use and recycling or scrapping of a product may affect the environment more than emissions during production. The goal of a lifecycle assessment is to give as full a picture as possible of how a product affects the environment. The ISO 14000 standard divides a lifecycle assessment into the following four steps:

1   *Defining goal and scope of the analysis*: definition of the system studied means determining its temporal and geographical limits.

2   *Inventory*: when the system limits are set, information is collected on the environmental impact of activities.

3   *Impact assessment*: an assessment of the system's environmental impact can be divided into a classification part and a characterisation part. Examples of classification categories are the consumption of resources, effects on health, greenhouse effects and acidification effects. Characterisation means weighing the total impact on each environmental category. For example, the total emissions of methane, carbon dioxide and nitrogen oxides are weighed to illustrate the system's total contribution to the greenhouse effect.

4   *Interpretation*: in this final step, the different environmental impacts are compared and interpreted.

A lifecycle assessment can also provide the answer to whether a product should be recycled or not. It may take more energy to recycle a product than it for example takes to burn it and manufacture a new product. It may sometimes be more environmentally friendly to throw a product on the tip than to recycle it.

6.6 Conclusion and Summary

This chapter has treated the logistics system's relationship with the environment. Different meanings of environmentally adapted logistics have been discussed. The point of departure was in what way transportation and packaging affects the environment. The potential for decreasing the logistics system's negative effects on the environment was taken up. Authorities' means of control through knowledge, finance and legislation was treated. The handling alternatives of the logistics system were discussed in terms of filtering, recycling, re-using and reduction in external transportation and packaging, and for materials supply, production and distribution systems. Finally, environment management systems and some principles for quantifying the environmental impact of a system were described.

 Key concepts

Congestion charge 131

Eco-cycle 129

Eco-labelling 131

Emission right 131

Emission standard 131

Environmental impact assessment
  (EIA) 128

Environmental management
  system 128

Environmental zone 131

Environmentally adapted
  logistics 128

EU flower 131

Green dispatch 136

ISO 14000 135

Lifecycle assessment (LCA) 141

Polluter pays principle 132

Recycling 132

Reducing 132

Return flow 137

Re-using 132

Reverse logistics 133

Vehice charge 131

Discussion Tasks

1 What is the role of consumers in the sustainable logistics system? Discuss the possible consumer impact as a result of increased affluence, changing lifestyles and taste, etc.

2 The environmental impact of the logistics system is partly a result of customers' requirements. Examples have been given in this chapter of how external customer requirements can give rise to negative environmental consequences. Customer requirements vary between products, markets and during the product lifecycle. Start with a product. Can it be expected that customers in the future will put different demands which will mean changes in environmental impact? Give examples of possible changes in requirements that may lead to increased or decreased environmental impact.

3 The environmental impacts of the logistics system can be partly reduced with the aid of information technology. Give some examples of how different IT solutions affect environmental impact.

4 The logistics system influences the environment in different ways, and there are a number of different possible measures to reduce its environmental impact. The different alternatives originate at different levels of an organisation and in different units in a company. Give examples of a number of measures with different characteristics and explain which organisational level (e.g. managing director, production manager, logistics manager, transportation purchaser, traffic planner, stores worker) and unit (e.g. purchasing, production, design, marketing) is responsible for each alternative.

5 A common transportation problem with obvious environmental impact is the absence of backload for vehicles, resulting in that they have to return back from the delivery destination to the starting point with empty loads. What factors may constrain backloading of trucks? Give examples of how to increase backloading and thereby decreasing empty running of trucks.

Further reading

Autry, C., Daugherty, P. and Richey, G. (2001), "The challenge of reverse logistics in catalog retailing", *International Journal of Physical Distribution and Logistics Management,* Vol. 31, No. 1, pp. 26–37.

Genes, R. (2002), "Smart ecology" *Manufacturing Engineer,* Vol. 81, No. 2, pp. 48–53.

May, G. (2005) "Transport in Europe: where are we going?", *Insight,* Vol. 7, No. 6, pp. 24–38.

McKinnon, A. (1998) "Logistics restructuring, freight traffic growth and the environment", in Banister, D. (ed.), *Transport policy and the environment,* Routledge, London, pp. 97–109.

McKinnon, A. and Ge, Y. (2006) "The potential for reducing empty running by trucks: a retrospective analysis", *International Journal of Physical Distribution and Logistics Management,* Vol. 36, No. 5, pp. 391–410.

Murphy, P. and Poist, R. (2003) "Green perspectives and practices: a 'comparative logistics' study", *Supply Chain Management: An International Journal,* Vol. 8, No. 2, pp. 122–131.

Pretty, J., Ball, A., Lang, T. and Morison, J. (2005) "Farm costs and food miles: an assessment of the full cost of the UK weekly food basket", *Food Policy,* Vol. 30, No. 1, pp. 1–19.

Rogers, D. and Tibben-Lembke, R. (1998) *Going backwards: reverse logistics trends and practices,* Reverse Logistics Executive Council, University of Nevada, Reno (http://www.rlec.org).

STEP, Sustainable education technology projects: http://www.stepin.org/casestudy.php?id= smartcar.

van Hoek, R. (1999) "From reversed logistics to green supply chains", *Supply Chain Management: An International Journal*, Vol. 4, No. 3, pp. 129–134.

Westermark, L. (2001) "Integrate the environmental dimension: visions for transport", *Environmental Management and Health*, Vol. 12, No. 2, pp. 175–180.

Wu, H.-J. and Dunn, S. (1995) "Environmentally responsible logistics systems", *International Journal of Physical Distribution and Logistics Management*, Vol. 25, No. 2, pp. 20–38.

PART 3
Logistics and Supply Chain Structures

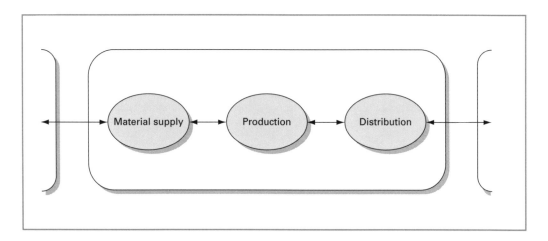

The third part deals with logistics and supply chain structures. Chapter 7, the first of four chapters concerns different design and structural aspects of the items and products in the supply chain. Chapter 8 deals with common sourcing strategies, design of supplier structures and their impact on a company and supply chain. Chapter 9 clarifies production conditions from a logistics point of view and how they impact on logistics and supply chain management. Chapter 10 about distribution structures concerns alternatives for distribution structure design and the role of distribution for supply chain value adding.

Part Contents

Products in the logistics system

It was stated in the first chapter that the aim of logistics is to achieve the efficient flow of materials. Naturally, materials themselves play a central role in the logistics system. Distribution companies refer to flows of products in and out of the company, whereas manufacturing companies use different terms depending on where the materials are located in the flow. In the outbound flow, i.e. the material flow to customers, materials are referred to as products, while the inbound flow consists of raw materials and components from suppliers. Materials flowing within the company, in which value is directly added, are called *manufactured parts* and *semi-finished products*. The concept of *item* is often used as a common term for all these aspects of materials. This chapter treats various aspects of the products and items which flow through the logistics systems of companies and supply chains.

The chapter is closely related to several other chapters in the book. There are direct links to Chapter 9 Production processes and layouts, Chapter 10 (especially Section 10.6 Postponement and speculation), Chapter 11 Demand management, Chapter 14 Transport planning and Chapter 16 (especially Section 16.4 Supply chain design).

7.1 Products, Product Groups and Product Ranges

Products in this context are physical objects that are sold and delivered to customers. However, it should be explained that the concept of product in general terms has a considerably wider meaning. For example, services of various kinds are referred to as products. For practical reasons products that are similar from the distribution and manufacturing viewpoints are often classified into **product groups**. Long-term forecasts and planning are often based on such classifications. A company's total number of products is called the *product portfolio* or **product range**.

Most companies have a large number of products whose material flows must be controlled. The number of items influences logistics work and the logistics system in various ways. The larger the number of items, the greater the workload required for their operative control, and the more complex and difficult to analyse the logistics system applied. In addition, the number of items has a considerable effect on profit variables which can and must be influenced by logistics measures; for example, capital tied up and delivery service. Most products are necessary for competitiveness on the market, but there are often products of dubious profitability which could be removed from the range without the company losing any competitiveness. Most companies have an almost constant stream of new products. To avoid having an unmanageably large range of products it is necessary to regularly phase out some products, especially those that are no longer justified in terms of the extra work and complexity of control required for their marketing.

The selection of a product range is strategically important for a company. A wide range may be important to spread risks or to even out demand for products with different seasonal variations. It may even be a prerequisite for competing at all – for example, when the market demands suppliers with complete product ranges. The positive effects of limiting the range of products are often so obvious, however, that logistics aspects should be considered in decisions made on retaining or phasing out an existing product.

A common approach to the issue of limiting product ranges is to use an ABC analysis as described in Appendix A. By ranking products in order of diminishing profit contribution, a clear picture is obtained of which products contribute most to the company's profitability. It is often the case that a small part of the range accounts for a large proportion of profit contribution. It is primarily these items that should be retained in the product range.

Limiting the product and **component range** has a number of effects on a company's logistics system. Range limitation always results in a decrease in the administration work required to control flows of materials. Fewer products simplify forecasting, and the quality of control systems can be improved by allocating more time to the most profitable products. This impacts on financial results in the form of less capital tied up, more efficient utilisation of resources and better delivery service.

A decrease in the number of similar products may also result in increased quantities of retained products manufactured, which provide other advantages from the logistics angle. For example, benefits of scale in production and fewer manufacturing orders will lead to less planning and follow-up work. Figure 7.1 illustrates two cases that show these relationships. In the first case, five similar products are manufactured in a certain production department: A, B, C, D and E. In the second case, the five products have been reduced to three: A, B and C. If the aggregate demand for the different products in the two cases remains unchanged and for simplicity's sake we assume that the production time per unit is also unchanged and that all products are

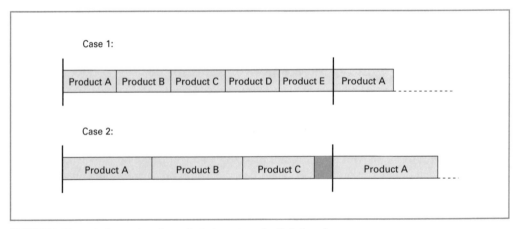

FIGURE 7.1 Change in the number of manufacturing orders after limitation of range
The rectangles represent manufacturing time for each product.

manufactured in all periods, the annual number of production orders can decrease by 40 per cent, from five to three in each period. Normally the total set-up time for starting a new order will also be reduced by the same amount since fewer modifications need to be made, resulting in less capacity required for production resources. The shaded area in case 2 represents the decrease in set-up time obtained when products D and E are removed from the range.

The decreased capacity required makes possible a reduction in manufacturing costs, or using the surplus capacity to increase production volumes – assuming that there is sufficient demand on the market. The surplus capacity can also be used to make more frequent set-ups, since more set-up time can be accepted within the framework of the existing capacity. It then becomes possible to manufacture smaller quantities each time, which gives gains in the form of less capital tied up in stocks and more flexibility for changes in customer demand.

Limiting the product range also gives positive effects on capital tied up. The following formula is usually applied to give a rough estimate of the relationship between capital tied up and the number of items. It is based on the formula for calculating economical order quantities as detailed in Chapter 12.

$$\text{Stock size} = \text{constant} \cdot \sqrt{\text{turnover} \cdot \text{number of products}}$$

If, for example, it is possible to reduce the number of items and retain the same overall turnover for a certain product group from 40 to 30, total stocks will be reduced to $\sqrt{¾} = 0.87$, i.e. by 13 per cent. The risk of obsolescence is also reduced with the number of products since products are removed from the low turnover and slow moving parts of the range.

7.2 Product Structures

Manufacturing companies make products by processing raw materials and assembling purchased components and their own semi-finished products. The material contents of such products are defined with the help of product structures, also called **bills-of-materials (BOM)**. A **product structure** specifies how a product is designed from raw materials and purchased components, through manufactured parts and semi-finished products, to the final manufacture or

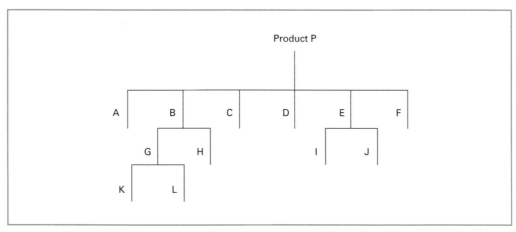

FIGURE 7.2 Illustration of a product structure
A to L refer to components included in product P.

assembly of a product. The structure also specifies quantities of each item included in the final product; for example, each chair has four legs.

A product structure may be illustrated in the form of a tree, as in Figure 7.2. The appearance of the tree indicates the complexity of the product. Product P in the figure consists of four structure levels. The upper structure level consists of six different items. The semi-finished product B consists of part G and component H, and the semi-finished product E and the components I and J. Part G consists of components K and L. The items A, C, D, F, H, I, J, K and L are purchased components which do not have their own product structures.

The structure information in the form of which and how many products and other manufactured items are included plays a decisive role for many functions in logistics. It provides a specification of how items and products are manufactured and it is the basis of product accounting. Component materials can be reserved by all the registration with the help of structures. Structures are also a prerequisite for the use of material planning methods based on material needs derived from forecasts of finished products: for example, material requirements planning which is described in Chapter 12.

The product structure determines the complexity of the product from a logistics viewpoint. Above all it is the product's structural depth and breadth that are decisive for its complexity. The structural depth of a product, i.e. the number of structural levels from raw material and purchased components to finished product, are first and foremost a consequence of its characteristics. The number of structural levels also depends to some extent on how it is designed and the technical production solutions for manufacturing it. The structural depth may also be influenced in this way. Deep structures arise as a result of numerous sub-stages in acquisition of materials and components, and manufacturing and assembly/final manufacture. Every sub-stage comprises one structural level and results in a separate item that must be planned, ordered to manufacture and delivered to stores and retrieved from stores for its use in other structural levels. Every node in the product structure is a planning point. The deeper the structure, the more planning points there are. For this reason the structural depth influences administration work required for controlling the flow of materials for each product. The number of structural levels in a manufacturing company normally lies between three and seven, but there are those with more than ten levels, especially in the mechanical engineering industry.

The structural depth is significant for the clarity and simplicity of the design of manufacturing and flow of materials. Large structural depth results in long leadtimes. Every planning point requires administration, causing another increment in leadtime. Less clarity and increased complexity in the flow of materials, which are part of deep structures, also extend the total leadtime for manufacturing products. Certainly, manufacturing in several structural stages is a necessity in most cases due to production economy. But by considering the logistics perspective and costs it is possible in many cases to achieve solutions which are more efficient in terms of the flow of materials as well as total costs.

A **product's complexity** in terms of breadth is related to the number of **items** at each structural level. In general it is the upper structural level which has the largest number of items. There may be hundreds of items at one structural level, and in many cases over a thousand. Again, the mechanical engineering industry tends to have many items in its products.

The significance of the breadth complexity for logistics applies especially to the operative control of materials. Broad structures mean that many items must be available simultaneously for the initiation of manufacturing at higher structural levels. For example, sufficient quantities of items A, B, C, D, E, and F in Figure 7.2 must be available for the manufacture of product P. The more items are involved, the more difficult and complex it is to handle the issue of co-ordination. These problems can be illustrated with the help of an example: assume that a product consists of 10 component items and that all of these have an inventory service level of 95 per cent, i.e. that in 95 per cent of cases there are sufficient items in stock. The probability of all items being available when manufacturing is to start will be $(0.95)^{10} = 0.60$, or only 60 per cent. The more items and the lower the inventory service levels, the higher is the probability of shortages when starting manufacturing, unless special material planning measures are taken.

In the same way as for deep structures, the structural breadth is to a large extent determined by the nature of the product. For example, a large number of items is unavoidable when assembling a car. There are certain options for reducing the structural breadth, however. One approach is to purchase ready-assembled, semi-finished products instead of purchasing all the individual components and assembling them in the plant prior to final assembly. This strategy involves selecting systems suppliers that deliver entire subsystems for the product instead of component suppliers.

Another way of reducing the number of component items is to integrate. This means that two or more items are replaced by one, or that two or more functions are integrated in one item. A simple example is that of replacing an item manufactured by welding together a number of steel parts by one cast item. The feasibility of achieving integration of different items is largely determined by developments in the production engineering area.

Product complexity from the logistics viewpoint is also affected by the size of the range of items, i.e. the quantities of raw materials, the number of purchased components and semi-finished products manufactured within the company. Limiting this range is a **standardisation** issue and depends on reducing the number of different dimensions, material qualities, shapes, colours and so on used in the design and manufacture of products. The strategy of limiting the range of components is called **component commonality** and means, for example, that instead of using different dimensions of screws each adapted for a specific purpose, one larger dimension is used for all purposes, even those that could have utilised a smaller screw dimension. The effects of component commonality are similar to the limitations on product range as described above.

7.3 Standard Products, Customer-Specific Products and Customer Order-Specific Products

In a manufacturing company, products can be categorised into standard products, more or less customer order-specific products, and customer-specific products. This division is related to the degree of customer order control in the manufacturing of products. The principal difference between product categories is related to where the **customer order decoupling point (CODP)** is located.

The customer order decoupling point is defined as the point in a product structure at which the product's manufacture and delivery is determined by a customer order. From this point on, manufacture is governed by the customer order, whereas manufacture and purchase of items at lower structural levels are governed by forecasts and must be based on estimated future needs. In the case of customer order decoupling points, the items in lower structure levels are generally kept in stock. One general example of the significance of the customer order decoupling point and the various control principles applied from each side of it are shown in Figure 7.3. The example refers to a personal computer, which is assembled and packaged for customer orders but whose components, such as the main unit, screen, mouse and packaging, are taken from stores. The inventory control of these components is governed by forecasts of expected future sales.

It is possible to differentiate between five different types of company when referring to where the customer order decoupling point is located in product structures, which determines the degree of customer order control. The different types are illustrated in Figure 7.4.

CASE STUDY 7.1: DESIGN FOR LOGISTICS – IKEA'S TABLE LACK (Baraldi, 2006)

In 1981 IKEA launched the small table "Lack". The goal was a price that no other competitor could ever come close to. This required IKEA to design a product that could be produced and transported as such a low cost that it would become the price leader. Compared to its competitors' products, the logistics costs would make a greater impact on Lack's value because of its low price and because Lack needed to be easy to handle by logistics personnel and by consumers taking it home, while minimising the risk of logistics damage.

In designing Lack, the following key logistics functions and features were considered: weight, shape/volume, service level and quantities/variants. The logistics goals are affected by the following functions and features:

- *Low weight*: reduced transport costs, reduced transport damage, easier physical goods handling, easier pick-ups by customers from IKEA's self-service warehouses.

- *Shape and volume*: Lack is packed in flat packets, as are all IKEA's products. This allows for high load utilisation in trucks, containers and pallets.

- *Service level*: Lack is one of the items requiring the highest delivery precision. It is assigned a 99 per cent service level at the warehouses. This may however require less than truck load deliveries to warehouses.

- *Quantities and variants*: it is more cost-efficient to keep the finished goods stock upstream in distribution centres or at the manufacturers. This has pressured IKEA to cut delivery leadtimes aggressively throughout the supply chain and to develop a global planning approach for planning and execution stock replenishment. The number of variants also drives costs which is why these have had to be kept at a minimum level.

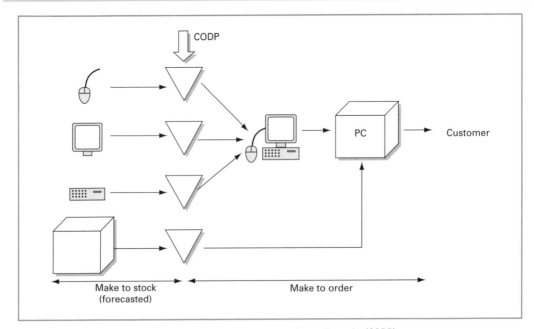

FIGURE 7.3 Control principles on each side of the customer order decoupling point (CODP)

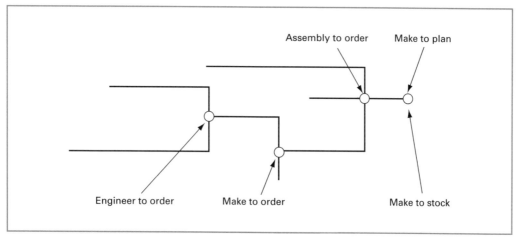

FIGURE 7.4 The location of the customer order point for different types of company

Engineer to order (ETO) means that the company's products are designed to customer order specifications to a greater or lesser degree. Design work, preparations for manufacture, materials sourcing and manufacturing are carried out and governed both in terms of time and content by customer orders received. The customer order decoupling point lies at a very low level, i.e. far down in the product structure. Stocks in this type of company consist of unsophisticated purchased components and raw materials.

Make to order (MTO) is similar to the above type, but in this case products are generally fully designed and ready for manufacture before customer orders are received. A large part of materials sourcing and manufacturing of parts and semi-finished products is carried out without any connection to specific customer orders. Some component manufacturing and all assembly/final manufacture are carried out directly to customer orders. Materials from external suppliers are also sourced to some extent to customer orders. The degree of integration of production and customer orders is thus less for this type of company than the previous type, and the customer order decoupling point lies higher in the product structure. Stocks consist mainly of purchased components, raw materials and components produced within the company.

Assembly to order (ATO) means in principle that all materials are sourced and all component manufacturing is carried out without connection to specific customer orders. The final form of the products and their characteristics are achieved through ordering variants when assembling/final manufacture to customer order. Apart from the final step of ordering variants, the products are completely standardised and defined and designed by the manufacturing company itself. The degree of integration is relatively low and the customer order decoupling point lies just under the final product's structure level. In this type of company stocks consist of all purchased components, raw materials, and components and semi-finished products that are produced within the company.

The remaining two types of company, **make to plan (MTP)** and **make to stock (MTS),** have the smallest correlation between manufacturing and customer orders. Products are fully known and specified when the customer order is placed, i.e. the customer order decoupling point lies after the level of final product in the product structure. In the case of make to stock, standard

Characteristics	Engineer to order	Make to order	Assembly to order	Make to plan	Make to stock
Delivery time to customer	Long	Medium	Short	Short	Very short
Typical production volumes	Very small	Small	Medium	Very large	Large
Product variants	Very much	Many	Many	Few	Few
Basis for planning	Customer order	Forecast/ Customer order	Forecast/ Customer order	Delivery plan	Forecast
Integration with customer	High	Medium	Low	High	No
Number of customer orders	Very few	Few	Medium	Few	Medium

TABLE 7.1 Characteristics of different company types

products are kept in stock awaiting customer orders. Make to plan may also refer to completely standardised products without any connection to specific customers but it may also refer to customer-specific products that are delivered to individual customers. Customer-specific products are designed for a particular customer, but the product is known when the customer order is received. Examples of this type of relationship are suppliers to the car industry and other repetitive industries. Instead of manufacturing activities being initiated by customer orders, delivery plans and forecasts respectively and stock levels initiate manufacturing in both of these types of company. Stocks in this case consist of end products and all purchased components, raw materials, and components and semi-finished products produced within the company.

A summary of the characteristics of these different company types is given in Table 7.1. The characteristics stated refer to commonly occurring and typical relationships for each type of company. Deviations may occur in individual companies. Integration with customers in this table describes to what degree the customer, through the customer order, affects the form of the product and thus its composition in terms of materials and manufacture.

7.4 Product Variants and Dealing with Variants

A range of products can be characterised in terms of breadth and depth. A broad range has many products which are not especially related to each other, while a deep range is characterised by a few basic types, each with a number of variants. Being able to supply many different qualities and variants of the same product is often a prerequisite for being able to compete on a market that is increasingly characterised by demands for satisfying individual customers' unique needs. From a marketing point of view it may be a drawback to have to limit the range by reducing the number of variants. However, a deep product range carries with it a number of problems from the logistics perspective, especially if the different variants are manufactured to stock. It is difficult to avoid large amounts of capital tied up, and also to avoid high obsolescence

A	Lamp shade	B	Foot	C	Cable
1	Cylindric	1	Cubic blue	1	Length 1 metre
2	Cone	2	Cubic red	2	Length 2 metre
3	Double cone	3	Cubic yellow	3	Length 3 metre
		4	Cylindric blue		
		5	Cylindric red		
		6	Cylindric yellow		

D	Plug	E	Switch	F	Bulb
1	Earthed	1	Two positions type	1	25 Watt
2	Unearthed	2	Three positions type	2	40 Watt
		3	Continuous type	3	60 Watt

TABLE 7.2 Options in the manufacture of a table lamp

costs, i.e. costs for scrapping products due to changes on the market or changing customer requirements reducing demand for them.

One simple example is sufficient to illustrate the fact that the number of variants can easily become unreasonable. Assume that a lamp company manufactures basic table lamps. The various options with regard to lampshade, foot and so on are shown in Table 7.2. This simple lamp has a total of 972 variants. Naturally, it is almost impossible to forecast demand for so many variants, and even more difficult to keep all in stock. Typical for this type of problem with variants is that the number rapidly increases with each option added. To give an example: if it was possible to choose between three colours of lampshade, the number of variants would increase to 3 times 972, or 2916.

One strategy which can be applied to this type of problem to make handling more efficient is called **postponement**. This means trying to avoid manufacturing products to stock. Instead, the component parts are stocked and the end product is not manufactured until a customer order is received specifying which variant is required. To create very short delivery times it is even possible to allow local distributors to carry out final assembly of the product after the customer has placed his order. For the postponement strategy to be possible, the leadtime for final assembly to customer order must be shorter than the delivery time required by the customer. The opposite strategy, *speculation*, means that variants are manufactured on the basis of forecasts, with the risk that there will be insufficient demand for certain variants.

There are two main alternatives for the application of postponement strategy to handling a large number of **product variants**. One is called basic version with accessories, and the other **modularisation**.

Basic version with accessories

The simplest alternative for dealing with a number of variants of standard products is to create variants by providing a number of basic versions with different types of accessories. Application of this principle means that demand for basic versions of the product is forecast and the products manufactured to stock. Manufacturing may also take place according to a production plan, i.e. a plan for the quantities manufactured in one week, or other time period. Incoming customer orders are then booked according to those quantities. The various optional accessories, which ideally can be easily added to the basic version of the product, are also manufactured separately

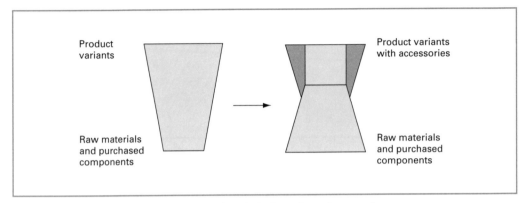

FIGURE 7.5 General illustration of dealing with variants by basic version and accessories
The breadth of the cones is proportional to the number of items. The shaded area represents items that are accessories.

to stock. When a customer order is received, the basic version is supplemented with those accessories desired by the customer. In the example of the lamp in Table 7.2, the bulb and the switch are assumed to be accessories. The number of variants is then reduced from 972 to 108, and the number of items which must be forecast and stocked will be these 108 variants plus 3 switches and 3 bulbs, i.e. a total of 114 items. It is still a large number, but the reduction is significant even in such a simple example.

The principle behind the use of basic version and accessories is illustrated in Figure 7.5. The breadth in the pictures is proportional to the number of different items that occur at different structure levels from raw materials and purchased components to finished products. The picture on the left represents the case of manufacture of all product variants to forecast, and on the right a limited number of basic versions manufactured to forecast and the remaining product variants created through supplementing basic versions with accessories of different sorts. The shaded areas in the picture on the right correspond to customer order specific variants created with these accessories.

A more far-reaching alternative is to arrange for the replacement of certain parts included in the basic version, i.e. to modify the basic version kept in stock. This could be the flexible cable in the example of the table lamp above. Assume that the basic version is a table lamp with a flexible cable 1m long, with an unearthed plug and a 25W bulb. If the customer wants any of the other lengths of flexible lead, switches or bulbs, these are changed at the time of the customer order. The number of variants which must be forecast has then been reduced to 54. In addition to this, 5 more items must be forecast and stocked, i.e. two and three-metre flexible cables, unearthed plugs and 40W and 60W bulbs.

Modularisation

A more radical method of solving the problem of variants is to modularise the products and create variants to customer order by combining variants of different modules. Modularisation means that the products are divided into well-defined and standardised parts which can be combined with each other. In the example of a lamp, the lampshade, foot, flexible cable, switch, and bulb would be modules. For the approach to be really efficient it is desirable that there are as few dependencies between the different modules as possible, and as few mutual restrictions as possible in the choice of different module variants. In the example of the lamp it is desirable that all switches can be used for all lengths of flexible cable.

CASE STUDY 7.2: USE OF THE CUSTOMER ORDER DECOUPLING POINT AT ALFA LAVAL CORP.

Alfa Laval AB is a global manufacturer of, for example, heat exchangers. A heat exchanger is made from a number of standard components made to stock. When a customer order is received, standard components are withdrawn from the component store, adjusted and assembled to a finished customer-specific heat exchanger. The customer order decoupling point is consequently at the component stock. The delivery time from customer order to delivery equals the assembly time from withdrawal of standard components to finished product.

Manufacturing of heat exchangers is described in the figure below. Triangles illustrate stock points and circles illustrate production operations.

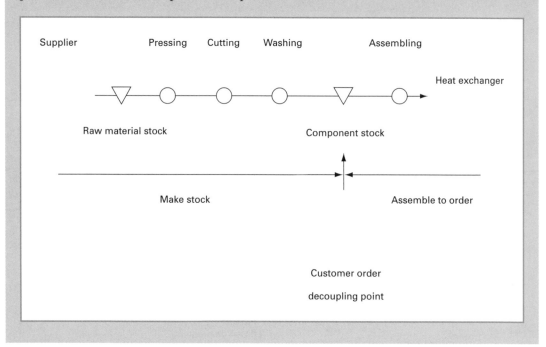

CASE STUDY 7.3: MODULAR DESIGN AT SCANIA TRUCKS

Scania Trucks is the fourth largest heavy truck manufacturer in the world, with plants in Europe, South America, Asia, Africa and Australia.

Scania's manufacturing system is based on a modular product design, allowing them to have fewer components in its assortment but without fewer product variants compared to its competitors. Each truck is based on a number of standardised modules. Engines, transmissions, axles and cabs are examples of such modules. Every module exists in a number of variants: for example, engines with different horsepower. It is possible to combine the different module variants into a very large number of possible truck configurations, even if the number of variants for each module is limited. Diagram of Scania's modularisation programme:

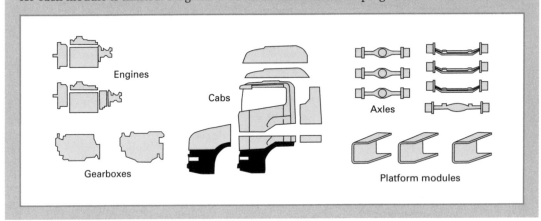

The different modules are forecast, planned and manufactured to stock, while the final composition of products is made to customer order. When processing customer orders, the customer's requirements are specified with respect to which variants are desired for each respective module, called *configuration*. If dealing with the issue of variants for the table lamp in Table

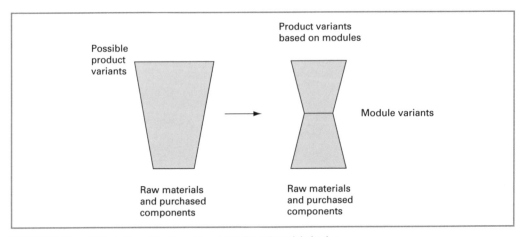

FIGURE 7.6 General illustration of dealing with variants through modularisation
The breadth of the cones is proportional to the number of items.

7.2 is based on modularisation, it is not necessary to stock any product variants. Instead, the different items which make up variants for each module are stocked. The total number of items which needs to be forecast and stocked will be reduced to only 20. In the same way as for the basic version and accessories, dealing with variants by modularisation is illustrated in Figure 7.6.

7.5 Product Lifecycle

The time during which it is financially defensible to sell a product on the market is limited. Terms used in this context are technical product life and financial product life. The sales volumes of a product normally vary in a very characteristic fashion during its lifespan, as illustrated in Figure 7.7, the **product lifecycle**.

It is possible to differentiate between a number of different phases in the product lifecycle. During the introduction phase, i.e. the period immediately after the product is launched on the market, the demand is often small and grows slowly due to buyers' resistance and the product remaining relatively unknown to customers on the market. During the growth phase, awareness of the product increases which, if its reception on the market is positive, leads to a rapid rise in sales. During the subsequent phases, maturity and saturation, sales reach their highest level. These phases are often considerably longer than the others. When the product is no longer able to attract the market sufficiently, a decrease in sales starts and the decline phase of the product lifecycle is initiated.

Where in its lifecycle a product is at any one time has a crucial effect on which logistics strategies should be chosen and which performance variables should be prioritised to work towards. The selection of suitable forecast and planning methods is also affected.

It is very important to get the product accepted during the introduction and growth phases, otherwise there is a risk that sales will never pick up properly. For this reason it is essential to be

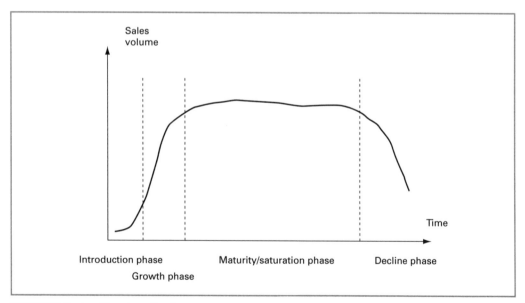

FIGURE 7.7 Product lifecycle and its phases
The curve shows how sales volumes vary during the product's life.

able to deliver as demand increases, and the focus of logistics must therefore be high delivery service. Missed delivery times or the incapacity to deliver from stock, if it is a stock item, will both decrease the probability of a customer placing repeat orders during these phases. It is also important during these phases to quickly raise sales volumes in order to capture market shares and establish the product on the market. This places great demands on the production and distribution systems and their flexibility.

The first two phases are further characterised by the extreme difficulty of predicting future demand. This depends not least on the fact that there is no sales history. Traditional forecast methods for predicting demands are not applicable, and companies are forced to rely largely on test sales, market research and assessments by experience. Due to the unreliability to which these difficulties in forecasting lead, there is a great risk that large stocks are built up which must be discarded if the product does not succeed on the market. To decrease this risk it may be advisable to manufacture smaller quantities at a time, or manufacture to customer orders as much as possible, even if order quantities are financially too small – provided that delivery times to customers are still competitive. If stocks must be accepted, the risks can be decreased by accepting stocks kept in a central warehouse and delivering directly to customers from this warehouse instead of establishing local warehouses for different markets, even though this may mean additional costs for transportation.

During the maturity and saturation phases, volumes are larger and more stable. The focus of logistics must therefore be aimed primarily at ensuring large volumes through stable material supplies from suppliers and stable flows of material in production, as well as stable deliveries to customers. Storage and distribution capacity must be expanded, and manufacturing methods and production planning must be adapted to high-volume production. Consideration of production and distribution costs is more important than during the two introductory phases.

Owing to the relatively even delivery volumes that normally occur during the maturity and saturation phases, forecasting of future demand can be based on historic values, and traditional forecast methods can be used. Since activities can be planned to a greater degree, material planning can be based on more long-term production plans. To be able to ensure delivery volumes, efficient long-term and medium-term capacity planning is important.

During the decline phase, the same type of problems arises as in the introduction and growth phases – unpredictability and difficulties in forecasting. In order to avoid unnecessarily high obsolescence costs for unsaleable products it is important that stocks are reduced as the rate of deliveries fall, both in terms of volume in stock and the number of storage points in the distribution network. The focus of logistics during this phase should be primarily aimed at decreasing the amount of capital tied up in different sections of the material flow.

If the products in question are capital goods, i.e. durable goods, the decline phase is also a period in which spare parts activities must be developed for the products that will later be phased out. In this context logistics plays a decisive role, not least because the aftermarket activities related to spare parts deliveries are generally very profitable. In addition, they are crucial to retaining customers and creating better conditions for succeeding with new products designed to replace them after they are phased out. An important focus for logistics in this case is on inventory service level and general customer service.

7.6 Conclusion and Summary

Products and their constituent items make up the flow of materials within and between companies, which is controlled by logistics processes. How efficiently these flows can be controlled with respect to costs, capital tied up and customer service depends also on how many products and items the company has and on the breadth and depth of the product and item ranges. In manufacturing companies, the control of the flow of materials also depends on the complexity of products' component parts, i.e. the complexity of the product structure.

Depending on where in the product structures the customer order decoupling point lies, different types of manufacturing may be categorised. Customer order decoupling points are the points from which manufacturing is governed by customer orders. The categories of usual manufacturing types are: *engineer to order, make to order, assembly to order, make to plan* and *make to stock.*

It is often impossible for companies that manufacture a large number of product variants to deliver finished products from stocks. Different approaches are used instead to create variants to order. Two different strategies for handling the issue of variants were described in this chapter: basic version with accessories and modularisation. Finally, the need to apply different logistics focuses in different phases of the product lifecycle was discussed.

🔓 **Key concepts**

Assembly to order (ATO) 153

Bill-of-material (BOM) 149

Component range 148

Component commonality 151

Customer order decoupling point
 (CODP) 151

Design for logistics 152

Engineer to order (ETO) 153

Item 150

Make to order (MTO) 153

Make to plan (MTP) 153

Make to stock (MTS) 153

Modularisation 155

Postponement 155

Product complexity 150

Product group 147

Product lifecycle 159

Product range 147

Product structure 149

Product variant 155

Standardisation 151

 ### Discussion Tasks

1 The customer order decoupling point is defined as the point in a product's structure from which manufacture and delivery are determined by customer orders. Does this mean that the product's appearance and performance must also be determined by customer orders, and if not, can we then talk about different types of decoupling points? What is the connection between them?

2 A company presently making products to stock consider switching to a make to order strategy. What positive and negative impact could such a switch result in?

3 Component commonality means eliminating the range of components used in products. A component commonality strategy may impact logistics in several ways. How

could a component commonality strategy be used within and affect a clothing manufacturing supply chain?

4 This chapter describes two main alternatives for manufacturing and delivering a large number of variants using postponement strategy. What aspects are involved in the choice between these two alternatives with respect to the number of possible variants, demands on the suitability of initial design, options for the customer to configure the variant designed, and demands for short delivery times?

5 The selection of a suitable logistics strategy is influenced by which phase of its lifecycle a product is in. Product lifespans in most industries have decreased over a number of years. How may this shortened life span influence logistics strategies in each phase of a product's lifecycle?

Further reading

Boraldi, E. (2006) "IKEA's lack table – a product designed for network-level logistics", in M. Jahre (ed.), *Resourcing in business logistics: the art of systematic combining*, Liber and Copenhagen Business School Press, Malmö.

Hopp, W. and Spearman, M. (2000) *Factory physics*, McGraw-Hill, New York.

Hayes, R. and Wheelwright, S. (1994) *Restoring our competitive edge: competing through manufacturing*, John Wiley & Sons, New York.

Slack, N., Chambers, S. and Johnston, R. (2007) *Operations management*, Prentice Hall, Essex.

Material supply structures

Raw materials and components purchased as input goods to a company's own production often account for more than 50 per cent of the cost of goods sold (COGS). In some industries, for example the electronics industry, it may be as high as 80–90 per cent. The proportion of costs for purchased items also tends to increase as a result of more extensive outsourcing. For whole-sale and retail companies, the proportion of purchase costs in the cost of goods sold is even higher. Under such conditions, the importance of working with optimal number of suppliers in parallel, with optimum geographic location, delivery patterns, relationships, etc. is clear. These issues that are partly overlapping and interrelated are making up a company's material supply structures.

A company's supply structures are not only significant from a cost viewpoint and the price of the company's products. Component and material supply is crucial for every company's competitiveness. For example, suppliers to a great extent also influence the quality of products, and have a large effect on the company's ability to keep promised delivery times to its customers and thereby maintain high delivery service. The shaping of a company's supply structures is decisive for an efficient and effective logistics system, and thus for a successful and competitive company.

Developing and introducing appropriate supply structures is both a strategic and a tactical issue. To oversimplify somewhat, we can say that these structures make up the framework for what is possible to achieve with the operative material supply processes. The potential for what is operatively possible is therefore largely determined by the supply structures.

This chapter deals with commonly occurring sourcing strategies and their significance for a company and its logistics system. Different aspects of the form and selection of supplier struc-tures are taken up. For example, issues related to the number of suppliers, distance to suppliers, supplier networks, alternative supply patterns and types of supplier relationships are discussed.

The chapter is closely related to several other chapters in the book. There are direct links to Chapter 15 The procurement process, Chapter 16 Emerging practices in supply chain manage-ment and Chapter 17 (especially Section 17.4 Electronic market places and businesses).

8.1 Sourcing Strategies

One very central issue in the shaping of sourcing strategies is the principle to be chosen regarding the number of **parallel suppliers** per item. Based on the number of parallel suppliers and the business relationships between these, it is possible to distinguish between variants of single, multiple and hybrid sourcing strategies.

Single vs multiple sourcing

The two basic sourcing strategy options consist of single sourcing and multiple sourcing, i.e. one supplier per item or several parallel suppliers per item.

Single sourcing means that a company only uses one supplier for a certain item, despite other suppliers being available on the market. In many cases the main motivation is that for the small purchase volumes involved, administration costs would be too high to use several suppliers. Other common reasons are the difficulty of finding equivalent alternatives, or that alternatives are difficult to find at a reasonable distance from the company. One further motivation is the company striving to create **partnership relations** and integrated co-operation with its suppliers. Deep partnership relations are difficult to maintain with more than one supplier per item, partly due to the resources demanded but also to avoid too much mistrust and competition in relationships. Single sourcing is more or less a prerequisite for being able to conduct mutual product and production development.

Multiple sourcing means that for every item, several alternative suppliers are used simultaneously and parallel. For a long time this has been the dominating supply strategy. The main purpose is to improve a company's negotiating leverage when prices and delivery conditions are being established. Using a number of suppliers also decreases risks; should one of the suppliers have delivery problems, another can be used to compensate. The strategy of multiple sourcing is based to a large extent on the notion that one supplier can be easily replaced by another. Thus, it is mostly applicable when switching costs are small, i.e. when the cost of changing from one supplier to another is low.

Many observers claim that the use of multiple sourcing is on the decline. The possible advantages involved in terms of influence on prices and decreased risks no longer balance the disadvantages involved when establishing **partnership suppliers**. Besides, there are other ways

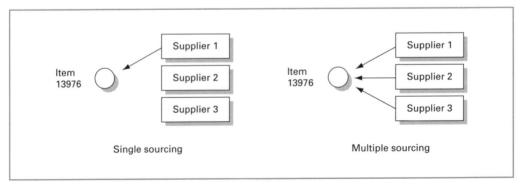

FIGURE 8.1 The sourcing strategies of single sourcing and multiple sourcing
Shaded areas represent active suppliers for the item 13976.

of controlling prices and decreasing risks. The price competition gained through multiple sourcing is more or less illusory since the purchase price is only one part of the total costs related to acquisition. Many of the other costs can be more effectively influenced in single sourcing relationships based on a partnership. The short and fragmentary contacts with suppliers obtained by a company using multiple sourcing also jeopardise the chances of carrying out continuous improvement work.

Of the two main alternatives, single sourcing has greater advantages than multiple sourcing when building up relationships with suppliers. The supplier is not subject to competition and is therefore more likely to share information and contribute to the customer company's activities. The negotiating situation which automatically follows with multiple sourcing also contributes to creating the feeling of both players being adversaries and competitors rather than partners. Multiple sourcing has a negative effect on the atmosphere of co-operation.

The use of the single sourcing strategy means that the total number of suppliers is smaller and it is possible to strive for and attain deeper integration. Procedures in the purchasing and supplying companies can be more closely adapted to each other, and conditions are better for reducing the amount of administrative work.

Since one of the main aims of multiple sourcing is to force suppliers to compete with each other to obtain negotiating advantages, it lies in the nature of things that relationships with parties involved cannot be secured in the long term. This strategy is, consequently, difficult to combine with partnership relations.

Among the advantages of the multiple sourcing strategy is that it can lead to a somewhat better capacity flexibility, since several suppliers' capacity can be utilised in times of high demand. It may also have benefits in terms of ensuring the supply of materials in times of transport disruptions, strikes and so on. On the other hand, the short-term delivery flexibility in single sourcing may be superior since it allows a more open and efficient exchange of information. In the same way, this improvement in efficient exchange of information may mean that short disruptions in the flow of materials are easier to avoid in single sourcing relationships.

Some of the important benefits and drawbacks of using these sourcing strategies are summarised in Table 8.1. In addition to that noted above, the following comments may be made with regard to the table: the reason for single sourcing being preferable from the quality viewpoint is that the strategy makes close and broad co-operation with a supplier more likely. This co-operation may extend to include product and production development. From the supplier's side there is not such a strong, single focus on manufacturing costs as in the more competitive case of multiple sourcing.

The fact that variations exist in what is delivered from a supplier is largely inevitable. This may include variations in product characteristics, delivery times and delivery precision. The more

	Single sourcing	Multiple sourcing
Product quality	+	–
Delivery variation	+	–
Risk of supply disruption	–	+
Partnership relation	+	–
Collaborative product development	+	–
Price	–	+
Costs for supplier relations	–	+

TABLE 8.1 Some benefits and drawbacks of single sourcing and multiple sourcing

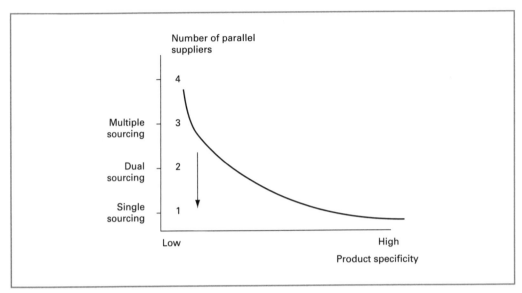

FIGURE 8.2 Single sourcing and multiple sourcing as a function of specificity
The arrow shows the development towards fewer parallel suppliers, even for items with low specificity.

parallel suppliers used, the greater will be these variations, partly as a result of more parties being involved in achieving the same objective and partly because single sourcing facilitates the achievement of close co-operation and efficient exchange of information, which can reduce the amount of variation.

The advantages that multiple sourcing may bring to prices are primarily in the case of standard items purchased on a well-developed market with many competitors. It is mainly in these conditions that the competition pressure brought about by multiple sourcing can result in lower prices. However, single sourcing has other advantages that can lead to lower prices. For example, it results in the selected supplier having greater volumes, and through economy of scale benefits more cost-effective manufacturing is possible. The greater security perceived in remaining a single source supplier may also motivate more investment in product development and rationalisation. This can further improve cost-effectiveness, which may then be passed on to the customer in terms of lower prices.

Maintaining good supplier relationships demands work and thus costs. Since single sourcing contributes to a decrease in the total number of suppliers, the strategy has a relative advantage in this respect too. Single sourcing also creates better conditions for making operative processes more efficient between the customer company and its suppliers. More efficient system solutions for the exchange of information can be developed and introduced when there are fewer relationships to maintain. Packaging, handling and transport solutions are more easily co-ordinated and are more cost-effective if only two parties are involved.

Single sourcing has traditionally been used in cases where the item purchased was specific to the purchasing company, i.e. has high specificity. The more the item was a commodity-type item, i.e. standardised and generally available on the market, the more common was multiple sourcing. However, now developments are towards using the strategy of single sourcing even for more standardised items. One important reason for this is the administration cost involved in dealing with many suppliers. This relationship is illustrated in Figure 8.2.

Variants of single and multiple sourcing

In addition to these two main alternative sourcing strategies, there are a number of variants of both single and multiple sourcing. **Sole sourcing** is one of these. Sole sourcing also means that only one supplier is used per item. It is, in other words, a special case of single sourcing. The difference is that in single sourcing the company freely chooses to work with one supplier, whereas in the case of sole sourcing it is a necessity since there is only one supplier available on the market. Sole sourcing situations may arise because the existing alternative suppliers have lost out in the face of competition, or have disappeared for other reasons. They may also arise because the customer company has had one supplier develop and manufacture a special item unique to the customer company. In this case the situation is self-inflicted. Sole sourcing has all the benefits and drawbacks of single sourcing. In addition, there is a greater dependency since alternatives do not exist in principle.

Single group sourcing is a sourcing strategy which may also be called a variant of single sourcing. Not only a single item is purchased from a single supplier, but an entire group of items with similar characteristics, e.g. all items with one and the same raw material. Single group sourcing means that the company becomes even more dependent on single suppliers than in the case of single sourcing. However, increased volumes brought about by this alternative mean that the supplier can achieve further economy-of-scale benefits and better conditions for well-developed customer co-operation, e.g. in issues related to development of materials and the development of new manufacturing technologies. The company will also become a larger customer of the supplier and can expect to be treated benevolently – for example, in the case of delivery problems. The difference between single sourcing and single group sourcing is illustrated in Figure 8.3.

Dual sourcing is a special case of multiple sourcing. Quite simply, the strategy involves using two parallel suppliers for each item. Another special case of multiple sourcing means that one of the suppliers in question for an item is appointed as the primary supplier or main supplier, while others act as secondary suppliers. The main suppliers account for the delivery of the majority of purchases and the secondary suppliers account for the remainder. For example, primary suppliers may account for 70 per cent of material flows and two secondary suppliers may account for 15 per cent each of the remainder. This strategy retains many of the advantages of single sourcing, such as the company acting as a large customer and the supplier gaining scale

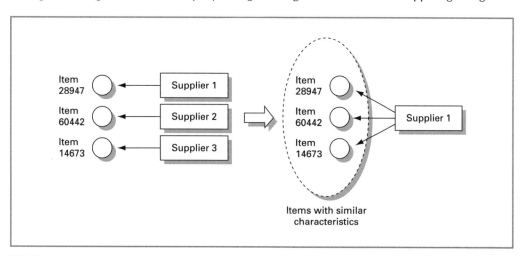

FIGURE 8.3 From single sourcing to single group sourcing

benefits through larger volumes, at the same time as disadvantages such as risk exposure to material flow disruptions are eliminated. The strategy, in contrast to single sourcing, also allows the company to maintain a certain price pressure on the primary supplier through the existence of secondary suppliers.

Hybrid sourcing

Hybrid sourcing is a group of supply strategies that can be described as combinations of single and multiple sourcing. In effect, it is a group of methods of getting the best from both strategies. One common form of hybrid sourcing is **parallel sourcing**, involving the use of multiple sourcing at the level of groups of items and single sourcing for the individual items in the groups. It is then possible to keep the advantages of single sourcing and at the same time decrease its disadvantages in the form of risks of delivery disruptions. If the supplier that normally delivers an item has delivery problems, another supplier within that group of items may temporarily take over deliveries. This approach works better for more uniform manufacturing technology used for items in each item group. The differences between single sourcing and parallel sourcing are illustrated in Figure 8.4.

One supply strategy closely related to parallel sourcing is *network sourcing*, which in addition to the above advantages includes the direct exchange of information and knowledge between suppliers.

One further hybrid is **triadic sourcing**. The name refers to one customer company co-operating with two suppliers and forming a triad for one group of items. The customer company makes the two suppliers compete for volumes and responsibility of development for each item. By forcing the suppliers to alternately, but in parallel, take responsibility for the development and production of different items and sometimes for "each other's" items, mutual dependency is created within the triad. Thus, the need to co-operate arises in the development of items, groups of items, products, and the development and operation of production processes and materials management. The triad can be developed internally through the coexistence of co-operation and competition, and externally through impulses from other business relationships. The incentive to

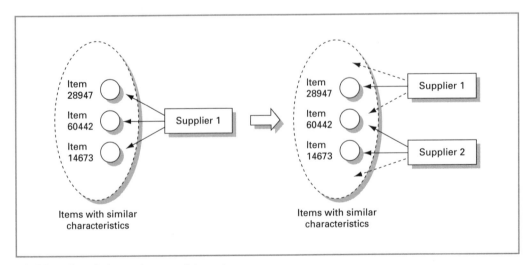

FIGURE 8.4 From single sourcing to parallel sourcing
The solid line refers to deliveries from the supplier. The broken line refers to possible deliveries that do not take place.

co-operate is produced by the continuity involved in the triad and the potential for utilising ideas in other customer relationships.

With respect to the conditions in supply chains, hybrid sourcing alternatives may be more advantageous than a strategy involving many suppliers for each item. Its benefits and drawbacks coincide in other respects with the single sourcing alternative. The same is true of single group sourcing. However, in one respect the single group sourcing alternative has advantages over hybrid sourcing: demand is more predictable and stable if all items within an item group are given to one supplier as opposed to individual items in the group being given to different suppliers.

8.2 Supplier Networks

The fact that suppliers often account for more than half a manufacturing company's added value, expressed as purchasing costs in relation to cost of goods sold, means that not only suppliers' performance is important to a company's competitiveness and efficiency. Supplier companies may have similar conditions in relation to their suppliers. With respect to a company's total costs, suppliers' suppliers may also be of interest, especially if the company is an Original Equipment Manufacturing (OEM) company, i.e. a company that manufactures a product which is sold on the end-customer market. The same is true of quality aspects of a company's products, since both the choice of materials and components and methods of manufacture used by the suppliers' suppliers may influence the quality and functional capabilities of the company's products. Consequently, in certain companies and industries it may be important to not only include in the **sourcing strategy** those aspects which affect direct suppliers, but also other suppliers in the network or hierarchy of suppliers which all companies have. For example, it could be a question of demanding approval of a suppliers' choice of suppliers, particularly for functionally critical and quality critical items.

Approved suppliers

There are two different contexts in which it is especially important to consider suppliers on second tier and further upstream in the supplier network. One of these relates to companies which manufacture complex products for which incorporated components must also be supplied as spare parts. These are conditions which prevail in mechanical engineering industries, for example. A component which is also a spare part may well be manufactured by a supplier's supplier. For a company to be able to take long-term responsibility for the sales of spare parts and future service, it must have an acceptable level of control over how these spare parts are manufactured and what quality they maintain. This is also the case if it is the company's first-tier suppliers that have direct responsibility for purchasing and mounting the items in their products. One consequence of this division of responsibility may be that the company must approve its first-tier suppliers' choice of suppliers in order to guarantee quality levels. The suppliers that are allowed to be used by the first-tier suppliers are called **approved suppliers**.

System and component suppliers

The second context in which a company must involve itself in the network of suppliers is the case of system deliveries and system suppliers. A system supplier refers to a supplier that is able to deliver complete subsystems, partial assemblies or other forms of semi-finished goods at a high level in the product structure. Its opposite, component suppliers, are suppliers that deliver

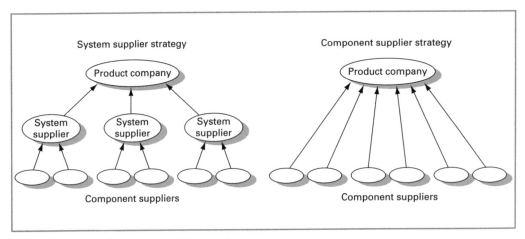

FIGURE 8.5 System and component supplier strategies

simple components or raw materials. Component suppliers may deliver to both the original equipment manufacturing company and system suppliers. System and component supplier strategies are illustrated in Figure 8.5.

If the strategy chosen is to use system suppliers, the hierarchy of suppliers becomes deeper. Suppliers at the highest level, i.e. system suppliers, represent the most complete suppliers. In addition to supplying an entire system, they often contribute to product development projects. The further down the supplier hierarchy one goes, the more specialised are the suppliers and the more limited are their areas of products and production technology.

To be able to use strategies based on system suppliers, it is often necessary for the company to take initiative and organise this type of company and the hierarchies of suppliers required at lower levels. System suppliers do not often arise by themselves. To take an example: large international companies in the Japanese automotive industry have taken the initiative to form and organise the various hierarchies of suppliers.

With respect to efficiency and integration in supply chains, the development towards system suppliers is of great significance. The use of system suppliers is one way to reduce the number of first-tier suppliers and thereby contribute to creating better conditions for establishing partnerships with a supplier base. It is also easier to establish a partnership with system suppliers since the companies have more points of contact, involving several people and functions in the companies, and more common interests. Conditions for a mutually rewarding exchange of competence, for example, are better. In addition, integration with system suppliers can be developed further than with component suppliers, not least regarding common product development.

8.3 Number of Suppliers

The number of first-tier suppliers is part of a company's sourcing strategy and impacts the purchasing strategy. The trend in most industries is towards decreasing the total supplier base but still there are situations where a large supplier base is preferable.

Why having a large supplier base?

Traditionally, purchasing departments of companies have seen as their primary task supplying the company with materials and components at the lowest possible prices. Quality aspects, delivery times and other factors have been given lower priority. As a natural consequence of the crucial influence of prices, most companies have a large number of suppliers and multiple sourcing has been the most common sourcing strategy. Even relatively small companies generally have several hundred more or less active suppliers. The fact that pricing has contributed and continues to contribute to the existence of many suppliers is related to the fact that pricing in a market economy is to a large extent determined by current competition relations. For purchasers to ensure that they gain the best possible price from suppliers, they must have relations with several different suppliers whose performances can be compared and who can be used against each other in negotiations.

The need to have a strong negotiating position in relation to suppliers in order to achieve low purchasing prices has possibly been the most important and common driving force behind the existence of many suppliers. However, there are other driving forces. Many companies lack a formally organised and consistently executed sourcing strategy. For reasons of tradition, it is easy that more than one supplier per item is always chosen. If new supplier alternatives arise, for reasons of routine the old ones are not removed at the same rate. Old established supplier relationships also have a conserving effect on the existing structure of suppliers.

Another decisive driver behind the existence of many suppliers is the company's need, through multiple sourcing, to ensure the long-term future supply of materials and components and decreased risks of disruption in the operative supply of materials. If several parallel suppliers of each item are chosen as a means of risk management, the total number of suppliers will naturally become larger.

The number of items that a company actively works with may be considered as the most basic reason for the number of suppliers required to ensure the supply of materials and components, since every item not produced within the company will, in principle, require a supplier. The lack of standardisation and low commonality leads to an extensive range of items and therefore constitutes one main reason for the company needing to maintain a large number of supplier relationships. Commonality means the extent to which items are used in several products at the same time. Low commonality means that every individual item in the input goods of a company's products is only included in one or few products. Lack of appropriate engineering and product development policies is one main reason behind low commonality and the subsequent tendency for raw materials and components to be chosen more or less every time a new product or product variant is produced. Commonality is described in more detail in chapter 7.

Drivers for supplier base reduction

In recent years the importance of developing more partner-like relationships with suppliers and more integrated activities with other companies as a means of making supply chains more efficient has been given increasing attention. Developing and maintaining such relationships with a large number of suppliers is, as will be discussed later in this chapter, neither practically feasible nor defensible in terms of cost-effectiveness. For this reason there has been a development towards reducing the number of suppliers, or in other words, to reduce the supplier base.

> ### CASE STUDY 8.1: SUPPLY BASE REDUCTION AT OUTOKUMPU (Lewis, 1995)
>
> Outokumpu is a Finnish stainless steel company making different types of metal products. Manufacturing is partly based on waste metal. The impurity of the waste metal could impact the product quality and consequently drives costs. In order to decrease the costs related to the impurity of the metal waste, it was considered necessary to improve the quality control of the bought material and the co-operation with the suppliers. Outokumpu reduced the number of metal waste suppliers from 186 to 50. This resulted in a decrease of the quality deficient metal waste from 10 to 0.2 per cent. The total purchasing costs were estimated to be reduced in the same extent.

This development has meant that the number of suppliers per company has fallen sharply over a number of years due to the creation of better conditions for achieving efficient flows in supply chains. This has been especially clear in, for example, the automotive industry, but extensive reductions in the supplier base have been carried out in other industries too. The results achieved in this respect are very tangible and are illustrated with examples from a number of well-known companies in Table 8.2.

Supplier base reduction methods

There are three principal methods of reducing the number of first-tier suppliers. One effective approach is to use more system suppliers responsible for fewer but more extensive parts of a product and who in turn administrate subsystem suppliers and component suppliers in a supplier hierarchy.

Another possible way is to carry out rationalisations in the range of products and standardise the range of items so that fewer items are needed, and thus fewer suppliers. The development of new production methods and the use of new materials may also contribute to a decrease in the number of items required to manufacture a product. An increase in the degree of commonality in the range of items will also lead to a reduction in the number of items.

Adaptation of the sourcing strategy is a third alternative. This may mean changing from single sourcing to single group sourcing and from multiple sourcing to single sourcing. In both cases there will be a reduction in the use of parallel suppliers per item. It is, for example, common that a company contains a large number of not frequently used suppliers, especially for low volume and value commodity items. Several of these could easily be eliminated.

Ford	35% in 3 years
Motorola	40% in 3 years
ABB	25% in 2 years
Xerox	94% in 4 years
3M	64% in 3 years

TABLE 8.2 Examples of reduction in the number of suppliers during the 1990s.
Source: Goldfeld, 1999, p.24.

8.4 Supplier Distance

An important issue regarding the choice of sourcing strategy and the forming of a supplier structure is the extent to which the company should strive to be supplied from local or global suppliers. The concept of global supply means that the company strives to establish supplier relationships over the entire world, in principle irrespective of the geographical distance involved, while local supply means that the company strives to maintain and establish supplier relationships only with suppliers at a short distance from the company.

Dimensions of supplier distance

The distance between the company and its suppliers is very relevant to achieving efficient supply chains. From the logistics perspective, its significance has three different dimensions:

- Spatial distance
- Time distance
- Cultural distance

The *spatial dimension* refers to geographical distance. Short distances to suppliers lead to lower transportation costs and enable more frequent deliveries of smaller quantities. They also make possible shorter delivery times. Short delivery distances are therefore almost a prerequisite for the application of a just-in-time philosophy and *kanban* suborders to suppliers as described in Chapter 12. Delivery flexibility between parties can also be improved. The distance between the customer company and the supplier company also plays a significant role in the conditions for establishing co-operation of the partnership type. This is related not least to the fact that short distances make frequent meetings possible, and the running of quality co-operation and other types of development projects together.

The *time dimension* refers to the difference in time between the purchasing and supplying companies. If there is a great distance between the parties they will be located in different time zones and will therefore have different working hours. The organisation of working hours during the day also varies considerably from one country to another. There are differences, too, in lunch breaks and other breaks. As a result of such conditions, the time window during one working day when a customer can be in contact with a supplier or vice versa may be during a limited number of hours, even if the companies are in time zones with only one or two hours' difference. This limits the possibilities of communication and flexibility in the relationship.

Also connected with the time dimension is the fact that different countries have different free days and the holidays are of different length and at different times. During these periods it may be impossible to contact a supplier and in many cases to have goods delivered. To avoid shortages, delivery times must be adapted and buffer stocks used with a subsequent decrease in efficiency of the supply chain.

The *cultural dimension* refers to the significance that differences in language may bring about when doing business with companies in other countries. Even though English is the international language of business, it is still not especially useful in a number of countries at lower levels in companies. Confusion as a result of different languages makes the exchange of information more difficult and increases the risks of misunderstandings and consequent disruptions in the flow of materials. The cultural dimension also includes differences in behaviour and attitudes when doing business, which exist between almost all countries. These differences are especially tricky when more partnership like relations are established.

Local and global sourcing

Local sourcing means, as explained above, that suppliers who have their business at a short distance from the customer company are given priority. The driving forces here are primarily the efficient exchange of information and personal contacts, and the achievement of high delivery flexibility and frequent deliveries. Another factor may be that the proximity to a customer facilitates the supply of service as a complement to the physical product.

The increasing proportion of customer-oriented products and production has in recent years influenced development towards the selection of local suppliers. Through customer-order orientation, warehouses are not able to separate to the same extent the supplier's and the company's activities, and instead the relationship of dependency in the flow of materials increases. These increasingly interdependent relationships are for natural reasons more difficult to manage over long distances. **Synchro-deliveries** to companies with repetitive manufacturing, such as car manufacturers, are one example of this phenomenon.

Syncro-deliveries means that individual items specific to one customer order must be delivered in exactly the same sequence as the assembly sequence at the receiving company. The flow of materials in the supplier company and the customer company must be completely synchronised. This means that the greater the distance between the supplier and customer companies, and thus the time-lag as a result of inevitable transportation time, the further in advance must the assembly sequence be established. As a result of this, the German car manufacturer BMW refuses to accept synchro-suppliers that are located more than 100 km from the assembly plant.

CASE STUDY 8.2: SUPPLIER PARK AND SEQUENCE DELIVERIES IN THE EUROPEAN CAR INDUSTRY

The Supplier park concept is common in the European automotive industry, especially in Germany where, for example, BMW runs a park in Wackersdorf, Ford in Saarlouis, DaimlerChrysler in Rastatt, Audi in Necarsulm and Ingolstadt, also in, for example, Belgium where Volvo, Mitsubishi and Volkswagen have supplier parks and in the European car manufacturer's assembly plants in South America.

The Volvo Gothenburg supplier park contains about 20 suppliers and is located 15 minutes transport distance from the assembly plant. The suppliers make different customer-specific systems for delivery and assembly in the cars. Each system is made up of a number of standard components. The suppliers carry out made-to-order manufacturing, initiated by so-called *synchro-orders* received from Volvo. The systems are delivered from the suppliers in the same sequence as they are to be assembled in the cars in the assembly plant.

During working hours Volvo continuously sends synchro-orders to the suppliers. Each order concerns a specific car and contains specifications about what system variants will be used in the final assembling of the car. The synchro-orders consequently contain information about what variants to make and in what sequence to put them in racks so that the Volvo personnel can pick them in the same order as they will be assembled in the cars. The time from receiving a synchro-order at the supplier's site to delivery varies between one and several hours depending on the system type. Loading, transport and off-loading at the assembly plant takes about 45 minutes. Deliveries from the suppliers to the assembly plant take place continuously during the day. With small buffers of systems at the assembly plant they can be assembled in the cars one to two hours after being manufactured at the supplier plants.

The establishment of supplier parks in the vicinity of final assembly plants is especially common in the car industry. Through the close proximity of suppliers, assembly plants and synchronised activities in supplier parks, short and frequent synchro-deliveries are guaranteed just-in-time to the assembly plants.

In spite of the importance of local sourcing and short distances to suppliers, there are a number of good reasons for **global sourcing**. Current development is towards increased global sourcing. One very common strategy behind global sourcing is that suppliers are selected on the basis of achieving the lowest possible purchase price. This approach means that suppliers to manufacturing companies in Europe are often selected from low-cost countries in Eastern Europe or in Asia. The strategy is particularly useful for purchasing low-value standard items. As such, this approach represents a typically traditional line of action for purchasing items.

Global sourcing may also be chosen for other reasons, however. The chances of finding local suppliers that represent world-class companies with respect to quality and competence are often small, and companies – especially in certain high-technology areas – are forced to seek suppliers from a more global market. The same need may arise during the changeover from component suppliers to system suppliers. The stability, size and resources for joint product development required from a system supplier are not especially easy to find among local suppliers. It is also common that purchasing companies with business activities in many countries wish to have the same supplier for all their plants.

8.5 Delivery Patterns

In most cases, if no deviations occur from plans and expectations, materials flow from supplier companies to customer companies downstream in the supply chain. For every supplier–customer pair, the flow starts by a supplier performing value-adding activities to make products and/or pick finished products from its stocks for delivery to the customer. Which of these alternatives is relevant from the supplier side depends on whether the customer company is a make to order or make to stock company, or a distribution company. The process ends where the customer is able to assimilate the delivered product, i.e. for storage in stocks, forwarding to customers or use in its own production, depending on whether it is a manufacturing or distribution company.

The flows of material from the supplier to the point where a customer will use or consume the material delivered may vary. Such variations are related to what extent the supplier or logistics service provider is responsible for activities required to ensure the flow of materials, and also to what extent the material flow corresponds to the customer company's direct needs. In this respect we can talk about different delivery patterns, which are a part of the supply structure, and selecting a pattern is also part of the company's sourcing strategy. Different types of delivery patterns used in industry are illustrated in Figure 8.6. Consideration is not given to which company is responsible for the physical transport from supplier to customer, i.e. whether it is the supplier, the customer or a logistics service provider. The following six patterns are described:

1 Batch delivery to stock
2 **Direct delivery** to production
3 Delivery through logistics centre
4 **Vendor-managed inventory**
5 **In-plant store**
6 Direct delivery to customer's customer

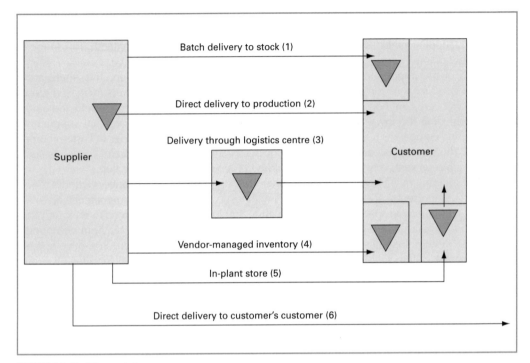

FIGURE 8.6 Six different delivery patterns
The triangles indicate the localisation of the warehouse for each delivery pattern.

Batch delivery to stock (delivery pattern 1) means that the supplier delivers some form of economic order quantity on order from the customer, which corresponds to the customer's estimated future need. A quantity is delivered to the customer's stocks for later retrieval and use.

Direct delivery to production (delivery pattern 2) is a more integrated delivery pattern. The supplier only delivers the quantity which the customer needs, irrespective of whether it is input items for production or for forwarding to a customer at the next level. This is described as a pull-driven delivery pattern. There are two variants within the framework of this alternative. One is when the delivered quantity is sent to goods reception and stores in the normal way and from there is transported on to the customer's production or dispatch. The normal quantity and quality controls are made at goods reception. The second variant is when the quantity is sent directly to the production department where the items will be used, i.e. to the consumption point, or directly to dispatch, called cross-docking. In this case the supplier takes responsibility for the delivery as far as the customer's consumption point. For this to be possible it may be necessary that the supplier is responsible for any quality control activities required.

If the supplier is responsible for the delivery of several items which are used to some extent in the same assembly or manufacturing process, the delivery undertaking may be extended so that the supplier does not only deliver individual items according to needs, but instead delivers more or less complete kits of items required to start production at the customer's, or to deliver an order with several order lines to a customer at the next level. Such options are available especially for wholesaler suppliers that are able to supply a reasonably wide range of items. This variant involves a further expansion of the supplier's function and responsibilities.

To ensure that complete kits of input materials can be delivered directly to production at a company, a logistics centre may be used. This third delivery pattern is called *delivery through logistics centre*. The centre may be administrated by a logistics service provider company, which then performs a consolidating function, meaning that it is responsible for stock-keeping, picking and delivery of everything, or almost everything, required for the manufacture of the company's products. The contents of the delivered kits correspond exactly to the needs stated in each manufacturing order. Manufacturing input items with low value is an example of material that may be cost-effective to exclude from the kits and can instead be delivered to stocks in quantities that correspond to a couple of weeks' continuous consumption.

One further type of delivery pattern is where the supplier does not only undertake to deliver material, but is also responsible for the size of stocks of the delivered material at the customer (delivery pattern 4). The difference from delivery pattern 1 is that the customer's inventory control

CASE STUDY 8.3: SOURCING STRATEGIES AT MACK, RENAULT AND VOLVO TRUCKS

Mack Trucks, Renault Trucks and Volvo Trucks belong to the Volvo Group. They have as an objective to develop common logistics and supply-chain strategies for all three manufacturers. The inbound material flow to the assembly plants is divided into three categories:

1 *Batch supply from local suppliers or consolidation points.* Items are delivered directly from suppliers if they are located within three days of normal transport time, according to FCA (Incoterm, 2000). Items are delivered through a consolidation point, often a Volvo Logistics terminal, if the suppliers are located within a transport time longer than three days. Ideally, the batches are delivered direct to point of use or, alternatively, to a raw material store. Invoicing is carried out at the same time as delivery. Steel beams and larger standardised components are example of items in this category.

2 *Modules and sequenced supplies from a nearby facility.* The target for this type of material flow is to receive the module components at the right time from the suppliers in line-sequence and in one single flow at the point of use. The supplier owns the items and is responsible for transportation, packaging, etc. to the point of use in the assembly plant. Payment should be triggered when the item is used, not when it is received. Sequencing can be achieved from the suppliers located within immediate range, defined as a maximum number of hours of transport time. If the supplier location is further away, the items can be distributed to and sequenced at a logistics service provider's terminal. The selection process of items suitable for this type of material flow is based on volume, available space, complexity, number of variants, handling and transport costs, supplier pre-requisites (e.g. quality and EDI), etc.

3 *Small parts supplies operated by one or very few suppliers.* This category is used for low-volume value items, such as fasterns, bolts, nuts, etc., used as input material in several products. The aim is that the supplier has the full responsibility for purchase, transport, storing the goods, and supplying in one single flow up to the agreed transfer point (preferably the final use point). There should be a very small number of active suppliers and only one point of contact and communication between the plant and the respective supplier. The materials planning could be conducted, for example, through *kanban*, re-order point or vendor-managed inventories.

activities are taken over by the supplier. This is usually called *vendor-managed inventories* and is described in more detail in Chapter 16. The stock is owned either by the customer or by the supplier.

In delivery pattern 4, the customer picks items from the stores which are controlled by the supplier. Other aspects of the physical stores are administrated by the customer. Delivery pattern 5 further adds to the supplier's responsibilities, which now include all materials handling and administration in the store including stocking, picking, dispatch and stocktaking. In other words, the supplier has his own personnel on site at the customer company. This type of supplier relation is called *in-plant store*. For this alternative to be applied in the case of a wide range of items without too many suppliers being directly involved, a logistics service provider may be used. A variant of delivery pattern 5 is when a logistics service provider company also takes over the purchasing function.

The sixth of these basic delivery patterns which is included here and illustrated in Figure 8.6 involves the delivery of items directly from the supplier to the customer company's customer, i.e. without going through the customer company at all. This delivery pattern is normally called *direct delivery to customer's customer*. One condition for using this alternative is that the quantity delivered by the supplier must correspond exactly to that ordered by the customer company's customer. There are variants of this delivery pattern which use logistics centres and logistics service providers, which then play a co-ordinating role and consolidate direct deliveries from several suppliers to one and the same customer.

8.6 Supplier Relations

A sourcing structure is not only characterised by the number of suppliers, the structure of the network hierarchy in which the suppliers are organised, the distances between the company and its suppliers, or delivery patterns. It is also characterised by the relationship of co-operation between the company and its suppliers, especially with respect to the choice of an appropriate level of relations for different types of suppliers.

Arm's-length relations between parties

One can say that the traditional attitude between customers and suppliers has the character of a relationship between legal parties. Customer companies talk about keeping suppliers at arm's length. Customers look for suppliers and negotiate conditions that are as favourable as possible. The time perspective is often short and is related to one deal at a time. The focus for the purchasing party is the lowest price possible rather than the lowest total cost and high delivery capability. To achieve this, companies use several parallel suppliers for the same items. Contacts between customer and supplier are infrequent and often limited to the companies' salesmen and purchasers. This traditional customer–supplier relationship can be characterised, if somewhat simplified, in the following way:

- Customer and supplier have a competitive relationship to each other.
- It is a win/lose game for both parties.
- Each party tries to reduce the opposing party's position of power.

Competition is over the profit margin in the supply chain, i.e. the surplus which arises on sale to the end-customer market when all costs are covered for the players involved in the process of creating value. The basic reasoning is "if the supplier charges more and has a higher profit margin, we will have higher costs and a lower profit margin".

In the face of such attitudes, the parties' behaviour is centred on trying to avoid a relationship of dependency and to reduce the power of the opposing party. For the customer it is desirable to have many suppliers, and that costs for discarding a supplier relationship should be low. This means, too, that integration upstream in the supply chain represents a threat, since it creates connections which may weaken the scope for negotiating. From a customer's perspective it is also desirable to avoid long agreements.

The supplying company tries to avoid having one dominant customer on which it may become dependent due to its large use of capacity. It will also try to achieve agreements with its customers to make their costs for defection as large as possible. Integration downstream in the supply chain is avoided.

The long-term risks in using this strategy for a customer company include the fragmentation and depletion of the supplier market. It may then develop into a number of small companies without the capacity to develop their products and technological competence. Supplier companies will be under continuous price pressure with the accompanying risk of decreased profit margins and consequently limited conditions for improving their competitiveness.

Such attitudes do not generally create good conditions for an efficient relationship between parties that is built on co-operation. Efficiency built on co-operation always involves bonds and interdependency to some extent, which are difficult to combine with the self-interest of individual companies involved.

Partnership relations

Influenced by just-in-time and the Toyota Production System philosophy, a different attitude between customers and suppliers has developed. For the purchasing party, the focus according to this philosophy is to develop close and intimate relations with a limited number of companies and through business agreements to achieve reasonable prices that are acceptable to both parties. Contacts between customer and supplier are more frequent than in traditional party relationships and involve more people than just the companies' purchasers and salesmen. This frame of mind, based on partnership, can be characterised in the following way:

- Customer and supplier have a partner relationship.
- It is a win/win game for both parties.
- The parties try together to increase the total competitiveness of the supply chain and in this way achieve improved profit margins for both.

This attitude means that the parties' behaviour will be characterised by attempting to achieve close co-operation and create a relationship of dependency, rather than avoiding it. For the customer, for example, it is desirable to have a small number of suppliers so that close co-operation can be established and maintained. Long agreements are desirable for both parties. With this type of arrangement it is also in the interest of suppliers to contribute to their customers' competitiveness.

The risk taken by the individual customer or supplier by being involved in this type of customer–supplier relationship is above all a strong dependency on the abilities of the partner. If the "wrong" partner is selected, the company risks its own existence since it will be difficult and time-consuming to break off and replace the co-operation invested in. The degree of risk varies with the type of co-operation. It is considerably larger if co-operation includes marketing and product development, for example, or if manufacturing technologies and choice of materials are adapted to each other instead of merely co-operating with respect to operative flows of materials.

The partnership perspective on the customer–supplier relationship corresponds far more closely to the demands required for developing more efficient logistics systems. It also supports, in a completely different way, a holistic perspective and the process orientation which characterises efficient logistics systems. From this viewpoint, it is the total competitiveness of the supply chain which is most significant for parties to be successful. It means, among other things, that performance measures which are positive for one individual company in the chain but which have strong negative consequences for other players in the chain will sooner or later have repercussions on the entire supply chain, since it is the aggregate costs for all value adding activities that the consuming end customer must pay for.

Balance of power and relationship of strength

Irrespective of whether the customer–supplier relationship is of the traditional type or of the partnership type, it is affected by the internal relationship of strength between the parties involved. We can talk about a balance of power which regulates the relationship between parties. With respect to the arm's-length type of customer–supplier relationship, it may manifest itself in the pricing and delivery conditions being influenced by or even decided by the stronger party. With respect to the partnership-type relationship, it is more often the case that the content and time period of agreements tend to be more in the interests of the stronger party.

In the balance of power between customers and suppliers, the supplier has a position of strength if the supply market is dominated by a few companies and the customer has few options to choose between. Likewise, the supplier's position is strengthened if the product he delivers is unique and for which there are few suitable substitutes. The relative strength of a supplier is also greater if the industry to which a customer belongs is of limited interest for the industry to which the supplier belongs, and if the suppliers' product is an important part of the customer's product in terms of either function or quality.

The power position of the customer company will be greater if it represents a considerable part of the supply company's turnover. The same is true if the products purchased are price-sensitive or the customer company belongs to an industry with low profit margins. The strength of the customer company increases if the supplier's products are standardised and of the commodity type, and if there are many alternative suppliers available. In the same way, customer strength will increase if costs associated with those changes required to place orders and receive deliveries from a different supplier are low. This is not the case in partnership relations.

Dependency and bonds

Partnership has been described as a prerequisite for creating efficient logistics systems and establishing successful activities in supply chains. However, partnerships involve interdependency between parties involved. Such relationships of dependency are necessary for successful partner relationships to be established. Successful partner relationships build on the fact that they are long term, which also creates interdependency.

Interdependent relationships and long-term relationships are therefore positive from this viewpoint. But from other viewpoints they may be negative. They may involve deadlocks and make rectifying actions difficult in terms of future events – for example if one party in the relationship no longer complies with reasonable demands and expectations required for successful co-operation. In the following three situations, strong interdependency may cause difficulties:

- When one party wishes to break off the relationship while the other wishes to extend it.

- When both parties wish to break off the relationship but it is not possible or is costly and time consuming due to strong interdependency.
- When both parties wish to break off the relationship but external factors make this impossible.

A partner relationship or similar may not always be positive in all situations. This is due to the risks and costs which are associated with the interdependency and bonds which partnerships can give rise to.

It is possible to distinguish between independent and dependent customer–supplier relationships. This means that in every relationship there are elements of common and conflicting interests, whether or not the relationship is a partnership type or not. That the supplier has a small proportion of the customer's total business, or the proportion of the total purchasing costs, that the risk exposure for the customer if the supplier fails is low, or if the costs of changing supplier are reasonable, are all indications of relationship dependence from the customer's perspective. The existence of many available supplier alternatives and small strategic significance is an indication of relationship independence.

From the supplier's perspective, relationship dependence is low if the customer accounts for a small proportion of the supplier's turnover, if the significance of the business is small even if the relationship should break off, or if the customer has little strategic importance. Few competitors, high differentiation in product and service range relative to competitors and being a price leader are indicators of low relationship dependence.

One important characteristic of the relationships which exist between customer and supplier companies is the concept of bonds. Bonds between companies can be of different types and have different functions. They also have different characters and different purposes. Bonds represent strong cohesive forces in the relationship, but they bring with them limitations to the freedom of movement of the companies involved, to a greater or lesser degree. It is possible to

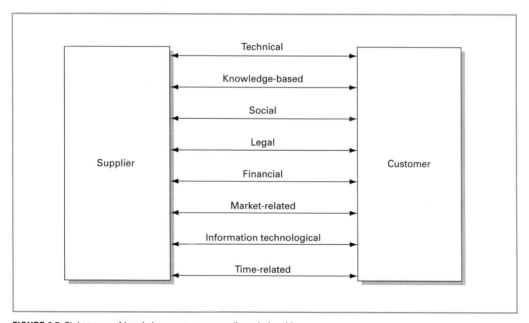

FIGURE 8.7 Eight types of bonds in a customer–supplier relationship

identify eight different types of bonds: technical, knowledge-based, social, legal, financial, market-related, IT and time-related (see Figure 8.7).

Technical bonds refer to bonds of a technical nature such as customer and supplier adapting their production equipment or their production methods to each other. The choice of materials, too, may be due to an agreement within the framework of co-operation between the companies.

Knowledge-based bonds arise through a customer and supplier building up knowledge of each other's activities and problems. This knowledge bank may be seen as an investment which represents a value, since it enables better adaptation to each other and may lead to opportunities in providing mutual support in problem solving if difficulties should arise.

The majority of all contacts between customer and supplier companies take place through individuals, which over a period of time result in the development of personal relationships. People learn who to contact to get a problem solved or to change procedures. Building up these contacts may be seen as an investment which facilitates co-operation, but it also involves a type of social bond. Moreover, a personal network means the growth of trust between parties involved.

Contracts and other agreements obviously represent legal bonds between customers and suppliers. Such legal forms of agreement also have the purpose of ensuring long-term commitment and can therefore be seen as de facto bonds between companies.

CASE STUDY 8.4: VIRTUAL AND EXTENDED ENTERPRISES IN THE GERMAN AUTOMOTIVE INDUSTRY (Binder and Clegg, 2006)

Inter-organisational collaboration is sometimes called *enterprise management*. A **virtual enterprise** is a temporary and flexible collaboration between companies with specific competences. The transaction costs are normally quite high because processes are not aligned. The switching costs are however low and the risks spread of several companies. An **extended enterprise** consists of partners with more mature competences and collaboration experiences. Any unsuccessful partners are excluded from the supply chain and the remaining companies try to align strategies and processes and create stable, connected and long-term collaboration.

BMW used a virtual enterprise structure for highly innovative technologies in the early stages of a joint product development process to increase collaboration with small and medium sized companies perceived as being innovative. This happened in the case of BMW's i-drive navigation system, where one small company identified the technology, another company developed the initial concept, and another partner conducted the industrialisation of the production-ready product. All the partners were co-ordinated by BMW.

VW is re-designing the structure of its product-development process using so called "Project Houses". These are totally autonomous but wholly owned subsidiaries of VW that compete directly with external suppliers for future development. For example, car models such as Golf and Passat each have a VW "Project House" and an external supplier competing for the business to develop new derivative models. This gives VW the option on a fair and planned basis to re-intermediate their position in the supply chain for any particular venture. The final decision on who wins the business is primarily based on maximising strategic supply chain advantage, and second on minimising transaction costs.

Examples of financial bonds are owner influence or help with financing. They may also involve bringing about common investments in market offers.

Market-related bonds also exist between companies. Such bonds may relate to the image and status of being the supplier of a well-known brand or company, which may contribute to good-will for the supplier.

IT bonds may be formed when a customer and supplier must invest in common equipment for the exchange of information or a communication standard. One example is EDI-based communication, which requires special adaptations of existing standards. Another example is that of software, such as customer and supplier both choosing the same CAD system to be able to exchange engineering drawings electronically.

Time-related bonds represent mainly operative aspects, such as co-ordinating activities in time in the supply chain and delivering in accordance with detailed predetermined points in time. This type of bond is relatively easy to break in comparison with other bond types, and does not tie customer and supplier to each other for longer periods of time. In general it is not especially costly to break off this type of bond in comparison with the other types.

Development of supplier relationships

Looking at the current extent of outsourcing in industry, a company's suppliers are very significant for its success. It is usually said that a company cannot become world class unless it has world-class suppliers. The choice of suppliers and the policy on the company's behaviour towards its suppliers, consequently, play a crucial role in the company's efficiency and competitiveness.

Even though the choice of supplier is felt by many to be important for a company, the approach and attitude towards suppliers is often considerably different from that towards customers. Put bluntly, a prevalent attitude is that it is easier to find new suppliers than new customers, and companies should consequently take more care of their customers than of their suppliers. Such behaviour could in some situations have detrimental effects on a company's performance.

Levels of relationships

The relationships between customers and their suppliers are spread along a scale from one extremity characterised by the exercise of power and directives to another extremity characterised by total partnership and mutual solidarity. For practical reasons it is appropriate to define some specific levels of these relationships.

In order to segment different categories of suppliers, there are three levels of relationship between a customer and its suppliers as identified in Figure 8.8. Suppliers at the lowest level are called conventional suppliers. This relationship is characterised by deliveries to single orders, prices being decisive for the supplier chosen, the company having its own quality control and the company guarding against disruptions in deliveries by keeping its own safety stocks.

Conventional suppliers can be divided into two main types with respect to continuity of the relationship. Type one is a relationship completely or largely of a one-off character, or of such low frequency that evaluation and selection of suppliers takes place on each procurement occasion. In the second type, relations are more frequent but procurement takes place without any particular evaluation and selection of supplier. Instead, suppliers are chosen as first alternatives until further notice, without the existence of any formalised co-operation or agreements.

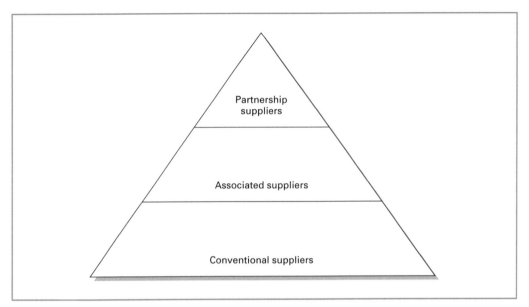

FIGURE 8.8 Three levels of customer–supplier relationship

Suppliers at the next relationship level are called **associated suppliers**. Relationships with them are long term and reviewed periodically. The supplier guarantees the quality of products delivered, which means that the customer company does not need to carry out quality controls on deliveries. Frequent sub-deliveries and deliveries take place and flows between the companies are as far as possible synchronised. In the ideal case, deliveries are made directly to the company's factory floor or distribution warehouse. Both companies work continuously to reduce stocks and leadtimes, and to eliminate buffering as a safeguard against disruptions. The supplier's prices are only one of several variables on which suppliers are assessed for selection.

At the highest relationship level are partnership suppliers. Relationships with them are largely similar to those with associated suppliers, but also include joint product development and frequent exchange of information on production processes, products and quality issues. They often involve joint investments in new technology. Measures for improvements are carried out together. Partnership suppliers are deeply integrated in a company's logistics processes. Contracts and other types of agreement on co-operation are often not limited in time.

Supplier segmentation and selection of relationship level

The different levels of relationship represent different degrees of partnership. It is obviously not realistic to talk about selecting and immediately initiating a long-term partner relationship with a supplier. It is about a more or less continuous process of developing a relationship with a supplier towards an increasing degree of partnership.

To develop and maintain partner relationships is demanding both in time and in resources. For this reason it is not feasible to establish partner relationships with a large number of suppliers. Neither is it appropriate practically, nor defensible financially, to integrate value-adding activities and material flows with a large number of suppliers.

For the increased integration of business between a company and its suppliers to have an impact on competitiveness and profitability, a minimum critical amount of the total material flow to a company must be involved. One way of achieving this is to limit the number of suppliers, as mentioned earlier in the chapter. It will then be easier to achieve a critical mass. One further option for achieving a minimum critical amount of the integrated flow of materials is to focus strictly on the introduction and development of partner relationships with those suppliers who account for the larger part of material flows.

By concentrating on relationships with major suppliers it is possible to include the most significant proportion of material flows in terms of volume with relatively limited efforts. It should be added that high volume values are not necessarily synonymous with high transaction volumes for high transaction costs. To attempt to solve the problem of too many suppliers by controlling the selection of established partnerships through volume values does not guarantee that the entire potential for efficiency will be achieved with suppliers. For this reason, selection should not take place on the basis of volume values alone. Other sub-suppliers should be included that are important to the company for various reasons – for example, the development of technology – and for which there are clear advantages associated with more long-term and close co-operation.

Segmentation based on significance and availability

In order to segment suppliers and select and develop suitable relationship levels with suppliers, a so-called Kraljic matrix may be used as shown in Figure 8.9. Purchased items are evaluated on the basis of their significance for the company and their availability on the market. High or low availability means roughly that there are few or many suppliers available on the market, while an item's significance may refer to both its influence on product costs and how critical it is for product quality and performance.

In each of the squares in the matrix, items are characterised and given a designation for their properties. For example, the designation of **leverage items** is given to items that are of great significance to the company and for which availability on the market is good. This group of items

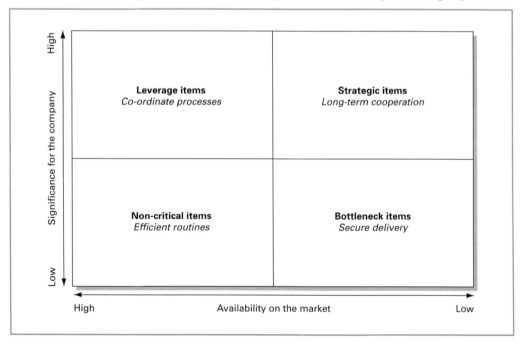

FIGURE 8.9 Kraljic's matrix for structuring procurement items and adapting supplier relationships
Source: Kraljic (1983).

normally includes a combination of standard and special items for which the annual purchasing costs are a significant proportion of the company's total purchasing costs. There is also a strategic significance stated in the squares of the matrix regarding supplier relationships. For example, a suitable strategy may be to create procedures which are as efficient as possible for items which have low significance to the company and for which there is high availability on the market.

The combination of large significance to the company and high availability of suppliers may be characterised as a buyer's market. With the relative strength which the purchasing company owns in such a procurement situation, there is no urgency to develop partnership relations. In many cases it may even be a disadvantage. A far-reaching partnership with its associated bonds runs the risk of reducing the purchasing company's opportunities of exploiting its market edge to gain good prices and delivery terms in general. Since there may be large flows of materials involved it may be more important in this case to have a strategy which focuses on co-ordination of flows of information and materials but which does not involve bonds, which are costly and time-consuming to break off. Both single and multiple sourcing may be appropriate for leverage items. Single sourcing allows for co-ordination and economy of scale, while multiple sourcing may reduce purchase price.

Items which are less significant for the company and for which availability on the market is good are called **non-critical items** and are not a primary target group for developing deeper partnerships. Consumables and cheap items such as screws and washers are examples of item types which belong to this group. In this case it is more important to establish simple forms of co-operation and agreements which make possible far-reaching simplification and optimisation of procurement procedures. Transaction costs for items in this category may be significant relative to purchase costs. It is not uncommon that as much as 80 per cent of the total administrative activities in purchasing are for this group of items. Elimination of a number of suppliers in this segment is important.

CASE STUDY 8.5: SUPPLY BASE RATIONALISATION AT CHEMICAL INC. (Dubois, 2003)

The company Chemical Inc. Corporation makes healthcare products, coatings and chemicals. The following project regarding MRO supply aiming at rationalising indirect purchasing costs was conducted at one of the company's subsidiaries.

The direct costs of MRO supplies amounted to about 4 MEuro and the indirect costs were estimated to be 3.2 MEuro. The indirect costs of MRO were consequently 80 per cent of direct costs, which was substantially more compared to other types purchasing items. For raw material, for example, the percentage was only 0.3 per cent.

The purchasing activities were divided into five activities with the following cost distribution (MEuro):

- Supplier handling 0.8
- Orders and call-offs 0.45
- Goods reception 0.4
- Payments 0.7
- Inventory 0.85
- Total 3.2

The following drivers for the indirect purchasing costs were identified:

- Large number of suppliers (10 000)

- Large number of deliveries per year (33 000)
- Large number of invoices per year (40 000)
- Large number of stocks (37)
- Large number of stock keeping units (10 000)
- Large number of cost centres (2300)
- Large number of small purchasing transactions (60 000 transaction with purchasing value under 10 Euro)

The managers of each cost centre put a great deal of effort into finding the cheapest source for each purchase. This buying behaviour was one of the reasons for the large number of suppliers. But it also impacted on the number of products, deliveries and invoices. It was also identified that the purchasing activities were not always conducted in the most efficient way. About 2 per cent of all invoices caused problems owing to insufficient or incorrect information, for example, regarding who actually ordered the product.

The number of suppliers was concluded to be the overall cost driver. It had a direct impact on supplier handling costs. But the number of suppliers also had indirect impact on all the other indirect costs. As long as the number of suppliers remained the same, it would be difficult to deal with the other cost drivers such as the number of purchasing items, stock keeping units, transactions, deliveries and invoices. In addition, educating the suppliers in order to improve the administrative processes to reduce the number of incomplete or incorrect documents would not be possible if the total number remained the same. Consequently, almost nothing could be done to reduce costs unless the number of suppliers was dramatically reduced.

In order to reduce the supplier base and deal with the indirect costs, five commodity groups responsible for different assortments were established and long-term relationships were established with a few numbers of suppliers. Each group identified one supplier as its key supplier. The purchase was concentrated as far as possible to these key suppliers but other suppliers were also used. An immediate effect of concentrating the purchases to five key suppliers was price reductions of 7–15 per cent as a direct consequence of economy of scale based cost reductions utilised by the suppliers. Another effect was that Chemical Inc. became one of the most important customers to the suppliers. Therefore, Chemical Inc. was given priority by the suppliers that further stimulated their general willingness to cooperate on adjustments of various kinds to potentially reduce costs further.

When key suppliers were chosen, commodity teams, consisting of representatives of the buyer and the supplier were put together. The working principles for the commodity teams focused on the common goal of reducing "the total cost of the exchange". Three general areas of rationalisation were identified from the commodity team work:

1 Some of the activities previously carried out by the buyer (e.g. stock-keeping) could be conducted more efficiently by the supplier.

2 Performance could be improved by increasing buyer–supplier co-ordination (e.g. administration of orders, invoices and payment).

3 Certain adjustments among the firms could reduce internal costs at both parties (e.g. bar-code communication, assortment adjustment, Extranet).

Those segments in the matrix where development towards a higher level of partnership may be most relevant are the two cases with low availability of suppliers. The aim, however, is somewhat different in the two cases. **Bottleneck items** with little significance to the company and low availability on the market could be certain electronic components, paint pigment, flavouring and so on, for which there is only one supplier. The primary aim of developing a partnership for this type of item is to ensure individual deliveries and avoid any delivery shortages. In this situation, the supplier governs the market, especially if there is only one possible supplier. The partner relationship is a way of ensuring delivery of these items. Another way is to search for and identify alternative methods of sourcing, such as through product development, which could possibly enable the replacement of the bottleneck item for another item with a lower delivery risk. If an item for which there are few alternative suppliers has great significance for a company – for example, as a result of large purchase volumes or because the item has been developed in co-operation with a supplier – the aim instead is to ensure future supplies and develop the partnership relationship since it is a **strategic item** on a seller's market.

Segmentation based on frequency and specificity

An alternative matrix model for supplier segmentation and selection of relationship type is shown in Figure 8.10. This matrix uses the procurement dimensions of frequency and customer-order-specific items. Within these two dimensions it is possible to distinguish between one-off procurement and repetitive procurement, and between standard items and order-specific items.

For every square in the matrix, generally appropriate procurement strategies are stated. The two cases of repetitive procurement are of greatest interest for establishing a partnership since they have an inbuilt time period, which means that supplier relations can be developed. The aims behind partnerships may be different, however. In the case of repetitive procurement of

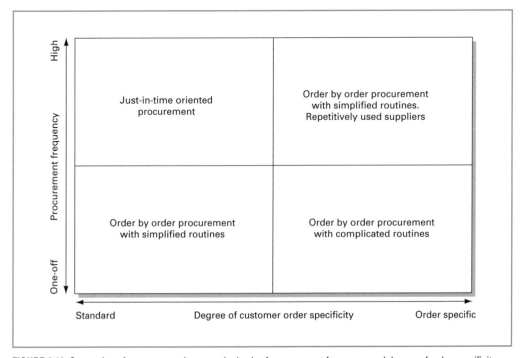

FIGURE 8.10 Structuring of procurement items on the basis of procurement frequency and degree of order specificity

standard items, the aim of a deeper relationship may be primarily to establish efficient procurement processes. For order-specific procurement it is more a question of deeper co-operation in the whole area of product development, including the development of common support for product specifications, transfer of engineering drawings and production instructions between customer and supplier, etc.

For one-off procurement of standard items, partnership-type relations are of lesser interest. In this case, simple agreements with suppliers may be sufficient, especially if they relate to items with limited significance for the company. For these, such as low-value items, it may be sufficient to have the internal guidelines for the selection of suppliers and to carry out procurement without performing an evaluation and selection between alternative suppliers on every occasion. For one-off procurement of order-specific items there are generally neither conditions nor reasons for entering into long-term partner relationships.

CASE STUDY 8.6: SOURCING STRATEGIES – ITT FLYGT

ITT Flygt is a global pump manufacturer. The products are submersible pumps and mixers. The company has its own foundry and engine factories but also purchases casting goods, engines and the other input items for assembling pumps. Different pump types are made in four different manufacturing divisions.

The central procurement department is responsible for supplier evaluations, supplier contracts, etc. Every manufacturing division has daily contact with suppliers and call-off of bought items is decentralised to the divisions. Relevant sourcing strategies can be identified by using the Kraljic matrix.

- Example of *strategic items*: casting goods and specialised cables. These are complex items with important impact on the product functionality and quality. For these items, close relationships are developed with a few suppliers.

- Some electronic items, which are complex but have low volume value, are considered *bottleneck items*. Focus is on securing supply.

- For simple high volume value items, for example, steel, there exist multiple suppliers in order to negotiate the lowest possible price or a single supplier in order to get quantity discount. These are examples of *leverage items*.

- Fasteners are examples of *non-critical items*. Focus is on simple administration. Vendor-managed inventories are used for controlling the supply of some fasteners.

8.7 Conclusion and Summary

This chapter has taken up common sourcing strategies and their significance to a company. Different aspects of the form and selection of supplier structure have been discussed. Sourcing strategies may take the form of sole sourcing, single sourcing, dual sourcing, multiple sourcing, single group sourcing and hybrid sourcing. Two main strategies for constructing a company's network or hierarchy of suppliers have also been treated: system and component supplier strategies. Strategies related to the number of suppliers, supplier distance and supplier patterns were included in the discussion.

A supply structure is dependent on the relationship between customers and suppliers. Different forms of customer–supplier relationships and their significance in the creation of efficient supply strategies were treated at the end of the chapter. Two supplier segmentation models were described which are aimed at structuring procurement items and the selection and development of suitable supplier relationships.

🛈 Key concepts

Approved suppliers 169	Parallel sourcing 168
Arm's-length relation 178	Parallel suppliers 164
Associated supplier 184	Partnership relations 164
Bottleneck items 188	Single sourcing 164
Direct delivery 175	Single group sourcing 167
Dual sourcing 167	Sole sourcing 167
Extended enterprise 182	Sourcing strategy 169
Global sourcing 175	Strategic items 188
Hybrid sourcing 168	Supplier segmentation 184
In-plant store 175	Synchro-deliveries 174
Leverage items 185	Triadic sourcing 168
Local sourcing 174	Vendor-managed inventory 175
Multiple sourcing 164	Virtual enterprise 182
Non-critical items 186	

Discussion Tasks

1 Figure 8.6 shows six possible delivery patterns. Try to identify one real case for each alternative.

2 Several positive and negative effects could be related to low-cost sourcing in geographically distant countries. Identify the most important issues for a company to consider before deciding about increasing its sourcing in low-cost countries.

3 A bakery produces bread, buns and cakes, amongst other items. Analyse the company's supplier strategy using Kraljic's matrix. What are suitable relationship levels for the different purchase items?

4 A company manufactures electric motors. Analyse the company's supply strategy using Kraljic's matrix. What are suitable relationship levels for different purchase items?

5 Use the alternative matrix (Figure 8.10) when analysing the sourcing strategy of the companies in tasks 3 and 4. Compare the findings.

Further reading

Axelsson, B., Rozenmeijer, F. and Wynstra, F. (2005) *Developing sourcing capabilities: creating strategic change in purchasing and supply management.* John Wiley & Sons, Chichester.

Binder, M. and Clegg, B. (2006) "A conceptual framework for enterprise management", *International Journal of Production Economics*, Vol. 44, No. 18–19, pp. 3813–3829.

Dubois, A. (2003) "Strategic cost management across boundaries of firms", *Industrial Marketing Management*, Vol. 32, pp. 365–374.

Gadde, L.-E. and Håkansson, H. (2001) *Supply network strategies.* John Wiley & Sons, Chichester.

Goldfeld, C. (1999) *Supplier strategies.* PT Publications, Miami.

Håkansson, H. and Ford, D. (2002) "How should companies interact in business networks?", *Journal of Business Research*, Vol. 55, pp. 133–139.

Kraljic, P. (1983) "Purchasing must become supply management", *Harvard Business Review*, Sept–Oct, pp. 109–117.

Lamming, R., Cousins, P. and Notman, D. (1996) "Beyond vendor assessment: relationship assessment programmes", *European Journal of Purchasing and Supply Management*, Vol. 2, No. 4, pp. 173–181.

Leenders, M., Johnson, F., Flynn, A. and Fearon, H. (2006) *Purchasing and supply management.* McGraw-Hill, New York.

Lewis, J. (1995) *The connected corporation: how leading companies with through customer – supplier alliances.* The Free Press, New York.

Van Weele, A. (2005) *Purchasing & supply chain management: Analysis, Strategy, Planning and Practice.* Thomson Learning, London.

Zeng, A. (2003) "Global sourcing: process and design for efficient management", *Supply Chain Management: an international journal*, Vol. 8, No. 4, pp. 367–379.

CHAPTER

09

Production processes and layouts

Organising and managing production resources is crucial to what can be achieved with the aid of logistics measures and logistics systems. Put simply, production structures set the limits for what is possible. Certainly, the options when selecting suitable production structures are rather strictly controlled by what the products are and what manufacturing technologies are financially realistic to use. Within the framework of these limitations there are alternatives which may be more or less appropriate from a logistics viewpoint. Material flow structures and how material flows should be most efficiently controlled through production is of great importance to logistics conditions. To clarify the prerequisites for production from the logistics perspective and their significance for achieving effective flows, this chapter takes up alternative methods of organising production and sizing resources used in production. The focus is on production processes and layouts.

The chapter is closely related to several other chapters in the book. There are direct links to Chapter 7 (especially Section 7.3 Standard products, customer specific products and customer order specific products) and Chapter 13 (especially Section 13.2 Capacity planning and Section 13.3 production activity control).

9.1 The Concept of Production

Production generally means a process for creating goods and services by combining materials, work and fixed capital. Using such a general definition, the concept includes such wide-ranging events as the manufacture of trucks, the distribution of beer, lectures in logistics, medical examinations and bank transactions. Thus, production takes place in all types of companies and organisations. Since this chapter is about value added in manufacturing companies, production here is viewed from a narrower perspective and only includes processes which create goods. This delimitation does not mean that there is a clear distinction between production of goods and production of services. Since consumption is the overall goal of all production, goods produced must be distributed in some way for consumption. Production of goods is in most cases not of interest unless it is combined with production of services. This relates above all to logistics services, which are always a necessary part of being able to distribute goods to customers.

The production of goods can be said to consist of a series of operations or stages of production, in which the original material is transformed from a given state to a desired one. This transformation can be achieved through the following five main methods, in many cases in combination with each other:

1 **Transformation through division**, mainly with an item as input and several different items as output from the production system. Examples of this type of transformation are sawing timber into different formats from logs, or the production of petrol and diesel from crude oil.

2 **Transformation through combination**, with several items as input and one item as output. The manufacture of machines and production of chemical products are examples in this category.

3 **Transformation through separation**, where the form of the input item is changed through the removal of material, such as in the manufacture of axles by turning on a lathe.

4 **Transformation through shaping**, where the shape of the input item is changed through re-forming the material mass. Examples of this type of transformation process are rolling of steel profiles from billets, and molding of plastic items.

5 **Transformation through adapation of properties**, meaning that the properties of the input item are changed without changing its form. Heat treatment and surface treatment are examples in this category.

9.2 Material Flow Structures in Production

In every manufacturing company, different material flow structures can be identified in the value adding which takes place from raw materials and purchased components to finished products. It is possible to distinguish between different basic types of material flows, called V, A, T , X and I types. All of these have a close connection with the different types of transformation used in production as described above. The type of flow in question is also influenced by how a product is designed and by its product structure. For example, the introduction of a modularised product structure will mean a transition from A type to X type material flow. In one and the same company, several types of flow may take place simultaneously and in many cases in combination with each other. The different types of material flow are illustrated in Figure 9.1, in which original materials and semi-finished products are symbolised by circles and finished products by squares.

V type material flow is characterised by diverging flows of material, and is found in companies where production takes place in the form of transformation through division. The dominating characteristic of this flow structure is the occurrence of divergence points at which one starting material is transformed into various finished products. The number of finished products may be large or extremely large relative to the number of raw materials and semi-finished products. Abattoirs and sawmills are examples of typical companies with diverging flows of material.

In contrast to V type all of the types A, T and X involve converging material flows. All of them represent transformation through combination. The differences between them are related to the number of final products in relation to the number of starting materials. A type material flow has a number of convergence points at which several input materials are combined into single-

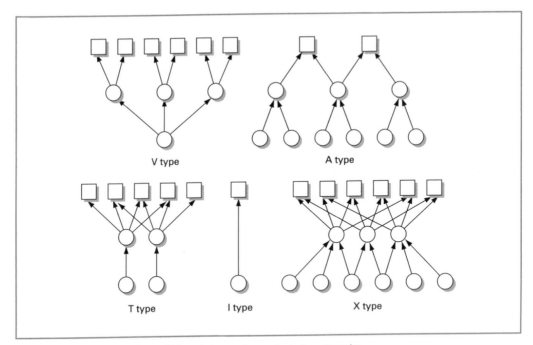

FIGURE 9.1 Different types of material flow that occur in manufacturing companies

Squares represent finished products and circles represent input raw materials and components either purchased or manufactured at the company.

output, semi-finished products, and finally into finished products. This type of flow is charac-terised by a small number of finished products in relation to the number of starting materials. Complex products manufactured in small volumes and a small number of variants such as air-craft engines and tool machines are examples of products whose manufacturing gives rise to A type material flows.

T type material flow has fewer convergence points than A type, and they are concentrated at the finished product level to a larger extent than is the case for A type. In other respects, the T type is characterised by an extremely large number of finished products in comparison with the number of starting materials. Product variants are created through the combination of different starting materials and semi-finished products. Most of the starting materials and semi-finished products are included in many products, i.e. they have a wider range of use as products than is the case for A and X types of material. Paint is one example of a product with T type material flow. A small number of basic colours are mixed in the retail store to a large number of customer-specific colours.

X type material flow also has several convergence points. The number of convergence points is greatest immediately under the finished product level. One characteristic for this type is that a large number of starting materials are combined into a limited number of semi-finished products, often in some form of standardised modules. These semi-finished products/modules can then be combined into an extremely large number of different finished products. A typical product which has X type material flows is a car, in which a large number of customer-specific finished prod-ucts are configured from a limited number of relatively complex modules.

I type material flow corresponds to transformation through separation, shaping and adaption of properties. This type is characterised above all by the fact that it has no real divergence or convergence points. In principle, one or a few starting materials result in a finished product. In terms of material control, I type is considerably easier to manage than the other types. The production of glasses by glass-blowing is an example of a process with this type of material flow.

9.3 Production Layout

The resources used in a company to achieve the transformation of raw materials and purchased components into finished products can be organised in a number of different ways. How this is done will result in a structure of production groups and work centres through and between which goods flow during the process of manufacturing. Four different basic types of production layout can normally be distinguished. The functional layout is **process-oriented**, i.e. organised by type of production process. Line and cellular layouts are **product-oriented** and focus on flow efficiency. The fixed position site layout is also product-oriented but has low flow efficiency. In every company there are generally combinations of these basic types. There are also a large number of variants of each basic type.

Functional production layout

A **functional production layout** is characterised by the various production resources being organised by function, i.e. all machines and other workstations are grouped and located in the factory according to their production functions. The materials to be used in the manufacturing are moved from group to group, and in principle there is one manufacturing step per group. In a mechanical workshop, for example, lathes (La), milling machines (Mi), grinders (Gr) and drills (Dr) are located in separate groups. The principle is illustrated in Figure 9.2. The line of arrows shows the path of raw materials through a production process consisting of the production steps of turning, drilling and milling.

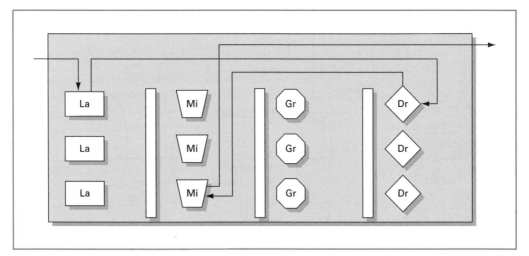

FIGURE 9.2 Illustration of a functional production layout. The figure illustrates the flow of materials through different work centres in the manufacturing process

The functionally based production layout is appropriate above all when the range of items manufactured is wide and every item is manufactured in relatively small numbers. The advantages of the production layout from a logistics viewpoint are primarily that it can be easily adapted to changes in product mix and variations in production volumes. In other words, it is very flexible.

CASE STUDY 9.1: FUNCTIONAL LAYOUT – GORDON & LUND

Gordon & Lund is a mechanical engineering company making metal components of various kinds to different OEM manufacturers. The input material is iron bars, iron sheet and wrought metals. The production contains processes such as cutting, lathing, drilling, milling, grinding, etc. Finishing is outsourced to a subcontractor.

The factory has a functional layout (see figure). Five operations are carried out when making a specific metal component. The five operations as described in the figure below are:

1 Goods reception

2 Laser cutting – the metal sheet is cut

3 Bending – the metal piece is bent

4 Welding – two metal pieces are welded on the bent metal sheet

5 Drilling – holes are drilled in the welded component

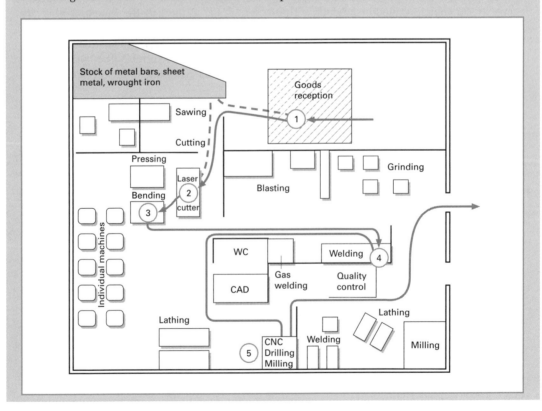

It is also generally less sensitive to disruptions than other types of production layout since there are alternative production resources available within every functional group if one unit should cease operations. The disadvantages of functional production layouts include the fact that internal transportation and materials handling is often extensive and flows of materials are complex and difficult to analyse. This means in turn that functional production layouts are unfavourable from the viewpoint of tied up capital and they make it difficult to avoid long leadtimes.

Line-shaped production layout

When items are manufactured continuously and/or in large quantities, the **line-shaped production layout** is often a better alternative. A line-shaped production layout is characterised by production resources being organised by product/item and located in the same sequence as the production steps which are carried out during manufacture. Instead of organising production resources by function, they are organised around the manufacturing sequence of the product itself. This alternative is sometimes referred to as **production layout** for this reason. Common examples of this type of production layout are assembly lines and complete process plants for chemical-technical production. The principle is illustrated in Figure 9.3.

There are many different types of line-shaped production layouts. A distinction is made between regulated and floating lines. In the former, the material flow is controlled mechanically, and all workstations along the line must have the same rate of production. In the latter there is no forced control, and buffers are allowed to exist between production stations to avoid short-term differences in rates of production that could disrupt previous and subsequent steps of production.

The line-shaped production layout corresponds well to a flow-oriented production system with straight and distinct flows of materials and opportunities for rational transportation solutions. Leadtimes can also be short, with queue times theoretically only at the beginning of the line. The line layout is thus favourable from the viewpoint of tied-up capital, even though buffer stocks must sometimes exist between production stations to avoid too many coupling and balancing problems. The largest disadvantage of the line layout is its sensitivity to disruptions. If one

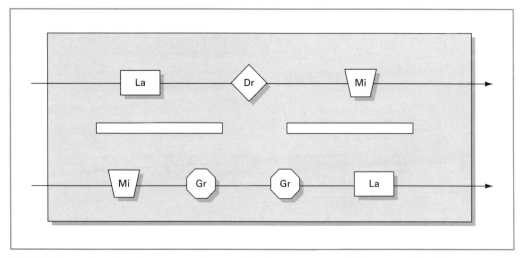

FIGURE 9.3 Ilustration of line-shaped production layout. The figure shows material flows through the different processing machines along a manufacturing line

workstation is down, the entire line comes to a standstill. A line-shaped production layout is also less flexible, especially with changes in product mix and design changes, since every change may force rebalancing the line so that the rate of production is the same for all workstations along the line.

CASE STUDY 9.2: LINE-SHAPED LAYOUT AT TOYOTA MOTOR COMPANY

Between 1990 and 2005 the assembly lines at the Toyota Motomachi and Tahara plants were changed in order to increase the total system capacity and to better handle variation in production. The assembly line layout now has the following characteristics:

1 The entire flow line is cut up and contains large buffer capacities of up to 15 cars between eight line segments (mini lines). The lofty ceiling makes the large buffers and clean floor possible. Each mini-line is entrusted to a group of operators which is responsible for completing a certain assembly function.

2 The individual operator can use at a minimum the double regular cycle time without disturbing any colleague and there are 30 minutes autonomy between the lines. Consequently, system variations can be absorbed by the average buffers of three to four cars.

3 The assembly density is low. On average there is one assembler per car, compared to about two workers per car in the European automotive industry.

4 Most parts to be assembled for each vehicle are delivered in baskets of material kits. The basket rides down the line with the car that gets the parts. Workers no longer have to rummage through numerous bins along the assembly line to find the right part.

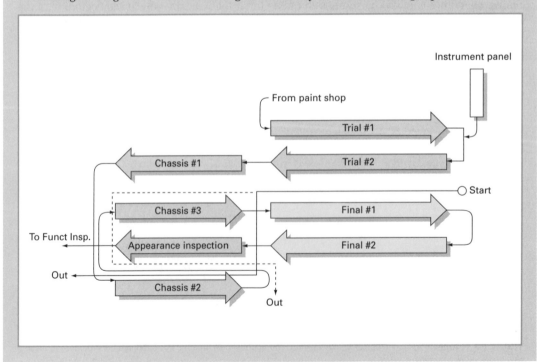

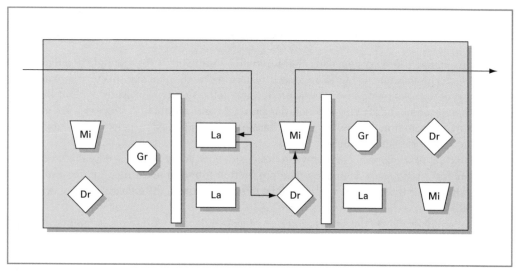

FIGURE 9.4 Ilustration of cellular production layout. The figure shows the flow of materials through different processing machines in a flow group

Cellular production layout

Organising production resources into groups called production cells is one way of achieving the advantages of the line-shaped production layout from the material flow viewpoint, even for the production of small quantities and without demands on continuity. The layout is built around grouping items by similarity of manufacture. For the manufacture of such a group of items, a group of machines and workstations is organised which, in the ideal case, can produce finished items within the group. The principle of **cellular production layout** is illustrated in Figure 9.4. The arrow shows the manufacture of an item in three different types of production resources. A flow group is characterised by the production resources being grouped around a group of items, and not by function as in functional manufacture. There are no general requirements that work-stations must be located in a fixed order of production steps, as in the line layout.

The production cell has many of the advantages of a line layout. It is generally possible to achieve short leadtimes and low levels of capital tied up. It is often easier to oversee the material flow than in a line layout. This alternative has more flexibility when there are changes in product mix and is less sensitive to disruptions when compared with a line layout. Product mix flexibility and disruption sensitivity are, however, worse than is normally the case for functionally shaped production layouts. The potential for efficient transportation solutions is considerably better than for functional production layouts, but is often not in the same class as line production layouts. One other disadvantage of production cells is that it is difficult to achieve an acceptably high utilisation of capacity for all machines and workstations in the cell.

CASE STUDY 9.3: CELLULAR MANUFACTURING – AUTOLIV, INC.

Autoliv makes safety systems for the automotive industry – for example, seatbelts and airbags. The manufacturing is organised according to cellular manufacturing principles. Different products are made in different production cells. In a typical Autoliv plant there are about 50 production cells. Cells with similar products and production processes are grouped into about 10 production groups. If necessary a product could "buy" capacity from another cell within the same production group.

The product lifecycle may vary between three and eight years, which is why the production cells are re-built with same frequency. The production rate (the takt time), i.e. the number of produced items per time unit in a cell could be varied by using a different number of operators in the cell.

The table below shows the production rate of a specific cell with four operations. The cell can be operated by one to three workers. The production rate is 24 items per hour with one operator, 40 items per hour with two operators and 61 items per hour with three operators.

		Minutes									No of operators	Min per item
	0	**36**	**60**	**96**	**111**	**120**	**126**	**129**	**150**	**171**		
No. of items	0	14	24	38	44	48	50	52	60	68	1	2.5
	0	24	40	64	74	80	84	86	100	114	2	3.0
	0	37	61	98	113	122	128	131	153	174	3	3.0

Fixed-position layout

For certain types of manufacturing, it is so difficult to change location of the product that it is not appropriate to move it during manufacture. This is the case, for example, in the manufacture of large turbines, aircraft and ships. In such cases, different forms of so called **fixed-position layouts** are used. This means that the gradually evolving product is located at a specified place and production resources are moved to that place and organised around the product. For this type of product and production there are seldom any alternatives. Realistically, then, it is not meaningful to talk about advantages or disadvantages from the viewpoint of logistics in comparison with other layout alternatives.

9.4 Production Layout from the Logistics Viewpoint

The previous section presented some alternative production layouts. They can be characterised as supporting various degrees of production volume and variety (see Figure 9.5). The layouts can also be differentiated from some other logistics viewpoints. Above all, the number of planning points affects the scope and complexity of planning work. In this context, a planning step is a production step in a manufacturing order. In principle, every step of production or operation must be planned, ordered, followed up and reported. Every separate operation can be considered as a **planning point**. If, for example, an axle is to be manufactured from a round bar, this will involve a turning operation. The lathe work must be planned in time, the execution of the work must be ordered in the workshop, and the progress of the work must be followed up. When

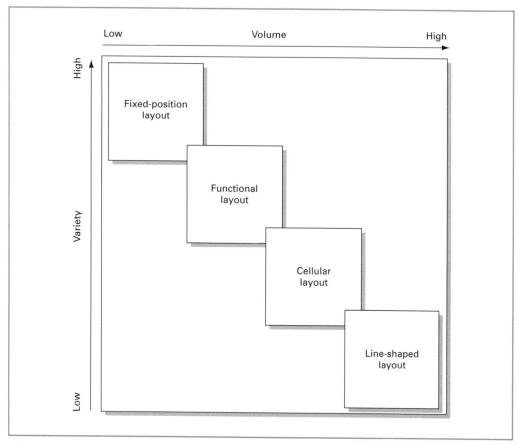

FIGURE 9.5 The volume-variety characteristics of production layouts

the work is completed it must be reported so that subsequent operations can be planned and prepared for.

The number of operations required to manufacture a finished product is determined primarily by the nature of the product and the possible technical solutions for its design and production. There is, however, a certain freedom of action involved and this should be exploited. Traditional technical production solutions often involve a detailed breakdown of the production at every stage, resulting in short production times. This striving to optimise the direct production time often leads to an increase in the number of operations. This not only causes more planning work; it is also significant for lead times, since each operation contributes to queue times in its production group. The number also affects delivery times and capital tied up. If, after the technical production solutions have been drawn up, the logistics effects are also taken into consideration, there may be financial advantages in reducing the number of operations instead. For example, the introduction of digitally controlled multifunction machines (CNC machines) in the workshop industry has led to the number of operations for cutting processes being radically reduced. The increase in the number of working operations per individual at manual workstations is another example of a reduction in the number of operations.

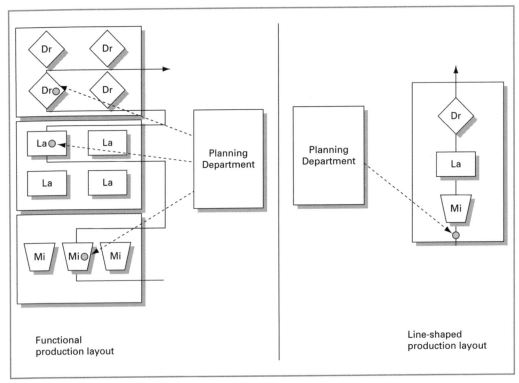

FIGURE 9.6 The number of planning points in different production layouts
The circles represent planning points required to initiate manufacture in both alternatives.

The various types of production layouts presented have different characteristics of complexity from the planning viewpoint. Both line-shaped production layouts and production cells lead to considerably fewer planning points than functional production layouts. In both cases, the manufacturing sequence for an entire line or group may be considered as one single joint operation from the point of view of planning. The number of planning points is thereby reduced to one, as illustrated in Figure 9.6. For line-shaped production layouts and production cells, the operation sequence is more or less fixed and defined by the production layout and/or the system used for materials handling and internal transportation in the line or cell. No planning or follow-up is required in the production system. In those cases where the sequence is not completely fixed, planning may be independently carried out by personnel working in the group. Given the simplicity and clarity of these types of production layout, this seldom causes any problems.

Viewpoints regarding the fixed-position production layout mainly relate to the degree of specialisation in the execution of production. If there is a great degree of specialisation, the number of operations and thus the number of personnel involved in production will increase. If an increase in leadtime is to be avoided, this means that more personnel must be able to work on the object at the same time. Due to the space requirements for executing such work, planning the sequence of operations may be more difficult. In many cases, detailed priority planning must be introduced so that those people who are working with the object do not disturb each other too much.

CASE STUDY 9.4: MANUFACTURING LEAD TIME REDUCTION AT HAVELOCK (Gunn, 1992)

Havelock Europe is a UK based manufacturer of retail store equipment such as counters and shelves. The process of building a sloping front counter for drugstores was analysed with the objective of reducing cycle times. Out of 116 steps in this manufacturing process, only 22 (19%) added any value to the product. During the seven weeks the sloping front counter was a work-in-process, value-adding activities only took place during 4.15 hours or 1.5% of the total throughput time. Havelock redesigned the process to have only a one week leadtime and 68 steps, and travel 18% of the distance it did before.

9.5 Planning the Dimensions of Production Capacity

Determining the capacity required in a production system is to a large extent a question of estimating future demand. The real result of production from a given capacity depends, however, on other factors connected with the structure of the production system and how the planning of its capacity has been carried out. In this section three characteristics of capacity in a production system will be treated: **capacity structures**, **functional flexibility** and capacity balancing. Their effects from the logistics viewpoint will also be discussed.

Capacity structures in production

When production resources are to be chosen and given the right dimensions to achieve a certain desired production capacity, there are two main alternative capacity structures to choose between. A single structure may be chosen, i.e. a production resource that has sufficient capacity alone to fulfil current demands. A second alternative is to choose a parallel structure, which means that several smaller production resources are selected which together have sufficient capacity to satisfy demand. For example, one machine with a very large capacity or several small machines with smaller individual capacities may be chosen. Traditionally, the choice has often been single-structure alternatives, since they have enabled a greater degree of automation and lower unit costs in production. If logistics aspects and flexibility are also taken into account, the choice is not so simple. The degree of sensitivity to disruption is also influenced by the alternative selected.

If the capacity of a machine in a single structure is 100 pcs/hour, two machines in a parallel structure each having a capacity of 50 pcs/hour will have the same aggregate capacity. The single-structure alternative, however, will run a considerably greater risk of disruptions in the flow of materials. Even though there is a production drop if one of two machines is down, the likelihood of at least being able to maintain some production is considerably greater.

The parallel principle also has advantages of flexibility. If for some reason demand increases, capacity investments can be made in incrementally smaller steps if a parallel structure is chosen. The exposure to risk is less if at a later stage the increase in demand was not as high as expected. Capacity reductions are also easier to handle with parallel structures since they can take place in small steps each time.

CASE STUDY 9.5: PARALLEL ASSEMBLY FLOWS AT THE VOLVO UDDEVALLA PLANT (CASE Written by Lars Medbo, Chalmers University of Technology)

Ever since Henry Ford introduced the line, cars have been assembled based on the assembly line principle. In the end of the 1980s Volvo Cars developed a new assembly plant in Uddevalla based on parallel product flows and group-based assembly. This was the first full-scale assembly plant based on parallel product flow. The factory was designed for making 40 000 products a year, which was a relatively low capacity compared to other car assembly plants in the world.

Volvo wanted to create an efficient and more worker-satisfactory production system compared to the traditional assembly line approach. The number of cars to assemble in parallel increased further downstream in the plant (see figure). To assemble cars in parallel decreased the dependencies between the operations and, consequently, the negative effects of disturbances in single operations were reduced. Upstream in the flow, where the level of parallel assembly was low, the automation could be high (e.g. using robots for assembling screens). Downstream in the flow, where the level of parallel assembly was high, the level of manual work was higher. Here groups of seven to nine operators assembled final cars.

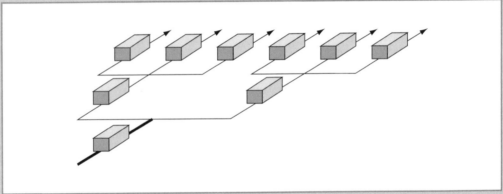

In this type of production system the throughput time is longer for a product variant containing a great deal of manual work content compared to a product variant with little manual work content. In the assembly line system all product variants get the same throughput time. Consequently, high volume and product mix flexibility was achieved in the plant. In the parallel production system, each assembled car passed through fewer workstations. This reduced the total waiting and idle times.

Another consequence was that the work content for an individual operator had more variety compared to that in an assembly line situation, and the group worked as an independent production cell within the factory.

Functional flexibility for production plants

Functional flexibility here means to what extent different workstations are multifunctional, i.e. can perform more than one manufacturing function. Using multifunctional workstations is more or less the opposite of specialisation. Better economy of production through more specialisation has often been a guiding star in the design of production systems. The more material flow aspects

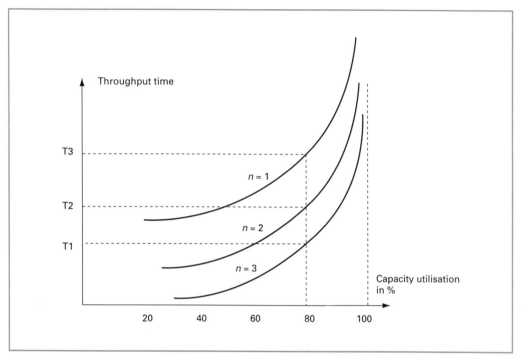

FIGURE 9.7 The dependency of leadtime on capacity utilisation for different numbers of alternative workstations

of various types are taken into consideration, the greater is the motivation for workstations with broad functionality and competence. The advent of different types of computer-controlled machines and production equipment has made it possible to have workstations with broader areas of use. Through different types of skills training, operators become more versatile and can master several types of tasks. This has often taken place in parallel with changes in the salary system so that labour versatility is rewarded. Salary scales have been introduced in which every additional task that a person can carry out leads to an increment in pay.

Introducing multifunctional workstations is very efficient from a capacity planning viewpoint. It provides an increase in flexibility which is able to absorb unpredictable capacity variations and contribute significantly to reduced leadtimes, improved delivery precision and reduced capital tied up in flows of materials. It is not difficult to realise that an increase in capacity flexibility is gained through decreased specialisation and increased versatility. If workstations are extremely specialised, some of them become easily overworked while others have little to do. If a worksta-tion with a low workload could also carry out the tasks of the overworked station, it would be possible to reduce queues to the overworked station and achieve a more even total use of capacity at the same time. It is possible to show in theory that the relationship between lead-times and utilisation of capacity in a production system with variations in possible workstations will look like Figure 9.7. In this figure, *n* is the number of workstations which can execute a certain manufacturing task. If there is only one workstation able to execute a manufacturing task and it is working at 80 per cent capacity, the leadtime on average will be T3. If instead there are two workstations each working at 80 per cent capacity which can perform the manufacturing task, the average leadtime will be reduced to T2, and if there are three parallel workstations able to do the job, it will be reduced to T1. The differences in leadtimes for a given utilisation of capacity are considerable. In addition to the reduction in leadtime, the increased versatility also provides a potential for increased production through the more even spread of workload between workstations. The risk of unexploited capacity during certain periods will be less.

Capacity balancing

It would be easy to imagine that with respect to utilisation of capacity, it is always optimal to balance capacity in production, i.e. that resources are sized so that all production groups and workstations are equally utilised. In the long term and as an approximation this is the case. In the short term, however, it is not always that obvious, especially as required quantities, manufacturing times and so on vary from time to time and disruptions in production and inbound deliveries cannot be completely avoided. It may sometimes even be motivated to deliberately create a certain imbalance between capacities in different parts of production. Two cases of deliberate imbalance between capacities are discussed here to illustrate the conditions.

In all production, real working time varies from one occasion to another. Only in cases of completely machine-controlled manufacturing rates can working time be expected to remain absolutely constant. Such time variations tend to lead to disruptions in subsequent steps in manufacture, and these disruptions grow at each step. In addition, various types of temporary capacity drops and other disruptions in production at workplaces propagate and expand along the flow of materials, resulting in workstations further downstream being subjected to more disruptions and thus more capacity drops than workstations at the beginning of the flow. These effects are often considerable in line-shaped production layouts, the main reason being that time lost in subsequent steps of manufacture due to waiting time caused by disruptions in the preceding step can never be regained. Unutilised capacity is lost forever.

To achieve material flows that are as uninterrupted as possible, a higher capacity should be planned for those workstations towards the end of the chain of production than those at the beginning of the chain. In this way it is possible to make up for delays in the later steps of man-

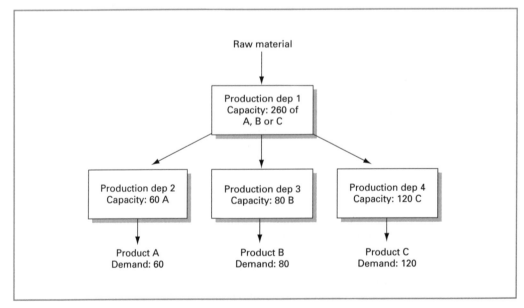

FIGURE 9.8 Illustration of capacity balancing for varying demand

ufacture that are caused by disruptions in earlier stages. The fact that the value of material towards the end of a production chain is greater than during the initial stages also motivates an accelerated flow in the later stages. It is sometimes described as a "pull" through the workshop.

Another reason for deliberately not balancing capacities in a production system is that the demand for a company's products normally varies. These variations can lead to the possible production not being equivalent to the existing capacity. To maximise the utilisation of capacity in a production system as a whole, it may be desirable to *under-dimension* certain production sections. A simplified example to illustrate this is given in Figure 9.8. Assume that a company has three different products, A, B and C, and four production departments for manufacturing them. All products are manufactured from the same raw materials, and the same production department is used for the first step of production. The second step of production is specific for each product. Product A is manufactured in department 2, product B in department 3 and product C in department 4.

Assume that the annual requirement for each product has been forecast at 60 pieces, 80 pieces and 120 pieces for A, B and C respectively, and that the capacity requirement in the common production department is the same for the three products. If the four production departments are sized exactly according to the forecast demand, their capacities will be 260 pieces, 60 pieces, 80 pieces and 120 pieces respectively. They are then, in theory, completely balanced.

Now assume that the total demand is correctly forecast but that the real demand for A, B and C is 70 pieces, 100 pieces and 90 pieces respectively. Since it is not possible to produce more than 60 pieces of A and 80 pieces of B, the total production cannot be more than 60 + 80 + 90 = 230 pieces. Thus, there is no point in having a capacity of 260 pieces in department 1. It will never be completely utilised. The conclusion to draw from this example is the following general rule for capacity balancing: always under-balance capacities in production departments that are common to several products relative to departments which are used for single products. To receive the best possible gain from capacity investments, avoid balancing different departments or workstations and instead deliberately over-balance and under-balance according to the above rule.

Instead of trying to balance capacities in the short term, companies should try to balance the flow through production. Balancing the flow instead of capacities is one part of the theory of constraints. According to this theory, imbalances in capacities should be accepted and the location of bottlenecks in the production system should be identified instead. A *bottleneck section* is a production group or workstation which is overloaded, i.e. has a capacity that is less than the current capacity requirement. This section will be the limiting factor for what is possible to produce in the whole production system. According to the theory of constraints, the company should strive as far as possible to utilise the bottleneck section and try to prevent any production disruptions and shortages of starting materials. The utilisation of other production groups and workstations should be subordinate to the bottleneck section and only utilised to the extent required to match volumes that can be produced in the bottleneck section. The subordination of the degree of utilisation of other production groups to that of the bottleneck section is the same as balancing flows through the production system.

9.6 Strategies for Capacity Adaptation

All companies experience fluctuations in demand, which cause imbalances between the capacity available for producing goods at the rate corresponding to current demand. To a certain extent these imbalances can be handled by increasing or decreasing the stock of products in the company that manufactures to stock, or by increasing or decreasing unfilled orders by changes

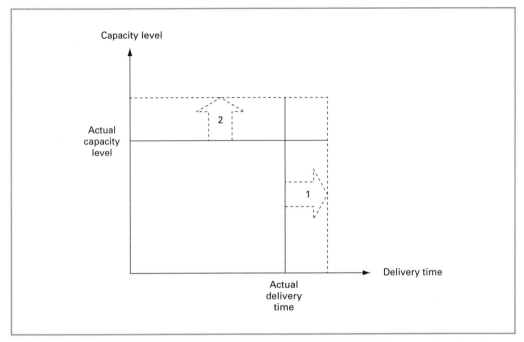

FIGURE 9.9 Stock levels, capacity and delivery time adaptation to increased demand. 1) Increased delivery time, 2) Increased capacity

in delivery time in the company that manufactures to customer order. If this is not possible, is not suitable or cannot be done on a sufficiently large scale, the capacity must be increased or the **capacity utilisation** must be decreased, depending on whether the demand is too large or too small in comparison with the production capacity available. Figure 9.9 describes the principles of increasing capacities or increasing delivery times when demand is increasing. The alternative to lengthen delivery time may not be sufficient in a business-to-business situation and the decreasing stock levels not possible when manufacturing to order.

There are two basic strategies for the adaptation of capacity to expected future needs: a *lead strategy* and a *lag strategy*. The alternatives are illustrated in Figure 9.10, in a case where demand is expected to rise in the future. The **capacity lead strategy** means that capacity is either increased or decreased before demand increases or decreases. It is a type of proactive strategy, in which the access to capacity is adapted before the need arises or disappears. In times of increased demand this strategy gives a volume flexibility that makes possible the capture of market shares and thus the ability to expand business activities. It also involves a larger risk exposure with respect to the utilisation of capacity invested in. If demand is on the decline the strategy may lead to a reinforcement of this decline, since it will be difficult to retain market shares due to shortage of capacity. The advantage is that the risk of being left with costs for underutilised capacity is less.

The **capacity lag strategy** is a reactive strategy which means that investments in new capacity cannot be carried out until a change in the size of demand is stated and real. This strategy results in low volume flexibility after rises in demand and puts higher demands on being able to work with large stocks, or the company allowing delivery times to increase to avoid losing sales and market shares. As such, the strategy may result in higher average stock levels and larger unfilled

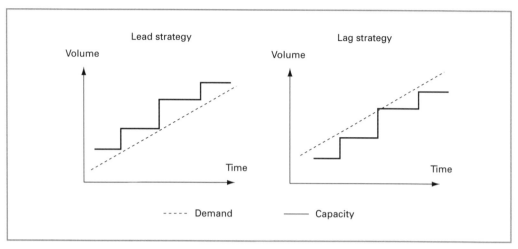

FIGURE 9.10 Illustration of different strategies for capacity adaptation

orders compared with the previous strategy. One advantage of the strategy is that the risk of landing in a situation with costly over-capacity is less, especially in those cases where there is some uncertainty regarding how large and enduring the rise in demand will be. In the case of declining demand, the opposite relationship applies.

These strategies represent two extremes. Both are characterised by the company having either a constant over-capacity or a constant under-capacity. In practice it is often a question of using a compromise, that is, to a greater or lesser extent switching between working with over-capacity and at other times with under-capacity.

9.7 Conclusion and Summary

In a manufacturing company, value is added from the flow of raw materials and purchased components to products through the company. Depending on the nature of the structures in the flow of materials under production, companies are categorised as having V type, A type, X type, T type and I type of flows. The methods of controlling flow vary between these different types.

Value adding is achieved with the help of different production resources. The methods of organising these resources plays a decisive role in what can be achieved with logistics measures and logistics systems. Four basic types of methods of organising production resources are normally listed: functional production layouts, line-shaped production layouts, group-organised production layouts and fixed-position production layouts. The sizing and adaptation of production resource capacity is very important to the efficiency of material flows and the optimal utilisation of resources, as is the choice between single structures and parallel structures and the extent to which workstations are functionally flexible.

Key concepts

Capacity lag strategy 208	Product-oriented layout 195
Capacity lead strategy 208	Production capacity 203
Capacity structures 203	Production layout 197
Capacity utilisation 208	Transformation through adaptation of properties 193
Cellular production layout 199	
Fixed-position layout 200	Transformation through combination 193
Functional flexibility 203	
Functional production layout 195	Transformation through division 193
Line-shaped layout 197	Transformation through separation 193
Planning point 200	Transformation through shaping 193
Process-oriented layout 195	

Discussion Tasks

1 For products with structures of the A type, it is possible to forecast final products and with the help of these forecasts to calculate the quantities of raw materials and purchased components that need to be sourced to manufacture and deliver the forecasted quantities. What would be the best methods of controlling deliveries of finished products and the sourcing of raw materials if the products were of the V type instead?

2 In this chapter there were three alternative production layouts mentioned in addition to the fixed-position layout. Which of these three alternatives do you think is most suitable for a company that manufactures a large number of steel items with short product lives and uneven demand; a company that manufactures a small number of different plastic items, each one in a large number of different colours; and a company that assembles printed circuit boards in large quantities whose structure is often changed by replacement of components? How would your choice be affected if there were large demands on low manufacturing costs and high utilisation of capacity, and if there were demands on short lead times?

3 It is common that a manufacturing company combines the different types of production layouts in the same factory. Give an example of an imaginary or real company that should benefit from combining production layouts. How could this be carried out?

4 According to the theory of constraints, the utilisation of machines and workstations that are not constricting sections in production should be subordinated to a constricting section. What is the reason for this and what would happen if this principle were not followed?

5 Capacity adaptation could concern the capacity needs of this week but it could also concern capacity needs several months from now. What strategies would be relevant for a manufacturing company wanting to change capacity within the existing weeks? What strategies would be relevant for a manufacturing company wanting to change capacity within the coming months?

Further reading

Anupini, R., Chopra, S., Deshmukh, S., van Mieghem, J. and Zemel, E. (1999) *Managing business process flow*. Prentice Hall, Upper Saddle River.

Gunn, T. (1992) *Century manufacturing – creating winning business performance*, Omneo, Essex pp. 60–61.

Hayes, R. and Wheelwright, S. (1994) *Restoring our competitive edge: competing through manufacturing*. John Wiley & Sons, New York.

Hopp, W. and Spearman, M. (2000). *Factory physics*. McGraw-Hill, New York.

Schmenner, R. (1994) *Plant and service tours in operations management*. Macmillan Publishing, New York.

Slack, N., Chambers, S. and Johnston, R. (2007) *Operations management*. Prentice Hall, Essex.

Vollmann, T., Berry, W., Whybark, C. and Jacobs, R. (2005), *Manufacturing planning and control for supply chain management*. McGraw-Hill, New York.

CHAPTER 10

Distribution structures

The supplier's distribution to many customers is divergent: i.e. products from a limited number of production and storage locations are distributed to a large number of customers. For several companies, the strategies for distributing products and their selection of distribution structures are crucial for their competitiveness and profitability. Products must be made available to the market in a cost-effective manner. The method of distribution also has great significance for the company's ability to keep short and reliable delivery times to customers; in other words, to maintain a high delivery service.

Developing and introducing appropriate distribution methods and distribution structures is both a strategic and a tactical issue. As is the case for strategies and structures on the supply side, described in Chapter 8, the company's strategies for distribution constitute the framework within which operative processes for marketing and delivering products to customers can take place. The potential for what is operatively possible to achieve is largely determined by the company's strategies and how the distribution system is structured.

This chapter treats the utility value which is contributed by distribution and the roles it plays in the logistic system. Different basic alternatives which can be applied to the planning of distribution structures are described, as well as aspects of choice and design of warehouse structures in the distribution system. Distribution aspects related to postponement strategies and speculation strategies, and the use of value-adding distributors and terminals' logistical roles in distribution structures, are also discussed.

The chapter is closely related to several other chapters in the book. There are direct links to Chapter 3 The flow of materials, Chapter 14 Transport planning, Chapter 16 (especially Section 16.3 Supply chain collaboration concepts and section 16.4 Supply chain design) and Chapter 17 (especially Section 17.2 information exchange and section 17.4 Electronic marketplaces and businesses)

10.1 Utilities, Gaps and Roles in Distribution

To be able to produce efficient distribution systems it is first necessary to understand what utility values distribution contributes to and what roles distribution companies play in supply chains. The starting point for consideration of these utility values and roles is the end consumer in the supply chain, whether it is a company that uses the products as input goods in production, a company that consumes products in its business activities, or an individual that consumes products.

The distribution utility values

As described earlier, activities in a supply chain are aimed at satisfying customers' needs by supplying various types of products. To achieve this, four different types of utility must be performed in the supply chain:

- Form utility, which represents the added value created through value refinement of input goods to finished products

- Place utility, which represents the added value created through making products available for acquisition at the right place

- Time utility, which represents the added value created through making products available for acquisition and at the right time

- Ownership utility, which represents the added value created when ownership rights or rights of use of a product delivered are transferred to a customer

Of these four utilities, a company's marketing and sales units traditionally account for ownership utility, its production unit for form utility, and its distribution unit for time utility and place utility. However, in recent years it has become increasingly common for distribution companies also to contribute to some degree in the process of creating form utility. This phenomenon will be discussed further in a later section in this chapter. In general, this book only discusses different ways of creating place and time utility.

The four utilities, as pointed out above, must always be provided for a supply chain to be able to fulfil its goal of satisfying customers. However, the division of the utility-performing activities among different resources can be made in a number of different ways. It is both a question of dividing them between different units in a company and between companies in the supply chain. Designing distribution structures is to a large extent concerned with this division, in order to obtain the most efficient distribution system possible. To illustrate this idea, we can look at how the furniture company IKEA works. The fact that customers drive to IKEA stores themselves to fetch their goods has transferred a number of activities for creating place utility to the customer. Similarly, a number of activities for creating form utility have been taken over by customers as they assemble furniture themselves. Time utility, on the other hand, is created by the warehouse function at IKEA stores, as is ownership utility by means of the cashier function at the stores.

The distribution gaps

The division of activities into different resources in the supply chain to create utility is one of the fundamental problems in the planning of distribution structures. Another is how to bridge the gaps which always exist between companies that produce products and customers that consume products by using **intermediaries** of different types. Examples of these are retailers, different agents, distributors and various other players. Bridging these gaps is a prerequisite for the supply chain being able to create the above four utilities for customers in a cost-effective way.

The gaps in question are as follows:

- The pace gap, that arises because customers do not acquire and consume at the same places, at the same times and at the same intervals as manufacturing companies produce
- The distance gap, that arises because producers are located in a few places whereas customers are more numerous and widespread on the market
- The quantity gap, that arises because companies for financial reasons produce and deliver in different quantities per time than individual customers purchase and consume
- The range gap, that arises because customers need a wider product range than individual manufacturers can supply in an economic fashion
- The variant gap, that arises because customers need access to more product variants than are financially justifiable for manufacturers to produce and transport to customers

The pace gap means that, for reasons of cost, the rate of flow outwards from production does not fully correspond to the pace in flow equivalent to customers' demand. To decouple these flows from each other, products are made to stock or customer order backlogs built up. A balance can then be achieved by increasing or decreasing the size of stocks, or by increasing or decreasing the delivery time and, through that, the size of customer order backlog. Seasonal stocks and campaign stocks are examples of this type of stockbuilding. Bridging the pace gap is essentially a task for production in a supply chain. Stocks and backlog are related to production. They are used to compensate for limitations in the flexibility of production to adapt to current demand. Distribution can only play a marginal role in bridging the pace gap.

The same relationship between stock size and delivery time is true for bridging that part of the quantity gap which is related to larger quantities being produced per time than the equivalent individual customer's needs. Manufacturing in economical order quantities that correspond to a number of customers' expected total needs per time is the normal way of bridging this gap. It is a purely production issue related to set-up costs in production, i.e. costs for the changeover from manufacturing one product for one customer to another product for another customer. But the bridging of that part of the quantity gap related to delivery quantities is an issue for distribution. Similarly, bridging the other three gaps largely affects distribution.

The intermediary roles

To the extent that a gap is controllable through distribution activities, different types of intermediaries are used to achieve cost-effective bridging. *Intermediaries* are players that carry out distribution functions between the producer and the consuming customers. It could be a distribution subsidiary, or another company. It is possible to identify five fundamental roles for intermediaries. Figure 10.1 illustrates the relationships between utilities, gaps and roles. Designing distribution structures is to a large extent a question of determining what roles these intermediaries will play and organising interaction between them. The five roles of intermediaries are:

- The aggregation role, which means that a distributor delivers quantities equivalent to each customer's individual needs
- The spreading role, which means that a distributor with stock-keeping function delivers with short delivery times

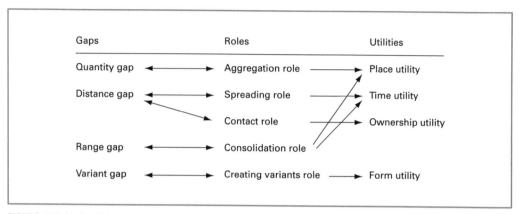

FIGURE 10.1 Model of the relationship between utilities, gaps and roles

- The contact role, which means that a distributor takes care of direct customer support
- The service-providing role, which means that a distributor carries out the final and customer-order-specific product configuration
- The consolidation role, which means that a distributor represents several companies and distribute their products

The *aggregation role* means that a local distributor close to the market delivers those quantities equivalent to each customer's individual needs (see Figure 10.2). The sum of the

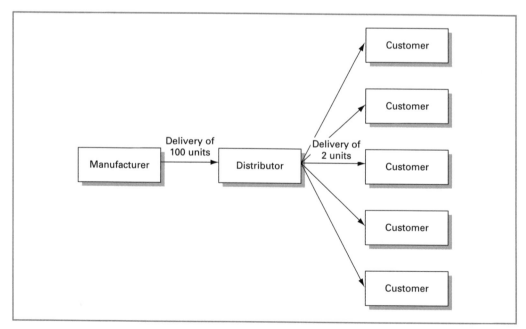

FIGURE 10.2 The aggregation role

Consignments in large quantities are delivered from the manufacturer to the distributor's warehouse, and small customer-specific quantities from the distributor's warehouses to customers.

individual customers' needs is delivered to the distributor directly from the production company or via a central distributor – a wholesaler – who serves several local distributors. Deliveries are made to the local distributor's warehouse in the case of standard products. The role of aggregation then includes responsibilities for inventory control, and deliveries to customers take place through withdrawals from stocks. Deliveries may also be customer-order controlled and destined for customers when they are transported from production to the distributor. They are then a combination of all the customer orders received during a period, for example, one week. Work by the distributor will be to break down the consignment from the manufacturing company and send individual orders on to each customer, i.e. to perform more or less advanced cross-docking activities. The quantity gap can be bridged with the help of intermediaries' aggregation role.

Another fundamental role played by intermediaries in a distribution system is the *spreading role* (see Figure 10.3). This is achieved by distributors with stock-keeping functions being placed close to the market so that they are able to deliver with sufficiently short delivery times, according to customer demands. The manufacturer or central warehouse will deliver to the local distributor's warehouse, and from there deliveries are made to customers. Thus, the spreading role also includes responsibilities for inventory control. The distance gap can be bridged with the help of intermediaries' spreading role.

The *contact role* is a third distribution role. It is achieved by having distributors close to the market who have units for technical support, application support and other types of customer support. Units for handling guarantee issues, service commitments and returns may also be included. The aim is to supply more efficient customer service through proximity to customers. The contact role is also a way of bridging the distance gap.

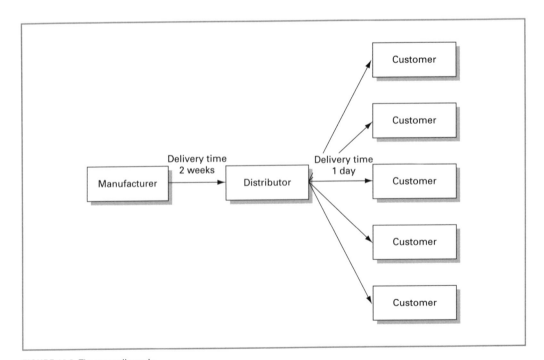

FIGURE 10.3 The spreading role

Infrequent deliveries from manufacturers to distributors' warehouses and frequent deliveries from distributors' warehouses to customers.

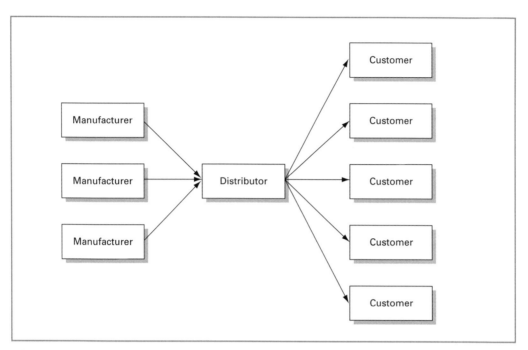

FIGURE 10.4 The consolidation role

Every customer has access to several manufacturers' ranges through one consolidating distributor.

Intermediates may also have the role of providing variants. This means that final and customer-order-specific product variants are created by an intermediary located close to the market. Basic products for customer adaptation or modules and standard components assembled to specific product variants are delivered to intermediaries from the manufacturing company. The aim is to avoid transportation of small quantities of product variants from manufacturers directly to customers. Another aim is to provide customer support to specify and configure product variants and achieve acceptably short delivery times through proximity to the market. The purpose of this role, creating variants, is primarily to bridge the variant gap, but it also contributes to bridging the quantity and distance gaps in make-to-order activities.

The *consolidation role* means that an intermediary may represent several different companies and distribute their products as illustrated in Figure 10.4. It may involve delivering the represented company's products from own stocks, or mediating transactions in which delivery takes place from the manufacturer directly to customers. The aim is to enable customers to buy many different products from the same supplier, or one-stop shopping. The consolidation role can bridge the range gap.

Through consolidation of this type, the number of contacts between manufacturers and consuming customers can be radically cut. For example, if five manufacturers each sell and deliver products to 100 different customers, the number of contact paths is 500. If an intermediary is used instead to deliver orders to customers, the number of contact paths will be 105, which means a reduction of almost 80 per cent. This is one of the most important reasons for using intermediaries in distribution.

10.2 Transactions in Distribution Channels

Distribution in this context means, somewhat simplified, tying together in supply chains the flow of materials and information between manufacturing companies and consuming customers. Obviously, the easiest way of achieving this is if the producing company takes orders directly from a customer and transports products in the desired quantities directly to the customer, i.e. use of a **distribution channel** which consists of two players and one single link. For different reasons this is seldom possible or financially justifiable. The gaps described in the previous section would be far too costly to bridge using this strategy. In most cases parties must use other more complicated distribution channels, including intermediaries of different types, to bridge the gaps. **Direct delivery** should be seen instead as one of several alternatives for distributing products to customers. There are several factors shown in Table 10.1 that indicate the pros of direct delivery and intermediaries respectively.

Transaction and material flow channels

Most distribution channels are comprised of networks of vertically co-operating companies. What is appropriate in the structure depends to a large extent on the products in question and the state of the market. It also depends on the nature of the business activities and their objectives. In other words, there are no best channel structures for all companies.

Since the purpose of a distribution channel is to bring together the flow of materials between manufacturers and consuming customers in supply chains with or without the use of intermediaries, it can be said that a distribution channel has two component parts: a **transaction channel** and a **material flow channel**. The transaction channel is related to the deal between the purchaser and the vendor, and covers the flow of information around the administrative parts of the order-to-delivery process, i.e. mainly receiving orders, confirming orders and invoicing. The material flow channel relates to the physical parts of the order-to-delivery process, i.e. delivery of products ordered. Since this part of the distribution channel affects the flow of materials, it is also associated with the extent to which intermediaries hold stocks.

The reason for considering the distribution channel as a transaction channel and a material flow channel is that both channels may have different paths through a distribution system. It is important to take this degree of freedom into consideration when designing an optimal distribution system. To make possible a separation of these two parts there must be an efficient exchange of information between the parties involved in the ordering and delivery processes; for example, the manufacturing company, the intermediary and the consuming customer. With all the new options of exchanging information provided by modern IT, the transfer of information between different players in supply chains is no longer a problem.

For direct deliveries	For intermediaries
Few consumers	Several small consumers
Make-to-order	Frequent customer orders
Tendering	Fast delivery requirements
Probable returns	Widespread customer base
Lack of industry wholesaler	Mature standard product

TABLE 10.1 Factors that indicate direct delivery or use of intermediaries

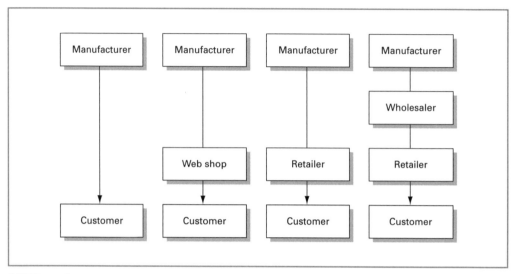

FIGURE 10.5 Four main types of commonly occurring distribution channels for consumer products of different types and with different intermediaries

This section deals with transaction channels. Descriptions are limited to a few main types of transaction channel, some for consumer products for which the purchasing customer is an individual, and some for industrial products where the purchasing customer is a company. The various main types of transaction channel can be used as a starting point for the design of a distribution channel.

Transaction channels for consumer products

Because of the wide distribution of small customers, the need for intermediaries is in general much larger for consumer products than for industrial products, and distribution channels are more complex. Demands on proximity and accessibility are also greater. If there are shortages of any products, there is a considerable risk that the customer will turn to another supplier. Four main types of commonly occurring transaction channels for consumer products are illustrated in Figure 10.5.

The most typical channel for this type of product consists of a manufacturing company, a wholesaler and retailer. Most fast-moving consumer goods are distributed in this manner. In those cases where retailers are involved, there are three possible cases. The retailer may be an independent company, it may be owned by the manufacturer or by the wholesaler. In the latter two cases we can describe it as a vertical integration in the supply chain. Wholesalers and retailers are often responsible for storing products. There are also cases where these intermediaries do not deliver from their own stocks, especially wholesalers.

Transaction channels for industrial goods

Conditions are different in many respects regarding industrial goods, as illustrated in Figure 10.6. There are fewer customers and proximity between distributor and customer is not as important. The element of customer-order-specific variants is considerably larger in this category of products. Order values for industrial products are generally a lot higher.

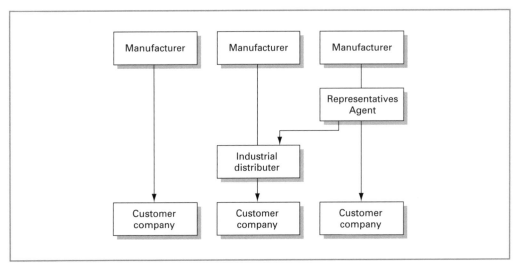

FIGURE 10.6 Three main types of distribution channels for industrial products with different numbers and types of intermediaries

The case of direct delivery in particular is more common for industrial products than for consumer products, not least regarding input goods for the purchasing company's own production. Differences between the two categories are smaller when different types of indirect material are involved.

Distribution through a company's own sales company can take place in combination with direct delivery from the manufacturing company or from stocks in hierarchies of varying complexity, via central warehouses, regional warehouses and local warehouses. The same relationship may be true for representatives and industrial distributors, even though the most typical case is when a representative does not keep stocks and deliver, in contrast to the industrial distributor, which has a stock-keeping and wholesaler-like function. In both cases, when it comes to direct deliveries, the representative and the industrial distributor are responsible for the transaction channel to the customer, while the manufacturing company is responsible for the material flow channel.

10.3 Material Flows in Distribution Channels

A distribution channel between the product manufacturing company and the consuming customer may also contain intermediaries that are responsible for administrating the flow of materials, keeping stocks and delivering physical products. There are a large number of different ways of designing such material flow channels and all of them are suitable to varying degrees, depending on the unique situation each company finds itself in.

Accordingly, in the same way as for transaction channels, there are no material flow channels which are optimal in all situations. Some main types of material flow channels will be described in this section. They can be used to select the type of distribution solution best suited to a specific situation. They serve as a starting point for adaptation and modification when designing a detailed and company-specific distribution channel. To give some structure to this process, we distinguish between cases in which the transaction channel and the material flow channel are in the same distribution channel, and cases where they are separate.

Separate transaction and material flow channels

When the transaction channel and the material flow channel are separated, there are two general alternatives:

- Direct material flow channel
- Direct transaction channel

Direct material flow channel

The first is where the transaction channel initially goes to an intermediary and then to a product-supplying company – for example, a manufacturing company or a distributing company in the distribution system. This alternative is illustrated in Figure 10.7a. In concrete terms this means that the intermediary, for example a sales company, receives and confirms orders and invoices the customer. The intermediary is also responsible for the supplying company being informed of what is to be delivered, when the delivery will take place and to whom. The delivery company is subsequently responsible for physical delivery to the consuming customer. The alternative can be described as direct delivery with respect to the material flow channel, but a delivery through intermediaries with respect to the transaction channel.

Using this alternative, the intermediary principally has a consolidation role with respect to the transaction channel, but not with respect to the material flow channel. This means that the intermediary may represent different suppliers at the time of sale and ordering, and as such provide a type of one-stop shop for the customer. But this does not mean that the intermediary can deliver the purchased products together and at the same time. This alternative can be applied for standard products which are delivered from stock, and for customer-order-specific products which are delivered directly from production.

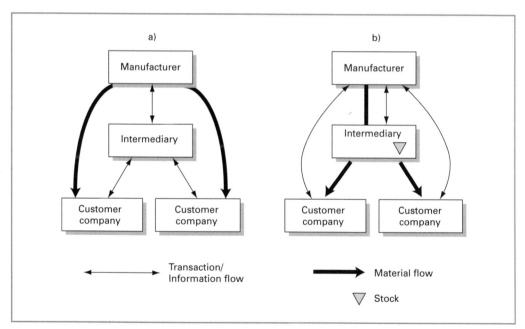

FIGURE 10.7 Alternative distribution channels in which the transaction channel and the material flow channel are separated

CASE STUDY 10.1: TRANSACTIONS AND MATERIAL FLOWS IN DISTRIBUTION CHANNELS – B&B TOOLS

B&B Tools provides the industry and the construction sector in northern, eastern and central Europe with tools, industrial consumables and industrial components. It has developed an Internet portal (www.toolstore.com) with product information about more than 100 000 products from a number of product manufacturers. Toolstore is used by retailers (e.g. hardware stores) to get access to inventory availability, register purchase orders, etc. The retailers can also let their customers log in and register their purchasing orders directly in the portal. The order information is then automatically communicated to the retailer and the product supplying company (B in the figure).

Luna is one of B&B Tools' product-supplying companies. It has an assortment with approximately 40 000 items in the machine and tool sector. It only sells products through about 600 local retailers. Three different information and material flow channels exist.

Material flow 1 means that the respective retailer has a local stock of products. The customer places an order to the retailer (information flow A). The product is picked in the retailer's stock and delivered to the customer. The retailer places purchasing orders to Luna to replenish its stock. This approach is used for the standard assortment on which very short delivery times are required.

Material flow 2 represents purchase and delivery of non-standard items in combination with standard items stored at the retailer. The customer places a purchasing order through Toolstore (B) or directly to the retailer (A). Non-standard items are delivered to the retailer where the ordered stored items are picked and the entire customer order is distributed to the customer. The non-standard items are not stored at the retailer but distribution is carried out through cross-docking at the retailer. The delivery time is less than six days, but one to two days are possible with express transport.

Material flow 3 means direct distribution from Luna to the customer. The retailer has the customer contact and is responsible for sales and invoicing, in the same way as for material flows 1 and 2. The customer normally places the purchasing order through Toolstore (B), but order direct to the retailer (A) is also possible. Large and bulky deliveries with short delivery time requirements of one to two days are normally delivered in this way.

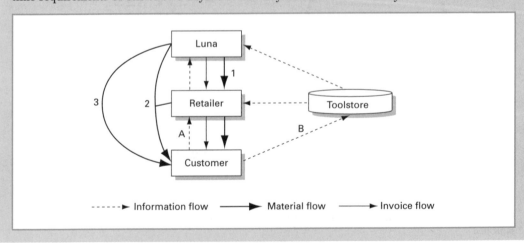

Direct transaction channel

The second alternative is characterised by the transaction channel initially going to the product-supplying company and subsequently to the intermediary company, while the material flow channel goes from the intermediary company to the consuming customer. In concrete terms this means that the product-supplying company itself receives orders, confirms them and invoices the end-customer. The delivery of the products ordered takes place from stocks at the intermediary company, however. The intermediary company in this case is in general a third-party logistics company (see Figure 10.7 b). This alternative does not allow the intermediary company to play a consolidation role, i.e. to deliver products from different suppliers at the same time.

For the intermediary to be able to deliver at the same rate as the supplying company receives orders, the distribution solution must also contain a transaction channel from the product supplier to the intermediary. This channel forwards picking and delivery commissions in accordance with customer orders received. A further pair made up of one transaction channel and one material flow channel, separated in time and quantity, also exists between the supplying company and the intermediary. These channels handle the replenishment of stocks at the intermediary. The product supplying company can manufacture to own stocks and deliver to the intermediary from these stocks or manufacture directly to stock replenishment at the intermediary.

Shared transaction and material flow channels

There are three general alternatives for cases in which transaction channels and material flow channels are shared:

- Traditional warehousing and distribution
- **Cross-docking** with sorting
- Direct cross-docking and **merge-in-transit**

What distinguishes the three alternatives is whether or not storage takes place in the material flow which passes the intermediary company. They are also different with respect to the position of the **customer order decoupling point (CODP)** in the supply chain. This is the point in the supply chain from which a product is destined to a certain customer. Downstream from this point, material flows are driven by customer orders, and upstream by forecasts and plans. The reason that the product is destined to one customer from this point may be that it is customer-specific from a certain stage in its refinement, be this for reasons of its unique product characteristics, unique packaging or goods marking. Another reason may be that manufacture and delivery is based on the just-in-time philosophy and in the exact quantities that correspond to a customer's needs.

Traditional warehousing and distribution

The most common and traditional alternative of these three types is where the intermediary is responsible for the entire warehousing and distribution function. It receives orders, confirms them, picks and delivers the order and invoices the consuming customer, as well as keeping stocks. This method is illustrated in Figure 10.8 a. The inventory control function may be with the intermediary or at the product supplying company. In the latter case we refer to vendor-managed inventories. The customer order decoupling point is in the intermediary company.

The intermediary company places its order with and receives its product supply from a manufacturing company, or from another supplying distribution company: for example a central warehouse or a wholesaler. Thus, there are parallel transaction channels and material

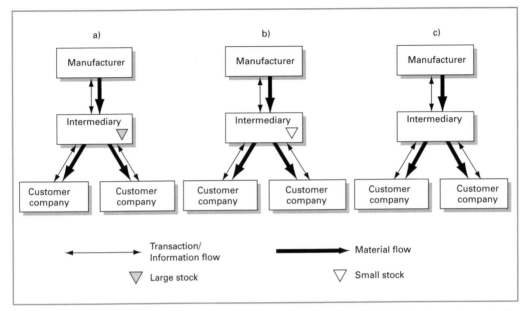

FIGURE 10.8 Alternative distribution channels in which the transaction channels and material flow channels are shared

flow channels, some between the product-supplying company and intermediary company and others between the consuming customer and the intermediary company. However, in contrast to the following alternatives, the channels on either side of the intermediary differ in time points and quantity since the product-supplying company delivers to stocks. This alternative enables the intermediary to play a consolidating role, i.e. to represent and deliver products from several manufacturing companies

Cross-docking with sorting

In the second basic alternative, where transaction channels and material flow channels are shared, the stock-keeping function of the intermediary is marginal. This alternative is almost identical to that previously described with respect to the channels between the intermediary and customer and between the intermediary and product supplying company (see Figure 10.8 b). The difference lies in the fact that both the channels on each side of the intermediary are interconnected to a larger extent in terms of quantity and time. The supplying company receives orders from the intermediary and delivers only what the intermediary has received in customer orders during a certain time period, possibly one day or one week. In each time period, needs from orders received from the intermediary's customers are aggregated, and these aggregate needs are delivered product by product from the supplying company. Deliveries from the supplying company are therefore not tied to customer orders, and for this reason we can say that the customer order decoupling point is located in the intermediary company in this case, too.

Complete orders are then picked at the intermediary company from deliveries received from the supplying company for delivery to customers. In other words, for reasons of co-ordination there is a store at the intermediary only during the period from inbound delivery until the orders have been picked and dispatched. There is no real inventory control. In principle this variant has an almost stockless flow of materials via an intermediary. The size of the stock depends on how well the intermediary succeeds in co-ordinating inbound delivers of the products and to what extent a company is prepared to accept not being able to deliver complete orders. The variant can be called *cross-docking with sorting*. In this case, too, the intermediary may play a consolidating role. Specific sorting and picking of complete orders relate to products from more than one supplier.

CASE STUDY 10.2: CROSS-DOCKING AT COCA-COLA

On the Swedish market, the Coca-Cola company has moved from a decentralised storage and distribution structure with four regional warehouses to one central warehouse at the factory site and 14 cross-docking terminals in different regional traffic areas. Originally the four warehouses were replenished from the factory and the stores were supplied from the warehouse responsible for the traffic area where the store was located.

In the new set-up, customer orders from stores are registered on a daily basis in Coca-Cola's central customer order management system at the central warehouse. Picking, sorting, packing loading and distribution of trucks to the respective cross-docking terminal is conducted once a day, based on the actual orders received. When a truck arrives at a cross-docking terminal, the goods are unloaded and put on distribution trucks for further distribution to stores along a specific route. The route planning for the individual distribution trucks are planned before the trucks' departure from the central warehouse. This means that the goods can be sorted and loaded on the trucks in order to minimise the handling and sorting activities and thus the unnecessary waiting time at the cross-docking terminals. The customer order decoupling point is consequently at the central warehouse and not at the cross-docking terminal.

Customer orders registered before the fixed stop times are delivered from the central warehouse the same day and reach the retailer stores within 24 hours. The stop times vary between traffic areas and are determined in order to have time for picking, sorting, packing, loading and transportation to the respective destination. About 70 per cent of the daily volumes reach the stores within 24 hours.

Direct cross-docking and merge-in-transit

The third basic alternative is identical to the previous one with respect to the general characteristics of the channels between the intermediary and the customer and between the intermediary and the product-supplying company. The alternative is illustrated in Figure 10.8 c. The difference compared with the previous alternative is that both channels on each side of the intermediary are completely interconnected in terms of quantity and time. The orders received by the intermediary from customers are forwarded line by line to the product supplying company, which then supplies exactly the product, in the quantity and point in time that corresponds to the consuming customer's order. It can be described as a *completely stockless flow of materials via an intermediary company*. Every delivery from the supplying company is completely consigned to a certain customer. Thus, the customer order decoupling point in this alternative lies in the product-supplying company. The alternative may be called *directly addressed cross-docking*. The role of the intermediary from the material flow viewpoint is limited to co-packing and co-loading the different products in packages or load carriers marked for and delivered to the same customer. Cross-docking is a commonly occurring distribution alternative for fast-moving consumer goods, for example. Large quantities are delivered daily from suppliers to regional cross-docking points where the goods are broken down into smaller customer order consignments and reloaded onto regional delivery trucks. Customers are normally retailers, which are then able to receive daily deliveries from regional delivery trucks without any storage being necessary in regional warehouses.

One variant of the third alternative is called *merge-in-transit*. In the case of traditional cross-docking, a larger delivery is broken down into smaller units and distributed directly to several customers without requiring any appreciable storage in the distribution warehouse. Achieving efficiency in this arrangement places high demands on co-ordination of inbound and outbound transportation to and from the cross-docking point. Merge-in-transit also involves larger consignments being broken down, sorted and reloaded for further distribution to customers without interim storage at the distributor. The difference from cross-docking is that goods from several different factories and suppliers are delivered in separate consignments to terminals, also refered to as *distribution centres*, where they are merged together and distributed to one or more customers. Co-ordination of inbound and outbound transportation is important also for merge-in-transit, but in addition there are high demands on the right information being available to enable the merging of correct items for customer-specific deliveries. The basic differences between cross-docking and merge-in-transit are described in Figure 10.9.

Merge-in-transit is, for example, used in the computer industry. When ordering a computer which is distributed using a merge-in-transit strategy, the order is registered as a customer order

CASE STUDY 10.3: MERGE-IN-TRANSIT AT DELL COMPUTER CORPORATION

Dell Computer Corporation does not distribute computers to retailers but assembles to end consumers' orders and distributes complete computer packages through merge-in-transit directly to the end consumers.

The customer places a purchasing order to Dell through phone or Dell's web portal. The order is automatically downloaded in the factory system in Dell's assembly plant in Limerick, Ireland, and sent to suppliers of accessories, such as computer monitors, speakers, etc. and to the logistics service providers, responsible for the outbound distribution and merge-in-transit activities. Within two hours, the raw materials come to the plant from an inbound logistics provider. The product will then be assembled according to the customer's order specifications, within two hours or maximum one day, and then packed, marked with the customer's order information and loaded on a truck for distribution to the merge-in-transit centre serving the market of the customer. At the same time the suppliers of accessories prepares deliveries of the order-related accessories to the same merge-in-transit centre.

When, for example, an order is placed from Scandinavia the merge-in-transit centre is in Copenhagen and the outbound activities managed by Schenker Stinnes Logistics. The transport time from Limerick to Copenhagen is three days and for suppliers of monitors and speakers in Tillburg, Holland, 12 hours. Deliveries of computers and accessories are planned to arrive at Copenhagen the same day, in order to minimize storage. In the Copenhagen terminal the received packages are sorted and merged into complete customer packages with computer and accessories. The complete customer packages are loaded on distribution vehicles for transport to the region where the customer is located. Vehicles with the complete customer packages depart from Copenhagen the same day as the different inbound packages arrive.

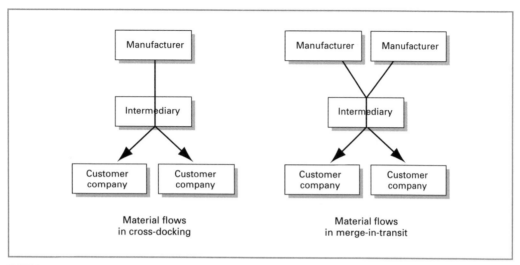

FIGURE 10.9 Material flows in cross-docking and merge-in-transit

in the computer manufacturer's system, which in turn generates an assembly order for the computer in question in the factory and the delivery of accessories required (e.g. screen, loudspeakers, keyboard) from each factory. All the computer parts included in the customer order are marked with the details of the customer order and delivered daily to a terminal which is managed by a distribution company. At goods reception in the terminal each package is identified to a customer order. A complete end-customer package is then picked and loaded onto the distribution vehicle for delivery to the customer's region without any interim storage in the terminal.

Since the customer order decoupling point in the third channel alternative in Figure 10.8 lies within the product-supplying company, customer-order-specific products can be distributed using this type of channel, in contrast to the two first alternatives. Products may be technically or functionally customer-order-specific, or even specific from the distribution viewpoint. For example, this alternative enables every end-customer to have its own specific labels on the products, or specific packaging provided by the manufacturing company, and even individual price marking may take place at the manufacturing company. The intermediary company is able to play a consolidating role, i.e. it can represent many suppliers.

This third alternative in Figure 10.8 is considerably more demanding in terms of information exchange between the players involved in the distribution channel than both of the previous alternatives, particularly when compared with the case in which the intermediary company also has stock-keeping functions. This is especially true of merge-in-transit. Transaction volumes are also greater, particularly between the intermediary and the product manufacturer. The higher costs incurred by this increase in transaction volumes may well be compensated for by decreased costs of capital tied up in stocks and decreased costs of handling materials in and out of stores.

10.4 Warehouse Structures

For a distribution system to be fully capable of managing its aggregation role and distribution role, it is not always sufficient to have one warehouse between the product manufacturing company and the consuming customer. In many cases it is necessary to have a hierarchy of warehouses. One example could be a central warehouse close to the production company, or a relocated warehouse which will cover the needs of a whole continent. A regional warehouse supplied by a central warehouse which serves a regional market is another possibility, or even a local warehouse supplied by a central warehouse or a regional warehouse, which delivers to customers in more local markets. The number of levels and warehouses in such hierarchies is a measurement of the degree of centralisation in the distribution channel. The fewer the levels and warehouses, the greater is the degree of centralisation. There are both disadvantages (−) and advantages (+) of a **centralised warehouse structure**:

- − Longer proximity to customers
- − Increased transport costs
- − Longer delivery times
- − Not local existence
- + Economy of scale
- + Reduced **bullwhip effect**
- + Reduced non-value activities
- + Reduced obsolescence risks

The advantage of a low degree of centralisation, i.e. disadvantage of a high degree of centralisation, is above all increased proximity to customers. This is particularly important for products which demand reliable and short delivery times. The same may be true for products which need customer access to user support and service. It is also generally accepted that there is a direct relationship between potential delivery service and the number of storage points in a distribution system. In all these cases it is a question of factors that influence a company's competitiveness and which therefore affect its revenues. High transport costs in relation to a product's value are a good reason for choosing a low degree of centralisation. Transportation costs are also significant on markets where customers buy frequently and in small quantities. Degrees of centralisation that are too low indicate a lack of suitable transport alternatives to reach local markets.

High degrees of centralisation, on the other hand, bring two main types of economy of scale to distribution. Fewer storage points mean that material flows will be greater at each place of storage. Conditions are then better for investments in high-efficiency automatic warehouses and automated handling systems, and thus an overall decrease in the total transportation and handling costs in the distribution system. The second type of economy of scale is related to the size of stocks required to maintain the desired delivery service level to customers. The fewer the places of storage used, the smaller will be the stocks required to maintain a specific service level. Conversely, the fewer the points of storage, the higher the level of service possible for a given size of stocks. The relationship between service level and size of stocks for high and low degrees of centralisation is illustrated in Figure 10.10. The cycle stock is also positively influenced by a higher degree of centralisation.

CASE STUDY 10.4: FROM DECENTRALISED TO CENTRALISED WAREHOUSING AT MICHELIN

Michelin makes tyres. In year 2000 the company restructured its tyre distribution in northern Europe. It went from a structure of 36 regional warehouses in Sweden, Denmark, Norway and Finland to a central warehouse in Sweden and a supporting warehouse in Finland. The delivery time from the central warehouse is 24 hours to all customers in Sweden, Denmark and most customers in Norway. Finland is reached within 48 hours from the central warehouse and within 24 hours from the Finnish support warehouse.

The effects of the centralisation are reduced inventory-carrying costs, improved inventory service level, partly because Michelin now only stores the items in one location, but also because the delivery services of the inbound flows from the factories have increased because the central warehouse has become an actor with larger demand and more frequent flows than before.

CASE STUDY 10.5: CENTRALISED DISTRIBUTION STRUCTURE AT PHILIPS (Schary and Skjøtt-Larsen, 1995)

Philips Consumer Electronics manufactures and markets a wide variety of electronic products. Philips decided in 1994 to develop a new distribution system and reduce the number of their warehouses. Their goal was to reduce inventories and increase cost efficiency.

The company separated physical distribution from their sales and marketing channels. The warehouses at Philips' national sales organisations were closed and replaced by a small number of logistics service centres. Each logistics service centre was intended to serve several national markets. Philips established a European distribution centre in Belgium to serve the logistics service centre with products common to most markets.

The influence of degree of centralisation on size of stocks and thus capital tied up in material flows can be estimated with the aid of a common rule of thumb, which is based on the formula for economic order quantities shown in Chapter 12. This rule of thumb states that, if the number of warehouses is reduced from n to m, the total volume of stock will be reduced by the factor $1 - \sqrt{\dfrac{m}{n}}$. A reduction from 10 warehouses to 1 will bring about a reduction in stocks of 68 per cent according to this rule.

Bullwhip effects, i.e. variations in demand which are amplified upstream in supply chains with storage points, are described in Chapter 16. Such variations in demand reduce the potential of maintaining a high delivery service and a high and even utilisation of capacity, if at the same time it is desirable to decrease capital tied up in stocks. Bullwhip effects have a direct relationship with the number of levels in the warehouse structure. Estimates have been made which indicate that variations are amplified by a factor of two for every level in the warehouse structure. An increase in the degree of centralisation by reducing the number of warehouse levels can result in a radical reduction of bullwhip effects.

Another advantage of a high degree of centralisation is that the number of non-value-adding activities will be reduced. This is especially true if the number of levels in the warehouse

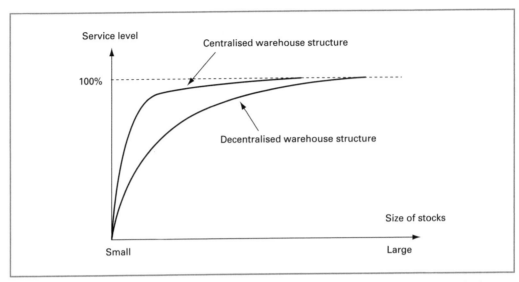

FIGURE 10.10 The relationship between service-level and size of stocks with high and low degrees of centralisation

structure is decreased. For example, one regional warehouse between a central warehouse and local warehouses will cause a lot of extra loading and unloading, unpacking and packing, compared with products being transported from a central warehouse directly to local warehouses. The number of put-aways and retrievals from stocks, and the administration required to perform and follow up the flow of materials, will also be significantly reduced. None of these activities create any added value for customers.

One further advantage of a high degree of centralisation is that the risks of obsolescence and incorrectly composed stocks will be reduced. Every time a quantity of products is transported from a central warehouse to warehouses on local markets, there is a risk that the products delivered will never be in demand, or that the demand will be considerably less than expected. At the same time, a large demand for the product may occur on another market and stocks in that area may be insufficient. Uneven distribution of this type between different warehouses leads to shortage situations and missed sales on certain markets. It can also lead to surplus stocks and the need to dispose of or return products from warehouses on other markets. Such risks are eliminated by not delivering from central stores until customer orders have been received. This aspect of the selection of degree of centralisation has become increasingly important in recent years with the accelerating rate of change of markets and difficulties in predicting future demand. Strategies in this area are discussed in a later section in this chapter.

The relationship between some of the logistics costs described above and the number of warehouses is illustrated in general terms in Figure 10.11. Storage costs in this figure represent costs for warehouses, handling equipment and personnel costs, while inventory-carrying costs for keeping goods in stock refer to capital costs, etc. for such products. The reduction in transportation costs that follows from an increased number of warehouses is thanks to the fact that geographical distances and therefore transportation distances to customers decrease as the number of warehouses increase. These cuts in costs more than offset the transportation costs that arise for replenishing local warehouses from a central warehouse, since stocks are replenished less frequently and with greater volumes per delivery.

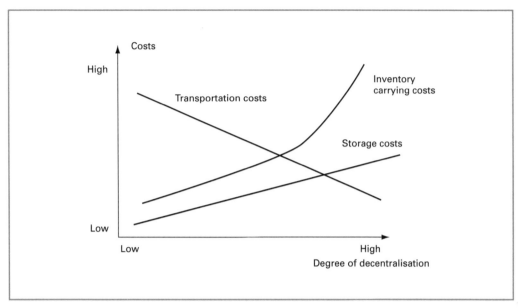

FIGURE 10.11 The relationship between different logistics costs and degree of decentralisation of warehouse structure

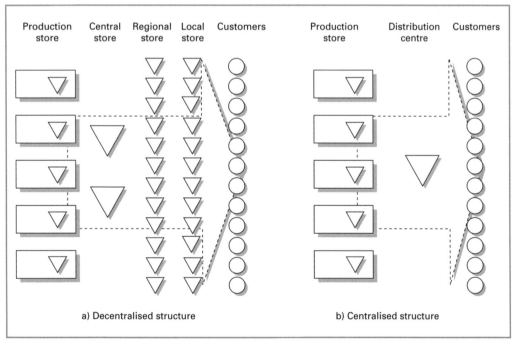

FIGURE 10.12 General differences between a) decentralised warehouse structure with a large number of warehouse levels and places and b) centralised warehouse structure with a smaller number of warehouse levels and places

For the same reasons as the design of distribution channels, there is no universally optimal solution for selecting the degree of centralisation. The appropriate degree of centralisation is always related to a specific situation, and it will be the situation on the market and the nature of the products which determine optimal warehouse structures. One consequence of this reasoning is that the degree of centralisation should not necessarily be the same for all products in a company. In general there are good reasons for differentiating warehouse structures for different products, just as there are for distribution channels, through direct delivery of certain products from a production warehouse and delivering others from decentralised warehouses on local markets, for example. For a number of years developments in Europe have been towards an increasing degree of centralisation. Another clear trend is to phase out national warehouses and introduce transnational regional warehouses at the European level, or in many cases one common central warehouse for the whole of Europe. A similar development is undertaken in the USA. The general differences between a centralised and decentralised distribution structure are shown in Figure 10.12. Figure 10.12a shows a **decentralised warehouse structure** with a large number of storage levels and parallel places of storage. Figure 10.12b shows a centralised structure with a smaller number of warehouses.

10.5 Changing Conditions for Intermediaries

Changes in the conditions for distribution lead to both reduced and increased needs for intermediaries. During the past decade the existence and value of intermediaries has been increasingly questioned. Different forms of intermediaries have also been eliminated as distribution systems have been made more efficient. This process has been called **disintermediation**. The question has arisen of what types of distribution companies will survive in the future. But new forms of intermediaries have evolved which have contributed to increased efficiency.

There are many ways of eliminating intermediaries in supply chains. In the case of consumer products this may take place as illustrated in Figure 10.13. The wholesaler, retailer, or both, may be eliminated. Which of these three alternatives is most likely is not possible to answer in general

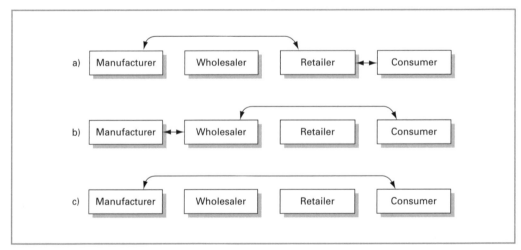

FIGURE 10.13 Different principles of eliminating intermediaries in supply chains. Elimination of a) the wholesaler, b) the retailer, c) the wholesaler and retailer

terms. It varies from industry to industry, from market to market, and from product to product. The only thing that can be generally stated is that an intermediary which contributes added value to the consuming customer in the supply chain always has a role to play and a justified existence.

To remove intermediaries in one of the ways shown in Figure 10.13 does not mean that the functions of the intermediary removed also disappear. The function of connecting the product manufacturing company to the consuming end-customer cannot generally be eliminated. But it may be transferred to other players along the supply chain, and even to the manufacturing company itself.

Developments in the area of IT and improved potential for communicating information between companies are among the main reasons for the rise in interest in eliminating intermediaries. This development has created completely new possibilities for the shaping of distribution channels and the need to use intermediaries to reach consuming customers. Trends towards greater demands for customer-order-specific products on the market and towards increased specialisation of manufacturing companies together with a narrower range of products also influence the need for intermediaries and their primary roles. From such starting points it is possible to analyse and evaluate the expected significance of distribution companies in the future in terms of the different distribution roles discussed above.

We may expect the significance of the role of aggregation for distribution companies to continue to decrease. The increased trend towards customer-order-specific products and the increasing range of product variants means that demand aggregation is no longer possible to the same extent as previously. Opportunities for transporting even small quantities at reasonable cost have improved as a result of IT development and better exchange of information between companies. Transportation companies have access to daily information about transport needs between supplying and purchasing companies, meaning that transportation can be co-ordinated in a completely different way from the past. It is now possible to achieve economy in transportation through sufficiently large quantities by consolidation and co-ordination of deliveries of different products to different recipients instead of consolidating the same product from the same supplier. In other words, it has become increasingly economical to deliver standard products in small quantities directly from the product manufacturer to consuming customers. The wider application of just-in-time thinking in industry and pull-based logistics solutions are also an important driving force behind the declining significance of the aggregation role of distributors.

Demands for shorter delivery times have shown a tendency to constantly increase, which speaks for an increasing significance of the spreading role of distributors. This is certainly the case in some industries. However, in the transportation and forwarding sector it has at the same time made it possible to deliver goods economically and rapidly to all parts of the world. Global companies such as UPS, Fedex and DHL and air freight which is becoming increasingly cost-effective, have together created new possibilities for rapid and direct deliveries over great distances. Developments in the area of IT have been significant in this context too, by enabling rapid and co-ordinated transportation as well as creating the conditions for almost continuous tracking and tracing of goods from supplier to customer. In this way the risks associated with delayed delivery times for long-distance transport can be reduced. The spreading role of distributors is declining for this reason in many industries and segments.

The contact role of distributors has remained important in many areas, especially in those cases where needs and demands for providing technical service and other assistance are important for competition and customer service. The contact role for providing information in conjunction with placing and receiving orders, however, has decreased significantly in many product areas. Opportunities for exchange of information via the Internet have meant that customers are easily able to obtain necessary information and place their orders over great distances. In many contexts the reliance on proximity has been considerably reduced and the distance gap has been largely bridged with the aid of IT-based solutions and Internet instead of local distribution companies.

On the other hand, the role of creating variants is undergoing an upswing. Increasing demands on a wide range of different product variants to remain competitive on the market, and consumer behaviour which is increasingly difficult to predict have driven this tendency. By only creating the final product variants after customer orders have been received at the local distributor, it is possible to decrease the risks of manufacturing product variants which will never be in demand and accumulating unmanageably large stocks. This **postponement** strategy is described in more detail in the next section. Through the increased use of this type of strategy, the distributors' role of creating variants will become increasingly significant. In this context we talk about **value-adding distributors**.

The role which in relative terms can be expected to increase most in the future is that of consolidation, i.e. the role which creates opportunities for customers to buy different products from several product manufacturers through one and the same supplier at the same time. There are two main reasons why this role is increasing in significance. The first is connected with economies of scale and leads to product manufacturing companies tending to become more specialised and having a narrower range of products. This development is illustrated in a simplified fashion in Figure 10.14.

From concentrating on supplying a wide range of products to a few markets, manufacturing companies have increasingly moved towards supplying a narrow range of products to many geographical markets. This strategic approach means that the purchaser must turn to more and more suppliers to satisfy his total purchasing needs. This is seen as costly, which leads to the second reason behind the growing significance of the consolidation role of distributors. Companies have reduced the number of their suppliers. The primary motivation behind this ambition is to reduce costs and to establish a deeper co-operation. There are considerable transaction costs associated with purchasing from many suppliers compared with applying a one-stop-shop strategy. Also it is costly in terms of expensive experts and practically difficult to establish a large number of deeper partner relationships aimed at integration with suppliers' activities.

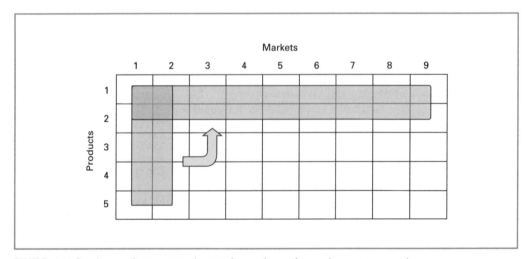

FIGURE 10.14 Development from many products on few markets to few products on many markets
The arrow illustrates the trend of development.

When referring to the role of consolidation, it is important to differentiate between its role in the transaction channel and in the material flow channel. As pointed out above, the flows of information and materials do not necessarily take the same paths through a distribution network, i.e. the transaction channel and the material flow channel do not necessarily share the same distribution channel. To enable a purchaser to acquire a broader range of products from one distributor, it is only necessary that the supplier has a consolidating role in the transaction channel. In practical terms this means that orders for a wide range of products can be placed with a single supplier and relations from the transaction viewpoints are limited to this distributor. Alternatively, deliveries can be made directly from the product manufacturer or consolidated at the order-processing distributor as described in some of the models in the section on material flows in distribution channels. In the first case above, the distributor may be considered as an information wholesaler.

10.6 Postponement and Speculation Strategies

There are two very central alternative strategies to choose between when creating distribution channels, especially for the material flow channel. The strategies are called *speculation* and *postponement*. Speculation in the context of supply chains means that value-adding or material-moving activities are carried out without any commitment from a customer in the form of an order, for example. Activities are initiated on the basis of anticipation and forecasts instead. Speculation, then, means that a company manufactures a finished product without having a customer order and/or that a company delivers a product from manufacturing or from a central warehouse to a warehouse at a local market without a customer order. We can speak of two dimensions of speculation: *manufacturing speculation* and *material flow speculation*.

Speculation strategy means risk exposure, namely the risk that the product variant as manufactured will never be in demand or will never be sold on the market to whose warehouse it has been transported. The products may then become obsolete or need to be transported back to production or to a central warehouse. The strategy also results in stocks building up and associated capital tied up and inventory carrying costs. The speculation strategy also has a number of advantages, however. It enables benefits of scale, when larger quantities of a product are manufactured and delivered than actually demanded at a point in time in the form of customer orders. Manufacturing costs and transportation costs can be reduced. Manufacturing and distribution on speculation also decreases the risks of shortages and delivery problems, and it contributes to decreasing delivery times to customers.

The opposite of speculation strategy is postponement strategy. This means waiting as long as possible before performing value-adding and material-moving activities in supply chains, preferably until customer orders have been received. In the same way as was the case with speculation, we can speak of *manufacturing postponement* and *material flow postponement*. Manufacturing postponement means that specific product variants, whether in terms of form, function or identity through labels and packaging, are not manufactured until a customer order is received for them. Material flow postponement means that products and starting materials of different types are not transported from central warehouses to local warehouses until there is a customer order for the goods. Postponement strategy provides advantages where speculation strategy has disadvantages, and vice versa.

Postponement strategy has become increasingly important and more widely used in recent years. The driving force is mostly a tendency towards more unpredictable customers and markets, and shorter product lifespans. As a result of this development, risk exposure has increased in the areas of manufacture and distribution when there is no guaranteed security in the form of a customer orders. Postponement strategies are an effective way of radically reducing this risk exposure. Thanks to developments in the IT area, flexible production and rapid deliveries, these strategies are feasible in quite a different manner than was previously possible.

Neither of the above strategies must be implemented alone. It is rather a question of greater or lesser emphasis on speculation or postponement. For example, keeping stocks at the central warehouse level, regional warehouse level, or local warehouse level will entail different degrees of speculation. In the same way, labelling and packaging to customer order of products manufactured to stock, assembly to customer order and manufacturing to customer order involve different degrees of postponement. In one specific case it may clarify matters more to characterise the strategies with respect to where the customer order decoupling point lies in the supply chain and the product structure. Speculation strategy means that the customer order decoupling point is moved downstream in the supply chain, or towards the finished product in the product structure, whereas postponement strategy means that the customer order decoupling point is moved upstream in the supply chain, or towards raw materials in the product structure.

Both the dimensions of speculation and postponement can be combined in different ways as shown in Figure 10.15. If speculation strategy is applied to both manufacture and material flow, this means that manufactured finished products are stocked at and delivered from downstream distributors. If postponement strategy is used for material flow in combination with speculation in manufacturing, manufactured finished products will be stocked at the manufacturer or upstream distributors and delivered on customer order from these stocks, either through downstream distributors or directly to consuming customers.

Manufacturing postponement in combination with material flow speculation means that items used in own semi-finished products and purchased components will be stocked at a downstream distributor. Specific product variants will be produced to customer order and delivered to customers. Finally, the case of both manufacturing and material flow postponement will lead to specific product variants being produced by the product-manufacturing company to customer order and delivered to customers. One type of this particular combination will mean that the variant-specific product is produced by a downstream distributor, but that own semi-finished

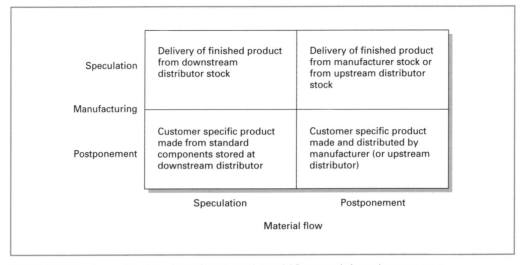

FIGURE 10.15 Possible combinations of manufacturing and material flow speculation and postponement

products and purchased components used will not be transported to the distributor before a customer order has been received and the material needs have been determined. The difference is whether the material flow postponement is related to the finished product manufactured or the materials used in the product.

10.7 Value-adding Distributors

The combination of material flow speculation and manufacturing postponement means that own semi-finished products incorporated and purchased components are transported downstream in the supply chain and stocked by distributors on local markets. Local distributors receive customer orders and assemble product variants corresponding to customer orders from these stocks of incorporated materials, and deliver them to the consuming customer. In other words, distributors supply form utility and play a variant-creating role. Such distributors are called *value-adding distributors*. In many cases, **terminals** act as an important value-adding resource.

The value-adding activity

The value adding which these distributors can achieve is of various types and involves different degrees of manufacturing in the traditional sense of the word. Among commonly occurring forms of value-adding activities, the following may be named:

- *Simple assembly* – some parts of assembly are postponed.
- *Supplementing with accessories* – supplementing the basic model in order to create customer-order-specific product variants is postponed. One example is composing a customer-specific computer package.
- *Mixing* – the final mixing/blending operation is postponed, for example in the case of paints.
- *Kitting* – picking of different items to a kit is postponed. For example, putting together an assembly kit for an assembled object which will then be forwarded to an assembly plant.
- *Sorting* – grading and sorting heterogeneous products for delivery to customer is postponed.
- *Sequencing* – in the case of delivery of components and semi-finished products to assembly plants with manufacture to customer order, it is common that items delivered must be in the same sequence as the recipient will assemble them in the object manufactured. Such sequential assembly of components and semi-finished products can be carried out by the distributor.
- *Adjustment* – settings of product characteristics are postponed, for example configuration of computers.
- *Packing* – packaging of the finished product is postponed, for example, so that customer specific and country specific packages can be used.
- *Labelling* – labelling and affixing trademarks are postponed.

  The value-adding activities carried out by distributors differ in a number of ways from traditional manufacturing. In general they require relatively few fixed assets, and the need for skilled labour and access to engineering qualifications is small. The "manufacturing" which is carried out is closely associated with sales and receipt of customer orders, and is often organised in conjunction with the warehouse and dispatch departments. In addition, simple planning systems can be used.

The use of value-adding distributors has increased significantly in many different industries during the last decade, not least as a consequence of market demands for more product variants and more customer-specific products. The increasing number of product variants brings with it greater difficulties in predicting future demands for each single variant. Risk exposure can be unacceptably high when using manufacturing-speculation strategies. At the same time, increased demands on the delivery of customer-specific variants with short delivery times means that materials incorporated may need to be transported and stocked for manufacturing finished products at local distributors and not at remote product manufacturers.

The role of terminals in distribution structures

A *terminal* is a plant to which goods are transported to be combined and/or split up into other consignments, given more value by another activity and reloaded for further transport to customers. Storage often occurs in the terminal or nearby. The terminal plays a central role in distribution structures since it enables the gap between producers and consumers to be decreased. One common terminal activity is sorting, which is the case at post office terminals where collected letters are sorted for further distribution to a terminal closer to the recipient, or directly to the recipient. Another is a repackaging into larger or smaller loads and reloading onto other means of transport. Some interim storage may be necessary at a terminal, since it is extremely difficult to synchronise all inbound and outbound transportation. It is also the physical unit where distributors' value-adding activities are carried out.

Unloading and loading are normally bottlenecks in terminal activities. This is particularly the case at truck terminals where there are often queues in the mornings and evenings. Due to this imbalance in workload, terminals may be forced to be extremely *over-dimensioned*, and loading and unloading times must be spread more evenly over the day, even if this is not always optimal from the transport-planning viewpoint.

The function of the terminal is the same, whether it is a land, sea, air or combined terminal, but the design will vary to adapt to handling the goods to and from the specific means of transport involved.

10.8 Conclusion and Summary

This chapter has dealt with different strategies for planning the structure of distribution systems. The starting point was the creation through distribution of utilities of form, place, time and ownership, and to bridge the gaps of pace, distance, quantity, range and variants between suppliers and customers. As an intermediary in a distribution structure, a distributor is able to influence these gaps and create utilities. The role of the intermediary may be to aggregate, spread or consolidate the flow of materials, but it may also be to create variants and make contacts between players in distribution channels.

A distribution channel aims at bringing together the flow of information and materials between manufacturers and consuming customers. The different principles for devising these channels and their associated flows have been described in this chapter, including cross-docking and merge-in-transit.

Other central issues discussed in the area of distribution structures were the consequences of centralised versus decentralised warehouse structures, the effects and possibilities of eliminating intermediaries in structures, strategies for postponing the creation of product variants and opportunities for distributors to be responsible for and to carry out the creation of variants.

🔑 Key concepts

Bullwhip effect 228	Intermediary 213
Centralised warehouse structure 228	Material flow channel 218
Cross-docking 223	Merge-in-transit 223
Customer order decoupling point (CODP) 223	Postponement 234
	Terminal 237
Decentralised warehouse structure 232	Transaction channel 218
Direct delivery 218	Value-adding distributor 234
Disintermediation 232	Warehouse structure 228
Distribution channel 218	

 Discussion Tasks

1 Discuss how distribution structures may be expected to differ between the distribution of components from subcontractors to finished product manufacturers in the car industry, foodstuffs from manufacturer to shop, and computers from manufacturer to private consumer.

2 Explain possible roles of intermediaries in the distribution channels of question 1 above.

3 Distributing companies can take the roles of aggregating, spreading, contacting, providing variants and consolidating. How could these roles be expected to change as a result of more customer-order oriented production and increased specialisation among manufacturing companies?

4 What effect on demands within the whole logistics system can be expected in the changeover from several regional warehouses to one central warehouse and no regional warehouses?

5 What new roles might we expect in the future to be played by distributors/third-party logistics companies? Discuss some of these possible roles.

Further reading

De Koster, M. and Warffemius, P. (2005) "American, Asian and third-party international warehouse operations in Europe: a performance comparison", *International Journal of Operations and Production Management*, Vol. 25, no. 8, pp. 762–780.

Gadde, L.-E. and Håkansson, H. (2001) *Supply network strategies*. John Wiley & Sons, Chichester.

Harrison, A. and van Hoek, R. (2004) *Logistics management and strategy*. Prentice Hall, Essex.

Kärkkäinen, M., Ala-Risku, T. and Holmström, J. (2003) "Increasing customer value and decreasing distribution costs with merge-in-transit", *International Journal of Physical Distribution and Logistics Management*, Vol. 33, No. 2, pp. 132–148.

Rabinovich, E. and Evers, P. (2003) "Postponement effects on inventory performance and the impact of information systems", *International Journal of Logistics Management*, Vol. 14, No. 1, pp. 33–48.

Schary, P. and Skjøtt-Larsen, T. (2001) *Managing the global supply chain*. Copenhagen Business School Press, Copenhagen.

Stern, L. and El-Ansary, A. (2001) *Marketing channels*. Pearson, London.

Van Hoek, R. (1998) "Logistics and virtual integration: postponement, outsourcing and the flow of information", *International Journal of Physical Distribution and Logistics Management*, Vol. 20, No. 7, pp. 508–523.

PART 4
Planning and Control of Logistics and Supply Chain Systems

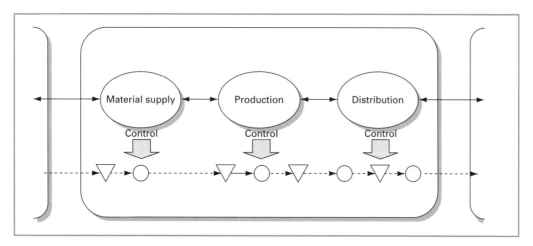

The fourth part contains five chapters. The first describes customer order processes and forecasting processes and methods. The second focuses on materials management and contains different planning methods for controlling material flows and inventories. Basic approaches and principles for planning and control and the decoupling functions of inventories are also discussed. The third and fourth chapters deal with planning and control issues specific for manufacturing and distributing companies, respectively. The last chapter deals with procurement from a logistics perspective.

Part Contents

Demand management

The aim of logistics and supply chain management is to control the flow of materials and the consumption of resources so that market demand for a company's products can be satisfied in the most efficient and effective manner. To achieve this there must be a balance between market demand for products and services on the one hand, and assets in the form of materials, production and distribution capacity and capital available in a company on the other. Thus, to achieve this balance it is necessary to be aware of or able to predict future demand to a reasonable extent.

The processes in a company related to administration of demand for the company's products are of two types: the customer order process and the forecast process. The **customer order process** covers the known part of demand, while the forecast process covers that part of demand which must be estimated in different ways. The role played by customer orders in relation to forecasts in gaining information about future demand depends to what extent the company's products are delivered directly from stocks or with delivery time. Both processes are described in this chapter, primarily from the viewpoint of their role in gathering information about future demand.

The chapter is closely related to several other chapters in the book. There are direct links to Chapter 13 Manufacturing planning and control, Chapter 16 (especially Section 16.1 negative effects in supply chains, 16.3 Supply chain collaboration concepts, 16.4 Supply chain design) and Chapter 17 (especially Section 17.1 Planning and execution systems, 17.2 Information exchange and 17.5 Information quality).

11.1 Customer Order Processes

A **customer order** represents a commitment from a customer to purchase certain quantities of a company's products at a certain point in time. Even though the quantities and delivery times of such customer orders may be changed, or the order may even be cancelled, in practical terms customer orders are still considered and treated as known information about future demand.

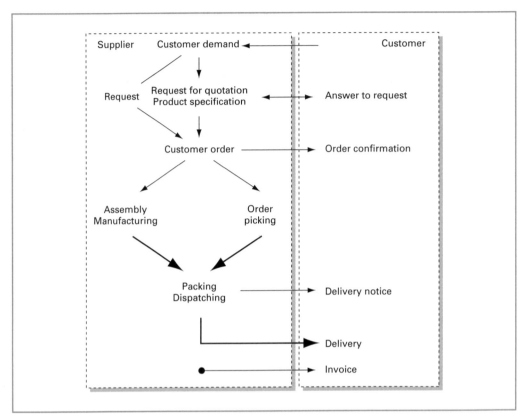

FIGURE 11.1 A simplified model of the customer order process in a company
Thin arrows indicate flow of information and thick arrows indicate flows of material.

Working methods applied to the processing of customer orders vary considerably between different types of company. From the logistics perspective and at an overall level of description, however, we still talk about the general customer order process with associated activities, irrespective of the type of company. One such general customer order process is illustrated in Figure 11.1. It may be seen as a simplified model of flows of information and materials during the customer order process from requirement to delivery.

In the first step of the customer order process there are two main alternatives, depending on what the customer demands. If a standard product is demanded, the customer's requirement after a simple inquiry may directly result in a customer order to the supplier. The inquiry may, for example, relate to price and possible delivery times. If instead it is a question about specific products that are produced to customer order, the process is more complex and may even include a **request for a quotation** with information about product performance, price, delivery conditions and other aspects which define the supplier's offer. The activities between a customer and supplier are also intended to specify and estimate the desired product. Determining a delivery time is considerably more complicated in this case. Some negotiations of prices and delivery conditions are also common. For specific products to customer orders there may well be extensive discussions and exchange of information before a customer order is completed.

When a supplier has received an order, it is often confirmed by sending an **order confirmation** to the customer. In straightforward cases, this means that the supplier confirms that he undertakes to deliver a certain quantity of a certain product at a certain point in time. In more complex cases, the order confirmation may also contain drawings, specifications, guaranteed performance and so on for the product to be supplied. In the simpler types of customer order, order confirmation is sometimes not sent and instead a procedure known as *tacit acceptance* is applied. This means that the customer order may automatically be considered as confirmed if the supplier has not been in contact within a certain time period, for example, one week.

If the customer order is for standard items in stock, a **picking list** is printed out when delivery is to take place and the stated quantities are picked. If the customer order refers to products to be manufactured, a *work order* is drawn up which is started in time for delivery to take place as agreed. Whether products are manufactured or picked from stocks, they are sent to be packed and dispatched to the customer. In some cases the supplier will send a **delivery notice** to the customer at the time of dispatch, informing him that the delivery is on the way.

Specification and registration of customer orders

In cases where customer orders are for standard products, they are fully known and defined by their product numbers. Specification is not required and the order can be registered directly in the supplier's ERP system (see Figure 11.2). At the time of registration, products are reserved in the quantities and times stated in the order. By making these reservations, the information on demand which the customer order represents is stored in the system so that consideration may be given to the need to deliver that amount when conducting materials planning.

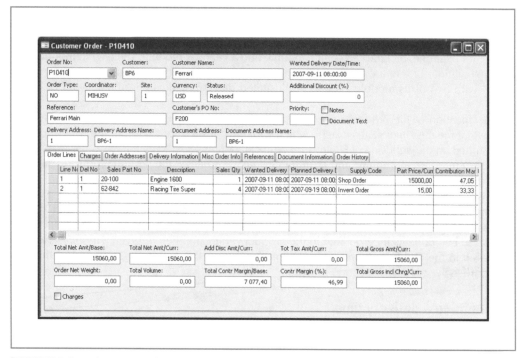

FIGURE 11.2 Example on screen of customer order registration

The picture illustrates the registration of two order lines, the first for one piece of item 20-100 and the second for four pieces of item 62-842, on the order number P10410 to customer BP6. The picture represents a function from the ERP system IFS Applications.

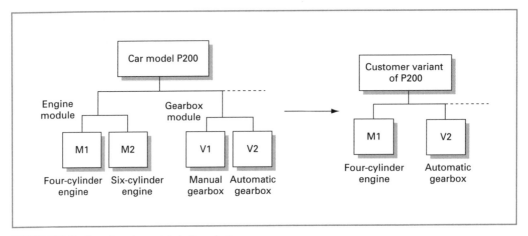

FIGURE 11.3 Configuration of a module-built product

If the customer order is for products made to customer order, they are not fully known on order intake and must be specified in consultation with the customer. However, semi-finished products and components used in the final product are often known and in many cases kept in stock. This is usually the case when products are configured and built from modules. The product variant ordered can then be manufactured by combining different variants from each of the modules incorporated in the product and can be specified with the aid of product configurators. Specification starts from the product model which the ordered variant belongs to and which represents all product variants that can be produced by combining different module variants. A car model, for example, includes an engine module and a gearbox module. The engine module may be a six-cylinder or a four-cylinder engine and the gearbox may be manual or automatic. A car model with two of its module variants is illustrated diagrammatically in the left part of Figure 11.3.

Specification of the product variant desired takes place at the time of customer order. This means that the customer states exactly which variant is desired for each module. This approach is illustrated on the right side of Figure 11.3. The car variant selected by the customer in this case includes a four-cylinder engine and an automatic gearbox. When the desired product variant has been specified and a possible delivery time determined, the customer order is registered.

A work order must be created in order to manufacture the product variant as specified on the customer order. This may take place automatically when the customer order is registered, or separately by manual registration. When the work order is registered, the semi-finished products and purchased components incorporated in the product variant are then reserved. These reservations are stored in the ERP system and make up information on the demand represented by the customer order.

Determining a delivery time

One central part of the customer order process is determining a **delivery time** for the customer order. Customers require information about the expected time of delivery, and information about demand must include both quantities to be delivered and the times at which deliveries will take place. Information about demand, in other words, must include a quantity dimension and a time dimension to be complete.

For standard products which are delivered directly from stocks or successively as they are planned for production, a delivery time is determined by calculating the earliest time at which there are available quantities to promise for delivery. Available quantities to deliver means in this case the quantity which at a given point in time can be delivered from stocks without negatively impacting on other customers' deliveries. For example, the fact that there are seven items of a product in stock is not the same as having seven items available for delivery. A number of them may be reserved for another customer.

Calculation of what is available for delivery is called **available to promise (ATP)** and is illustrated by means of an example in Table 11.1. The first row in the table refers to the total quantities reserved from customer orders on hand. A **reservation** is a booking of a certain quantity for delivery at a later date. The second row refers to expected inbound deliveries from ongoing or planned work orders, or purchase orders if it is a purchased product. Stock balance is 47 pieces, and line 3 illustrates how stock development is calculated when outbound deliveries to customer orders on hand or inbound deliveries from work orders successively take place. The fourth and last row shows how much that accumulated remains in stock for possible delivery to a new customer. Note that 17 pieces are not available to promise in week 1, even though there are 17 pieces remaining in stock when the week is over. If these 17 pieces were to be delivered to a new customer, deliveries of a total of 15 pieces promised to customers in week 2 would not be possible. If the company receives an enquiry from a customer regarding the earliest delivery date for 10 pieces, the answer must be in week 3.

The question of when it is possible to deliver a certain quantity of customer-order-specific products is somewhat more complicated to calculate than the delivery of standard products from stocks, since available to promise must include both capacity and availability of materials. Consideration must be paid to available capacity, since this is related to manufacturing in the form of assembly or final manufacture taking place to customer order. Determination of delivery time must therefore take into account what capacity is available for manufacturing. One method is by continuously updating current production capacity as orders are received. Real-time information is obtained on how much capacity is available for further customer orders. When a new order is received, a calculation of the number of hours required to manufacture the product ordered is made and when they will be earliest available in the production groups used for the manufacture.

In order to manufacture a product, in addition to available capacity there must also be sufficient quantities available of semi-finished products and components incorporated in the specified product variant. Available to promise must also be calculated for these items. The same approach as described above for standard products can be used. The items incorporated which are last available will determine the point in time when the work order attached to the customer

Week		1	2	3	4	5	6
Reservations		30	15	21	12	7	0
Planned manufacturing order		–	–	50	–	–	50
Projected available inventory	47	17	2	31	19	12	62
Available to promise		2	2	12	12	12	62

TABLE 11.1 Example of calculation of available to promise (ATP)
Stock balance is 47 pieces.

order can be started. This point in time, plus the leadtime for manufacturing, will determine when the customer order can be delivered with respect to materials availability.

As an alternative to determining possible delivery times to customers with the aid of available to promise calculations as above, many companies apply a more or less fixed policy delivery time. This is generally based on experience. The disadvantage of fixed delivery times is that they must always be sufficiently long to work when the workload is temporarily higher than normal. The advantage is that the principle is simple to apply and that delivery times can be very quickly given to potential customers.

Picking, manufacturing, packaging and delivery

When the delivery time for a customer order arrives and products ordered are in stock ready for delivery, a picking list is printed. The products are picked from stocks, packed and sent to the customer. At the time of picking, the quantity withdrawn for the customer order is deducted from the stock balance. Reservations are removed at the same time so that available quantities in stocks remain correct. If the quantities in stock at the time of picking are not sufficient, either the delivery must be delayed or part delivery of the order must take place. Part delivery means that a certain proportion of the quantities promised are noted as back-orders and delivered at a later date, while the quantity available is delivered immediately. In the case of back-orders, reservations are retained for the relevant quantity.

When manufacturing customer-order-specific products, the work order is started in good time so that manufacturing can be completed within the framework of the total delivery time to the customer. When the work order is started, the semi-finished products and purchased components required for the product variant in question are picked from stocks. As they are picked, the stock balance for each item is decreased and the reservations registered for the work order in the ERP system are removed since they no longer represent future demand.

Customer orders in the form of delivery plans

The description above applies to cases where there are customer orders that define when a certain product will be delivered and in what quantity, i.e. information is provided on future demand which the company intends to satisfy. For companies that manufacture and deliver to **delivery plans** (also called **delivery schedules**), conditions are somewhat different. In this case it is a question of standard products which are fully known at the time of order. The difference when compared with delivery from stock is that manufacture and/or delivery take place according to a delivery plan, or the quantities to be delivered periodically during the coming weeks or months. Quantities manufactured can be delivered directly to customers in accordance with the delivery plan or delivered to stock, and later delivered from stock to the customer as stated in the delivery plan.

A delivery plan often consists of three parts, as shown in Figure 11.4. The first part is a **call-off** for delivery and may be considered as a clear order from the customer. Normally this part will take anything from one or two days to a week or so. The time period depends on current delivery times and the delivery agreement between the parties which regulates how delivery plans are interpreted and processed. This first part also constitutes a fixed part of the delivery plan and may not be changed by the customer without good reason from one delivery plan to the next. The agreement between the parties regulates to what extent changes may take place in this fixed part of the plan. The sub-order part of the delivery plan may be seen as a reservation and is therefore a type of unfilled order. It also defines delivery times for the supplier.

CASE STUDY 11.1: DEMAND INFORMATION TO SUPPLIERS IN THE AUTOMOTIVE INDUSTRY – VOLVO CAR CORPORATION

Volvo Car Corporation assembles the majority of cars to order. The suppliers make customer-specific variants of systems and deliver them to the Volvo Assembly plant in the right sequence and just-in-time for assembling. Forecasts, delivery plans and so-called *synchro-orders* are communicated to the suppliers upstream in the supply chain. Forecasts are sent once a month and contain production plans expressed as number of demanded components per week for the next 60 weeks. Delivery plans are sent daily and contain the daily demand of the respective component for the next 30 days. Synchro-orders are sent continuously during the day, containing exact specifications of what customer specific systems for a supplier to make from standard components and deliver the same day.

The extent the delivery plans for the components are allowed to vary depends on the annual demand and the time horizon. For components used in more than 80 per cent of all car variants, for example, the weekly as well as monthly demand are allowed to vary +/−10 per cent. For components used in 1 to 10 per cent of all car variants the plans are allowed to vary between 100 and +150 per cent between weeks and +/−50 per cent between months. For all components, the plans are fixed within the next eight days and cannot be changed.

The subsequent part of the delivery plan concerns the quantities which are expected to be called off. These expected sub-orders are not a full and fixed commitment from the customer for actual sub-orders. However, there is often some form of undertaking from the customer – for example in the form of paying costs for raw materials and components that the supplier must order in advance to be able to manufacture in time when the sub-order is placed. For the supplier, the most distant part of the delivery plan is only a forecast of needs for future deliveries based on the customer's assessments.

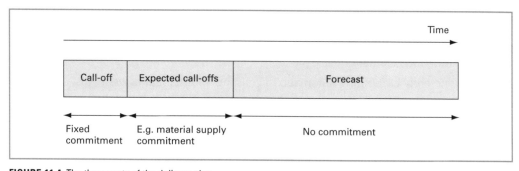

FIGURE 11.4 The three parts of the delivery plan

11.2 Forecast Processes

To be able to efficiently balance supply and demand for a company's products, information is required about what needs may be expected as far in the future as it takes to carry out adaptations of resources available. For example, it may be a question of the time it takes to acquire raw materials for manufacture, or the time needed to increase production and distribution capacity if demand increases. The information about future demand provided by current customer orders does not often stretch far enough into the future for sufficient planning. For this reason it is more or less necessary to estimate future demand with the help of forecasts.

Forecasts in a company may be thought of as strategic, tactical or operative decisions. In this chapter forecasts are only described in terms of tactical and operative issues. Forecasts are closely tied to decisions about acquisition and use of resources, but also for current operative activities. In this context it is mainly a question of estimates of future demand for the company's products, and so they may be described as demand forecasts. The size of demand is completely decisive for both the flow of materials and production. As an example of situations where demand forecasts influence tactical and operative decisions, the following questions may be asked:

- What capacity of personnel and machines are required for next year's production plan?
- What quantities of item XX are estimated to be required for purchase next year as a basis for entering into sub-order agreements with suppliers?
- What quantities of item YY are estimated to be consumed next year as a basis for determining suitable order quantities?
- How long will stocks last and when must replenishments be ordered?

Defective forecasts

Since a forecast is an assessment of future demand, in principle it will never coincide exactly with real demand. A forecast, by definition, will always contain some degree of error. In other words, defective forecasts must be accepted, but the defects must be minimised.

There may be a number of different reasons for a forecast being defective and **forecast errors** being unacceptably large. Some common reasons for low forecast accuracy are:

- Ineffective forecasting methods
- Misleading forecast data
- Not sufficiently combining automatic forecasting and manual assessments
- Unrealistic expectations
- Low acceptance level
- Conflicting interests
- Lack of forecast responsibility and **forecast monitoring**

One reason may be that the forecasting methods used are not efficient enough. This may be true for computerised and automatic forecasting methods as well as procedures and approaches used with manual forecasting that are based more on experience and estimation. Another reason for defective forecasts is that the factual bases for forecast calculations are misleading, such as when deliveries of a large one-off order are allowed to influence usage statistics and thus influence forecast calculations and forecast estimates.

Automatically calculated demand forecasts of the type described here are always built on projecting the future through events in the past, or retrospective thinking. In an environment with volatile demand it is difficult, and in some cases almost impossible, to obtain good forecasts only through automatic calculations based on historic demand. By combining manual future assessments, for example at the product group level, with automatic calculations based on historic facts it is possible to achieve higher forecast accuracy.

Defective forecasts are not generally only the result of error. There are also a number of psychological reasons involved in this context, such as unrealistic expectations. As mentioned above, forecasts are by definition erroneous. It is pointless to expect anything else and to make plans as if forecasts were exact.

Another reason why forecast accuracy is not, or is not perceived as, satisfactory may be that there is a vicious circle. If, for whatever reason, personnel begin to doubt the quality of forecasts and start making their own forecasts instead, there is a risk that the entire forecasting procedure will degenerate and the acceptance level will be low. The personnel whose job it is to make forecasts, in the marketing department for example, will have less motivation to produce good forecasts. The result is that forecasts become even worse and that even fewer personnel use them. It is not unusual in industry that planning and production personnel make parallel forecasts for just this reason.

One further reason for defective forecasts is the conflict in interests which may exist between different departments in a company. The company's sales department may have an interest in submitting over-optimistic forecasts as a means of ensuring that production can deliver the quantities which they thought they could sell and deliver. The production department, on the other hand, may have an interest in keeping forecasts low to avoid risking low workloads on production resources sized on the basis of high forecasts. Overall forecasting and processes for master production schedules are important to avoid this type of problem, and should be considered a process of strategic importance with clear responsibility and improvement emphasis.

Forecast data and forecast patterns

To facilitate the forecasting of future demand, access to information on historic demand is required. The compilation of real historic demand is not entirely straightforward, however. The historic data which are normally available in an ERP system consist of delivery statistics and invoicing statistics, but that does not completely represent real demand. For example, differences may arise when shortages of stocks lead to loss of sales or delayed deliveries. There may also be differences between desired, promised and real delivery times, while delivery statistics as a rule only provide data on real delivery times. For practical reasons companies are usually forced to use delivery or invoicing statistics. Which of these types of statistics should be chosen as an approximation of historic demand must be determined from case to case. If a company has rapid

January	25 pcs	July	13 pcs
February	19 pcs	August	18 pcs
March	21 pcs	September	24 pcs
April	26 pcs	October	25 pcs
May	12 pcs	November	19 pcs
June	15 pcs	December	23 pcs

TABLE 11.2 Historic demand data as a time series

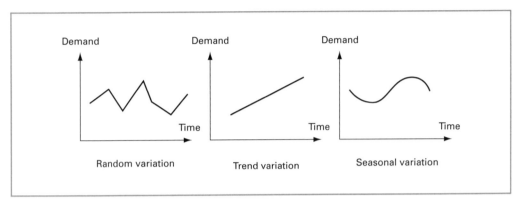

FIGURE 11.5 Illustration of three commonly occurring demand patterns

invoicing procedures, invoiced volumes will generally correspond to delivered volumes with only one or two days' difference. Slower invoicing procedures, i.e. when there is a longer time between deliveries and invoicing, will make delivery statistics preferable.

Historic demand is reported for forecasting purposes in time series, or compiled historic demand data that shows historic demand volume period for period. More strictly defined, a time series may be said to be a succession of chronologically ordered data with constant periodicity. One example of this is shown in Table 11.2. The time series refers to deliveries per month of a certain product. The total quantity delivered during the year was 240 pieces, and the delivered quantities on average per month were 20 pieces.

When working with such time series as a basis for forecasting, it is important to distinguish between demand patterns which are hidden in the sequence of demand data. Common examples of demand patterns may be random variations around a mainly unchanging demand, trend changes, i.e. when demand increases or decreases period by period, or seasonal variations, meaning that demand varies regularly at different times of the year. These three demand patterns are illustrated in Figure 11.5.

When forecasting several years ahead, it may also be necessary to take into account cyclical demand variation, which depends on more general changes in the business cycle.

Forecasting with qualitative methods

Methods used for forecasting demand can be roughly divided into *qualitative methods* and *quantitative methods*. Qualitative methods are generally based on individuals' experiences and more or less well-considered personal assessments of future demand. They are also characterised by few or no formal calculations on the basis of demand statistics and other data. Methods in this group range from simple intuitive estimates by a sales manager to detailed formal procedures and approaches with many individuals involved.

In comparison with quantitative methods, qualitative methods are generally preferable in situations where the number of products and number of periods to be forecast are small, such as forecasting annual rather than weekly demand. Qualitative methods are more often used if it is necessary to make them far in advance, and if demand is influenced to a large extent by the company's various marketing activities. In general, qualitative methods are appropriate for products being introduced on the market or being discontinued, since during these phases there is a limited amount of data on which to base demand calculations.

Period	Forecast	Demand	Deviation
0701 January	200	256	+ 56
0702 February	200	197	− 3
0703 March	200	294	+ 94
0704 April	225	267	+ 42
0705 May	225	246	+ 21
0706 June	225		
0707 July	250		
0708 Augusti	250		
0709 September	250		
0710 October	300		

TABLE 11.3 Example of information used as a basis for individual forecasting

Even though qualitative methods of forecasting do not generally use any automatic calculation procedures, various forms of computer systems support may be applied in order to supply demand information rationally for assessment and to facilitate the various types of calculations required. Table 11.3 and Figure 11.6 show two examples illustrating such computer systems support. Table 11.3 shows examples of forecasting data in the form of an earlier forecast, actual demand, and deviations between forecast and actual demand during earlier periods. The data may be presented on a monitor. Graphically processed assessment information is often used to facilitate forecast work.

In Figure 11.6 an example is shown of how calculation support for forecasting is used in an ERP system. The example illustrates how an individually prepared annual forecast can be divided into periods with the aid of a distribution curve which shows the percentage of the total annual demand in each of the year's twelve months. Aids of this type make it possible to utilise individual assessment methods for forecasting to a greater extent, since it is sufficient to make forecasts on an annual basis for each product. Distribution curves may be common to all products within one product group, and can be produced automatically from stored delivery

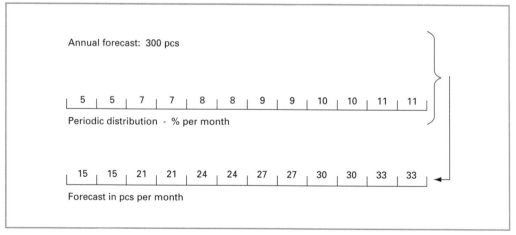

FIGURE 11.6 Distribution of annual forecast with the aid of a distribution curve

statistics. One special case of distribution of annual forecast into periods is that used for seasonal variations in demand.

Forecasting with quantitative methods

Quantitative methods for forecasting are based almost entirely on mathematical calculations starting with time series of sales, consumption or other types of demand history. In this context a distinction is made between **extrinsic** and **intrinsic** quantitative methods. Intrinsic quantitative methods are characterised by forecasts being expressed in the same variable as the time series calculations are based – for example, that both the forecast and the time series behind it refer to sales of a certain product. Extrinsic quantitative methods are based instead on time series that refer to some other explanatory variable than the one to be forecast. For example, demand for electric cable is extremely dependent on housing construction, and demand for ice cream is dependent on the weather temperature. Only two of the commonly occurring intrinsic quantitative methods for operative forecasting will be taken up here: **moving average** and **exponential smoothing**.

Moving average

The simplest form of intrinsic quantitative methods is, quite simply, to assume that demand in the next period will be equivalent to that of the most recent period. However, such a method risks being too sensitive to random variations, especially if the forecast period is short. If the lengths of periods are quarters or more, it may be useful.

   If the average value of demand during a number of periods is taken instead as a measurement of demand in future periods, a method is obtained which complies with greater demands on stability. The number of periods that should be included in calculating the average must be determined from case to case, depending on the length of the periods and the size of variation in demand. In general terms, demand values based on many periods will provide better stability against random fluctuations but at the same time poorer sensitivity to trends and other systematic changes. The longer the forecast periods used, the fewer are the number of periods that need to be included.

Example 11.1

Monthly sales of a product during the previous year are shown in figures in Table 11.2. The company uses 12-month moving average to forecast future sales. The forecast for January the following year will be 20 pieces, i.e. equivalent to the average value of the previous 12 months' demand. If the real demand for January the following year is 19 pieces, the forecast for February will be one twelfth of the sum of demand values from February in the previous year until and including January in the current year. One way of calculating this forecast value is to deduct the previous January figure from the new figure, divide it by 12 and add this amount as a forecast adjustment to the old forecast. The following calculations have then been carried out:

Forecast adjustment $= \dfrac{19 - 25}{12} = -0.5$

New forecast $= 20 - 0.5 = 19.5$

It is clear from this type of calculation that the forecast method involves the successive replacement of the oldest period's demand value with that of the latest period's. The method is called moving average for this reason.

Exponential smoothing

The moving average method means that all demand values are assigned the same weight in calculations, irrespective of their age. This in itself indicates that other weightings are possible, such as recent demand values – which in theory should have a higher information value – being assigned a greater weight than older values. In principle, forecast calculations could be made in the same way as in the previous section, except that each single demand value would be multiplied by a certain weighting before being totalled. This type of calculation is rather lengthy, however. It also places large requirements on the storage of historic demand data, especially if there are many periods in the calculation.

If the relationship between two consecutive weights is constant, this is called an *exponential weighting distribution*. For example, with a ratio of 0.5 a weighting distribution is obtained as follows:

$$0.5 - 0.25 - 0.125 - 0.062 - 0.031 \text{ etc.}$$

This is the series of numbers whose sum is equal to 1 if the sum of the highest weight and the constant weighting relationship is equal to 1. As a designation of this constant relationship, the Greek letter α is normally used. Note that α must always be less than or equal to 1. From this relationship, the following formula for forecast calculations can be derived:

$$F(t + 1) = \alpha \cdot D(t) + (1 - \alpha) \cdot F(t)$$

Where $F(t + 1)$ = forecast demand for period $t + 1$
　　　　　$D(t)$ = real demand during period t
　　　　　α = the **smoothing constant**

As is evident from the formula, only the latest real demand value and the preceding forecast need to be saved. The method using exponential smoothing is in this respect considerably more attractive than the moving average method.

CASE STUDY 11.2: FORECASTING OF BEVERAGE AT CARLSBERG

One of Carlsberg Breweries' European subsidiaries makes beer, water and soda to stock based on forecast. The forecasting method exponential smoothing (with an alpha value of 0.1) is used to develop weekly forecasts per product group. Daily forecasts are developed by dividing the weekly forecasts by 5. To consider daily sales variations, the deviation between actual sales and forecast for a day is added to the next day's forecast. For example, the part of Monday's forecast that is not sold on Monday is added to the forecast of Tuesday. Quantities can only be moved to the next day within the same week, i.e. forecast adjustments are only conducted within the respective week.

The forecast error is followed up and evaluated at the end of each week. The causes of deviations are analysed if the deviation between forecast and sales is large. If accumulated deviations are identified, the forecasts are adjusted manually. The forecast goal is to have daily forecast errors (deviation between forecast and sales) below 5 per cent.

Somewhat simplified, exponential smoothing means that if, for example, α is selected at 0.2, the most recent demand value will be assigned a 20 per cent weighting, while the older forecast will be assigned an 80 per cent weighting. The selection of the α value has the same significance as the selection of the number of periods when using the moving average method. A high α value provides better flexibility for systematic demand changes, but also causes larger instability with random demand variations. In practical applications, selected α values normally lie between 0.1 and 0.3.

Example 11.2

In Example 11.1, the forecast for January in year 2 was 20 pieces and the real demand for the same month was 19 pieces. Using the exponential smoothing method and $\alpha = 0.3$, the forecast for February is as follows:

New forecast $= 0.3 \cdot 19 + 0.7 \cdot 20 = 19.7$ pieces

Consideration of trends and seasonal variations

If systematic trends in changes are more than negligible, the forecast methods of moving average and exponential smoothing need to be supplemented by different types of **trend** corrections. They may result in a faster accuracy of forecast when real demand shows changes that follow a trend.

Taking consideration of trends is especially important if forecast values are extrapolated far into the future, i.e. when the forecast is not only used for the subsequent period. For example, if a forecast is to be made each month during the next 12 months, it is often necessary to take into consideration any existing trends to gain reasonable forecasting precision. This type of extrapolating forecast is especially useful when long-term production plans are being drawn up.

It is possible to compensate for trend changes when calculating long-term periodic forecasts by adding an estimated trend correction to each period. If the forecast obtained by using the moving average value or exponential smoothing method is called the basic forecast, the extrapolated forecast for the period n will be as follows:

$$\text{Forecast for period n} = \text{Basic forecast} + (n - 1) \cdot \text{Trend}$$

Table 11.4 illustrates an extrapolated forecast with a basic forecast of 290 pieces and a trend of 5 pieces per period. If $n = 2$ then the forecast will be $290 + (2 - 1) \cdot 5 = 295$ pieces.

In the same way, forecasts made using the moving average or exponential smoothing methods may need to be supplemented when there are seasonal variations in demand. To achieve this, a seasonal index is estimated which expresses the magnitude of the **seasonal variation**. The **seasonal index** for any particular month refers to the normal demand during the month in relation to the average demand for all months during the year. If, for example, demand during recent years was 72 pieces on average during the month of April and average demand during all months of the year was 60 pieces, the seasonal index for April will be $72 / 60 = 1.2$.

The principal for calculating a seasonal index is shown in Figure 11.7, in which D(i) is the demand in period i and D(a) the average demand during the year. After the seasonal indexes have been estimated they are normalised, i.e. rounded off and adjusted so that the sum of all seasonal indexes will be equivalent to the number of periods during the year.

Period	1	2	3	4	5	6	7
Demand	290	295	300	305	310	315	320

TABLE 11.4 Illustration of extrapolated forecast with trend

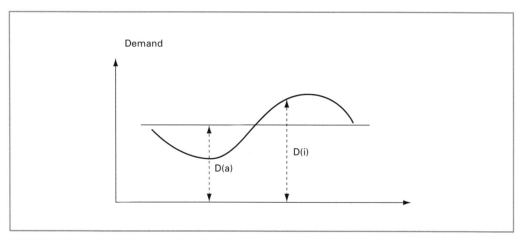

FIGURE 11.7 Illustration of the principal for calculating a seasonal index

When the seasonal index for all periods has been determined, consideration can be taken of the effects of seasonal variations by multiplying the basic forecast by the seasonal index for each period in the same way as for trend correction. If, for example, demand in the month of April is forecast at 65 pieces without consideration to seasonal variations, the forecast adjusted for seasonal variations will be $1.2 \cdot 65$, or 78 pieces.

Example 11.3

Quarterly demand for the three previous years is shown in the table below. Using exponential smoothing, $\alpha = 0.3$ for forecasting and the forecast for quarter 4 in year 3 being 73 pieces, the forecast for quarter 1 in year 4 will be as follows:

| | \multicolumn{4}{c}{Quarter} | Total |
	Q1	Q2	Q3	Q4	
Year 1	100	121	105	74	400
Year 2	96	119	105	80	400
Year 3	95	120	114	71	400
Average per quarter	97	120	108	75	400
Seasonal index	0.97	1.20	1.08	0.75	

No trend can be identified in historic demand, but there are seasonal variations between the four quarters. The seasonal index is obtained by calculating the relationship between the average demand for each quarter and one quarter of the annual consumption (400/4 = 100 pieces). For quarter 1 the seasonal index will be 0.97 (97/100).

To make a forecast for the next quarter, a forecast is first made based on demand without seasonal variation, which is then adjusted by the seasonal index. The forecast for quarter 1 in year 4 will be 94 pieces and is calculated as follows:

Non-seasonal demand for quarter 4 in year 3: 71/0.75 = 94.7 pieces

Non-seasonal forecast for quarter 4 in year 3: 73/0.75 = 97.3 pieces

Non-seasonal forecast for quarter 1 in year 4: $94.7 \cdot 0.3 + 97.3 \cdot 0.7 = 96.5$ pieces

Forecast for quarter 1 in year 4: $96.5 \cdot 0.97 = 94$ pieces

Forecast errors and forecast monitoring

Forecasts calculated using the above methods will always have certain inaccuracies. There is therefore good reason to calculate forecast errors and carry out continuous monitoring of forecasts to keep them within acceptable margins of error. This is especially relevant for automatic forecasting, using either moving average or exponential smoothing methods. There is otherwise a risk of losing control over forecasts, which can have serious consequences for materials management.

Basic to all forecast monitoring is the measurement of forecast errors. Continuous measurement of forecast errors should therefore be an integral part of the forecasting system. The aim is partly to identify individual, random errors and partly to identify systematic errors, i.e. that the forecast is systematically too high or too low. As described in the Chapter 12 on materials management, random forecast errors are also used as a basis for determining the size of safety stocks.

Forecast errors are measured for each period and may be defined as the difference between the forecast for a period and the actual demand for the same period. A positive forecast error means that the forecast was too high, and a negative forecast error means that it was too low in relation to actual demand. To continuously monitor forecast errors, the average forecast error is used to measure if the forecast is systematically incorrect or not. The average forecast error in absolute values, i.e. without taking into consideration whether the forecast is higher or lower than the actual demand, is used to measure the random variation. The latter measurement of the spread of forecast demand relative to actual demand is usually called **mean absolute deviation (MAD)**. A low MAD value is consequently not sufficient as a measurement of good quality forecasts. A good forecast method should also result in small average forecast errors in the long term, i.e. equally often provide forecasts which are too high and forecasts which are too low. An ideally functioning forecast method will result in an average forecast error of zero.

Example 11.4

With forecasts and actual demand as shown in the two first columns of the table below, the MAD will be 7.3 pieces (73/10) and the average error −1.9 pieces (−19/10) for each period, calculated from the 10 periods reported. The example consequently contains both random and systematic forecast errors.

	Demand	Forecast	Forecast error	Absolute error
Period 1	50	55	+5	5
Period 2	52	55	+3	3
Period 3	70	55	−15	15
Period 4	50	55	+5	5
Period 5	60	55	−5	5
Period 6	65	55	−10	10
Period 7	46	55	+9	9
Period 8	66	55	−11	11
Period 9	60	55	−5	5
Period 10	50	55	+5	5
Total			−19	73

11.3 Conclusion and Summary

To be able to control the flow of materials and consumption of resources in an efficient manner, there must be a balance between market demand on the one hand and the company's assets in the form of materials, production capacity and distribution capacity on the other hand. It is therefore essential to be able to predict future demand with a reasonable degree of accuracy. Customer orders and forecasting processes enable this to be achieved at a company.

A customer order represents an undertaking from a customer to purchase certain quantities of the company's products. Customer orders may therefore be said to constitute the known part of demand. Customer order processes vary between different companies, not least depending on their type of manufacturing. However, important activities which are virtually always included in customer order processes in all types of company include product specification, order registration, delivery specification, picking, packing and delivery. Customer orders also exist in the form of delivery plans.

Forecasting processes are used to estimate the unknown part of demand for future sales. Tools used in forecasting are qualitative methods and quantitative methods, examples of the latter being moving average and exponential smoothing. In some forecasting contexts it is also necessary to take into consideration existing trends and seasonal variations. Since forecasts by definition involve some inaccuracies, forecast error calculation and forecast monitoring must be an integral part of any forecasting system.

🔑 Key concepts

Available to promise (ATP) 247	Intrinsic forecasting method 254
Call-off 248	Mean absolute deviation (MAD) 258
Customer order 243	Moving average 254
Customer order process 243	Order confirmation 244
Delivery notice 245	Picking list 245
Delivery plan 248	Request for quotation 244
Delivery schedule 248	Reservation 247
Delivery time 246	Seasonal index 256
Exponential smoothing 254	Seasonal variation 256
Extrinsic forecasting method 254	Smoothing constant 255
Forecast error 250	Trend 256
Forecast monitoring 250	

Discussion Tasks

1 What are the similarities and differences between a customer order and a delivery plan?

2 Why do most companies claim that their forecasts are not good enough? Identify possible reasons.

3 Forecasting may be carried out using qualitative methods or quantitative methods. It is often advantageous to use them simultaneously. In what way can a qualitative method be a complement to the use of a quantitative method and vice versa?

4 What are the motives for following up current forecast errors when making manual forecasts and when using automatic forecasting methods?

5 What are the relationships between the customer order process and the customer's procurement process?

Exercises

Exercise 11.1

At a company which manufactures cement mixers, sales of a newly introduced product variant during a six-month period were as follows:

January	February	March	April	May	June
45 pcs	78 pcs	67 pcs	116 pcs	105 pcs	94 pcs

a) What will the sales forecast be during July if the moving average method is used for six months?

b) How large will forecast sales be during July if exponential smoothing is used instead with $\alpha = 0.4$ and if the forecast for January was 50 pcs?

c) What are the reasons for using so few periods when the moving average value method is used for forecasting as opposed to such a high α value in exponential smoothing?

d) How large will the MAD be for the forecast error during the above six months if exponential smoothing is used as a forecasting method?

Exercise 11.2

A golf shop sells complete golf equipment sets, among other products. Average sales per quarter over the last three years for one of these golfing sets are shown in the table below:

Quarter 1	Quarter 2	Quarter 3	Quarter 4
22 pcs	47 pcs	32 pcs	11 pcs

During the previous year, a total of 137 golfing sets were sold compared with an annual forecast of 109. Forecasts are used to place long-term preliminary orders to suppliers.

a) Calculate the seasonal index for each of the four quarters.

b) Which sales can be expected per quarter during the coming year if exponential smoothing is used with an α value equal to 0.5?

c) Forecasts are only made of expected sales for one year ahead in the golf shop. Bearing this in mind, what may be the reason for using such a relatively high α value?

Further reading

Bowersox, D., Closs, D. and Cooper, B. (2002) *Supply chain logistics management.* McGraw-Hill, New York.

Brander, A. (1995) *Forecasting and customer service management.* Helbing & Lichtenhahn, Basel.

Crum, C. and Palmatier, G. (2003) *Demand management best practices: Process, principles and collaboration.* J. Ross Publishing, Boca Raton (FL).

Lewis, C. (1998) *Demand forecasting and inventory control.* John Wiley & Sons, New York.

Makridakis, S., Wheelwright, S. and Hyndman, R. (1997) *Forecasting methods and applications.* John Wiley & Sons, New York.

Silver, E., Pyke, D. and Peterson, R. (1998) *Inventory management and production planning and scheduling.* John Wiley & Sons, New York.

Schönsleben, P. (2000) *Integral logistics management,* St. Lucie Press, New York.

Wilson, H. and Keating, B. (2002) *Business forecasting.* McGraw-Hill, New York.

CHAPTER 12

Materials management

Companies may be characterised by flows of materials from suppliers into the company, flows of material within the company during the manufacturing process if it is a manufacturing company, and flows of material in the form of finished products from the company to its customers. These flows are initiated by various types of orders. Each of these orders, and the resulting flow of material, is defined by the quantity to be transferred from a supplying unit to a consuming unit and by the point in time when the specified quantity must be available at the consuming unit. Material flows cause an increase in stocks of material through inbound flows from supplying units, and a decrease through consumption. Different methods of managing the flow of materials and thus the size of stocks are presented in this chapter. Some general and fundamental principles for this management and the decoupling functions which different types of stocks have in the flow of materials are discussed.

The chapter is closely related to several other chapters in the book. There are direct links to Chapter 4 (especially Section 4.3 Delivery service elements), Chapter 5 (especially Section 5.1 Logistics costs), Chapter 8 (especially Section 8.5 Delivery patterns), Chapter 16 (especially Section 16.1 Negative effects in supply chains and Section 16.3 Supply chain collaboration concepts) and Chapter 17 (especially Section 17.1 Planning and execution systems, Section 17.2 Information exchange, Section 17.3 Data capture systems and Section 17.5 Information quality).

12.1 Basic Principles for Materials Management

Manufacturing orders and purchasing orders are created with the purpose of initiating flows of materials and satisfying current requirements. Materials management aims at determining quantities and time points for all items' manufacturing and purchasing orders. The goal is to achieve these material flows as efficiently as possible with respect to capital tied up, delivery service and the utilisation of resources. For these reasons, materials management should be able to answer the following four fundamental questions:

1 For which items must new orders be planned (item question)?

2 What quantity must be stated in the order for each item (quantity question)?

3 When must the order for each item be delivered to stock, directly to production or directly to the customer (delivery time question)?

4 When must the order for each item be transferred to the supplier, or when must it be initiated in internal production (start time question)?

The different materials planning methods which are applied in companies all provide data used as a basis for answering these questions. How these data are created and how the questions are answered varies between the different methods.

Independent and dependent demand

From the viewpoint of materials management, it is possible to distinguish between **independent** and **dependent demand**. This distinction is fundamental in understanding how material flows are connected, and for the selection of suitable materials planning methods. Independent demand for an item refers to demand that has no direct connection with the demand for other items. Items stocked for delivery to customers as a rule have independent demand. These are mainly finished standard products.

Dependent demand, in contrast to independent demand, means that the demand for an item may be traced from the demand for another item. Items that are incorporated as input materials in the production of other items have dependent demand. Under such circumstances demand forecasts for items are not necessary, but may be calculated from the demand for the principal item. For example, if there are 32 spokes in a bicycle wheel, and sales forecast is 50 per week for bicycles (with two wheels), it can be calculated that the demand for spokes will be 3200 per week.

Many items with dependent demand may also have a certain proportion of independent demand. This will be the case if an item is used as incorporated material in the manufacture of another product and is also sold separately as a spare part. The bicycle spokes above is an example of such an item. A certain proportion of independent demand may also arise for other reasons. Scrap items are for example part of independent demand since a certain proportion of the quantity picked from stocks cannot be used in production and must be scrapped.

Balancing demand and supplies

In principle, materials management involves balancing requirements of materials with availability of materials as cost-effectively as possible. If supply is less than required demand, the flow of materials must be increased by planning new manufacturing orders or purchasing orders. If, on the other hand, supply is larger than demand, inbound deliveries of already **planned** and **released orders** must be delayed or demand influenced as much as possible, possibly through sales campaigns of different types. Imbalances between supplies and demand will lead to large stocks if supplies are too large, or shortage situations and poor delivery capacity if demand is too large.

A primary function of stocks is to decouple processes so that unacceptably costly relationships of dependence do not arise. In the short term, for example within the coming week or month, there may be reasons for not maintaining an exact balance between supply and demand. For reasons of cost it may be preferable to manufacture or purchase quantities that are larger than the immediate demand. From a long-term perspective, however, there must always be a balance between supply and demand; if this is not the case and accumulated supplies have become too large, balance must be restored by scrapping or selling off surplus stocks. If accumulated demand outstrips supplies, balance may be forcibly restored through the loss of sales and customers.

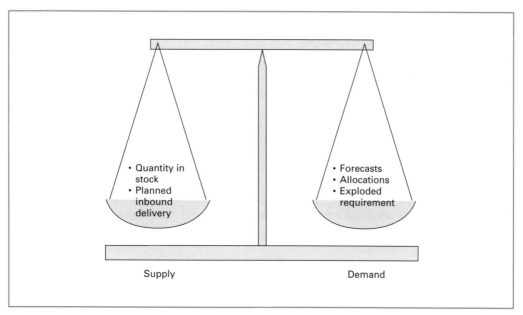

FIGURE 12.1 Balancing of supplies and requirements in materials management

In operative materials management, supplies are the sum of those quantities which are in stock and the quantities in planned and released purchasing and manufacturing orders which are to be delivered. Stocks represent current supply, while planned inbound delivery is a supply that is expected to be accessible at a certain future point in time. Demand is expressed in different form, e.g. as forecasts, exploded from aggregated **gross requirement**, customer allocations and allocations for manufacturing orders. Refer to the illustration in Figure 12.1. Of the different types of requirement, forecasts represent the least certain and reliable information about future requirements and allocations represent the most certain, since they are based on decisions made by customers or result from the company's own planning. **Exploded material requirements** lie between these two from the information reliability viewpoint. These requirements are obtained with the aid of product structures, also called **bill-of-materials (BOM)**, in calculating requirements of incorporated material from plans for volumes of products the company intends to manufacture.

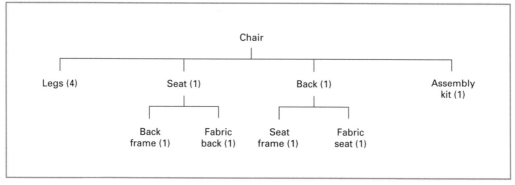

FIGURE 12.2 Bill-of-material for a chair

To give an example: if a company plans to manufacture 100 chairs with four legs each, 400 legs will be required. Figure 12.2 contains a simplified bill-of-material for the chair showing the parts (with number of parts in brackets) required to make the chair. The finished product is shown in the top of the structure and different levels of assembly are shown below. For obvious reasons, materials management should be based on allocations as much as possible since the quality of information is highest in this type of demand information.

Another factor that divides different types of requirements is the time span within which materials are used. For products kept in stock, short-term customer allocations are used in the coming days or week, while forecasts or plans are used for events further in the future. For items which are input materials for production, conditions are slightly different depending on the current planning environment and which planning methods are used. Allocations for short-term manufacturing orders are mainly used in the short term, and exploded requirements or forecasts are used for the longer term. If these items are also sold and delivered directly to customers, such as for spare parts, allocations for customer orders are also used as information on which to base materials management.

Synchronisation of material flows

As explained above, materials management aims at balancing supplies of materials and demand of materials in a cost-effective manner. This process of balancing has a quantity dimension and a time dimension in accordance with the fundamental questions described in the beginning of this chapter. Thus, supply quantities must correspond to demand quantities, but supplies must also be available at the point in time when demand requirements arise. Balancing the time and quantity of the material flow according to its demand and supply is called synchronisation of material flows. The balancing of quantities is in this context less of a problem compared to the time dimension. Somewhat simplified we can say that it is either a question of producing and delivering those quantities which are immediately needed at each separate time of demand, or

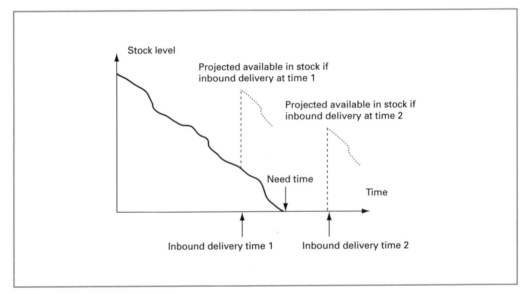

FIGURE 12.3 Synchronisation of requirements and supplies in the flow of materials
Broken lines show how stock levels would have changed if deliveries had taken place at time 1 and time 2.

producing and delivering a quantity which is the equivalent of a calculated economic order quantity and which will cover a number of expected future demand requirements. Financial motives for manufacturing and delivering more than the immediate needs are described in section 12.4 about lot sizing.

Synchronising points in time for supplies and points in time for demand requirements represents a considerably larger challenge. It is a question of making supplies and thus inbound delivery times for an order of an item to coincide as closely as possible with the times when the item is needed. If delivery takes place too early, it will lead to capital being unnecessarily tied up, and if deliveries are too late there will be shortages, resulting in disruptions of production and poorer delivery service to customers. Figure 12.3 illustrates this relationship in a stock which, due to expected retrievals, gradually becomes empty. At that point in time there will be a need to replenish the stock, i.e. it is the expected time point for material to flow into the stock. If inbound delivery takes place at time 1, there will be unnecessary capital tied up, and if it takes place at time 2 there will be shortages in the stock. Efficient materials management involves being able to foresee and calculate as certainly and exactly as possible when demand requirements will arise, and to ensure that inbound deliveries take place as closely to these required time points as possible.

The difficulties involved in achieving synchronisation are also affected by the fact that it is seldom possible to consider items as isolated events from the point of view of planning. It is necessary also to take into account how other items are managed. In most cases, material flows for different items are dependent on each other and demand for them are interconnected. For this reason they must be managed as a whole. If, for example, the final manufacturing or assembly of a product is to be carried out, the supply of many input items is required simultaneously, and for a customer order with several order lines to be delivered it is necessary to have supplies of all of the products specified in the order. The flows of materials must be as synchronised as possible with each other regarding the time and with the nodes in material flow structures which represent manufacturing order start and picking for customer orders.

What occurs if this synchronisation does not take place is illustrated in Figure 12.4 for a manufacturing order of product P consisting of the three items A, B and C. If the need for any of these items has been planned to fall too late, as is the case for item C in the picture on the left of the figure, the manufacturing order start for item P will be later than planned. This means that other material will remain in stock waiting for the delayed item. If, instead, the need for an item has been planned to fall too early, as in item A in the right-hand picture of the figure, the item will remain in stock and have to wait until the order for P is planned to start.

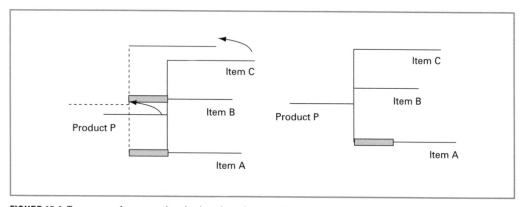

FIGURE 12.4 Two cases of poor synchronisation of requirement times at nodes in a material flow structure

To achieve perfectly timed and synchronised flows of materials it is not sufficient to merely synchronise requirement times at the planning stage. For perfect synchronisation, the flow of materials must also be synchronised from the supply side, implying that consideration must be given to capacity shortfalls and disruptions in the inbound flow of materials. If, for example, due to lack of capacity in the company's own production, it is not possible to deliver a certain in-house manufactured component to final manufacturing at the point in time when final manufacturing has been planned to start, there may be reasons to delay the inbound delivery of other items required for manufacture. By such delaying of other items and the synchronisation of their flows of materials and those of the delayed item, it is possible to avoid unnecessary tied-up capital. Conditions are similar when a supplier cannot deliver a purchased item in time.

Ideal materials management synchronises the flows of materials both with respect to demand and supply during the planning stage of manufacturing orders and purchasing orders. To the extent that requirements are changed or disruptions occur in the flow of materials on the supply side after the order has been planned, synchronisation is restored if possible through re-planning. Such an ideal condition is in general not possible to achieve completely in reality. The stock that arises as a result of incomplete synchronisation is called **synchronisation stock**. It arises whether or not the lack of synchronisation relates to requirement or supply of single items, or whether it is related to the synchronisation of several items' material flows towards common nodes in the material flow structures.

Push- and pull-based materials management

One common way of characterising materials management is to differentiate between so-called **push**- and **pull**-based management, or put another way, to distinguish between materials management based on the suction of requirements or the pressure of planning. There are different conceptions of what is meant by push and pull. The concepts are defined here in the following way:

- Materials management is of the pull type if manufacturing and the movement of materials only take place on the initiative of and authorised by the consuming unit in the flow of materials.
- Materials management is of the push type if manufacturing and movement of materials take place without the consuming unit authorising the activities, i.e. they have been initiated by the supplying unit itself or by a central planning unit in the form of plans or direct orders.

The principles are illustrated in Figure 12.5. The decisive difference between the two methods of initiating the flow of materials is: who authorises that the value adding and material movement processes should take place? The pull principle means, in contrast to the push principle, that no such activities may take place without the party that is the recipient and consumer of the material ordering them. Material flows that are directly initiated by customer orders or sub-orders of different types may be considered as pull-based planning. The concept of pull, however, also includes the fact that quantities ordered for manufacture or movement are small and correspond as closely as possible to single, direct and immediate material requirements, i.e. do not constitute an economic order quantity in the traditional sense.

It is not the materials planning methods in themselves which are of a pull or push character, but rather their application, which determines whether flows of material are pull- or push-based. Most materials planning methods may be used with either pull- or push-based management. For

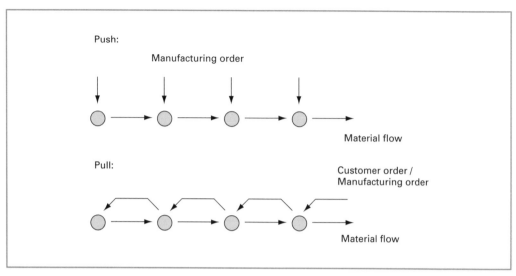

FIGURE 12.5 Illustration of push- and pull-based management

example, a re-order point method (see section 12.3) can be used by a consuming unit to order the replenishment of materials, i.e. as a pull application. The system can also be used by a central materials management department to initiate manufacturing to stock for future sales, i.e. used in the form of a push application.

12.2 Stock Functions

The flow of materials is a question of moving raw materials, materials in various degrees of processing, and products. An ideal flow of materials is made up of the continuous movement of material, including processing, from suppliers to customers in supply chains. For various reasons, such ideal flows are not possible to achieve in practice. There are differences in the speed of flows in different parts of the overall flow, since the rate of supply is not the same as the rate of consumption. In addition, flows are seldom continuous: there are generally interruptions between successive movements. Different sub-flows must be decoupled from each other, partly as a result of lack of continuity and partly to avoid inevitable disruptions in one sub-flow propagating into another sub-flow. The primary function of stocks is to achieve this decoupling. Stocks of various sorts, then, may be considered as an integrated part of the total material flow system. The relationship may be compared to ponds and lakes that serve as water reservoirs for a river whose flow varies with the time of year and whose total water system is used to generate electricity.

With respect to the type of decoupling function, we can distinguish between the following types of stocks:

- **Cycle stocks**
- **Safety stocks**
- **Levelling stocks**
- **Work in process (WIP)**

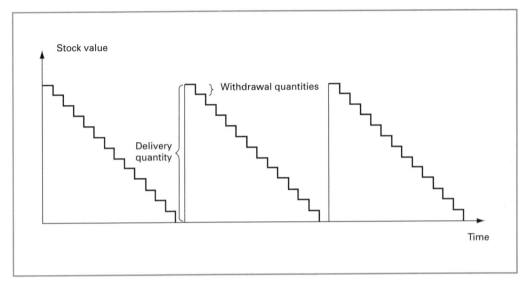

FIGURE 12.6 The origin of cycle stock

- **Co-ordination stocks**
- Synchronisation stocks
- **Speculation stocks**
- **Obsolescence stocks**

Cycle stock refers to that part of stocks which arise because inbound deliveries take place at a different pace and in larger quantities than consumption. In Figure 12.6 cycle stock is caused by the delivered quantity corresponding to 13 different withdrawals from stocks. Decoupling

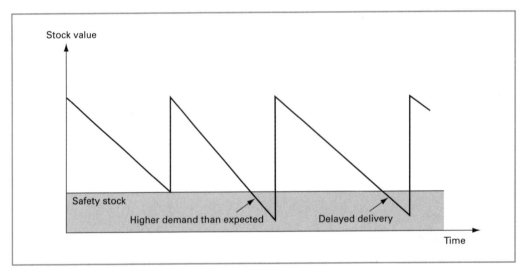

FIGURE 12.7 Safety stock functions

between stock replenishment and consumption is motivated by the fact that every order, transportation and delivery is associated with **ordering costs**, irrespective of the quantity. The larger the order quantity, the less the ordering cost per unit.

Disruptions in stock replenishment are inevitable in a material flow system. For example, inbound deliveries may be delayed, and inbound quantities may be less than expected, nor is it possible to predict future consumption perfectly. If demand is greater than predicted, the stock will be depleted earlier than expected. To decouple different processes along the flow of materials so that disruptions and the effects of delays in deliveries and unpredictable increases in demand do not propagate and result in shortages, safety stocks are used. The function of *safety stocks* is illustrated in Figure 12.7.

In many cases the consumption of goods is strongly dependent on the season, i.e. more consumption takes place during certain periods of the year. It may still be favourable to produce the goods relatively evenly – for example, to achieve an even utilisation of capacity and thereby to decrease capacity costs. In a similar way, production may be seasonal, as is the case for agricultural products even though consumption is relatively even. This is the reason for using *levelling stocks*, also called *anticipation stock*. The function of a levelling stock is thus to decouple the rate of production from the rate of consumption and allowing for a levelled production or sales plan.

Work-in-process (WIP) refers to stocks of material in the process of being manufactured in or between two consecutive production resources. This means that the different manufacturing steps involved are decoupled from each other, which makes possible different rates of manufacture in different parts of the production system. This decoupling function can be used to limit the extent of production disruptions propagating to other steps in manufacture in production processes. Work-in-process also arises due to the fact that production processes take time to be carried out.

Managing the flows of materials in a manufacturing company is a difficult task, especially if it involves complex products. It demands a lot from planning methods and working procedures to achieve the necessary co-ordination of the different sub-flows along the path to the finished product. Two types of stocks arise as a result of these difficulties. The one type, called *co-ordination stocks*, is a deliberately created stock whose purpose is to couple parallel flows of material and to gain benefits of consolidation. Co-ordination stocks arise in the case of simultaneous ordering of several items, and when ordering or delivery is regulated through a timetable. An example could be simultaneous inbound delivery of several items from the same supplier to decrease transportation costs, or simultaneous ordering for manufacture to decrease set-up costs in production resources. The other type of stock arises unintentionally and may be called *synchronisation stocks*, since their size is related to imperfections in synchronising supply, demand and material flows. In this case, too, certain items must wait for others to achieve simultaneous availability. A common example of this type of stock is items which are needed simultaneously for final assembly or packaging, but which must wait in stock for the start of assembly owing to another item being delayed in delivery or shortages in stocks. When a computer is being delivered to a customer, for example, the main unit, the keyboard and the monitor and mouse may come from different suppliers. One of them may be delayed and packaging must then be postponed, and delivery to the customer will also be delayed.

A special type of decoupling is achieved with the aid of so-called *speculation stocks*. A speculation stocking is a type of cycle stock, but its turnover is completely decoupled from short-term expected consumption. The motivation for building up a speculation stock is expected future price increases or possible market shortage of raw material.

Obsolescence stock is a further type of stock, sometimes also known as inactive stock. It means a stock of goods which is no longer expected to be consumed. In principle, the stock will be accounted for as scrap. The decoupling that takes place in obsolescence stock can be described as definite and complete decoupling from active material flows.

12.3 Materials Planning Methods

The balance between supplies and demand requirements can be maintained by new manufacturing orders and purchasing orders being planned. Different materials planning methods can be applied as a support in achieving this so that material flows are synchronised as much as possible. These methods have different characteristics and are more or less suitable for application in different planning environments. They all have in common that they respond to the materials management questions and, in different ways, the two time questions (i.e. when the order will start or be sent to the supplier, and when inbound delivery will take place) stated in the beginning of this chapter. Here we provide an overview of the most commonly used methods.

Re-order point method

A **re-order point method**, also called order point method, is a materials planning method built on comparisons made between the quantity available in stock and a reference quantity called a re-order point. When stocks fall below this reference quantity, an order is sent to replenish the stock, i.e. a manufacturing process or a replenishment process is initiated to manufacture or acquire the desired stock replenishment quantity. The principle is illustrated in Figure 12.8. The vertical lines in the figure indicate stock replenishment.

The quantity which corresponds to the re-order point refers to expected demand during the lead time for replenishment plus a safety stock quantity to protect against unpredictable variations

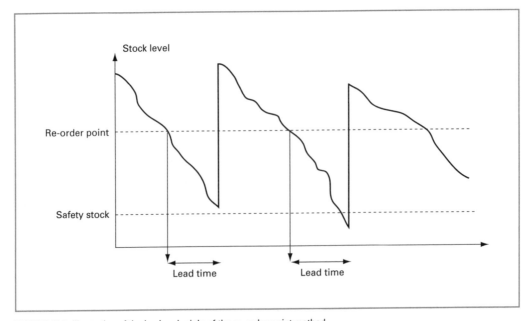

FIGURE 12.8 Illustration of the basic principle of the re-order point method

in demand. Thus the re-order point represents the forecast of demand during time, as well as the safety stock. Expected demand may be determined by using consumption statistics, forecasts or summarised gross requirements by breaking down production plans to the actual item level.

The following formula is used to calculate order points:

$$OP = SS + D \cdot LT$$

Where   OP = re-order point
           SS = safety stocks
           D = demand per time period
           LT = leadtime

Two main types of re-order point methods exist, depending on when the comparison between the re-order point and **stock balance** is made: systems with continuous comparison and systems with comparisons at predetermined constant intervals. The type that uses continuous comparison corresponds to the original re-order point method. In its practical application, comparisons are made on the basis of transactions, i.e. after every stock transaction that decreases the stock. The method using comparisons at constant intervals corresponds to the so-called **periodic review system**. Comparisons between the current stock balance and the re-order point are made after each time interval. If the value falls below the re-order point at the time of inspection, an order proposal is created, otherwise not. In its practical application this method is achieved by periodically, for example each week, running a re-order point programme in the ERP-system and from this programme obtaining order proposals for items whose stock balance falls below the actual re-order point.

By using the periodic review system, planning of new orders can be carried out as an integrated measure at regularly recurring intervals for several items at the same time, thereby making administration more efficient. Using the transaction-oriented system, the work of planning new orders is more divided and spread over time in a less controlled fashion. The periodic review system enables, to a completely different extent, consolidated ordering and consolidated delivery of items from the same supplier, which is one way of decreasing the ordering costs and transportation costs. The safety stock in the periodic review system does however need to be larger than in the transaction-oriented system.

Example 12.1

A re-order point method is used for materials management of a purchased item. Consumption of the item during leadtime has been estimated at 30 pieces on average, and the safety stock has been calculated at 8 pieces. At a certain day the stock balance is 35 pieces. Should a new purchase order be placed for the item?

With the information given about the item, the re-order point is equal to 30 + 8 = 38 pieces. Since the stock balance is 35 pieces, i.e. less than the re-order point, a new order should be placed to the supplier.

Run-out time planning

When the re-order point method is used, the re-order point is determined excluding the safety stock so that the quantity available in stock when it falls below the re-order point is calculated to cover future requirements during the replenishment leadtime. The coverage of requirements determined for a re-order point method is thus expressed as a quantity. As an alternative, it is natural to express coverage of requirements as a time instead of a quantity. **Run-out time planning** is a materials planning method that uses this concept. The method is therefore closely related to the re-order point method.

Run-out time planning, sometimes called **cover-time planning**, is the time for which available stocks, i.e. physically present stocks plus planned inbound deliveries, are expected to last. It is calculated by dividing the available stocks with expected demand per time unit. In the same way as for the re-order point method, expected demand can be determined on the basis of consumption statistics, forecasts or aggregate gross requirements by breaking down production plans to the actual item level.

In run-out time planning, a safety time is used to protect against uncertainty and variations in demand during the replenishment time. This safety time multiplied by demand per time unit is equivalent to the safety stock that is used in the re-order point method. The decision rule is to plan a new order if the run-out period is less than the replenishment time plus safety time. The delivery time is the day's date plus the item's leadtime.

In a similar way to the re-order point method, run-out time comparisons can be made when stock transactions take place or periodically in the form of joint processing of the entire range of items. Run-out time planning can, in other words, be transaction oriented or periodically recurrent. Both alternatives have the same advantages and disadvantages as the re-order point method.

Example 12.2

Run-out time planning is used as a materials planning method for planning a range of manufacturing items. The consumption of one of these items on average per week has been estimated at 15 pieces. The item's leadtime is 3 weeks and due to uncertainty of consumption one extra week's requirement is kept in stock. At a certain point in time the balance of the item is 75 pieces. Should a new manufacturing order be planned?

Since the stock balance is 75 pieces, it may be calculated that these stocks will be sufficient for a further 75 / 15 = 5 weeks. This supply time is larger than the leadtime plus the safety time, 3 + 1 = 4 weeks. Consequently, the release of a new manufacturing order can be postponed one week.

Kanban

One group of materials planning methods is characterised by the material requirement which arises in a consuming unit more or less directly initiating manufacture and/or delivery from a materials-supplying unit. The degree of direct initiation is dependent on the size of the buffer stock which for different reasons must be used. Examples of these reasons include leadtimes being too long to order with immediate delivery or that set-up or order preparation costs are too high to financially motivate manufacture and/or transportation of the direct requirement. Restrictions of this type force companies to some extent to manufacture and/or delivery quantities which cover several direct requirements.

For the majority of all materials planning methods, planned orders are registered in an ERP-system, although this is not the case for methods belonging to the **kanban** category. Instead direct call-offs are sent from consuming units to supplying units without any orders in the traditional sense. The methods are thus a reasonably pure example of a pull system.

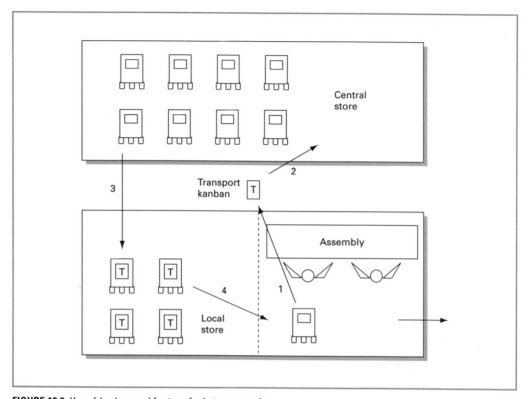

FIGURE 12.9 Use of *kanban* card for transfer between stocks

The figure shows how pallets, with transport *kanban* cards affixed, are transferred from central stores to local stores where assembly takes place.

There are two main types of *kanban* method: those based on some form of physical and visual initiation of new orders, and those based on some form of administrative initiation. Traditional *kanban* is an example of the first type. In the second type, initiation is carried out through a computerised planning system. Terms such as *electronic kanban* are used for this type. If a fax is used to send *kanban* cards, the system is called *faxban*.

The method that employs *kanban* cards is based on a limited number of cards being in circulation, that all full load carriers must contain a predefined standard quantity stated on the *kanban* card, and that all load carriers that contain materials must have a *kanban* card affixed to them. With the aid of these rules, the amount of materials in stock and in transportation or production can be controlled. The *kanban* principle for initiation of transfer of materials from stocks to an assembly unit is illustrated in Figure 12.9. The *kanban* principle is in the figure illustrated as containing four steps. When a new package of material is withdrawn from the local store, the transport *kanban* card attached to the package is removed from the package (1) and sent to the central store (2). The empty card is a signal to the central store to replenish the local store with a full package according to the instructions on the card. The card is attached to a full package at the central store and the package is moved to the local store (3) where the package with the attached card is stored until moved to the assembly station (4).

The required number of *kanban* cards is calculated by taking into consideration current lead-times for replenishment and for any safety stocks desired to protect against demand variations and other uncertainties. In the ideal case, the manufacturing order quantity and transport quantity is equivalent to the quantity on a standard load carrier used and stated on the *kanban* card. If this is not possible due to high ordering costs, multiples of these standard quantities are either manufactured or transported instead. The smallest number of cards to start manufacturing or transport is then stated on the *kanban* cards.

A large number of *kanban* variants exist. It is mainly the physical medium of the load carrier which distinguishes these variants from each other. They may be light signals, sound signals, balls, pallets or other load carriers. The traditional *kanban* method is built on the use of *kanban* cards. Manufacturing *kanban* is used to order manufacturing, and transport *kanban* is used to order movement or transportation. Two *kanban* card systems combine manufacturing and transportation *kanban*. There are also single card systems, in which the *kanban* card initiates both manufacturing and transportation.

Material requirements planning (MRP)

The above materials planning methods are based on the principle that new orders are planned when consumption has taken place, i.e. they are consumption initiated. **Material requirements planning (MRP)** is a materials planning method that is instead based on the points in time when net requirement of materials arises, i.e. when future calculated stock availability becomes negative. MRP is thus a requirement-initiated materials-planning method. The principle is illustrated in Table 12.1. As is clear from the table, stocks are estimated to become negative in week 6. A new order must therefore be planned for delivery during that week to avoid shortages. In the example in the table, the order quantity is 60 pieces and the leadtime 3 weeks, which means that the manufacturing order must start or the purchasing order must be registered in week 3.

Protection against uncertainty in the requirements and supplies that are part of material requirements planning can be achieved with the aid of safety stocks or safety time. If safety stocks are used, the starting stock availability is reduced by the selected safety stock quantity before the calculation of net requirements is started. If safety time is used instead, the point in time of delivery for the planned order is the same as the calculated requirement time minus the selected safety time.

MRP is applicable to dependent and independent requirements. When it is used for planning independent materials requirements, the method is called **time-phased order point**. It may be regarded as an alternative to the traditional re-order point method.

Week		1	2	3	4	5	6	7
Forecast/requirement		15	15	15	20	20	20	20
Projected available inventory	40	25	70	55	35	15	−5	−25
Planned order delivery			60					
Planned order start				60 ◄				

TABLE 12.1 Calculation method for material requirements planning
Starting stocks are 40 pieces in the calculation example.

Calculating MRP plans

If MRP is used for items with dependent and traced requirements, i.e. for materials incorporated in products, a requirements breakdown is included in the method with the help of bill-of-materials (see Figure 12.2). This breakdown procedure using bill-of-materials is called **explosion**. The starting point for MRP is a production plan stating in what quantities and when a company's final products are to be manufactured and delivered to stock or to customers. From this production plan, material requirements are exploded to underlying structural levels. Requirements are "netted" to available stock balance and already planned deliveries. To cover residual **net requirements**, new orders are planned. From planned orders the explosion continues through levels of product structures as far as raw materials and purchased items at the lowest structural levels. Irrespective of the structural level, net requirements are calculated for each item in periods and new orders are planned in the same way as when the method is applied to items with independent requirements. The real difference is that in the case of independent requirements, the calculation is based on some form of forecast, while the calculation for items with traced requirements is based on requirements traced and calculated from manufacturing orders for higher levels in the bill-of-materials.

The explosion from a production plan and MRP of incorporated components is illustrated in Figure 12.10. According to the production plan, a manufacturing order for 250 chairs of model A will be started in week 5 and a manufacturing order of 100 chairs of model B in weeks 4, 5 and 6. For models A and B, four chair legs of the same type are used. The gross requirement of chair legs during weeks 4, 5 and 6 will then be as shown in the lower part of the figure. The stock of 1890 legs available will cover requirements for weeks 4 and 5, but to manage the assembly requirement in week 6 the new order for manufacturing chair legs must be planned at the start of week 4 for delivery in week 6, since the leadtime is two weeks. This procedure is called leadtime offsetting. The order created for 1800 chair legs generates in turn a purchase order for raw materials at a lower structural level.

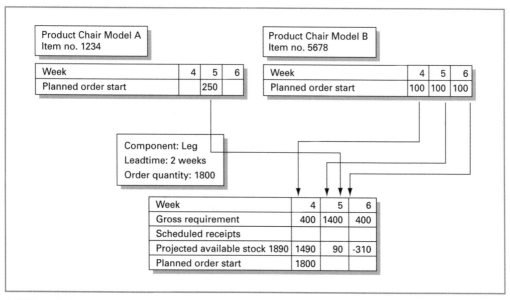

FIGURE 12.10 Breakdown from production plan and MRP

Distribution requirements planning (DRP)

The principle of MRP can also be used to control material flows between stocks in distribution networks. We then talk about **distribution requirements planning (DRP)**. In common with MRP, DRP is based on the principle that material flows should not be estimated from forecasts if they can be calculated from demand instead. In a distribution network, demand normally needs to be forecast only for end customers. Demand from a consuming stock to a supplying stock can be calculated on the basis of planned stock replenishment orders. One prerequisite for DRP is that the distribution structures in the network can be specified in the same way as bill-of-materials used for MRP. Such distribution structures state, among other things, which stocks supply which other stocks, and how long the leadtime is for transportation between stocks in the network.

The principle of DRP is illustrated with the aid of the example in Table 12.2. Three local stores, A, B and C, are supplied from a central store. Demand has been forecast for each local stock. With the aid of these forecasts and DRP, the requirements of new stock replenishment orders for each of the other stores have been calculated. The leadtime for replenishment from the central store is two weeks in all cases. The three stock replenishment orders created constitute traced demand on the central store. With the aid of this traced demand, orders for replenishing the central store can be planned; in the example, a stock replenishment order of 1200 pieces for delivery in week 5. The leadtime for replenishing the central store is four weeks.

12.4 Lot Sizing

Materials planning methods treat the time dimension of materials management, i.e. they support calculation of when manufacturing orders will start or items be delivered from suppliers. As described, the balancing of supplies and requirements contains not only a time dimension but also a quantity dimension. It means that the quantity to be delivered must be determined for every order planned in the flow of materials. In an ideally synchronised flow, this order quantity is equal to the quantity for which there is a current requirement, i.e. if there is a

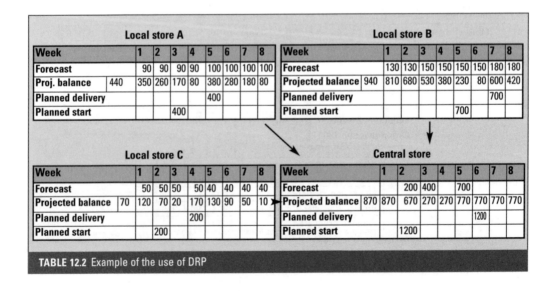

Local store A

Week		1	2	3	4	5	6	7	8
Forecast		90	90	90	90	100	100	100	100
Proj. balance	440	350	260	170	80	380	280	180	80
Planned delivery					400				
Planned start				400					

Local store B

Week		1	2	3	4	5	6	7	8
Forecast		130	130	150	150	150	150	180	180
Projected balance	940	810	680	530	380	230	80	600	420
Planned delivery								700	
Planned start						700			

Local store C

Week		1	2	3	4	5	6	7	8
Forecast		50	50	50	50	40	40	40	40
Projected balance	70	120	70	20	170	130	90	50	10
Planned delivery					200				
Planned start				200					

Central store

Week		1	2	3	4	5	6	7	8
Forecast			200	400		700			
Projected balance	870	870	670	270	270	770	770	770	770
Planned delivery						1200			
Planned start		1200							

TABLE 12.2 Example of the use of DRP

The figure shows the percentage of manufacturing companies using different material planning methods according to a survey conducted among manufacturing companies in different industries.

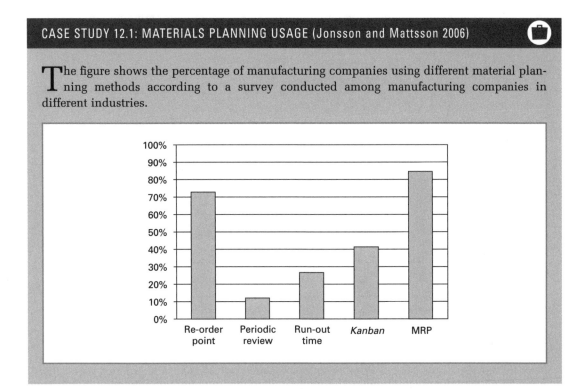

requirement for three pieces of a certain item on a certain day, these three pieces are delivered on that day. Under such conditions there is no need for any stocks to decouple the flow of supplies from the flow of consumption.

For different reasons it is often not suitable or even possible to only manufacture and deliver the quantity of goods required at any single point in time. Requirements from a number of consumption or delivery events must be consolidated into larger quantities. This consolidation process is called **lot sizing**, or establishing appropriate order quantities. Manufacturing and acquiring larger quantities than immediate requirements dictate result in cycle stocks. This also means that the planning of material flow has an element of push, even though it is the consuming unit which initiates the material flow.

The reasons for lot sizing can be roughly divided into financial and non-financial types. Non-financial types are characterised by the suitability and in certain cases even necessity of manufacturing or acquiring larger quantities than required for the moment, even though there is no financial motivation. As an example, when acquiring goods it is often necessary to accept one whole package quantity or one full pallet. The manufacturing process in use may be forced to use a certain quantity, such as a vessel for mixing and boiling a chemical product or a foodstuffs product must be utilised at its full volume.

Financial motivation for lot sizing

A decisive reason for determining a lot size that deviates from the direct requirements quantity is of a financial nature. Every order and delivery is associated with ordering costs, i.e. all the incremental costs which are associated with executing an order process for the acquisition of

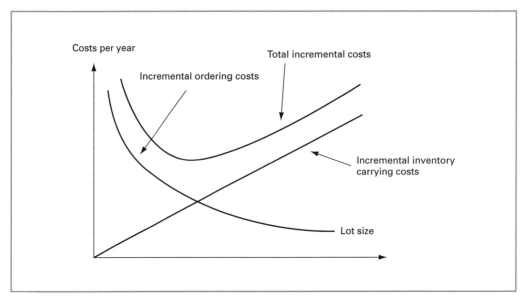

FIGURE 12.11 Relationship between ordering costs and incremental inventory carrying costs

items from external suppliers, or from the company's own manufacture. The ordering cost is the sum of the re-tooling and dismantling (set-up) costs, costs for capacity losses, material handling costs and order processing costs at a specific ordering occasion (the ordering costs are described in more detail in Chapter 5). Depending on the ordering situation, certain of these costs are incremental costs and must be included in the ordering costs used in lot sizing. In general, these incremental costs are independent of the quantities ordered. The larger the order quantity is, the lower the incremental ordering cost per unit will be. This relationship obviously indicates large order quantities.

If, however, order quantities are larger than those needed for immediate requirements, the excess quantity will have to be stored until it is consumed or delivered. This results in increased **incremental inventory carrying costs** (as defined in Appendix B). The incremental inventory carrying costs can in general be assumed to be proportional to the value of the stock, i.e. the quantity stored multiplied by the standard price or average price for the item in question. In other words, the incremental inventory carrying costs increase at the same rate as the quantity stored.

The relationship between lot size, incremental ordering costs and incremental inventory carrying costs respectively is shown in Figure 12.11. Since incremental inventory carrying costs increase and incremental ordering costs per item decrease with increasing lot sizes, the selection of a suitable lot size is obviously determined by balancing these two cost items. Determining a suitable lot size is thus a question of optimising the sum of incremental inventory carrying and ordering costs, and the term used for this is **economic order quantity (EOQ)**. The majority of all lot-sizing methods for the calculation of economically optimum order quantities are based on this type of balance.

The cost curve in Figure 12.11 is reasonably level. This means that additional costs will not be especially large if for various reasons a company needs to deviate from the economically optimum order quantity. Due to this relationship, it is possible to round off calculated quantities to even figures – for example, to round up an order quantity to 200 even though the economic order quantity has been calculated at 181. It is also acceptable to round off calculated economic order quantities to multiples of packaging quantities, full load bearers and so on. Finally, it is acceptable to a certain extent to adapt order quantities to the price and discount structure of a supplier. If the order quantity is of great significance for the price or discount available, it may be more suitable to use lot-sizing methods for calculating economic order quantities, which can take into consideration existing price and discount structures.

Lot-sizing methods

Many lot-sizing methods have been developed and used since the first method for calculating economic order quantities was presented at the start of the twentieth century. Here some of the more commonly used methods are described.

Estimated order quantity

This lot-sizing method could be called estimated order quantity and means that the selection of an order quantity is based on a manual and experienced assessment of what is a suitable quantity to manufacture or acquire each time. The assessment is based on estimated annual consumption, price, how resource-demanding the order process is, risk of obsolescence, and so on.

Economic order quantity

Order quantities can also be calculated by the trade-off between incremental ordering costs and incremental inventory carrying costs. Through the relationship illustrated in Figure 12.11 and the optimisation of total incremental costs, the following formula for calculating economic order quantity (EOQ) may be derived:

$$EOQ = \sqrt{\frac{2 \cdot D \cdot O}{i \cdot c}}$$

Where   D = demand per time unit
   O = incremental ordering or set-up cost per order event
   i = incremental inventory carrying cost in % per item and time unit
   c = unit cost/goods value per item

This formula is often called the *Wilson formula* or the *square root formula*. The derivation of the formula is shown in Appendix C. There are a number of reasonably simple assumptions behind the derivation: the delivery of whole-order quantities takes place instantaneously, unit price is not affected by order quantity, and shortages do not occur. There is no optimisation in a strict sense with respect to the relationships in a normally occurring planning situation. Considering the rather level total cost curve, the formula provides a satisfactory basis for decisions to determine suitable order quantities from a cost perspective. The formula is widely used in industry. In addition to being able to take into consideration costs associated with material flows, the lot-sizing method compared with estimated order quantity also has the advantage of automatic calculation and storage in the ERP-system. It is then easier and more rational to update what constitutes suitable order quantities when conditions in the planning environment change: for example, when demand increases or decreases.

Example 12.3

For lot sizing a purchased item, the economic order quantity is calculated using Wilson's formula. The incremental ordering costs have been estimated for executing a replenishment of Euro 400, the purchase price of the item is Euro 100, and the annual incremental inventory carrying costs have been determined as 25 per cent of the item unit cost. The annual demand for the item has been estimated at 2000 pieces, and the package size provided by the supplier contains 50 pieces. How large should the order quantity be for each replenishment?

Using Wilson's formula, we obtain

$$EOQ = \sqrt{\frac{2 \cdot 2\,000 \cdot 400}{100 \cdot 0.25}} = 252 \; pieces$$

Since the package contains 50 pieces, the order quantity is rounded off to 250 pieces.

Both the estimated order quantity and the economic order quantity mean in principle that a fixed order quantity is used. What the use of a fixed order quantity entails can be illustrated with the aid of Table 12.3. This reflects the situation for an item that is included in a product, in the case that materials management is based on MRP and that consequently there is information on expected future requirements. The fixed order quantity for the item is 30 pieces.

Week	1	2	3	4	5	6	7	8	9
Net requirement	10	6	19	8	13	27	17	12	6
Order quantity	30		30			30	30		
Projected available inventory	20	14	25	17	4	7	20	8	2

TABLE 12.3 Stock development when using fixed order quantities

Lot-for-lot

The lot-sizing method **lot-for-lot** means that orders are created for each requirement and that the different order quantities are equal to each required quantity. This means that there is no real lot sizing, since order quantities correspond to required quantities, and no requirement consolidation or storage occurs as in the case of cycle stock. The method may be considered as a special case of the next lot sizing methods, i.e. **periodic order quantity** with a period length of one period.

Lot for lot is primarily used for customer order controlled material flows, expensive products and components in planning environments with small set-up costs. When planning for items that make up semi-finished goods and purchased components, it is more commonly used at the upper structural levels, i.e. close to the finished product in the product structure, than at the lower structural levels.

Estimated run-out time

The lot-sizing method estimated run-out time means that the order quantity is chosen to cover a whole number of planning periods, for example, weeks or days. In the same way as for estimated order quantity, the selection of the number of periods is based on a manual and experienced assessment of what may be a suitable time period to cover on each occasion. Assessments are based here, too, on estimated annual consumption, price, how resource-demanding it is to execute the order process, risk of obsolescence, and so on.

Irrespective of whether the run-out-time is manually estimated or economically calculated, the order quantity is stated as a run-out time expressed in a number of periods. The order quantity is calculated on each order occasion, based on the number of periods and the current requirements during those periods. Two alternatives exist. In the material requirements planning environment, the order quantity is calculated by adding together forecast requirements, reservations and material requirements broken down from upper structural levels over the number of periods selected. If consumption-initiated methods are used instead, e.g. the re-order point method, the order quantity is calculated as the number of periods multiplied by the forecast average demand per period.

Economic run-out time

As an alternative, the run-out time can also be calculated as a trade-off between incremental ordering costs and incremental carrying costs, i.e. so that the total incremental costs associated with storage are optimised. This can be done by first calculating the economic order quantity (EOQ) and subsequently the economic run-out time in periods (ECT), with the aid of the following formula:

$$ECT = \frac{EOQ}{D}$$

where D = average demand per period.

By calculating the run-out time in this way, the average order quantities will be equal to the economic order quantity. The use of the lot-sizing method "run-out time" is illustrated in Table 12.4, with the same demand data as for the example in Table 12.3. The run-out time in the example is three weeks. Note that the order quantities in this planning environment are completely adapted to whole weeks' requirements.

Week	1	2	3	4	5	6	7	8	9
Net requirement	10	6	19	8	13	27	17	12	6
Order quantity	35			48			35		
Projected available inventory	25	19	0	40	27	0	18	6	0

TABLE 12.4 Stock development using the lot-sizing method "run-out time"

Example 12.4

At a company, a number of items are purchased from the same supplier. To be able to consolidate inbound deliveries, lot sizing is used with the aid of economic run-out time. Deliveries are wanted only every second, every fourth or every eighth week. For one of the items, the economic order quantity has been calculated using Wilson's formula at 700 pieces, and the average demand per week has been estimated to 170 pieces. How long should the run-out time period for each item be?

The economic run-out time for the item is equal to 700 / 170 = 4.12 weeks. For reasons of consolidated deliveries, the run-out time is rounded off to four weeks.

One of the advantages of using lot-sizing techniques based on run-out time is that order sizes to a certain extent automatically adjust to changes in demand, and thus it is not necessary to update run-out times as frequently as order quantities. If, for example, demand increases, the quantity required during the run-out time will increase and thus the order quantity will increase too, which is entirely reasonable considering the increase in demand.

CASE STUDY 12.2: LOT-SIZING METHODS USED (Jonsson and Mattsson, 2006)

The figure shows the usage of lot-sizing methods when conducting materials planning using the MRP method, according to a survey conducted among manufacturing companies in different industries.

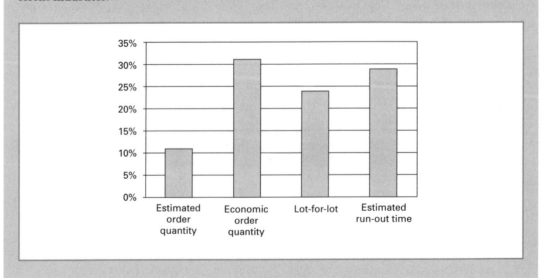

12.5 Safety Stock Determination

Supplies and demand requirements in material flows can never be completely synchronised. It is especially difficult with respect to the time dimension, i.e. to co-ordinate inbound deliveries of materials in time with outbound deliveries governed by demand. In all material flows, some materials requirements uncertainties exist. Disruptions in the flows which occur for different reasons from supplying units to consuming units also make the supply situation uncertain. Thus, there are elements of uncertainty in material flows regarding both requirement and supplies, and these are made up of quantity uncertainties and time uncertainties. To control these elements of uncertainty, companies must use different types of safety mechanisms, primarily safety stocks and **safety times**.

Uncertainties of future requirements are primarily quantity uncertainties, i.e. uncertainties regarding what quantities may be consumed or demanded in the future. At the product level, this uncertainty may relate to volumes of a unique product or product models, but also uncertainties regarding the distribution of demand for different variants of a certain product model.

On the supply side, uncertainties relate primarily to errors in the current stock balance, to what extent suppliers will deliver the quantities ordered, and to what extent quantities delivered to the company must be scrapped due to non-compliance with stipulated quality demands. Compared with the uncertainties on the demand side, these uncertainties are in general relatively small. The greatest uncertainties on the supply side are instead related to time, i.e. uncertainty regarding when an expected delivery will really become available. This time uncertainty is connected to the supplier's and own production's deficiencies in always delivering on time.

Uncertainty hedging

There are two principally different approaches to uncertainty hedging: *quantity hedging* and *time hedging*. Quantity hedging means that a company tries to have larger quantities available than what are really expected to be required. These are called safety stocks. The second approach is time hedging, meaning that inbound deliveries are deliberately placed earlier in relation to requirement times. In this case it is called safety time instead of safety stocks. Irrespective of whether safety stocks or safety time is used to hedge against uncertainties, the use of these strategies will result in larger stocks than otherwise. This type of stock is called safety stock.

An illustration of the difference between quantity hedging and time hedging is shown in Table 12.5. In the upper case, quantity hedging is used in the form of safety stock, and this safety stock is subtracted from the stock balance of 60 pieces before available stocks are calculated week by week. The calculations result in a new order being planned for delivery in week 5, so that the 10 units in the safety stock can be used without a shortage arising. In the lower case, time hedging is used. There is no deduction of the safety stock in this case. Instead, inbound deliveries are planned one week before stockout to hedge against the risk of a delayed delivery. In both cases the planned order has the same delivery time, since the safety stock in the upper case is equivalent to one week's consumption and thus causes a shift in delivery time of one week.

In general, quantity hedging is to be preferred if there is an issue of quantity uncertainty, and time hedging in the case of time uncertainty. Quantity hedging can also work well against time uncertainty if the individual material requirement that occurs is small in relation to the annual consumption. The safety stock used in such conditions may cover several periods' requirements if a delay in delivery should occur. The larger the individual period's requirements are in relation

Week		1	2	3	4	5	6	7
Requirement		10	10	10	10	10	10	10
Projected available inv.	60–10	40	30	20	10	0 ↓		
Planned receipt						40		
Week		1	2	3	4	5	6	7
Requirement		10	10	10	10	10	10	10
Projected available inv.	60	50	40	30	20	10	0	
Planned receipt						40 ←		

TABLE 12.5 Quantity guarding as compared with time guarding against uncertainties

to annual consumption, the lower are the possibilities of hedging against time uncertainties using quantity-based safety stocks. Very large safety stocks would be required.

Financial motives for safety stocks and safety leadtimes

Econmic order quantities are determined by balancing ordering costs and inventory carrying costs. Similarly, safety stocks can be determined by balancing shortage costs and inventory carrying costs. The larger the safety stock is, the lower the shortage costs and the higher the inventory carrying costs are. The economically optimum safety stock could consequently be obtained by minimising the sum of these two costs.

All costs that arise as a result of a demanded product or other item not being in stock when required are called *shortage costs*. There may be loss of income due to unrealised sales, damages for delayed delivery, or costs for back-orders and extra transportation. Shortage costs may also be costs for production disruptions and reduced utilisation of capacity as a result of lack of start-up materials. In general it is very difficult to estimate shortage costs satisfactorily. They are seldom predictable, and their size depends to a large extent on the situation when the shortage occurs. For this reason shortage costs and economic optimisation are seldom used to determine the size of safety stocks. To achieve a balance between shortage costs and inventory carrying costs, policy-determined **service levels** are used instead. An inventory service level is a measurement of the extent to which shortages in stocks can be avoided. It is stated as a percentage and can be defined in different ways, as described in Chapter 4.

The use of safety stocks and safety times will incur costs and sacrifice resources. There are often good reasons for distinguishing between the size of safety stocks and safety times so that the maximum utility effect of a given resource is achieved, for example in the form of tied-up capital. With the aid of some of the safety stock methods presented in the next section, this is achieved by taking into account variations in demand, forecast errors, leadtimes, etc. Such considerations are individually oriented and relate to individual items. In many contexts there may be reasons for differentiating of safety stocks and safety times from a holistic perspective. For products sold to customers, for example, it may be justified to have relatively large safety stocks of those products that are sold in large volumes or which have high profit contribution. Similarly, it may be justified to have larger safety stocks of spare parts which are critical components for customers' plants or which are under fierce competition from pirate manufacturers. It may also be justified to have longer safety times for suppliers that have previously proved to be unreliable in their delivery times.

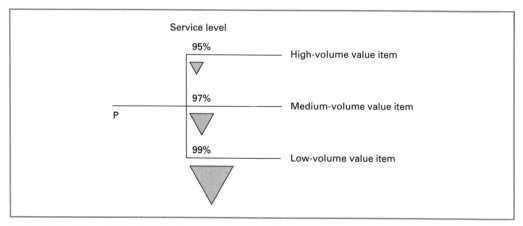

FIGURE 12.12 Differentiation of service levels related to item volume value
The size of the triangles represents different safety stock sizes.

Differentiating safety stocks and safety times is also justified for items that are in the production process and whose material flows converge at nodes in product structures. Hedging against uncertainties in this context is one way of handling the problems associated with synchronisation of material flows, which were discussed earlier in this chapter. For items whose material flows meet at such nodes, shortage costs may be the same irrespective of the cost of each item. Disruption in production may occur whether it is a cheap or expensive item missing, and shortage costs are more connected with the disruption in production than which item is missing. To allocate safety stocks as economically as possible to hedge against such disruptions, the safety stock should be sized higher for low-volume value items than for high-volume value items. This may take place by differentiating between service levels in relation to item volume value, for example using an ABC analysis using volume value (see Appendix A). For the same reason, safety times can be differentiated so that high-volume value items will be given shorter safety times than low-volume value items. The principle for differentiating safety stocks is illustrated with the aid of an example in Figure 12.12. The example refers to a product P that consists of three different incorporated items: one high-volume value item with a service level of 95 per cent, one medium-volume value item with a service level of 97 per cent, and one low-volume value item with a service level of 99 per cent.

Safety stock methods

To determine safety stocks, there are a number of different methods developed and used in industry. The most common are described below.

Manually estimated safety stocks or safety times

A simple approach to determining safety stocks and safety times is to make manual estimates on the basis of experience. In such estimates consideration should be taken to the effect on tied-up capital and storage costs, as well us to the consequences of any shortage in stocks or delayed deliveries. The estimated safety stocks and safety times must be manually registered in the ERP-system database. It is thus relatively labour-intensive and not rational to revise safety stocks and safety times so that they reflect changing conditions in the planning environment – for example, in changes to demand variations, changes in scrapping rates, or supplier behaviour.

Item A:
Demand per week: 18 – 21 – 19 – 20 – 20 – 18 – 22 – 20 – 19 – 23
Mean demand per week: 20 pcs

Item B:
Demand per week: 44 – 0 – 4 – 8 – 12 – 0 – 48 – 20 – 0 – 64
Mean demand per week: 20 pcs

TABLE 12.6 Example of items with different variations in demand but with the same average demand

Safety stocks as a percentage of leadtime demand

Another simplified method for calculating safety stocks is to size the stock as a percentage of the **leadtime** demand. The safety stock size will then be coupled to the size of demand and the lead-time. The safety stock can then easily be updated as changes in demand and leadtime arise. The method also enables the sizes of safety stocks to be systematically differentiated by using different percentages for different item groups. The disadvantage is that this method does not take into consideration variations in demand or forecast errors. The consequences are illustrated in Table 12.6. The time series for both items refers to historic demand per week over a 10 week period. Since they have the same average demand per week, they will have equally large safety stocks if they have the same leadtimes. The variation in demand for item B is considerably larger than that of item A. Thus, there should be a larger safety stock of item B than of item A to achieve the same safeguard against shortages with future variations in demand.

Safety stocks calculated by desired service level

Determining safety stocks on the basis of desired inventory service levels and variations in demand for each item is the most correct approach. It is then possible to couple sizing of safety stocks to overall goals for service levels to customers, and the level of disruptions in the flow of materials that are unacceptable in production. In the same way, the size of safety stocks will be adapted to the degree of uncertainty for each item. Basing safety stock calculation on selected service levels also enables safety stocks to be differentiated on the basis of relevant relationships for each item, for example, through different service levels for different groups of items.

To size safety stocks with the aid of this method, the following formula may be used:

$$SS = k \cdot \sigma$$

Where   SS = safety stock
           k   = safety factor calculated by desired service level
           σ   = standard deviation of demand during leadtime, i.e. measurement of how much demand varies during the time it takes to replenish stocks

The theoretical background to the formula is illustrated in Figure 12.13. Curve A shows the maximum conceivable consumption during the leadtime, curve B shows the most probable consumption, and curve C shows the smallest conceivable consumption. Curve D represents the probability of consumption lying between maximum and minimum values. By setting the safety stock at $k \cdot \sigma$, demand during the leadtime to replenish the stock will be at most equivalent to the average leadtime consumption plus the safety stock at a probability level equivalent to the desired service level. The standard deviation of demand can be calculated by multiplying the mean absolute deviation (MAD) by a factor of 1.25. For the situation in the example in 11.4, the standard deviation of demand will be 9.3 pieces (7.3 multiplied by 1.25) per period. If the lead-time variation is small or the leadtime short, uncertainties in leadtime may be ignored and the standard deviation for demand during leadtime may be calculated using the formula below:

$$\sigma = \sigma_t \cdot \sqrt{LT}$$

σ = standard deviation of demand during leadtime
σ_t = standard deviation of demand per time unit
LT = leadtime mean value

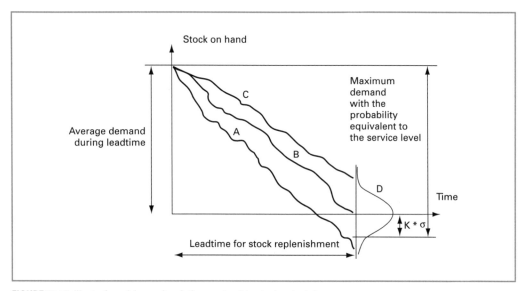

FIGURE 12.13 Illustration of demand variations and safety stock calculation

It can often be assumed that the variation in demand has a normal distribution. If the service level is defined as the probability of not having a shortage during one inventory cycle, the safety factor can be determined directly using a normal distribution table, and safety stocks necessary to achieve the desired service level can be calculated with the aid of the above formula. The inventory cycle is defined as the time between two consecutive inbound deliveries. The service level defined in this way is often referred to as **cycle service**. An extract from a normal distri-bution table is shown in Appendix D.

Example 12.5

Demand for an item can be assumed to be normally distributed with an average value of 2000 pieces per week and a standard deviation of 500 pieces per week. The leadtime on average is two weeks. How large must the safety stock be to achieve a service level of 95 per cent?

According to the normal distribution table in Appendix D, a service level of 95 per cent corresponds to a **safety factor** of 1.65. This means that the safety stock will be equal to

$$1.65 \cdot 500 \cdot \sqrt{2} = 1667 \text{ pieces}$$

The service level can also be defined as the proportion of demand that can be satisfied directly from stocks. This service level is often called **demand fill rate**. When this service level definition is used, the **service function** must first be calculated using the following formula:

$$E(z) = \frac{(1 - FR) \cdot Q}{\sigma}$$

Where σ = standard deviation of demand during leadtime
Q = order quantity on average
FR = demand fill rate

When the value of the service function has been calculated, the corresponding safety factor can be read off in a service function table, and the safety stock calculated with the aid of the above formula. An extract from a service function table is shown in Appendix E.

Example 12.6

The demand for an item is normally distributed with an average value of 2000 pieces per week and a standard deviation of 1000 pieces per week. The leadtime is one week. The order quantity for replenishment of stocks is 10 000 pieces. How large must the safety stock be to achieve a service level of 98 per cent? The service level is defined as the proportion of demand that can be satisfied directly from stocks (i.e. demand fill rate).

Using the formula for service function, $E(z) = (1 - 0.98) \cdot 10\,000 / 1000 = 0.20$.

From the table in Appendix E, it can be seen that the safety factor k is equal to 0.49. Consequently, the safety stock will be equal to $0.49 \cdot 1000 = 490$ pieces.

Safety stocks expressed as time

In the same way as for order quantities, safety stocks can be expressed in the form of run-out time. Time in periods, for example days or weeks, is calculated by dividing the safety stock quantity already determined by the average demand per period, i.e. in the same way that run-out time was calculated for lot sizing. The time calculated is stored in the ERP system database. On each material planning occasion for which information on current safety stocks is required, the time is multiplied by the current average demand per time unit. This way of expressing safety stocks has the advantage that the size of stocks is automatically adjusted to changes in the size of demand, for example, in the case of seasonal variations. Safety stocks, in contrast, do not adjust to changes in demand variations. It should be noted that the calculated time is not the same as a safety time. It is merely another way of expressing a safety stock in the form of a time.

Example 12.7

For an item with seasonal variation in demand, the size of the safety stock is expressed in the form of a desired run-out time which has been set at 2 weeks. During the two months of the year in which demand is highest, this is 200 pieces per week, whereas for the two months with lowest demand the figure is 50 pieces per week. How large will the safety stock be on average during the high season months and low season months respectively?

During the high season months, the safety stock will be $2 \cdot 200 = 400$ pieces, and during the low season months it will be $2 \cdot 50 = 100$ pieces.

12.6 Stock Accounting

Access to materials is made up of the quantities in stock at a company, among other things. To make it possible to take into consideration such stocks when managing materials, the quantities in stock must be known and so there must be some form of **stock accounting**, i.e. a unit which keeps track of the current stock balance.

There are two methods of accounting stock balance in a company: transactional stock accounting and periodic stock accounting. Transactional stock accounting is the more common of the two and means that the stock balance is updated as transactions take place that affect the balance. When inbound deliveries are made, these are added to the balance, and when items are withdrawn they are subtracted from the balance. Periodic stock accounting means that the balance is only updated when required, by physically counting the remaining quantity in stock.

Inbound deliveries

Inbound deliveries, from the stock accounting point of view, mean that the quantity in stock increases by the quantity delivered. Such deliveries may be of different types. It may be a question of deliveries from an external supplier, or from the company's own workshop, depending on whether the items are purchased or manufactured internally. There may also be transfers from another storage place or from one location to another in the same stores. Finally, there may be a return delivery from an external customer who has made a complaint, or from the company workshop because too large a quantity has been withdrawn.

Irrespective of the type of inbound delivery, it is important that the delivered quantity goes through quality control before it is placed in stock. This quality control is carried out on reception of goods or directly after production in an internal or external workshop. The aim of quality control is to ascertain as far as possible that the quantities in stock are satisfactory for production or outbound delivery to customers, otherwise the analyses of available to promise as described in Chapter 11 will provide incorrect information. Other problems may also occur as a result of shortages that arise.

Stock withdrawals

Withdrawals from stock are the opposite of deliveries, i.e. the stock balance decreases through withdrawal transactions, which may be of five different types. Withdrawals may take place through customer orders or manufacturing orders. Withdrawals may also take place in conjunction with transfer of quantities from one storage point to another, and from one location in a store to another location. Finally, withdrawals may be of the indirect type, i.e. withdrawals for unspecified consumption.

Customer order withdrawals are reported in order lines, the stock balance being updated at the same time. There are three different types of withdrawal to manufacturing order. One involves every withdrawal of material being reported and the stock balance updated at the same time. Another means that the stock balance of incoming material is automatically updated with the aid of product structures as finished items are reported in. For example, if there is an order for the manufacture of four-legged chairs and 100 chairs are reported as finished, the stock balance for legs will be decreased by 400 pieces. This approach is illustrated in Figure 12.14. **Back flushing** is a common term for this type of automatic stock balance updating.

Automatic stock balance updating in conjunction with reporting of manufacturing orders means that the stock balance for input items is not updated in conjunction with actual withdrawals from stocks when picking takes place. The physical stock balance will therefore be lower in certain periods than the administrative stock balance as shown by the stock accounting system. Available to promise will still be correct, however, since reservations for manufacturing orders will remain until stock balances are updated.

The third main alternative for withdrawals, reporting to manufacturing order, means that withdrawals take place for consumption in general, without being reported to or debited from any particular manufacturing order. Withdrawals from stocks are accounted as costs on the general expense account when the stock balance is updated. The application of this third alternative means that quantities are withdrawn from stocks to cover current requirements during a certain period, for example one week or one month, irrespective of which manufacturing order

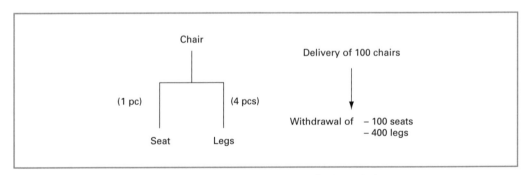

FIGURE 12.14 Stock balance updating with the aid of product structures (back flushing)

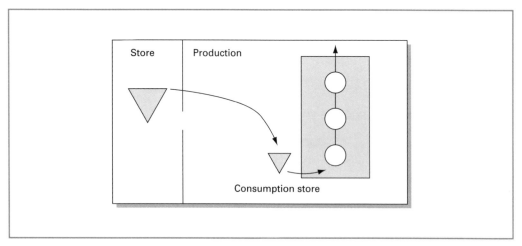

FIGURE 12.15 Withdrawals from stock to a consumption store in the production department

they relate to. The quantities are " stored" in the factory next to production in a general consumption store, also called floor stocks, hand stocks or weekly consumption stocks.

The principle is illustrated in Figure 12.15. Withdrawals from consumption stocks are not reported, the stock is not included in stock accounts and it does not represent any value entered in the accounts. This alternative is primarily useful for low-value items that would need to be picked and reported often if they were handled using the two previous methods.

The three alternatives for stock accounting can also be used in combination with each other. For example, in the case of high-value items it is possible to pick and report every withdrawal for manufacturing orders while low-value items are withdrawn from consumption stock without being associated with any particular manufacturing order.

Cycle counting

Using the materials planning methods outlined above presupposes that information is available on the current stock balance at the time of planning. These stock balances are updated through reporting of withdrawals and deliveries. For various reasons, there may still be differences between the stock balance shown in the system and the real, physical stock balance. Examples of such reasons are errors made in reporting, wastage or stock movements not reported through forgetfulness. **Cycle counting** is an administrative process aimed at correcting any errors that may have arisen, i.e. tallying the reported stock balance with the real, physical stock balance.

Cycle counting is carried out by counting the quantities of the various items in stock and correcting the reported stock balance so that it corresponds to the quantities counted. As an aid to this work, the cycle count request from the ERP-system may be printed out as in the illustration in Figure 12.16.

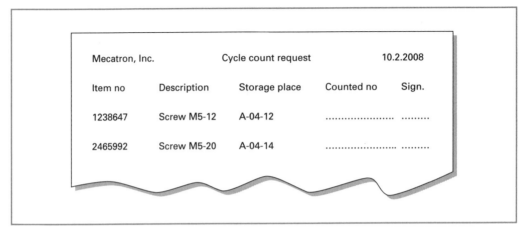

FIGURE 12.16 Example of cycle count request

12.7 Conclusion and Summary

Materials management is aimed at planning manufacturing orders and purchasing orders so that materials are available when required. This takes place through the determination of quantities ordered and delivery times for each order. How it is achieved depends to a certain extent on whether the requirements to be satisfied are independent or dependent, and if they are related to push- or pull-based control.

There are a large number of methods available for determining delivery times. For example, the re-order point method, run-out time planning, *kanban*, and materials requirements planning. There are also different methods for determining order quantities, or lot-sizing methods. Economic order quantities and run-out times are examples of these. They are based on minimising the sum of incremental inventory carrying costs and incremental ordering costs.

As a result of uncertainties in requirements and supplies, it is not possible to fully determine when inbound delivery will take place. To compensate for this uncertainty, safety stocks are used, which are sized on the basis of experience or for a desired service level. If materials management relates to items in stock, there must be information about what quantities are in stock for the desired delivery times to be calculated. For this purpose, all inbound deliveries and withdrawals are reported from the stores. Stock accounting also includes cycle counting, to check from time to time that real quantities in stock correspond with quantity information in the ERP-system, which materials management is based on.

🔓 Key concepts

Back flushing 292

Bill-of-material (BOM) 265

Co-ordination stock 270

Cover-time planning 274

Cycle counting 293

Cycle service 289

Cycle stock 269

Demand fill rate 290

Dependent demand 264

Distribution requirements planning
    (DRP) 278

Economic order quantity (EOQ) 280

Exploded material requirement 265

Explosion 277

Gross requirement 265

Incremental inventory carrying cost 280

Independent demand 264

Kanban 274

Leadtime 288

Levelling stock 269

Lot-for-lot 282

Lot sizing 279

Material requirements planning
    (MRP) 276

Net requirement 277

Obsolescence stock 270

Ordering cost 271

Periodic order quantity (POQ) 282

Periodic review system 273

Pull 268

Push 268

Planned order 264

Projected available inventory 282

Released order 264

Re-order point method 272

Run-out time planning 274

Safety factor 290

Safety stock 269

Safety time 285

Service function 290

Service level 286

Speculation stock 270

Stock accounting 291

Stock balance 273

Stock withdrawal 292

Synchronisation stock 268

Time-phased order point 276

Work in process (WIP) 269

Discussion Tasks

1 Materials planning methods are usually divided into consumption-replacing and requirements-initiated systems. In the former system, new orders are initiated as a result of materials being used, whereas in the latter system new orders are initiated on the basis of real or forecast requirements. Which of these systems fall into the categories of re-order point system, run-out time planning, *kanban* and material requirements planning?

2 In the derivation of the Wilson formula for economic order quantity, it is assumed that the order quantity does not affect tied-up capital in work in process (for internally produced items), that the price is not affected by the order quantity (for purchased items), that inbound deliveries of the whole order quantity take place instantaneously, and that shortages do not arise. How would order quantity be influenced if these assumptions were not fulfilled?

3 In the calculation of safety stocks using the formulas described in this chapter, it is assumed that leadtime is constant. How would safety stocks be influenced if leadtime varies? Is there any difference if demand during leadtime is large or small?

4 The different material planning methods have different characteristics, which make them more or less suitable to use in different situations, i.e. situations with various demand patterns, leadtimes, etc. Identify and compare some characteristic situations for the MRP, re-order point and *kanban* methods.

5 It is normally not enough to match materials planning method with appropriate planning situation. The method also has to be designed and used in appropriate way, i.e. with appropriate user skills, planning organisation, software support, etc. Discuss how the user situation may impact MRP usage.

Exercises

Exercise 12.1

A wholesaler purchases two different items, A and B, from the same supplier. The following information applies to both items:

	Item A	Item B
Annual demand	2400 pcs	1500 pcs
Ordering cost per order	€200	€350
Purchase price	€180	€120

The larger ordering cost for item B is due to more extensive quality control necessary for each consignment delivered. An incremental inventory carrying cost in percentage of the unit cost of 25 per cent is applied at the company.

a) How large is the economic order quantity for each item?

b) How often per year must each item be ordered if these order quantities are used?

c) How large will the total cycle stock be for each item if the company chooses the use the economic order quantities?

d) To decrease the annual ordering costs, the company is considering always ordering the two items at the same time. In this case, the shared ordering cost will be €425. How much will the sum of incremental inventory carrying cost and ordering costs change per year if both items are ordered as often per year as item A in task b) above? How large will the corresponding changes in cost be if both items are ordered as often as item B in task b) above? Which alternative should be chosen?

Exercise 12.2

A manufacturer of lawnmowers markets one of their product models in northern Europe. In recent years, sales per month have been on average 65 during the period from October to March and 310 during the period from April to September, i.e. 2250 per year on average. The following information applies to the lawnmower model:

Ordering costs per manufacturing order, including testing: €670. Manufacturing cost for the model: €560.

Incremental inventory carrying costs for the company are calculated to be 25 per cent of the manufacturing cost per year. So far the company has chosen to have the same fixed manufacturing order quantities during the whole year. The economic order quantity used has been 150 pieces. Since the testing and control equipment has a capacity to check 10 lawnmowers at a time, it is most practical to choose order quantities that are whole multiples of 10.

a) The company is considering applying different order quantities during the summer and winter seasons. How large would the economic order quantities then be?

b) Since the current model of lawnmower is relatively new and subject to recurring design changes, there is a risk that components must be replaced in products already assembled if stocks are too large. This has caused large costs and also some obsolescence. The policy has now been introduced to limit manufacturing to four months' demand at a time. How will this policy affect the choice of economic order quantity?

c) By how much could the annual ordering costs and inventory carrying costs be reduced if the alternative was chosen to manufacture different sizes of order quantities during the winter and summer seasons?

Exercise 12.3

A wholesaling company buys six products from a supplier. The estimated annual demand is:

Product	Annual demand (units)	Unit price
A	10 000	10
B	5000	5
C	1000	50
D	50 000	20
E	25 000	10
F	2000	100

The freight cost is €200 per delivery plus €2 per kilogram. The ordering cost of the company is €100 per order. The incremental inventory carrying cost is 25 per cent of the stored item value per year. How often should the company buy, and how much of each product should on average be delivered each time?

Exercise 12.4

A company consumed 25 000 kilograms of a certain raw material every year. This raw material is used in production, and is consumed evenly during the year. The price is €120 per kilogram, to be paid cash on delivery. With every purchase the company sends an engineer to deal and inspect the raw material. These trips are necessary and each trip costs €900.

The company has its inventory insured. The insurance premium is 2 per cent of the value of the average inventory. The total cost for inventory (rents and personnel) is €24 000 per year. These costs are not affected by variations in the inventory level within the interval 1000 to 8000 kilograms. The company demands an 8 per cent yield on invested capital.

The freight costs are best illustrated by the following extract from the freight rates: 1000 kg = €700; 2000 kg = €800; 3000 kg = €900; 4000 kg = €1000; etc.

Calculate the optimum number of purchases per year.

Exercise 12.5

Consider that an economic order quantity calculation is carried out. The question is "how is the EOQ affected if the following events occur one at a time?"

Events		EOQ	
	–	0	+
1. The annual demand increases			
2. Increased leadtimes to customers			
3. The inventory carrying cost increases			
4. Increased time for production planning			
5. Decreased set-up cost per batch			
6. Increased sales price			
7. Decreased cost of raw materials			

Exercise 12.6

A company expects a constant demand of 10 000 units a month for a specific item. Ordering cost per purchase is €250, no matter quantity per purchase. The incremental inventory carrying costs are estimated to €0.05 per unit stored per month. The price of the item is €0.65 if less than 20 000 units are purchased at a given occasion, but there is a discount of 3 per cent on quantities larger than 20 000 units.

What is the optimum purchasing quantity?

Exercise 12.7

A small brewery is using sugar continuously in its production of soft drinks at a steady rate of 1000 tons per year. The supplier gives you two options. Either the sugar is delivered in sacks on pallets or by a bulk truck. The price in the first case is €4000 per ton and in the latter case €3800 per ton.

In any case the cost at the procurement department is €200 per delivery. Transportation cost for sugar on pallets is €300 per delivery + €100 per ton. The cost of a bulk transport is €2000 per delivery + €60 per ton. The maximum quantity per delivery equals a full truck with a trailer or about 25 tons (10 tons on the truck and 15 tons on the trailer).

Handling time (unloading and transfer to the storage area) of pallets on arrival is 1 hour per delivery + 0.1 hour per ton. Actual cost per man-hour is €150. The annual cost of keeping one ton of sugar in sacks in stock is estimated to 25 per cent of its value.

The corresponding figure for sugar delivered in bulk is 20 per cent. In the latter case it is necessary for the brewery to lease a silo for storing the sugar. The yearly cost for this is €65 000. The silo could hold 40 tons of sugar.

a) Calculate the optimal delivery quantity in each case.

b) Compare the annual costs of the two alternatives.

Exercise 12.8

The following information applies to a spare part which is distributed from spare parts stocks:

Forecast annual consumption: 120 pieces
Delivery time from supplier: 2 weeks
Order quantity from supplier: 20 pieces
Standard deviation of demand per 4 weeks: 5 pieces

Inventory management in the spare parts stores is carried out with the aid of a re-order point method. Outbound deliveries take place during 48 weeks of the year and may be considered as normally distributed. The item in question has a service level defined as a probability set at 96 per cent that there will be no shortage during one inventory cycle.

a) Calculate how large the re-order point should be to achieve the service level set.

b) At present there is a daily check made on whether stocks are below the re-order point. To make work placing new orders to replenish stocks more efficient, the company is considering only checking stocks once a week. What impact would this change have on the size of the re-order point and safety stock for the spare part in question?

c) How much will the size of the safety stock be affected if the company chooses to use another supplier that has a delivery time of five weeks?

d) How much will the safety stock be affected if the new supplier does not want to deliver smaller order quantities than 30 pieces?

Exercise 12.9

A retailer of imported household products uses a re-order point method for its inventory management. Sales per week for one of its products are on average 50 pieces, with a standard deviation of 16. The order quantity to replenish stocks is 200 pieces, and the delivery time is three weeks. The company applies a service level definition of the proportion of demand which can be satisfied directly from stocks, and the service level defined in this way has been set at 98 per cent.

a) Calculate how large the re-order point must be for the company to achieve the established service level for the product in question.

b) To decrease capital tied up in stocks, the company is considering choosing another supplier who is willing to deliver 100 pieces each time. How much will the total capital tied up in cycle stocks and safety stocks be affected by such a measure?

c) On average the company's customers order three pieces of this product each time. To increase sales, the company is considering offering discounts to customers who order more than 10 pieces at a time. What effect will this have on the size of safety stocks if the set service level is maintained?

Exercise 12.10

A toy distributor delivers its products to shops over the whole country from four different regional warehouses. Annual sales from the regional warehouses are assumed to be normally distributed and independent of each other. For one of the products, the purchase price from the supplier was €75 and the demand per four-week period for the previous year was 230 pieces for regional warehouse A, 450 pieces for warehouse B, 360 pieces for warehouse C, and 510 pieces for warehouse D. The standard deviation during leadtime for replenishing each warehouse was 137 pieces, 256 pieces, 179 pieces, and 278 pieces respectively. The leadtime for warehouse replenishment was three weeks each for warehouses A, B and C, and two weeks for warehouse D. The inventory carrying factor at the company is 25 per cent. The company applies a service level of 90 per cent defined as the probability of not having a shortage situation during one inventory cycle. Outbound deliveries from the four regional warehouses take place during 48 weeks of the year.

In the current situation, each regional warehouse orders replenishments from the same supplier. The order quantities which have been used are 300 pieces, 430 pieces, 370 pieces and 450 pieces respectively. The company is considering replacing the regional warehouses with one central warehouse which will supply the whole country. Ordering costs for replenishments of this warehouse have been estimated at €300 and the delivery time from the supplier at two weeks. The standard deviation of demand during lead time has been calculated at 440 pieces if all deliveries take place from a central warehouse.

a) How much could the service level be improved if the four regional warehouses were replaced by one central warehouse, on the condition that at the same time tied-up capital will be reduced by 30 per cent compared with the current level in the four regional warehouses?

b) What other disadvantages are introduced by centralising activities to one central warehouse in this way?

Exercise 12.11

A company manufactures plastic stools in different models and colours to stock. One plastic injection moulding machine per model is used for manufacture. A certain model is manufactured in three different colours: black, blue and red. The capacity of the moulding machine for this model is 200 pieces per day. In addition to the plastic injection moulding, after treatment, surface treatment and control are included in the whole process of manufacturing a stool. These different operations are carried out in production groups which are common for all models manufactured. The leadtime using in planning the manufacturing order is in all cases five days plus production time in the moulding machine. In general, the following information applies to these three products:

	Black	**Blue**	**Red**
Sales per week	240 pcs	500 pcs	150 pcs
Standard deviation in leadtime	96 pcs	140 pcs	110 pcs
Manufacturing order quantity	500 pcs	1500 pcs	300 pcs
Safety stocks	125 pcs	180 pcs	140 pcs

At a certain point in time there are 853, 1080 and 290 pieces respectively in stock of the black, blue and red versions of this model. The company uses run-out time planning to plan new manufacturing orders. Manufacturing takes place five days a week.

a) For which of the products must new manufacturing orders be planned?

b) Which of the products for which manufacturing orders must be planned should be started first, considering the stock situation?

c) Which of the products for which manufacturing orders must be planned should be started first, if consideration is also given to production time in the moulding machine and the order quantity to be manufactured? When the one colour variant has been completed in the moulding machine, manufacturing of the next colour variant can be started immediately.

Exercise 12.12

A company manufactures two different models of desk, LX and NO. Both models consist of a desktop, a supporting frame in steel, steel legs and a number of screws. All these components are purchased from external suppliers. Assembly of the two models takes place in batches of 50 and 120 respectively each time. On a certain date, an assembly plan as shown in the following figure was produced, in which the quantities refer to assembled desks ready for delivery. The leadtime for assembly is two days for model NO and one day for model LX.

Day	1	2	3	4	5	6	7	8	9	10	11	12	13	14	15
LX				50					50					50	
NO			120				120				120				120

Both models use the same legs, but in model LX there are five legs and in model NO four legs. These legs are also purchased and delivered to an associated company in quantities of 80 pieces every fifth day, i.e. days 5, 10 and 15. On one planning occasion there are 890 legs in stock and a purchase order of 1200 legs is expected for delivery during day 4.

a) On which day must a new purchase order be placed to avoid any shortages in stock? The order quantity is 1200 pieces and the delivery time is 7 days.

b) What should have been done if the stock balance had been 690 pieces instead of 890 pieces?

c) According to the calculations made in task a) above, there was no consideration given to safety stocks to safeguard against rejects and uncertainties in requirements from the associated company. When must a purchasing order be placed if the safety stock is set at 100 pieces?

Further reading

Fogerty, D., Blackstone, J. and Hoffman, T. (1991) *Production and inventory management.* South-West Publishing, Cincinnati.

Hopp, W. and Spearman, M. (2000) *Factory physics.* McGraw-Hill, New York.

Jonsson. P. and Mattsson, S-A. (2006) "A longitudinal study of material planning applications in manufacturing companies", *International Journal of Operations and Production Management,* Vol. 26, No. 9, pp. 971–995.

Landvater, D. (1997) *World class production and inventory management.* John Wiley & Sons, Essex.

Martin, A. (1993) *Distribution resource planning: the gateway to true quick response and continuous replenishment.* Oliver Wight Publications, Essex.

Silver, E., Peterson, R. and Pyke, D. (1998) *Inventory management and production planning and scheduling.* John Wiley & Sons, New York.

Vollmann, T, Berry, W., Whybark, C. and Jacobs, R. (2005) *Manufacturing planning and control for supply chain management.* McGraw-Hill, New York.

Wild, T. (2002) *Best practice in inventory management.* Butterworth Heinemann, Oxford.

CHAPTER

13

Manufacturing planning and control

The materials planning methods described in the previous chapter are to a large extent the same whether the company in question is a distribution company or a manufacturing company. With regard to the materials management, it is the value added in the flow during manufacture which distinguishes the two types of company. The use of resources required to achieve this value added must also be planned, monitored and followed up, which is the reason for some form of production management being required parallel with materials management. Since the flow of materials and the use of resources are closely tied to each other, materials management and production management are considered to be a joint process. This chapter deals with manufacturing planning and control, i.e. the various aspects of materials management and production management that are specific to manufacturing companies.

The chapter is closely related to several other chapters in the book. There are direct links to Chapter 8 Production processes and layouts, Chapter 11 Demand management, Chapter 12 Materials management and Chapter 17 (especially Section 17.1 Planning and execution systems).

13.1 A Structure for Manufacturing Planning and Control

Planning involves making decisions about future activities and events. For manufacturing activities, such decisions may relate to the coming days or the coming hours: for example, when a new manufacturing order will start in production. However, decisions may also concern activities and events which lie six months or more in the future: for example, when decisions are made to hire more staff or invest in new machines.

Decision situations which arise do not only differ in their time perspective, but also with regard to the level of precision and detail required for the information on which decisions are based. To be able to start a new order within a few hours, exact information is required about the quantities to be manufactured, whereas the decision to expand capacity in 12 months' time may be made even though the quantitative information on which the decision is based is only approximate.

Planning level	Planning object	Horizon	Period length	Re-planning
Strategic network planning	Supply chain links and nodes	Several years	Quarter/Year	Yearly
Sales and operations planning	Product group	1–2 years	Quarter/Month	Quarterly/ Monthly
Master production scheduling	Product within product group	0.5–1 year	Month/Week	Monthly/Weekly
Order planning	Item in product	1–6 months	Week/Day	Weekly/Daily
Production activity control	Operation for order on item	1–4 weeks	Day/Hour	Daily

TABLE 13.1 Planning functions in a manufacturing company

In practical terms, the problem of different time perspectives and details required is dealt with by planning material flows and production successively in a hierarchical structure of planning functions. For planning functions in long-term planning, low precision and detail levels may be acceptable, while short-term planning will demand a high precision and level of detail. The planning structure often used in manufacturing companies contains the following four planning functions:

1 **sales and operations planning**
2 **master production scheduling**
3 **order planning**
4 **production activity control.**

A fifth and more long-term planning function than all four traditional functions is sometimes also used. This function is called **strategic network planning**. A summary of the characteristics of these different planning functions is shown in Table 13.1.

Strategic network planning

The four traditional manufacturing planning and control functions refer to the tactical and operative level of planning. To be able to carry out such planning and taking the entire supply chain into consideration, the structure of the network between plants, suppliers and customers must be determined, how products will flow between these players and the capacities and utilisation of these capacities. In many cases this network and the flows involved are clear from the start and cannot be influenced in the foreseeable future, but in many situations it is possible to question, and to a certain extent modify, existing structures. This is, for example, the case when establishing new plants. In larger companies with global production and distribution, evaluations are made of possible flows when products are distributed to new markets, when new products are distributed or when other conditions for logistics undergo changes.

Network planning involves making decisions about the number, geographical location and capacity of plants such as factories and distribution centres, about which specific products will flow, where products will be stored, from which plants different customers will be served and what means of transport will be used between plants. Figure 13.1 provides an example of a

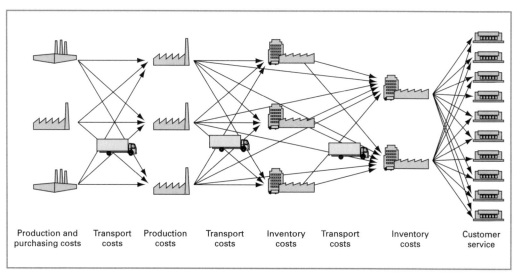

FIGURE 13.1 Example of material flows and related costs in a network of factories, warehouses and transportation

network consisting of several storage points which are supplied from different storage points or factories via transportation. There are several possible solutions regarding localisation and flow paths for networks in the figure. Planning is carried out using aggregate data – product groups and product types rather than individual products – and with as long-term perspective as possible, preferably several years.

Re-planning usually takes place annually or even less frequently. Planning is normally supported by some form of mathematical calculation model which, on the basis of the network's customer service goals, production costs, purchasing costs, inventory carrying costs and transportation costs will evaluate the current situation, identify a theoretically optimal solution and make possible comparisons between various structures. Since many practical restrictions on localisation cannot be included in calculation methods, in practical terms it is often most appropriate to make analyses by only comparing feasible structures. This may be carried out with the aid of scenario analysis in which the effects of using different structures in different environments and with different levels of demand are compared.

The goal in strategic network planning is normally to minimise total logistics costs at the same time as ensuring that delivery service exceeds levels set. There may be other goals, such as maximising the delivery service at the same time as total logistics costs are held under a set level. Another possible goal is to maximise profits by maximising the difference between expected revenues generated by a certain level of delivery service and the costs which are incurred in achieving that service. However, models aimed at profit maximisation are often difficult to transfer since it is not easy to predict the influence of their structure on revenues, and different countries have different regulations, including taxation of profits.

Sales and operations planning

The upper of the four traditional planning levels is called *sales and operations planning*. This level has the longest time perspective and lowest precision and level of detail among these four levels. It is a process at the management level of the company, aimed at producing and establishing overall plans for sales, supply and production.

The guiding principle for sales and operations planning is the company's business concept, its operational strategies and its overall business goals. Starting with forecasts and other assessments of future demand for the company's products, plans are made for expected sales and production. After consideration of stock on hand, these plans represent a requirement to produce, and are thus the starting point for overall sales and production plans. Planning at this level is often carried out for entire product groups, and plans are normally expressed in monetary terms. Typical time scales are one to two years. In many companies, plans produced relate to the production budgets used for the financial management of the company. An example of a sales and operations plan at a furniture company regarding planned production per month during one quarter is shown in the upper section of Table 13.2. The plans are for product groups of chairs and tables.

CASE STUDY 13.1: MASTER PLANNING AT BRIO TOYS

Brio Toys Supply is a European toy manufacturer. Once a month it receives forecasts from its subsidiaries around the world. These are weekly forecasts per product for the coming 12 months. Some subsidiaries make the forecasts available online, while others send them to the manufacturer through email-attached Excel documents.

Brio Toys Supply makes no distinction between sales and operations planning and master production scheduling, but these two planning functions are integrated in a common function called *master planning*. The master planning function makes some manual adjustments to the forecasts of new and phased-out products. Thereafter, a forecast software (Demand planner) aggregates the forecasts to cumulative forecasts per product and calculates the production need during the year. The annual demand is used for updating economic order quantities and safety stocks in the ERP system. It is also used to calculate the planned production load and related capacity need in production.

When this is done, a master planning meeting (called "priority meeting") is held. Here, representatives from the planning and production departments review the planned production load and capacity. They analyse the need for adjusting the capacity in order to fulfil the expected production. Examples of strategies used for balancing capacity and production load are to add another shift in critical resources or to produce in advance in order to even out periods with peak load. If these capacity and load adjustments are not enough to meet the demand, the product volumes produced are allocated to the different subsidiaries serving different markets. This process generates the master plan at Brio Toys Supply that is the plan of what to make during the coming 12 months.

Master production scheduling

The next planning level down is called *master production scheduling (MPS)*. At this level, sales plans and production plans for the company's products are made, based on current customer orders and/or forecasts and taking into consideration any stock on hand. The products are planning objects, and a typical time scale for master scheduling is between six and 12 months. Production plans relate to quantities to be produced and delivered during each planning period, for example a week, and for each product as shown in the lower section of Table 13.2. These

Sales and operations planning Quarter 1			
Month	Jan	Feb	Mar
Product group Chairs	1800	1600	1900
Product group Tables	2700	2400	2200

Master scheduling – February				
Week	5	6	7	8
Product Model A	250		250	
Product Model B	100	100	100	100
Product Model C	50		50	
Product Model D		300		300
Product group Chairs	400	400	400	400

TABLE 13.2 Relationships between sales and operations planning and master scheduling

plans are produced within the framework of the overall production plan for each product group, as determined by sales and operations planning. The relationships between these two planning functions are also illustrated in the table. The sum of products in the product group, Chairs, planned to be produced in February is 1600 pieces, as stipulated in the production plan at the master scheduling level. This is the same quantity as in the production plan at the sales and operations planning level for the same month and for the same product group, Chairs. In practice, deviations between these quantities are acceptable within certain tolerances.

Order planning

Order planning is the planning level for materials supply, i.e. raw materials, purchased components, small items and semi-finished products to be purchased or manufactured at the company in such quantities and at such times that production plans drawn up under master production scheduling can be fulfilled. Planning objects are those items included in the products, and the result is material plans in the form of planned manufacturing orders and purchasing orders for each of these items in order to ensure the material supply. In the case of repetitive manufacturing, it may also refer to manufacturing rates per day and item instead of orders. The time scale for planning at this level is often between two and six months.

The relationship between master production scheduling and order planning was illustrated in Figure 12.10 (see previous chapter). According to the master schedule in the figure, 250 Chairs A must be ready for delivery in week 5 and 100 Chairs B each in weeks 4, 5 and 6 respectively. This triggers a new order for the manufacture of 1800 chair legs to start in week 4 for delivery in week 6.

Production activity control

Materials planning methods as described in Chapter 12 can be used for order planning. For purchase items, the purchase order is sent to the supplier on the basis of purchase order proposals created by these methods, or alternatively a call-off is made from previously communicated delivery plans. For items manufactured internally, available capacity must be considered and the various stages of manufacture planned in more detail. This planning of manufacturing orders takes place at the production activity control level. The planning objects are manufacturing orders and the operations which must be carried out to produce the finished item. The operations are planned in between the planned start date and delivery date for the order in question. The *production activity control* function also includes planning the release of new orders to the workshop, including verification that start-up materials are there, and planning of the sequence in which released orders and operations must be carried out. The time scale for planning at the production activity control level is days or weeks. Production activity control is described in more detail later in this chapter.

13.2 Capacity Planning

To achieve added value in a manufacturing company, production resources of various types are required. Capacity is a measurement of the extent to which these production capacities can achieve added value.

A certain production capacity at the company will entail costs, whether or not the capacity is utilised. It also entails costs in the form of loss of earnings if there is a larger demand for the company's products than the quantities that can be produced using existing resources. Thus it is

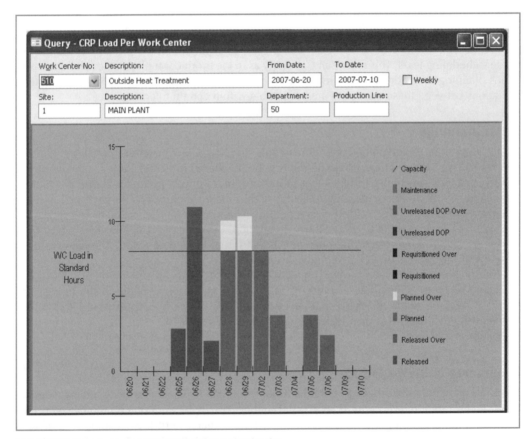

FIGURE 13.2 Example on computer monitor of capacity planning

The picture shows workload and capacity for work centre no 510. The graphic display also shows types of workload. The illustration shows one function of the ERP system IFS Applications.

in the company's interest to balance access to capacity with need for capacity. The unit in a company that deals with activities designed to balance access to capacity and need for capacity is called **capacity planning**. Capacity planning is relevant at all planning levels as described earlier in this chapter. Software support for such capacity planning exists in the ERP systems used by companies. One example is illustrated in Figure 13.2.

Calculation of capacity and capacity requirements

The capacity to produce is calculated or estimated for each production group or other planning unit at the company, and is a measurement of how much each group can produce. The most commonly used units for capacity are man-hours per time period, or machine-hours per time period. In other words, these units state how many hours production are expected to be carried out during a certain time period. The choice between machine-hours or man-hours depends on how machine-intensive or labour-intensive the manufacturing process is. Other capacity units such as number of items, kilograms or monetary units per time period also exist. The most important thing is that the unit selected is representative of the activities of each production group and that the operation times for the manufacturing operations which are carried out in the group and which represent **capacity requirements** are expressed in the same unit.

The theoretically maximum capacity of a production group is the capacity that could be achieved if production continued round-the-clock every day of the year. This is seldom the case, and so this capacity figure is rarely of interest. Instead, the calculation of available capacity is based on what capacity can normally be used. This so-called nominal capacity is often stated in the form of four variables: number of machines or other production units in the group, number of shifts per day, number of hours per shift, and number of working days in each planning period. The nominal capacity can be calculated from these variables.

Example 13.1

There are four machines in the production group at a company. Work takes place in the group in two shifts, and each shift consists of 7.5 hours. One week contains five working days. The nominal capacity of the production group will then be $4 \cdot 2 \cdot 7.5 \cdot 5 = 300$ hours per week.

In general, the nominal capacity cannot be fully utilised and an estimation of the available capacity must take into account different forms of capacity drops (see illustration in Figure 13.3). For example, there may be drops in capacity as a result of machine breakdown, short-term absence, maintenance activities and so on. After deducting such capacity drops, we can then talk about remaining gross capacity. However, various types of indirect but unavoidable downtime must also be taken into account during which no direct production can take place. It may be waiting time for materials, time for reviews with supervisors, small breaks in work or such like. Capacity may also be required for non-planned manufacturing such as repairs after items have been rejected or urgent orders of different sorts. After having adjusted the nominal capacity by such factors we arrive at something called *net capacity*, which represents the capacity estimated to be at the company's disposal to carry out planned production activities.

To be able to calculate the capacity requirements from quantities in production plans drawn up in sales and operations planning and master production scheduling from quantities on manufacturing orders created by materials management, these quantities must be translated in a

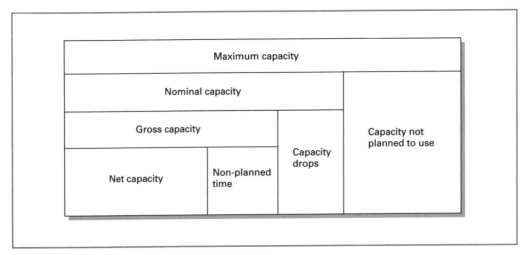

FIGURE 13.3 Capacity levels and capacity drops in a production group

uniform fashion into capacity requirements – for example, man-hours or machine-hours. The capacity requirements for manufacturing a product are generally retrieved from operation times which are stored in the ERP system database.

To meet current throughput times, capacity requirements must also be placed correctly on a time scale in relation to when the equivalent planning activities or order quantities must be manufactured. For example, if the throughput time for a manufacturing order is four weeks and it is to be delivered in week 38, the capacity requirements for the first operation must be planned in week 35.

Alternative measures for capacity planning

The purpose of capacity planning is to reconcile requirements for capacity and access to capacity for individual time periods – for example, week by week, as well as accumulated over time. To make these two tally, estimated capacity requirements are compared with estimated capacity available period by period as well as accumulated. *Accumulated conformity* means a situation in which the accumulated available capacity corresponds with the accumulated capacity requirements over the entire planning time scale. In other words, the total capacity requirement during all planning periods is of the same order of magnitude as the total availability of capacity during the same time periods. *Periodic conformity* means that there is a balance between capacity requirements and capacity availability within each planning period. In the ideal situation for capacity planning, conformity would be achieved within each period and over the entire planning time scale. If this conformity does not exist, different measures must be taken to achieve it as far as possible.

In principle there are *four different approaches* to achieving conformity between capacity availability and capacity requirements:

1 Increase/decrease accessibility to capacity.

2 Reallocate current capacity between different departments and production groups.

Type of measures	Long-term	Short-term
Increase/decrease capacity	Hire/lay off personnel New machines Number of shifts/short week Subcontracting	Overtime Postponed maintenance Subcontracting
Reallocate capacity	Moving capacity between departments	Moving capacity between departments
Increase/decrease capacity requirement	Change production plans Marketing activities	
Reallocate capacity requirement	Changed delivery times Increase/decrease stock	Advance/postpone order Change order quantity Alternative production groups

TABLE 13.3 Summary of alternative measures to create conformity between capacity availability and capacity requirements

3 Increase/decrease the requirement for capacity.

4 Reallocate the requirement for capacity between different time periods.

A summary of the various measures involved in each of these approaches is shown in Table 13.3. The table also illustrates the time scale for which it is possible to apply each measure.

To increase available capacity, it is possible to hire more personnel or use temporary staff if the shortage in capacity is not expected to be sustained. Investment in new machines or other production equipment is another possibility. Increasing the number of shifts is another measure for increasing capacity which also involves increasing the utilisation of machines at the same time as labour utilisation is unchanged. Increasing the number of shifts will require new employees. Finally, capacity can be increased by subcontracting or outsourcing, i.e. letting an external supplier take over some of the manufacturing process for shorter or longer periods of time. Capacity can be decreased by taking opposite measures, such as decreasing the number of shifts, introducing short weeks, laying off personnel or taking on previously outsourced work.

Short-term capacity adaptation to achieve conformity between capacity availability and capacity requirements means increasing or decreasing available capacity in the short term, i.e. for a number of weeks. Using overtime is one such alternative. In contrast to introducing more than one shift, the degree of utilisation will increase both for labour and for machines. The option of using overtime is limited by labour legislation, however. Measures such as postponement of service and maintenance of machines also belong to short-term adaptation, and that type of activity may instead be carried out during periods of low capacity requirements. In some contexts outsourcing may also be used for short-term capacity adaptation.

The reallocation of capacity to adapt to current capacity requirements, which may be used for balancing capacity utilisation between different planning periods, is one measure that may be used in the short term as well as the long term. For example, it is possible to transfer production personnel from departments with low workloads to departments with high workloads. For this to be possible in the short term, either the work must have low competence requirements or the workforce must be trained for multi-tasking in advance.

Decreasing or increasing capacity requirements when there is no accumulated conformity between capacity availability and capacity requirements is primarily a question of adapting the company's production plans, i.e. adapting the quantities planned to be manufactured. A decrease in the capacity requirements may be achieved by deliberately allowing production plans to state smaller volumes than those demanded by the market. Capacity requirements in production may be increased in a similar manner by increasing demand with the aid of campaigns or other marketing measures.

CASE STUDY 13.2: CAPACITY FLEXIBILITY AT ERICSSON RADIO SYSTEMS

Ericsson Radio Systems makes telecommunication systems. In one of its factories about 350 radio base stations, with some 3000 possible product configurations, were distributed each day to customers in 70 countries.

Ericsson wanted to keep a fixed order-to-delivery cycle of five days, at the same time as they faced high demand variation. They therefore developed a volume flexibility strategy, based on a combination of Ericsson employees and temporary contract workers. During peak demand periods more than half of the 500–600 workers could be temporary contractors. The volume flexibility strategy was based on the following principles:

♦ Production equipment should always have 15–20 per cent over-capacity.

♦ Ericsson's own personnel would be used for production of the "base volume", i.e. non-peak volumes.

♦ Temporary contract workers are used for peak and seasonal production volumes.

♦ All temporary workers have to finish internal education and training.

♦ 2-shift is used for "normal" production volumes. Night shift and weekends are only used as extra capacity and production in high-volume periods.

♦ Overtime is only used when there are internal or supply process disruptions, and cannot be used as planned extra capacity.

Examples of applying the strategy for manufacturing of a specific radio base station are:

♦ Increasing production volume from 110 to 150 products per day is possible within two weeks with 25 extra temporary workers.

♦ Increasing production volume from 150 to 195 products per day is possible within two weeks with 30 extra temporary workers and use of two expansion areas in the factory.

♦ Increasing production volume from 195 to 275 products per day is possible within eight weeks with 70 extra temporary workers, for night-shift work.

♦ The capacity can be decreased to the base level within one week.

For companies that manufacture to stock, the reallocation of capacity requirements in the medium term may be achieved by decreasing capacity requirements during the high season by delivering from stock and increasing capacity requirements during the low season by producing to stock. This alternative means that seasonal stocks are used to even out variations in demand. For companies that manufacture to customer order, capacity requirement may be adapted by changing delivery times, i.e. by extending them in times of high demand and decreasing them

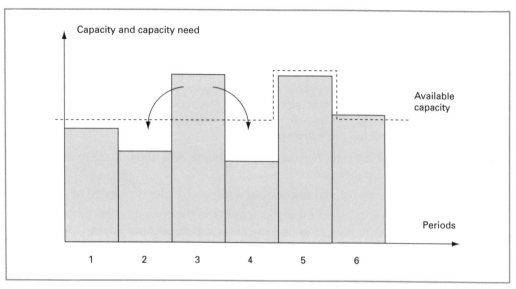

FIGURE 13.4 Adaptation of capacity and capacity requirements through short-term capacity increase and reallocation of capacity requirements respectively
The arrows represent bringing forward or postponing capacity requirements.

when demand declines. Short-term reallocation of capacity requirements involves a number of different possibilities. The principle is illustrated in Figure 13.4, which shows the case of accumulated but not periodic conformity between capacity availability and capacity requirements. The overload problem in period 3 can be solved by advancing or postponing a certain amount of production to periods 2 or 4 respectively. In period 5, the problem has been solved by temporary capacity adaptation.

Postponing and bringing forward manufacturing, compared with the ideal case, should take place as a main alternative for reallocation of capacity requirements. It is achieved by changing the start-up time and completion time for planned manufacturing orders. To be able to advance manufacturing, start-up materials must be available earlier than originally planned, and this alternative will lead to increased tied-up capital since the manufactured items will be finished earlier than they need to be. Postponement may cause shortages of incorporated materials in final manufacture/assembly.

Other methods of reallocating capacity requirements involve using alternative production groups or alternative operation sequences, thus reducing the load on production resources which are overloaded and loading those which are not. Increasing and decreasing order quantities are also methods of reallocating capacity requirements. For example, by decreasing order quantities fewer products will be manufactured during a certain period and more must be manufactured at a later date to be able to satisfy total demand.

13.3 Production Activity Control

To gain efficient utilisation of capacity and at the same time short throughput times, a balance is required between available manufacturing capacity and planned orders and capacity requirements for operations. Releasing more orders to the workshop than there is capacity to cover will only create long queues and capital tied up in work-in-process. Start-up materials must also be available for orders to be executed in an uninterrupted and cost-effective manner. Releasing manufacturing orders that are not completely materials-ready will create unnecessary administrative work and efficiency losses in production. Alternative sequences may be chosen for priorities among orders released. This prioritisation and minimising of queues may be more or less effective with respect to throughput times and delivery times. Such prioritisation is dealt with in the most detailed planning function, the production activity control. For efficient production activity control there must be suitable procedures, regulations and methods. Consequently, production activity control has three main purposes:

1 to release orders at the rate that capacity conditions will allow them to be executed with reasonable throughput times

2 to ensure that start-up material is available when each order is planned to start

3 to ensure that orders released for manufacturing in the workshop are completed in a suitable sequence with respect to delivery times and throughput times.

The first two purposes concern **order release** control and **material availability checking**. Together they precede the actual release of the manufacturing order to the workshop. The third purpose refers to priority control and involves detailed control of orders released for the relevant production groups. In addition to managing these tasks, production activity control also includes labour reporting from the manufacturing process and final reporting of completed manufacturing orders.

Order release control

Order release control means determining when the manufacturing order will be released to be started in the workshop, taking into consideration capacity conditions and the probability of executing the order with a reasonable throughput time. The point of departure is the start date as determined at the top planning level, normally with the aid of a materials planning method. When the order is released, the extent of currently available capacity must also be considered. On release, the order status changes from being a planned order to a released order.

Material availability check

Manufacturing orders cannot be started until materials are available. The process of verifying this in order to start an order is called *material availability checking*. Its purpose is to avoid orders with material shortages being released for manufacture in the workshop.

Material shortages may be caused by disruptions in the company's own production, delayed or incorrect delivery from a supplier, or a discrepancy between the real stock balance and the balance as reported in the ERP system. If during material availability checking it becomes clear that material is not available and will not arrive in time, corrective measures will be necessary. This may mean persuading a supplier to deliver materials, postponing the completion date for the order, shortening the throughput time or decreasing the order quantity.

Priority control

The purpose of **priority control** is to ensure that orders released for manufacture in the workshop are executed in a suitable sequence with respect to delivery times and throughput times.

Time plans for orders and operations determined before the order release may have been too approximate, stated in days or weeks, or production conditions used as a basis for the plans may have changed. More orders may have joined the queue for the same production group. Priority control will determine in which order the queued orders must be executed. Conditions are created for planning to influence the sequence of manufacturing orders so that there are as few disruptions as possible in the flow of materials. The selected sequence of orders will also affect the amount of work-in-process.

Priority control may be carried out by using priority rules, also called **sequencing rules**, or with the help of dispatch lists. Priority rules guide the selection of priorities among a number of orders which are available for start-up in a production group. The order which has the highest priority is selected first, according to these rules. Examples of common priority rules are: shortest operation time first, first in/first out, planned start time for operation and planned completion time for order. The shortest operation time first means that out of a number of possible orders to start, the one with the shortest operation time is selected first. First in/first out means executing the orders in the same order as they came to the production group in question. Both of these are examples of general priority rules, and are not related to any specific planning situation.

The other two priority rules are planning-based, i.e. they are connected with how orders and operations have been planned in time. The rule for planned start time for operation means that orders are executed according to their planned operation start times. Planned completion times for orders means that orders planned to be completed earliest are selected first out of all orders which are selectable.

A *dispatch list* is a list of operations for each production group in the order of priority in which they will be executed. An example of this is illustrated in Figure 13.5. In contrast to the

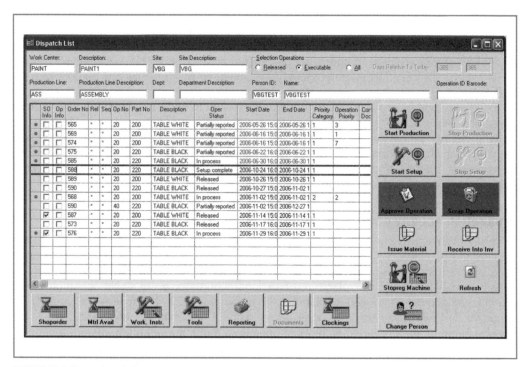

FIGURE 13.5 Illustration of dispatch list

The figure shows the sequence of execution of 13 orders in the work centre PAINT. It also shows for each order its order status, start and end date, priority category, etc. The picture represents a function from the ERP system IFS Applications.

method of priority rules, in which workshop personnel select the order of execution with the aid of established rules, dispatching means that a suitable order of priority is communicated directly to the workshop in the form of printed papers or via display screens from the ERP system.

Priority control using dispatch lists requires more computer system support than general priority rules. In other aspects it is just as straightforward to use. Since dispatch lists can be generated and distributed daily, and if presented on monitors at the same time as planned operations are carried out and new ones are planned, manufacturing can be carried out in the sequence which almost always reflects current materials requirements.

Feedback reporting

Planning of manufacturing orders and operations in time is no guarantee that they will always start or be completed at the times stipulated. During the process of planning it is impossible to completely predict access to materials and capacity. Some changes in comparison with how orders have been planned for production are therefore inevitable. It is not always possible to avoid all types of disruption, for example in the form of production disruptions and delays in promised deliveries of start-up materials. There is thus good reason for monitoring and following up how orders released are actually executed in the workshop. One of the purposes of feedback is to convey information used as the basis for monitoring and follow-up of released manufacturing orders. It is then possible at an early stage to make corrective measures if deviations should arise, and to minimise any negative consequences that may occur.

In order to plan manufacturing orders, it is necessary at every step to have information on what resources are available, primarily in the form of start-up materials and manufacturing capacity. Since these resources are gradually consumed, it is necessary that information on their consumption is fed back so that current resource availability can be kept updated. It could be a matter of reporting materials withdrawn from stocks, or reporting work completed so that the workload of current production groups can be documented. This is the second purpose of **feedback reporting**.

Real consumption of materials and the use of capacity in executing a manufacturing order are seldom exactly as large as those calculated and planned, as reflected in the information stored in the ERP system database. More or less material may be consumed than estimated, and the same is true of working hours. To make cost-accounting calculations for products or items, there must be information on real consumption. The supply of information on real resource consumption is the third purpose of feedback.

Production activity control for different production layouts

The production activity control process may differ considerably between environments with different production layouts. Above all, differences arise between functional workshops on the one hand, and cellular or line-oriented manufacturing layouts on the other.

When manufacturing takes place in a functional workshop, every single operation in the manufacturing order is treated separately. All production-control activities are roughly as important and extensive. After the order release control and material availability check, the manufacturing order is released to the first operation. Since queues often arise in functional workshops, a detailed dispatch list is generally required to allocate priorities to orders released. To be able to apply advanced priority rules in priority control, some form of computer support must be used and feedback of order status must be carried out continuously and with greater detail.

A cellular or production line is characterised by high volumes of few or similar products, as well as short **set-up times** and **leadtimes**. The focus in these environments is on the manufacture rate in the whole process. The order release control and priority control takes place more or less at the same time.

Priority control is considerably simpler than manufacturing in a functional workshop since there is only one **order point**, i.e. the group/line as a whole and not the separate machines or workstations is included in the group. The operational sequences for all manufacturing orders are in principle identical and are determined to a large extent by the physical manufacturing layout. The order sequence for executing released orders is not determined at the workshop level, but by the order in which the manufacturing orders are released, i.e. in accordance with the priority rule first in/first out. Queues within the groups/lines are normally negligible or very small.

In the case of repetitive manufacturing, especially for planning of final product manufacture in cellular or assembly line layouts, **rate-based scheduling** without manufacturing orders is normally applied. *Rate-based scheduling*, also called *tact time scheduling*, is built on compliance with a predetermined production rate expressed as total quantities to be produced per day or per hour. The rate, or tact, of production is determined so that it is equivalent to the desired outbound delivery volume. Which product variants are to be assembled and in what sequence is determined by the current stock and order stock. Since manufacturing based on production rates is not administrated via manufacturing orders, feedback cannot be based on manufacturing orders. For the purposes of stock reports, in this type of planning environment material withdrawals are usually reported in the form of automatic stock deductions with the help of product structures. Orders are checked off as products and are reported as completed at the end of the assembly line. For example, if a dishwasher is reported as completed, the withdrawal of two hinges is reported from stocks. This principle is called **back flushing**. This type of production activity control approach was developed as part of the Toyota Production System and is often included in lean manufacturing strategies.

13.4 Conclusion and Summary

The transformation and value creation of raw materials and purchased components takes place in a manufacturing company during the assembly of finished products. For this reason it is necessary to manage the use of resources in the value-adding process in this type of company. This production management must take place in parallel with materials management, since value is added during the flow of materials. Materials management and production management are terms often used in the context of manufacturing companies.

In the manufacturing planning and control, work takes place at different planning levels which differ from each other with respect to the time scale in which planning takes place and at what level of detail. Common levels of planning are strategic network planning, sales and operations planning, master production scheduling, order planning and production activity control. The planning of material flows and capacity of production resources take place at all levels. The management of materials is generally the same as described in the previous chapter, while the capacity planning dimension is particular to manufacturing companies.

Capacity planning aims at balancing supply and capacity requirements. It takes place primarily at the top planning levels, since these are involved in long-term planning.

At a more detailed level, the capacity dimension is taken care of by production activity control. The short-term aspect of production activity control makes this more a question of managing production and value creation within the framework of a given capacity than adapting to available capacity. Order release control, priority control and feedback reporting are examples of typical production activity control functions. In the case of repetitive manufacturing, rate-based scheduling may be applied without manufacturing orders.

🔑 Key concepts

Back flushing 317	Order release 314
Capacity planning 309	Priority control 314
Capacity requirement 309	Production activity control 304
Feedback reporting 316	Rate-based scheduling 317
Leadtime 317	Sales and operations planning 304
Master production scheduling 304	Sequencing rules 315
Material availability check 314	Set-up time 317
Order planning 304	Strategic network planning 304
Order point 317	

 ## Discussion Tasks

1 Why is it important in manufacturing planning and control that decisions at a certain level of planning are made within the framework of decisions made at higher planning levels?

2 The objective in long-term as well as short-term planning is to achieve conformity between capacity availability and capacity requirements. But how will the capacity focus and capacity planning importance vary between long-term and short-term planning?

3 In this chapter four different ways of achieving conformity between capacity availability and capacity requirements are discussed. Which alternatives are most suitable if the company is operating in a market where delivery problems cause loss of market share, or if the company delivers products with uncertain demand and short product lifespan from stock? Which alternative is most suitable if the company manufactures customer order determined products and competes primarily on the basis of low prices?

4 How is capital tied up in stocks and the utilisation of capacity in production affected by the shortage in stock of an incorporated component or raw material at the start of a manufacturing order?

5 Manufacturing planning and control is to great extent dependent on software support. Still, several planning tasks could be carried out manually. Discuss what planning functions and problems could be manual and what need software support.

Further reading

Fogerty, D., Blackstone, J. and Hoffman, T. (1991) *Production and inventory management.* South-West Publishing, Cincinnati.

Hamilton, S. (2003) *Maximizing your ERP system: a practical guide for managers.* McGraw-Hill, London.

Hopp, W. and Spearman, M. (2000) *Factory physics.* McGraw-Hill, New York.

Landvater, D. (1997) *World class production and inventory management.* John Wiley & Sons, Essex.

Ling, C. and Goddard, W. (1998) *Orchestrating success: improve control of the business with sales and operations planning.* John Wiley & Sons, New York.

Silver, E., Peterson, R. and Pyke, D. (1998) *Inventory management and production planning and scheduling.* John Wiley & Sons, New York.

Stadtler, H. and Kilger, C. (eds) (2005) *Supply chain management and advanced planning: concepts, models, software and case studies.* Springer Verlag, Berlin.

Vollmann, T., Berry, W., Whybark, C. and Jacobs, R. (2005) *Manufacturing planning and control for supply chain management.* McGraw-Hill, New York.

CHAPTER

14

Transport planning

Network planning and materials management is performed in the same way in distribution companies as in manufacturing companies, but a distribution company is also responsible for transportation activities. Transportation incurs costs. The choice of suitable transportation patterns will influence environmental concerns, delivery time, frequency and quantity, and thus tied-up capital and delivery service. Transportation patterns are also significant for the extent to which different material flows between suppliers and customers must be co-ordinated in terms of deliveries and production. The use of resources required to achieve these transportation activities and patterns must therefore be planned. Transport planning is carried out at all planning levels. Strategic planning consists of determining the structure of transport networks and how the traffic will flow. This planning includes deciding what and where to locate terminal nodes, what traffic modes to link the nodes with and what capacities to assign nodes and links. This strategic transport network planning could be conducted in a similar way as the strategic network planning of manufacturing companies described in Chapter 13. At the tactical and operative level, planning involves consolidation of deliveries, selecting distribution paths between terminals or directly between firms, planning aggregated transport quantities and frequencies on these paths, route planning within traffic areas, vehicle loading, vehicle scheduling and tracking and tracing goods in delivery. This chapter covers different transport planning problems and the basis for pricing transportation services.

The chapter is closely related to several other chapters in the book. There are direct links to Chapter 3 (especially Section 3.3 Freight transportation), Chapter 10 Distribution structures and Chapter 17 (especially Section 17.1 Planning and execution systems, Section 17.2 Information exchange and Section 17.3 Data capture systems).

14.1 Consolidation of Deliveries

The simplest and most traditional form of transportation pattern is where materials are transported directly from supplier to customer order by order, without any co-ordination with other customers' or suppliers' transportation. Each individual delivery is optimised, and the time of transport can be chosen for the order in question. The need for co-ordination is less and the potential for keeping delivery times is very favourable. There will also be relatively high delivery flexibility, and re-planning can easily be adapted to the current supply situation. The need for co-ordination in flows arises when it is desired to co-ordinate deliveries of several products to a customer to achieve a higher fill rate in the vehicle used for transportation. It also occurs when there are periodic deliveries to replenish all stocks of products supplied.

Transportation costs depend on the utilisation of capacity, i.e. to the extent to which the vehicle is utilised for transportation and the extent to which its load space is filled with goods. The greatest disadvantage of direct transportation is, therefore, its relatively high cost. It makes the frequent delivery of small quantities more difficult, i.e. the application of a just-in-time approach to material flows, with daily deliveries. One way of improving the utilisation of capacity and thereby reducing transportation costs per transported weight unit is to co-ordinate many small consignments into fewer but larger consignments. Co-ordinating small consignments into larger flows is called consolidation of deliveries and can be carried out in the following ways:

- Deliveries to **storage points**
- Fixed delivery days
- **Breakpoint distribution** and **hub-and-spoke** systems
- **Milk runs**
- **Consolidated distribution**
- **Return flows**

Deliveries to storage points

Stores may have a consolidating function. By delivering a batch size to a store and then emptying the store as demand arises, the delivered batch size can be made larger and possibly the equivalent of a **full truck load**. The gains made through consolidated deliveries must then be weighed against extra storage costs.

Fixed delivery days

It is also possible to gather customer orders for a certain region or customer and provide transportation on fixed delivery days. In this way, many small deliveries to the same destination may be avoided. The disadvantage is that delivery will sometimes take a few extra days. Delivery precision cannot normally be improved, however, since deliveries take place at fixed points in time and often with very short delivery windows, i.e. short time intervals within which deliveries must arrive and depart.

Breakpoint distribution and hub-and-spoke systems

Breakpoint distribution means that many flows of goods are co-ordinated between breakpoints, where large loads are broken down for onward transportation. Hub-and-spoke systems mean that a large number of inbound and outbound flows converge on a hub where the goods are broken down and consolidated. The breakpoint, or the hub, consists of a terminal which enables sorting, interim storage and reloading. Smaller batches from different suppliers are delivered to the terminal where they are consolidated with other batches and transported to either a customer or another breakpoint. They are then either reloaded for delivery to yet another breakpoint or to their final destination. By building up a network of breakpoints with local collection and

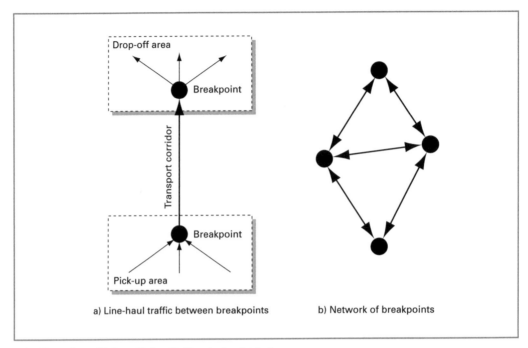

a) Line-haul traffic between breakpoints   b) Network of breakpoints

FIGURE 14.1 Consolidation with the aid of breakpoint distribution

distribution areas, high-frequency transportation of full loads may be established between these points. Frequent deliveries can also be made to a large number of local final destinations. One prerequisite for breakpoint distribution is that volumes to be transported are large enough to justify the desired transport frequencies in both directions with full loads. This alternative may incur somewhat higher handling costs when compared with direct deliveries since it requires extra reloading activities. For the method to be as advantageous as possible, the consolidation point should be located centrally in the area in the proximity of a number of suppliers. Breakpoint distribution is illustrated in Figure 14.1. Planning of regular traffic between break-points is described later in the chapter.

Milk runs

Another way of consolidating deliveries is to fill a vehicle by making several loading stops along a transportation loop within a limited area for onward transportation to a breakpoint for reloading or to a common customer in the same or different region. It is also possible to arrange the loop from one supplier directly to several customers, i.e. with several unloading stops of materials from a common supplier. Milk runs with several loading and unloading stops also occur. The aim of choosing a transportation pattern based on transport routes with several suppliers or customers involved is to radically decrease order quantities and increase delivery frequencies in comparison with direct deliveries. This principle of distribution is called a *milk run* or *shuttle traffic*.

It is the customer company that has the responsibility of co-ordinating supplier delivery routes, and it is the supplier company that has the corresponding responsibility for customer routes. In both cases, the transportation itself may be arranged by a logistics service provider company. If supplier routes are used, there will be a need for external co-ordination of material

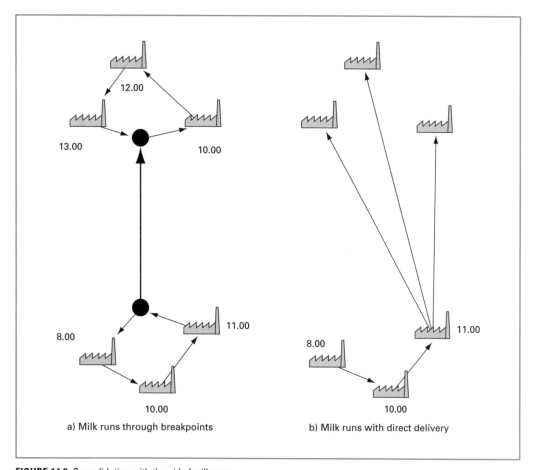

FIGURE 14.2 Consolidation with the aid of milk runs

a) Timetabled collection and delivery rounds via breakpoint, b) Time-governed collection rounds with direct delivery to individual customers.

flows, i.e. the supplier company must adapt production, picking, packing and other activities to be able to deliver at times when the shared transport will depart. This makes demands on planning and delivery times, but at the same time creates good opportunities for very frequent deliveries of the just-in-time type. The co-ordination requirement when using customer routes is similar, but in this case it is the customers that must adapt their orders and activities to the times when the shared transport arrives. For the supplying company there may also be the need for internal co-ordination if customer orders contain several order lines.

A milk run is governed by a timetable with the aim of loading or unloading goods at several customers. Figure 14.2 illustrates such timetabled transport routes. In Figure 14.2a, local milk runs are described which deliver to or from a consolidating centre which operates as a breakpoint. Figure 14.2b illustrates milk runs which go from several suppliers to individual customers. The problem with milk runs which do not deliver to a breakpoint but instead go directly to geographically remote customers is that the vehicle may need to drive back empty after the last unloading. In the case of long transportation distances it may therefore be more efficient to transport via breakpoints. The principles for determining suitable routes are discussed later in the chapter.

CASE STUDY 14.1: TRANSPORT SYSTEMS AND BUSINESS PROCESSES OF VOLVO LOGISTICS

Volvo Logistics is a logistics service provider in the automotive, transport and aerospace industries. It provides services for the Volvo Group, including Volvo Truck, Volvo Buses, Volvo Construction Equipment, Volvo Aero, and Volvo Penta, across Europe, North and South

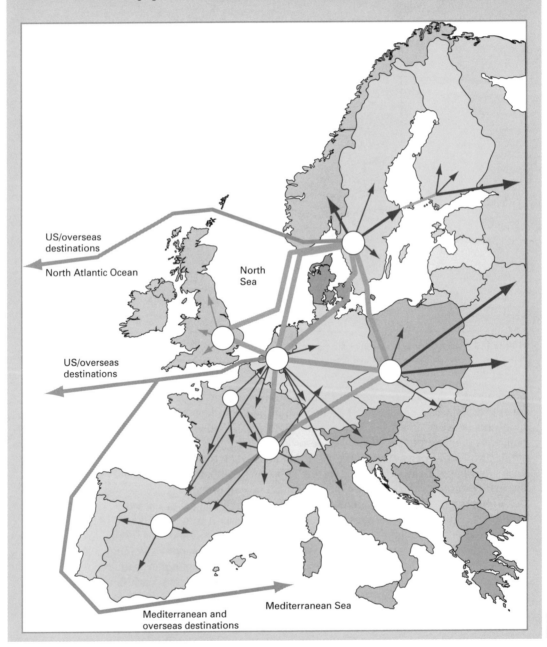

America, and Asia. It also provides services for Volvo Car Corporation and Ford Motor Company. It has defined and works with three major business processes: inbound, outbound and packaging. Inbound processes start at dispatch from supplier and end at agreed point of use at a customer's manufacturing plant. Outbound processes start at dispatch from a customer's plant with finished units and end at agreed point of use, at the manufacturer's customer. Packaging processes mainly supply the inbound processes with packaging material.

The transport system set-up for managing the inbound and outbound processes includes several different transport modes, hubs and links as illustrated in the figure to the left.

The inbound transport system consists of:

- *Full load systems*: trailers are fully filled at one supplier and are sent directly to one receiver.
- *Groupage systems*: carriers pick up parts at several supplier sites and combine these shipments so that the trailer is fully utilised.
- *Parcel systems*: Small shipments build up like the Groupage system, but are operated in a different way.

Milk-run pick-up is used for the Groupage and Parcel systems. Carriers follow transport routes between several suppliers and deliver to a Volvo Logistics cross-dock terminal, where the goods are sorted and loaded on carriers for distribution to the customers. The timetables are designed and maintained by a transport planner. Information about the routes and timetables are available for customers on an Internet portal. For some customers, the information is automatically communicated to their ERP system every night.

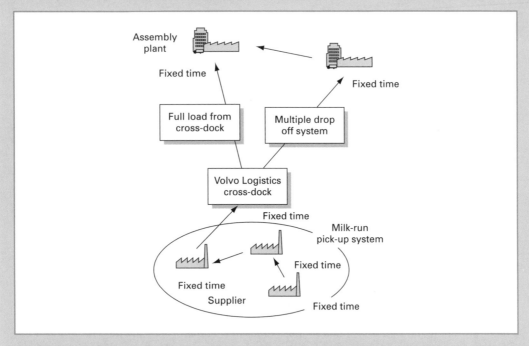

The timetable below includes milk-run information for a group of suppliers to different Volvo manufacturing plants. The lower part of the table shows when the carrier will pick up goods at the respective supplier and when it will arrive at the Volvo Logistics terminal. The upper part shows when the goods will be available at the customer. For deliveries, for example, from Svenska Adja AB to Volvo Olofström, the goods are picked up on Thursday 9 am, arrive at the Volvo Logistics terminal at 7.20 pm and are delivered to Volvo Olofström at 7 am on Friday morning.

VOLVO	Information	Timetable	Suppliers	Instructions	Latest Update

Material Supply Timetable

Area Småland 1 (1,1)

		Arrival	Time	VLCArrival	Time	VLC
	VTV	07:00	+1	Lindesberg	07:00	+2
	VCP	07:00	+1	Olofström	07:00	+1
	Tuve	10:00	+1	Tanum	11:00	+1
	Uddevalla	08:00	+1	Umeå	06:00	+2
	Borås	12:30	+1	Vara	08:00	+2
	ECT/CCT	07:00	+1	Skövde	11:30	+1
	Köping	07:00	+1			

Volvo Logistics

Transporter: Schenker

Booking Fax: 0370-699175

Home
Sweden
Småland 1
Småland 1 (1)
Småland 1 (2)

			Loading day									Arrival Volvo Logistics							
Supp ID	GSDB ID	Supp Name	M	T	W	T	F	S	su	Time	M	T	W	T	F	S	su	Day	Time
000007		Svenska Adja AB				4				9:00				4				0	19:30
000013	BHEDA	Thor Ahlgren AB	1	2		4				3:30	1	2		4				0	19:30
000018		Krahner AB		2		4				9:00		2		4				0	19:30
000029	BQEFA	Gnosjöplast AB	1	2	3	4	5			9:00	1	2	3	4	5			0	19:30
000064	BKR3A	Recticel AB	1							12:00	1							0	19:30
000082	C61MA	ABA of Sweden AB				4				10:00				4				0	19:30
000114		Hordagruppen			3		5			9:00			3		5			0	19:30
000114	BQAHA	Trelleborg Horda AB	1	2	3	4	5			9:00	1	2	3	4	5			0	19:30

The outbound process focuses on ensuring that undamaged vehicles reach every recipient on the promised date, mainly through direct deliveries, and according to the delivery terms CIP/DDU (Incoterms, 2000).

The packaging system consists of flows to the assembly plants with parts in packaging material and flows from the assembly plants with used packaging systems. Some of the packaging material is very expensive, bulky and designed for unique components. The efficiencies of the packaging flows are therefore very important. The European packaging system consists of six packaging pools (terminals) and 30 packaging depots (small terminals) with packaging material.

Consolidated distribution

Consolidated distribution means that small batches of goods from several different suppliers and/or shippers are transported together in the same vehicle. This may mean that a load to a low population area is filled with goods of different types from different suppliers to different customers, so the quantity of goods that is transported to a certain company may be less and the transportation may take place more frequently than would otherwise be possible. Consolidated delivery takes place between two consolidation terminals where the goods are sorted and repacked.

Balanced flows

If the quantity of goods to be transported to a region is not as large as the quantity of goods coming out from that region, there will be an imbalance between inbound and outbound transportation. An imbalance in flows may also arise, for example, when empty, specially designed load carriers take a large part of the load space during return flows. In such situations it is difficult to achieve transportation with high fill rates in both directions. Trying to decrease these imbalances as much as possible will also involve a form of consolidation of deliveries with the aim of reducing transport costs per transported weight unit.

All the above transportation patterns are characterised by their fixed structures. By using logistics service provider companies, it is possible to achieve consolidation of transportation requirements without having fixed structures. This type of transport pattern means that transport routes are always optimised on the basis of transportation requirements of all customer and supplier companies that are customers of the logistics service provider company. In comparison with traditional transport patterns, there is a co-ordinated optimisation of the total known transportation requirements instead of individually for each separate transport. For this to be possible there must be continuous access to information regarding existing transport requirements and available transport capacity, both time-wise and geographically.

The demands on external co-ordination will be smaller since the logistics service provider company can in principle adapt its collection and unloading times to the supplier companies' or the customer companies' desires. This alternative is particularly useful when there are large distances between suppliers and customers and when the transported volumes in question are small.

14.2 Regular Traffic Between Terminals

As explained earlier in the book, the flows of materials between geographically separated suppliers and customers may take place directly or via one or more terminals. When using a layout involving terminals, transportation takes place between different terminals as well as within the traffic area for which each terminal is responsible. It is also possible to have several levels of terminals, i.e. to group together geographically adjacent traffic areas into one planning unit with several terminals. Distribution via terminals thus demands both planning of transportation between terminals and within the traffic area around each terminal. The principles for planning within a terminal's traffic area are treated in the next section which deals with **route planning**.

The flows between terminals are normally structured around regular traffic. The average daily flow of goods is the basis for sizing transport capacity and transport frequency between different traffic areas. When planning regular traffic, it is necessary to take into account capacity restrictions caused by the limited load capacity of vehicles used and time restrictions caused by transportation times. If time restrictions governing the requirement for short delivery times are high, it may be difficult to achieve high load utilisation of vehicles.

Regular traffic planning dictates which inbound and outbound distance routes are used, as well as planned delivery and dispatch days and necessary capacity requirements for the number and sizes of vehicles for all routes. This planning is the basis of the timetable that will be followed by regular traffic.

For timetabled, regular traffic to be efficient, it is necessary that the demand for transportation is even over time. If there are variations in the flow of goods over time, there are different options available. One is to size the regular traffic capacity on peaks, which means that there

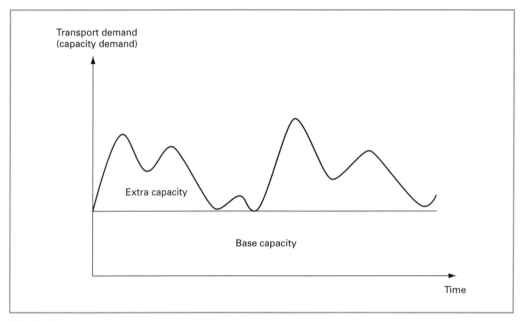

FIGURE 14.3 Transport planning using base capacity and extra capacity

will be a lower utilisation of capacity in periods with lower demands for transportation. If the variations are of a long-term and seasonal nature, specific timetables can be produced for time periods with different capacity requirements. If the variations are of a more short-term character and vary between days and weeks, it is not possible to adapt to different timetables. In such situations it is better to adapt regular traffic to time periods with lower capacity requirements. Regular traffic then constitutes a basic capacity. Capacity peaks are handled instead by using extra capacity in the form of vehicles which are not tied to any particular route but which are available within the terminal's transportation area. This extra capacity is also used for urgent deliveries such as spare parts. The principle for planning using base capacity and extra capacity is shown in Figure 14.3. In the case of a large short-term variation in the flow of goods, a low base capacity is organised with a high extra capacity. Smaller short-term variations allow for a higher base capacity and lower extra capacity, however.

For regular traffic between terminals and long-distance transportation directly between customers and suppliers, decisions on suitable transport routes are a planning problem. This problem is solved by using a calculation methods similar to those described in the later section on route planning.

14.3 Planning Within a Traffic Area

Planning transportation within a terminal's **traffic area** consists of decisions on daily transport routes from the terminal to a large number of customers spread out within the traffic area. It also involves decisions on which vehicles will be used for each route, how the goods will be loaded onto the vehicles to achieve the best load rate, and planning of loading and unloading

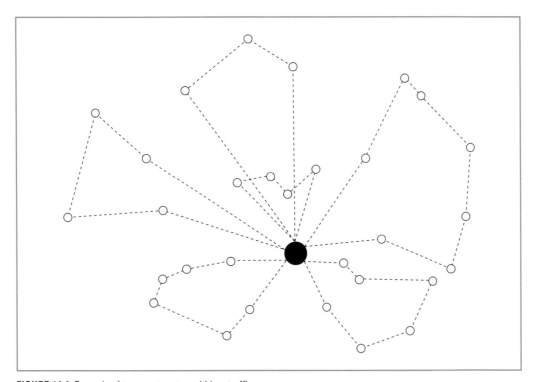

FIGURE 14.4 Example of transport routes within a traffic area

Broken lines illustrate six transport routes from a common terminal. The number of loading and/or unloading points per loop varies between three and seven.

times at the terminal. Software support for this type of planning is called **transport management system** and is described in Chapter 17.

Route planning

In a network of several terminals and traffic areas, it may happen that a customer has the same distance to more than one terminal. The first step is to decide which traffic area each customer belongs to. On the basis of known demand and customers, the next step is to determine the number of routes, the number of vehicles necessary, which customers to include on each route, and the sequence of stops on the route. When there are a large number of customers to serve, there is an almost infinite number of possible route combinations for them. The task of finding suitable routes quickly becomes complex and requires software support, normally included in transport management systems.

A number of heuristic methods have been developed to handle this complexity. These methods support re-planning in different situations. The aim of route planning is to determine routes which will provide the highest overall capacity utilisation of vehicles, as many customer visits and the largest amount of goods delivered as possible, at the same time as the total distance covered, time taken and delivery time to customers are minimised. Other goals such as a maximum number of vehicles, consolidation possibilities and so on may also be taken into account in route planning. Advanced route planning could take specific input factors into account – for example, road conditions, traffic conditions (e.g. speed limits, peak hours),

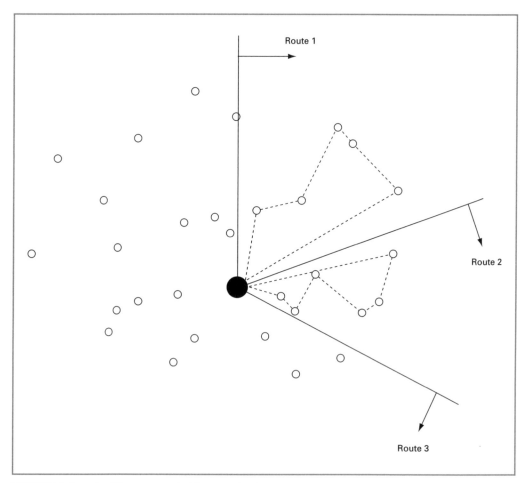

FIGURE 14.5 Example of the sweep method for route planning

weather, etc. Figure 14.4 shows how a transport solution with six routes and one terminal may be structured after calculations have been made using a planning method.

Route planning using the sweep method

The *sweep method* is an example of a simple route-planning method. A geographical sweep is conducted, for example, clockwise in relation to the terminal. The sweep continues until any one of the current constraints is met, for example, that the vehicle is full or maximum driving time is reached. Figure 14.5 illustrates the principles of the sweep method.

Route planning using the savings matrix method

The **savings matrix method** is also called the **Clark-Wright method** and is a simple route-planning algorithm. It contains four steps which are described below and exemplified in Example 14.1.

   1 *Identifying FTL deliveries*: Customers with demand that exceed the capacity of one vehicle are provided with the necessary number of vehicles for full truck load (FTL) deliveries. Demand fulfilled with FTL is excluded from the route-planning calculation but eventual remaining demand from these customers is included in the iterative route-planning procedure described in the following three steps.

2 *Develop a distance matrix:* A distance matrix shows the geographical distance, time distance or cost to travel between every pair of customer nodes to be visited. If accurate distances or travelling costs are not known between the terminal and all customers to be visited, the matrix can be derived from a map with x- and y-co-ordinates using the following formula:

$$\text{Distance (A,B)} = \sqrt{(x_A - x_B)^2 + (y_A - y_B)^2}$$

3 *Develop a savings matrix:* The savings matrix represents the distance or cost savings that occur if, instead of driving directly to single customers, two customers are consolidated on the same route. The savings involved in, for example, combining a direct trip from the terminal to customer A and back with a direct trip from the terminal to customer B and back into a new combined trip from the terminal to customer A, further to customer B and back to the terminal can be calculated using the following formula:

Savings (A,B) = Distance (Terminal to Customer A) + Distance (Terminal to Customer B) − Distance (Customer A to Customer B)

4 *Assign and sequence customer nodes to routes:* The objective when assigning customer nodes to routes is to maximise savings in distance or cost. This is done in an iterative procedure of pairwise combining of routes. The procedure starts by combining the two routes that result in the highest saving and ends when no more combination results in positive saving. Vehicle and driving restrictions like maximum driving hours, maximum vehicle load capacity, etc. must be considered when combining and assigning new routes. When designing a route, it is extended step-wise, with the customer node that belongs to a customer pair containing one of the customers at either end of the route. The route is thereby built up from the centre towards the periphery. The customer to add to a route is always the one with highest savings value. Adding customer nodes with highest savings value to a route is continued as long as there are no vehicle restrictions. Also the difference in vehicle types must be considered. A normal simplification is to assume that all customer goods can be loaded on all vehicles. It can often also be assumed that the largest vehicles, if used to the full, will have the lowest transport cost per goods unit. A good rule-of-thumb method is therefore to start filling the largest vehicle, and then continue with the second largest, etc.

Example 14.1

The Farmer Association distributes fodder and other supplies from a depot to six farms (customers). The customers' demand varies from day to day. Daily route planning therefore has to be carried out in order to manage efficient distribution with a limited number of vehicles. A distribution vehicle can carry 12 tons of fodder. For a specific day the distribution vehicle shall deliver the following quantities to the six farms:

Farm	Quantity (tons)
1	1.2
2	2.0
3	1.8
4	1.5
5	2.5
6	2.0

Distances in kilometres (km) between the depot and farms are:

	Depot	Farm 1	Farm 2	Farm 3	Farm 4	Farm 5	Farm 6
Depot	-						
Farm 1	27	-					
Farm 2	15	21	-				
Farm 3	24	51	34	-			
Farm 4	27	39	18	30	-		
Farm 5	28	27	13	41	14	-	
Farm 6	29	12	14	53	29	10	

Use the savings matrix method to determine a route schedule for Farmer Association. Consider the vehicle capacity restriction of 12 tons but not any maximum driving hour restriction when determining the maximum route length.

No farmer demands 12 tons or more. No FTL delivery is therefore scheduled and all demand is included in the route planning procedure.

The distance matrix (step 2) is given above. Therefore, the next step (step 3) in the procedure is to develop the savings matrix with savings values for each customer pair. The savings value for customer pair 1-2 is 21 (27+15−21), for pair 1-3 it is 0 (27+24−51), for pair 2-3 it is 5 (15+24−34), etc. The savings values for all customer pairs are consequently:

	Farm 1	Farm 2	Farm 3	Farm 4	Farm 5	Farm 6
Farm 1	0					
Farm 2	21	0				
Farm 3	0	5	0			
Farm 4	15	24	21	0		
Farm 5	28	30	11	41	0	
Farm 6	44	30	0	27	47	0

Step 4 in the routing procedure is to assign customer nodes to routes. Because this is done in a sequence starting with the customer pair with the highest savings value, the pair-wise savings values are first sorted in descending order:

Customer pair	Savings value
5-6	47
1-6	44
4-5	41
2-5	30
2-6	30
1-5	28
4-6	27
2-4	24
1-2	21
3-4	21
1-3	15
3-5	11
2-3	5
1-3	0
3-6	0

- The customer pair with the highest savings value of 47 is 5 and 6. These two are therefore the first to combine into a common route (Route: Depot-5-6-Depot). The combined route is feasible because the total load is $2.5 + 2.0 = 4.5$ tons, which is below the maximum vehicle load of 12 tons.
- The second highest savings value is 44 for combining customers 1 and 6. Combining customer 1 to the route for customer 6 (Route: Depot-5-6-1-depot) is feasible because it results in a total load of 5.7 tons $(2.5+2.0+1.2)$, which is below 12 tons.
- Customer pair 4-5 is the next customer pair in the descending list of savings values. Customer 5 is part of the existing route and at one "end" of it (next to the depot stop). Therefore, customer 4 can be added (Route: Depot-4-5-6-1-Depot). This is feasible because it results in a total load of 7.2 tons $(5.7+1.5)$, which is below 12 tons.
- Next customer pair in the savings value list is customers 2 and 5. But, customer 2 cannot be added to customer 5 because customer 5 is not located next to a depot stop. Instead, a customer pair including customers 1 or 4 must be identified, because these customers are in the ends of the route. The pair with highest savings value including customers 1 or 4 and customers 2 or 3, which are the only customers not yet in the route, is pair 2-4. Including customer 2 (Route: Depot-0-2-4-5-6-1-depot) is feasible because the total load will be 9.2 tons $(7.2+2.0)$.
- Now only customer 3 remains. The savings values are used to identify in what end of the route the customer should be added. Customer pair 2-3 has a savings value of 5 and pair 1-3 has a savings value of 0. Customer 3 is then added to customer 2 in the route (Route: Depot-3-2-4-5-6-1-depot). This route is feasible because the total vehicle load becomes 11 tons $(9.2+1.8)$, which is below the vehicle capacity of 12 tons.

The demand of all customers could be fulfilled by one route. The suggested route sequence (Depot-3-2-4-5-6-1-Depot) has a total travelling distance of $24+34+18+14+10+12+27=139$ km.

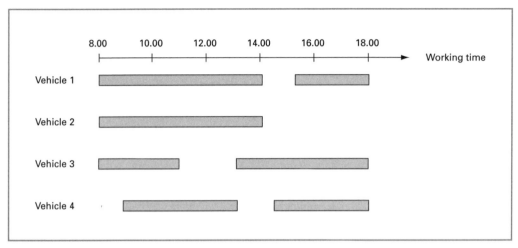

FIGURE 14.6 Example of route sequencing. Planning of four vehicles for seven routes during one day

Sequencing of routes

Route planning does not necessarily mean that the devised route will require a vehicle for the whole day. If a route only takes part of the day, the use of vehicles for each route must be planned to achieve the shortest waiting time between two routes and thus the maximum utilisation of time. This planning is called sequencing of routes and is carried out every day for routes which do not take whole days and over longer time periods for routes which are not used daily. Figure 14.6 shows an example of daily sequencing of vehicles not used for whole-day routes.

Load planning

To achieve the maximum utilisation of capacity possible for a vehicle, it is not only a question of using it as many hours as possible but also of using as much of its load capacity as possible. This is generally called **fill rate** and is measured in terms of the utilised proportion of the total available load volume, load area, or maximum weight. The fill rate will vary depending on which definition is used. For road transport, the load volume or load area is usually the *limiting factor*, rather than weight. Full load utilisation with respect to volume may mean less than full utilisation of weight. In calculating fill rate it is also important to take into account return flows. If a vehicle has a 100 per cent fill rate when it is loaded for transportation to a consignee and returns empty, the total fill rate will only be 50 per cent.

Loading and unloading times

Transportation via terminals, in addition to planning routes and utilisation of vehicles, requires planning of terminals' capacity utilisation. The seasonally related and daily distribution of the number of loading and unloading events at a terminal is the basis of this planning. Figure 14.7 shows how this distribution could be arranged. Handling equipment needs to be of the correct dimensions to manage capacity peaks. For long-term capacity planning, it is possible to even out capacity requirements by moving personnel between loading and unloading. For short-term planning, or daily planning, it is possible to distribute unloading events more evenly over time by allocating arriving vehicles specific unloading times, called *slots*. If possible, outbound deliveries should also be planned for time periods when the incoming flow is less.

Facts and figures 14.1: Fill rate according to weight, volume and number of pallets (Lumsden, 2004)

A study of carriers of long-haul distribution in Europe compared the fill rate of 137 transports. Three measures of fill rate were calculated and compared. The first was constrained by the weight, the second by the volume and the third by pallet capacity. The results show that long-haul transportation in Europe is capacity constrained regarding pallet capacity and volume but the total weight capacity is seldom fully utilised (see figure).

- Of 137 transports studied, about 40 per cent utilised the full pallet volume and 2/3 used at least 90 per cent of the volume. No transport had less pallet utilisation than 55 per cent.

- The average fill rate in terms of load volume was 82 per cent. About half of the transports had about 90 per cent fill rate. None had a lower fill rate than 38 per cent.

- The average fill rate in terms of weight was 57 per cent. Fewer than 10 out of 137 transports fully used the weight capacity. No transport had lower weight utilisation than 10 per cent.

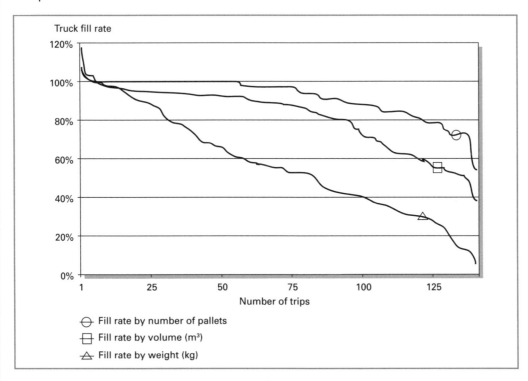

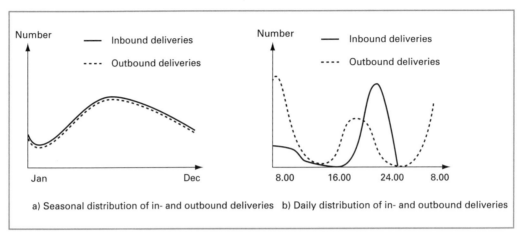

a) Seasonal distribution of in- and outbound deliveries   b) Daily distribution of in- and outbound deliveries

FIGURE 14.7 Example of distribution of loading and unloading events at a terminal over one year and one day respectively

14.4 Tracking and Tracing

Tracking means following a physical unit along the flow of materials, while **tracing** means finding a unit that has disappeared or has been lost in the flow of materials. There are many reasons for deliveries being delayed, and since a delayed delivery may have serious consequences for customers it is important to identify changes in delivery times as early as possible and communicate them to customers. Information technology available provides good support for tracking and tracing.

Tracking and tracing systems may be active or passive. In an active system, the status of a unit is registered when it arrives at or leaves an identification point and is compared with planned status. Any deviations are reported to the parties involved. In a passive system, status information is registered and saved but not compared automatically with planned values. If an enquiry is made into the status of a unit, its position in relation to identification points can be established.

A physical unit can be continuously followed, or at discrete times or points along the flow of materials. A truck or load carrier can be followed continuously using satellite navigation. In this way it is always possible to know where different vehicles are. It is also possible to have telephone contact with the driver at specific times. With the aid of identification systems such as barcodes and **RFID**, the goods on a truck may also be followed via the discrete points in time and place where they are handled during the flow of materials (for example, when loading or unloading). Information systems for tracking and tracing are further described in Chapter 17.

14.5 Pricing Transportation

Pricing transportation services depends on market forces and the costs incurred by transportation. For transport repeated at certain time intervals, a **freight tariff** is normally applied. This is a price list with fixed rates for different types of transportation. Prices in the tariff vary according to the transportation distances involved, the volume to be shipped, the density of the goods, the physical shape of the goods, the risks attached to the goods, and the supply and demand of transportation.

- *Transportation distance* – This is decisive for the price of transport. Longer distances will mean higher costs for fuel, longer working hours and more wear and tear on vehicles, etc.

- *Shipped volume* – As described in an earlier section on consolidation, a shipment that fills a whole vehicle is more cost-effective to transport than a shipment which only fills part of that vehicle. The costs for loading, unloading, handling and administration will be relatively speaking higher at small load volumes. This is either due to more handling required to fill a vehicle with several smaller loads, or because the fill rate is lower and handling costs must be allocated to smaller shipping volumes.

- *Density of goods* – the weight of goods per unit volume. The price for transportation over a specified distance is normally expressed in a rate per weight unit (for example, Euro per ton). Vehicles are normally more limited with respect to volume than weight. Since the cost for transportation is not greatly influenced by the weight of a load, a shipment with a high weight means that the higher the density of the goods, the lower will be the transportation cost per weight unit. For this reason it is desirable to distinguish between goods with high or low densities. Goods with a density under a certain limit are normally called *bulky goods* and are priced according to volume.

- *Physical shape of the goods* – meaning how easy it is to load the goods in the load space of the vehicle. The aim is to obtain as high a fill rate as possible. This is easier to achieve if goods are packed in rectangular packages rather than cylindrical, for example. Units that are too small may make good fill rates difficult to achieve. Goods with unusual physical shapes may also require special handling equipment to load and unload them, which could make transportation even more costly.

- *Cooling and heating* – goods which must be kept at a certain temperature during transportation and handling may require special cooling or heating systems, which can increase transportation costs.

- *High-risk goods* – certain goods are particularly sensitive to damage in transit, have a very high value, are theft prone, or are dangerous in that a transport accident could have very serious consequences. Transportation of this type of goods is more costly than others since it will require special measures during loading, transportation and unloading. They also incur higher insurance costs, etc.

- *Supply and demand of transportation* – the cost of transportation between two places is affected by the degree to which the return transport can be carried out with a fully loaded vehicle. The vehicle must come back to its point of origin after delivering its shipment. If the return journey takes place with an empty vehicle, the cost for this must also be carried by the goods in the outbound transport. The optimal situation is obviously to have full loads in both directions, but this is not always possible. For transportation to and from places with a large, frequent and continuous supply and demand of goods it can be achieved. If the supply and demand is not balanced though, there is a risk that empty vehicles will be travelling in one direction. Imbalances may be continuous or seasonal, such as those caused by agricultural harvesting times.

On the basis of the goods' density, physical shape and risk, products can be grouped into different classes. The aim is to enable differentiation of prices for products which incur different

Freight tariff for transportation between area A and area B	
Weight (tons)	Product class A (Euro per 100 kg)
50	150
40	185
25	245
10	295
5	445
1	600
0.5	745
0.25	895

TABLE 14.1 General appearance of a freight tariff table for transportation between area A and area B for a certain class of products

transportation costs. In a similar way, prices are also differentiated with respect to shipping volumes. Other characteristics may also be used as a basis for differentiating prices for transportation between two places. One example of a freight tariff is shown in Table 14.1. Transport costs are stated per 100 kg for the product class in question and total shipping weight.

The use of freight tariffs is not the only way to price transportation services. Purchasers and vendors may also reach an agreement on a price for the service. Freight tariffs are not used when the distance for the goods to be transported is not defined in the tariff, or when the carrier takes greater responsibility for the purchasing company's arrangements. Even when special agreements are made between shippers and carriers, previously described characteristics of transportation are still used as a basis for pricing.

14.6 Conclusion and Summary

Tactical transport planning includes co-ordination of deliveries with the aim of balancing transportation costs and delivery service achieved. The following six different principles for this consolidation of transports were treated in the chapter: deliveries to storage points, fixed delivery days, breakpoint distribution and hub-and-spoke systems, milk runs, consolidated distribution and return flows. It also involves planning of regular traffic between terminals and route planning within regional traffic areas. Capacity planning of vehicles concerns their time utilisation and load utilisation. Transport planning also involves planning loading and unloading times to achieve optimal utilisation of capacity at terminals. The bases and principles of producing freight tariffs for transportation services were also discussed.

ⓘ Key concepts

Breakpoint distribution 321

Clark-Wright method 330

Consolidated distribution 321

Fill rate 334

Freight tariff 336

Full truck load (FTL) 321

Hub and spoke 321

Milk run 321

Return flow 321

RFID 336

Route planning 327

Savings matrix method 330

Storage point 321

Tracking and tracing 336

Traffic area 328

Transport management system
  (TMS) 329

Discussion Tasks

1 One important reason for consolidation of deliveries is to minimise transportation costs. What other effects and advantages may be expected from consolidation?

2 Air traffic is based on hub-and-spoke systems. Identify a specific airline's hubs and spokes. Also discuss strategies for increasing capacity in the identified system.

3 It is not uncommon to encounter low fill rates on return flows. One reason for this is that distribution and transportation systems are not well adapted to return flows. Give some examples of items with adapted return flows and others where return flows do not exist.

4 The savings matrix method is a simple route planning method. Discuss possible limitations of the method.

5 Tracking and tracing systems are common services in transportation. What advantages can a manufacturing company expect to gain from such systems when items are delivered from China to Europe?

Exercises

Exercise 14.1

The following amount of goods is to be delivered from a distribution centre to eight customers. The same type of goods is delivered to all customers.

Customer	Quantity (tons)
1	3
2	2
3	1
4	6
5	2
6	15
7	5
8	4

Deliveries are made by three vehicles with the following capacities:

Vehicle	Max load (tons)	Max operating time (min/day)
A	9	200
B	9	200
C	12	200

Transport time (one way in minutes) between the distribution centre and customers are:

				Customer					
	DC	1	2	3	4	5	6	7	8
DC	0								
Customer 1	20	0							
Customer 2	28	48	0						
Customer 3	30	23	31	0					
Customer 4	32	33	60	56	0				
Customer 5	40	60	32	63	51	0			
Customer 6	45	65	17	48	74	41	0		
Customer 7	47	27	75	50	50	86	85	0	
Customer 8	53	73	34	65	75	26	23	99	0

Determine a route schedule using the savings matrix method, i.e. determine which vehicle shall visit what customers and in what sequence. Also specify how much the respective vehicle is used (in minutes).

Exercise 14.2

The following amount of goods is to be delivered from a distribution centre to 13 customers. The same type of goods is delivered to all customers.

Customer	Quantity (tons)
1	12
2	5
3	2
4	3
5	2
6	11
7	1
8	5
9	4
10	2
11	3
12	5
13	4

Deliveries are made by three vehicles with the following capacities:

Vehicle	Max load (tons)	Max operating time (min/day)
A	10	330
B	10	330
C	10	330

Transport time (one way in minutes) between the distribution centre and customers are:

						Customers								
	DC	1	2	3	4	5	6	7	8	9	10	11	12	13
DC	0													
Customer 1	83	0												
Customer 2	50	38	0											
Customer 3	47	58	20	0										
Customer 4	58	74	46	26	0									
Customer 5	55	28	21	41	67	0								
Customer 6	34	54	16	27	52	30	0							
Customer 7	30	64	26	17	42	40	10	0						
Customer 8	38	84	48	39	20	60	30	22	0					
Customer 9	27	93	70	61	42	82	52	44	22	0				
Customer 10	57	116	88	68	42	109	82	72	52	30	0			
Customer 11	39	113	89	81	62	94	72	64	42	20	43	0		
Customer 12	47	106	85	94	99	90	69	77	79	57	80	37	0	
Customer 13	22	89	60	69	80	55	44	52	60	41	71	53	25	0

Determine a route schedule using the savings matrix method, i.e. determine which vehicle shall visit what customers and in what sequence. Also specify how much the respective vehicle is used (in minutes).

Further reading

Banister, D. (2002) *Transport planning: an international appraisal.* Taylor & Francis, London.

Bardi, E., Novack, R. and Coyle, J. (2004) *Transportation.* Thomson Learning, London.

Bowersox, D., Closs, D. and Cooper, B. (2002) *Supply chain logistics management.* McGraw-Hill, New York.

Chopra, S. and Meindl, P. (2004) *Supply chain management: strategy, planning and operation.* Prentice Hall, Upper Saddle River.

Lumsden, K. (2004) *Truck masses and dimensions – impact on transport efficiency.* ACEA report, work in process paper, Division of logistics and transportation, Chalmers University of Technology, Gothenburg, Sweden.

Murphy, P. and Wood, D. (2004) *Contemporary logistics.* Prentice Hall, Upper Saddle River.

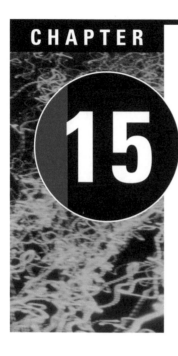

The procurement process

The procurement of materials concerns both preparation and execution of procurement. Procurement may also relate to services and fixed assets, but those aspects are not dealt with here. Procurement may be seen as a process consisting of a sequence of activities which are carried out by the purchasing company. The process initiates a customer order process in the selling company. The two processes take place in parallel and involve frequent exchanges between the companies.

In this chapter, the procurement process is described from the logistics perspective. Also described is how the process is designed for the procurement of different types of items. The concluding section treats different types of supply contracts and the economic significance of procurement, as well as the principles for supplier evaluation. Procurement as described here is synonymous to purchasing. Both terms are used in the chapter.

The chapter is closely related to several other chapters in the book. There are direct links to Chapter 8 Material supply structures, Chapter 16 (especially Section 16.3 Supply chain collaboration concepts and Section 16.5 Supply chain risk management strategies) and Chapter 17 (especially Section 17.2 Information exchange and Section 17.4 Electronic market places and business).

15.1 Procurement from a Logistics Perspective

The procurement process varies, depending on what type of item is being purchased, whether it takes place from an existing or a new supplier, the nature of the supplier relationship and what IT support is available. It is also influenced by whether the supplier manufactures the item to stock or plan, or if it is assembled, manufactured or engineered to customer order. Irrespective of which unique conditions apply, and how the procurement unit is organised, the procurement process always contains certain general activities. Figure 15.1 shows a general materials procurement process. Activities associated with invoicing, invoice control and payment have not been included since the focus here is not on the monetary flow.

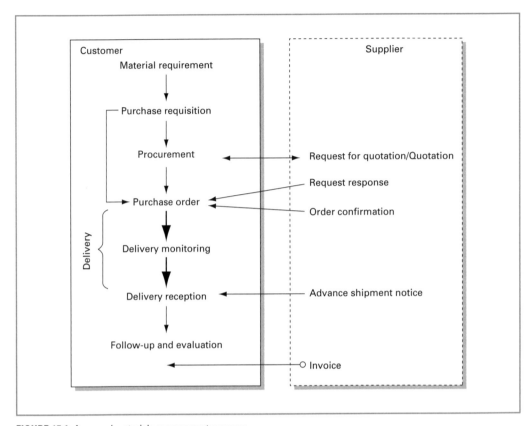

FIGURE 15.1 A general materials procurement process
Thin arrows indicate flow of information and thick arrows indicate flow of materials.

Specification of purchasing requirements

Expected future materials requirements are always the basis of procurement. These are identified by planned orders or order proposals being generated from a material requirements planning system or from a re-order point system. Order proposals in the form of **purchasing requisitions** from the unit that requires materials at the company may also be created manually. This is the case in one-off purchases of a product manufactured to customer order and when procuring indirect materials.

An order proposal or a purchasing requisition is a request to the purchasing unit to send a corresponding purchase order to a supplier. The purchasing request is, thus, a document or signal for procurement which passes on the commission to the purchasing unit to create a purchase order and execute the purchase.

Procurement

The procurement activity in the procurement process refers to selecting a supplier and drawing up a purchase agreement. Purchasing is either from a supplier with which the company has had previous business relations, or from a new supplier. If the existing or previously used supplier is an approved supplier, then it has showed a high and stable product quality and delivery quality which have fulfilled expectations over a long period of time. Using approved suppliers therefore means greater security and enables some simplification of the procurement process. If the purchase is of an item for which there is no previous relation with any supplier, enquiries must be made at potential suppliers, and possibly formal offers requested so that the company in question is able to choose a suitable supplier.

When complex items are procured, clear requirement specifications must always be drawn up and a more extensive offering procedure is carried out. This is also the case if procurement is for large amounts of an item and there will be recurring deliveries of large volumes over a long period in the future. **Request for information (RFI)** means requesting information about a possible supplier, for example, to be able to compare and select suppliers that will be allowed to give offers. **Request for quotation (RFQ)** is a request for a business offer from the supplier. It is normally used where the need can be clearly described, for example, in terms of a specific material or stock-keeping unit. The RFQ will then basically bring the supplier comparison to one of price. When the procurement needs are more difficult to specify and the supplier may have to be involved in developing and proposing a detailed solution, then a request for proposal (RFP) would be appropriate. It means that the supplier gets information about the buyer's needs and is requested to propose a solution. The aim of RFI, RFQ and RFP is to compare potential suppliers with respect to factors that affect the total cost, quality and delivery service for the procured materials. However, many purchases are of a straightforward nature and do not require full RFI, RFQ or RFP processes for selecting a supplier.

Procurement activities may also include drawing up agreements with selected suppliers with the aim of securing future deliveries and also to be able to negotiate better price and delivery benefits. A supply agreement may be drawn up in many different ways and may refer to areas of responsibility for the supplier and the customer, key persons in different areas of responsibility, standards for the exchange of information, order quantities, unit loads, prices, quantity discounts, packaging specifications, goods marking and transport documentation, product performance, quality levels, capacity availability, delivery terms etc. Delivery terms may include times when the goods are to be delivered, who pays for freight costs, who pays for loading at the place of supply, how long the vendor is responsible for the goods, when the purchaser takes over responsibility for the goods, who is responsible for customs clearance and any customs duties etc. Different types of agreement are covered later in the chapter.

If a supplier relation is established for an item and there is already a delivery agreement, it is not necessary to go through an RFQ procedure or other type of extensive procurement process. A purchase request can be directly transformed into a **purchase order**. This also applies for the purchase of standard items in smaller quantities and of a one-off nature. Agreements can then quickly be made at the time of purchase.

Purchase orders

A purchase order is the document which authorises the supplier to deliver. It defines the relevant item, what quantity is to be delivered, when, and the price of the item. Current delivery conditions are also specified in the purchase order. Figure 15.2 shows an example of purchase order information

A long-term agreement may exist with a supplier for material against which short-term releases will be generated to satisfy the requirements. If such a delivery agreement exists, the parties have already negotiated and agreed on delivery times, quantities, quality levels, prices etc. A simplified purchase order procedure in the form of a **call-off** from an already valid agreement can then be applied. In such cases the supplier usually has access to a delivery plan as the basis for short-term deliveries and for more long-term materials planning. The **delivery plan** states quantities required of the item for future time periods. The format and use of delivery plans is described in Chapter 11.

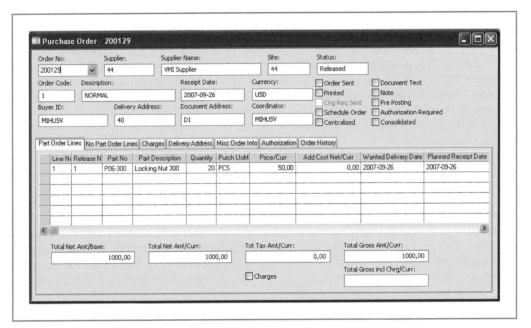

FIGURE 15.2 Example of a purchase order list and details

The illustration shows purchase order number 200129 to supplier number 44. The order contains one order line of 20 pieces of part no P06-300. The picture represents a function from the ERP system IFS Applications.

The method of applying delivery agreements in combination with call-offs means, in principle, that the procurement process is divided up into one process for drawing up the agreement itself, and another routine process for call-offs. The agreement process is of a more strategic nature and should be dealt with by the purchasing department. The call-off process, on the other hand, is operative in nature and can be delegated to materials planners or even automated and executed by the planning system.

Order confirmation

To ensure that the conditions for a purchase order have been approved by the supplier, the order is normally confirmed. An **order confirmation** from the supplier means that the order has been received and the quantities and delivery times accepted, among other things. Confirmation may also contain changes made to the customer's order, for example a delivery time that has been changed.

When call-offs are made from a delivery plan, as a general rule there are no order confirmations made. In other contexts, too, companies may not require or send order confirmations.

Delivery monitoring

Delivery monitoring means checking that deliveries take place at agreed times. This means that information is sent to the supplier about when the delivery is expected to take place according to the agreement made at the time of order. A late delivery may result in production disruptions, dissatisfied customers and loss of sales. A delivery made too early will cause unnecessary tied-up capital, disturb the normal flow of materials and require unnecessary storage space.

Follow-up and checking may take place before and after an agreed delivery time. Checking in advance means that the supplier is notified that the delivery is expected to take place in accordance with the relevant purchase order. The aim is to increase the probability that delivery really will take place as agreed. Delivery checking before the agreed time is generally only carried out selectively. Checking may be limited to including items or groups of items for which it is especially important to avoid shortages, or to suppliers that have previously shown low delivery precision.

Checking after an agreed delivery time is a measure to hasten an already delayed delivery, and then takes on the nature of a delivery reminder. Such pressure on the supplier to deliver is called *expediting*. The aim is to minimise the effects of an already late delivery and may involve threats of order cancellation or withdrawal of future business if the supplier cannot meet the agreement. In this case, too, the process may be carried out selectively. Selective expediting means that reminders are only sent if the delay has already led to a shortage, or will lead to a shortage in the near future. Accordingly, reminders are not normally sent if there are sufficient quantities in stock to cope with requirements for a while.

Tracking and tracing systems are examples of systems for delivery checking.

Delivery notification

In some situations a supplier will notify a customer that a delivery is on the way. This is done by sending **delivery notification**, also called **advanced shipment notice**. The aim of the information is to give notice of imminent delivery so that goods reception and quality control can be prepared. The aim is also to transfer information about loading and packing so that the identification, reception control and possibly onward transport can be made easier. Delivery notification is mostly used by suppliers to companies with repetitive manufacturing – for example, the automobile industry and the white goods industry.

Delivery reception

Delivery reception and inspection control means that the goods have been received and checked to ensure that the delivery was correct and in agreement with the relevant order. The delivery is reported at goods reception and information from the goods delivery note is read off and registered. In some cases, the goods are reloaded to pallets or other packages. Controls may include a visual control to check that the goods are not visibly damaged, quantity control and quality control. Any deviations are noted and will form the basis of complaints.

How extensive the inspection of goods at the reception is and how it is carried out varies a great deal from situation to situation. In some cases, for example of materials from approved and partner suppliers, the company may rely on the supplier to guarantee the quality, which means that the goods inspection at reception can be eliminated and the material sent directly to point of use. Inspection always cost money, takes time and may damage the inspected goods, so the ideal situation is not to have any inspection. Some suppliers, however, have lower reliability, and inspection is necessary for assuring that these have delivered corresponding to the agreements. If quality control is carried out, it may either be complete, meaning examination of all units of the delivered item, or it may be a random check or test on a small sample of items in a large batch, in which case conclusions will be drawn for the whole batch on the basis of the results of the checks.

The quantity-approved and quality-approved delivery is then put into stock or transported directly to the place of consumption in the workshop.

Follow-up and evaluation

In the same way that a supplier evaluation is carried out to select a suitable supplier, an evaluation of current suppliers is carried out to follow up their delivery performance. Evaluation of individual suppliers is done to follow up whether they have complied with agreements made. For current suppliers that are used continuously, supplier evaluations are carried out with a certain frequency – for example, every year. Evaluations may be more or less extensive and cover anything from direct delivery performance, customer service and product quality to the company as a whole, including its financial position, management, organisation, research and development, environment policy, experience, reputation etc.

Supplier evaluations are the basis for considerations regarding future relations with the company. They may identify areas which need improving which can help the supplier to improve its future performance. They may also be the basis for a decision made to leave an existing supplier, or to identify successful suppliers for rewards. Suppliers which over a long time have fulfilled requirements set for delivery service performance and product quality are usually called *approved suppliers*. It is primarily purchasing processes with approved suppliers that can be simplified – for example, through the delegation of the call-off process to departments outside the purchasing department, or the simplification and in certain cases even elimination of quality control.

15.2 Procurement of Different Types of Items

Purchased items can normally be divided into three types: **components**, **raw materials**, and **consumables**. The process of procurement is slightly different depending on what type of item is purchased. Procurement of equipment, which is a fourth item type, is not covered here.

Components

Components refer to semi-finished products and sub-systems which are incorporated in start-up materials in the purchasing company's manufacturing process. Components can either be *special* or *standard* (also called *commodity*). Large volumes of standard components are usually purchased and handled. Product quality is of central importance in purchasing components. Accordingly, it is important to gain detailed knowledge of the supplier's production process and quality system in the procurement phase. Quality control and delivery follow-up are normally extensive.

In the case of standard components, purchasing is normally repetitive and therefore relatively simple. No extensive procurement procedure is required and it is normally possible to draw up long-term delivery agreements and apply a simplified call-off procedure. Especially in the case of purchases from approved suppliers, quality control at goods reception can be either eliminated or drastically simplified. Transaction costs in connection with repetitive purchases of components can be minimised through automatic generation and transfer of demand information (for example forecasts, delivery plans and call-offs) directly from the purchasing company to the vendor's ERP system, for example via electronic data interchange (EDI).

Purchase of special components, on the other hand, requires extensive procurement activities since detailed requirement specifications must be drawn up for the item to be purchased. Several of the purchasing company's departments are involved in this procedure, such as production, product development and marketing departments. In some cases the supplier is also involved. Activities related to purchase orders, quality control and follow-up are normally extensive too.

Raw materials

Raw materials consist of, e.g., metals, timber and other materials at low refinement levels which are included as part of the company's refinement process. They are normally purchased in large volumes. Since prices can fluctuate over time, speculative purchases are sometimes made with large stocks as a result. Raw materials are often physically large and heavy, and handling issues may be of central importance. For this reason, materials handling personnel should be involved in the procurement process. Production personnel should normally be involved, too. By adapting raw materials to the specific production requirements it may be possible to simplify the company's own production process and thereby reduce wastage and eliminate some operations in manufacturing.

Raw materials are in some respects more straightforward as purchased products than are components, and this fact affects the procurement process. For example, drawing up requirement specifications and quality control is simplified. Raw materials often constitute a large part of the total purchase value, but there may well be several possible suppliers. For this reason they are placed in the upper left-hand quadrant of the Kraljic matrix, as was shown in Figure 8.9. This means that procurement may be more difficult, since it could be necessary to request offers from several suppliers to identify and negotiate the lowest purchase price. Since the price is in focus for this type of item, Internet-based markets for auctions between buyers and sellers may be one way to simplify procurement, see Chapter 17.

Consumables

Consumables include purchase products such as spare parts, cleaning and sanitary items, office items and so on. Procurement of consumables differs from procurement of most other types of items. There are many special types of items within the group spare parts, which have low and variable demand. Purchasing therefore takes place irregularly, in some cases from existing suppliers and in other cases from new suppliers. None of the activities in procurement will then be able to be simplified. Delivery monitoring will be of central importance in the express delivery of a spare part, for example.

There are also consumables which are continuously used up and purchased with more continuity and in larger volumes than spare parts. They have a large number of items with a relatively low purchase price. It is normally possible to buy these consumables from a large number of suppliers, and for this reason they are usually classified as non-critical items in the lower left-hand quadrant of the Kraljic matrix. Transaction costs caused by many purchasing events must be minimised by using a limited number of contract suppliers and rationalising procedures for purchase orders and deliveries.

Procedures can be rationalised in different ways. An internal website could have a purchasing portal for contract suppliers. Purchase orders can then be placed by personnel in need of an item. The purchasing department need never be involved in daily purchasing work. Purchasing via wholesalers' web shops is also a solution which simplifies purchasing administration. Invoicing and payment procedures can be simplified by the supplier sending a collective invoice once a month instead of on every purchase occasion. This is a solution which could also be applied to repetitive purchases of components.

CASE STUDY 15.1: REDUCING STOCKS OF PURCHASED ITEMS AT CIRCUITS ATLANTA (Weng, 1998)

Circuits Atlanta is a printed circuit-board manufacturer. To be able to reduce the inventory of purchased parts, the company had to reduce uncertainty about their suppliers' leadtime. To accomplish this they introduced the following principles:

◆ Use local suppliers as much as possible to reduce transportation times and risk of disruptions.

◆ Offer a premium to suppliers that deliver on time.

◆ Pick up hazardous goods themselves to eliminate the paperwork needed with the Environmental Protection Agency when using third-party logistics service companies.

15.3 Supply Contracts

A buyer–supplier business relationship could to varying degrees be regulated by a **supply contract**. A contract could clarify and regulate anything that is of importance for the buying or selling firm: for example, technical specifications, prices and terms of delivery, terms of payment, penalty clauses, warranty conditions, or product return policies. Some contracts are about **risk** and gain **sharing** between buyers and sellers with the objective of improving their total performance. Specific terms and conditions will vary between business relationships and for different types of purchase items. This limits the use of standard purchase contracts.

Supply contracts and business relationship

The following four types of business relationships can be distinguished by the type and degree of contract and agreements between purchasers and vendors:

- Procurement in direct competition
- Procurement through contracts in direct competition
- Procurement through operative contracts
- Procurement through strategic contracts

The most traditional type of supplier relationship is called *procurement in direct competition*, which means that the supplier is subjected to competition in principle on every purchase occasion. This type is also characterised by the lack of any form of contract or other agreement between the parties to regulate the procurement process and the conditions under which successive business deals take place. Evaluation and selection of suppliers and negotiations on price and delivery terms are an integral part of the procurement process. Transaction costs are generally high in this type of supplier relationship. Through the large and ever-present element of competition, information exchange between customer and suppliers is very limited and generally only covers short-term and commercial aspects. Information exchange is mainly limited to the time period from the enquiry to order confirmation.

The second type of supplier relationship is characterised by some form of simple general agreement that regulates the procurement process between purchaser and vendor. It may be called *procurement through contracts in competition*. Agreements in this context regulate prices and delivery terms. They may also contain aspects of performance such as clauses stipulating minimum quantities per year which the customer undertakes to purchase, or undertakings by the supplier of minimum quantities per year delivered. Such agreements help to shed certain parts of the procurement process when compared with "Procurement in direct competition". Transaction costs can in many cases be reduced by applying this type of supplier relationship.

The element of competition is relevant when contracts are entered into. The purchasing company, however, is not necessarily obliged to purchase from one supplier only. A number of valid contracts may be made with alternative suppliers at the same time, which means that competition is present during the entire contract period. In addition to contacts made in connection with contract negotiations, the exchange of information in this type of supplier relationship is relatively limited and mainly covers the period from order to order confirmation.

The third type of supplier relationship, called *procurement through* operative contracts, is also contract based, but agreements are wider in scope than the above type and refer to medium-term operative co-operation. Contracts are renegotiated at regular intervals, the negotiations do not generally take place in competitive conditions with other suppliers and they seldom result in change of supplier. The element of competition with other suppliers is rather indirect during renegotiations. Procurement or call-offs from the contract do not take place in competition, as in the above case. It is either a question of single sourcing, or having two or more suppliers, and contracts stating fixed allocations of volumes purchased. A supplier may have an agreement to

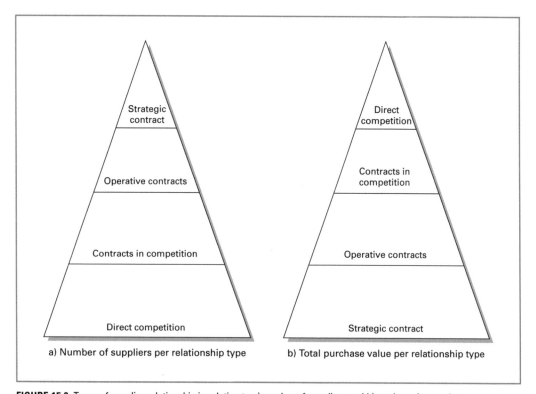

FIGURE 15.3 Types of supplier relationship in relation to a) number of suppliers and b) total purchase value

deliver 70 per cent of the total purchasing requirements of an item, while another supplier has an agreement to deliver the remaining 30 per cent.

Since the suppliers in this type of supplier relationship are less subject to competition, there are better opportunities for more extensive and frequent exchange of information than in both the previous cases. The procurement process can also be made simpler and more rational, since contracts entered into regulate virtually all issues except for quantities and times of individual purchases or call-offs. The higher degree of long-term commitment and stability made possible through these contracts also means that functional systems and forms of co-operation can be built up to make the flow of information and materials more efficient between purchasers and suppliers. There are good opportunities to further reduce transaction costs in the supply chains. The use of delivery plans is common in this type of supplier relationship.

The type of supplier relationship which is built on the most extensive and far reaching contracts may be called *procurement through* strategic contracts. In this case contracts do not only have operative elements, as in the previous type. They also have elements of co-operation in a wider sense, and they have a wider scope than the procurement process. They may include collaboration involving quality, product development and production development. In addition, the contracts cover long-term commitments such as securing the supply of materials in the long term or access to production capacity. Forecasts and planning work are often included within the framework of "Procurement through strategic contracts".

Contracts associated with this type of supplier relationship are long term. In many cases there are no clauses regarding termination time. There is often only one supplier, so this is a case of single sourcing. The element of competition is achieved through annual price negotiations. Compared with the previous type of relationship, there are even better conditions for creating an efficient exchange of information and materials and integrated collaboration between customers and suppliers in the supply chain.

The most common supplier relationships are of the type "Procurement in direct competition" and the least common are of the type "Procurement through strategic contracts" and other forms of long-term supplier relationships (see Figure 15.3). The distribution by purchase value is different. Only a small proportion of the purchase value is normally delivered by suppliers of the type "Procurement in direct competition", whereas suppliers with business relationships of the type "Procurement through strategic contracts" account for a large proportion of delivered value. For items purchased from the greater proportion of suppliers, in which there is procurement in direct competition, administrative costs in relation to the purchase value are high.

Types of supply contract

We can distinguish between supply contracts mainly focusing on price agreements, minimum purchase commitment, quantity flexibility, allocation rules, buyback or return policies and revenue sharing. Often a contract includes several types of agreements. These are examples of commonly used agreement types included in supply contracts:

- *Fixed price plus incentive fee*: A fixed price is agreed on but the supplier is rewarded if performing above the agreed standards. It can, for example, relate to better delivery service or product quality.

- *Cost-related contract*: A fixed price is not agreed on, normally because it is not possible to specify the supplier's work and costs adequately. Instead, the price is being related to the supplier's costs, for example, based on fixed hourly rates for labour and equipment. Incentive fees and penalty clauses are normally included in these contracts in order to provide incentives for the supplier to focus on costs and customer service.

- *Price protection clause*: A price protection clause may be included in a long-term supply contract in order to make it possible for the buyer to accept a low price offer from another supplier or to force the contracted supplier to sell at a lower price if the buyer is offered this from another supplier.

- *Escalation clause*: An escalation clause provides for an increase or decrease in price if costs change. Such a clause is used when a long-term agreement exists for market-sensitive materials and where the future costs of the supply are considered very uncertain. The price is linked to a price adjustment formula, including external factors such as changes in raw material price, labour costs, etc.

- *Quantity flexibility contract*: In situations of uncertain demand the supplier may want the buyer to order in advance for efficient raw material supply and resource utilisation, while the buyer would like to adjust its orders when necessary in order to reduce obsolescence risks. The buyer may consequently want the supplier to guarantee a certain delivery flexibility. A quantity flexibility contract is normally based on a fixed price for a certain purchasing volume and an upward or downward adjustment parameter that changes the price if the purchasing volume increases or decreases. The quantity flexibility contract may also include a commitment of the buyer to buy a fixed quantity or monetary value in each period and get a penalty cost if not buying this committed quantity. The contract may also include a commitment of the supplier to have a back-up of additional units or capacity and guarantee the availability of additional units for the buyer. Such commitment increases the supplier's risk. Therefore, purchase from back-up capacity or volumes may have higher agreed prices and longer delivery times.

- *Buy-back contract*: The buyer agrees to buy back unsold items from the buyer for a pre-determined price. The buyer reduces its obsolescence risk and is motivated to buy larger quantities. The seller takes a risk of having to buy back items but is also able to sell more items to full price and in large order quantities. The buyer needs an efficient reverse logistics system.

- *Revenue-sharing contract*: The seller agrees to reduce the price at the same time as the buyer shares some of its revenue from the actual products with the seller. The idea is that the buyer will afford to keep higher stock levels and thereby reducing the stock-out risks, and also lower sales prices which may increase the total sales and revenues to share between the two parts. However, if the buyer doesn't manage to increase sales, the seller will not gain from this agreement.

- *Sales rebate contract*: A sales rebate contract gives the buyer a rebate on the purchase price for volumes above a certain volume. It is consequently a type of quantity flexibility contract. This volume is determined as a total volume for a certain time period and does not concern the unique order quantity at a specific purchasing occasion. A sales rebate contract consequently gives the buyer the incentive to sell more products and if doing so it will decrease its purchasing cost per item. Also the seller will gain by increasing its sales.

CASE STUDY 15.2: RISK-SHARING CONTRACT AT AGILENT TECHNOLOGIES (Case written by Andreas Norrman, Lund University and based on Norrman, 2006)

Agilent is a global high-tech company delivering capital equipment to semiconductor manufacturers. Some units of Agilent have a supply chain that is almost fully outsourced, and where contract manufacturers put together the entire system for them while final integration and testing is done in-house. Second-tier suppliers provide circuit boards, cables, etc.

Two major uncertainties Agilent faces are volatile demand and the risk of allocation of their suppliers. The net revenue could vary by 50–80 per cent between years. In addition to the volatile business, a high percentage of its revenue is generated from sales with a seasonal pattern. In terms of uncertain supply, allocation is very common regarding ASICs (Application-Specific Integrated Circuits) and semiconductor products. When the industry tightens up, everyone starts clambering for various types of semiconductors. That Agilent sometimes has suffered allocation problems and had to buy on the spot was one of the main reasons for Agilent to implement structured contractural mechanisms for risk sharing.

Agilent has previously tried to reduce uncertainty by improving forecast accuracy and sharing real-time data, but now finds greater potential in trying to prepare for uncertainty. This includes working with so called "range forecasts", i.e. a point forecast with expected range between minimum and maximum volumes, and using structured contractural mechanisms to better co-ordinate with suppliers, sharing risk and securing cost-effective levels of supply availability and responsiveness.

The main thrust of the contract is that Agilent first develops an internal range forecast of expected demand. Then Agilent tries to get the supplier to guarantee supply and availability, especially for demand at the high end in the range forecast, as well as leadtimes and prices. Suppliers will secure clearer planning information, a price tied to flexibility, and a purchase commitment, although the commitment is a liability since Agilent specifies minimum purchase quantity. Another ingredient is to be explicit about who is liable for what, as liability was previously not very well defined.

The contract provides an opportunity to differentiate between more or less unexpected scenarios within the contract. Levels of various contract parameters could also differ over time. In the example in the figure to the right, levels are set for the four coming quarters, and they all differ. For volumes and leadtimes, a standard short leadtime could be agreed on (based on vendor-managed inventories in the example in the figure) for the "standard" demand, while additional demand must be called off with longer leadtime. For both these categories, the price per unit differs. In addition, a minimum purchase commitment is part of the agreement. This liability, the minimum purchase commitment, often has a longer time horizon than the other parts of the contract, but involves a lower quantity. Duration of commitment differs, e.g. specific quantities are defined for short leadtime (VMI), and long leadtime (flexibility) for quarters 1 and 2, while the minimum purchase commitment is given for the next four quarters. Typically the length of a minimum purchase commitment is 6 to 9 months, but is agreed upon three months in advance, which makes it a 3–12 months commitment. The purchase commitment is a major change from how Agilent previously did business. In addition to volume/capacity, lead time, price and liabilities, penalties are part of the contract.

The price for different flexibility levels (leadtime and volume) could differ. Increased availability and flexibility normally drive the suppliers to increase inventory of raw materials, etc.,

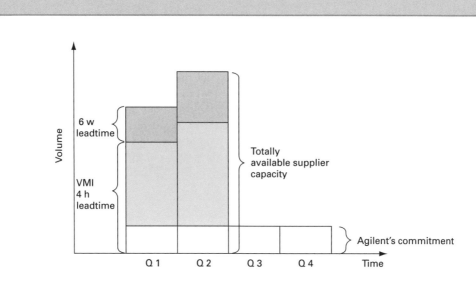

SUPPLIER AVAILABILITY AND RESPONSIVENESS	PRICE
Quantities guaranteed available with 4 hours leadtime (VMI) Q1 1700 units per week Q2 2000 units per week	$1800 per unit
Additional quantities guaranteed available with 6 weeks leadtime Q1 500 units per week Q2 700 units per week	$1750 per unit

AGILENT'S LIABAILITY (COMMITMENT)	PRICE
Quantities Agilent commits to buy Q1 400 units per week Q2 400 units per week Q3 400 units per week Q4 400 units per week	$1700 per unit

NON-PERFORMANCE
Price reduction of 1% per day late, up to 15%, for units not delivered on time.

and they would like these costs compensated by higher prices. Prices are also dependent on Agilent's liability; with no commitment the supplier takes all the risk of supply obsolescence and inventory holding. On the other hand, if Agilent accepts all liability directly for all material put into the supply chain, then the supplier takes a limited risk and could tend to give a lower unit price. In reality, the prices for the different options are often set equal due to difficulties in implementing different values in the ERP system.

The range forecasts are normally not shared, but Agilent shares the maximum availability and the purchase commitment, and sometimes the expected run rate. This information, which is not intended to be used for planning, gives signals for pricing. Normally there will be an interrelation between the ratio of availability to liability and prices. The lower the ratio, the better price the buyer could get, as the uncertainty for the supplier decreases. Some suppliers are willing to take higher ratios, and Agilent will try to keep the minimum purchase commitments low, typically because that assures that Agilent does not have to take on inventory in case of a downturn. Upturns and downturns are fairly large in their magnitudes, so it helps Agilent to have low levels of minimum purchase commitment and high levels of availability – even if that means that purchase commitment has to stretch out for a fairly long time.

Incoterms

Incoterms stands for *international commerce terms*. They are normally parts of a supply contract and constitute an international standard which regulates the distribution of freight costs, risk undertakings and drawing up of documentation between purchasers and vendors in the context of deliveries. In total there are 13 Incoterms, which distinguish between modes of transport and where responsibility is transferred during delivery from vendor to purchaser (see Table 15.1).

Incoterms are organised into four groups – E, F, C and D, where the vendor's responsibility gradually decreases and the purchaser's increases from E towards D. The only E coded term is EXW. This means that the purchaser is responsible for the entire delivery from when the supplier made the goods available to the purchaser at the factory, store or on board a ship. FOB, FAS and FCA belong to group B and mean that the supplier will deliver goods to the quay or load them onto a vehicle, after which the purchaser will bear all costs and risks. CIF, CFR, CPT and CIP belong to the C group and are variations on regulations under which the supplier bears transportation costs to an agreed place. The differences between CIF and CFR, and CPT and CIP respectively consist of which party has responsibility for transportation risks. The fourth D group of Incoterms indicates that the supplier is responsible for delivery as far as the customer's plant.

Type of transport	Transfer of responsibility			
	With vendor	*On quay/vehicle*	*After transport*	*With purchaser*
Sea transport	EXW, Ex works	FOB, Free on board	CIF, Cost insurance freight	DES, Delivered ex ship
		FAS, Free alongside ship	CFR, Cost and freight	DEQ, Delivered ex quay
Other transport type	EXW, Ex works	FCA, Free carrier	CPT, Carriage paid to	DAF, Delivered at frontier
			CIP, Carriage & insurance paid to	DDU, Delivered duty unpaid
				DDP, Delivered duty paid

TABLE 15.1 Incoterms 2000. Transfer of responsibility for different Incoterms

The different categories differentiate which party is responsible for Customs clearance, amongst other things. DDU, for example, means that the vendor does not pay Customs duties but will bear the costs for transportation to the customer's plant.

15.4 Financial Considerations in Procurement of Materials

Materials procured often account for a large proportion of manufactured products' cost price. For this reason it is important to consider and decrease the total cost effects of procurement. Purchasing larger quantities may gain quantity discounts and lower purchase prices, but will mean higher storage costs and risks of obsolescence. A decision to purchase not only influences the purchasing company's costs but also the supplier's costs if forced to deliver smaller batches that can be manufactured.

Costs can be shared between purchaser and vendor by some sort of agreement, as discussed earlier in this chapter. It is important that both partners in a long-term supplier relationship are as successful as possible, share any risks and make similar financial gains. The traditional focus on purchasing has not been based on common interests and the total costs of the supply chain, but has more to do with the purchaser minimising the purchase price as much as possible.

The approach of concentrating less on the purchase price and more on the total costs of procurement has sometimes been called **total cost of ownership (TCO)**. Cost items usually involve direct procurement costs, i.e. the purchase price, transportation costs and Customs duties, plus indirect costs including order administration and invoicing costs, costs related to flow of materials and quality control, storage, materials handling and return flows, as well as more long-term preventive costs for supplier evaluations, supplier development, quality systems, etc. It is not uncommon for the indirect procurement costs to exceed direct costs. This is often the case when procuring equipment for which operating, maintenance and phasing-out costs during the

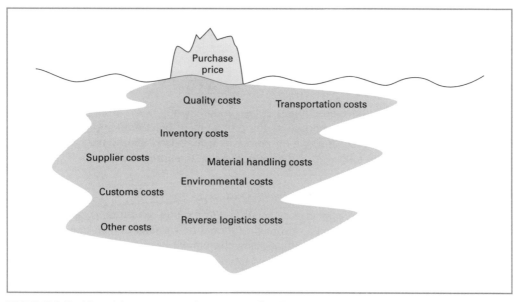

FIGURE 15.4 Total financial consequences of procurement. The direct costs are visible like the tip of an iceberg, while indirect costs are hidden beneath the water

whole lifespan of the equipment are added to the purchase price. Even the procurement of components, raw materials and consumables can incur significant indirect costs. The total costs of the product and all logistics-related activities are often called *total landed cost* or just **landed cost**. Figure 15.4 illustrates the relationship between direct and indirect procurement costs. The direct costs are visible rather like the tip of an iceberg, while the indirect costs are hidden beneath the water level.

Minimising the total procurement costs means as far as possible minimising activities which generate costs but which do not add any extra value. The role of efficiency in cutting total costs has been described earlier in this and other chapters. This may mean simplifying, automating or transferring activities to the other party, or eliminating those which do not add any value. An example of such measures is transferring quality control from purchaser to supplier, the latter applying quality assurance to processes and decreasing total quality-related costs. In addition, storage costs can be cut by more frequent inbound deliveries, provided that the supplier's production process can be adapted to smaller batch sizes. Administration costs for generating, transferring and receiving customer orders can be minimised through automation and EDI between systems. Invoicing can be simplified by issuing collective invoices once a month, or allowing the purchasing company to pay for registered delivered quantities without issuing an invoice. Cost savings at the supplier can also be achieved by the customer company providing the supplier with future forecasts and delivery plans for expected procurement volumes.

One way of preventing high total costs from ever arising is to consider them at the product development phase. **Target costing** is a concept applied to this end. Instead of allowing costs to be the result of design, the starting point is the expected sales price of the product. By subtracting the desired profit margin from the price a maximum cost per item is obtained, known as a *target cost*. If the estimated cost of the product is higher than the calculated target cost, an analysis is made of the project group with the aim of identifying cost-minimising measures. A similar approach can be applied to the purchaser–vendor relationship with the goal of continuously decreasing the total procurement costs and achieving a certain target value for total costs. This can be achieved by the purchaser providing the supplier with a target price which the purchaser is prepared to pay. The two parties then discuss how that price level can be achieved through cost rationalisations and what profit margin it would result in.

15.5 Supplier Evaluations

As is apparent from the above description of the procurement process, a supplier evaluation has different purposes. It may be part of the procurement procedure and be the basis of choosing a new supplier, either for a one-off purchase or for a long-term future relationship. It may also be the basis of the follow-up and development of an existing supplier.

Criteria for supplier evaluations

The criteria used to evaluate a supplier vary according to the purpose of the evaluation. If the object is to choose a supplier, a broader evaluation should be carried out than one based only on criteria related to the delivery itself. Situations with frequent product introductions will put demands on the supplier being able quickly to adapt to new requirements for costs, quality and product design, to produce new products in time, to swiftly increase capacity to meet increases in demand for certain products, to have the necessary knowledge and technology to develop, manufacture and solve problems in conjunction with new product designs, and so on. To gain an impression of a supplier's capabilities in these respects, the evaluation should also include such criteria as the company's financial situation, corporate culture, quality system, technological know-how, IT maturity, etc. If, on the other hand, the object is to evaluate an existing supplier, then the customer service dimension will be more significant. If it is a question of development at an existing supplier then direct performance will be measured, but it is also important in that situation to have a picture of the underlying reasons for the present and potential future performance in the same way as when making a choice between suppliers. Supplier evaluations can be an important input to the supplying company's constant improvement of its logistics-related processes. The following are examples of commonly occurring evaluation criteria:

- significance of the deal for the company
- financial position
- quality and process development
- environmental policy
- technological status and know-how
- corporate culture, work organisation and management
- procurement process
- manufacturing process
- distribution process
- customer service performance

Supplier evaluation process

Supplier evaluation can be carried out with the help of self-evaluation. This means that the supplier fills in a self-evaluation form containing the most fundamental evaluation criteria. Other possible approaches are to pay a personal visit to suppliers to collect requested information, or to outsource the entire evaluation process to a third party. Personal visits normally provide an opportunity of gaining an impression of more subjective criteria such as attitudes and policies. Such criteria especially influence the potential for developing partner relationships. It is also possible to use a combination of self-evaluation and personal visits.

It is common to use some sort of classification system to rate and categorise suppliers with varying performances into different groups. The principle for such a rating system could be to use a *weighted point-evaluation system*. It weights different criteria according to their significance, for example on a scale of one to three. Either a point is gained if the criterion is considered to be fulfilled, or the degree of fulfilment may be judged on a scale of zero to two points. In the latter case, total points per criterion are calculated by multiplying the criterion's weight by assessed fulfilment. If one criterion is regarded as very important and has been assigned a weighting of three, at the same time as the supplier's performance has been assessed as average and has been given one point, the result will be three points out of a total of six. Points obtained for each criterion are then added together to give a total, which could be the basis of an ABC classification of suppliers as described in Appendix A.

If it is an existing supplier that is being evaluated, the focus is on tracking actual performance over time. The aim may be to identify areas which can and should be improved so that the total efficiency of the supply chain can be improved. Regulations describing how suppliers' processes must be developed and their performances improved could be in the form of an action plan drawn up to describe measures that must be taken for all criteria whose minimum level has not been achieved. The evaluation could also underlie some sort of supplier reward system, possibly based on the ABC group (see Appendix A) in which the suppliers have been placed. Also, when a new order is about to be placed, the past supplier evaluation records can be used to assess whether the actual supplier should be considered or not.

15.6 Strategic and Operative Procurement

The procurement process is no longer a purely operative process only consisting of transactions; it also includes the establishment and development of relations and more or less strategic business agreements. As procurement has become more strategic and global, procurement activities have become more diversified. We can distinguish between strategic procurement activities which are organised by purchasing managers or a strategic procurement unit, and operative procurement activities which are organised by operative purchasers, materials planners or automatically in an ERP system. Figure 15.5 illustrates how procurement activities may be distributed between strategic and operative personnel.

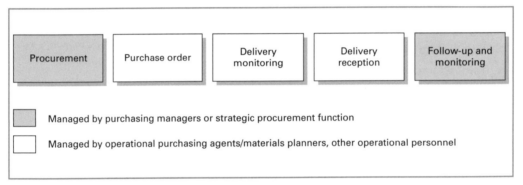

FIGURE 15.5 Strategic and operative procurement activities

15.7 Conclusion and Summary

The general materials procurement process consists of specification of purchasing requirements, procurement, purchasing orders, order confirmation, delivery monitoring, delivery notification, goods reception, follow-up and evaluation. The different parts of the process have different scope and significance in different purchasing situations. Opportunities and methods of making the process more efficient will therefore vary between different situations. The possibility of dividing the process into two sub-processes has been described, one for strategic activities run by the procurement department and one for operative activities which can be decentralised to locally consuming departments.

Different types of items place different requirements on the procurement process, whose characteristics and structure have been studied with respect to three different types of items: components, raw materials and consumables. The chapter described different types of supply contracts in the procurement process, and how Incoterms are used to regulate undertakings between purchasers and vendors during delivery. In the context of materials procurement, it is important to consider all financial consequences. To describe this, the concepts of total cost of ownership, landed cost and target costing were introduced. The principles of supplier evaluation and strategic versus operative procurement were discussed at the end of the chapter.

🔓 Key concepts

Advance shipment notice 347	Purchase order 345
Call-off 345	Purchase requisition 344
Components 348	Raw material 348
Consumables 349	Request for information (RFI) 345
Delivery monitoring 346	Request for quotation (RFQ) 345
Delivery notification 347	Risk-sharing contract 350
Delivery plan 345	Supplier evaluation 348
Delivery reception 347	Supply contract 350
Incoterm 356	Target costing 358
Landed cost 358	Total cost of ownership (TCO) 357
Order confirmation 346	

Discussion Tasks

1 One part of the procurement process is to identify possible suppliers of an item. Identify at least five criteria which can be used to qualify a potential supplier.

2 Delivery checking can be carried out in a number of different ways. Discuss the advantages and disadvantages of the different methods of monitoring deliveries. Give some examples of situations where each method of monitoring is preferable.

3 Some supplier contracts contain paragraphs describing penalties/sanctions if the supplier of goods does not fulfil agreed specifications, such as delivery times or quality of items. What advantages and disadvantages can you see in this procedure?

4 Supplier evaluation and rating can have several different objectives. How could the evaluation process differ when evaluating a potentially new supplier and an existing supplier?

5 Why are companies distinguishing between operative and strategic procurement? What benefits could be expected from making this distinguishing?

Further reading

Cousins, P., Lawson, B. and Squire, B. (2006) "An empirical taxonomy of purchasing functions", *International Journal of Operations and Production Management*, Vol. 26, No. 7, pp. 775–794.

Gadde, L.-E. and Håkansson, H. (2001) *Supply network strategies*. John Wiley & Sons, Chichester.

Leenders, M., Johnson, F., Flynn, A. and Fearon, H. (2006) *Purchasing and supply management*. McGraw-Hill, New York.

Mol, M. (2003) "Purchasing's strategic relevance", *Journal of Purchasing & Supply Management*, Vol. 9, No. 1, pp. 43–50.

Norrman, A. (2006) "Supply chain risk sharing contracts from buyers' perspective: content and experiences, *Proceedings of the 18th Annual Nofoma Conference*.

Ramsay, J. (2001) "Purchasing's strategic irrelevance", *European Journal of Purchasing and Supply Management*, Vol. 7, No. 4, pp. 257–263.

Simchi-Levi, D., Kaminsky, P. and Simchi-Levi, E. (2008) *Designing & managing the supply chain: concepts, strategies & case studies*. McGraw-Hill, New York.

Tang, C. (2006) "Perspective in supply chain risk management", *International Journal of Production Economics,* Vol. 103, pp. 451–488.

Tsay, A., Nahmias, S. and Agrawal, N. (1998) "Modelling supply chain contracts: a review", in S. Tayur, R. Ganeshan and M. Magazine (eds), *Quantitative models for supply chain management*. Kluwer Academic, Norwell, pp. 299–336.

Van Weele, A. (2005) *Purchasing & supply chain management: analysis, strategy, planning and practice*. Thomson Learning, London.

Weng, K. (1998) "Lead-time management in a make-to-order manufacturing firm", *Production and Inventory Management Journal*, 2nd Q, 1998, pp. 38–41.

PART 5
Supply Chain, IT and Improvement Aspects of Logistics

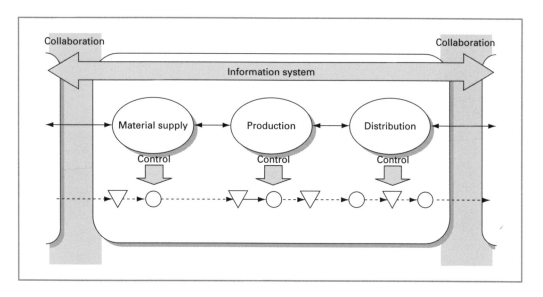

The last part of the book contains two chapters. The first extends the supply chain perspective and describes different collaboration approaches and supply chain strategies. The second focuses on information technology in logistics and supply chain management. It covers planning and executions systems, communication systems, data capture and e-business.

16 Emerging practices in supply chain management

Logistics has traditionally focused to a large extent on processes within companies, and in general the focus for making the flow of information and materials more efficient has been on the logistics system that coincides with the company's system boundaries. Even though consideration has always been given to customers and suppliers, the perspective has still to a large extent been internally oriented and it has been primarily the interests of the company itself that have been decisive for the approach and execution of performance measures. It was emphasised in the first chapter that developments during the last decade have led to an increasing need to consider and co-operate with customers and suppliers in joint inter-organisational processes. It is no longer enough to be individually efficient; collective efficiency in the entire supply chain is now required. Supply chain issues are dealt with in all chapters but this chapter puts a special emphasis on supply chain management as an inter-organisational issue.

The chapter presents some of the logistics related effects which occur in supply chains and which are specifically associated with the supply chain consisting of sequences of companies which together create and distribute products to consuming end customers. We look at the driving forces which have led to the increased significance of co-operation in supply chains. Also discussed are a number of concepts and approaches for achieving this co-operation which have been introduced in a large number of companies over the entire world. Some different types of supply chains and supply chain design strategies are introduced. Finally, the principles of managing risks in supply chains are presented.

The chapter is closely related to several other chapters in the book. There are direct links to Chapter 7 Products in the supply chain, Chapter 10 Distribution structures, Chapter 11 Demand management, Chapter 12 Materials management, Chapter 15 The procurement process and Chapter 17 Information systems for logistics and supply chain management.

16.1 Negative Effects in Supply Chains

In every supply chain, the individual company is influenced by a number of characteristic effects linked to the fact that the company, its customers and suppliers are all part of supply chains. These effects can be related to 1) variations in demand, 2) time delays, and 3) long delivery time and delivery precision inaccuracy. They always occur whether it is a question of small and simple chains of companies or complex and long chains. The significance of the effects from the viewpoint of management and financial impact increases with the complexity and the length of the supply chains.

Variations in demand

In most areas of business, the short-term variations in demand which occur in companies delivering to end customer markets are rather moderate, with the exception of seasonal fluctuations. Short-term variations in demand tend to be considerably larger for companies upstream in the supply chain, i.e. raw material producers at an earlier stage in the supply chain. These variations in demand are reinforced for different reasons in the direction of the raw materials producers. Such amplifications are to a large extent generated by companies' behaviour in relation to each other. The amplification effect on demand increases at each step in the supply chain and, consequently, the longer the supply chains, the greater the problem. Rough estimates indicate that variations in demand double with each step in the supply chain. *Cascade effects* or **bullwhip effects** are terms used to describe this. The bullwhip effects are illustrated in general terms in Figure 16.1. The figure shows how small demand variations at the local store tend to amplify into larger demand variations further upstream in regional and central stores. The main reasons for the bullwhip effect are:

- Large order quantities
- Few customers
- Long leadtimes
- Non-aligned planning and control
- Not sharing **point-of-sales (POS) data**
- Price fluctuations and promotions
- Rationing and shortage gaming

Amplification of variations in demand from company to company upstream in supply chains depends to a large extent on *large order quantities*. A materials planning method generates a purchase order proposal of a certain quantity when the stock balance is below a certain level. A more-or-less even end-consumer demand at the retailer could thus generate lumpy demand for the supplier. Order quantities tend to increase further upstream in the supply chain when purchase items become more standardised, which further adds to the bullwhip effect. The demand variations become larger as order quantities increase in size.

The current development towards fewer and fewer production units due to economies of scale has led to suppliers having *fewer customers*, which in turn may further increase variations in demand. Many small customers will always give a more even demand than a few large customers. Larger customers in general have larger order quantities, which for the same reason will increase variations in demand.

The length of leadtime also affects the size of variations in demand. *Long leadtimes* always lead to larger variations than shorter leadtimes. If order cycle times become longer, order quan-

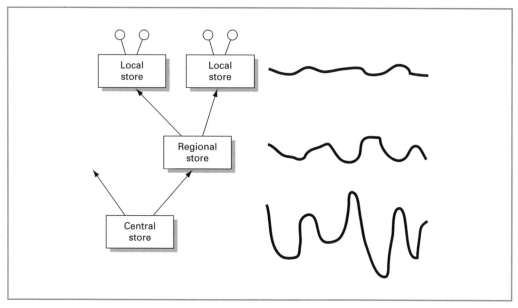

FIGURE 16.1 Bullwhip effects in supply chains

tities and safety stocks increase too, which exacerbates the bullwhip effect on demand. Long leadtimes are also obstacles for fast response to sudden demand changes.

Non-aligned planning and control activities between customers and suppliers also contribute to increasing variations in demand in supply chains. If a method is used to calculate economic order quantities, and a new calculation is made on each ordering occasion, self-propagating oscillations will occur in the supply chain. Assume that an upward trend in demand has been identified. The materials management system does not only try to deal with the increase in itself, but also tries to increase the size of stock so that it will measure up to the new demand level. If the EOQ formula is used to calculate the economic order quantity, a 20 per cent increase in demand will lead to an approximately 10 per cent increase in order quantity, i.e. the total increase in demand before the system has adjusted to it will be around 30 per cent. Similar effects occur if safety stock quantities are calculated dynamically at the same rate as demand changes. The materials management system does not only try to replenish stocks on the basis of a new level of demand; in addition, it strives towards increasing the size of the safety stock for the new demand, which is momentarily perceived as an increase in demand and by extrapolation results in forecasts which are higher than real demand. Re-planning a company's activities also contributes to creating instability and changes in demand upstream in the supply chain. Even relatively small changes in current production plans can cause large disturbances in the supply chain, especially if the exchange of information between supplying and consuming parties is limited and changes in plans are communicated less frequently. In order to synchronise the material flow in the supply chain, the materials management should be aligned between several actors in the supply chain. This could, for example, be conducting using **vendor-managed inventories (VMI)** or **customer-managed ordering (CMO)** as described later in this chapter.

Another reason for the bullwhip effect is when a supply chain actor only reacts on the orders placed by its immediate customers. The received customer order information is used to update forecasts, but the company has little knowledge about what has actually triggered the order at the customer and what the true end consumer demand actually is. If information about the reasons for demand changes is communicated upstream in a supply chain, there is a lesser risk that this will give rise to incorrect forecasts, temporary overstocking and resulting bullwhip effects. Communicating daily electronic *point-of-sales (POS) data*, as discussed later in this chapter, from retailers and upstream the supply chain is an example of making more accurate demand information available in the supply chain.

Temporary sales price changes or sales promotions can increase sales volumes in the short term. If price discounts take place frequently, buyers will stop buying when prices are high, only buying again when discount prices are offered. This will, for example, result in capacity costs for overtime and undertime for employees and machines, require large warehouse volumes and inventory carrying costs because of large purchasing quantities when buying, further contributing to the bullwhip effect. Eliminating sales price fluctuations may decrease several of the above-mentioned effects. Many retailers have therefore adopted a constant, so-called *everyday low price*.

Another source of demand variations being generated in supply chains is *rationing and shortage gaming*, which is of a more psychological nature and is caused by poor communications between customers and suppliers. If a temporary increase in demand occurs and a company is forced to extend delivery times to adapt to this, customers will perceive this as the supplier having a delivery problem. To safeguard against this, companies then order larger quantities than usual and/or place their orders earlier. Without information about the real cause of demand, the supplier sees events as an increase in demand. When the supplier is able to resume more normal delivery times after increasing production capacity, many customers try to cut down on their orders on hand, or quite simply cancel them. Other customers, by accepting what they have ordered, will have covered their requirements for far into the future, since the increased order quantities were not matched by a real increase in demand from the end-customer market. The whole sequence of events was principally a result of lack of relevant information and an imagined risk of not being able to secure required future supplies. This customer behaviour leads to demand being perceived by suppliers as declining, which in this case does not correspond to conditions on the end-customer market.

Time delays

Another characteristic effect in supply chains is the time delays which arise in the transfer of information on market demand. The longer the supply chains, and the higher the rate of change, the more conditions for achieving efficient material flows are affected. The effects are closely related to the methods of information exchange between customers and suppliers.

Demand between customers and suppliers has traditionally been communicated in most companies through purchase orders. This transfer of information risks delays and distortion on the way from the real market through the supply chain to the production units. Methods of communicating demand information can be illustrated as in Figure 16.2.

The figure illustrates a supply chain with four companies. To make things simpler, assume that replenishments of stocks from one company to another takes place once a month, i.e. that order quantities for deliveries in the chain are equivalent to approximately one month's requirements and that ordering takes place once a month on average. For the example in the figure this means that it takes approximately three months before the supplier receives information about demand on the end-customer market. A number of sequential orders will be required to be able to identify changes in demand, which means that in this example there will be a time delay of several months between demand changes on the market and their reasonable certain identification by the supplier.

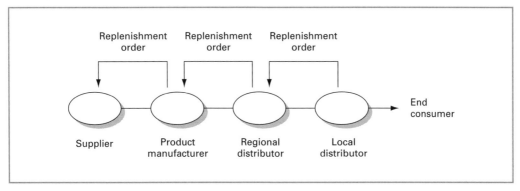

FIGURE 16.2 Transfer of demand information in a supply chain

True demand arises when customers in the end-customer market want to buy products, not when a distributor wants to replenish stocks. Communicating demand through purchase orders does not only mean that there will be time delays in the transfer of information. Information also becomes distorted upstream in the supply chain since it tends to reflect intermediary players' needs to replenish stocks rather than actual consumption by end-customers.

It is in general easier to achieve a faster and more efficient exchange of information when it is operative information, i.e. different types of information about when goods ordered are available for a customer, as long as manufacturing takes place in the company's own factory. In the case of outsourcing and logistics flows in external supply chains, the information system is a key to success.

Delivery times and delivery precision

For a number of years there has been a development towards make-to-order production. This development has meant that suppliers can be involved in the process of adding value which

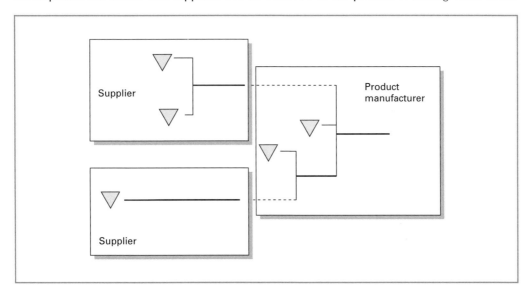

FIGURE 16.3 Supplier influence on delivery times in make-to-order production

takes place in conjunction with customer orders. The length of delivery times and delivery precision will also be influenced by the structure of relationships in the supply chain.

In most supply chains value-adding activities only take place during a small part of the total leadtime. The proportion of time when no value is added often arises in transitions between sequential value-adding resources – for example when the flow of materials crosses departmental boundaries within the company, and even more so when it crosses company boundaries. The structures of co-operation and exchange of information have great significance for the length of leadtimes, and thus for delivery times to customers. The larger the degree of outsourcing, the more time delays will arise if procedures and forms of co-operation between companies involved are not highly developed.

The significance of suppliers for the length of delivery time and delivery precision in make-to-order production is illustrated in Figure 16.3. The product structure is drawn in a time scale and the items driven by customer orders are drawn in thick lines. The items made to orders for which suppliers are responsible have a direct influence on both potential delivery times and delivery precision if there are no intermediate points of storage.

Suppliers influence delivery precision even if their items are made to stock. The larger the number of suppliers involved in the value-adding activities in production, the more uncertainties will arise and the greater the risk of disruptions, which will decrease the chances of delivering to customers as agreed. The variations which inevitably arise in every link of the supply chain are cumulative, and when more players are involved, the total variation will be larger – for example, in the form of changes in delivery times to customers. It is these variations which cause poor delivery precision.

16.2 Driving Forces Towards Increased Co-operation in Supply Chains

In addition to eliminating the logistics effects in supply chains as described in section 16.1, there are primarily three driving forces which have resulted in a shift from an intra-organisational focus towards an inter-organisational perspective, to increased efficiency and co-operation between customers and suppliers in supply chains. These are:

- Uncertain demand
- Operative dependency relationships
- Outsourcing and transaction costs

Uncertain demand

The primary force for change is the increasing difficulty of predicting future demand, not least due to the increasing rate of change in the market and ever-shorter product lifecycles. The requirement to react faster to market changes has become more and more tangible. Development has led to an increased importance of avoiding time delays in supply chains, in flows of information and of materials towards the end customer. This can only be achieved to a limited extent within individual companies' organisations, resources and processes.

Operative dependency relationships

The second decisive force is caused by operative dependency relationships between activities and material flows in companies and corresponding activities and material flows in other companies in a supply chain. These interdependencies have always existed and will always exist between customers and suppliers in supply chains. It is the amount of interdependency which has increased considerably in recent years.

There are a number of important reasons behind this development towards increased operative dependency between companies in supply chains. One reason is that companies increasingly avoid different types of buffers in material and information flows, primarily in the form of stocks and lengthened leadtimes. One of the functions of stocks is to decouple flows, i.e. to make them less dependent on each other. Stocks of finished goods decouple demand from production, and stocks of raw materials and purchased components will decouple material supply flows from consumption in production. The smaller the order quantities in manufacturing and customer order deliveries become, and the smaller the stocks kept by companies, the stronger are the ties between direct requirements in the procuring company and events in the supplying company. Requirements and needs are consequently growing for tighter co-ordination of temporal activities between companies in a supply chain.

Increased operative dependencies have also arisen as a result of an increase in production driven by customer orders. The more customer-order-specific products there are, the less it is possible to decouple material flows between customers by using capacity balancing buffer stocks of different types. With the increasing significance of short delivery times in maintaining high competitiveness, it has become far more difficult to decrease operative dependencies with the help of leadtime buffers.

More efficiency in material flows in supply chains with strong dependency relationships between companies involved is only possible if it takes place in a spirit of mutual consideration and co-operation between companies.

Outsourcing and transaction costs

A third significant driving force is connected with the increasing amount of outsourcing – the fact that suppliers account for larger proportions of manufacturing. With this growth in external value-adding processes, the degree of self-sufficiency has fallen in many companies. Products today are more often created through co-operation in networks rather than through individual companies' own efforts. The number of transactions required to do business in these networks and to control the flow of materials, information, and money has soared. There are transactions such as orders from customers to suppliers, order confirmation from suppliers to customers, and invoices from suppliers to customers. There are also material transactions in conjunction with the physical delivery of goods.

Transactions between producing and consuming units may become more complex and costly if they are carried out between external companies' customers and suppliers, rather than between customers and suppliers in the same company. There can be very simple administrative procedures between a company's assembly department and component manufacturing department for ordering and replenishing stocks of components, for example using a *kanban* card. The situation is very different if component manufacturing is outsourced. There are more transactions and, in addition, they are more complex. Administrative transactions may in a normal case include orders, order confirmation, delivery notification and invoices: that is, four relatively complex transactions compared with one simple transaction when manufacturing takes place in the company's own factory.

The transition to external suppliers may consequently cause material transactions to become more complex and extensive. They may also include control activities and packing/unpacking activities which would not have been necessary, had production been carried out internally.

Transaction costs between customers and suppliers in supply chains also influence the ongoing development towards increasingly smaller quantities. If the order quantity for a certain item is changed from 100 pieces to 10 pieces, the number of transactions between the customer and the supplier will be multiplied by 10. If the procedures used are not changed at the same time, by eliminating unnecessary activities and automating other activities, transaction costs will be 10 times higher.

The number of transactions in the supply chain is also affected by the development towards the use of value-adding distributors. If, instead of delivering a finished product to a distributor, it is decided to deliver incorporated standard components, the number of items delivered will increase and with that administrative transactions and the number of material transactions.

Total transaction costs are also influenced by increasing labour costs. The result is that in many companies there are items that cost more to procure and administrate than their equivalent cost price.

Transactions in supply chains are a shared issue in every customer/supplier relationship and must be tackled from a joint perspective to become really efficient.

16.3 Supply Chain Collaboration Concepts

Collaboration is key to creating efficient supply chains. There are different methods of collaboration, and here we describe five central concepts which can be divided into two main types. From the point of view of collaboration, *customer-managed order (CMO)* processes and *vendor-managed inventory (VMI)* can be described as attempts to achieve more optimal allocation of administrative work and materials management work associated with the dyad process, which includes the order-to-delivery process in the supplier company and the procurement process in the customer company. The other three concepts for collaboration between companies in supply chains, **Quick Response (QR)**, **Efficient Consumer Response (ECR)** and **Collaborative Planning Forecasting and Replenishment (CPFR)**, are characterised by a striving to co-ordinate and synchronise joint flows of materials to achieve the most efficient utilisation of resources possible. The application of these concepts often involves more than two companies in supply chains.

Customer-managed ordering

Of the basic types of processes described in Chapter 2, the order-to-delivery process and the procurement process are the most central and significant for operative flows of information and material in supply chains. Traditionally, they have been considered as two individual processes within a company and this attitude has remained in the work carried out to find newer and more efficient supply chain process structures. However, if they are considered from a customer/supplier perspective, it becomes clear that they are not two separate processes at all, but one process which is shared between the customer company and the supplier company as illustrated in Figure 16.4. The circles signify activities which are included in the processes.

Somewhat simplified, the shared inter-organisational business process or inter-company process may be said to have the following sequence: it starts with the identification of material requirements at the customer company. This leads to activities at the supplier company in the form of withdrawals from stock and delivery if it is a company that delivers from stock, or in the form of manufacture and delivery if it is a manufacturing company that manufactures to customer orders. The process is completed when the requirement is satisfied at the customer company. Since the process connects activities in the customer company with activities in the supplier company, it is an inter-company process. The procurement process in the customer

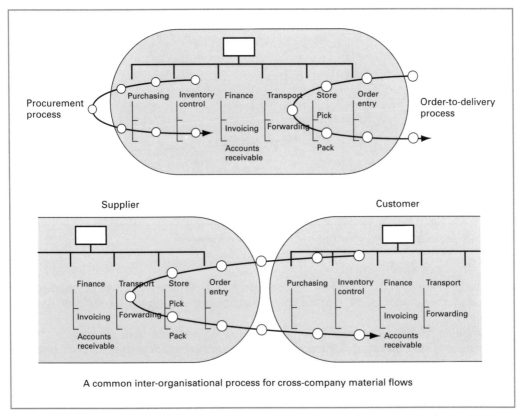

A common inter-organisational process for cross-company material flows

FIGURE 16.4 The order-to-delivery process and the procurement process as one common inter-organisational process

company and the order-to-delivery process in the supplier company can thus be considered as sub-processes in the inter-company process which results in material flows between companies in supply chains. The process may be called a *dyad process* since it comprises one dyad in a supply chain, i.e. a customer and supplier pair.

By collaborating and allocating activities in the shared process between both companies involved instead of performing the sub-processes separately at each company, the total amount of administrative work and leadtime in the processes can be reduced. One way of achieving this is to have the customer company's personnel plan and register orders directly in the supplier's ERP system when requirements arise, instead of the supplier's own personnel performing order-processing work at the customer's request. In practical terms this may mean that a purchaser at the customer company places an order or, if the processes are integrated even further, the materials planner who has a requirement for procurement places an order in the system himself. A similar approach is of course feasible when the customer is an individual end consumer. This form of collaboration may be called a *customer-managed ordering process*, and the principle is illustrated in Figure 16.5.

To be able to introduce customer-managed ordering processes, the customer connects with the supplier's ERP system. This can be in the form of a traditional online solution through a dial-up connection or fixed telephone line, or through an extranet solution and a web server provided by the supplier. There are two main alternatives. In the first, the customer can only register orders

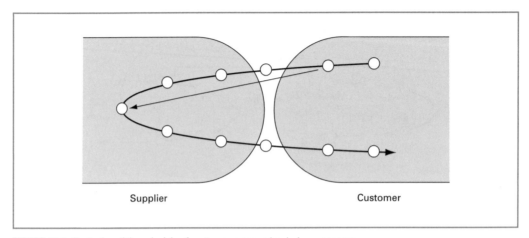

FIGURE 16.5 Illustration of the principle of customer-managed ordering processes

in the supplier's system. These orders are considered as preliminary and will be checked and modified after registration by the supplier's personnel before they are given the status of accepted and definite.

In addition to the decrease in total order registration work for both companies and the improvement in data quality, this solution has a number of other advantages for both customer and supplier. The customer can manage more of the order processing himself. By working in the supplier's system, he has direct access to information on prices, available stock, current delivery times and so on without needing to contact the supplier by telephone or fax. This saves work, both for the customer and the supplier. The access to information, in contrast to telephone contacts, is independent of any differences in working time between the customer and supplier companies – an aspect which has become increasingly important in these times of global trade.

A more radical alternative from the perspective of integration is to have the customer complete the entire order registration process himself, including the establishment of a delivery time. If the items to be ordered are standard, he can allocate materials for the order, whereas if they are customer-order-specific products, both allocations of incorporated materials and of capacity for final manufacture/assembly will be determined. One condition for the customer being able to complete order registration is naturally that sufficient materials and capacity are available and that different prices and delivery terms are fulfilled. In other cases, the supplier must be contacted.

The consequences of the latter alternative are more far-reaching than the former. In principle, the customer takes over the entire order processing task, and the supplier need not be involved at all. Since the customer can complete the entire process, it is not necessary for the vendor to confirm the order, so the order confirmation process can be eliminated completely.

CASE STUDY 16.1: CUSTOMER-MANAGED ORDERING AT SIBA AND HEINEKEN
(Mattsson, 2000)

Siba is a chain of retailers selling consumer electronic goods and operating in Scandinavia. Order Hemelektronik is one of their major wholesalers. The two companies use a system that integrates the order fulfilment process between the end-customers and the wholesalers. The goal is to reduce administrative costs and inventory, and improve customer service.

Customers who access the homepage of their Siba retailer are automatically linked to the order entry system of the company's wholesaler, Order Hemelektronik. However, the Siba logo and design has been retained. Using a Web browser, customers have access to information about prices, product availability, etc. Customers can also enter orders directly into the system.

Ordered products are shipped directly from the wholesaler to the end-customer. The only part of the order-fulfilment process performed by Siba is sending invoices to the end-customer. Invoicing is based on a corresponding invoice from Order Hemelektronik to the Siba retailer.

Another example of customer-managed ordering is at Heineken USA, the largest importer of beer in the United States. The company encountered distribution problems that to a large extent were due to long cycle times to the distributors across the country. To solve this, Heineken decided to implement a new system to reduce the time between order placement and delivery from 10 weeks to 4 weeks.

A network based on Internet technology was implemented to connect Heineken to its distributors. The ordering process is now carried out through a customised website and with standard browser techniques. On this website the distributors can modify and submit orders as well as review forecasts for planning processes.

Vendor-managed inventory

The use of customer-managed ordering processes means, as described above, that the customer can take over work in the joint dyad process from the vendor. In the opposite case, the vendor relieves the customer of work in the process. This could be called *vendor-managed order processes*, but since it is related to administration of customer stocks, the term used is *vendor-managed inventory (VMI)*.

Traditionally, ownership and the physical holding and control of stocks have been within the same organisation. Application of VMI means a change in this approach so that responsibility for and performance of the three functions of owning, holding and controlling is divided organisationally and lies with different legal entities. The implications of VMI are illustrated in Figure 16.6.

There are a number of applications for VMI. One of the most decisive differences between them is who owns the stock that the vendor manages, or – expressed differently – when the ownership rights of supplied products are transferred from vendor to customer. Irrespective of which alternative is applied, the vendor must have access to information from the customer regarding quantities in stock and current sales, forecasts, delivery plans or other types of demand information – in principle, the same type of information that the customer's own personnel access when they administrate their stocks.

Applying VMI means that the supplier, or vendor, on the basis of received stock balance and demand information, manages the customer stock and continuously plans new replenishment

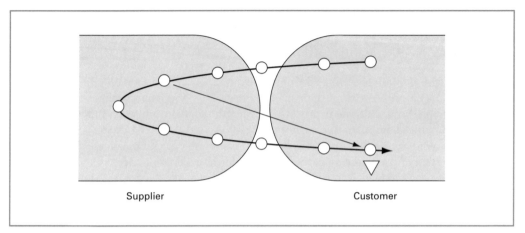

FIGURE 16.6 Illustration of the principle of VMI

orders, effectively placing purchasing orders in his customer's ERP system. If the customer owns the stocks, the vendor's deliveries are usually regulated by an agreement between the parties which defines the minimum and maximum limits for quantities in the customer stock which must be adhered to. These limits are set using the customer's desired inventory service levels and the size of stocks the customer is willing to pay for. Within the minimum and maximum limits the supplier has virtually full freedom of decision. He can select delivery times and order quantities to suit his own workload and stock situation.

If, on the other hand, the supplier owns stocks which are physically held with the customer, it may be said that he, the supplier, has taken complete responsibility for materials management. The collaboration contracts that are the basis of applying VMI include terms related to inventory service levels which the vendor undertakes to fulfil for the customer. In other respects, the vendor has full freedom to determine materials management and choose delivery times and order quantities according to his own desires and the capacity conditions and access to stock he has at each replenishment time. The vendor has the opportunity to optimise the allocation of stock quantities between his own finished stocks and customer stocks by moving the concentration of stock upstream or downstream in the supply chain. Contracted rules governing minimum and maximum limits for stock levels are often agreed on as a complement in cases where the vendor owns the stock.

Since the vendor owns the stock, the contract governing VMI must also include rules governing which party will conduct inventory counting, and which party will stand for inventory record discrepancies, wastage and scrapping. Normally the vendor will invoice the customer when products are withdrawn from the customer's stocks.

The exchange of information between customer and vendor which is required for VMI can be based on online communications or batch transfer of data using EDI, for example. Online communications basically means that the vendor has access to the customer's ERP system via the Internet or a telephone line, and performs materials management work directly in the system. If there is a need for real-time information or supplementary information in connection with materials management work, IT solutions of this type may be preferable. One disadvantage is that the vendor's personnel must learn to master the customer's ERP system. This may be a problem if the vendor uses VMI for many customers.

If batch transfer of data is used instead between a customer and vendor, every customer can be treated as a point of storage and the vendor can perform materials management work completely in his own ERP system. Information transferred from customers may consist of stock balances, historic consumption, forecasts and information about planned campaigns. The information transferred from vendor to customers consists primarily of planned stock replenishment orders and notification of imminent deliveries.

CASE STUDY 16.2: VENDOR-MANAGED INVENTORY AT STABBURET – PROCORDIA FOOD

Stabburet AS is one of the largest Norwegian food manufacturers and Procordia Food is one of several suppliers to Stabburet. Stabburet does not place purchasing orders with Procordia but Procordia is responsible for replenishing Stabburet's stocks, i.e. through a vendor-managed inventory strategy. Procordia receives daily forecasts of the expected weekly demand during the coming 12 months. It also received daily information about inventory balances. Information about planned replenishment orders and advanced shipment notices are sent from Procordia to Stabburet. The information exchange is conducted using EDI/Edifact. Stabburet owns the stock, which means that Procordia invoices Stabburet when the stock is replenished. Minimum and maximum stock levels, priority rules if lack of capacity, targeted runout time in stock, forecast accuracy, etc. are regulated in a collaboration agreement.

Quick Response

Quick Response (QR) is a concept for collaboration and exchange of information between manufacturers, wholesalers and retailers in supply chains. It normally involves more than two companies in a supply chain. In a similar fashion to that in the two subsequent concepts, it strives to co-ordinate and synchronise the common flow of materials to achieve the most efficient utilisation of resources possible. Its primary purpose is to enable a company to react faster to market changes and run operations in a more cost-effective manner to be able to better satisfy end consumers' needs. It was originally developed in the textile and clothing industry in USA at the end of the 1980s to compete with inexpensive imported clothes. It has since been developed and is now used to a varying degree and in different ways in a number of industries around the world, primarily in the consumer goods sector and on the distribution side of finished-product manufacturing companies.

The concept of Quick Response is built on and characterised by the following principles:

- Activities that influence the flow of materials and are carried out in a company must as far as possible be tied in with the customers' needs and behaviour. Flows of material along supply chains must as far as possible be synchronised with end-customers' demand. It is these customers' demand that must drive activities in all companies in the supply chain.

- Quick Response emphasises the holistic view of the supply chain and the significance of the consuming end-customer. In this respect it can be considered as a concept based on supply chain management. The difference in relation to traditional supply chain management is that Quick Response focuses on the synchronisation of requirements and supplies to a much larger extent. In that respect it may be considered as a just-in-time application in the distribution sector.

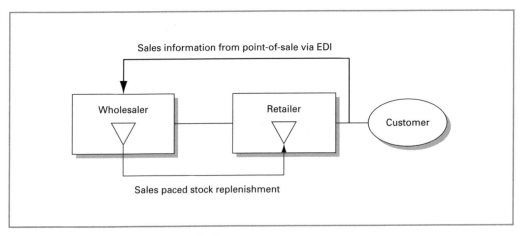

FIGURE 16.7 Example of Quick Response application

- Time used and time reduction plays a critical role for activities based on Quick Response. It is by reducing leadtimes in all parts of the supply chain that really large competitive advantages are obtained. In this way, Quick Response can be seen as an approach to time competition.

- Access to information and the willingness to exchange information between companies in supply chains, customers as well as suppliers, is one of the keystones in the entire Quick Response concept. It is built on trust and openness between the companies involved.

The developments within the area of IT have been a decisive prerequisite for the development and use of Quick Response. The concept builds on EDI or similar technologies for transferring information upstream in the supply chain from the point-of-sale (POS). It is also built on the use of automatic identification systems, such as bar codes and RFID, to quickly and cost-effectively identify current sales volumes at points-of-sale to end-customers. Figure 16.7 shows a simple example of a Quick Response application between a wholesaler and a retailer. Information about current sales is sent periodically, daily or weekly, via EDI to the wholesaler. On the basis of this information the wholesaler will replenish the retailer's stocks with quantities sold during the previous period. In other words, a consumption-replacing system is used to replenish stocks.

Efficient Consumer Response

Efficient Consumer Response (ECR) is closely related to Quick Response, but is a more wide-ranging concept for collaboration and exchange of information in supply chains. It was developed by a group of companies in the fast moving consumer goods industry in the USA in the beginning of the 1990s. ECR is used in a growing number of companies to varying extents and in different ways, but primarily between product manufacturers, wholesalers and retail companies working with foodstuffs and other fast moving consumer goods.

The organisation ECR Europe defines ECR as:

A joint initiative by members of the supply chain to work to improve and optimise aspects of

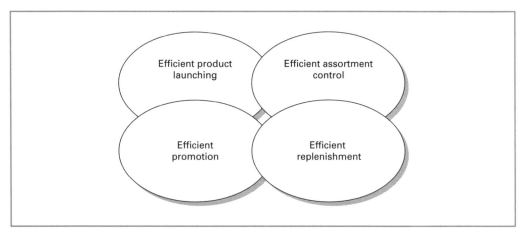

FIGURE 16.8 Main areas of the ECR concept

the supply chain and demand management to create benefits for the consumer e.g. lower prices, more choice of varieties, and better product availability. The mission of ECR Europe is 'To serve the consumer better, faster and at lower costs'. (ECR Europe Glossary, http://www.ecrnet.org, 20070508)

In comparison with Quick Response, ECR has a considerably broader approach in bringing more efficiency to supply chains. ECR also has more strategic and tactical dimensions. However, similarities are considerable with respect to basic approach and aims.

The four main areas of efficiency work within the ECR concept can be identified as follows: efficient launching of products, efficient promotion, efficient product range control and efficient supply of goods (see Figure 16.8). Each of these areas has its own goals within the framework of the overall aim of introducing and using ECR.

Efficient launching of products is aimed at increasing accuracy when introducing new products, and reducing launch costs. It represents a strategy for how vendors can collaborate with retailers with the purpose of developing and introducing new products to the market. From the logistics point of view, efficient launching of products includes co-ordinating manufacturing and distribution in time with marketing campaigns so that goods are in place as closely as possible to the time at which demand arises.

The goal of efficient promotion is to achieve more efficient marketing towards the consumer and to decrease costs of canvassing the market for different players in the supply chain. Through the exchange of information and collaboration, effective promotion also aims at managing material flows so that manufacturing and distribution can be efficiently adapted to the effects on demand caused by campaigns of different types, without the need for large excess stocks in any part of the supply chain. In other words, the flow of materials must be as synchronised and pull-driven as possible even during campaign periods.

Efficient assortment control refers to composing a range of products based on consumer demand which will optimise the use of available stock and sales space. Activities are aimed at improving profitability for retailers and different categories of suppliers. Since different products have different levels of profitability for players in the supply chain, the choice of product ranges must be made in collaboration between parties involved. Category management is an important part of efficient range control. In this case, collaboration strategies and product range issues affect whole categories or groups of goods.

The part of the ECR concept which is most similar to Quick Response is the efficient replanishment. This aims at optimising the flow of goods from the manufacturer, via any intermediaries, to the shelf in a shop. In the same way as Quick Response, it may be seen as a pull strategy since it too strives for synchronised and demand-driven material flows as much as possible. This is achieved by communicating point-of-sale information upstream in the supply chain and by using consumption replacing materials planning methods for stock replenishment.

In the same way as Quick Response, development in the IT area has been crucial for the application of ECR. Access to EDI or similar technologies is required to obtain a sufficiently rapid and cost-effective exchange of information between companies in a supply chain, from producer to retailer and the reverse. The use of bar codes or RFID for rapid and accurate identification of current sales volumes at points-of-sale is another prerequisite.

Collaborative planning, forecasting and replenishment

Both Quick Response and Efficient Consumer Response are to a large degree built on information exchange and collaboration between players in a supply chain. *Collaborative Planning Forecasting and Replenishment (CPFR)* is a concept which includes further steps in this direction. It may be seen as a logical further development of both Quick Response and ECR. Just like both the other collaboration concepts, it was developed in the USA by players in the fast moving consumer goods trade. Among the pioneers were large multinational companies such as Proctor & Gamble and Wal-Mart, both also experienced users of ECR.

CPFR is aimed at creating collaborative relationships between suppliers and customers through common processes and a structured exchange of information to achieve increased sales, more cost-effective material flows and less tied-up capital. The concept is built on the following five principles:

1 Collaboration within the framework of partnership relations and mutual trust. For such collaboration to take place, it must be based on overall common goals and activity plans.

2 Using common and agreed forecasts which both parties in the customer and supplier relationship use as a basis for their planning and activities. This is an important prerequisite for synchronising material flows between the companies.

3 Exploiting core competencies in the supply chain irrespective of which company they are located in. The party most suited to performing an activity in a chain of refinement should do that, no matter which company owns the resource. Use of vendor-managed inventory is an example of this procedure.

4 Using a common performance measurement system in the entire supply chain, which is based on customer demands. This creates a uniform and shared focus for all companies to serve the consuming customer.

5 Sharing risks and utilities which arise in the supply chain. This is not only a consequence of far-reaching collaboration and commitments to other companies – it also brings about positive mutual influence on behaviour in companies involved. If the total tied-up capital in a supply chain is reduced, retailers are motivated to improve their forecasting accuracy. Correspondingly, manufacturers are motivated to improve their delivery precision.

CPFR can be said to represent a relatively new management philosophy. Different companies have traditionally created their own individual forecasts and plans, and there have not been any

Retailer tasks	Collaboration tasks	Manufacturer tasks
Strategy and planning		
Vendor management Category management	Collaboration arrangement Joint business plan	Account planning Market planning
Demand and supply management		
POS forecasting Replenishment planning	Sales forecasting Order planning/forecasting	Market data analysis Demand planning
Execution		
Buying/re-buying Logistics/Distribution	Order generation Order fulfilment	Production and supply planning Logistics/Distribution
Analysis		
Store execution Supplier scorecard	Exception management Performance assessment	Execution monitoring Customer scorecard

FIGURE 16.9 The four activities in CPFR and the eight collaboration tasks
Source: APICS (2005) and VICS (www.vics.org).

mechanisms to ensure that they correspond to those of other companies. The chances of synchronising processes and material flows have not been great. CPFR, if implemented well and used efficiently, can change this.

A standardised model for successfully implementing CPFR has been produced, as shown in Figure 16.9. It includes four activities and eight collaboration tasks for members of the supply chain. The activities are strategy and planning, demand and supply management, execution, and analysis. Strategy and planning is aimed at determining rules for collaboration and contains collaboration arrangement and joint business planning. Demand and supply management projects customer demand and contains information on sales forecasting and order planning/forecasting. Execution corresponds to the order-to-cash cycle and contains information on order generation and order fulfilment. Analysis consists of the collaboration tasks of exception management and performance assessment.

The process for achieving shared handling of plans and forecasts may be practically applied in the following way: the retailer shares his historic sales statistics which are obtained by reading off bar codes. The information is transferred via EDI or equivalent technology upstream in the supply chain. The retailer also shares information on planned campaigns and other activities which may be expected to influence future demand. The forecasts which the retailer produces are also transferred to the supplier, and these forecasts are compared with the supplier's own order forecast. Any discrepancies are discussed by the two parties and adjustments made so that both forecasts completely correspond with each other. This procedure ensures that companies involved can use one single forecast throughout the entire supply chain.

16.4 Supply Chain Design

Supply chains can be designed in a number of basic ways. The degree of owner influence is one way of distinguishing between different chains. A vertically integrated supply chain has realised collaboration and integration through the purchase and involvement of several plants within one organisation. A laterally integrated supply chain, on the other hand, is built on collaboration and integration between several business units without any owner influence. Another point of departure for the design of supply chains is market demands and product characteristics. Within this approach, supply chains are designed to be market-responsive or physically efficient. The former can rapidly and flexibly respond to unpredictable market changes, while the latter operates to supply relatively predictable and stable market demand in a resource-efficient manner.

Vertically vs. laterally integrated supply chains

In a vertically integrated supply chain, one party has ownership influence over the parts of the chain; see Figure 16.10a. The main advantages of **vertical integration** are control, visibility, and the possibilities of collaboration and synchronisation of material flows. A management unit may have access to information from the entire chain, and control and optimise the flows of materials centrally. Uncertainties are small since the supply of raw materials and availability of capacity are well known and not subjected to any competition. But there are also conditions of high

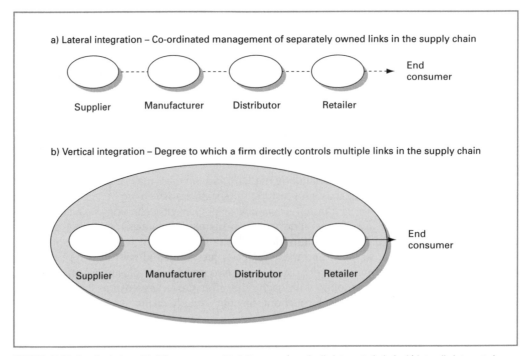

FIGURE 16.10 Supply chains with different ownership influence, a) vertically integrated chain, b) laterally integrated chain
Source: based on APICS (2005).

uncertainty, since it is difficult to adapt to changing demands which may require different competence and capacity than that existing within the chain.

A *vertically integrated supply chain* can either be built up through internal growth or through mergers and acquisitions of organisations. Possibly the best-known example of a vertically integrated supply chain is the Ford Motor Company's organisation at the beginning and middle of the twentieth century. With the aim of becoming self-sufficient and independent of other parties, Ford gained ownership of as many as possible of the other organisations in the supply chain, including mines, steelworks, factories, means of transport and showrooms. Vertical integration is considerably less common today than it was previously, however. Ford and many other companies that once owned large parts of their chains have now outsourced most of the processes they once owned.

Companies that work with fast-moving consumer goods, such as the Spanish clothes company Zara and the Swedish furniture company IKEA, build their supply chains on vertical integration to some extent. They have limited ownership control of production processes, but own warehouses and retail outlets. Ownership of production facilities secures availability of capacity. Through their control of retail outlets, communication of point-of-sales data upstream in the supply chain is made simpler, as are replenishments of products to shops.

Supply chains that are structured around several independent organisations in collaboration are usually called *lateral supply chains* (see Figure 16.10b). This type of supply chain is by far the most common at the moment. One main advantage is that each organisation can focus on its core activities and obtain economies of scale. In a vertically integrated supply chain, each process may be carried out satisfactorily, but it is very difficult to be extremely good at several processes, or indeed all. Not having ownership control of processes in the supply chain means that suppliers also deliver to competitors, which can lead to confidentiality problems and a reluctance to share information and collaborate. Another advantage of **lateral integration** compared with vertical integration is its flexibility; it is easier to change business direction, suppliers and so on.

Laterally integrated supply chains place high demands on the exchange of information and collaboration, and the synchronisation of joint material flows. Thanks to developments in the area of IT, the potential for achieving these is much greater than it was in the past, but it is still far from simple. What a laterally integrated supply chain gains in core competence focus, economies of scale and flexibility, it may in some situations lose several times over in lack of understanding and control of the supply chain as a whole.

Responsive vs. physically efficient supply chains

It is possible to categorise a company's products with respect to their demand pattern, including the products' lifecycle length, demand uncertainty and market demands on short leadtimes. Products with different demand patterns require different types of supply chain characteristics. Marshall Fisher (Fisher, 1997) presented in his article "What is the right supply chain for your product?" a model for designing supply chains based on existing product characteristics. According to Fisher's model, products can be categorised as either *functional* or *innovative*.

Table 16.1 describes characteristic properties for these two product types. Functional products refer to commodities with few variants which are sold in high volumes through many market channels to many different customers. These products do not change much over time and have a stable and predictable demand. They have many suppliers, however, which results in low profit margins and a focus on low costs. It is possible to forecast demand for the products with high precision and to manufacture products to stock without risking high costs for stock shortages or obsolescence.

Aspects of demand	Functional (predictable demand)	Innovative (unpredictable demand)
Typical products	Commodities	Fashion goods
Product lifecycle	Long	Short
Profit margin	Low	High
Product variety	Low	High
Marketplace demand	Predictable	Volatile
Stockout rate	Low	High
Forced end-of-season markdown (obsolescence)	Low	High
Leadtime required for made-to-order products	Long	Short
Order winner	Cost	Service level

TABLE 16.1 Demand comparison for functional and innovative products
Source: Based on Fisher, 1997 and Mason-Jones et al., 2000.

Innovative products are those which compete through their unique design or basis on a unique concept. Fashion clothes are a typical example of an innovative product. They have many variants and short product lifecycles. The profit margin is considerably higher compared with functional products, but so is the risk of stockout and obsolescence, meaning that products in stock must be scrapped or sold at reduced prices of the end of the sale season. It is not possible accurately to predict demand for innovative products. Manufacture of innovative products to stock is not a viable strategy for this reason. It is more important to be able to adapt quickly to

	Physical efficient supply chain	Market-responsive supply chain
Primary purpose	Supply predictable demand efficiently at the lowest possible cost	Respond quickly to unpredictable demand in order to minimise stockouts, forced markdowns and obsolete inventories
Manufacturing focus	Maintain high average utilisation rate	Deploy excess buffer capacity
Inventory strategy	Generate high turns and minimise inventory throughout the chain	Deploy significant buffer stocks of parts or finished goods
Leadtime focus	Shorten leadtimes as long as they do not increase costs	Invest aggressively in ways to reduce leadtimes
Approach to choosing suppliers	Select primarily for cost and quality	Select primarily for speed, flexibility and quality
Forecasting	Forecast product variants	Forecast capacity need
Product-design strategy	Maximise performance and minimise cost	Use modular design in order to postpone product differentiation for as long as possible
Information exchange	Highly desirable	Obligatory

TABLE 16.2 Comparison of physical efficient and market-responsive supply chains
Based on Fisher, 1997.

changes in volumes and variants demanded and to supply the market with correct volumes and variants with short leadtimes.

The two types of products thus place different demands on supply chain processes. According to Fisher's model, functional products demand physically efficient supply chains and innovative products demand market-**responsive supply chains** (see Table 16.2). Physically efficient chains do not support innovative products, and market-responsive chains do not support functional products. Therefore it is necessary to match market and product characteristics with supply chain characteristics, as shown in Figure 16.11.

Physically efficient supply chains are also called **lean supply chains**. In a physically efficient or lean process, value is created and costs minimised through elimination of all waste. Market-responsive supply chains are sometimes called **agile supply chains**, which expresses their ability to adapt quickly and flexibly to changing requirements. The two types of supply chain differ with respect to cost focus and adaptability. The physical costs of production, transportation and storage are dominant in physically efficient supply chains. They can be minimised by high utilisation of capacity in production and reducing stocks in the whole supply chain. In market-responsive supply chains, **market mediating costs** are dominant, meaning costs for stock shortages and obsolescence. The focus for production and storage in this type of supply chain is not to minimise all costs, but to determine where in the chain it is best to have storage and extra production capacity to best satisfy the unpredictable demand at the lowest possible cost.

Both types of supply chain require short leadtimes. To quickly satisfy changing customer demands for innovative products in market-responsive supply chains, total lead times from customer orders placed to delivery of product to customers must be short. Short leadtimes are also necessary in physically efficient supply chains, but for a different reason. Long leadtimes always cause high costs, often consisting of partly unnecessary activities or waste.

Suppliers in physically efficient supply chains are chosen for their capacity to eliminate waste and minimise total costs. In market-responsive chains it is more important to have flexible suppliers that can adapt to changing volumes and variants with short leadtimes.

Physically efficient supply chains are dependent on good forecasts at the product variant level. The long product lifecycles and the predictable demand often make it possible to base forecasts on historic sales statistics. This is neither possible nor appropriate for innovative products. Forecasts are nevertheless important for innovative product and market-responsive supply chains, but in this case to forecast the total future capacity requirements and trends for variants based on the first days' or weeks' sales.

Product design is important in both types of supply chains. In physically efficient chains it is important to decrease the number of variants at the component and product level in order to simplify forecasting and management and to minimise tied-up capital and costs. In market-responsive chains it is necessary to have product structures which enable postponement of product configuration. By postponing the configuration of customer specific variants based on standard components and modularisation, both physical and market mediating costs can be minimised at the same time as volatile demand is satisfied. Information exchange is important in physically efficient supply chains to minimise bullwhip effects and unnecessary stocks, among other things. In market-responsive supply chains, the exchange of real-time information, for example, in the form of capacity requirements forecast to suppliers is absolutely crucial to succeed in exploiting short leadtimes and flexible processes and to react sufficiently quickly and efficiently to rapid market changes.

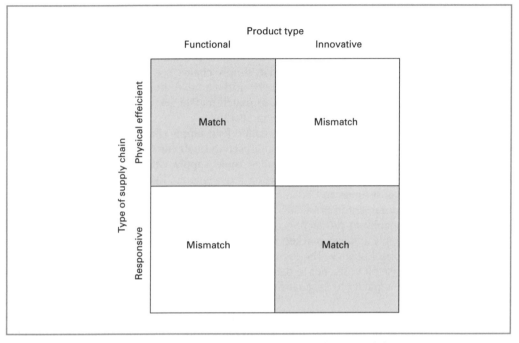

FIGURE 16.11 Matching market and product characteristics with supply chain characteristics
Source: Fisher (1997).

CASE STUDY 16.3: ZARA'S QUICKNESS AND RESPONSIVENESS CONCEPT (Ferdows et al., 2004)

The profit in the clothing industry is closely tied to the percentage of products a company can sell to full price. The Spanish clothing manufacturer Zara has developed a business concept based on quickness and responsiveness for maximising full price sales. It can design, produce and deliver a new garment based on the latest trends and put it in stores worldwide in 15 days. This responsiveness and quickness allows them to introduce more than twice as many products as its competitors each year. A product may only be on the market for a couple of weeks before it is exchanged; thus, it works with some twenty "seasons" a year. The relentless introduction of new products in small quantities reduces the costs of shortages, because the item can be considered outdated when it is sold out. The short market windows of the products motivate its customers to visit Zara shops more frequently than they might other shops. This reduces the need for advertising. Zara spends only 0.3 per cent of its turnover on ads, compared to 3 to 4 per cent among its competitors. Because of this responsiveness and quickness Zara can sell about 85 per cent of its products at full price, compared to the industry average of 60 to 70 per cent. But how can then Zara be so responsive and quick?

The information exchange throughout the supply chain, between customers, store managers, designers, production staff, buyers, warehouse managers, distributors, etc., is the cornerstone of Zara's business concept. All information exchange between stores and the head quarters in La Coruna is simplified and speeded up as much as possible. The stores frequently transmit information about possible future sales, such as point-of-sales data, forecasts and informal customer reactions to different garments, models and styles. The actual assortment is communicated from La Coruna to the stores 24 hours before ordering. Replenishment orders from store managers to central product managers are done at strictly enforced deadlines twice a week for each product using "hand beamers".

Zara has a single centralised design and production centre in La Coruna, Spain. Three design teams (for women's, men's and children's lines), procurement and production planners are located close together and work as cross-functional teams which allows for both high speed and quality in the design, purchasing and production process. They could, for example, examine prototypes, choose design, and commit resources for its production in a few hours.

At the central warehouse in La Coruna the items are prepriced, tagged and mostly hung up on racks so they can be displayed in the stores as fast as possible after delivery. Truck and air deliveries from the central warehouse in La Coruna reach the stores twice a week. In Europe most stores are reached within 24 hours, in the US within 48 hours and in Asia within 72 hours. This fast and responsive distribution strategy drives high costs due to expensive traffic modes (truck and air instead of ships and trains), frequent deliveries (twice a week) and low warehouse utilisation and transport fill rates (clothes stored and transported hanging on racks instead of packed in tight packages). However, these costs are justified since they result in greater benefits in terms of lower inventory carrying costs, lower obsolescence risks and shorter time to market.

Compared to its competitors, Zara is to a greater extent vertically integrated in the supply chain. It owns all its stores, which simplifies the information exchange and the centralised planning. It produces about half of its products in its own factories in Spain and Lithuania and buys a large proportion of its fabrics and dyestuff from own suppliers. The high degree of vertical integration reduces the possibilities of gaining from economy of scale but gives better control of the capacity. The access to extra production, warehousing and transportation capacity when needed is a necessity for carrying out its quick and responsive strategy successfully. Most facilities, for example, are scheduled for one shift and can quickly ramp up and down production of specific garments.

Zara's entire supply chain is, however, not quick and responsive. About half of the products are simple, standard products or base volumes of products which are easier to forecast and for which the time factor is not considered as important as the costs. Physically efficient rather than responsive supply chains are suitable for these products. Production of these is outsourced to low-cost producers in Europe, North Africa and Asia to allow for more physically efficient supply. The postponement of fabric dying is another issue allowing for both physical efficiency and responsiveness. More than half of its fabrics are bought and stored undyed. This allows for purchase and storage of a limited number of standard fabrics in a physically efficient manner. It consequently reduces the obsolescence risks of stored fabric and aligns the reaction time to colour and pattern changes.

Multiple supply chains

Most companies have more than one supply chain since they have different types of products and supply different markets. A company may purchase different items from several suppliers to manufacture a product with a complex product structure. Purchased items can vary from cheap commodities to specially designed and customer-unique components. This means that physically efficient supply chains may be preferable for some items while market-responsive chains are more suitable for other items. It may be an advantage to combine physically efficient and market-responsive characteristics in the same supply chain, or to combine physically efficient and market-responsive supply chains for the same product.

One way of combining physically efficient and market-responsive supply chains is to differentiate supply chains before and after the **customer order decoupling point (CODP)**, as shown in Figure 16.12. This is synonymous with applying postponement, or keeping stocks of standard items and modules and only configuring and assembling customer-specific variants when customer requirements are known. Items kept in stock have more or less functional characteristics and are supplied by physically efficient supply chains. Flows from the storage point to the market, on the other hand, must be market-responsive and quickly satisfy unpredictable demand. Differentiating supply chains before and after the decoupling point is a commonly applied strategy in the computer and automotive industries, where a large number of customer-specific variants are based on a limited number of standard components.

Another way of combining physically efficient and market-responsive supply chains is to design different chains for the demand which may be characterised as *base* or *surge* respectively. In many situations it is possible to identify a **base demand** for a product which is predictable and which can be forecast, and a **surge demand** which is unpredictable and uncertain. The base demand corresponds to market conditions for a functional product and is best satisfied by a physically efficient supply chain. Surge demand reflects conditions for an inno-

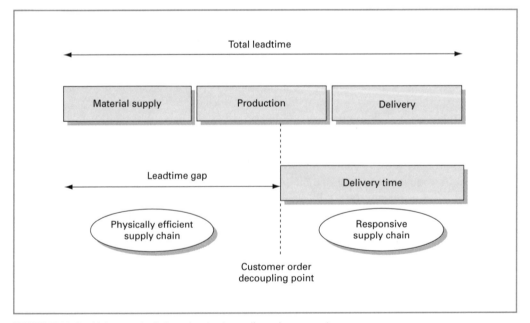

FIGURE 16.12 Combining supply chains using the decoupling point approach

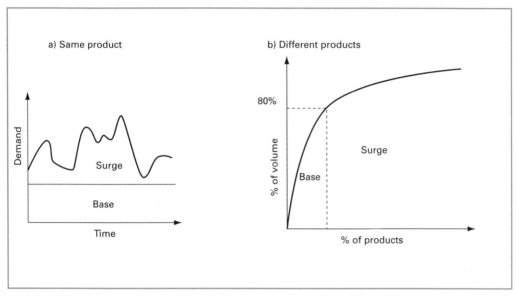

FIGURE 16.13 Combining supply chains by separating *base* and *surge* demand, a) combination through separate production lines or plants, b) combination through different priorities
Source: Christopher and Towill (2001).

vative product and as such is best satisfied by a market-responsive supply chain. Supplying base and surge demand from separate supply chains is a common strategy in the textile industry, for example. The predictable base demand is forecast and manufactured to stock in low-cost countries, thus minimising physical costs. The unpredictable surge demand is then manufactured locally at a higher cost but with better chances of quickly satisfying volatile demand, thus minimising the market mediating costs. Combining supply chains for base and surge demand can be achieved either by having separate production lines or geographically separate plants. Base and surge demand could also be separated between different products based on ABC analysis. A few prodcuts with high volume and even demand could then be made to stock based on forecast. Low volume products, on the other hand, could get high priority and be made to order. Figure 16.13 illustrates the two strategies for combining supply chains with respect to base and surge demand.

16.5 Supply Chain Risk-Management Strategies

All activities are subject to risks. This is also the case for supply chains. A supply chain aims at creating the largest possible value for the end consumer by facilitating the material, information and monetary flows along the whole path from the original raw materials producer to the end customer, and where appropriate, reverse flow. The risks that exist in the supply chain are, consequently, any events which may disturb these different flows. As companies develop closer business relationships with their customers, suppliers and logistics service providers and become increasingly dependent on information systems, there is an increased risk of disruptions which start with one player or system and spread to other systems and players in the supply chain. A process for developing **supply chain risk-management strategy** can be described as consisting of the following activities: 1) risk identification, 2) risk analysis, 3) development of risk management strategy.

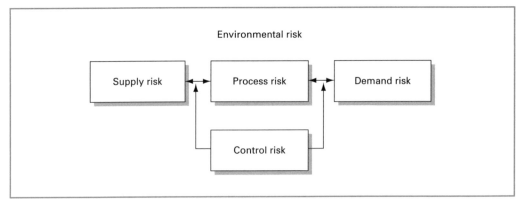

FIGURE 16.14 Sources of risk in supply chains
Source: Mason-Jones and Towill (1988).

Risk identification

The first step in being able to manage risks is to be aware of them and their sources. Risks in a supply chain can be defined as environmental risks, supply risks, demand risks, process risks and control risks, as illustrated in Figure 16.14.

The sources of environmental risks are external and outside the company's or supply chain's system limits, while the sources of the other risks are considered to be internal, and can thus be influenced by the company itself or the supply chain.

Environmental risks: the origins of environmental risks are external and cannot be influenced by the company or the supply chain, since they arise outside the sphere of influence of the company and the supply chain. External risks may be political (e.g. regulations, environment taxes), environment related (e.g. fires, storms, earthquakes), or social (e.g. terrorist attacks).

Supply risks: Supply risks are related to supply activities and supplier relationships. The source of the risk is the supplier or the supplier's supplier. Single and global sourcing strategies increase dependence on individual suppliers, and thus risks that disruptions at the supplier may spread to the company itself. Supply risks may be caused by external risks, so damage due to lightning at a supplier may result in delivery disruptions to downstream customer companies. Supply risks are not necessarily associated with a particular supplier: they may be of a general nature and applied to a whole line of industry or type of supplier. This is the case when there are general shortages in capacity or raw materials.

Demand risks: demand risks are created by flows to and relations with customers. They could include seasonal variations, changing customer behaviour and preferences, changes in design or short product lifecycles.

Process risk: Process risks arise as a result of bottlenecks, variations or defects in internal processes such as materials handling, quality control or production processes. As well as being a source of risk, internal processes can either absorb or amplify risks which occur at suppliers, customers or in the environment. Excess capacity in an internal process may mean that the effects of delayed delivery to a customer is minimised, for example.

Control risks: Control risks are caused by the internal planning and control system and rules for making decisions. This could be related to materials planning methods, or the size of safety stocks which may in themselves cause problems that are difficult to handle, or that may increase or decrease the consequences of supply and demand risks.

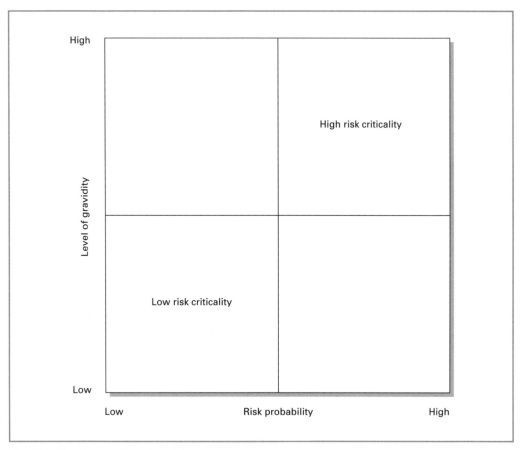

FIGURE 16.15 Risk probability and level of gravity

Risk analysis

Risk analysis is aimed at defining critical paths amongst all identified risks where particular attention needs to be paid. The critical rating of the risk is determined by the probability of it occurring
and the gravity of the consequences if it occurred. Risks with high probability of occurring and
grave consequences if they occur are the most critical types, as shown in Figure 16.15.

There are tools produced and used within the area of Total Quality Management to analyse
the consequence of risks and reasons for them. *FMECA (Failure Mode Effect and Criticality
Analysis)* is a tool for 1) systematically mapping possible failure modes in a system, 2) identifying
the potential effects of failures on the performance of the system 3) quantifying the likelihood of
the failure occurring, 4) quantifying the criticality of the consequences and 5) quantifying the
level of difficulty in discovering failures before their consequences affect a customer. The
Ishikawa diagram and Five Why's are methods of identifying the underlying reasons for a failure
or problem. These tools could be used for risk analysis in supply chains. Figure 16.16 describes
an FMECA table and an Ishikawa diagram.

a) FMECA

Process/ system/ item	Potential risk (failure mode)	Failure effect	Severity if occurance (1-10)	Potential causes of failure	Probability of occurance (1-10)	Current process control detection	Difficulty of detection (1-10)	RPN (1-1000)	Recommended action	Responsibility & target completion date	Action taken
Process X	Risk 1										
	Risk 2										
	Risk n										
Process Y											

RPN = Risk priority number (Severity x Occurancy x Detection)

a) Ishikawa diagram

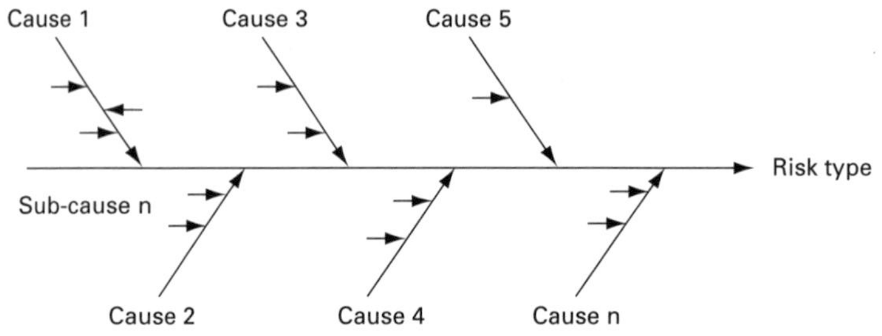

FIGURE 16.16 (a) FMECA and (b) Ishikawa diagram for the analysis of risks in supply chains

Development of risk management strategy

There are two basic methods of handling critical risks. Either a company focuses on process improvements with the aim of eliminating or at least decreasing the probability of risks, or safety mechanisms and buffer strategies are introduced to decrease the criticality of risk consequences. In reality, both methods are necessary since it is neither practical nor economically feasible to eliminate all risks.

The development of risk strategies is not a one-time activity. Effective risk management demands continuous visualisation and monitoring of existing critical risks, and analysis to identify new risks and to reassess existing critical paths.

CASE STUDY 16.4: SUPPLY CHAIN RISK MANAGEMENT AT ERICSSON AND NOKIA (Latour, 2001)

In March 2000 lightning struck a Philips Electronics semiconductor manufacturing plant in Albequerqy, New Mexico. The lightning caused a fire for some minutes and shut down the plant for a couple of weeks. The plant was the sole source for a critical component for Nokia's and Ericsson's mobile phone handsets.

At Nokia the fire in the Philips plant was recognised immediately and resulted in activities to secure the necessary supply from alternative sources. As a result, Nokia's production was only marginally affected by the event.

At Ericsson it took weeks to recognise that the fire had occurred and to realise that it would affect its supply of components. This delay was partly due to high stock levels in the supply chain. When the company realised the global supply shortage of the critical component, it was already too late to do anything about it. With a better visibility in the supply chain and a clearer and faster supply chain risk management plan Ericsson could have secured the supply in the same way as Nokia. The business impact on Ericsson was enormous, with large revenue and market share losses. Later, Ericsson outsourced production to Flextronics and merged the cellphone business with Sony in the new SonyEricsson cellphone company.

16.6 Conclusion and Summary

In the last few decades logistics has developed to include far more than traditional business processes within a company. To achieve efficient flows of materials and information in supply chains, a company must also collaborate with customers and suppliers in joint inter-organisational processes. Increased operative dependence relationships between companies, increasingly unpredictable future demand, increasingly volatile markets and the growing number of transactions and thus transaction costs are the main forces that have driven this development.

There is a growing tendency to introduce solutions such as customer-managed ordering processing and vendor-managed inventory as methods of achieving a more optimal work distribution between customer companies and supplier companies in the inter-organisational processes that achieve material flows between partners. Collaboration in inter-organisational processes also benefits co-ordination and synchronisation of material flows and resource utilisation in companies along the same supply chain. Applications of this type often include more than two companies. Common examples of such applications are Quick Response, Efficient Consumer Response and Collaborative Planning, Forecasting and Replenishment. This is especially appropriate for fast moving consumer goods but also for several other industries.

Design of supply chains can result in different types of chains. Vertically and laterally integrated supply chains differ from each other in the degree of owner control. Physically efficient and market-responsive supply chains have their primary advantages in minimising physical costs and market mediating costs respectively.

With increasing interdependencies between players and supply chains, vulnerability to disruptions becomes greater. The chapter therefore concluded with a discussion on the principles of supply chain risk management.

Key concepts

Agile supply chains 385	Market mediating cost 385
Base demand 388	Physically efficient supply chain 385
Bullwhip effect 366	Point-of-sales (POS) data 366
Collaborative Planning Forecasting and Replenishment (CPFR) 372	Quick Response (QR) 372
	Responsive supply chain 385
Customer-managed ordering (CMO) 367	Supply chain risk management 389
Customer order decoupling point (CODP) 388	Surge demand 388
	Transaction costs 371
Efficient Consumer Response (ECR) 372	Vendor-managed inventories (VMI) 367
Lateral integration 383	Vertical integration 382
Lean supply chains 385	

Discussion Tasks

1 Collaboration between companies in supply chains creates favourable conditions for increased efficiency in those companies. However, there may be problems associated with introducing different forms of collaboration, and it may have some inherent disadvantages. Discuss some conceivable difficulties and disadvantages involved in collaboration.

2 What types of products are first and foremost suitable for customer-managed ordering processing between companies, or business-to-business applications (B2B)? Would they be low-price or high-price items, items in stock or manufactured to customer order, items with short or long leadtimes, repetitive high turnover items or low-frequency, low-turnover items?

3 In the application of vendor-managed inventory, either the customer or the vendor may own the store of goods. Discuss the consequences of both these alternatives with respect to settlement procedures, accounting and closing the books, and the contracts which regulate collaboration between both parties involved.

4 Consider a manufacturer of wooden toys. Discuss how it could gain from combining physical efficient and market responsive supply chains.

5 All companies face some types of supply chain risks. Discuss different supply chain risk types for an importer of fresh fruits.

Further reading

APICS (2005) *Building competitive operations, planning and logistics.* APICS certified supply chain professional learning system Module 2, APICS, Alexandria.

Christopher, M. (2005) *Logistics and supply chain management.* McGraw-Hill, New York.

Christopher, M. and Lee, H. (2004) "Mitigating supply chain risk through improved confidence", *International Journal of Physical Distribution and Logistics Management,* Vol. 34, No. 5, pp. 388–396.

Christopher, M. and Towill, D. (2001) "An integrated model for the design of agile supply chains", *International Journal of Physical Distribution and Logistics Management,* Vol. 31, No. 4, pp. 235–246.

Disney, S. and Towill, D. (2003) "Vendor-managed inventory and bullwhip reduction in a two-level supply chain", *International Journal of Operations and Production Management,* Vol. 23, No. 6, pp. 625–651.

Ferdows, K., Lewis, M. and Machuca, J. (2004) "Rapid-fire fulfillment", *Harvard Business Review,* November, pp. 1–6.

Fisher, M. (1997) "What is the right supply chain for your product? A simple framework can help you figure out the answer", *Harvard Business Review,* March-April, pp. 105–116.

Frohlich, M. and Westbrook, R. (2001) "Arcs of integration: an international study of supply chain strategies", *Journal of Operations Management,* Vol. 19, pp. 185–200.

Kotzab, H. (1999) "Improving supply chain performance by efficient consumer response? A critical comparison of existing ECR approaches", *Journal of Business & Industrial Marketing,* Vol. 14, No. 5/6, pp. 364–377.

Latour, A. (2001) "A blaze in Alburquerque sets off major crisis for cell-phone giants", *Wall Street Journal,* 29 January, section A, p. 1.

Lee, H. (2002) "Aligning supply chain strategies with product uncertainties", *California Management Review,* Vol. 44, No. 3, pp. 105–119.

Lee, H., Padmanabhan, V. and Whang, S. (1997) "The bullwhip effect in supply chains", *Sloan Management Review,* Spring, pp. 93–102.

Mason-Jones, R. and Towill, D.R. (1988) "Shrinking the supply chain uncertainty cycle", *Control,* September, pp. 17–22.

Mason-Jones, R. and Towill, D. (1997) "Information enrichment: designing the supply chain for competitive advantage", *Supply Chain Management,* Vol. 2, No. 4, pp. 137–148.

Mattsson, S.-A. (2000) *Embracing change: Management strategies in the e-economy era.* Intentia International, Stockholm.

Pohlen, T. and Goldsby, T. (2003) "VMI and SMI programs: how economic value added can help sell the change", *International Journal of Physical Distribution and Logistics Management,* Vol. 33, No. 7, pp. 565–581.

Skjoett-Larsen, T., Thernoe, C. and Andresen, C. (2003) "Supply chain collaboration: theoretical perspectives and empirical evidence", *International Journal of Physical Distribution and Logistics Management,* Vol. 33, No. 6, pp. 531–549.

Småros, J. and Holmström, J. (2000) "Viewpoint: reaching the customer through e-grocery VMI", *International Journal of Retail & Distribution Management*, Vol. 28, No. 2, pp. 55–61.

Smith, I. (2006) "West Marine: a CPFR success story", *Supply Chain Management Review*, Vol. 10, No. 2, pp. 29–36.

CHAPTER 17

Information systems for logistics and supply chain management

A prerequisite for rational decision-making is access to complete, up-to-date and correct information. Such information is also essential for managing industrial activities and for the efficient flow of materials and use of resources. Different types of information systems are used as tools to collect, process and transmit information as a basis for the operative management of resources and material flows. Information systems are required to process information and provide a basis for decisions. The different information systems used in logistics and supply chain management can be divided into four main groups as shown in Figure 17.1:

1 *Planning and execution systems*, which contain databases and software for providing information and data for decisions to support ongoing business processes in the company.

2 *Communication systems* that relate to different methods aimed at communicating information within and between companies, such as between customer companies and supplier companies and between trucks and stationary distribution systems.

3 *Identification systems*, used to identify goods in the flow of materials, such as items delivered to stock.

4 *Electronic marketplaces*, used to facilitate communications and transactions between, e.g., purchasing and selling parties.

In this chapter, the relevant aspects of planning and execution systems, communication systems, identification systems and electronic marketplaces are described from perspectives of logistics and SCM. The concept of information quality is introduced, and a discussion follows on how the information system influences this information quality.

The chapter is closely related to several other chapters in the book. There are direct links to Chapter 11 Demand management, Chapter 12 Materials management, Chapter 13 Manufacturing planning and control, Chapter 14 Transport planning, Chapter 15 The procurement process and Chapter 16 Emerging practices in supply chain management.

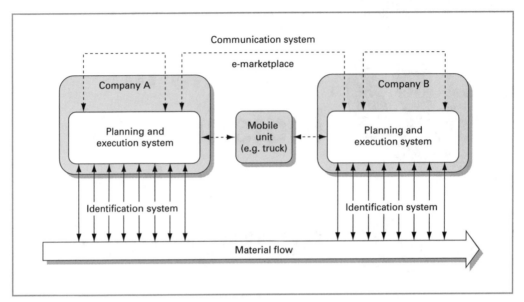

FIGURE 17.1 The logistics information system consists of planning and execution systems, communication systems, identification systems and electronic marketplaces

17.1 Planning and Execution Systems

There are two main types of planning and execution systems: enterprise resource planning systems and different types of specialised and advanced planning systems. The **enterprise resource planning system (ERP)** usually contains computer systems support for all business processes in the company, not only those units which are directly connected with logistics and supply chain management but also units such as marketing and sales, financial management and accounting, and human resources. ERP is characterised by its capacity to store large amounts of data and handle large volumes of transactions. The data-processing carried out is relatively simple.

Specialised and advanced planning systems are intended for more specific applications. In many cases they do not have their own databases, but utilise data stored in a parallel ERP system. The systems are characterised by advanced data-processing, in many cases based on operations research methods. To a greater degree than the ERP system, they provide complete data for decisions related to the planning or execution of different types of measures. In recent years, specialised and advanced types of systems applications have been developed as integrated parts of ERP. In addition to ERP systems, the principles for **warehouse management systems (WMS)**, **transport management systems (TMS)** and **advanced planning and scheduling** systems (**APS**) will be described.

Enterprise resource planning systems

An ERP system is a database and a collection of software programs which provide and process information required for administrative management and control of activities in a company. Most ERP systems on the market are so general and have such wide-ranging functionalities that they are applicable to most types of companies. There are also systems which to a greater or lesser degree are specially designed for certain trades, and there are systems which are primarily intended for trading companies or service companies. The same designation, ERP, is used for all these systems.

In general, an ERP system includes a database which is shared between all program functions and which can provide the necessary information for all business processes. This is called an *integrated system*. Using this system's architecture, every user has online access to all the information which they need to carry out their parts of enterprise resource planning, and personnel can work in one and the same system without problems with different interfaces – which is often the case if several different functional systems are involved.

CASE STUDY 17.1: STRUCTURE AND FUNCTIONALITY OF IFS APPLICATIONS

IFS is an ERP vendor. Its ERP system is used by mid-sized and large companies. The ERP system contains several modules. They are grouped in the eight business areas: financials, human resources, sales and service, engineering, manufacturing, distribution, maintenance and business enablers. In addition, there are a number of modules (business performance, document management, etc.)

				DEMAND PLANNING			
				CONSTRAINT BASED SCHEDULING			
ENTERPRISE STOREFRONT				COSTING			
WEBSTORE	FINANCIAL LEDGER			SHOP FLOOR REPORTING	PAYROLL ADMINISTRATION		VEHICLE INFORMATION MANAGEMENT
ePROCUREMENT	REPORT GENERATOR		SUPPLIER SCHEDULING	CRP/MRP	EXPENSE REPORTING	SCHEDULING	PROCESS DESIGN
eMARKETS	CONSOLIDATED ACCOUNTS	FIELD SERVICE & OPERATIONS	CUSTOMER SCHEDULING	SHOP ORDER	TIME & ATTENDANCE	PREVENTIVE MAINTENANCE	INSTRUMENTATION DESIGN
CONTACT CENTRE	FIXED ASSETS	PROPOSAL GENRATION	CUSTOMER ORDERS	MAKE TO ORDER	PROJECT REPORTING	WORK ORDER	ELECTRICAL DESIGN
COLLABORATION	ACCOUNTS RECEIVABLE	SALES CONFIGURATOR	INVOICING	ASSEMBLE TO ORDER	RECRUITMENT	EQUIPMENT	PLANT LAYOUT & PIPPING DESIGN
EMPLOYEE PORTALS	ACCOUNTS PAYABLE	SALES & MARKETING	PURCHASING	REPETITIVE PRODUCTION	EMPLOYEE DEVELOPMENT	EQUIPMENT PERFORMANCE	PROJEST DELIVERY
WIRELESS SERVICES	GENERAL LEDGER	MARKETING ENCYCLOPEDIA	INVENTORY	MASTER SCHEDULING	SKILLS & QUALIFICATIONS	EQUIPMENT MONITORING	PDM CONFIGURATION
IFS eBUSINESS	IFS FINANCIALS	IFS FRONT OFFICE	IFS DISTRIBUTION	IFS MANUFACTURING	IFS HUMAN RESOURCES	IFS MAINTENANCE	IFS ENGINEERING
PERSONAL PORTAL MANAGEMENT	PROJECT		QUALITY MANAGEMENT	ACCOUNTING RULES		DOCUMENT MANAGEMENT	BUSINESS PERFORMANCE
IFS Foundation1 v5							

Of the different parts of the ERP database related to logistics and supply-chain activities, we can distinguish between a *basic database*, a *transaction database* and a *planning database*. The basic database contains information about products which are manufactured and distributed and the items included in products, the structure of the products, how they are manufactured and what resources are required for their manufacture. The basic database stores information about the manufacturing and distribution resources at the company and what storage places and storage positions there are. It also contains information about customers and suppliers with which the company deals and between which there are materials, information and monetary flows.

In all manufacturing and distributing operations there are large volumes of different types of transactions taking place all the time. Information on these must be processed and stored for it to be used in management and follow-up of operations. This storage is in the part of the ERP database called the transaction database. Transactions may be purchase orders, manufacturing orders, customer orders or transport orders. They may relate to inbound deliveries to stock and withdrawal from stock, or they may refer to product manufacturing or transportation carried out. They include suppliers' invoices and customers' invoices, and can store information about settlement of these invoices.

By processing and storing information about transactions carried out, access is gained to current information on resources available in operations. This may relate to what quantities of a certain item are available in stock, what capacity remains to be utilised in a certain work centre, or how large the remaining storage and transportation capacity in a certain distribution centre is. The transaction database also provides historic data for follow-up purposes and for planning future operations. Forecasts and plans for future use of resources and flows of material provided with the aid of the ERP system are stored in a planning database. This may include forecasts of future demand for the company's products, plans for quantities intended to be delivered to different distribution centres, and plans for volumes intended to be manufactured.

In general, ERP systems are divided into modules which in turn may be grouped into different application areas. Commonly occurring application areas are finance, production, marketing/sales, distribution and human resources. Each application area contains several modules. The modules included in an ERP system can be selected at will for the requirements of the company. The system can thus be configured so that it fulfils company-specific requirements of information access and information processing.

Certain modules are of direct significance for a company's logistics activities. The basic data module contains software for structuring and maintaining basic data required for different applications in the ERP system. It also contains software for performing different types of analyses, such as which items are incorporated in which products, leadtime analysis and ABC analysis. The purchasing module contains support for processing requests for quotations, registration of purchase orders, delivery monitoring, goods reception and evaluation of suppliers.

The materials planning module is a central module in the ERP system. It contains functions for stock accounting, handling of inbound deliveries and withdrawals from stocks, and support for stocktaking. The model also contains systems support for materials planning and inventory management. In general it contains a number of different methods for materials planning, such as re-order points, run-out time and material requirements planning. There is also support for calculation of economic order quantities and safety stocks. Special forecasting modules are usually included in ERP systems. They provide forecast methods such as moving average and exponential smoothing, and there are functions for forecast control and forecast follow-up.

For the manufacturing company there is a master planning module and a production activity control module. The master planning module contains functions for creating and maintaining master production schedules and for rough-cut capacity planning. In the production activity control module there is support for planning and registering manufacturing orders, reporting withdrawals of materials and work carried out, and for reporting inbound deliveries of finished items. It also contains functions for short-term capacity planning and dispatch.

The ERP system includes a customer-order module, which contains system functions to support registration of customer orders, allocations of materials, print-outs of order confirmations, print-outs of picking lists and transportation documents, and invoicing. Administration of delivery plans is usually included. System support normally included in customer order modules also has functions for incoming orders and outbound deliveries statistics. There is often support for **electronic data interchange (EDI)** or Internet communication with customers and suppliers in customer-order modules and purchasing modules.

Other modules in an ERP system have less direct significance for the logistics system and the management of supply chains. The finance module, for example, provides data for stock valuation and cost calculations, while the sales ledger and suppliers' ledger module manages settlement of invoices from the customer-order module and the purchasing module respectively. The after-market module can process claims and spare parts administration. The personnel module contains data for salary payment and information on working hours and attendance figures of different sorts, which can be used for capacity planning and cost calculations.

In later versions of ERP systems, the basic modules have been supplemented with modules which support more performance measurements, alternative production strategies such as make-to-order and *kanban*, integration with other planning and execution systems, tools for co-ordinated planning, electronic commerce, etc. The ERP system has changed from being a more-or-less closed system which focused on optimising one company's activities to an open one aimed at creating value through integration with processes in other companies. The new generation of ERP systems are sometimes called ERP II.

Warehouse management systems

ERP systems support both planning and execution of material flows. Since they are standard software intended to support all processes in most companies, in certain situations they do not have sufficient detail support. They can then be supplemented with specialised programs designed to support more specific planning needs.

Warehouse management system (WMS) is an example of such a system. It contains support for storage related activities. Originally, WMS only supported operative storage activities, but the range of the system has been expanded in a similar way to the ERP system. They now often contain support for simple manufacturing, transportation planning, finance and order administration. Some of the common functions in the WMS are:

- *Goods reception* – registration of incoming goods. Automatic matching of purchase orders and advance shipment notice. Keeps track of whether incoming goods should be placed in stores or as backorders to be delivered directly to a customer.

- *Putting in stores* – calculations can be made to identify the optimal location for each package to be stored.

- *Stock management* – the system updates stock balance after withdrawals and through information generated in the stocktaking processes. It keeps track of where stock goods are located and enables tracking of goods, with respect to date of expiry, for example.

- *Order reception and order picking* – the system can automatically generate picking orders and advance shipment notices when internal or external parties signal demands or orders.

- *Dispatch* – when goods are withdrawn from stocks, picking orders are generated by the system and during dispatch labels and other documentation to follow packages when shipped out are printed.

- *Materials management* – activities such as re-order point calculations and generation of purchase orders can be carried out.

In addition to traditional stores and materials handling activities, the system may contain planning support for different terminal activities such as sorting, sequencing, cross-docking, etc, as well as personnel planning and management of return flows. To enable the efficient use of WMS and other execution systems they are normally integrated with systems for automatic data capture such as **bar codes** and **radio-frequency identification (RFID)**, as well as electronic communication such as **Web-based EDI** for receiving advance shipment notices and Web portals for creating visibility through making stock balances available to external co-operating parties.

Transport management systems

Transport management system (TMS) is another type of software. It supports transport planning with the aim of optimising total costs and delivery service requirements which are affected by how goods are transported between different points in the supply chain. The following are examples of functions in a TMS:

- *Design of transport network* – strategic planning means that when major structural changes are made such as acquisitions, new markets or new large customers, it will identify the optimal location of transport hubs and how the flows of transport between these hubs should be best sized.

- *Transport optimisation* – means at a tactical level, within the framework of the existing transportation network, matching available capacity with expected demand by determining optimal use of different traffic modes for different flows and routes.

- Route planning – means at an operative level determining optimal transport routes for different traffic modes and types of delivery, such as which stops are suitable for delivering and collecting goods. Sequencing of routes, or which routes are optimal for a given vehicle, is included in route planning.

- *Load planning* – means determining which combination of goods is optimal to send in one load. It includes consideration of different demands for goods, such as hazardous materials or perishable goods.

- *Manifesting* – means generating and printing out necessary and desirable delivery documents.

- *Tracking & tracing* – communicates with vehicles and supports tracking and tracing goods in transit. Tracking and tracing systems are often Web-based and enable shippers to follow and receive information about any disruptions in the delivery of their goods.

Advanced planning & scheduling systems

APS is often used as an acronym for *Advanced Planning & Scheduling*. Other terms used include *Advanced Planning & Optimisation (APO)*, *Advanced Planning Systems (APS)* and *Supply Chain Planning (SCP)*, the latter since several of the systems modules are aimed at supporting planning of material flows in the whole supply chain. There are many factors which distinguish APS from the traditional ERP system, but APS can be seen as a natural development of ERP and incorporates recent knowledge and development from logistics, planning, mathematics, IT, computer hardware and so on. The following are some of the basic principles of APS systems:

- They allow very frequent re-planning to enable adaptation to changes in planning conditions.
- They make concurrent priority and capacity planning with the aim of identifying possible and feasible plans.
- The decision engine is based on advanced mathematics and logical algorithms.
- Optimisation tools can be included as part of planning/decision tools with the aim of identifying best possible plans, based on cost minimisation or profit maximisation, for example.
- They support planning that considers business limitations in planning processes (such as capacity, material flows, business goals).
- They support scenario simulation and "what if" analyses.
- They support multi-site available to promise in real time.
- In the planning process, consideration is taken of stock levels and utilisation of resources in multiple sites and processes external to the company and plans are generated which result in best total efficiency.

Different APS systems on the market have slightly different areas of focus but are built on roughly the same structure, as illustrated in Figure 17.2.

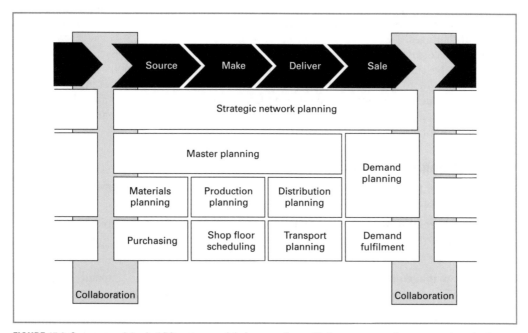

FIGURE 17.2 Common modules in APS systems and their connections with the processes of procurement, production, distribution and order-to-delivery

Source: Stadtler and Kilger (2005).

The modules included in an APS system contain different planning timescales and different business processes. The names of each module sometimes vary between different systems. There may also be several industry-specific variants of each module produced by the same supplier.

Supply-chain design refers to support for strategic decisions. It includes selection of suppliers, network planning (localisation of plants and suitable distribution structures), long-term forecasting, etc. If there is a situation where manufacturing takes place in three geographically separated locations which supply customers globally, the module can be used to calculate the cost effects of different distribution structures. It is possible to compare the effects of using different storage points and terminals, different modes of transport and different factories supplying different markets.

Materials planning, master planning and *distribution planning* in this context refer to support for material requirements planning, master production scheduling (including capacity planning) and aggregated distribution planning at the tactical planning level. These planning modules involve simultaneous planning of several processes and/or production plants with the aim of identifying optimal utilisation of different resources in different time periods. *Demand planning* refers to forecasting and dispatch planning at the tactical and operative level, but also short-term determination of the earliest delivery date for customer orders – available-to-promise.

Transport planning includes support for daily route planning, taking into consideration time and cost optimisation. Shop floor scheduling supports the execution of operative material flows during production from released manufacturing orders to finished products, based on finite and constraint-based planning. It also supports short-term planning of personnel on the shopfloor and operative materials procurement.

The APS system also includes support for planning co-operation with customers and suppliers. Customer collaboration includes support for co-ordination and adjustment of forecasts. Support is also available for investigating options of creating alternative product configurations, delivery times and prices in short-term shortage situations. Joint production of purchase plans with suppliers is enabled to provide them with better planning conditions and minimise the risks of material shortages.

It is not necessary to implement all of the APS modules described above. Individual APS modules can be combined with modules from an ERP system, for example. There are also a number of even more specialised independent software programs that support individual business processes such as inventory management, forecasting, constraint-based capacity planning and vendor-managed inventory. These programs are also a type of APS system in that they are advanced optimisation systems for supply chains.

Other planning and execution systems

In addition to the planning and execution systems described above, the following system types support logistics and SCM:

- **Customer relationship management (CRM)** system is another example of the type of system that can be independent or incorporated in an ERP system. It mainly supports marketing and sales processes in different ways.
- **Labour management system (LMS)** manages planning of demand, capacity and use of personnel, considering working times, workstations, shifts, breaks, etc.
- **Product content data management system (PCDM)** manages product data and enables several business units and organisations to work with a joint database using unique item numbers.

- **Supply-chain event management (SCEM)** is a system that enables users to set parameters which will trigger messages if a certain event occurs or if deviations from normal procedure arise. In this way it is possible to focus on daily planning and react to deviations when they occur.

- **Supply-chain visibility (SCV)** system is a group of tools for showing information on stock levels, production status, delivery status, deviations, etc, with the help of graphics, colours and sounds. Many SCV tools are also built in to other planning and execution systems, especially in SCEM.

Nine examples of different designations and functionalities in planning and execution systems have been provided above (ERP, WMS, TMS, APS, CRM, LMS, PCDM, SCEM and SCV). Different systems vendors give different names to the systems, and functionalities in different vendors' systems vary considerably. Solutions on the market have similarities and differences in functions and appearance. Some of the functionality in one vendor's WMS system may be found in another vendor's TMS system. There may also be an amount of overlapping between APS and TMS systems, which are both built on optimisation. Tools from SCV systems are gradually being implemented into other systems and ERP systems can be continually expanded with more functionality which has only previously been found in various specialised systems.

17.2 Information Exchange

The information which is required to manage material flows in, through and out of a company in a supply chain is either generated internally or externally. External information comes from the world outside the company, primarily its customers and suppliers. As such it must be com-

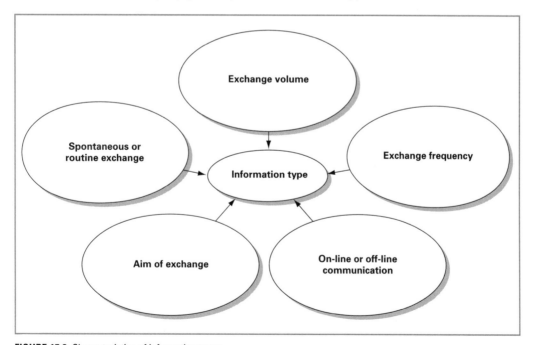

FIGURE 17.3 Characteristics of information types

municated between companies with the aid of a communication system. The internally generated information is created within the company, such as information reporting finished production units, items put into storage etc. Internal information may also be the result of decisions and processing of externally generated information. Incoming order statistics are an example of internally generated information created through the processing of externally generated information. The generation of a production plan from the delivery plan received from a customer is another example. Externally generated information is used together with internally generated information to manage flows in the company, but it is also communicated further in the supply chain and then becomes externally generated information for other companies.

Examples of types of information exchanged between companies are requests for quotations, offers, orders, order confirmations, advance shipment notices, invoices, payment notifications, payment reminders, delivery plans, consumption history, forecasts, stock status, product specifications, price lists, delivery terms, requests for delivery times, tracking of goods delivered, etc. This externally generated information exchanged between companies varies in character and puts different demands on information systems and communication methods. To understand in what ways specific types of information put demands on information systems and communication methods in connection with the exchange of information between companies, they may be distinguished in terms of whether they give rise to spontaneous exchange or routine exchange, high or low volumes, are frequent or infrequent, require on-line communication with the other party, and the aim of the exchange (Figure 17.3). Depending on the characteristics of the information type, different communication methods are more suitable or less suitable for transmitting information between companies.

Types of information exchange

Spontaneous exchange and routine exchange may be distinguished in information exchange between companies. Spontaneous exchange refers to the exchange of information in which the need arises spontaneously, i.e. is not planned in advance. It may be spontaneous in time and arise on unpredictable occasions, or it may be spontaneous in terms of its content. Examples of spontaneous exchanges are requests for quotations, requests for available stocks and requests for the estimated delivery time of goods ordered. Routine information exchange refers to exchange of a standardised character which often takes place regularly or in conjunction with specific activities. Sending order confirmations and invoices from supplier to customer and delivery plans from customer to supplier are examples of routine information exchange. Routine exchange enables the use of communications methods built on standardised and automated transfer of information. This is not normally the case with spontaneous exchange, where manual communication methods may be necessary.

It is also important to distinguish whether the exchange of information contains large or small quantities of data and if it takes place frequently or infrequently. Large quantities of data, such as drawings and databases for sales history, require different methods of communication than small quantities of data, such as order confirmation. Every exchange of information gives rise to a transaction cost, and so high-frequency exchanges require more automated and cost-effective communications methods than low-frequency exchanges.

Information processing can take place online or offline. Information transfer online means that the transmitting party is in direct contact with the receiving party during the whole of the information-processing session. Information transfer and information processing may take place momentarily and simultaneously. Information processing online is also interactive, which means that the transmitter can receive an immediate reaction from the receiver. Offline means that the transmitter and receiver are not in direct contact with each other during all of the information-processing session. Information transfer is then separated from information processing. Transmitter and receiver cannot control when transfer and processing take place. Events which give rise to information processing cannot be completed simultaneously and instantly, but must be completed in discrete steps with intervals between the steps.

Information exchange between companies can also have the following aims: requests, updating and transfer. In the case of requests, one company receives information from the other but neither company's own systems are updated as a result of the request. Customer request for delivery time is one example. In the updating type of information exchange, one party's information system is directly affected by the other party when information is exchanged. Online customer registration of an order in his supplier's ERP system is an example of this type of information effect. Transfer-type information exchange means that the content of information is transferred from one company's information system to another company's information system. Transfer of a delivery plan from a customer to a supplier is one example of this type of information exchange.

Information communication methods

Communications methods enable the exchange of information between individual and individual, between planning systems and an individual, and directly between planning systems. There are a number of different principles and technical solutions for communicating information which are dependent to a greater or lesser degree on the requirements and conditions in a certain situation. For this reason, many of them are used in parallel in a company.

Certain methods only enable information exchange between stationary units, while others enable information exchange to and from mobile units, such as trucks. Available systems are more or less suitable for spontaneous information exchange compared with routine information exchange, and for unstructured information exchange compared with well-structured and predefined information exchange. They are also more or less suitable for large and high-frequency quantities of information compared with small and low-frequency quantities. One other difference between communication methods is the extent to which they allow information processing online or offline. In addition, their implementation requires different levels of investment, and they may be more or less suitable for temporary information exchange needs as opposed to continuous and long-term.

Below follows a description of the communication methods EDI types, EDA, Internet, telephone, letter, fax, email, radio-frequency communication and satellite communication.

EDI, Web-EDI and XML

EDI stands for Electronic Data Interchange and means that data are transferred from one computer system to another in a predefined and standardised format and in such a way that the receiving system can interpret and process the information. There are different EDI standards, including Edifact which stands for electronic data interchange for administration, commerce and transport, Odette and Ansi X.12. Edifact is a UN standard. Odette is used within the automobile industry, and Ansi X.12 is an American EDI standard. The Edifact standard contains around 180 standardised messages which can be used within different areas of business and for different purposes, such as purchase orders, invoices and delivery plans. Figure 17.4 shows some common EDI messages. Letter combinations in brackets in the figure are the standardised abbreviations for message types. DELFOR stands for delivery forecast, for example.

A simplified picture of how EDI communication operates is shown in Figure 17.5. The information to be transferred is generated in a file in the transmitting ERP system. A special EDI software then translates the file's contents into the Edifact standard format. This file is transferred

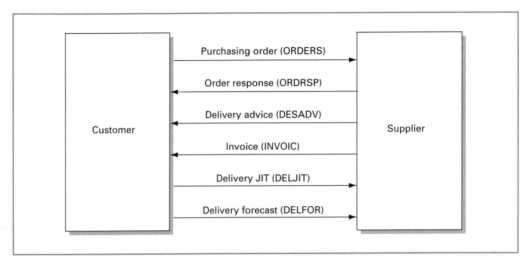

FIGURE 17.4 Examples of common EDI messages between customers and suppliers

via the telecommunications network to the receiving system. There it is converted into the format used in that system. The converted file then updates the ERP system register with the aid of a batch program. EDI uses offline communication; information transfer is separated from information processing. This takes place in batches at certain predefined points in time or when certain events have occurred.

EDI is mainly used between companies and organisations that have a regular and recurring exchange of structured information. Introduction of EDI requires large investments and running

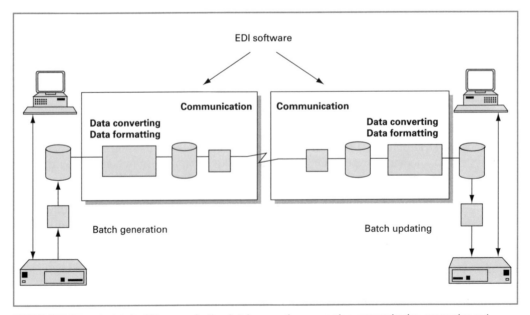

FIGURE 17.5 Flow principle for EDI communication: batch generation, conversion, communication, conversion and updating of databases

costs are relatively high. EDI is also a relatively complex method of communication which requires high IT competence to be operated. For these reasons EDI is used mainly in large companies.

The information exchange in the VMI collaboration described in case study 16.2 is automated using the following Edifact messages:

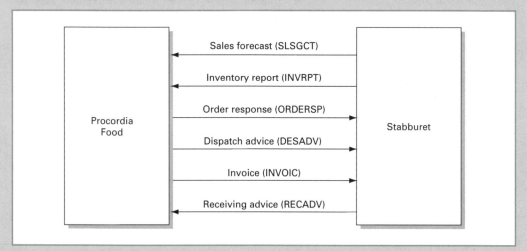

FIGURE I EDIFACT messages between Procordia Food and Stabburet

Sales forecasts (SLSFCT) of the expected weekly demand and inventory reports (INVRPT) with information about actual inventory balances are sent from Stabburet's to Procordia Food's ERP system on a daily basis. The information is collected in Stabburet's system at a specific time every day and automatically updates the Procordia Food databases. This information is input to the replenishment planning at Procordia Food. Information about planned replenishment orders (ORDRSP) is generated in Procordia Food's ERP system and automatically communicated to Stabburet's system. When registering a delivery to Stabburet, the system generates dispatch advice message (DESADV) and an invoice (INVOIC) that are sent to Stabburet's ERP system. The DESADV creates a purchasing order in Stabburet's system. At the same time a customer order is generated in the own (Procordia Food) system. When the goods are received and registered at Stabburet an automatic comparison with the invoice and purchasing order is conducted. If these tally, an accounts payable ledger for payment is automatically generated. If they fail to tally, the invoice is sent to an email box for manual handling. A receiving advice (RECADV) is also generated and sent to Procordia Food.

To create better conditions for companies to communicate efficiently with small customers and suppliers, system solutions built on a combination of EDI and Internet have been developed, so-called *web-based EDI systems*. Using these solutions, companies involved can work with the technology which suits each company best. For a small company, a Web browser is sufficient, and a larger company can still achieve complete systems integration in their ERP system with the help of a traditional EDI solution. A major customer can generate delivery plans which are sent as Edifact messages to suppliers. Suppliers with EDI can then automatically read in information in their ERP systems and automatically update their registers with new or modified information. Smaller suppliers without EDI have the message converted into a form on a Web server in an extranet solution to which the supplier has access and from which he can download information using a Web browser. On the same Web there are associated forms for order confirmation, advance shipment notice, and invoicing. Much of the information in these forms is already filled in by the customer in advance, and the remaining information is filled in by the supplier. Information is sent as an EDI message back to the customer's ERP system.

To obtain the greatest benefits of electronic information communication between different companies' systems, the generation, transfer and reception of information should be automated. EDI enables automatic generation and transfer, but not necessarily automatic reception of messages. If the receiver can only receive and print out the electronic message locally at his own company, many of the advantages of the EDI system are lost. Information must then be registered manually in the receiver's ERP system using hard copies. This is done in small companies without full EDI support.

XML is another technology for file transfer, which may supplement or replace EDI. XML stands for *eXtensible Markup Language* and is a language for building Web pages that are independent of platforms, i.e. hardware independent. XML can also be used to send structured business information via Internet. The information consists of content and tags which can be identified by the user. This option gives more flexibility than EDI. It is then possible to use general elements from the Edifact standard, which makes easier the replacement of the existing EDI solution or the use of XML parallel with EDI for customers and suppliers that do not have EDI support in their ERP systems.

EDA

EDA stands for **electronic data access** and means that a company makes parts of the information contents of its ERP system accessible to its customers or suppliers. In this way, external partners are provided with the option of online communication with the company's databases. It enables customers and suppliers to enter and maintain data about their own companies and products in their suppliers' and customers' systems. It is possible for customers to enter orders in the supplier's system, and suppliers can administrate their customers' stocks. Companies can also book transportation directly in logistics service provider companies' systems.

Compared with EDI, investment costs for this type of communication system are low. In principle no more than a computer and modem are required for a customer or supplier to connect to the system. A large advantage compared with EDI is that the method allows an interactive work process and thus can reduce the number of separate activities in enterprise resource planning, and can thereby reduce cycle times and time delays. It also has considerably fewer limitations than EDI when providing spontaneous information requirements in enterprise resource planning, both in terms of time and content. The only real limitation is the restrictions on access to information set by the company to which connection is being made.

Internet

Internet is a public and international network of local computer networks. There are a number of Internet services. Of these, the World Wide Web allow simple access to information on websites which are stored on servers connected to the Internet. Internet sites with limited access to certain customers or other business partners are usually called *extranet*. Websites with the aim of conveying specifically updated information are called **portals**, which may be accessible to the public; if they contain business data they are often only accessible to people within the company, suppliers or customers with special authorities. Information on a portal can quickly be updated and made accessible to the parties involved. Suppliers can have continuous access to customer companies' stock levels, forecasts, delivery service measurements and so on by logging into a special supplier portal.

CASE STUDY 17.3: SUPPLIER WEB PORTAL AT VOLVO CONSTRUCTION EQUIPMENT

The Hauler Lauder Division within Volvo Construction Equipment has developed a Web portal for communication with its suppliers. Suppliers are able to read, download and comment on figures on the portal. The portal contains the following information:

♦ *Supplier information*: ABC, items, shortage list, stock levels, etc.

♦ *Quality*: charts and inspection reports

♦ *Delivery*: weekly consumption, actual delays, order history, delivery service charts and open orders information

♦ *Capacity*: suppliers, items, programmes, etc.

♦ *Visual stock*: Stock and need information for suppliers to replenish stocks based on VMI

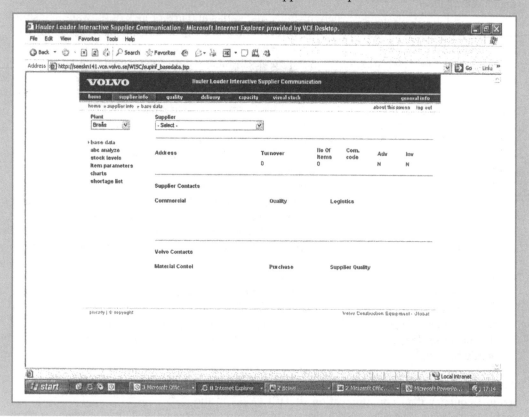

By exchanging data between these websites and the company's ERP system, there are great opportunities for rational communications between companies. In principle, the method has the same character as EDA and can be characterised as an interactive online method of communication. However, the Internet offers considerably larger possibilities for establishing contact with an almost infinite number of customers and suppliers. Web-based communication is also very simple to use and relatively inexpensive to establish. In general it is sufficient to have a computer connected to the Internet and a Web browser. In contrast to EDI and EDA, Web-based communication is also usable between individuals and companies, not only between companies. One weakness in relation to EDA is that of certain security problems.

Telephone, letter, fax and email

Telephone, letter, fax and email communication systems have their greatest strengths in unstructured and spontaneous exchange of information. However, they are still used to a large extent even for routine exchanges such as sending a purchase order to a supplier.

Telephone communication takes place through fixed lines or the mobile telephone network. Communication via mobile telephones is a simple way of communicating with mobile units such as the driver of a truck or personnel in a warehouse.

Letters were a routine method of communication before electronic communication systems became common. Invoices and order confirmation are still often sent by letter, even though this procedure is fast becoming digitalised. Letters are appropriate when there are large demands on freedom of content and form of information, or when for some reason it is not possible to send digital information.

Letters still have advantages when, owing to different standards or lack of software, transmitting and receiving information systems cannot exchange digital documents. The options of automatic registration of information in a letter are generally fewer.

Fax is a system which transfers information electronically but not in digital form. It is fundamentally a paper-based system and therefore has the same general characteristics as letters. The difference is that a letter is transferred via a postal system whereas a fax is transferred via the telephone network. A big advantage of fax compared with letters is that fax transfer takes only a few minutes compared with up to a week by letter. The printed document is normally put in a fax machine which then sends it to a receiving fax machine for printing. ERP systems can also automatically produce and send faxes directly to a fax machine or to another computer system for printing out.

With email it is possible to transfer unstructured and structured text from a transmitting computer system via the Internet to a receiving computer system. The system is in some ways similar to a fax. One difference is that computers are used to transfer information and that the message is presented on a monitor or as a hard copy. Computer support allows considerably more rational handling of information transfer both for creating, storing and sending as well as answering messages. Another difference is that attachments can be sent with emails. These attachments may be normal letters, or they may be files with predefined formats and forms which are systems-readable. This means that they can be interpreted by the receiver's computer and processed without information needing to be registered again. A customer may send delivery plans to his supplier in the form of Excel files as attachments to an email. In this way, email can be used as a carrier for EDI messages. In general, all information which used to be sent by fax can now be sent more efficiently by email.

Radio-frequency communication

Radio-frequency data communication (RFDC) works in the same way as communication via mobile telephones. The difference is that another technology is used. It is the traditional method of communicating within distribution and taxi industries, but also indoors in large warehouse and factory environments. Radio-frequency communication is also common with the police, emergency services, at sea and between military units. It is the least expensive communication method in many situations since there are no subscription charges. To communicate via RFDC, users must agree on a common radio-frequency (channel). This creates a limitation within the system, since it is not possible to communicate with those who do not know or use that frequency. Traditional radio-frequency communication is analogue. Digital systems exist and are under development and with the advent of these systems the limitation of only communicating with those who have the same radio-frequency set will disappear. In principle they work in the same way as mobile telephones. Data transfer is possible using digital systems.

Satellite communication

Satellite communication means that information is communicated via a number of satellites. It is a means of communication used instead of the terrestrial telephone network or a mobile telephone network where the normal network has no coverage, such as at sea. A satellite telephone looks like and works in the same way as a mobile telephone. The disadvantage is that it is a relatively expensive method of communication.

17.3 Data Capture Systems

Identification systems are used to enable automatic data capture, or to identify objects, capture information about them and transfer that information to a computer system without any manual inputs being required. The advantages of automatic data capture include the speed of registering an object, fewer faulty registrations compared with manual registration, and releasing personnel from registration work. Identification systems differ in the degree to which they can operate automatically, and how much and what type of information they can convey. The fact that they are built on different technologies makes them more appropriate in some situations than others, and investment costs vary considerably.

Bar codes

The bar-code system is the most common system for automatic object identification. It consists of bar codes and bar-code readers. Bar codes are printed as a series of vertical lines with different thicknesses and gaps, and attached to the object to be identified.

Bar codes are structured on line symbols that represent different alphanumeric or numeric characters. There are several hundred different types of bar codes. EAN (European Article Numbering) and UPC (Universal Product Code) are the most common codes for marking and identifying consumer products. Code 128 is a more advanced code that can contain 128 characters and includes alphanumeric characters without requiring further space.

If a large amount of information needs to be conveyed, two-dimensional bar codes can be used. They can convey an amount of information approximately equivalent to one A4 page of text. They also enable storage of other types of information such as graphics and photographs. The codes can be used for the identification of consignment notes and delivery notes in transportation and work descriptions in production. The two-dimensional codes contain a vertical and horizontal bar code on the same label. PDF 417 is the most common two-dimensional bar code. It is self-verifying and self-correcting, which means that through its algorithm it can correct certain faulty codes. Thus, despite a damaged code, it is still possible to interpret the entire contents of the code. In addition to its higher information capacity,

FIGURE 17.6 EAN13 code and PDF 417-kod

PDF 417 has higher security levels than one-dimensional bar codes. Examples of bar codes are shown in Figure 17.6.

Bar codes are read with the help of different sorts of bar-code readers. For straightforward bar codes, manual laser scanners can be used, as when material handlers and operators register order confirmations, goods received, supplier invoices, inputs and withdrawals from stores, ready times for manufacturing operations etc. Two-dimensional codes are normally photographed with a camera, but some codes can also be read using a laser scanner. Another bar-code application is where a fixed bar-code reader at the end of a conveyor belt, for example, automatically reads bar codes on ready packages as they leave the belt. For such a system to work, the bar codes must always be placed at the same height and on the same side of the packages, and the packages must always have the same orientation on the conveyor belt. There must be free line of sight between the bar codes and the bar-code reader. Most bar-code readers do not require physical contact with the bar code; proximity is sufficient.

RFID

RFID stands for Radio-frequency identification. This is a system which uses radio waves for automatic identification of objects. Information is stored in a microchip in an RFID tag or in RFID transponders, which are affixed to the object to be identified. This enables the transfer of identification information to the reader, which converts the radio waves from the RFID tag into a format which can be relayed to a computer for further processing.

RFID systems differ from bar-code systems and other identification systems in three respects. Since they use microchips, it is possible to store considerably more data. By using radio waves for identification, line of sight is not required between the reader and the object, even though certain substances such as water or metals may interfere with communication. The time taken for reading an object is normally less than for other identification systems. All packages in a truckload can be identified at the same time using an RFID system.

RFID tags vary in terms of memory functions and range. Memory functions may be of the type read only, meaning that the memory is factory programmed or that the user puts in information once only. The permanently stored information can then be read on many occasions. Write and read memory is another type of memory functionality which supports changing tag information on several occasions. The range of the RFID tag is determined by its power source. Active tags are equipped with batteries and normally have a range of 30 m or more. Due to battery discharge, however, active tags have a limited active life. Passive tags are more common than active tags. They are powered externally by radio frequency energy which is emitted from the reader. They are smaller, lighter and cheaper than active tags, and moreover have a virtually unlimited life. The range is shorter though, normally between 0.5 and 10 m.

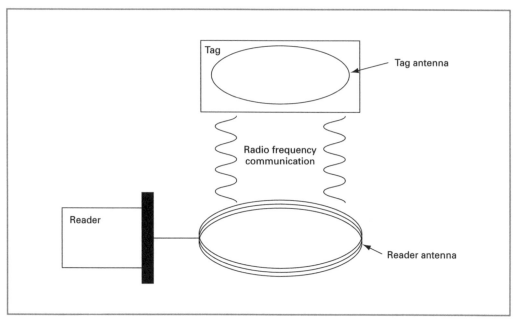

FIGURE 17.7 Principles of communication between an RFID reader and tag

---

CASE STUDY 17.4: RFID AT SACHSENMILCH AG'S WAREHOUSE ("Safety for dairy products...with RFID", White paper published by Dematic GmbH & Co, Öffenbach, Germany, www.dematic.com/rfid, Date: 2007-09-10)

Sachsenmilch AG is the leading dairy company in Germany. They have implemented RFID to support the storage and retrieval in the finished-goods warehouse for dry substances. The warehouse contains 420 individual channels where pallets are stored. Each of these channels is equipped with RFID tags. RFID readers are mounted on the forklift trucks. The pallets contain no RFID tags but are marked with bar codes.

When pallets are received, forklift truck operators read the bar code on the pallet. The warehouse management system (WMS) automatically generates a transport order to a specific storage channel. This is acknowledged by the RFID at the actual storage position when the forklift places the pallet in the channel. The pallet is thereby booked to the destination channel in the WMS. The position management in the WMS makes it possible to see which pallet is in which position of the channel at any time.

Retrieval is verified in two steps. Firstly, the slot where the pallet is stored is acknowledged via the automatic transponder. The unique bar-code label is then scanned and registered. This two-step identification process identifies possible incorrect storage and allows for the correct retrieval of goods.

A radio-frequency reader is required to identify an RFID tag and transfer the information to the reader (refer to Figure 17.7). To be able to interpret an RFID message, standardised communication protocols and radio frequencies are required. The EPC standard is a commonly used RFID standard, but there is only one unique product number in the tag. Any further product information must be retrieved from an underlying database. An RFID system may include a database in the tag itself, thereby providing independence from an external database. A number of ISO standards exist for different RFID applications.

The price for RFID tags is still an obstacle for widespread use of the technology. In 2003 major retailers including Wal-Mart and Tesco declared that their major suppliers were required to provide pallets and cases with passive RFID tags. Since then, there has been a heavy focus on RFID usage.

Other identification systems

In addition to bar codes, which currently represent the commonest identification system, and RFID, which is about to take off as the costs of tags decrease, there are a number of other automatic data identification systems for applications within logistics and SCM.

Magnetic strips are used on bank cards. They are water and dirt resistant. It is possible to charge the strips with new data on an almost infinite number of occasions. Magnetic strips are used in industrial applications on smart cards. By swiping the card through a reader, current information is displayed on a monitor. Smart cards can be used for identifying personnel authorisation for registering data, goods on a truck, or information about items and suitable paths for picking orders.

Optical character recognition (OCR) is an identification system consisting of alphanumeric character series. The OCR number can be read by an optical scanner similar to those used for reading bar codes. OCR numbers are used as reference numbers for bank payment slips, for example. The system is not as widely used in industry. The advantage of the OCR system is that it can be read and registered either manually or automatically.

Identification systems can also be designed for *light* or *voice transfer*. A voice transfer system for item picking requires materials handlers to be equipped with a headset and microphone. Picking instructions are conveyed by a synthetic voice to the materials handler, who reports when an activity is completed by speaking a commando (live voice instruction) such as "picking ready", upon which new instructions are given.

Global positioning system (GPS) is an identification system which uses satellites for identifying mobile units such as trucks and containers. The driver of a truck knows exactly where he is by using this system. This information can also be transferred to a stationary traffic centre which then registers where different trucks are located. The transfer of localisation information from the mobile unit is normally relayed through other media such as mobile telephones or communications radios, and not by satellite communication. Localisation information can then be used as the basis of traffic planning and to follow up and track goods in transit, and as support for tracking and tracing systems. GPS technology can be used for following and tracking load carriers in the supply chain.

17.4 Electronic Marketplaces and Businesses

Electronic businesses, also called *e-commerce* or *e-businesses*, sometimes replace physical processes for communicating and doing business between purchasers and vendors. E-commerce used for facilitating interactions between the company and individuals is called *business-to-consumer (B2C)*. For interaction between companies and companies it is called *business-to-business (B2B)*. Electronic methods of exchanging information as described in section 17.2, i.e. EDI, EDA, Internet and email, are important elements in e-commerce, as are electronic marketplaces and portals.

An **electronic marketplace** or *exchange* is an Internet-based solution which enables purchasing and selling activities between companies and other companies. It operates as a hub, around which one or more purchasers and one or more vendors collect to exchange information and do business.

By buying and selling production materials indirectly or directly via an electronic marketplace, it is possible to work together without a large number of paired interfaces created between players. In this way efficiency can be improved by forms of collaboration and transactions being simplified, automated and co-ordinated.

An electronic marketplace must take into consideration both purchasers' and sellers' needs and conditions. A number of different types of marketplaces have been developed which are specialised in different types of businesses. Traditionally, trading through marketplaces has focused on minimising costs. Marketplaces were initially places of trade for commodities and MRO items. The area of use has since expanded, and today e-marketplaces are also used for systematic purchasing and sales of indirect materials as well as direct production materials.

An electronic marketplace may mean that sales companies upload product catalogue information to an exchange. Purchasing companies conduct searches on the site and identify products to buy, and then complete the purchase. Exchanges can also enable the identification of possible suppliers, execution of tendering, closing of business deals and electronic auctions.

We can differentiate between vertical and horizontal marketplaces. A *vertical marketplace* co-ordinates and enables the exchange of information and transactions between several sellers and purchasers from the same industry. It is often used for transactions involving direct production material, and may be the basis of long-term purchases of items or one-off purchases. Covisint (www.covisint.com) is one example of a vertical marketplace for companies in the automobile and medical care industries. A *horizontal marketplace* focuses not so much on exchange within a certain industry, but rather the co-ordination of buyers and sellers from different industries. They aim primarily at decreasing total costs for purchasing commodities, indirect materials and services. An example of a horizontal marketplace is MRO.com (www.mro.com).

Auctions are another application area for marketplaces. Several sellers or purchasers can make offers for a deal and the one making the highest offer gains the contract. Auctions focus on lowest prices, which means that they are primarily for trading with commodities and not for items where product quality and delivery service are order winners. The following are common types of auctions:

Forward auctions: **Forward auctions** have one seller and many potential purchasers. The seller normally states a starting price or target price. Purchasers bid over each other until the highest bidder purchases the item. Forward auctions are normally used for sales of excess stock or obsolete items.

Reverse auction: **Reverse auctions** have one buyer and several potential sellers who make decreasing offers until the one with the lowest offer sells his goods. The auction is normally preceded by the purchaser sending out a request for information (RFI) to potential sellers. Those that fulfil demands set for delivery performance, product quality, financial status and so on may then join the auction and bid. Then they bid under each other until the lowest sales price bid gains the contract to supply. The purchaser can allow all bids to be visible for all vendors, or only the current lowest bid. Another alternative is that each vendor can see his ranking among current bids. Reverse auction is the most common form of electronic auction and can be used

CASE STUDY 17.5: REVERSE AUCTION AT AUSBUYER (Stein and Hawking, 2003)

In order to reduce purchasing costs of commodities, the Australian manufacturer AusBuyer turned to Auction.com, a company specialising in e-procurement and auctions, to conduct a reverse auction event. The commodity contract that was to be auctioned was worth about $1.6 million per year. At present, 20 per cent of this volume was bought from a small "micro-business" company with only a few employees and 80 per cent from a larger company. From the bidders' perspective the auction event contained the stages: qualification, auction strategy and auction event.

1 *Qualification:* The two existing suppliers were pre-qualified for the auction but also other bidders were identified and qualified, in order to ensure an adequate number of bidders to create the auction dynamic. Auction.com set the switching cost at $1.3 million, the price when AusBuyer would consider awarding the contract away from the existing suppliers. The existing contract was worth approximately $1.6 million, so the difference between the existing contract and the switching cost was about 18 per cent. In order to prepare for the auction, the bidders may spend considerable resources in this pre-auction phase. The small company with 20 per cent of the contract before the auction event, for example, spent considerable time on sub-contractor meetings, phone calls, emails, managing director time, consultancy time, etc.

2 *Supplier's auction strategy:* The small company developed the following auction strategies: the entry-strategy was to enter the auction with a $2 million bid, which was equivalent with the estimated costs plus a margin. They then should maintain control on the screen and drive the bids down in a controlled manner. The only strategy for the end was to be in the game, and if they didn't win they wanted to be under the $1.3 million switching cost at the end.

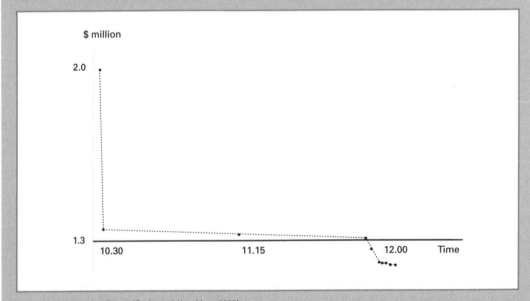

Reverse action at AusBuyer (Stein and Hawking, 2003)

3 *The auction event:* The auction event was determined to last for 1.5 hours, but a bid during the last seven minutes would extend the auction with one minute. All bidders had online connection with the auction site and could see the other bids. They could, however, not see who put a bid. When the auction event started, four actors immediately entered bids. The small company with 20 per cent of the contract started with its $2.0 million bid, but one of the other bidders came in with a bid right on the switching cost ($1.3 million). After about half an hour a fifth bidder came in and started to drive down the bids. There were three bidders left when seven minutes remained. The remaining bidders were very active during the last seven minutes, and the auction dynamic drew down the price $90 000 in these minutes. The number of bids in the last seven minutes tripled all bids in the previous 1.5 hours. The figure to the left shows how the lowest bid changed during the 1.5-hour auction event.

In order to not lose to the other bidders, the small company reduced its low margin from 12 to 5 per cent during the last minutes of the auction. This was, however, not enough. The company was in the game in the end, drew down the price for the other bidders, but did not win the auction and lost the 20 per cent of the contract they had at the start. AusBuyer received a 20 per cent reduction in its purchasing price for the actual commodities. This was what they aimed at when initiating the auction. Questions remain, however, about the service they will receive, whether contracts will be adhered to and what sort of supplier relationship they will enjoy in the contract period.

for purchasing high-value items that are easy to define and do not require long-term supplier relationships. Normally, reverse auctions result in drastically reduced purchase prices.

Dutch auction: **Dutch auctions** have one vendor and many purchasers. The vendor states a high starting price which is then decreased until a purchaser accepts it. Dutch auctions are used for items whose demand varies and for which there is a risk of shortage. They enable the vendor to gain the highest price possible.

Depending on the number of purchasers and vendors involved in a deal, it is possible to distinguish between four types of business situations as shown in Figure 17.8. The different variants of electronic marketplaces have their advantages since either more purchasers or more vendors are involved in the exchange of information and business. When purchasing activities take place between individual vendors and purchasers, integrated solutions such as those built on EDI are normally preferable.

The situation called *e-market solutions* is characterised by many purchasers and many vendors being involved. Catalogue buying through vertical and horizontal marketplaces is appropriate here. If several purchasers but only a few vendors are involved, the situation is called *sell-centric*. Normal and Dutch auctions are suitable marketplace solutions with the aim of obtaining the highest possible sales price for the vendor. When there are many vendors and only a few purchasers, a reverse auction helps the purchaser to pressure suppliers into selling at low prices. This situation is called *buy-centric*.

Tendering is sometimes included as part of the purchasing process. **E-tendering** means that activities and exchange of necessary documents in the tendering process with suppliers is automated and takes place electronically (often through an Internet solution). The following activities may be involved in e-tendering:

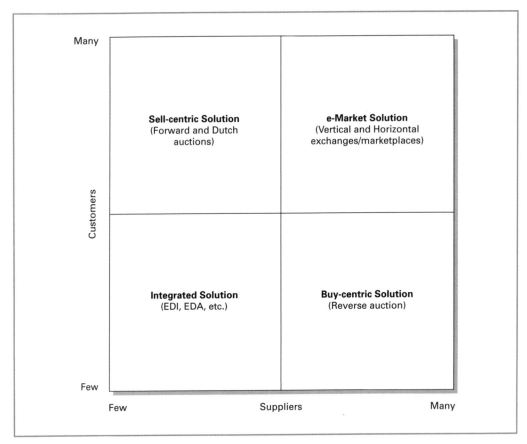

FIGURE 17.8 Types of business situations

- advertising the requirements for goods and services. This often includes sending requests for information (RFI) to potential suppliers.
- automatically evaluating, selecting and registering approved suppliers to co-operate with.
- issuing documents for request for quotation (RFQ) to qualified suppliers
- receiving tender documents from suppliers
- automatically evaluating tenders received
- automatically selecting suppliers
- automatically offering a contract to the selected supplier

The principle of e-tendering is that all necessary documents are communicated electronically. The degree of automation of the different activities in the processes varies. Evaluation and selection of suppliers is not usually done automatically since it often requires manual involvement.

Purchasing on e-marketplaces may result in clear cost cuts for purchasing parties since they can press prices, but it may also include risks caused by low-quality products, high distribution costs and the fact that each new transaction is made with a new and unknown supplier. As regards suppliers, trading on e-marketplaces means often that they are forced to sell at a lower price than they had anticipated. They may expect to decrease their administrative costs, but often suppliers that win a bid in an auction are forced to accept such a low sales price that it results in a negative profit contribution. Extra administration work may arise with e-commerce. Purchasers are often forced to spend more time preparing requests for information and quotations than in a more manually arranged procedure. The supplier's work with answering requests for tendering can also be more time-consuming. The supplier is forced to do a large amount of preparatory work in conjunction with replying to an RFI. E-marketplaces simplify the process for a supplier to gain new contracts, though. Trading on e-marketplaces means that relationships between purchasers and vendors are temporary and at arm's-length. Trading on e-marketplaces is therefore only appropriate when arm's-length is a suitable type of relationship.

17.5 Information Quality

Information collected and transferred within or between companies is used as a basis for analyses and decisions. The quality of these analyses and decisions is therefore influenced by the quality in the internally and externally generated information used as input in the processes. **Information quality** is a generic term and has several different dimensions. Normally, distinctions are made between the extent to which information is valid, reliable, timely, complete and straightforward to understand and use (Figure 17.9).

That information is valid means that it conveys what it is intended to convey. An agreement between a customer and supplier company that the supplier will deliver at a certain point in time may mean several things. The supplier may mean the time when the goods are ready for dispatch from his factory, while the customer may mean the time when the goods are available at the customer's goods reception, or when they have been checked and accepted for reception. If the parties have not specified exactly which time is referred to, the information is not valid. Validity is a prerequisite for high information quality. The validity of information is to a large extent influenced by how much the sending and receiving parties collaborate, communicate and agree upon common definitions for what the information is intended to represent.

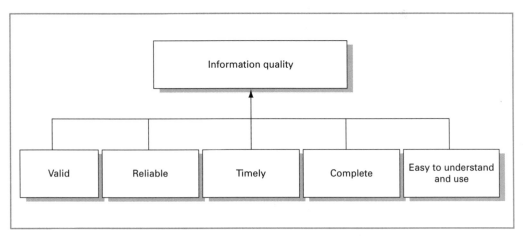

FIGURE 17.9 The five dimensions of information quality

The reliability of information refers to the extent to which it may be expected to be true. If the customer and supplier company have ensured that delivery precision is measured in the same way, but the probability of the deliveries taking place at the time agreed is small, then the quality of information is low. This is called *poor reliability*. To minimise disruptions in production processes and deliveries to customers, unreliable forecasts, delivery times and so on must be absorbed by safety mechanisms, such as safety stocks. There is a direct correlation between the reliability of information and the system's costs, tied-up capital and customer service. The way in which data is registered may influence its reliability. There is a risk of errors during manual registration of items when put in stock: wrong item number, wrong number of units, wrong store location and so on, which can give rise to an unreliable stock balance. Using automatic data capture with the aid of bar codes and RFID in principle eliminates risks of registration errors.

The third dimension of information quality is how current it is, in other words, the information is up to date or out of date. If information is out of date it no longer represents the point in time when it is intended to be used in an analysis or for making a decision. Information on current stock balance is no longer valuable if it refers to the stock balance one week ago. The consequences of out-of-date information depend on the type of information and the decision situation. A one-week-old stock balance can in certain situations be sufficient information, while in other situations it has no value at all. One-week delayed information about last year's sale statistics will have no serious consequences. If the new decision situation has arisen during the information delay time, however, the information may be completely irrelevant. If an order confirmation stating that a purchase order has been received and accepted arrives at the customer company after the goods ordered have been delivered, the information is of marginal interest. The degree of time delay is determined to a certain extent by how the information is exchanged. Virtually automated data exchange such as EDI can decrease the risks of time delays before information is sent and before it is read by the receiving party, which may be the case with email communication.

Complete information means that all details and underlying data requested has really been exchanged. The capacity of the information system may set limitations for the quantity and type of information that can be communicated. How complete transferred information is may also be a question of attitudes and the willingness to share information.

Valid, reliable and complete information may be available at the right time, but despite all these characteristics it may be considered to be of poor quality it is difficult to understand or if it requires a lot of work before it can be used. If an Excel file containing complete sales history for a certain period is sent to a supplier, but the supplier finds it difficult to understand which columns refer to the item in question, there is a deficiency in information quality. The same is true if the supplier can easily identify the relevant data but cannot upload it in his own ERP system and is forced to register the data manually in his own system. Then, the information is not easy to use.

17.6 Conclusion and Summary

Information systems for logistics and supply chain management are built on four types of system: planning and execution systems, communication systems, identification systems and electronic marketplaces. This chapter has described information systems used in each of these four types. Depending on the application situation, they can be used and combined in different ways to create efficient flows of information.

Enterprise resource planning (ERP) systems are the most common planning and execution systems, but there are also WMS, TMS, APS and other specialised planning and execution systems. The common aim is to perform planning and support execution of material flows in the supply chain. To provide planning and execution systems with data, communication and identification systems are required. EDI, EDA, Internet, telephone, letter, fax, email, radio-frequency communication and satellite communication are commonly occurring communication systems. Bar codes and RFID are examples of identification systems which allow automatic data capture. An electronic marketplace is an Internet-based solution that enables business-to-business purchasing and selling activities. Different types of marketplaces were described in the chapter, including vertical and horizontal marketplaces and e-auctions, as well as e-tendering as a part of the procurement process.

Information exchanged may be of poor quality in different respects. Quality of information is the degree to which it is valid, reliable, up to date, complete and simple to understand and use. For information to be used as the basis of correct analyses and decisions it must have high information quality, often in all dimensions at the same time. The structure of the information system influences the quality of information to a large degree.

🔑 Key concepts

Advanced planning and scheduling (APS) 398

Bar codes 402

Customer relationship management (CRM) 404

Dutch auction 419

Electronic data access (EDA) 410

Electronic data interchange (EDI) 401

Electronic marketplaces 417

E-tendering 419

Enterprise resource planning (ERP) 398

Forward auction 417

Global positioning systems (GPS) 416

Information quality 421

Labour management system (LMS) 404

Portal 411

Product content data management (PCDM) 404

Radio-frequency communication (RFDC) 412

Radio-frequency identification (RFID) 402

Reverse auction 417

Satellite communication 413

Supply-chain event management (SCEM) 405

Supply-chain visibility (SCV) 405

Transport management system (TMS) 398

Warehouse management system (WMS) 398

Web-based EDI 402

XML 410

 ## Discussion Tasks

1 Identify, by searching on the Internet for example, some different suppliers of ERP systems. Is it possible to identify what functions different suppliers' software have? In what ways are they similar and/or different?

2 The APS system is often called the new generation planning system, but despite this there are few companies that use the APS system to any significant extent. This is

particularly the case in long-term design and master production scheduling of supply chains involving multiple factories, warehouses, etc. What barriers are there when implementing and using APS for long-term planning of supply chains?

3 What has been the significance of the development of the Internet for logistics and SCM? Discuss some ways in which Internet can create opportunities for efficient logistics and supply chain solutions.

4 RFID is one of several systems for automatic data capture. Sometimes RFID is referred to as a component which enables the goods to become "intelligent" and "smart" so that they can "communicate" with their surroundings. Compare bar codes and RFID and give some examples of situations where you believe that RFID has advantages compared with bar codes.

5 Study the procurement process in Chapter 15. Identify how information systems can be used and how they can influence efficiency in different activities in the process and for different types of items.

Further reading

APICS (2007) *Using information technology to enable supply chain management.* APICS certified supply chain professional learning system Module 4, APICS, Alexandria.

Bowersox, D., Closs, D. and Cooper, B. (2002) *Supply chain logistics management.* McGraw-Hill, New York.

Hamilton, S. (2003) *Maximizing your ERP system: a practical guide for managers.* McGraw-Hill, London.

Ross, D. (2003) *Introduction to e-Supply Chain Management: engaging technology to build market-winning business partnerships.* St. Lucie Press, Boca Raton.

Simchi-Levi, D., Kaminsky, P. and Simchi-Levi, E. (2008) *Designing & managing the supply chain: concepts, strategies and case studies.* McGraw-Hill, New York.

Stadtler, H. and Kilger, C. (eds) (2005) *Supply chain management and advanced planning: concepts, models, software and case studies.* Springer Verlag, Berlin.

Stein, A. and Hawking, P. (2003) "The 20% solution? A case study on the efficacy of reverse auctions", *Management Research News*, Vol. 26, No. 5, pp. 1–20.

Appendix A

ABC analysis

In order to utilise a company's resources as much as possible for measures which will give the largest effect in relation to investments made, and which will have the greatest significance for business operations, it is often appropriate to differentiate logistics measures in the company. It may be a question of having a larger safety stock of products which give the highest profit contribution, and whose delivery will be ensured above others. ABC classification is a tool used to achieve such differentiation.

ABC classification involves a division of items, customers, suppliers and other objects into different classes. The different classes are often called A, B, C, D etc. Different criteria are used as the basis for the classification carried out, examples being volume value per item, profit contribution per product, turnover per customer, or purchase value per supplier. Volume value means the annual consumption multiplied by the unit price or unit cost. ABC classification is one application of the minority principle, meaning that in every group of objects there is a small number which accounts for a large proportion of the profit. In the case of volume value, the principal means that in every range of items there is a small number of items that account for most of the material flows measured in volumetric values. In the description of ABC classification that follows below, the only case treated is volume value, but the principle is identical for any object and criterion chosen as a basis for the classification.

The following working method may be applied to the calculation of volume value and determination of ABC class based on the criterion of volume value:

1 Calculate the annual consumption of each of the items to be included in the ABC classification.

2 Calculate the volume value for each of the items by multiplying its annual consumption with its sales price or standard cost/average cost.

3 Calculate the sum of the volume values for all items.

4 Calculate the percentage volume value of the total volume value for every item, i.e. each item's proportion of the total volume value.

5 Rank the items according to their percentage of the total volume value, from highest to lowest.

6 Analyse the distribution of items and divide them into a suitable number of different groups by specifying the number of different volume value brackets. Each bracket will correspond to one class: A, B, C, etc.

7 Each item will then be allotted to the ABC class which is the equivalent of its volume value.

In most planning systems there is system support for carrying out a volume value analysis of the above type.

Example

A group of 10 items has the following volume value expressed in Euros and volume value proportions expressed as a percentage, as stated in the table below. The items are ranked according to their proportion of the total volume value.

Item	Volume value	Percentage	Accumulated percentage
7	34 000	46.7	46.7
1	25 000	34.3	81.0
9	4500	6.2	87.2
5	3360	4.6	91.8
2	2200	3.0	94.8
6	1950	2.7	97.5
3	640	0.9	98.4
4	560	0.8	99.2
10	480	0.6	99.8
8	120	0.3	100.0

Based on the above volume value calculation, three different volume and value brackets can be defined: A is equivalent to a volume value larger than €10 000, B is equivalent to a volume value between €1000 and €10 000, and C is equivalent to a volume value less than €1000. An ABC classification is then obtained for the 10 items as in the following table.

Class	Items	Proportion of items %	Proportion of volume value %
A	7,1	20	81.0
B	9,5,2,6	40	17.5
C	3,4,10,8	40	2.5

As indicated in the table, those 40 per cent of items which were classified as C items account for only 2.5 per cent of the total volume value, while the 20 per cent of items classified as A items account for 81 per cent. Figure A.1 shows a graphic volume value distribution for the items in the example.

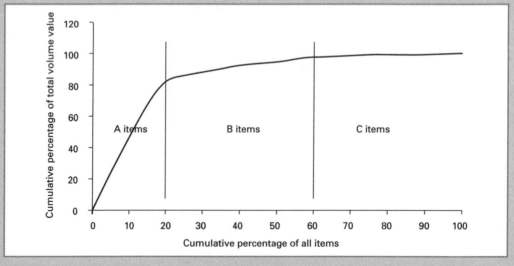

FIGURE A.1 Volume value distribution for items in the example

Exercises

Exercise A.1

Perform an ABC analysis of the items in the table below.

Item	Turnover (pieces/year)	Value/unit	Contribution margin %	Picking events/year
A	100	2	70	100
B	30	59	65	15
C	50	65	85	50
D	2000	0.50	70	1000
E	100	5	75	25
F	3000	0.50	50	115
G	5000	1	65	1000
H	1500	6	70	450
I	2000	1	80	400
J	500	19	75	190
K	2000	2	45	550
L	300	43	65	75
M	2000	1	70	650
N	1500	1.50	75	420
O	2000	2	80	1100

a) Assume that the items are purchased items kept in factory stores and used as start-up materials for internal production. The purpose of the analysis is to determine safety stock levels for the items.

b) Assume that the items are products that are stocked in finished goods stores. The purpose of the analysis is to divide the warehouse into zones for picking work.

c) Assume that the items are products that are stocked for sales in a finished goods store. The purpose of the analysis is to determine safety stock levels for the items.

Appendix B

Incremental inventory carrying costs

Incremental inventory carrying costs are one part of inventory carrying costs (capital costs, storage costs, and uncertainty costs) and can be expressed as the product of the value of items in stock and the *inventory carrying interest rate* (also called *inventory carrying charge* or *inventory carrying factor*). To obtain a correct value for the incremental inventory carrying costs, it is necessary to distinguish between incremental costs and common costs related to storing an extra unit, to select and use one principle for stock valuation, and to set a value for inventory carrying interest.

Incremental costs and common costs

It is possible to distinguish between incremental costs and common costs. Incremental costs are those costs which arise or decrease as the result of a decision – in this case, the decision to increase or decrease average stock volumes. For a company that rents pallet spaces in a storage hotel, an increase in average stock volume means that more pallet places must be rented, thus increasing storage costs. Wastage also tends to increase when average stock volumes are larger. These costs are thus incremental ones. Inventory carrying costs that do not change when stock volumes vary are defined as common costs.

The entire capital costs and uncertainty costs are normally incremental costs in this respect; that is, they change when stock volumes vary. Storage costs such as rent, depreciation, energy and personnel costs may in some situations be incremental costs which vary with different volumes stored, and in other situations they may be common costs which do not change. If a

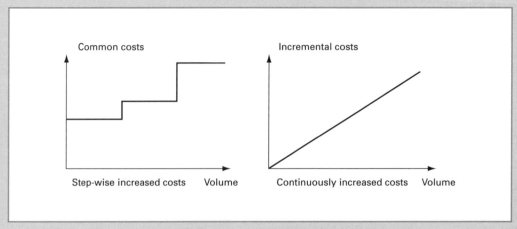

FIGURE B.1 Discrete versus continuous increases in common costs and specific costs

company owns a warehouse which is not utilised at its full capacity, increased stocks will not cause any further costs. In this case, rental cost is a common cost. If, on the other hand, the company has already filled its warehouse, increased stocks will mean that a new warehouse must be built or more storage space must be rented. If a new warehouse is built, common costs will increase, but that part of incremental costs which is related to storage will still be zero as long as there is unexploited storage space in the new warehouse. Increases in volumes will thus raise common costs when further capacity investments are necessary, while incremental costs increase in proportion to the rise in volumes, as illustrated in Figure B.1.

When rented space increases, common costs will be unchanged, but the additional rental cost is dependent on the number of pallets stored. The cost for renting additional pallet places is thus an incremental cost. The same conditions apply to costs for heating, handling equipment and personnel. If a warehouse that is not fully exploited is heated, there are no additional heating costs if the volume of stocks increases. If parts of the warehouse are unheated but must be heated when additional storage space is used, common costs will increase, but not incremental costs. It is the total inventory carrying costs which are used when making decisions on batch sizing and optimisation. That is why it is necessary to distinguish between incremental costs and common costs.

Stock valuation

The costs for carrying inventory are influenced by the value of items in stock. Yield requirements in euros will be higher for high-value items than for low-value items. Goods value refers to the accumulated costs which have been added to the item during its value refinement (including purchase, transportation, handling, production, etc.) i.e. the cost price of the item. All units of each item type kept in stock (stock-keeping unit, SKU) have probably not been put in the store at the same time, but have been purchased on different occasions, transported in different consignments and/or processed in different manufacturing batches. This means that the costs added to each unit are not exactly the same for all units of the same type of item. To determine a uniform value for all SKUs, it is necessary to use a principle for estimating the unit value of each individual item. Some common principles for this purpose are presented below.

Standard price: a standard price is a unit price that is calculated and determined to be valid during a certain time, often one year. It is used to prevent short-term variations in prices and costs from influencing product calculations and thereby item value.

Valuation to standard price is often used only for internally manufactured items. It is then estimated as a calculated cost based on standard prices of materials, standard salary costs and different increments. If it is used for purchased items it is often set at the expected purchase price for the coming year.

Average price: It is more common to use the average price for the valuation of purchased items. This average price is often calculated on a continuous basis by calculating a weighted price at each inbound delivery from the current average price for the quantity in stock and the purchase price for the quantity which has just been delivered. If there are 10 items already in stock when a delivery is made, and the current average unit price of the item is €15, and the delivered quantity is 50 pieces with a purchase unit price of €16, the new average price will be $(10 \cdot 15 + 50 \cdot 16) / 60 = €15.83$.

Price according to the first-come-first-serve principle (FCFS): in many cases the FCFS principle is used to valuate purchased items, which means that the first delivered quantity of an item is assumed to be dispatched first. If items of the same type are put in stock on different occasions, those that remain in stock are assumed to be those which were purchased most recently. In terms of valuation, this means that if the stock at a certain time contains a larger quantity than that of the latest delivery, some of the items will be valued at the purchase price for the latest delivery while others will be valued at the purchase price that was a valid at the time of earlier deliveries. If there are 60 pieces of a certain item in stock at a certain time, and the latest delivered quantity was 50 pieces at a price of €16 each, there were 10 pieces in stock at the time of delivery, and the previous delivery was of 40 pieces at the unit price of €15, the FCFS price will be (10 · 15 + 50 · 16) / 60 = €15.83.

Inventory carrying interest

As described above, the total incremental inventory carrying cost is the cost for storing one additional unit of an item. It is the sum of incremental costs for yield on capital, storage and uncertainty. It is often expressed as inventory carrying interest and refers to the annual incremental cost in per cent of the average stock value. To calculate this percentage, the average annual stock value must be estimated. The average inventory carrying interest for a company can then be calculated by using the following formula:

$$\text{Inventory carrying interest} = \frac{\Sigma \text{ incremental capital cost} + \Sigma \text{ incremental storage cost} + \Sigma \text{ incremental uncertainty cost}}{\text{average stock value}}$$

Since the incremental inventory carrying cost is an expression of the cost for increases and decreases in stocks, and not keeping stocks as opposed to not keeping stocks, it is only marginally affected by storage costs. Instead it is normally capital costs and uncertainty costs which dominate the incremental inventory carrying cost. In certain situations, however, the incremental inventory carrying cost may be high, as in the case of very voluminous goods or when a company rents pallet space.

Incremental storage costs and incremental uncertainty incremental costs usually vary between items in stock. For this reason it is not completely correct to apply the same inventory interest to the whole range of SKUs. A company may differentiate units the interest for different SKUs, or use an average cost for all units, or use the highest cost for all units. For practical reasons it is not common to use the same interest for all SKUs. For units with inventory interests that should be much higher than average (for example, voluminous goods) the effects on stock levels of inventory interest that is too low can be adjusted by also stating maximum permitted order quantities. For SKUs with a high obsolescence risk, a shorter maximum holding time (and thus a lower maximum order quantity) may be stated than for units with a lower obsolescence risk. Since uncertainty costs are normally very difficult to estimate, this procedure using supplementary rules may sometimes be the most practical and feasible alternative.

Example 1

A company manufactures paper forms to stock. The finished forms are put into packages of 750. The cost price for one package is €72. 56 packages can be put onto one EUR pallet. The storage of finished forms incurs the following costs, among others:

Handling, loading and unloading	€75 per pallet
Alternative cost for invested capital	10%
Obsolescence and insurance	€3 per package and year

The company also has a shortage of pallet places in its finished stocks and must rent extra storage space. This service costs €2.10 per pallet place and day (1 year = 365 days). What are the incremental inventory carrying costs per package and the inventory carrying interest for the form in question?

The incremental costs for storing every additional package for one year are calculated as follows:

Alternative cost for invested capital	72 · €0.10 = €7.20
Uncertainty and insurance costs	€3
Costs for space	2.10 € 365/56 = €14
Total incremental inventory carrying costs	€24.20 per package and year
Inventory carrying interest	24.20/72 = 34%

If the storage space is not an incremental cost and the item is stored in the company's own premises with free space, the inventory carrying interest will be 10.20/72 = 14%.

Appendix C

Derivation of the formula for economic order quantity (EOQ)

The formula for calculating economic order quantity (EOQ) is built on the following assumptions:

- Demand per time unit (D) is constant and known.
- Leadtime for stock replenishment is constant and known.
- Stocks are replenished momentarily with the entire order quantity on inbound delivery.
- Incremental ordering or set-up cost per event or occasion (O) is constant and known, and is independent of order quantity.
- Incremental inventory carrying costs per unit and time unit are constant and known, and independent of order quantity $(i \cdot c)$.
- The price or cost for the item ordered (c) is constant and known, and independent of order quantity and purchase occasion/manufacture occasion.

In stores with constant demand and momentary replenishment of the entire order quantity, stock level development will have the appearance of a sawtooth pattern, as in Figure C.1.

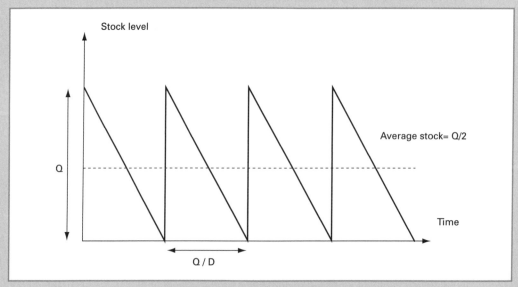

FIGURE C.1 Stock level development under the relevant assumptions for the EOQ formula

The maximum stock level will be the equivalent of the order quantity Q and the average half stock order quantity, i.e. Q / 2. Since the demand per time unit is D, one order quantity will be consumed during the time period Q / D, which is equivalent to the replenishment period or the order cycle. The number of stock replenishment occasions per year is thus D / Q.

With the above assumptions, the annual incremental inventory carrying cost is equal to the average stock (Q / 2) multiplied by the incremental inventory carrying cost per stored unit and year (i · c). The variation of annual incremental inventory carrying cost with order quantity is illustrated in Figure C.2. As the figure shows, the cost is proportional to the order quantity.

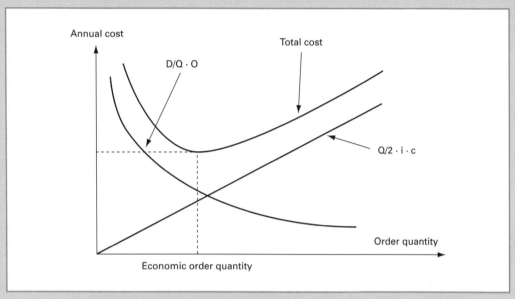

FIGURE C.2 Relationship between order quantities incremental and ordering costs, incremental inventory carrying costs and total incremental costs for ordering and carrying inventory

Correspondingly, the annual or incremental cost will be equal to the number of orders per year (D / Q), multiplied by the incremental ordering cost per order occasion. Consequently, a smaller number of order occasions will cause the annual incremental ordering costs to decrease. In other words, the larger the order quantities, the lower the incremental ordering costs per year. This relationship is also illustrated in Figure C.2.

The annual total incremental cost for carrying inventory and orders may be expressed with the help of the formula below. Its relationship with order quantity is illustrated in Figure C.2. The order quantity at the local minimum point is the economically optimal quantity, or the economic order quantity, EOQ.

Total incremental cost for carrying inventory and ordering $= TC = \dfrac{Q}{2} \cdot i{\cdot}c + \dfrac{D}{Q}{\cdot}O$

A formula for calculating the optimal order quantity is obtained by derivating the total cost function with respect to the order quantity.

$$\frac{dTC}{dQ} = \frac{i \cdot c}{2} - \frac{D}{Q^2} \cdot O = 0$$

$$\frac{i \cdot c}{2} - \frac{D}{Q^2} \cdot O$$

$$Q = \pm \sqrt{\frac{2 \cdot D \cdot O}{i \cdot c}}$$

$$Q_{opt} = \sqrt{\frac{2 \cdot D \cdot O}{i \cdot c}}$$

where   D = demand per time unit
          O = ordering cost per order occasion
          i   = incremental inventory carrying cost interest (in per cent)
          c = item value per stock unit

Appendix D

Normal distribution function

Safety factor	Service level %	Safety factor	Service level %	Safety factor	Service level %	Safety factor	Service level %
0.00	50.0	0.72	76.4	1.44	92.5	2.16	98.5
0.02	50.8	0.74	77.0	1.46	92.8	2.18	98.5
0.04	51.6	0.76	77.6	1.48	93.1	2.20	98.6
0.06	52.4	0.78	78.2	1.50	93.3	2.22	98.7
0.08	53.2	0.80	78.8	1.52	93.6	2.24	98.7
0.10	54.0	0.82	79.4	1.54	93.8	2.26	98.8
0.12	54.8	0.84	80.0	1.56	94.1	2.28	98.9
0.14	55.6	0.86	80.5	1.58	94.3	2.30	98.9
0.16	56.4	0.88	81.0	1.60	94.5	2.32	99.0
0.18	57.1	0.90	81.6	1.62	94.7	2.34	99.0
0.20	57.9	0.92	82.1	1.64	94.9	2.36	99.1
0.22	58.7	0.94	82.6	1.66	95.2	2.38	99.1
0.24	59.5	0.96	83.1	1.68	95.4	2.40	99.2
0.26	60.3	0.98	83.6	1.70	95.5	2.42	99.2
0.28	61.0	1.00	84.1	1.72	95.7	2.44	99.3
0.30	61.8	1.02	84.6	1.74	95.9	2.46	99.3
0.32	62.6	1.04	85.1	1.76	96.1	2.48	99.3
0.34	63.3	1.06	85.5	1.78	96.2	2.50	99.4
0.36	64.1	1.08	86.0	1.80	96.4	2.52	99.4
0.38	64.8	1.10	86.4	1.82	96.6	2.54	99.4
0.40	65.5	1.12	86.9	1.84	96.7	2.56	99.5
0.42	66.3	1.14	87.3	1.86	96.9	2.58	99.5
0.44	67.0	1.16	87.7	1.88	97.0	2.60	99.5
0.46	67.7	1.18	88.1	1.90	97.1	2.62	99.6
0.48	68.4	1.20	88.5	1.92	97.3	2.64	99.6
0.50	69.1	1.22	88.9	1.94	97.4	2.66	99.6
0.52	69.8	1.24	89.3	1.96	97.5	2.68	99.6
0.54	70.5	1.26	89.6	1.98	97.6	2.70	99.7
0.56	71.2	1.28	90.0	2.00	97.7	2.72	99.7
0.58	71.9	1.30	90.3	2.02	97.8	2.74	99.7
0.60	72.6	1.32	90.7	2.04	97.9	2.76	99.7
0.62	73.2	1.34	91.0	2.06	98.0	2.78	99.7
0.64	73.9	1.36	91.3	2.08	98.1	2.80	99.7
0.66	74.5	1.38	91.6	2.10	98.2	2.82	99.8
0.68	75.2	1.40	91.9	2.12	98.3	2.84	99.8
0.70	75.8	1.42	92.2	2.14	98.4	2.86	99.8

Appendix E

Service loss function

Safety factor	Service function	Safety factor	Service function	Safety factor	Service function	Safety factor	Service function
0.00	0.3989	0.72	0.1381	1.44	0.0336	2.16	0.0055
0.02	0.3890	0.74	0.1334	1.46	0.0321	2.18	0.0052
0.04	0.3793	0.76	0.1289	1.48	0.0307	2.20	0.0049
0.06	0.3699	0.78	0.1245	1.50	0.0293	2.22	0.0046
0.08	0.3602	0.80	0.1202	1.52	0.0280	2.24	0.0044
0.10	0.3509	0.82	0.1160	1.54	0.0267	2.26	0.0041
0.12	0.3418	0.84	0.1120	1.56	0.0255	2.28	0.0039
0.14	0.3328	0.86	0.1080	1.58	0.0244	2.30	0.0037
0.16	0.3240	0.88	0.1042	1.60	0.0232	2.32	0.0035
0.18	0.3154	0.90	0.1004	1.62	0.0222	2.34	0.0033
0.20	0.3069	0.92	0.0968	1.64	0.0211	2.36	0.0031
0.22	0.2986	0.94	0.0933	1.66	0.0201	2.38	0.0029
0.24	0.2904	0.96	0.0899	1.68	0.0192	2.40	0.0027
0.26	0.2824	0.98	0.0865	1.70	0.0183	2.42	0.0026
0.28	0.2745	1.00	0.0833	1.72	0.0174	2.44	0.0024
0.30	0.2668	1.02	0.0802	1.74	0.0166	2.46	0.0023
0.32	0.2592	1.04	0.0772	1.76	0.0158	2.48	0.0021
0.34	0.2518	1.06	0.0742	1.78	0.0150	2.50	0.0020
0.36	0.2445	1.08	0.0714	1.80	0.0143	2.52	0.0019
0.38	0.2374	1.10	0.0686	1.82	0.0136	2.54	0.0018
0.40	0.2304	1.12	0.0660	1.84	0.0129	2.56	0.0017
0.42	0.2236	1.14	0.0634	1.86	0.0123	2.58	0.0016
0.44	0.2169	1.16	0.0609	1.88	0.0116	2.60	0.0015
0.46	0.2104	1.18	0.0584	1.90	0.0111	2.62	0.0014
0.48	0.2040	1.20	0.0561	1.92	0.0105	2.64	0.0013
0.50	0.1978	1.22	0.0538	1.94	0.0100	2.66	0.0012
0.52	0.1917	1.24	0.0517	1.96	0.0094	2.68	0.0011
0.54	0.1857	1.26	0.0495	1.98	0.0090	2.70	0.0011
0.56	0.1799	1.28	0.0475	2.00	0.0085	2.72	0.0010
0.58	0.1742	1.30	0.0455	2.02	0.0080	2.74	0.0009
0.60	0.1687	1.32	0.0437	2.04	0.0076	2.76	0.0009
0.62	0.1633	1.34	0.0418	2.06	0.0072	2.78	0.0008
0.64	0.1580	1.36	0.0400	2.08	0.0068	2.80	0.0008
0.66	0.1528	1.38	0.0383	2.10	0.0065	2.82	0.0007
0.68	0.1478	1.40	0.0367	2.12	0.0061	2.84	0.0007
0.70	0.1429	1.42	0.0351	2.14	0.0058	2.86	0.0006

Appendix F

Exercises – solutions to problems

Exercise 4.1

			Service level			
	50%	**60%**	**70%**	**80%**	**90%**	**95%**
Revenue	45	50	60	70	90	110
Distribution cost	15	17	19	20	26	47
Profit	30	33	41	50	64	63

↑
Maximum profit

Exercise 4.2

Customer service =
(number of complete order lines for product X)/(total number of order lines for X)

Product	Frequency · Fill rate
A	0.05 · 0.95
B	0.01 · 0.92
C	0.01 · 0.89
D	0.02 · 0.85
E	0.01 · 0.86
All five	0.5 · 0.95 · 0.92 · 0.89 · 0.85
A+B+C	0.2 · 0.95 · 0.92 · 0.89
A+B+D	0.10 · 0.95 · 0.92 · 0.85
A+B	0.05 · 0.95 · 0.92
B+D	0.05 · 0.92 · 0.85

Exercise 4.3

Product	Sales	Contribution margin	Sales	Cummulative contribution margin	Cummulative percentage of total	ABC classification
C	7500	0.5	3750	3750	39.47%	A
I	4503	0.5	2251.5	6001.5	63.17%	A
F	5213	0.3	1563.9	7565.4	79.63%	A
B	920	0.7	644	8209.4	86.41%	B
K	712	0.7	498.4	8707.8	91.65%	B
L	2342	0.1	234.2	8942	94.12%	B
N	900	0.25	225	9167	96.49%	B
H	245	0.5	122.5	9289.5	97.77%	C
M	150	0.5	75	9364.5	98.56%	C
O	7000	0.01	70	9434.5	99.30%	C
D	176	0.3	52.8	9487.3	99.86%	C
A	62	0.6	37.2	9524.5	100.25%	C
G	8200	0.002	16.4	9540.9	100.42%	C
J	200	−0.05	−10	9530.9	100.32%	C
E	300	−0.1	−30	9500.9	100.00%	C
			Total:	9500.9	100.00%	

Exercise 5.1

The demand of 513 for the last five months is expressed as demand per year by multiplying with a $\frac{12}{5}$ factor. The average stock balance is determined as the mean of the six counted stock balances. The inventory turnover rate (ITR) could then be calculated as:

$$ITR = \frac{513 \cdot \frac{12}{5}}{\dfrac{(282 + 175 + 620 + 340 + 243 + 195)}{6}} = 4.0$$

Exercise 5.2

The flow consists of the sub-flows 1) finished goods stock, 2) rail transport, 3) terminal ware-house, 4) truck transport and 5) storage in distribution centre. The calculation of tied-up capital, costs for tied-up capital and throughput time for each sub-flow are as follows:

1 Stocks of finished goods:

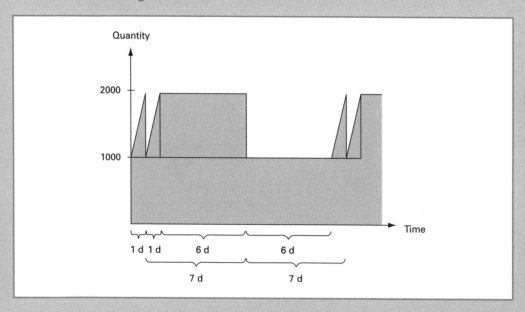

$$\text{Average stocks} = 1000 + \frac{\dfrac{1000}{2} \cdot 1 + \dfrac{1000}{2} \cdot 1 + 1000 \cdot 6 + 0 \cdot 6}{14} \quad 1500 \text{ pcs}$$

Average tied-up capital $= 1500 \cdot 1000 = €1500\,000$

Costs for tied-up capital $= 1\,500\,000 \cdot 0.15 = 225\,000$ €/year

2 Rail transport:

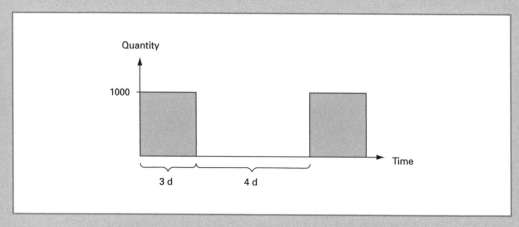

$$\text{Average stocks} = 1000 \cdot \frac{3}{7} = 429 \text{ pcs}$$

$$\text{Average value per piece} = \frac{1000 + 1100}{2} = \text{€}1050$$

$$\text{Average tied-up capital} = 429 \cdot 1050 = \text{€}450\,450$$

$$\text{Costs for tied-up capital} = 450\,450 \cdot 0.17 = 76\,576 \text{ €/year}$$

3 Storage at terminal:

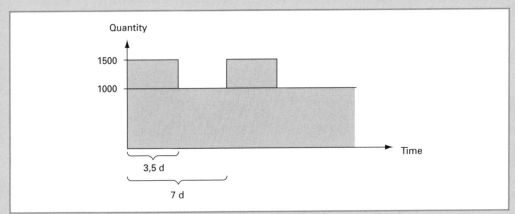

$$\text{Average stocks} = \frac{1500 \cdot 3.5 + 1000 \cdot 3.5}{7} = 1250 \text{ pcs}$$

$$\text{Average tied-up capital} = 1250 \cdot 1.100 = \text{€}1\,375\,000$$

$$\text{Costs for tied-up capital} = 1\,375\,000 \cdot 0.15 = 206\,250 \text{ €/year}$$

4 Truck transport

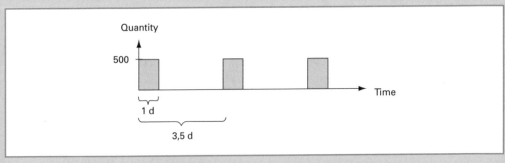

$$\text{Average stocks} = 500 \cdot \frac{1}{3.5} = 143 \text{ pcs}$$

$$\text{Average value per piece} = \frac{1100 + 1200}{2} = \text{€}1150$$

$$\text{Average tied-up capital} = 143 \cdot 1150 = \text{€}164\,450$$

$$\text{Costs for tied-up capital} = 164\,450 \cdot 0.15 = 24\,667 \text{ €/year}$$

6 Distribution centre:

$$\text{Average stocks} = \frac{52\,000}{8} = 6500 \text{ pcs}$$

$$\text{Average tied-up capital} = 6500 \cdot 1200 = €7\,800\,000$$

$$\text{Costs for tied-up capital} = 7\,800\,000 \cdot 0.15 = 1\,170\,000 \text{ €/year}$$

Total tied-up capital, costs for tied-up capital and throughput time in whole flow:

	Tied-up capital €	Costs, tied-up capital €	Throughput time
Finished goods stock	1 500 000	225 000	9 days
Rail transport	450 450	76 576	3 days
Terminal	1 375 000	206 250	9 days
Truck	164 450	24 668	1 day
Distribution stock	7 800 000	1 170 000	46 days
Total	11 289 900	1 702 494	68 days

Exercise 5.3

Rail:

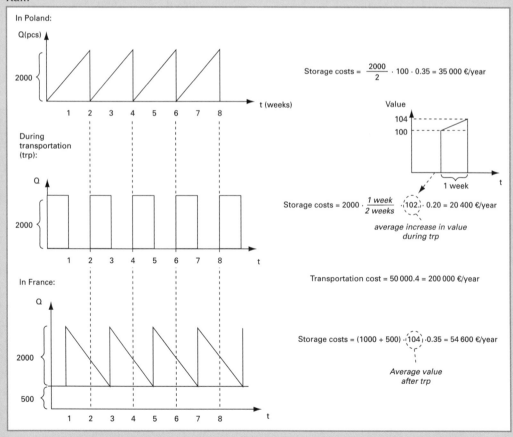

Total cost = 35 000 + 20 400 + 200 000 + 54 600 = 310 000 €/year

Truck:

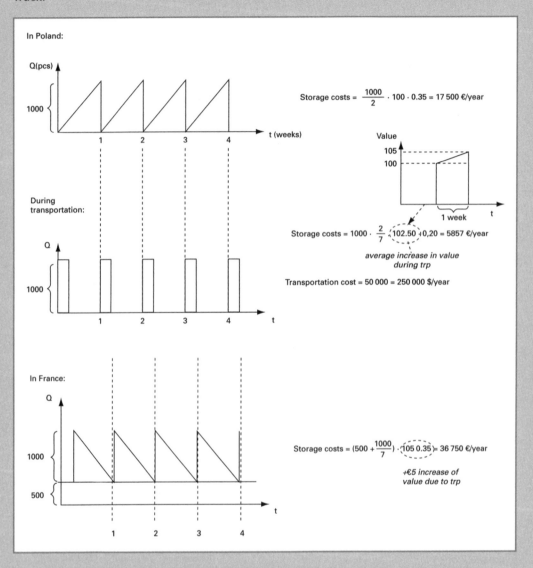

Total cost = 17 500 + 5 857 + 250 000 + 36 750 = 310 107 €/year

The total costs are almost the same for the rail and truck alternatives. Other issues, such as delivery service and environmental implications should be considered when making the decision.

Exercise 5.4

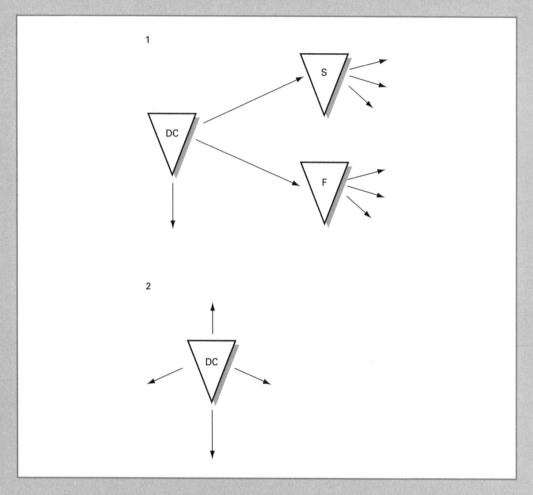

1

Tied-up capital, Netherlands: $\frac{330 \cdot 0.82}{6.5}^{*} \cdot 0.20 = 8.3$ M€

Tied-up capital, Sweden: $\frac{55 \cdot 0.82}{7.5} \cdot 0.20 = 1.2$ M€

Tied-up capital, France: $\frac{120 \cdot 0.82}{9.5} \cdot 0.20 = 2.1$ M€

Salaries:	$4.8 + 1.2 + 2.9$	$= 8.9$
Rental costs:	$5.6 + 1.8 + 4.5$	$= 11.9$
Transportation costs:		$= 15.5$
Other costs:		$= 3.7$
Total costs:		$= $ **51.6 M€/year**

*Contribution margin $= 1.00 - 0.18 = 0.82$

2

Tied-up capital, Netherlands: $\dfrac{330 \cdot 0.82}{9} = 6.0 \ M€$

Salaries: 5.2
Rental costs: 5.6
Transportation costs: 16.5
Other costs: 2.9

Order system: $\dfrac{2.9}{4} + \left(2.9 - \dfrac{2.9}{4} \cdot \dfrac{1}{2}\right) \cdot 0.2 = 1.2$

Total costs: 37.1 M€/year

Exercise 11.1

a) The forecast for July, using the moving average, will be equal to

$$(45 + 78 + 70 + 115 + 105 + 97) / 6 = 510 / 6 = 85 \ \text{pcs}$$

b) Using exponential smoothing, forecasts will be as follows:

for February = $0.4 \cdot 45 + 0.6 \cdot 50 = 48.0$ pcs
for March = $0.4 \cdot 78 + 0.6 \cdot 48.0 = 60.0$ pcs
for April = $0.4 \cdot 70 + 0.6 \cdot 60.0 = 64.0$ pcs
for May = $0.4 \cdot 115 + 0.6 \cdot 64.0 = 84.4$ pcs
for June = $0.4 \cdot 105 + 0.6 \cdot 84.4 = 92.6$ pcs
and for July = $0.4 \cdot 97 + 0.6 \cdot 92.6 = 94.4$ pcs

c) Since it is a new product, sales can be expected to increase rapidly during the introduction phase. For the forecasts to react sufficiently quickly to such a systematic sales growth, fewer periods than usual must be used in the moving average calculation, and a larger α value than normal when using exponential smoothing.

d) If the forecasts are rounded off to whole numbers, the forecast error for January will be $50 - 45 = 5$ pcs, for February $48 - 78 = -30$ pcs, for March $60 - 70 = -10$ pcs, for April $64 - 115 = -51$ pcs, for May $84 - 105 = -21$ pcs and for June $93 - 97 = -4$ pcs. MAD will then be equal to $(5 + 30 + 10 + 51 + 21 + 4) / 6 = 20.2$ pcs.

Exercise 11.2

a) Average sales per quarter over the last three years were $(17 + 47 + 32 + 16) / 4 = 28$ pcs. This means that the seasonal index for quarter 1 will be $22 / 28 = 0.79$, for quarter 2, $47 / 28 = 1.68$, for quarter 3, $32 / 28 = 1.14$ and for quarter 4, $11 / 28 = 0.39$.

b) Forecast sales for the coming year, calculated with exponential smoothing, are $0.5 \cdot 137 + 0.5 \cdot 109 = 123$ pcs. This means that forecast sales in quarter 1 will be $123 \cdot 0.79 / 4 = 24$ pcs, in quarter 2, $123 \cdot 1.68 / 4 = 52$ pcs, in quarter 3, $123 \cdot 1.14 / 4 = 35$ pcs and in quarter 4, $123 \cdot 0.39 / 4 = 12$ pcs.

c) The longer the forecast period is, the smaller will be random variations relatively speaking. The instability which may arise in forecasts with high α values due to random influence will be limited when working with a whole year as a forecast period. It is therefore possible to allow high α values so that the forecasts will be more responsive to systematic variations in demand.

Exercise 12.1

a) The economic order quantity, calculated with the aid of Wilson's formula, will be as follows for each item:

$$EOQ(A) = \sqrt{\frac{2 \cdot 2\,400 \cdot 200}{0.25 \cdot 180}} = 146 \text{ pcs}$$

$$EOQ(B) = \sqrt{\frac{2 \cdot 1\,500 \cdot 350}{0.25 \cdot 120}} = 187 \text{ pcs}$$

b) The number of times per year that each item is ordered will be:

$$\text{Item A: } \frac{2400}{146} = 16 \text{ times}$$

$$\text{Item B: } \frac{1500}{187} = 8 \text{ times}$$

c) The cycle stock for an item is on average half the order quantity. For both the items, the cycle stock will then be:

$$\frac{146}{2} \cdot 180 + \frac{187}{2} \cdot 120 = €24\,360$$

d) If the ordering frequency is determined by item A and both items are ordered 16 times per year, the annual ordering cost will be €16 · 425 = €6800. Since the order quantity for item B is halved when orders are doubled in frequency, the annual inventory carrying cost will be $(\frac{146}{2} \cdot 180 + \frac{187}{2 \cdot 2} \cdot 120) \cdot 0.25 = €4687$. The total costs will thus be 6800 + 4687 = €11 487.

   If the order frequency is determined by item B, then both the items are ordered 8 times a year instead and the annual ordering cost will be €8 · 425 = €3400. Since the order quantity for item A is doubled when orders are halved in frequency, the annual inventory carrying cost will be (2 · 146 / 2 · 180 + 187 / 2 · 120) · 0.25 = €9375. The total incremental costs will thus be 3400 + 9375 = €12 775.

   If both items are ordered individually according to the calculated economic order quantity, the annual ordering cost will be 16 · 200 + 8 · 350 = €6000, while inventory carrying costs will be 24 360 · 0.25 = 6090. The total costs will thus be 6000 + 6090 = 12 090. Ordering 16 times per year will lead to a reduction in costs of 12 090 − 11 487 = €603, while ordering 8 times per year will give a cost increase of 12 775 − 12 090 = €685. The alternative, ordering both items the number of times per year that is economically optimal for item A, should be selected.

Exercise 12.2

a) For the winter half of the year, the economic order quantity is $= \sqrt{\dfrac{2 \cdot 2 \cdot 6 \cdot 65 \cdot 670}{560 \cdot 0.25}}$

$= 86$ pcs and for the summer half of the year, $= \sqrt{\dfrac{2 \cdot 2 \cdot 6 \cdot 310 \cdot 670}{560 \cdot 0.25}} = 189$ pcs.

Since the order quantity should be rounded off to whole tens due to the testing equipment, the most economic order quantity during the winter half of the year is 90 pcs and during the summer half of the year it will be 190 pcs.

b) During the winter half of the year the economic order quantity will cover needs for 90 / 65 = 1.38 months. Since the company policy is not to manufacture more than one month's need at a time, the order quantity must be reduced to 60 pcs. For the summer half of the year the economic order quantity will cover 190 / 310 = 0.61 months, which is within the framework for the rule of a maximum of one month's sales in stock.

c) Using the existing strategy, the annual ordering costs and incremental inventory

carrying costs are equal to $\dfrac{2250}{150} \cdot 670 + \dfrac{150}{2} \cdot 560 \cdot 0.25 = €20\,550$. If different

order quantities are applied in the winter and summer halves of the year, the annual

cost will be $\left(\dfrac{6 \cdot 65}{60} + \dfrac{6 \cdot 310}{190}\right) \cdot 670 + \dfrac{60}{2} \cdot 560 \cdot \dfrac{0.25}{2} + \dfrac{190}{2} \cdot 560 \cdot \dfrac{0.25}{2} =$

€19 664. Cost savings of 20 550 − 19 664 = €886 are thus obtained.

Exercise 12.3

O = 100 + 200€
i = 25%
[Q] = €

$$Q_{opt} = \sqrt{\dfrac{2DO}{i \cdot c}} \rightarrow$$

$$Q_{opt} = \sqrt{\dfrac{2 \cdot (10000 \cdot 10 + 5000 \cdot 5 + 1000 \cdot 50 + 50000 \cdot 20 + 25000 \cdot 10 + 2000 \cdot 100)(200 + 100)}{0.25}} = 62\,450$$

$$\dfrac{D}{Q} = \dfrac{1625000}{62450} = 26 \rightarrow \text{Delivery 26 times/year}$$

$$Q_A = 10000/26$$

$$Q_B = 5000/26 \text{ etc.}$$

Exercise 12.4

Transportation costs:

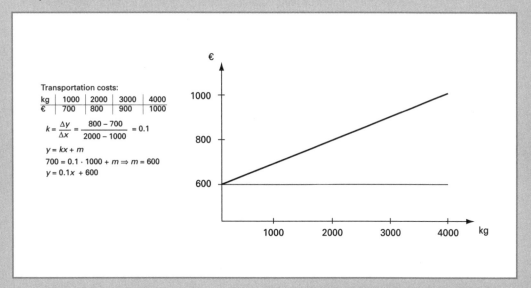

Transportation costs:

kg	1000	2000	3000	4000
€	700	800	900	1000

$$k = \frac{\Delta y}{\Delta x} = \frac{800 - 700}{2000 - 1000} = 0.1$$

$$y = kx + m$$

$$700 = 0.1 \cdot 1000 + m \Rightarrow m = 600$$

$$y = 0.1x + 600$$

Minimum ordering costs at minimum weight;
O = 900 + 600 = 1500

$$Q_{opt} = \sqrt{\frac{2 \cdot D \cdot O}{i \cdot c}} = \sqrt{\frac{2 \cdot 25000 \cdot 1500}{0.1 \cdot 120}} = 2500$$

Demand per year = 25000 → Purchase = 10 times per year

Exercise 12.5

Events		EOQ	
	−	0	+
1. The annual demand increases			+
2. Increased leadtimes to customers		0	
3. The inventory carrying cost increases	−		
4. Increased time for production planning		0	
5. Decreased set-up cost per batch	−		
6. Increased sales price		0	
7. Decreased cost of raw materials	−		

Exercise 12.6

D = 10 000 pcs/month = 120 000 pcs/year
O = €250
Inventory carrying costs = 0.05 € /piece and month = 0.60 €/piece and year
c = 0.65 if fewer than 20 000 are ordered

Without discount:

$$Q_{opt} = \sqrt{\frac{2 \cdot 120\,000 \cdot 250}{0.60}} = 10\,000 \text{ pcs}$$

$$TC_{opt1} = \frac{D}{Q} \cdot O + \frac{Q}{2} \cdot i \cdot c = \frac{120\,000}{10\,000} \cdot 250 + \frac{10\,000}{2} \cdot 0.6 = 6000 \text{ €/year}$$

EOQ:

$$Q_{opt} = \sqrt{\frac{2 \cdot 120\,000 \cdot 250}{0.60 \cdot 0.97}} = 10\,153 \text{ pcs} - \text{does not give discount}$$

$$TC_{20000} = \frac{Q}{2} \cdot i \cdot c + \frac{D}{Q} \cdot O - discount =$$

$$= \frac{20\,000}{2} \cdot 0.6 \cdot 0.97 + \frac{120\,000}{20\,000} \cdot 250 - 0.65 \cdot 0.03 \cdot 120\,000 = 4980 \text{ €/year}$$

Conclusion: Order 20 000 pieces with discount

Exercise 12.7

D = 1000 tons/year

Pallet

C = 4000 + 100 + 0.1 · 150 = 4115 €/year
    Price + Trp cost + Handing cost

O = 200 + 300 + 150
    Purchasing cost + Trp cost + Handling cost

i = 0.25
Q ≤ 25 tons

$$Q_{opt} = \sqrt{\frac{2 \cdot D \cdot S}{i \cdot c}} \cdot = \sqrt{\frac{2 \cdot 1000 \cdot 650}{0.25 \cdot 4115}} \cdot = 35.6$$

$$\rightarrow Q_{opt} = 25 \text{ ton}$$

Annual costs:

Trp: $\frac{1000}{25} \cdot 300 + 100 \cdot 1000 = 112\,000$

Purch: $\frac{1000}{25} \cdot 200 = 8000$

Handl: $\frac{1000}{25} \cdot 150 + 0.1 \cdot 150 \cdot 1000 = 21\,000$

Storage: $\frac{25}{2} \cdot 4115 \cdot 0.25 = 12\,860$

Purch: 4000 · 1000 = 4 000 000

Total annual costs = 112 000 + 8000 + 21 000 + 12860 + 4 000 000 = **4 153 000€**

Bulk

C = 3800 + 60 = 3860 €/ton
O = 200 + 2000 = 2200 €/ton
i = 0.20
Leasing cost = 65000 €/year
$Q \le 40$ tons (silo)
$Q \le 25$ tons (truck)

$$Q_{opt} = \sqrt{\frac{2 \cdot 1000 \cdot 2200}{0.2 \cdot 3860}} = 75.5 \text{ tons}$$

$$\rightarrow Q_{opt} = 25 \text{ tons}$$

Annual costs:

Trp: $\frac{1000}{25} \cdot 2000 + 60 \cdot 1000 = 140\,000$

Purch: $\frac{1000}{25} \cdot 200 = 8000$

Storage: $\frac{25}{2} \cdot 3860 \cdot 0{,}20 = 9650$

Silo: 65 000

Purch: $4000 \cdot 1000 = 4\,000\,000$

Total annual costs = 140 000 + 8000 + 9650 + 65 000 + 3 800 000 = **4 023 000 SEK**

Conclusion: Bulk is cheapest

Exercise 12.8

a) With the selected service level definition, the safety factor will be equal to 1.75 according to the normal distribution table. The standard deviation of demand will be $\frac{5}{\sqrt{4}}$ per weekly period and thus the safety stock will be $1.75 \cdot 5 \cdot \sqrt{\frac{2}{4}} = 6.2$ pcs. The re-order point will then be $\frac{120}{48} \cdot 2 + 6.2 = 11.2$ pcs, which is rounded up to 12 pcs to ensure the selected service level.

b) If the stocks are only checked once a week, the lead time will increase on average by half a week. The safety stock will then be $= 1.75 \cdot 5 \cdot \sqrt{\frac{2.5}{4}} = 6.9$ pcs and the re-order point $= \frac{120}{48} \cdot 2.5 + 6.9 = 13.2$ pcs, which is rounded up to 14 pcs. In other words, capital tied up in safety stocks will increase by $6.9 - 6.2 = 0.7$ pcs, or 11%.

c) With 5 weeks' delivery time the safety stock will be $= 1.75 \cdot 5 \cdot \sqrt{\frac{5}{4}} = 9.8$ pcs. If this supplier is selected the safety stock will increase by $9.8 - 6.2 = 3.6$ pcs, or 58%.

d) With this service level definition, the safety stock will not be affected at all.

Exercise 12.9

a) Using the figures stated, the service function will be $E(z) = (1 - 0.980) \cdot \dfrac{200}{16 \cdot \sqrt{3}} =$

0.1443. According to the service function table, this is equivalent to a safety factor of 0.69. The safety stock will thus be $= 0.69 \cdot 16 \cdot \sqrt{3} = 19.2$ pcs, and the re-order point will be $50 \cdot 3 + 19.2 = 169.2$ pcs, which is rounded up to 170 pcs.

b) If an alternative supplier delivers 100 pcs each time instead of 200 pcs, the cycle stock will decrease from $200 / 2 = 100$ pcs to $100 / 2 = 50$ pcs, i.e. by 50 pcs. The service

function will be $\dfrac{(1 - 0.98) \cdot 100}{16 \cdot \sqrt{3}} = 0.0722$, equivalent to a safety factor of 1.07.

Accordingly, the safety stock in this case will be $1.07 \cdot 16 \cdot \sqrt{3} = 29.7$ pcs compared with 19.2 pcs for the existing supplier, or an increase of $29.7 - 19.2 = 10.5$ pcs. In total, then, the stock will be reduced on average by $50 - 10.5 = 39.5$ pcs.

c) The larger the quantities ordered by customers each time, the more demand will vary from week to week. Thus, the safety stock will increase if the company wishes to maintain the existing service level.

Exercise 12.10

a) The total cycle stock in the four regional warehouses is $(\dfrac{300}{2} + \dfrac{430}{2} + \dfrac{370}{2} + \dfrac{450}{2}) \cdot$

€75 = €58 125. Using the normal distribution table, it can be seen that the safety factor in the four regional warehouses must be 1.28 to achieve a service level of 90%. This means that the safety stock in warehouse A will be $1.28 \cdot 137 = 176$ pcs, in warehouse B $1.28 \cdot 256 = 328$ pcs, in warehouse C $1.28 \cdot 179 = 230$ pcs and in warehouse D $1.28 \cdot 278 = 356$ pcs. The total theoretical capital tied up in the current regional warehouses will thus be $(176 + 328 + 230 + 356) \cdot 75 = $ €81 750 in safety stocks and in total $58\,125 + 81\,750 = $ €139 875. The target stock for central stock-keeping will then be $0.7 \cdot 139\,875 = $ €97 912.

If instead the product is distributed from a central warehouse, the order quantity

according to Wilson's formula will be $\sqrt{\dfrac{2 \cdot (230 + 450 + 360 + 510) \cdot 12 \cdot 300}{0.25 \cdot 75}} = 771$

pcs. This means that the cycle stock for the central warehouse case can be estimated at $771 \cdot 75 / 2 = $ €28 913. Assuming stocks remain unchanged, approximately $98\,280 - 28\,913 = $ €69 000 or 920 pcs will remain for the safety stock. This safety stock corresponds to a safety factor of $920 / 440 = 2.09$. The service level using a central warehouse will be approximately 98% as indicated in the normal distribution table, as compared with the original 90%.

b) Since the distance to customers increases, transportation costs will rise. Delivery times to customers in more remote parts of the country may also become longer.

Exercise 12.11

a) The run-out time for each paint, if plans are made to avoid using safety stocks, will be $5 \cdot (853 - 125) / 240 = 15.2$ days for the black stool, $5 \cdot (1\,080 - 180) / 500 = 9$ days for the blue stool and $5 \cdot (290 - 140) / 150 = 5$ days for the red stool. Since the lead-time is equal to $5 + 500 / 200 = 7.5$ days for the black stool, and thus less that the run-out time, no orders need to be planned for the black stool. The leadtime for the blue stool is $5 + 1\,500 / 200 = 12.5$ days and the leadtime for the red stool is $5 + 300 / 200 = 6.5$ days. In both cases, leadtimes are longer than the respective run-out times. New orders should therefore be planned for the blue and red stools.

b) The leadtime for the blue stool is $12.5 - 9 = 3.5$ days longer than the current run-out time, while for the red stool it is $6.5 - 5 = 1.5$ days longer than the current run-out time. The difference between the leadtime and the run-out time is thus greater for the blue stool. Manufacture of the blue stool should be planned before the manufacture of the red stool on the basis of the current stock situation.

c) Manufacture of the blue stool takes much longer in the injection mould than manufacture of the red stool since its economic order quantity is greater, $1500 / 200 = 7.5$ days compared with $300 / 200 = 1.5$ days. If it is decided to manufacture the blue stool first, it can be completed after 12.5 days, i.e. there will be a shortage in stocks for 3.5 days. The moulding of the red stool will not be able to be started until after 7.5 days and it will not be able to be delivered until after $7.5 + 1.5 + 5 = 14$ days, i.e. 9 days too late. If the red stool is manufactured first, it can be ready after 6.5 days, and there will only be 1.5 days with shortages. In this case the blue stool can start to be manufactured after 1.5 days and thus can be ready for delivery after $1.5 + 12.5 = 14$ days, i.e. 5 days too late. The total number of days with shortages in stocks for both products if the blue stool is manufactured first will be $3.5 + 9 = 12.5$ days, while the number of days with shortages of stocks will be $1.5 + 5 = 6.5$ days if the red stool is manufactured first. If the shortage cost per day for both stools is equal, it will be advantageous to manufacture the red stool first.

Exercise 12.12

a) The aggregate requirement of legs to fulfil the assembly plan and to be able to deliver agreed quantities to the associated company will be as in the table below:

Day	1	2	3	4	5	6	7	8	9	10	11	12	13	14	15
LX			250					250					250		
NO	480				480				480				480		
Other					80					80					80
Total	480		250		560			250	480	80			730		80

The calculation of how stocks successively decrease and the times of first net requirement are shown in the table below:

Day	1	2	3	4	5	6	7	8	9	10	11	12
Needs	480		250		560			250	480	80		
Delivered				1 200								
Stock	410	410	160	1 360	800	800	800	550	70	−10	−10	−10

As described in the table, the first net requirement arises on day 10. Inbound delivery of a new order must take place on that day. Since delivery time is 7 days, a new purchase order must be made to the supplier on day 3.

b) If the stock were 690 pcs instead of 890 pcs, there would be a shortage as early as day 3. The most suitable measure is to try to bring forward the outstanding purchase order by one day and place the new purchase order for delivery on day 9.

c) If safety stocks are used, the delivery must be received when the safety stock falls short. According to the table above, this will take place on day 9. Accordingly, a new purchase order must be placed on day 2.

Exercise 14.1

Step 1, Identifying FTL deliveries: Customer 6 demands 15 tons, which is more than the maximum 12 tons that the largest vehicle C can manage. The *first route* is then a FTL delivery of 12 tons to customer 6. The driving time is 45 + 45 minutes which is feasible because the maximum driving time was 250 minutes. The remaining 3 tons are added to the route calculations. The reason for choosing vehicle C for the FTL delivery is that it has the largest capacity of all vehicles. This minimises driving time usage and it is usually easier to fit a 3 ton demand in the route calculation than a 6 ton demand (as would have been the case if using vehicles A or B).

Step 2, Develop a distance matrix: This is given in the exercise.

Step 3, Develop a savings matrix: Savings values in descending order:

Customer pair	Savings value
6-8	$(45+53-23) = 75$
5-8	$(40+53-26) = 67$
2-6	$(28+45-17) = 56$
2-8	$(28+53-34) = 47$
5-6	$(40+45-41) = 44$
1-7	$(20+47-27) = 40$
2-5	$(28+40-32) = 36$
4-7	$(32+47-50) = 29$
1-3	$(20+30-23) = 27$
2-3	$(28+30-31) = 27$
3-6	$(30+45-48) = 27$
3-7	$(30+47-50) = 27$
4-5	$(32+40-51) = 21$
1-4	$(20+32-33) = 19$
3-8	$(30+53-65) = 18$
4-8	$(32+53-75) = 10$
3-5	$(30+40-63) = 7$
6-7	$(45+47-85) = 7$
3-4	$(30+32-56) = 6$
4-6	$(32+45-74) = 3$
5-7	$(40+47-86) = 1$
7-8	$(47+53-99) = 1$
1-2	$(20+28-48) = 0$
1-5	$(20+40-60) = 0$
1-6	$(20+45-65) = 0$
1-8	$(20+53-73) = 0$
2-4	$(28+32-60) = 0$
2-7	$(28+47-75) = 0$

Step 4, Assign and sequence customer nodes to routes: Consideration is taken to the time and load restrictions when conducting route planning. Here, we continue scheduling routes for vehicle C until all its time and load capacity is used. After step 1 where the first route was identified, customer 6 has a remaining demand of 6 tons and vehicle C has $250 - 90 = 160$ minutes left in operating time.

Second route:

- The highest savings value (75) has customer pair 6-8, so these are first linked together into a common route (Route: Depot-6-8-Depot). The combined route is feasible. The total load is $3 + 4 = 7$ tons, which is below the maximum vehicle load of 12 tons. The total driving time for vehicle C is 121 minutes ($45 + 23 + 53$) which is below the remaining 160 minutes operating time for the vehicle.

- Second highest savings value is 67, for customer pair 5-8. Since customer 8 is in the route and at the end of it, we can add customer 5 (New route: Depot-6-8-5-Depot). The combined route is feasible. The total load is $7 + 2 = 9$ tons, which is below the maximum vehicle load of 12 tons. The total driving time for vehicle C is 134 minutes ($45 + 23 + 26 + 40$) which is below the remaining 160 minutes operating time for the vehicle.

- Next in the savings value list is customer pair 2-6. Customer 6 is in the route and at one end of it, so customer 2 can be added to the route (New route: Depot-2-6-8-5-Depot). The combined route is feasible. The total load is $9 + 2 = 11$ tons, which is below the maximum vehicle load of 12 tons. The total driving time for vehicle C is 134 minutes $(28 + 17 + 23 + 26 + 40)$ which is below the remaining 160 minutes operating time for the vehicle.

- Next in the savings value list is pair 2-8 but since both of these are already included in the route, we have to continue downwards in the list looking for a customer pair containing customer 2 or 5 and one customer that isn't in the route yet. At savings value 27 we find customer pair 2-3, which fits the description. Adding customer 3 (to a new route Depot-3-2-6-8-5-depot) is feasible regarding the load restriction ($11+1 = 12$ ton which is okay) but not feasible regarding the operating time restriction. The suggested route results in 167 $(30 + 31 + 17 + 23 + 26 + 40)$ minutes driving time which is more than the remaining 160 minutes for vehicle C. Therefore, customer 3 cannot be added to the route. No other customer can be added because there is only 1 ton left in vehicle C and customer 1 demands 3 tons, customer 4 demands 6 tons and customer 7 demands 5 tons. This means we have to start another route, starting with the customer pair with the highest savings value but does not contain any of the suppliers in the previous route.

Third route:

- Customer pair 1-7 has a savings value of 40. Neither customer has been supplied with their demand yet, so we can start du design the third route from this pair (Route: Depot-1-7-Depot). Since all off vehicle C's operating time has been used, we need to use another vehicle for this route. We use vehicle A. The combined route is feasible. The total load is $3 + 5 = 8$ tons, which is below the maximum vehicle load of 9 tons. The total driving time for vehicle A is 94 minutes $(20 + 27 + 47)$ which is below the 200 minutes operating time for the vehicle.

- Next in the savings value list is pair 1-3 with a value of 27, which is equal to the savings value of pair 3-7, so it doesn't matter which end we add customer 3 to. The new route (Depot-3-1-7-Depot) is feasible. The total load is $8 + 1 = 9$ tons, which is equivalent with the maximum vehicle load of 9 tons. The total driving time for vehicle A is 127 minutes $(30 + 23 + 27 + 47)$ which is below the 200 minutes operating time for the vehicle. Vehicle A has now reached its maximum load capacity, so we cannot add another customer to this route. Remaining time capacity of vehicle A is 73 minutes.

- Only customer 4 remains so we have to make a new route containing only this customer. This route (Depot-4-Depot) is feasible. The total load is 6 tons, which is below the maximum vehicle load of 9 tons. The total driving time for vehicle A is 64 minutes which is below the remaining 73 minutes operating time for the vehicle.

Route solutions:

Routes	Vehicle	Driving time
Depot-6-Depot	C	90 minutes
D-2-6-8-5-D	C	134 minutes
D-3-1-7-D	A	127 minutes
D-4-D	A	64 minutes

Vehicle C is used for $90 + 134 = 224$ minutes
Vehicle A is used for $127 + 64 = 191$ minutes

Exercise 14.2

Step 1:

Routes	Vehicle	Used capacity	
		Load	Time
Route 1: Depot-1-Depot	A	10 tons	166 min
Route 2: Depot-6-Depot	A	10 tons	68 min

Capacity left in vehicle A: 96 minutes.

Step 2: This is given in the exercise

Step 3: Savings values in descending order:

Customer pair	Savings value	Customer pair	Savings value
1-5	110	1-8	37
1-2	95	3-10	36
2-5	84	4-11	35
3-4	79	8-11	35
2-3	77	5-8	33
4-8	76	1-10	24
4-10	73	1-12	24
1-3	72	10-12	24
2-6	68	5-13	22
1-4	67	2-10	19
1-6	63	1-9	17
2-4	62	9-12	17
3-5	61	1-13	16
3-7	60	7-10	15
5-6	59	3-9	13
2-7	54	7-9	13
3-6	54	2-12	12
6-7	54	2-13	12
9-10	54	5-12	12
10-11	53	6-12	12
1-7	49	6-13	12
11-12	49	1-11	9
3-8	46	6-9	9
4-5	46	6-10	9
4-7	46	9-13	8
7-8	46	10-13	8
9-11	46	11-13	8
5-7	45	2-9	7
12-13	44	4-12	6
4-9	43	8-12	6
8-9	43	3-11	5
8-10	43	7-11	5
6-8	42	5-10	3
2-8	40	6-11	1
4-6	40		

Step 4:

Third route:

- Customer pair 1-5 has the highest savings value. The combined route (Depot-1-5-Depot) is feasible. The total load is 4 tons, which is below the maximum vehicle load of 10 tons. The total driving time is 166 minutes which is below the 330 minutes operating time for vehicles A and B, but more than the remaining 96 minutes for vehicle A. We therefore assign vehicle B for this route.

- Next in the savings value list is pair 1-2. The combined route (Depot-2-1-5-Depot) is feasible. The total load is 9 tons, which is below the maximum vehicle load of 10 tons. The total driving time is 171 minutes which is below the 330 minutes operating time for vehicle B.

- There is 1 ton left to max-load. Customer pair 3-4 which has the highest savings value may not be linked since none of these customers is in the route. Customer pair 2-3 has the highest value but the load capacity will be exceeded. We may link customer pair 2-6. The combined route (Depot-6-2-1-5-Depot) is feasible. The total load is 10 tons, which is equal to the maximum vehicle load of 10 tons. The total driving time is 171 minutes which is below the 330 minutes operating time. As the maximal tonnage capacity of 10 tons is met we fix the route. 159 minutes of operating time of vehicle B remains.

Fourth route:

- Customer pair 3-4 now has the highest savings value. The route Depot-3-4-Depot is feasible. The total load is 5 tons, which is below the maximum vehicle load of 10 tons. The total driving time is 131 minutes which is below the 159 remaining minutes operating time for vehicles B.

- We then try with 4-8. The route Depot-3-4-8-Depot is feasible. The total load is 10 tons, which is equal to the maximum vehicle load of 10 tons. The total driving time is 131 minutes which is below the 159 remaining minutes operating time for vehicles B. As the maximum tonnage capacity is 10 tons, we fix the route.

Fifth route:

- Customer pair 9-10 now has the highest savings value. The route Depot-9-10-Depot is feasible. The total load is 6 tons, which is below the maximum vehicle load of 10 tons. The total driving time is 114 minutes which is below the 330 minutes operating time for vehicle C but more than the remaining 96 minutes for vehicle A and 28 minutes for vehicle B. We therefore assign vehicle C to this route.

- We then try with 4-8. The route Depot-9-10-11-Depot is feasible. The total load is 9 tons, which is below the maximum vehicle load of 10 tons. The total driving time is 139 minutes which is below the 330 minutes operating time for vehicles C. As the maximum tonnage capacity is 10 tons, we fix the route.

- Customer pair (with the next highest savings value) to be added to the route is 7-9 since customer 7 needs exactly 1 ton. The route Depot-7-9-10-11-Depot is feasible. The total load is 10 tons, which is equal to the maximum vehicle load of 10 tons. The total driving time is 186 minutes which is below the 330 minutes operating time for vehicles C. As the maximum tonnage capacity is 10 tons, we fix the route.

Sixth route:

- Only customer pair (12-13) remains so we have to make a new route containing only this pair. This route (Depot-12-13-Depot) is feasible. The total load is 9 tons, which is below the maximum vehicle load of 10 tons. The total driving time is 94 minutes which is below the remaining 96 minutes operating time for the vehicle A and the remaining 144 minutes for vehicle C. We assign vehicle A to the route.

Route solutions:

Routes	Vehicle	Used capacity Load	Time
Route 1: D-1-D	A	10 tons	166 min
Route 2: D-6-D	A	10 tons	68 min
Route 3: D-6-2-1-5-D	B	10 tons	171 min
Route 4: D-3-4-8-D	B	10 tons	131 min
Route 5: D-7-9-10-11-D	B	10 tons	186 min
Route 6: D-12-13-D	A	9 tons	94 min

Vehicle A is used for 328 minutes
Vehicle B is used 302 minutes
Vehicle C is used 186 minutes

Exercise A.1

Item	Turnover (pcs/year)	Value/pcs	Profit margin %	Picking freq/year
A	100	2	70	100
B	30	59	65	15
C	50	65	85	50
D	2000	0.50	70	1000
E	100	5	75	25
F	3000	0.50	50	115
G	5000	1	65	1000
H	1500	6	70	450
I	2000	1	80	400
J	500	19	75	190
K	2000	2	45	550
L	300	43	65	75
M	2000	1	70	650
N	1500	1.50	75	420
O	2000	2	80	1100

a) Sort by volume value: A – E – D – F – B – I – M – N – C – K – O – G – H – J – L, Highest
service level to items with lowest volume value, e.g. Lowest service level 0–60%: L – J
– H, Medium-high service level 60–90%: G – O – K – C – N – M, Highest service level
90–100%: I – B – F – D – E – A.

b) Sort by picking events, O – D – G – M – K – H – N – I – J – F – A – L – C – E – B, Shortest
moving distance for items with highest picking frequencies, e.g. Zone with shortest
moving frequency 0–60%: O – D – G, Zone with medium moving frequency 60–90%:
M – K – H – N, Zone with lowest moving frequency 90–100% (I – J – F – A – L – C –
E – B)

c) Sort by profit contribution/year: L – J – H – G – O – C – K – N – I – M – B – F – D – E
– A, Highest service level to items with highest profit contribution, e.g.: Highest service
level 0–60%: L – J – H, Medium-high service level 60–90%: G – O – C – K – N – I,
Lowest service level 90–100%: M – B – F – D – E – A.

Glossary

ABC analysis   A method for dividing items, customers, suppliers and other objects into different classes based on specific criteria, e.g. volume value per item, profit contribution per product, turnover per customer, purchase value per supplier. ABC analysis is an application of the minority principle, meaning that in every group of objects there is a small number which accounts for a large proportion of the value. ABC analysis is also called the 80/20 rule.

Advance shipment notice   A notification sent by the supplier to notify the customer that a delivery is on the way.

Advanced planning and scheduling (APS)**   Techniques that deal with analysis and planning of logistics and manufacturing over the short, intermediate, and long-term time periods. APS describes any computer program that uses advanced mathematical algorithms or logic to perform optimisation or simulation on finite capacity scheduling, sourcing, capital planning, resource planning, forecasting, demand management, and others. The five main components of APS systems are demand planning, production planning, production scheduling, distribution planning, and transportation planning.

After sales process   From delivered product or service performed to expiry of guarantee or agreement.

Agility**   The ability to successfully manufacture and market a broad range of low-cost, high-quality products and services with short leadtimes and varying volumes that provides enhanced value to customers through customisation.

Allocation*   The process of designating stock for a specific order or schedule. Also called reservation.

Approved supplier   A supplier allowed to be used by the first tier supplier.

Arm's length relation   It is a type of relation between parties in which the parties' behaviour is centred on trying to avoid a relationship of dependence and to reduce the power of the opposing party.

Assembly to order (ATO)*   A production environment where a good or service can be assembled after receipt of a customer's order. The key components used in the assembly or finishing process are planned and possibly stocked in anticipation of a customer order.

Associated supplier   A level of customer–supplier relationships in which the relationship is long-term and reviewed periodically. Product quality is guaranteed by the supplier. Flows between the companies are as far as possible synchronised. Both companies work continuously to reduce stocks and leadtimes, and to eliminate buffering as a safeguard against disruptions. The supplier's prices are not the only variables on which suppliers are assessed.

Automated storage and retrieval system (AS/RS)**   A high-density rack inventory storage system with unmanned vehicles automatically loading and unloading products to/from the racks.

Automatic guided vehicle system (AGVS)**   A transportation network that automatically routes one or more material handling devices, such as carts or pallet trucks, and positions them at predetermined destinations without operator intervention.

Available to promise (ATP)*   The uncommitted portion of a company's inventory and planned production, maintained in the master schedule to support customer order promising.

Back flushing*   The deduction from inventory records of the component parts used in an assembly or subassembly by exploding the bill-of-materials by the production count of assemblies produced.

Bar codes**   A symbol consisting of a series of printed bars representing values. A system of optical character reading, scanning, and tracking of units by reading a series of printed bars for translation into a numeric or alphanumeric identification code.

Base demand**   The percentage of a company's demand that is derived from continuing contracts and/or existing customers.

Batch delivery   Supplier delivers some type of economic order quantity on order from the customer.

Batching**   Practice of compiling and collecting orders before they are sent in to the manufacturer.

Bill-of-material (BOM)*   A listing of all subassemblies, intermediates, parts, and raw materials that go into a parent assembly showing the quantity of each required to make an assembly. Also called product structure.

Bottleneck items   Items with little significance to the company and low availability on the market.

Breakpoint distribution   A way of consolidating deliveries in which many flows of goods are co-ordinated between breakpoints, where large loads are broken down for onward transportation.

Bullwhip effect   Variations in demand which are amplified upstream in supply chains with storage points.

Call-off   The part of the delivery plan furthest in time. It is normally considered as a clear order from the customer.

Capacity lag strategy   A reactive capacity planning strategy in which the capacity is either increased or decreased after demand increases or decreases.

Capacity lead strategy   A proactive capacity planning strategy in which the capacity is either increased or decreased before demand increases or decreases.

Capacity planning**   Assuring that needed resources (e.g. manufacturing capacity, distribution centre capacity, transportation vehicles, etc.) will be available at the right time and place to meet logistics and supply chain needs.

Capacity requirement   Needed resources during a time period.

Capacity utilisation   The extent to which the available capacity (e.g. work centre, machine, truck, etc.) is used.

Carousel store   An automated form of storing items from opened packages. Also called paternoster store.

Cellular production layout   A production layout in which production resources are organised into groups called production cells. The layout is built around grouping items by similarity of manufacture.

Centralised warehouse structure   A warehouse structure with a low number of levels and warehouses.

Clark-Wright method   Also known as savings matrix method, is a route planning algorithm.

Collaborative planning forecasting and replenishment (CPFR)**   A collaboration process whereby supply chain trading partners can jointly plan key supply chain activities from production and delivery of raw materials to production and delivery of final products to end customers.

Combined transport   Any single journey that uses a combination of several traffic modes, for example rail and road transport

Component commonality   Eliminating the range of components used in products.

Component range   The total number of components used to make a company's products.

Components*   The raw material, part, or subassembly that goes into a higher level assembly, compound, or other item.

Congestion charge   Congestion charges are fees that are levied during time periods when the road network is most used, in order to even out the density of traffic at different times of the day.

Consolidated distribution   A way of consolidating deliveries in which the small batches of goods from several different suppliers and/or shippers are transported together in the same vehicle.

Consumables   Purchase items such as spare parts, cleaning and sanitary items, office items, etc.

Continual supply   A principle used to retrieve materials for supply of input material to a manufacturing process, in which small packages of a large number of items are moved to the production unit

Conveyor system   A mechanical handling equipment that moves materials from one location to another.

Co-ordination stock   An intentionally created stock whose purpose is to couple parallel flows of material and to gain benefits of consolidation.

Cost/Revenue analysis   An economic tool used in the decision making process to analyse the cost effectiveness of different alternatives by quantifying their costs and benefits. Also known as cost–benefit analysis.

Counterbalance truck   A truck type used for heavy lifts.

Cover time   Average tied up capital in flows divided by delivery value per year, week or day. Also called run-out time.

Cover time planning   Also known as run-out time planning, is the time for which available stocks, i.e. physically present stocks plus planned inbound deliveries, are expected to last.

Critical value analysis**   A modified ABC analysis in which a subjective value of criticalness is assigned to each item.

Cross-docking   A strategy where items from an inbound truck or rail are unloaded and loaded on outbound trucks or rail cars, with little or no storage in between.

Customer managed ordering (CMO)   The customer plan and register order directly in the supplier's system.

Customer order decoupling point (CODP)   The point in a product's product structure at which the product's manufacture and delivery is determined by a customer order. Activities before the customer order decoupling point is controlled by forecast.

Customer order process   One of the two processes in a company that in related to demand management for the company's products. It covers the known part of demand and the forecast process covers that part of demand which must be estimated in different ways.

Customer order**   An order from a customer for a particular product or a number of products. It is often referred to as an actual demand to distinguish it from a forecasted demand.

Customer relationship management (CRM)**   An information systems that help sales and marketing functions, as opposed to the ERP (Enterprise Resource Planning), which is for back-end integration.

Customer service**   Activities between the buyer and seller that enhance or facilitate the sale or use of the seller's products or services.

Cycle counting   An administrative process aimed at correcting any errors that may have arisen in the stock balance, i.e. tallying the reported stock balance with the real, physical stock balance.

Cycle service   The probability of not having a shortage during one cycle of storage.

Cycle stock   The part of stocks which arise because inbound deliveries take place at a different pace and in larger quantities than consumption.

Decentralised warehouse structure   A warehouse structure with a high number of levels and warehouses.

Delivery flexibility   The capacity to adapt to and comply with changed customer requirements in agreed and ongoing orders.

Delivery monitoring   Checking that deliveries take place at agreed times. In this process information is sent to the supplier about when the delivery is expected to take place according to the agreement made at the time of order.

Delivery notice   A notice to informing the customer that the delivery is on the way.

Delivery notification   A notification sent by supplier to customer to notify them that a delivery is on the way.

Delivery plan   Information on delivery time and quantity of future demand which the company intends to buy. Also called delivery schedule.

Delivery precision   The extent to which the delivery takes place at the delivery time agreed with the customer. Also called on-time delivery.

Delivery reception   Receiving, checking and registering an inbound goods delivery.

Delivery reliability   A measurement of the quality of delivery in terms of the right product being delivered in the right quantity.

Delivery schedule   See delivery plan.

Delivery service   Service related to carrying out the order-to-delivery processes. It takes place primarily during the phases order-to-delivery and delivery itself.

Delivery service index   An index that is the result of multiplying the percentages of delivery precision and delivery reliability, and possibly other relevant delivery service elements.

Delivery time   The time elapsed from receipt of customer order to delivery.

Demand fill rate   The proportion of demand that can be satisfied directly from stocks.

Dependent demand   Means that the demand for an item may be derived from the demand for another item, using a bill-of-material. Also called derived material requirement.

Depth stacking   To stack packages in depth and on each other.

Derived material requirement   See dependent demand.

Design for logistics   A product design approach that takes logistics consequences into consideration and thus helps to control logistics costs and increase customer service levels.

Direct delivery   **Direct delivery to production** is a pull-driven delivery pattern in which the supplier only delivers the quantity which the customer needs, irrespective of whether it is input items for production or for forwarding to a customer at the next level.   **Direct delivery to customer** is a distribution strategy where items are delivered directly from the supplier to the customer company's customer. Also called direct distribution.

Direct distribution   See direct delivery.

Disintermediation   The removal of intermediaries in a supply chain.

Disposable package   A package designed and intended for short-term, often single, use.

Distribution channel   A set of independent organisations involved in the process of making a product or service accessible for consumption by the final user.

Distribution process   The process from physically accessible product to distribution of product on site to customer.

Distribution requirement planning (DRP)*   The function of determining the need to replenish inventory at branch warehouses. A time-phased order point approach is used where the planned orders at the branch warehouse level are "exploded" via MRP logic to become gross requirements on the supplying source.

Distribution system   A subsystem of the logistics system. It contains the downstream environment – the customers.

Dual sourcing   A special case of multiple sourcing where two parallel suppliers are used for each item.

Durable package   A package that does not quickly wear out. It is designed and intended for being used several times and during long time.

Dutch auction   A type of auction in which there is one vendor and many purchasers. The vendor states a high starting price which is then decreased until a purchaser accepts it.

Eco-cycle   Is when natural resources are returned to the environment at the same rate as they are extracted.

Eco-labelling   Eco-labelling is a system in which the producer can apply for its products to be environmentally approved and marked with an eco-symbol.

Economic order quantity (EOQ)   A fixed order quantity method which optimises the incremental inventory carrying and ordering costs when deciding optimum order quantity.

Economic run-out time   A lot-sizing method in which the order quantity is chosen to cover a whole number of planning periods. It is calculated as the trade-off between incremental ordering and inventory carrying costs.

Efficient consumer response (ECR)**   A demand driven replenishment system designed to link all parties in the logistics channel to create a massive flow-through distribution network.

Electronic data interchange (EDI)   A communication method in which the data is transferred from one computer system to another in a predefined and standardised format and in such a way that the receiving system can interpret and process the information.

Electronic marketplaces   An Internet-based solution which enables purchasing and selling activities between companies and other companies. It operates as a hub, around which one or more purchasers and one or more vendors collect to exchange information and do business.

Emission right   A financial measure to reduce emission of pollutants.

Emission standard   Requirements that set specific limits to the amount of pollutants that can be released into the environment.

Engineer to order (ETO)   A production environment in which company's products are designed to customer order specifications to a greater or lesser degree. Design work, preparations for manufacture, materials sourcing and manufacturing is carried out and governed both in terms of time and content by customer orders received.

Enterprise resource planning (ERP)**   A class of software for planning and managing "enterprise-wide" the resources needed to take customer orders, ship them, account for them and replenish all needed goods according to customer orders and forecasts.

Environmental impact assessment (EIA)   The process of identifying, predicting, evaluating and mitigating the environmental impact of a product or system.

Environmental management system   An environment management system is a tool to organise environmental work in a company.

Environmental zone   Zones in which only vehicles with special conditions are allowed to drive.

Environmentally adapted logistics   Logistics that is adapted to the environment. It has several different aspects, depending on which factor set limits for what is regarded as being environmentally adapted, e.g. the environment, finance, technology or social conditions.

e-tendering   A tender in which all the activities and exchange of necessary documents in the tendering process with suppliers is automated and takes place electronically (often through an Internet solution).

EU flower   A standard eco-label within the EU.

EUR pallet   A European standard sized pallet. Also known as Europallet.

Explosion*   The process of calculating the demand for the components of a parent item by multiplying the parent item requirements by the component usage quantity specified in the bill-of-material. Also called requirements explosion.

Exponential smoothing   A quantitative forecasting method based on historical data.

Extended enterprise**   The notion that supply chain partners form a larger entity which works together as though it were a single unit.

Extrinsic forecasting method   Quantitative forecasting methods that are based on data that refer to some other explanatory variable than the one to be forecast.

Feedback reporting   A production activity control function, consisting of feedback from the manufacturing process and final reporting of completed manufacturing orders.

Fill rate**   **Demand fill rate:** The percentage of order items that the picking operation actually fills within a given period of time. **Load fill rate:** The utilised proportion of the total available load volume, load area, or maximum weight.

Fixed location storage**   A method of storage in which a relatively permanent location is assigned for the storage of each item in a storeroom or warehouse.

Fixed-position layout   A production layout in which the product is located at a specified place and production resources are moved to that place and are organised around the product.

Flow charts   A scaled down drawing of a workshop or supply chain. The drawing includes the different activities in the flow, e.g. operation, transport, storing, control and waiting.

Forecast error   Deviation between forecast and actual demand. The error can be systematic or random.

Forecast monitoring   Monitoring forecast error in order to identify random and systematic variations.

Forward auction   A type of auction in which there is one seller and many potential purchasers. The seller normally states a starting price or target price. Purchasers bid over each other until the highest bidder purchases the item.

Forwarder   A forwarder operates as a mediator of transport services, i.e. it identifies and enters into agreements for transportation services on behalf of the shipper.

Fourth-party logistics provider (4PL)   A term coined by the consulting firm Accenture, a 4PL is an integrator that assembles the resources, capabilities, and technology of its own organisation and other organisations to design, build and run comprehensive supply chain solutions.

Free stacking   To stack packages freely on each other.

Freight forwarder   An organisation that subcontracts services from different asset based transport carriers and arranges space for those shipments.

Freight tariff   A price list with fixed rates for different types of transportation, according to the transportation distances involved, the volume to be shipped, the density of the goods, the physical shape of the goods, the risks attached to the goods, and the supply and demand of transportation.

Freight transport   Transportation between geographically separated plants, but not internal transport within a plant.

Full truck load (FTL)**   A term which defines a shipment which occupies at least one complete truck trailer, or allows for no other shippers goods to be carried at the same time.

Function flow chart   A tool for mapping and analysing business processes.

Functional flexibility   The extent to which different workstations are multifunctional, i.e. can perform more than one manufacturing function.

Functional production layout   A production layout in which the various production resources are organised by function, i.e. all machines and workstations are grouped and located in the factory according to their production functions and the materials to be used in the manufacturing are moved from group to group.

Global positioning systems (GPS)**   A system which uses satellites to precisely locate an object on earth. Used by trucking companies to locate over-the-road equipment.

Global sourcing   A procurement strategy where suppliers are located geographically far away.

Goods mover   The player responsible for performing processes in the logistics system.

Goods owner   The player who owns the goods which are produced, stored and transported in the logistics system. Manufacturers and distributing companies are normally goods owners.

Green dispatch   A transportation system strategy in which the distributor delivers goods to the customer company when they have space in the vehicle going to the place in question.

Green energy   Energy that is produced using only environmental friendly methods.

Gross requirement*   The total of independent and dependent demand for a component before the netting of on-hand inventory and scheduled receipts.

Group-organised production layout   See Cellular production layout.

GSCF process   A process model for describing and supporting the design of supply chains. Developed by the Global Supply Chain Forum (GSCF).

Hub and spoke   Hub-and-spoke systems mean that a large number of inbound and outbound flows (spokes) converge on a hub where the goods are broken down and consolidated.

Hybrid sourcing   A group of supply strategies that can be described as combinations of single and multiple sourcing. Parallel sourcing is a common form of hybrid sourcing.

In plant store   Is a delivery pattern in which the supplier has his own personnel on site at the customer company and is responsible for all materials handling and administration in the store including stocking, picking, dispatch and stocktaking

Incoterm   Stands for international commerce terms. There are 13 Incoterms which distinguish between modes of transport and where responsibility is transferred during delivery from vendor to purchaser.

Incremental costs   The costs of making or storing extra units above the number already planned.

Incremental inventory carrying cost   The costs of storing an extra unit.

Independent demand   Independent demand for an item refers to demand that has no direct connection with the demand for other items in the bill-of-materials.

Information exchange service   Logistics information that may provide added value to the customer.

Information quality   The extent to which information is valid, reliable, up-to-date, complete and straightforward to understand and use.

Infrastructure provider   The organisation responsible for providing the necessary infrastructure prerequisite for carrying out transportation.

Integrated logistics support (ILS)   An approach to ensure that the supportability of an equipment is considered during its design and development.

Intermediary   A supply chain actor that carries out distribution functions between the producer and the consuming customers.

Intermodal transport   A type of combined transport where the successive movement of goods between modes of transport is carried out in a single loading unit without handling the goods themselves.

Intrinsic forecasting method   A forecast method based on historical time series data. Forecast is being expressed in the same variable as the time series calculations are based on.

Inventory carrying costs   The costs for keeping goods in stock. It is made up of a financial fraction, a physical fraction and an uncertainty fraction.

Inventory graph   A graphical illustration of tied-up capital with stock level on the Y-axis and throughput time on the X-axis.

Inventory service level   Measure of the probability that a stock item is available in stock when demanded. Also called service level, demand fill rate or inventory fill rate.

Inventory turnover rate (ITR)   The annual number of units consumed divided by the average number of units in stock. Shows how many times per year average stocks are "turned over".

ISO 14000   ISO 14000 is an extension of the quality standard ISO 9000 and relates to the work in designing, executing, following up and improving environment management systems.

Item picking   Picking strategy where the daily requirement of each item is retrieved from a warehouse to one location. The items are then transported to a sorting site where items for each customer order are identified and packed.

Item* Any unique manufactured or purchased part, material, intermediate, subassembly, or product.

Just-in-time (JIT)* A philosophy of manufacturing based on planned elimination of all waste and on continuous improvement of productivity.

Kanban A materials planning method. Japanese word for "visible record", loosely translated means card, billboard or sign.

Kitting Putting components of a parent item into a kit, a package of items to be used in production

Labour management system (LMS) An information system that manages planning of demand, capacity and use of personnel, considering working times, workstations, shifts, breaks, etc.

Landed cost** Cost of product plus relevant logistics costs such as transportation, warehousing, handling, etc. Also called total landed cost or net landed costs.

Lateral integration Integration through co-operation between entities with different ownership.

Leadtime* The span of time required to perform a process or series of operations. In a logistics context, the time between recognition of the need for an order and the receipt of goods.

Levelling stock Stock function to decouple the rate of production from the rate of consumption and allowing for a levelled production or sales plan. Also called anticipation stock.

Leverage items The items that are of great significance to the company and for which availability on the market is good.

Lifecycle assessment (LCA) A tool used to create a picture of the total environmental impact of a product, "from the cradle to the grave", or its total lifecycle.

Line-shaped layout A production layout in which the production resources are organised by product/item and are located in the same sequence as the production steps which are carried out during manufacture.

Local sourcing Suppliers have their business at a short distance from the customer company.

Logistics engineering A discipline based on systems engineering where reliability, maintainability, and availability are designed into products or systems. It includes logistics and supply chain as well as reliability engineering considerations.

Logistics service provider (LSP) A logistics service provider normally has no own transportation resources. Its role is to arrange and execute logistics by planning and subcontracting necessary logistics resources. A third party logistics provider is an example of a logistics service provider.

Logistics** The process of planning, implementing, and controlling procedures for the efficient and effective transportation and storage of goods including services, and related information from the point of origin to the point of consumption for the purpose of confirming to customer requirements. This definition includes inbound, outbound, internal, and external movements.

Lot-for-lot** A lot-sizing technique that generates planned orders in quantities equal to the net requirements in each period.

Lot sizing The process of establishing appropriate order quantities.

Make to order (MTO)* A production environment where a good or service can be made after receipt of customer's order.

Make to plan (MTP) A production environment in which customer specific products are designed for a particular customer, but the product is known when the customer order is received.

Make to stock (MTS) A production environment in which products are made to and kept in stock awaiting customer orders.

Manufacturing process From identified need to performed, accessible and approved added value to material and components.

Market mediating cost Costs for stock shortages and obsolescence. They are dominant in responsive supply chain.

Master production scheduling (MPS) The process of generating master production schedule.

Material administration Study of the entire flow of materials from the generation of raw materials to the end-user. See also logistics.

Material availability check The process of verifying the availability of materials in order to start an order.

Material flow channel The physical parts of the order-to-delivery process, i.e. delivery of products ordered.

Material requirements planning (MRP)   A materials planning method that uses bill of materials, explosion and lead time offsetting to generate quantities and times of material requirement.

Materials   A term used for different types of physical substances used by an organisation.

Mean absolute deviation (MAD)   The mean absolute deviation of forecast demand relative to actual demand.

Merge-in-transit   The process of combining or "merging" shipments from multiple suppliers at an interim terminal point. The inbound deliveries are unloaded, sorted and merged with other items to be delivered to a specific customer. A customer-specific "package" of items is formed and loaded on outbound trucks or rail without storage in between.

Milk run   A way of consolidating deliveries in which the vehicle is filled by making several loading stops along a transportation loop within a limited area for onward transportation to a breakpoint for reloading or to a common customer in the same or different region.

Modularisation   An approach aiming to dividing the product into well-defined and a limited number of standardised parts which can be combined into several end products when configuring customer specific products.

Moving average   A forecasting method based on historical data.

Multiple sourcing   Several alternative suppliers of an individual item are used simultaneously and in parallel.

Net requirement*   In MRP, the net requirements for a part or an assembly are derived as a result of applying gross requirements and allocations against inventory on hand, scheduled receipts, and safety stock.

Non-critical items   Items which are not very significant for the company and for which availability on the market is good.

Obsolescence stock   Also known as inactive stock, is a stock of goods which is no longer expected to be consumed.

On-time delivery   See Delivery precision.

Operations management*   A field of studies that focuses on the effective planning, scheduling, use and control of a manufacturing or service organisation

Order confirmation   A note by which the supplier confirms that he undertakes to deliver a certain quantity of a certain product at a certain point in time.

Order confirmation   A notice from the supplier indicating that order has been received and the quantities and delivery times are accepted.

Order line   Each unique item on an order represents an order line.

Order picking**   Selecting or "picking" the required quantity of specific items for movement to a packaging area and documenting that the item was moved from one location to shipping.

Order planning   The planning level for materials supply, i.e. raw materials, purchased components, small items and semi-finished products to be purchased or manufactured at the company in such quantities and at such times that production plans drawn up under master production scheduling can be fulfilled.

Order point   A point in the re-order point method. A set inventory level where, if the total stock on hand plus order falls to or below that point, action is taken to replenish stock. Also called re-order point.

Order qualifier   Competitive variables which make a company a viable competitor on the market but which in themselves do not mean that a customer buys a product.

Order release*   The activity of releasing materials to a production process to support a manufacturing order.

Order winner   Competitive variables which are decisive for a customer choosing a company's product over those of the competitors.

Ordering cost   All the incremental costs which are associated with executing an order process for the acquisition of items from external suppliers, or from the company's own manufacture.

Order-to-delivery process   From customer order received to invoiced dispatch.

Pallet truck   A small truck used to moving pallets.

Pallet**   The platform which cartons are stacked on and then used for shipment or movement as a group. Pallets may be made of wood or composite materials.

Parallel sourcing   A common form of hybrid sourcing that involves the use of multiple sourcing at the level of groups of items and single sourcing for the individual items in the groups.

Partnership relation**   A long-term relationship between a buyer and a supplier characterised by teamwork and mutual confidence. The supplier is considered an extension of the buyer's organisation.

Paternoster store   An automated form of storing items from opened packages. Also called carousel store.

Perfect delivery service   The order is delivered at the agreed time and contains no quantity errors or quality faults.

Periodic review method   The re-order point method in which comparisons are made between the current stock balance and the re-order point after each time interval.

Physical efficient supply chain   Also called lean supply chain, is a supply chain in which value is created and costs minimised through elimination of all waste.

Picking list   A list that is printed out when a customer order is for standard items in stock. It is printed when delivery is to take place and the stated quantities are to be picked.

Planned order*   A suggested order quantity, release date, and due date created by the planning system's logic when it encounters net requirements in processing MRP.

Planning point   Every step of production or operation must be planned, ordered, followed up and reported. Every separate operation requiring separate planning decision can be considered as a planning point.

Point-of-sales (POS) data**   Price and quantity data from retail locations as sales transactions occur.

Polluter pays principle   A principle meaning that the party responsible for pollution must also be responsible for dealing with it and paying for its environmental consequences.

Portal**   Websites that serve as starting points to other destinations or activities on the Internet. Initially thought of as a "home base" type of web page, portals attempt to provide all Internet needs in one location. Portals commonly provide services such as email, online chat forums, shopping, searching, content, and news feeds.

Postponement   Waiting as long as possible before performing value-adding and material-moving activities in supply chains, preferably until customer orders have been received.

Priority control   A production activity control function to ensure that orders released for manufacture in the workshop are executed in a suitable sequence with respect to delivery times and throughput times.

Process analysis chart   A tool used for mapping and documenting which activities are carried out in the process and in which order they are performed.

Process oriented layout   A production layout that groups together machines and workstations that undertake similar processes. Functional production layout is a process oriented layout.

Product complexity   The width, number of items at each structural level, and depth, number of structural levels, of the product structure.

Product content data management (PCDM)   An information system that manages product data and enables several business units and organisations to work with a joint database using unique item numbers.

Product group   A group of products which are similar from the demand, distribution and manufacturing viewpoints.

Product lifecycle   All phases in the life of the product from initial development, production, marketing and distribution until the product's discontinuation.

Product mix flexibility   The ability within the existing capacity to rapidly adapt production and material supplies to shifts in demand between existing products and product variants.

Product oriented layout   A production layout where the position of machines and workstations is organised to suit the flow of items and operations to undertake. A line-shaped layout is product oriented.

Product range   A company's total number of products is called the product portfolio or product range.

Product structure   See Bill-of-material.

Product variant   Variant of a basic product type.

Production activity control*   The function of routing and dispatching the work to be accomplished through the production facility and of performing supplier control.

Production capacity** Measure of how much production volume may be experienced over a set period of time.

Production layout The structure of production groups and workstations through and between which goods flow during the process of manufacturing.

Production system A subsystem of the logistics system. It is the structures and systems that control the flow of materials in production through supplying production resources with information on where and how much is to be produced by machines and personnel, and to ensure access to materials and components.

Products* Any good or service produced for sale, barter, or internal use.

Projected available inventory* An inventory balance projected into the future.

Pull A characteristic of materials management, meaning that the manufacturing and the movement of materials only take place on the initiative of and authorised by the consuming unit in the flow of materials.

Purchase order** The purchaser's authorisation used to formalise a purchase transaction with a supplier. The physical form or electronic transaction a buyer uses when placing order for merchandise.

Purchase requisition A request to the purchasing unit to send a corresponding purchase order to a supplier. The purchasing request is, thus, a document or signal for procurement which passes on the commission to the purchasing unit to create a purchase order and execute the purchase.

Purchasing contract See Supply contract.

Push A characteristic of materials management, meaning that manufacturing and movement of materials is initiated without the consuming unit authorising the activities, i.e. they have been initiated by the supplying unit itself or by a central planning unit.

Quick Response (QR)** A partnership strategy in which suppliers and retailers work together to respond more rapidly to the consumer by sharing point-of-sale scan data, enabling both to forecast replenishment needs.

Rack storage A system in which items are stored on a load carrier or a pallet, which is located in slots in a special construction, called a pallet rack.

Radio-frequency communication (RFDC) A communication method in which users agree on a common radio-frequency (channel) that they use to transfer data.

Radio-frequency identification (RFID) A system which uses radio waves for automatic identification of objects. Information is stored in a microchip in an RFID tag or in RFID transponders, which are affixed to the object to be identified.

Random location storage** A storage technique in which parts are placed in any space that is empty when they arrive at the storeroom.

Rate-based scheduling** A method for scheduling and producing based on a periodic rate, e.g. daily, weekly, or monthly. This method has traditionally been applied to high-volume and process industries. The concept has recently been applied within job shops using cellular layouts and mixed model level schedules where the production rate is matched to the selling rate.

Raw material** Crude or processed material that can be converted by manufacturing, processing, or combination into a new and useful product.

Recycling Processing a product into recycled material which can be used in the production of a new product.

Reducing A preventive environmental measure that aims at minimising the use of resources and the creation of residual products.

Released order* An open order that has an assigned due date. Also called open order or scheduled receipt.

Re-order point method Also called order point method, is a materials planning method built on comparisons made between the quantity available in stock and a reference quantity called a re-order point.

Request for information (RFI)** A document used to solicit information about vendors, products, and services prior to a formal RFQ process.

Request for proposal (RFP) A document used to solicit information about vendors offer prior to a formal RFQ process.

Request for quotation (RFQ)** A document used to solicit vendor responses when a product has been selected and price quotations are needed from several vendors.

Reservation* The process of designating stock for a specific order or schedule. Also called allocation.

Responsive supply chain Also known as agile supply chain, is a supply chain that is able to quickly and flexibly adapt to changing requirements.

Return flow Balancing return flows is a transportation system strategy in which the goal is to balance the inbound and outbound goods transported in and out of a region in order to decrease the total transport kilometres.

Return flow Goods carried on a backhaul route.

Return of capital employed (ROCE) Annual profits in relation to its total capital employed

Return process From identification of return need to received return consignment at recipient.

Re-using Re-using is a preventive environmental measure that aims at designing products in a manner that its materials and components can easily be separated and re-used, or designing products that can be easily upgraded and in this way given an extended lifespan.

Reverse auction A type of auction in which there is one buyer and several potential sellers who make decreasing offers until the one with the lowest offer sells his goods.

Reverse logistics** A specialised segment of logistics focusing on the movement and management of products and resources after the sale and after delivery to the customer. Includes product returns for repair and/or credit.

Risk sharing contract Contract about risk and gain sharing between buyers and sellers with the objective of improving their total performance.

Route planning The process of determining routes which will provide the highest overall capacity utilisation of vehicles, as many customer visits and the largest amount of goods delivered as possible, at the same time as the total distance covered, time taken and delivery time to customers are minimised.

Run-out time See cover time.

Run-out time planning Also known as cover-time planning, is the time for which available stocks, i.e. physically present stocks plus planned inbound deliveries, are expected to last.

Safety factor A factor used when determining safety stock based on determined service level.

Safety stock** The inventory a company holds above normal needs as a buffer against delays in receipt of supply or changes in customer demand.

Safety time An approach in hedging against uncertainty, meaning that inbound deliveries are deliberately placed earlier in relation to requirement times.

Sales and operations planning (S&OP)** A strategic planning process that reconciles conflicting business objectives and plans future supply chain actions. S&OP Planning usually involves various business functions such as sales, operations and finance working together to agree on a single plan/forecast that can be used to drive the entire business.

Satellite communication A communication method in which the information is communicated via satellites.

Savings matrix method Also known as Clark-Wright method, is a route planning method.

SCOR model Supply-Chain Operations Reference-model (SCOR) is a process model to describe, measure and evaluate supply chains.

Seasonal index An index for any particular month (or other time period) that refers to the normal demand during the month (or other time period) in relation to the average demand for all months during the year.

Seasonal variation The demand varies regularly at different times of the year.

Sequencing rules** Also known as priority rules, are rules that guide the selection of priorities among a number of orders which are available for start-up in a production group.

Service function Function used for determining safety stock based on demand fill rate.

Service level** A measure (usually expressed as a percentage) of satisfying demand through inventory or by the current production schedule in time to satisfy the customer's requested delivery dates and quantities.

Set-up time* The time required for a specific machine, resource, work centre, process, or line to convert from the production of the last good piece of item A to the first good piece of item B.

Shelving section storage   A storage system that enables items to be stored in boxes or compartments in a shelf construction.

Shipper   The actor buying transport and logistics services.

Single group sourcing   A variant of single sourcing, in which an entire group of items with similar characteristics are purchased from a single supplier.

Single sourcing   A sourcing strategy in which the company only uses one supplier for a certain item, despite other suppliers being available on the market.

Smoothing constant   An index used in exponential smoothing forecasting technique.

Sole sourcing**   When there is only one supplier for a product or service, and no alternate suppliers are available.

Sourcing strategy   The strategy that determines the number of suppliers in parallel, the suppliers' geographic location, supply delivery patterns, supplier relationships, etc.

Speculation stock   A type of cycle stock, which turnover is completely decoupled from short-term expected consumption.

Standardisation   An approach for increasing commonality of items in a product and product group. Standardisation enables postponed manufacturing and procurement decisions and reduces the number of stock keeping units (SKUs).

Stock accounting   The process of keeping track of the current stock balance.

Stock balance   The quantity of items available in stock.

Stock-keeping unit (SKU)*   An item at a particular geographic location. For example, one product stocked at the plant and at six different distribution centres would represent seven SKUs.

Stock retrieval   The retrieval frequency for each stock item refers to how many times per unit of time an item is removed from the store.

Stock throughput time   The average stock throughput time is the average tied up capital in flows (stocks) divided by delivery value per time unit (year or week). Also known as average cover time or average runout time.

Stock withdrawal*   The opposite of deliveries, i.e. the stock balance decreases through withdrawal transactions.

Storage point   A physical point of storage, e.g. warehouse or raw material stock.

Storage system   The equipment used for the physical storage of items in a warehouse.

Storage zone   A store can be divided into a number of smaller stores, called zones.

Strategic items   Items for which there are few alternative suppliers and have great significance for a company.

Strategic network planning   Making decisions about the number, geographical location and capacity of plants such as factories and distribution centres, about which specific products will flow, where products will be stored, from which plants' different customers will be served and what means of transport will be used between plants.

Supplier evaluation   An evaluation process that can be the basis for choosing a new supplier or for follow up and development of an existing supplier.

Supplier relationship management (SRM)   Activities aimed at developing long-term relationships with suppliers.

Supplier segmentation   Differentiating suppliers regarding characteristics and performance.

Supply chain event management (SCEM)   An information system that enables users to set parameters which will trigger messages if a certain event occurs or if deviations from normal procedure arise.

Supply chain management (SCM)**   Planning and management of all activities involved in sourcing and procurement, conversion, and all logistics management activities.

Supply chain risk management   A supply chain strategy involving risk identification, risk analysis and development of risk management strategy.

Supply chain visibility (SCV)   An information system that consists of a group of tools for showing information on stock levels, production status, delivery status, deviations etc. with the help of graphics, colours and sounds.

Supply contract   A contract to regulate the buyer–supplier business relationship to various degrees. It can clarify and regulate anything that is of importance for the buying or selling firm.

Supply process   From identified material need to received and approved delivery.

Supply system   A subsystem of the logistics system. It supplies the production system with raw materials and components.

Surge demand   The percentage of a customer's demand that is unpredictable and uncertain and not derived from continuing contracts and/or existing customers.

Synchro-delivery   Individual items specific to one customer order are delivered in exactly the same sequence as the assembly sequence at the receiving company. The flow of materials in the supplier company and the customer company must be completely synchronised.

Synchronisation stock   The unintentional stock that arises when certain items must wait for others to achieve simultaneous availability. Their size is related to imperfections in synchronising supply, demand and material flows.

Target costing**   A method used in the analysis of product design that involves estimating a target cost and then designing the product/service to meet that cost. A target cost is calculated by subtracting a desired profit margin from an estimated or a market-based price to arrive at a desired production, engineering, or marketing cost.

Terminal   A plant to which goods are transported to be combined and/or split up into other consignments, given more value by another activity and reloaded for further transport to customers.

Third-party logistics provider (3PL)**   A firm which provides multiple logistics services for use by customers. Preferably, these services are integrated, or "bundled" together by the provider. These firms facilitate the movement of parts and materials from suppliers to manufacturers, and finished products from manufacturers to distributors and retailers. Among the services which they provide are transportation, warehousing, cross-docking, inventory management, packaging, and freight forwarding.

Tied up capital   The capital tied in the flow of materials, that is, materials that are held in raw material and component stocks, in production, in finished stocks or distribution stocks and in transport.

Time-to-customer (TTC)   Time from order received to delivery to customer. Also called delivery time.

Time-to-market (TTM)   The time from product concept to product launch.

Time-phased order point   When MRP is used for planning independent materials requirements.

Total cost of ownership (TCO)*   The total cost of ownership of the supply delivery system is the sum of all the costs associated with every activity of the supply stream.

Total logistics cost analysis**   A decision-making approach that considers minimisation of total costs of a logistics system and recognises the interrelationship among system variables such as transportation, warehousing, inventory, and customer service.

Total logistics costs   The cost of all activities carried out in the logistics system.

Toyota production system   The logistics and production philosophy at Toyota.

Tracking and tracing**   Monitoring and recording shipment movements from origin to destination.

Traffic area   A geographical area supplied with goods from a specific terminal.

Traffic modes   Types of transport, for example, truck, rail, ship and air. Also called transport modes.

Transaction channel   One of the components of a distribution channel that covers the flow of information around the administrative parts of the order-to-delivery process, i.e. mainly receiving orders, confirming orders and invoicing.

Transaction costs   Costs related to a transaction, e.g. order, receipt, adjustment.

Transformation through adaptation   When the properties of the input item are changed without changing its form.

Transformation through combination   When there are several items as input and one item as output from the production system.

Transformation through division   When there is one item as input and several different items as output from the production system.

Transformation through separation   When the form of the input item is changed through the removal of material.

Transformation through shaping   When the shape of the input item is changed through re-forming the material mass.

Transport aisle   A corridor, aisle, in a warehouse where trucks and pickers can move.

Transport management system (TMS)   A computer system designed to provide optimised transportation management in various modes along with associated activities, including managing shipping units, labor planning and building, shipment scheduling through inbound, outbound, intra-company, shipments, documentation management (especially when international shipping is involved), and third-party logistics management.

Transport operators   The operators that carry out the transportation.

Trend   General upward or downward demand change over time.

Triadic sourcing   A customer company cooperates with two suppliers for one group of items. The customer company makes the two suppliers compete for volumes and responsibility of development for each item.

Unit load   Large standardised packages which can be handled as single units.

Value-adding distributor   The distributors that supply form utility and play a variant-creating role. They can have various value adding activities. Examples of value adding distribution activities: simple assembly, supplementing with accessories, mixing, kitting, sorting, sequencing, adjusting, packing, labelling.

Warehouse management system (WMS)   A system that contains support for storage related activities. They often also contain support for simple manufacturing, transportation planning, finance and order administration.

Warehouse structure   The number of levels and warehouses in the hierarchy of central, regional and local warehouses.

Web-EDI   A combination of EDI and Internet where EDI messages are transferred using Internet.

Vehicle charge   Special charges that drivers of vehicles which do not comply with specified environment classification requirements may be forced to pay.

Vendor-managed inventory (VMI)   A type of delivery pattern and materials management where the supplier decides when and how much to deliver of an item to a stock located at the customer's site.

Vertical integration**   The degree to which a firm has decided to directly produce multiple value-adding stages from raw material to the sale of the product to the ultimate consumer.

Virtual enterprise   A temporary alliance of enterprises that come together to share skills or core competencies and resources in order to better respond to business opportunities.

Volume flexibility   The ability to rapidly increase or decrease production and delivery volumes independently of any simultaneous mix changes.

Work in process (WIP)**   Parts and subassemblies in the process of becoming completed finished goods, including all of the material, labor and overhead charged against a production order which has not been absorbed back into inventory through receipt of completed products.

XML   A technology for file transfer. It stands for eXtensible Markup Language and is a language that is independent of platforms, i.e. hardware independent. XML can be used to send structured business information via Internet. The information consists of content and tags which can be identified by the user.

Zone picking**   A method of subdividing a picking list by areas within a storeroom for more efficient and rapid order picking.

Notes:
*Adapted from Cox, J. and Blackstone, J. (eds), (1998) *APICS Dictionary*, 9th edition, APICS, Fall Church.

**ADAPTED FROM CSCMP (2006) *SUPPLY CHAIN AND LOGISTICS*

References

Alvarado, U. and Kotzab, H. (2001) "Supply chain management: the integration of logistics in marketing", *Industrial Marketing Management,* Vol. 30, pp. 183–198.

Anupini, R., Chopra, S., Deshmukh, S., van Mieghem, J. and Zemel, E. (1999) *Managing business process flow.* Prentice Hall, Upper Saddle River.

APICS (2005), *Building competitive operations, planning and logistics.* APICS certified supply chain professional learning system Module 2, APICS, Alexandria.

Autry, C., Daugherty, P. and Richey, G. (2001) "The challenge of reverse logistics in catalog retailing", *International Journal of Physical Distribution and Logistics Management,* Vol. 31, No. 1, pp. 26–37.

Axelsson, B., Rozenmeijer, F. and Wynstra, F. (2005) *Developing sourcing capabilities: creating strategic change in purchasing and supply management.* John Wiley & Sons, Chichester.

Ballou, R. (2007) "The evolution and future of logistics and supply chain management", *European Business Review,* Vol. 19, No. 4, pp. 332–347.

Ballou, R. (2006) "Revenue estimation for logistics customer service offerings", *International Journal of Logistics Management,* Vol. 17, No. 1, pp. 21–37.

Banister, D. (2002) *Transport planning: an international appraisal.* Taylor & Francis, London.

Baraldi, E. (2006) "IKEA's lack table – a product design for network-level logistics" . In Jahre. M. (ed.) *Resourcing in business logistics: the art of systematic combining.* Liber & Copenhagen Business School Press, Malmö.

Bardi, E., Novack, R. and Coyle, J. (2004) *Transportation.* Thomson Learning, London.

Bergman, B. and Klefsjö, B. (2004) *Quality from customer needs to customer satisfaction.* Studentlitteratur, Lund.

Binder, M. and Clegg, B. (2006) "A conceptual framework for enterprise management", *International Journal of Production Economics,* Vol. 44, No. 18–19, pp. 3813–3829.

Bowersox, D., Closs, D. and Cooper, B. (2002) *Supply chain logistics management.* McGraw-Hill, New York (NY).

Brander, A. (1995) *Forecasting and customer service management.* Helbing & Lichtenhahn, Basel.

Chopra, S. and Meindl, P. (2004), *Supply chain management: strategy, planning and operation.* Prentice Hall, Upper Saddle River.

Christopher, M. (2005) *Logistics and supply chain management.* Prentice Hall, London.

Christopher, M. and Lee, H. (2004) "Mitigating supply chain risk through improved confidence", *International Journal of Physical Distribution and Logistics Management,* Vol. 34, No. 5, pp. 388–396.

Christopher, M. and Peck, H. (2003) *Marketing logistics.* Butterworth-Heinemann, London.

Christopher, M. and Towill, D. (2001) "An integrated model for the design of agile supply chains", *International Journal of Physical Distribution and Logistics Management*, Vol. 31, No. 4, pp. 235–246.

Cooper, M., Lambert, D. and Pagh, J. (1997) "Supply chain management: more than a new name for logistics", *International Journal of Logistics Management*, Vol. 8, No. 1, pp. 1–13.

Cousins, P., Lawson, B. and Squire, B. (2006) "An empirical taxonomy of purchasing functions", *International Journal of Operations and Production Management*, Vol. 26, No. 7, pp. 775–794.

Croxton, K., Garcia-Dastogue, S. and Lambert, D. (2001) "The supply chain management process", *International Journal of Logistics Management*, Vol. 12, No. 2, pp. 13–36.

Crum, C. and Palmatier, G. (2003) *Demand management best practices: process, principles and collaboration.* J. Ross Publishing, Boca Raton (FL).

De Koster, M. and Warffemius, P. (2005) "American, Asian and third-party international warehouse operations in Europe: a performance comparison", *International Journal of Operations and Production Management*, Vol. 25, no. 8, pp. 762–780.

Disney, S. and Towill, D. (2003) "Vendor-managed inventory and bullwhip reduction in a two-level supply chain", *International Journal of Operations and Production Management*, Vol. 23, No. 6, pp. 625–651.

Dubois, A. (2003) "Strategic cost management across boundaries of firms", *Industrial Marketing Management*, Vol. 32, pp. 365–374.

European Commission (2005) *European Union – Energy and transport in figures 2005.* Directorate-general for Energy and Transport in co-operation with Eurostat.

Ferdows, K., Lewis, M. and Machuca, J. (2004) "Rapid-fire fulfillment", *Harvard Business Review*, November, pp. 1–6.

Fisher, M. (1997) "What is the right supply chain for your product?" *Harvard Business Review*, March–April, pp. 105–116.

Fogerty, D., Blackstone, J. and Hoffman, T. (1991) *Production and inventory management.* South-West Publishing, Cincinnati.

Forslund, H. and Jonsson, P. (2007) "Dyadic integration of the performance management process: a delivery service case study", *International Journal of Physical Distribution and Logistics Management*. Vol. 37, No. 7, pp. 546–567.

Frohlich, M. and Westbrook, R. (2001) "Arcs of integration: an international study of supply chain strategies", *Journal of Operations Management*, Vol. 19, pp. 185–200.

Gadde, L.-E. and Håkansson, H. (2001) *Supply network strategies.* John Wiley & Sons, Chichester.

Genes, R. (2002) "Smart ecology", *Manufacturing Engineer*, Vol. 81, No. 2, pp. 48–53.

Goldfeld, C. (1999) *Supplier strategies.* PT Publications, Miami.

Gunn, T. (1992) *Century manufacturing – creating winning business performance.* Omneo, Essex, pp. 60–61.

Hamilton, S. (2003) *Maximizing your ERP system: a practical guide for managers.* McGraw-Hill, London.

Harrington, J., Esseling, E. and Nimwegen, H. (1997) *Business process improvement workbook.* McGraw-Hill Professional, New York.

Harrison, A. and van Hoek, R. (2004) *Logistics management and strategy.* Prentice Hall, Essex.

Hayes, R. and Wheelwright, S. (1994) *Restoring our competitive edge: competing through manufacturing.* John Wiley & Sons, New York.

Hill, T. (1999) *Manufacturing strategy.* McGraw-Hill, New York.

Hinkka, V. and Lehtinen, J. (2006) "Testing voice technology in the supply chain" . In Arlbjörn, J. (ed.) *Nordic case reader in logistics and supply chain management.* The Nordic Logistics Research Network, University Press of Southern Denmark, Odense.

Hopp, W. and Spearman, M. (2000) *Factory physics.* McGraw-Hill, New York.

Håkansson, H. and Ford, D. (2002) "How should companies interact in business networks?" *Journal of Business Research,* Vol. 55, pp. 133–139.

Jonsson. P. and Mattsson, S.-A. (2006) "A longitudinal study of material planning applications in manufacturing companies", *International Journal of Operations and Production Management,* Vol. 26, No. 9, pp. 971–995.

Kotzab, H. (1999) "Improving supply chain performance by efficient consumer response? A critical comparison of existing ECR approaches", *Journal of Business & Industrial Marketing,* Vol. 14, No. 5/6, pp. 364–377.

Kraljic, P. (1983) "Purchasing must become supply management", *Harvard Business Review,* Sep–Oct, pp. 109–117.

Kärkkäinen, M., Ala-Risku, T. and Holmström, J. (2003) "Increasing customer value and decreasing distribution costs with merge-in-transit", *International Journal of Physical Distribution and Logistics Management,* Vol. 33, No. 2, pp. 132–148.

Lambert, D. (2004) "The eight essential supply chain management processes", *Supply Chain Management Review,* Vol. 8, No. 4, pp. 18–26.

Lambert, D., Cooper, M. and Pagh, J. (1998) "Supply chain management: implementation issues and research opportunities", *International Journal of Logistics Management,* Vol. 9, No. 2, pp. 1–19.

Lambert, D. and Stock, J. (2001), *Strategic logistics management.* McGraw-Hill, New York.

Lamming, R., Cousins, P. and Notman, D. (1996), "Beyond vendor assessment: relationship assessment programmes", *European Journal of Purchasing and Supply Management,* Vol. 2, No. 4, pp. 173–181.

Landvater, D. (1997) *World class production and inventory management.* John Wiley & Sons, Essex.

Larson, P. and Halldorsson, A. (2002) "What is SCM? And, where is it?", *Journal of Supply Chain Management,* Vol. 38, No. 4, pp. 36–44.

Latour, A. (2001) "A blaze in Albuquerque sets off major crisis for cell-phone giants", *Wall Street Journal,* 29 January, section A, p. 1.

Lee, H., Padmanabhan, V. and Whang, S. (1997), "The bullwhip effect in supply chains", *Sloan Management Review,* Spring, pp. 93–102.

Lee, H. (2002) "Aligning supply chain strategies with product uncertainties", *California Management Review,* Vol. 44, No. 3, pp. 105–119.

Leenders, M., Johnson, F., Flynn, A. and Fearon, H. (2006) *Purchasing and supply management.* McGraw-Hill, New York.

Lewis, C. (1998) *Demand forecasting and inventory control.* John Wiley & Sons, New York (NY).

Lewis, J. (1995) *The connected corporation: how leading companies with through customer – supplier alliances.* The Free Press, New York.

Ling, C. and Goddard, W. (1998) *Orchestrating success: improve control of the business with sales and operations planning.* John Wiley & Sons, New York.

Lumsden, K. (2004) *Truck Masses and Dimensions – Impact on Transport Efficiency.* ACEA report, Work in process paper, Division of logistics and transportation, Chalmers University of Technology, Gothenburg, Sweden.

May, G. (2005) "Transport in Europe: where are we going?", *Insight,* Vol. 7, No. 6, pp. 24–38.

Makridakis, S., Wheelwright, S. and Hyndman, R. (1997) *Forecasting methods and applications.* John Wiley & Sons, New York (NY).

Martin, A. (1993) *Distribution resource planning: the gateway to true quick response and continuous replenishment.* Oliver Wight Publications, Essex.

Mason-Jones, R. and Towill, D. (1997) "Information enrichment: designing the supply chain for competitive advantage", *Supply Chain Management,* Vol. 2, No. 4, pp. 137–148.

Mattsson, S.-A. (2000) *Embracing change: management strategies in the e-economy era.* Intentia International, Stockholm.

McKinnon, A. (1998) "Logistics restructuring, freight traffic growth and the environment". In Banister, D. (ed.) *Transport policy and the environment,* Routledge, London, pp. 97–109.

McKinnon, A. and Ge, Y. (2006) "The potential for reducing empty running by trucks: a retrospective analysis", *International Journal of Physical Distribution and Logistics Management,* Vol. 36, No. 5, pp. 391–410.

Mentzer, J., Flint, D. and Kent, J. (2001) "Logistics service quality as a segment-customized product", *Journal of Marketing,* Vol. 65, pp. 82–104.

Mentzer, J., Min, S. and Bobbitt, M. (2004) "Toward a unified theory of logistics", *International Journal of Physical Distribution and Logistics Management,* Vol. 34, no. 8, pp. 606–627.

Mol, M. (2003) "Purchasing's strategic relevance", *Journal of Purchasing & Supply Management,* Vol. 9, No. 1, pp. 43–50.

Murphy, P. and Poist, R. (2003) "Green perspectives and practices: a 'comparative logistics' study", *Supply Chain Management: An international journal,* Vol. 8, No. 2, pp. 122–131.

Murphy, P. and Wood, D. (2004) *Contemporary logistics.* Prentice Hall, Upper Saddle River.

Norrman, A. (2006) "Supply chain risk sharing contracts from buyers' perspective: content and experiences", *Proceedings of the 18th Annual Nofoma Conference.*

Pohlen, T. and Goldsby, T. (2003) "VMI and SMI programs: how economiuc value added can help sell the change*", International Journal of Physical Distribution and Logistics Management,* Vol. 33, No. 7, pp. 565–581.

Pretty, J., Ball, A., Lang, T. and Morison, J. (2005) "Farm costs and food miles: an assessment of the full cost of the UK weekly food basket", *Food Policy,* Vol. 30, No. 1, pp. 1–19.

Rabinovich, E. and Evers, P. (2003) "Postponement effects on inventory performance and the impact of information systems", *International Journal of Logistics Management,* Vol. 14, No. 1, pp. 33–48.

Ramsay, J. (2001) "Purchasing's strategic irrelevance", *European Journal of Purchasing and Supply Management,* Vol. 7, No. 4, pp. 257–263.

Rogers, D. and Tibben-Lembke, R. (1998) *Going backwards: reverse logistics trends and practices.* Reverse logistics executive council, University of Nevada, Reno (http://www.rlec.org)

Ross, D. (2003) *Introduction to e-Supply Chain Management: engaging technology to build market-winning business partnerships.* St. Lucie Press, Boca Raton.

Schary, P. and Skjøtt-Larsen, T. (2001) *Managing the global supply chain.* Copenhagen Business School Press, Copenhagen.

Schmenner, R. (1994) *Plant and service tours in operations management.* Macmillan Publishing, New York.

Schönsleben, P. (2000) *Integral logistics management.* St. Lucie Press, New York.

Silver, E., Peterson, R. and Pyke, D. (1998) *Inventory management and production planning and scheduling.* John Wiley & Sons, New York.

Simchi-Levi, D., Kaminsky, P. and Simchi-Levi, E. (2008) *Designing & managing the supply chain: concepts, strategies & case studies.* McGraw-Hill, New York.

Skjoett-Larsen, T., Thernoe, C. and Andresen, C. (2003) "Supply chain collaboration: theoretical perspectives and empirical evidence", *International Journal of Physical Distribution and Logistics Management,* Vol. 33, No. 6, pp. 531–549.

Slack, N., Chambers, S. and Johnston, R. (2007) *Operations management.* Prentice Hall, Essex.

Smith, I. (2006) "West Marine: a CPFR success story", *Supply Chain Management Review,* Vol. 10, No. 2, pp. 29–36.

Småros, J. and Holmström, J. (2000) "Viewpoint: reaching the customer through e-grocery VMI", *International Journal of Retail & Distribution Management,* Vol. 28, No. 2, pp. 55–61.

Stadtler, H. and Kilger, C. (eds) (2005) *Supply chain management and advanced planning: concepts, models, software and case studies.* Springer Verlag, Berlin.

Stefansson, G. (2006) "Collaborative logistics management and the role of third-party service providers", *International Journal of Physical Distribution and Logistics Management*, Vol. 36, No. 2, pp. 76–92.

Stein, A. and Hawking, P. (2003) "The 20% solution? A case study on the efficacy of reverse auctions", *Management Research News*, Vol. 26, No. 5, pp. 1–20.

Stern, L. and El-Ansary, A. (2001) *Marketing channels.* Pearson, London.

Supply-Chain Council (2005) *Supply-chain operations reference-model: SCOR version 7.0 overview.* Supply-Chain Council, Brussels.

Tang, C. (2006) "Perspective in supply chain risk management", *International Journal of Production Economics,* Vol. 103, pp. 451–488.

Tsay, A., Nahmias, S. and Agrawal, N. (1998) "Modelling supply chain contracts: a review", in Tayur, S., Ganeshan, R. and Magazine, M. (eds), *Quantitative models for supply chain management.* Kluwer Academic, Norwell, pp. 299–336.

Van Hoek, R. (1998) "Logistics and virtual integration: postponement, outsourcing and the flow of information", *International Journal of Physical Distribution and Logistics Management*, Vol. 20, No. 7, pp. 508–523.

van Hoek, R. (1999) "From reversed logistics to green supply chains", *Supply Chain Management: an international journal*, Vol. 4, No. 3, pp. 129–134.

Van Weele, A. (2005) *Purchasing & supply chain management: analysis, strategy, planning and practice.* Thomson Learning, London.

Vollmann, T., Berry, W., Whybark, C. and Jacobs, R. (2005) *Manufacturing planning and control for supply chain management.* McGraw-Hill, New York.

Westermark, L. (2001) "Integrate the environmental dimension: visions for transport", *Environmental Management and Health*, Vol. 12, No. 2, pp. 175–180.

Weng, K. (1998) "Lead-time management in a make-to-order manufacturing firm", *Production and Inventory Management Journal*, 2nd Q, 1998, pp. 38–41.

Wild, T. (2002) *Best practice in inventory management.* Butterworth Heinemann, Oxford.

Wilson, H. and Keating, B. (2002) *Business forecasting.* McGraw-Hill, New York.

Woxenius, J. and Bärthel, F. (2007) "Intermodal road-rail transport in the European Union" . In Konings, R., Priemus, H. and Nijkamp, P. (eds) *The future of intermodal freight transport: concepts, design and implementation*, Edward Elgar Publishing, Cheltenham.

Wu, H.-J. and Dunn, S. (1995) "Environmentally responsible logistics systems", *International Journal of Physical Distribution and Logistics Management*, Vol. 25, No. 2, pp. 20–38.

Zeng, A. (2003) "Global sourcing: process and design for efficient management", *Supply Chain Management: an international journal*, Vol. 8, No. 4, pp. 367–379.

Index